LOVE

What Your Birthday Reveals About You and Your Personal Relationships

CARDS

ROBERT LEE CAMP

sourcebooks

Published by Sourcebooks, Inc.
P.O. Box 4410, Naperville, Illinois 60567-4410
(630) 961-3900
Fax: (630) 961-2168
www.sourcebooks.com

Library of Congress Cataloging-in-Publication Data

Camp, Robert (Robert L.)
  Love cards : what your birthday reveals about you and your personal relationships / Robert Lee Camp. -- [Rev. edition].
      pages cm
  Includes indexes.
  (pbk. : alk. paper) 1. Fortune-telling by cards. 2. Fortune-telling by birthdays. I. Title.
  BF1878.C27 2014
  133.3'242--dc23

                    2013041323

            Printed and bound in the United States of America.
                  BB 10 9 8 7 6

This book is dedicated to all seekers of truth who are willing to look where others fear to tread. May this book deepen your connection to yourself and to life here on this beautiful planet as it really is.

Contents

Introduction

I have always been a student of life and I have always wanted to know what is the 'Key to Happiness.' Perhaps it is this eternal quest that led me to the discovery of this most amazing system. When a friend handed me an old book about the cards and said, "Here, look up your card and see what it says about you," I was doubtful. How could any system based solely upon my birthday have anything relevant to say about me? I was an astrologer after all, and as many people know, an astrology chart requires the date, time, and place of our birth to be accurate. Still, I was interested and read a small section about my Birth Card. I was stunned a little after reading it. First of all, it was telling me things about myself that were true, but they were qualities that I hadn't accepted about myself. I felt the book was a little negative on my card, the Queen of Diamonds, but I had to admit that it was an accurate portrayal. Something inside told me that I had stumbled upon a gemstone of knowledge. My second sense about books and information has always been accurate and I knew then and there that this information came from a high and genuine source of spiritual truth.

I immediately acquired a copy of that book, called *Sacred Symbols of the Ancients*, and began reading up on everyone I knew. My thirst for more information was growing each day. But as I searched and searched, I could find no other books about this mysterious card system. There were lots of books on reading playing cards, but none gave me the feeling this book did. After about a year, I finally gave up searching, resigning myself to the reality that there really were no other books on this subject.

A couple of months later I made a big move to Los Angeles. Strangely enough, within two weeks of moving there a friend came over and noticed *Sacred Symbols* on my book shelf. "You have that book too?" she said. "Did you know there is a man in town who has written another book about the cards? His name is Arne Lein and he has been teaching classes about it." To make a long story short, I met Arne Lein, took classes from him, and received my initiation into this wonderful body of information. Over a year later, after Arne passed away, I dedicated myself to introducing this system to the world and began writing my first book about it.

About six years ago I had a reading done by a prominent psychic in Los Angeles. Most of the reading was useless mumbo jumbo, but at one point in the reading the psychic stopped what he was talking about and said, "Your deceased aunt, Elizabeth, wants to tell you something and she won't leave me alone until I tell you this." I told him to go ahead and he said, "She was an author herself. She knows you are writing books and she wanted me to tell you that when you write your book, think about creating a book that would be the book you have been looking for your entire life. Think about what book would make you feel like you had found the most valuable treasure in the world. Then, go out and write that book."

I took some notes and he went on with the rest of his reading. But that one message made a lasting impression on me. The feeling Aunt Elizabeth described is how I felt when I discovered *Sacred Symbols*. Honestly, there have been several other books that have made me feel that way and each one of them proved to be invaluable in my life, giving me priceless information that helped me to transform aspects of my life. I hope *Love Cards* has that impact for you.

When I meet people today, I immediately ask them their birthday. Once I know their birthday, I usually know more about them than they know about themselves. I constantly study people and learn more and more about them through the use of this system. This knowledge gives a certain kind of power. I can make predictions about people that come true 90 percent of the time. Knowing a person's card tells what to expect from them and gives an idea of how we will relate with one another. It gives an understanding of life that brings great joy.

It has also helped me to understand and accept myself. Much of the pain and suffering of my early life is gone, partly because I am no longer fighting with myself so much. I have come to accept myself in areas where I used to be in turmoil and conflict. And I believe this is one of the most priceless gifts this system has to offer. If you read this book and are able to understand and accept yourself a little more, then I have been successful.

But the potential is here for much more than that. There are literally hundreds of uses for this information, all of which will help your life and the life of those you love. The truth is really a loving thing. It spreads light wherever it goes, releasing much of the tension we experience from misunderstandings and inner conflicts. And as the wise man Swami Kripalu Vanandji once said:

Where there is darkness, let there be light.
  Where there is sadness, let there be joy.
    Where there is ignorance, let there be truth.
      Where there is hate and anger, let there be love.

Best wishes in your personal path to light, joy, truth, and love.

Robert Lee Camp

Chapter One

In the Beginning, Was a Card

This book has two main purposes, each of which are somewhat connected. The first purpose is to present information about each birthday of the year from the perspective of this system, which I call the Book of Destiny. Along these lines, you will find detailed information about your Birth Card and Planetary Ruling Card, both of which come from your birthday. You will learn how to look up anyone's Birth Card and Planetary Ruling Card and be able to read important and useful information about them that will reveal much about their personality and karmic destiny. I define our karmic destiny as a path in life that we will take by virtue of choices we made prior to coming into this life.

To get the most of this first feature of this book, you will have to learn the meaning of a Birth Card, Planetary Ruling Card, Karma Card, and Personality Card. You will learn how to look them up and how each of them reflects on aspects of our personality. It is not as complicated as it may sound, but if you want to really get the most use from this system, I suggest you take the time to read through this chapter carefully, because this is where we will go over all of these things step-by-step.

The second purpose of this book is to give you unique insight into your personal relationships, particularly your intimate relationships. Chapter Two takes you step-by-step through the process of doing what I call a Complete Relationship Reading between any two people. You will learn even more about yourself as you study the cards of the people with whom you have been intimately involved. After all, our relationships are the clearest mirrors of ourselves that we can find.

So these are the two main features of this book, although there are many other things presented here that you will find useful in terms of information about you, your life and your relationships. So please, take your time and go through each section carefully so that you are familiar with the terminology used and what the different cards are. It is like learning a new language, but one that comes fairly easily once you get into it.

OUR PERSONAL SIGNIFICATORS

In the Book of Destiny system there are many cards that act as symbols of who we are. We will discuss each one individually, but just to get an overview, what follows shows their relative importance in the overall scheme of things:

Birth Card

Most important of all the Personal Significators. Our Soul's Identity in the current lifetime.

Planetary Ruling Card

Next most important of the Personal Significators. The card that we express ourselves through in our work and life.

Karma Cards

Reflect past-life gifts and areas where we have spiritual growth and challenge (except for the special family of 7 cards—see below).

Personality Cards

Roles that we can choose to play at any time in our life, but not a strong identity unless we make it so. Can change at will. Optional identities.

OUR BIRTH CARD

In this system, each day of the year is assigned one of the 52 cards in the deck. Actually, there are 53, because December 31st belongs to the Joker. But we won't talk about the Joker too much, because that card stands mysteriously apart for many reasons and cannot be used like the others. There is a discussion of the Joker later in the book if you would like to learn more about it. For the rest of the birthdays, one card rules each day in an uneven distribution. Look at the Birth Card Chart on the inside back cover of this book and you can quickly find your Birth Card. You will also see that there doesn't seem to be any definable system for determining which card falls upon each day. For example, there are roughly twice as many Diamond and Club birthdays as there are Hearts and Spades. Also, some cards such as the K♠ and

A♥ have only one birthday, while others such as the K♣ and A♦ have twelve. In reality there is a very particular system and reasoning behind which cards fall on each day, but that is a subject best covered in another book. For now, just begin looking up the birthdays of people you know and see what their Birth Card is.

The Birth Card can also be called the Sun Card, much like our Sun Sign in astrology. It is the card that ruled our planet on the day we were born. People born under a certain card's rulership will all share some distinguishing traits, though there is some variety in the ways these traits may be expressed. I am of the belief that we all choose the day we will be born. Choosing a certain Birth Card can be seen as a limitation, sort of a box that we place ourselves in for an entire lifetime. Some people may not like this notion, but like it or not, it affects you daily. Every choice in life can be viewed as a limitation, because any choice we make automatically excludes other choices.

The Birth Card is the strongest and most important symbol of who we are in this lifetime. There are other cards we will also talk about, but know that your Birth Card is the most significant. Never lose sight of that one detail. If you studied only people's Birth Cards, you would have a wealth of information. The Birth Card is our soul's essence. It is the card with which we most strongly identify ourselves. All Queens, for example, see themselves as mothers of one sort or another. They will be motherly, nurturing people throughout their entire life. It is part of their innermost identity. As you read about your Birth Card, see if you can recognize parts of yourself. Each card has a high and low expression. Even though you may be choosing to manifest the highest qualities of your Birth Card, you still have the lowest qualities within you. We are the sum total of our Birth Card, not just one side of it. It is our choice as to which sides of it to present to the world. Later, you may discover that you have had significant relationships with people that are your mirror, card-wise. In these cases, the partners often manifest opposite qualities of the same card expression. For now, just be open to what may be represented about you in the Birth Card description, and reserve judgment until you have had time to see the entire picture.

The Birth Card descriptions are listed in groups of four. The Aces are together, followed by the Twos, etc. Preceding each group is a page or two that talks about the qualities that all the cards in that group share. Read those pages as well and you will receive further insight into yourself, perhaps some things that may have been missed in the actual description of your Birth Card.

Each Birth Card also has an article or profile that more vividly illustrates the natures of that Birth Card. Be sure to read yours as you make a study of your Birth Card.

BORN AROUND MIDNIGHT? GUESS WHAT?

Here's an important note for those of you who were born close to midnight. You may not be the card you think you are! The understanding behind which card governs each day of the year is very particular and specific. It uses what is known as True Solar Time to determine your time and day of birth. If you were born within an hour of midnight in a place that was observing Daylight Savings Time, or if the location of your birthplace is far away (East or West) from the Standard Time Meridian for the Time Zone in which you were born, your actual time of birth may put you a day ahead or behind what was recorded on your birth certificate.

We use a system called Time Zones whereby everybody within a certain geographical 'band' observes the same time on their watches. However, the sun could care less about the time on your watch. It is moving along, and when it is directly overhead, it is noon, regardless of what your watch may say. Its time is what we call True Solar Time, as opposed to the observed time that everyone in your time zone has agreed to call accurate. In many cases, there can be a wide variance between the True Solar Time and the observed time, since some time zones are quite wide. This can throw off the time of your birth, Sun-wise, by as much as an hour. In addition, Daylight Savings Time throws another monkey wrench into the calculations. You could have another hour difference in your actual time of birth versus the old tried and true sundial time. The Book of Destiny system strictly uses True Solar Time, so if you are thinking that your Birth Card description just doesn't fit you and you know you were born close to midnight, it would be worth investigating.

Our Planetary Ruling Card(s)

Your Planetary Ruling Card is derived from your birthday, but also involves knowing your astrological Sun Sign. This card is the second most important card that represents you. It acts in many ways like a second Birth Card, or like the Rising Sign or Ascendant in astrological terms.

Some birthdays do not have a separate Planetary Ruling Card. For example, the Planetary Ruling Card for people born under the sign of Leo is the same as their Birth Card. Leos are like a 'super-charged' version of their Birth Card. Whatever the qualities of their Birth Card, they will dramatize and emphasize the Birth Card and empower it with all of the power of their dynamic Sun energy. The result can be good or bad, of course. Leos may feel a little let down in discovering they have no different Planetary Ruling Card, but if they did, they probably wouldn't have as much personal power as they do.

At any rate, your Planetary Ruling Card will tell you even more about yourself. It is another symbol of what we identify ourselves to be, but more in an external way. It probably is more related to our Midheaven in astrological terms than our Ascendant, since the Midheaven is a symbol of how we present ourselves to the world, or how the world sees us. But these are subtle distinctions that may not make a difference in practical use. The bottom line is that we act very much out of our Planetary Ruling Card and very much identify with it. When you get someone's birthday, always determine their Planetary Ruling Card along with their Birth Card. These two will be all you need to know to learn as much about them as you want.

The table below shows the Sun Signs and the Planets that rule them. If you compare the Planets in this table with the cards in your Life Spread and the Life Spreads of others, you will quickly see how the Planetary Ruling Card is derived.

Sun Sign	Ruling Planet	Sun Sign	Ruling Planet
Aries	Mars	Libra	Venus
Taurus	Venus	Scorpio	Pluto, Mars*
Gemini	Mercury	Sagittarius	Jupiter
Cancer	Moon	Capricorn	Saturn
Leo	The Sun	Aquarius	Uranus
Virgo	Mercury	Pisces	Neptune

* Mars is the secondary ruler of Scorpio

To learn more about your Planetary Ruling Card and the qualities it may bestow upon you, first read the short description of each of them provided in Chapter Four. In addition, you can also read the information about the Birth Card of the same card. For example, if your birthday is March 27th, your Birth Card is the 9♣ and your Planetary Ruling Card is the K♥. Reading the description of the K♥ Birth Card will teach you more about your Planetary Ruling Card.

For Those Born on the Cusps

The Planetary Ruling Card is based upon your Birth Card and your Sun Sign, so you must be absolutely sure of your Sun Sign to know your Planetary Ruling Card. Many people are born on what we call a 'cusp date' in which they could one of two signs. Each month of the year has a couple of days, usually 2-4, where the sun

changes from one sign to the next. Because of leap year and other considerations, this can occur within a 3-4 day range each year. When you are born on one of these cusp days, you will probably need to have a professional astrological chart in order to determine exactly which sign you are. If you are born on a cusp day, you will find an 'OR' statement between which two Planetary Ruling Cards you may be, depending upon your Sun Sign. First, you must settle the question of your Sun Sign. This information is very important, and you will want to be accurate about this if at all possible.

Scorpios Take Note

Scorpios are another exception to this Planetary Ruling Card situation. Because Scorpio is ruled by both Pluto and Mars, we have to consider the Planetary Ruling Cards for both planets when we study their personalities.

Scorpios have both qualities within them. They usually choose to focus most of their attention to one Ruling Planet at a time, but both are always present to some degree. I chose the Pluto rulership first, which is the second Planetary Ruling Card listed in the book, but ultimately you should look at both of them. Don't you Scorpios like the fact that you are more complex than other cards? It may take the rest of us a little longer to figure out all of your little secrets.

The Birth Card and Planetary Ruling Card Are Usually All You Need

In 90 percent of the studies and readings that I do with people, I only use the Birth Card and the Planetary Ruling Card. The Karma Card influences, which we will discuss next, are already included in the descriptions of the Birth Cards found in this book. That is that each Birth Card has inherent in it the influence of its two Karma Cards. You can study your Karma Cards a little for more information about yourself, because they do act as mirrors of certain aspects of your personality. However, the descriptions I have written for each Birth Card already take into account the influence of the Karma Cards. So, for your purposes, you really only need to study the Birth and Planetary Ruling Cards to get a fairly complete picture of a person. I rarely use the Personality Card influences and only in specific situations that I will describe later in that section.

Our Karma Cards

Karma Cards serve a dual purpose in the magical world of cards, and it is important to understand these two separate functions. First of all, our Karma Cards represent different aspects of our own personality, much like our Birth and Planetary Ruling Cards. However, the Karma Card characteristics are usually those which are not apparent when we first meet someone. They are traits and characteristics that are not often shown to other people, but are there just the same. For example, the Q♦ Birth Card has a 3♦ as its first Karma Card. Some of the outstanding qualities of the 3♦ are worrying about finances and feeling that there just isn't enough—enough money, enough love, and so on. When you first meet a Q♦ person, you may not be aware that they have such an insecurity within them. However, if you spend some time with them, it will become apparent that this is a major factor in their life.

Most people have two Karma Cards. Specifically, 45 of the 52 Birth Cards have two Karma Cards. For these Birth Cards, the first Karma Card listed for them represents hidden qualities that are areas of growth for that card, while the second Karma Card represents hidden qualities that are natural gifts and abilities they have. Both Karma Card influences in these cases are past-life karmic influences, the first Karma Card being more of a negative karmic influence, while the second Karma Card is more of a positive karmic influence. Keep this in mind as you find out what your Karma Cards are.

The Special Family of Seven

The remaining seven Birth Cards fall into two categories. Among these seven cards are four that are called the Semi-Fixed Cards, and three that are called the Fixed Cards. The three Fixed Cards are the J♥, 8♣, and K♠. The six Karma Cards listed for these Birth Cards have no reflection on their personal characteristics whatsoever. The only thing these three cards have in common is that they are fixed in their natures. Beyond that, they do not share anything significant, nor do they act as mirrors of any characteristics between them. The four Semi-Fixed Cards are actually two pairs of cards that are strongly linked to each other. The first pair is the A♣ and 2♥. These two are perfect mirrors of each other, each having many of the qualities of the other. The A♣ has just as much of a yearning for love (2♥) as the 2♥ has a desire for knowledge (A♣). The other Semi-Fixed pair is the 7♦ and 9♥, which have just as much in common as the first pair have with each other. I have come to call these pairs Cosmic Soul Twins, because out of all of the cards of the deck, these are the only ones that have another card that is so intimately connected to themselves. We will talk more about this special family of seven cards later. For now, just remember that only the two Semi-Fixed pairs act as mirrors of each other's characteristics.

I mentioned earlier that Karma Cards serve two purposes. We have discussed at length their first purpose, which is to be mirrors of some of our qualities, usually those not readily perceived by others. Their second function is to tell us about certain people in our life with whom we have strong karmic ties from previous lifetimes. Karma Cards are not the only people that we have past-life connections to, but they are among the most significant. Relationships with people who are one of our Karma Cards will usually be significant in an important way—during the course of that relationship there will be some debt paid off that was incurred in a previous lifetime.

In most cases we have two Karma Cards—one that we owe something to and another who owes us something and from who we will collect in this lifetime. This is how it is between the 45 cards that are not part of the special family of seven. For example, if your Birth Card is a 10♣, you owe something to the J♠ and will receive something from the 4♠, your two Karma Cards. When you read to find out who your Karma Cards are, the first one listed is always the one you owe something to, and the second one listed is the one that comes to pay you something. You can learn more about this by reading up on the Karma Card connection (KRMA) found in the connections chapter.

Among the family of three Fixed and four Semi-Fixed Cards, the story is quite different. They are all connected together karmically in some way. You will notice that these people are usually found together. For example, most 7♦ people are close to a J♥, A♣, or 8♣. These cards are all bound to be together by some mysterious past-life energy that draws them to each other. However, I have not been able to observe any implied direction of exchange between them. You will see them living together in different fashions but may not be able to determine which one of them, if any, is paying the other. It seems to work in both directions. They are found together a lot more frequently than mere averages would account for, and thus there must be something special about their interaction. In *Sacred Symbols*, Florence Campbell and Edith Randall don't say much about it, except about the three Fixed Cards. About them, they say that when any two of these Birth Cards get together, a powerful force is created that, if properly channeled, could change the world. This I have confirmed with my own studies, and thus in this book you will find the Power Connection (POWR), which only exists between those Fixed Birth Cards.

Our Personality Cards

Personality Cards sit at the bottom of the pile as far as their importance in the overall scheme of things. However, there will be instances where their importance will be noticed in certain individuals. It is good to think of the Personality Cards as 'hats' that we can wear for different occasions. They are roles that we can put on or take off at will. They are not really us at all, but we each have the capacity to breathe life into these roles by virtue of our God-given powers. The Personality Cards are the Jacks, Queens, and Kings of our Birth Card's suit. Each of them has a personality all of its own, a set of characteristics that we inherit when we play that role, whether we are conscious of it or not. Regardless of your sex, you can be any of your Personality Cards. However, the norm is for women to play as the Queen of their suit and for men to play as the Jack. Let's discuss them individually and see how they work.

The Jack

When a man is young, let's say up until age 21 on average, or when a man of any age is romantically involved, he is probably playing the role of the Jack of his suit. Jacks in this role are of the sort who would say anything, do anything or be anything just to win over a woman.

Most men may be embarrassed to admit it and most women may hesitate to acknowledge it, but this is how men are during many romantic periods of their life. The archetype of the Jack is the fast-talking, charming, creative, romantic, and fun person. Most salespeople are playing through their Jacks. Indeed, you will discover that many of them are Jack Birth Cards. The same holds true for artists, musicians, creative types, and politicians. Are we seeing a pattern here? I certainly hope so. It must be noted that Jacks possess another, equally significant side to their personalities. This is the part that is immature, irresponsible, unreliable, and untruthful. It comes with the territory, and you cannot have one without the other. It is no coincidence that these professions are at the bottom of bankers' lists when people apply for loans or credit cards. So a man is a Jack when he is in love, working as a salesman, musician, artist, or politician. Keep that in mind. And when he is playing that role, he inherits all of the Jack's personality traits, both good and bad. As an aside, you will notice that most men in these roles choose to use a more familiar, child-like version of their given name. John will call himself Jack, William becomes Bill, Robert becomes Bob, and so forth. You can usually know which role a man is playing by which name he asks you to call him.

Women can be Jacks as well, but not when they are romantically involved. A woman would be playing a Jack role if she was in a Jack occupation. As mentioned earlier, these occupations would include sales and all of the creative pursuits—painting, jewelry making, music, sculpting, etc. When a woman is involved in one of these occupations, she will have many or all of the Jack qualities mentioned earlier. It may be true that some gay women are playing the Jack role. This would probably be true if this particular gay woman were playing the more masculine role, as such. Many gay women choose to dress and act out of their masculine nature, and I would imagine that in these cases the Jack would be appropriate for them.

The Queen

The woman's most commonly used Personality Card would be the Queen of her Birth Card's suit. The Queen represents her role as a mother, wife, or romantic partner. So, when in love, the man becomes his Jack and the woman her Queen. The Queens do not have the reputation of dishonesty and immaturity that the Jacks do. However, if we take a good look at the four Queens, we see that these Birth Cards individually are often fairly challenged in the relationship department. The Q♣ and Q♦ are two of the most romantically indecisive and uncertain cards in the deck. The Q♥ is one of the most codependent and emotionally addictive cards, while the Q♠ is often mired in struggle and mediocrity. When a woman falls in love, she inherits many of the qualities of her Queen, and in many cases those qualities are more of a liability than a blessing. In *Sacred Symbols of the Ancients*, Florence Campbell and Edith Randall admonish most of the Club and Diamond women to never rely on their personalities (which is what happens when they play the Queen role) to get by in life. Some Birth Cards are very powerful and successful in themselves and lose much of their power when they instead choose to operate as one of their Personality Cards. This is usually true in the case of

the Queens. But, it would be difficult for a woman not to act as her Queen. If you are a woman, the very act of falling in love means that your relationship with someone else has become prominent in your list of priorities. When the personal relationship assumes this much importance, you are the Queen and must deal with her individual karma as part of your own. This will become clearer as you study this system more. For now, it would be a good idea to familiarize yourself with the description of your Queen's Birth Card. Like it or not, you share some of her traits when you are in love.

The more positive traits of the Queen are her motherly and protective nature, and often a strong creative or artistic side, much like the Jack's. The Queen has strong management and organization skills that can be applied to creating and maintaining a nice home life for her family. The Queen is also very competent in what she does and can assume authority with ease. Remember that the Queen's power is second only to the King, and in many ways she is more powerful. She doesn't have to make things happen in a forceful manner. She attracts whatever she needs to herself and uses her intuition to know what is really going on around her.

A man could end up in the role of the Queen if he is a single parent or involved in work that is motherly in nature. This is usually a rare occurrence. Gay men may qualify as the Queen of their suit, and many are attracted to more effeminate occupations such as hair dresser, make-up artist, clothing designer, and the like. It may or may not fit a gay man to be a Queen, and you would have to examine each person individually to make that determination.

The King

The King Personality Card is reserved for those whose lifestyle or occupation places them in a responsible role overseeing or managing others. Men and women both can be Kings. Traditionally, Kingship was designated for men alone and every man was given his King as a Personality Card at age 36. However, my research has shown that becoming a King is reserved for those who play the real role of the King, not just given to someone by virtue of his or her sex or age. Anyone is playing the role of a King when they are managing others, leading others and taking responsibility for others. This, of course, would naturally fall into the lap of a man who is the father of a family in the traditional sense. He would be working all day while his wife raised the children and took care of the home duties. In the current age, however, these traditional roles have lost their importance, and either of the sexes can play the role of the King. Single mothers can be called Kings, because often they play the roles of both father and mother to their children. One must become familiar with how Kings operate to make a determination in some cases.

The King is authoritative and disciplinary in nature. He usually doesn't ask for things but demands them. The wise King leads with compassion and wisdom, but there are many dominating and arrogant Kings to be found as well. In the domestic scene, it may be a little harder to determine who is a King, but in the work scene it is fairly easy. If someone is managing others, they are the King. If you are given the responsibility to direct others' work or efforts, you are probably playing the role of a King whether your official job title says so or not.

One thing that can help you know whether or not a man is operating from his King is what name he wants to be called. Just as Jacks usually prefer the boyish, familiar name, a King will usually want to be called his full, formal name, such as William instead of Bill or Michael instead of Mike. If they ask you to call them 'Mister So-and-So,' you know they are probably operating as their King.

Of primary importance in using Personality Cards is ascertaining whether or not the person you are reading for is playing one of these roles in a prominent way. Some people, of course, have a Jack, Queen, or King Birth Card. When this is the case, they are acting as that card their entire life. That is their identity. They can still choose to be another Personality Card for any period of time but can never escape from their Birth Card's meaning. Most K♠ men, for example, act as the Jack of their suit. They usually are actors, musicians, gamblers, or salesmen. If a man or woman's occupation identifies them strongly with one of their Personality Cards, you must assume that they are exhibiting many of those characteristics in their life. If someone is a full-time car salesman, for example, you know that they are doing the Jack in a big way. You can bet that they have both the good and bad sides of their Jack. Can you trust them or trust that what they say is true? Maybe, and maybe not. That would depend upon which qualities of

the Jack they were allowing to come through. Will they rip you off? It's possible. Will they be romantic and fun to hang out with? Probably. Jacks love to have fun and have tremendous charm.

When anyone spends a large portion of their day in a particular role, be it Jack, Queen, or King, this is the case when the Personality Card becomes important. This is when you should use this Personality Card as a means to study this person, and also use it as part of your relationship readings for that person. Otherwise, don't place too much importance in it.

Keep in mind one other point as well. Many Birth Cards have influences of their own that are like the Jack, Queen, or King, and just because they have the same occupation, they may or may not be actually playing through those Personality Cards. The Threes, for example, are all very creative. Just because you meet a Three person who is an artist doesn't necessarily mean they are playing the Jack. Whenever there is a doubt about it, assume that they are not playing the role of the Personality Card. Remember that these Personality Cards are just temporary masks that we wear and have nothing to do with the real us.

MORE ABOUT TAKING ON THE KARMA OF OUR PERSONALITY CARDS

When we act as one of our Personality Cards, we inherit, for better or worse, some of the traits associated with that card. For example, all women of the Club suit inherit some of the Q♣ impatience and quick temper when they are operating as that Queen. That is because those are some of the basic qualities of the Q♣. As a matter of fact, it is advisable in some cases to avoid acting out of the role of your Personality Card, because to do so would lessen your power or good fortune. For example, most women of the Diamond suit are better off avoiding contact with their Queen, the Q♦, because the Q♦ Birth Card is one of the most indecisive and troublesome cards in the deck, especially in the area of relationships. If we examine this a little further, we can deduce that whenever any Diamond female gets involved romantically, she ends up having more difficulties in her life because of the difficult karmic burden that is associated with the Q♦. It is therefore difficult for all Diamond women to find happiness in love and romance. This sounds strange, but my studies have found it to be accurate. Much the same can be said for Club women as well.

But does this mean that all Diamond and Club women are doomed to never having any success or happiness in personal relationships? No, this is not quite the case. However, it is something to be aware of. Any of the problems or challenges associated with a Birth Card can be overcome through self-awareness and conscious effort. The Q♦ and Q♣ are two of the most difficult cards in the deck romantically speaking. But these difficulties can be traced to fears, negative associations with bad relationships from the past, and a tendency to want to escape when the going gets tough emotionally. Many people of these cards have gone on to make beautiful lives for themselves once they faced the many fears that controlled their choices in the past.

In cases where your Birth Card is one of power and strength, such as the 8♣ or K♦, the woman experiences a loss of power when she plays her Queen. Does she abandon her feminine side altogether? No, but she must find a way to integrate her personal relationships into her life in such a way that they do not become the most important thing in her life. Women who are power cards (Jacks, Queens, Kings, Eights, and Tens, for the most part) need to have a career and feel that they are contributing something of value to the world outside of their immediate family. If their marriage or love affair intercedes and prevents them from accomplishing their life's work, they become unhappy. They have to find a way to have their intimate relationships fit into their life without stealing their attention away from their work.

If you would like to learn more about the qualities of your Personality Cards, read the individual descriptions of those cards as if they were your Birth Card and you may discover more about yourself. You may even discover that you operate through one of your Personality Cards most of the time. Whenever we operate as one of our Personality Cards, we inherit some of his or her qualities and karma, both good and bad.

What If My Birth Card Is Already a Jack, Queen, or King?

Many people are born with a Jack, Queen, or King Birth Card. These people are acting as that particular Birth Card, which is one of the Personality Cards, most of the time. A person with a Jack Birth Card will act as a Jack all their life, for better or worse. The same holds true for the Queens and Kings. However, they still have the potential to operate as their other Personality Cards. I am a Q♦, for example. As a male Q♦, I retain some of the feminine and motherly characteristics of that Queen. I am sensitive and enjoy mothering people to a certain degree. However, I can still choose to operate as the J♦ or K♦ any time I choose.

Steps for Self-Study

Here I present a recap of this chapter, offering a step-by-step program for learning as much as you can about yourself using this wonderful system of self-understanding. In the beginning you will just be doing a lot of reading, but as you interact with this system a while and study the Birth Cards of people you are or have been close to, many more answers will come to you about you, your life and life itself. It is a wonderful path of discovery and I hope you enjoy it all.

1. First, read about your Birth Card. Read the chapter about your Birth Card, including the profile that pertains to your Birth Card. Remember to also read the section about the *number* of your Birth Card that appears at the beginning of the section. If you are a 7♦ Birth Card, read about the Sevens at the beginning of that section.

2. Read about your Planetary Ruling Card. Find your Planetary Ruling Card in your Life Spread (see Chapter Three). Read the short description of it in Chapter Four. Then read more about people whose Birth Card is the same as your Planetary Ruling Card. How many of those traits do you see manifested in your own life?

3. Determine whether or not you are spending a lot of time playing the role of any of the Personality Cards. If so, read up on that card to find out the positive and negative traits of that card that will be a part of your life while you play that role.

4. For a even more in-depth analysis, you can delve into examining the cards in your Life Path. Chapter Three presents enough of an introduction to this subject to explore these on your own. Your Life Path Cards are as much a part

of you as your Birth Card. They are intimately connected.

5. Study the pattern of your relationships as a mirror to yourself. As you read Chapter Two and begin doing relationship comparisons, you will probably notice patterns emerging from the choices you have made in your personal relationships (such as every man you have been with is the same Birth Card as your mother or father). Assume that each choice you made was a mirror of an important part of yourself. What does that tell you about yourself? Can you identify the path you are taking toward more self awareness by seeing a progression in these choices? Can you see where you are on that path and what your next steps might be?

6. Finally, read the articles in Chapter Eight that reveal some of the underlying truths of love and life. Perhaps you will find some reflection of yourself there and a new way of looking at that part of yourself which will bring more clarity and understanding.

With all of these tools and sources of information, you are likely to have many realizations about yourself while studying this book. Hopefully these will bring you more opportunities for love, fun, and happiness. For now, maybe you are ready to find out more about your personal relationships. The next chapter is going to open up many new doors of understanding. Though it may seem complicated at first glance, if you follow the simple steps involved, you will be doing readings in a matter of minutes. You already have a good foundation and now can begin applying this information in different ways.

When you are ready for additional information about this system, your Life Path Cards and relationship issues, turn to Chapter Seven, which has several informative articles that will help your understanding of this system and yourself. If you are ready to do your first relationship reading, proceed to Chapter Two.

Chapter Two

How to Do a Relationship Reading between Two People in Love

In this chapter we will cover a step-by-step process of doing a relationship reading between two people. The technique that you will learn will reveal all of the intimate details of your relationships and those of people you know. Every card in the deck has energetic 'connections' with every other card in the deck. There are no two cards that are entirely unrelated. The connections you look up and read about will tell you what is going on behind the scenes in your relationships, often revealing the underlying reasons why you are drawn to be with a certain person.

A complete relationship reading consists of two basic elements. The first element is understanding each individual separately. Every card has a certain approach to relationships or certain predictable patterns of behavior that will tell you a lot about any relationship they are involved in. So you must first get to know each of the people for whom you are doing the reading as individuals, before examining the interaction of their two Birth Cards as indicated by the connections between them. Study their Birth Cards and Planetary Ruling Cards. Read all about them and look for things pertaining to their relationship issues and patterns.

Once that is done, you can complete the second element of examining their connections. Was it sexual attraction or some past-life unfinished business that attracted the two? Is there really any compatibility between the two or is it all an illusion? The connections between cards will reveal all of this and much more—in intimate detail.

To make the entire process of doing a reading more understandable and easier to learn, it is divided into four distinct steps. If you follow these steps carefully, you will know what is going on between any two people in an intimate relationship. The fourth step is optional, one that you will do in specific situations where one or both of the partners is spending a lot of time acting out of one of their Personality Cards. More on this later.

The four steps you will learn to do are as follows:

1. Step One—Read about their Birth Card, Planetary Ruling Card, and Personality Cards
2. Step Two—The Birth Card Reading
3. Step Three—The Planetary Ruling Card Reading
4. Step Four—The Personality Card Reading

STEP ONE—READ ABOUT THEIR BIRTH CARD, PLANETARY RULING CARD, AND PERSONALITY CARDS

Before you begin doing a relationship reading between two people, you should familiarize yourself with the different cards that signify them. Some Birth Cards prefer more freedom in their personal relationships while others need more security. Some have a hard time with commitment while others have good marriage karma. Some have unusually high sex drives while others make their work and career the most important things in their life. It will be beneficial for you to know as much about the two people involved in the reading before reading about how they fit together. The success or failure of any relationship often depends more upon the general nature of the two individuals than it does upon how well they fit together. For example, no matter how compatible two people are, if one or both of them are averse to commitment, the relationship will be transitory at best. Many people are actually averse to commitment, even though they may not show it at first. The Birth Card, Planetary Ruling Card, and Personality Cards of each person will reveal information that will answer many of your questions about them and their patterns in the area of personal relationships. So what you will be doing in this step is learning all about both of the partners by studying their cards. The most important of the three is the Birth Card, next is the Planetary Ruling Card, and, finally, the Personality Card(s). Here are the things you should read to familiarize yourself with each person that you are reading for:

1. Read about both persons' Birth Cards.

   To begin, turn to this book's inside back cover and look up the Birth Cards of both people according to their birthday. Next, turn to Chapter Three and read the description of their Birth Cards. Be sure to read the entire description, especially the part about how they tend to act in relationships. The Birth Card description is the most important, as you will see later. The profiles about the Birth Cards of the two people for whom you are reading may shed more light on them, giving you further insight into their personalities and traits.

2. Read about both persons' Planetary Ruling Cards.

On the third page of the four-page section for each Birth Card, you will find a list of the Planetary Ruling Cards for that Birth Card, listed by the birth dates. Look up the Planetary Ruling Cards for the couple in question, and then find these cards in Chapter Three and read their meaning just as you did the Birth Cards. So, if your Birth Card is the A♠ and your Planetary Ruling Card is the 7♦, you would first look up and read about the A♠ Birth Card and then look up the 7♦ Birth Card and read that as well. Even though you are technically not a 7♦ Birth Card, the description of that card will reveal some pertinent information about you since your Planetary Ruling Card is a 7♦. Chapter Four has sections entitled '___ as Your Planetary Ruler.' Read the section pertaining to your card. To learn more about the importance of the Planetary Ruling Card and how it is used, turn to page 16. For now, consider it to be like a second Birth Card that gives additional information on how we act.

3. Read about their Personality Cards, if appropriate.

The Personality Cards are the next place we look for information about two people in love. However, we only look at these in certain situations. Read the section in Chapter One about the Personality Cards and how to find them. If, after reading this section, you think one or both of the people in this relationship are acting out of one of their Personality Cards, then go ahead and read up on that card as you did with the Birth Card and Planetary Ruling Card. However, in most cases this last step will not be necessary. The Birth Card and Planetary Ruling Card usually provide a complete description and understanding of a person's characteristics.

4. Check out the Marriageability Factor of each person's Birth Card and Planetary Ruling Card.

Finally you may want to read about the Marriageability Factor related to each card. Based upon my experience and knowledge of this system, I have developed a scale of marriageability that tells you just how marriageable each of the Birth Cards and Planetary Ruling

Cards are. If you are one of the 'unmarriageables' or if you are dating one of them, whatever relationship you are in will more or less be transitory. Knowing this in advance can save a lot of time and energy. At the beginning of Chapter Seven is everything you need to know about this factor and the table for all the Birth Cards. You should compare each person's Birth Cards and Planetary Ruling Cards in this table to see how they rate. The Birth Card values and Planetary Ruling Card values should be used together. Both are important, and one may balance out the other.

As you read about the two people in any given relationship, you are assessing their qualities and patterns as individuals. Just knowing about their Birth Cards will often reveal what is going on and what will happen. For example, if both of the partners are unmarriageable, this relationship probably will not last long. I also find it extremely helpful to find out something about their past histories in relationships. If we are anything, we are creatures of habit when it comes to love. Our past relationships tell us a lot about our personalities and what is important to us.

So, this is where we always must start. Assess each individual separately. Read carefully what is written about them. There are no wasted words in the descriptions—if a particular pattern is mentioned, pay attention. It may prove to be more prominent or important than you think. Once you have studied the Birth Cards of the two people involved, you are ready to do one or more of the Relationship Readings. Now, you have a better handle on just who these two people are.

STEP TWO—THE BIRTH CARD READING

This step has a few important parts. First, we will look up the connections that exist between the Birth Cards of the two people and then read the Index Ratings. When you are done with this step, you will have already done a fairly complete relationship reading that you can use to judge two people's overall compatibility and issues together. You could stop here if you like. You will have a pretty accurate assessment of the connections between these two people that will tell you a lot about how they will each experience being together. Later, if you want to get into the most detail possible, you can do Step Three with the Planetary Ruling Cards. This third step can be important, because some of our most significant connections are often found between one person's Birth Card and the other's Planetary Ruling Card, or vice versa.

Exploring the Connections That Exist between Two People

On the page immediately following the description of your Birth Card and your Life Spread, you will find a list of the 'Relationship Connections' between your Birth Card and that of all the other Birth Cards. These connections pages are really the heart of the techniques of comparison, the results of years of research, applying the original methods of this system to the areas of personal relationships. If you scan down this list and locate the Birth Card of someone you know in the left column, you will find, going across from left to right, abbreviations for the 3–5 most significant connections between your card and theirs. In over 98 percent of the cases, there are five connections. A few combinations of Birth Cards yield only four connections and even fewer yield three.

These connections represent vibrational energies between you and another person. Some are harmonious and easy, while others produce a lot of energy or tension. Each plays an important role in the overall makeup of your relationship and constitutes a different aspect of how the two of you relate. What you will do in this step is look up the meaning of each of these connections one by one, keeping a few things in mind as you do.

The first thing I want to emphasize is that these connections are from the point of view of the card whose page you are on, and not vice versa. This means that if you are reading for the 10♣ and 9♣, and you are currently reading the connections found on the 10♣ page, then these connections represent the way the 10♣ person is experiencing the relationship and not the other way around. To find out how the 9♣ is experiencing the

relationship, we must turn to the 9♣ page and look at it from their point of view. The relationship is always experienced in a slightly different way by each of the partners. After you have done a couple of readings, you will notice that two people often share the same connections, but even then, there are separate interpretations for these connections depending upon whose point of view you are looking at it from. There are always some minor differences and sometimes some major differences between your point of view and the other person's. If you are my Venus Card in the Life Spread, for example, the adoration quality of Venus occurs more from me to you than vice versa. In a sense, you represent that which I adore, not necessarily the other way around. Still, if I am adoring you, you are bound to enjoy that and thus you get a certain kind of experience from being the one who is adored that you reflect back to me.

The next thing to keep in mind is that the connections are always listed in the order of their importance. This means that 'Con1,' which stands for Connection One, is the most important, again from the point of view of the person for whom you are reading. Each connection listed after Con1 decreases in importance but still has some effect. Even the last connection will be felt and experienced by the partners at one time or another. It just will not be as significant as the first or second.

After the list of the individual connections for each relationship, there are three numbers, ranging from -10 to +10, called the Overall Index Ratings. These index values quantify the relationship in three important areas: Attraction, Intensity, and Compatibility. We will discuss their significance later in this chapter.

Let's examine the connections between a 10♣ and a 9♣ to better understand how this works and how this information is arranged. If we turn to page 199 that describes the 10♣ connections, we can scan the list for the one with the 9♣. It looks like this:

10♣ with	Con1	Con2	Con3	Con4	Con5	Attraction	Intensity	Compatibility
9♣	MOFS	VEM	MOF	CRFS	PLR	8	-2	8

This listing tells us that the first, and most significant, connection (Con1) between the 10♣ and the 9♣ is the 'MOFS' connection. MOFS is an abbreviation for 'They are your Moon Card in the Spiritual Spread,' which you can look up in Chapter Five. As mentioned earlier, this first connection is the strongest one between these two people and accounts for a large part of what they experience together. The connections that follow are in decreasing order of strength and importance, Con5 being the least significant connection between two people.

Reading the Descriptions
of the Relationship Connections

At this point you don't know what these connections mean. However, there are complete descriptions of each of the connections given in the 'Descriptions of the Connections' in Chapter Five. In that chapter you will find all the connections listed along with complete descriptions. To quickly find the page with the description of any connection you want to read, just turn to the very last page in the book to the Relationship Connections Quick Reference Page. Here you will see each connection listed in alphabetical order along with its complete name and the page number where its description is located. Go ahead and look up the first connection between the two people you are reading now.

When you read the descriptions you will understand all the significance, general and specific, of this connection and how it affects the partner for whom you are reading. In the above example, we found out that MOFS stands for 'They are Your Moon Card in the Spiritual Spread.' If we read the detailed description of what that means on page 278, we will understand exactly what the most important influence is in this relationship from the point of view of the 10♣ person.

Each successive connection you read will be slightly less important than the first. However, don't think that they are not important at all. As a matter of fact, there are many relationships where there are actually ten or more connections between the partners. I have chosen to list only the first five. These, in my opinion, are the most important ones, and account for 90 percent or more of what that relationship is about. Any connections beyond the first five are negligible in their effect on either of the partners. In cases where there are only three or four connections given, they become even more important. This means that the ones listed are the *only* ones between these two cards. Each one of these connections would share a greater proportion of importance than if there were five total connections.

Reading the Affirmations for the Connections

At the very end of the description of each of the connections is an affirmation for that connection. The affirmation given is one that puts that connection into its highest light. It illustrates the way in which that connection could contribute to the relationship if the person having it were to take it in the most positive and constructive way. These affirmations may indeed show why you chose that relationship or, at the very least, point to the way in which you can get the most out of it. Often the only difference between something being a good thing and a bad thing in our life is our point of view. These affirmations point toward the point of view that will encourage more gratitude and appreciation for what this relationship is for each partner. This sort of gratitude will greatly increase the chances of long–term success in this relationship.

It is interesting to note that people who are in an unfulfilling relationship that went sour years earlier have forgotten the feelings they had for each other when they first met. These affirmations often reveal those initial feelings they shared when their appreciation for each other was so strong. Mutual appreciation is the very heart of any good relationship. Without it, the couple probably will not have the strength to go through the challenges that life and the relationship are bound to bring their way. It is entirely possible that a couple could rekindle that kind of appreciation if they were to read these affirmations, take them to heart, and then look at the things that have caused their flow of appreciation to become blocked. A relationship is never really over until both parties say it is and mean it.

The Overall Index Rating of the Relationship

In the example above, the number appearing below the headings Attraction, Intensity, and Compatibility are called the Overall Index Ratings of that particular relationship from the point of view of the person you are comparing it from. These ratings are meant to give you a quick overview of the relationship as it would manifest in the majority of cases. It may not accurately reflect how partners experience the relationship because of the many individual factors involved. However, it is a good overall guideline and will apply accurately in most cases. It makes for a lot of fun for those who are dating, giving them a quick overview of the relationship. Serious relationships always require a more in-depth analysis, but this is a good place to start.

These index numbers are the result of adding together the sum total of the same index values for each of the connections listed. In other words, if you have five connections, each of them has their own individual index values in these three categories. I have used a formula to get an average for these connections, giving more weight to the first connections and decreasing the percentage of the overall value for each successive connection. This gives a fairly accurate assessment that will apply in the majority of cases. The descriptions that follow give more details about the individual indexes.

The Separate Index Ratings for Each Connection

The Index Ratings listed with each connection tell how much that particular connection tends to add to or subtract from the Overall Index Ratings of the relationship. In the example above, we see that the Overall Index Ratings between the 10♣ and the 9♣ are: Attraction: 8, Intensity: -2, and Compatibility: 8. However, the Indexes for the MOFS connection by itself are: Attraction: 8, Intensity: -4, and Compatibility: 10. We can see from this example that there must be other connections in the relationship that add to and subtract from the values of the MOFS connection to give us the Overall Index Rating. However, because this MOFS is the very first connection, it is stronger than the others. Its influence accounts for a greater percentage of the overall Index Ratings than any of the other connections that follow it.

The Attraction Index tells you how much that connection adds to your desire to be with your partner. This is also how much physical, emotional, psychic, and sexual attraction you share. Moon, Venus, Mars, Neptune, and Pluto connections represent the most Attraction between people. Some connections, such as Saturn, actually produce a negative Attraction or 'repulsion' that will be reflected in these ratings. A relationship with a high Attraction rating will have a lot of energy in it, energy that must be used constructively if the relationship is to survive. If not handled with awareness, the energy will actually be a major factor in the destruction of the relationship. Those of us who choose relationships with a high Attraction Index are usually working out anger and sexual issues in that relationship. High Attraction relationships will stimulate us to take action in our life and could be vital to our personal development.

The Intensity Index tells you how much each connection adds to the drama, excitement and challenge of the relationship. This can also indicate how much 'spiritual or personal growth' the relationship engenders. High Intensity means high growth and personal development. Connections such as Mars, Saturn, and Pluto contribute to high Intensity. Venus and Moon connections will reduce Intensity. A relationship with high Intensity may be too much for the average person. A high Intensity relationship will tend to be challenging and confrontational on a continual basis. If there is not some degree of Compatibility with it, a high Intensity relationship is not likely to last very long. It might just be too intense to deal with on a long–term basis. On the other hand, some people grew up in a high intensity environment and feel more comfortable with that level of growth and challenge.

The Compatibility Index tells you how much each of your connections adds to or subtracts from your overall compatibility and ability to live together for extended periods of time. Compatibility is the 'ease' of being together. Anything over 0 is considered favorable in the Compatibility area, and anything over a 2 is favorable for marriage. Venus, Jupiter, and Moon-based connections contribute the most to Compatibility, while Saturn connections usually detract a great deal from it. Few people choose high Compatibility relationships early in their life. It usually takes us a long time to realize that high Compatibility is best for a long–term relationship. High Compatibility means a 'good fit,' someone with whom we can coexist peacefully.

Each of us may like certain kinds of relationships. For example, I tend to like ones where the Attraction Index is high, the Intensity low, and the Compatibility high, such as a 5, 1, 5. As you study the patterns in your relationships, you will find the Index connections that work or do not work for you.

Once you have read these Indexes, you have completed the first and most important part of a complete relationship reading. Now, you can do the same thing from the point of view of the second person in the relationship by looking up the connections and Indexes listed on the page following their Birth Card description. Turn to this page, find the Birth Card of the first person listed on their Relationship Connections page and look up the connections, one by one, from their point of view. Then you will have a fairly detailed and accurate picture of this relationship and what it means to both partners.

Tips on Combining Separate Connections Influences for a Total Picture of the Relationship

The descriptions for each connection are detailed and accurate. However, you must keep them all in mind as you consider what this relationship is or may be like. Sometimes one connection will help offset another. For example, you may find two people who share a strong Saturn connection. This connection would usually make a certain aspect of the relationship very difficult for one or both of the partners. One of the two people would tend to be critical or demanding of the other. However, suppose there was also a strong Venus connection between the same two people. In this case, there would be a great deal of love and caring between them that would help offset the harshness of the Saturn connection. The criticism or harshness of Saturn may still be there, but it will be tempered with the love and caring of Venus.

Because the two connections are so different, one might think that they cancel each other out. On the contrary, they are both experienced simultaneously by the partners. Each connection is a vital part of the relationship and its influence on the relationship can be readily experienced by the two people involved. It is just that the other, apparently opposite part, helps to mitigate its effect on the relationship by adding another facet to the relationship that the partners can choose to focus on. In our example, if I am both Saturn and Venus to someone, I may sense that it is my duty to point out their shortcomings to them. However, the Venus connection gives me the compassion to put that awareness into loving words or helps me to express my love for them at the same time that I am apparently criticizing them. If I did express some form of criticism, the chances are better that they would not take it so hard because the Venus reminds them that I love them and that I am not doing it just to be hateful. Also, my partner may choose to focus much of their attention on how much I love them instead of the occasional suggestions I may make for their improvement. This is an example of how some of the diverse connections interact with each other within the same relationship.

STEP THREE—THE PLANETARY RULING CARD READING

This step is optional in a way. Once you have completed Step Two, you have a pretty good idea of what this relationship is all about. You could stop there if you are satisfied with what you have learned. However, this next step will reveal some things you wouldn't want to miss. In many cases, some really important connections will come from the connections with the Planetary Ruling Cards. Doing the Planetary Ruling Card reading is more complicated than the Birth Card reading. It involves more cards and more connections to look up. However, if you have decided to be as complete as you can in this reading, you will be well rewarded for your efforts to learn this next part. Take your time as you learn it and pay attention to the example reading so that you understand how it works as much as possible.

Doing the Comparison between Planetary Ruling Cards

The Planetary Ruling Card Reading is done exactly like the Birth Card Reading except for two things. First, of course, we are using the Planetary Ruling Cards as well as the Birth Cards. Secondly, in each comparison we only look at the first two connections between them, instead of looking at all three to five connections that are listed for the Birth Cards. The reason we only use the first two connections is that the connections you see listed are not just for the Birth Cards involved but also for their Karma Cards. It would not be as accurate to use the Karma Cards for the Planetary Ruling Cards to do relationship readings. It is one step too far removed from the cards involved. Using just the first two connections decreases the chances that you are reading connections between Karma Cards or the Planetary Ruling Cards, instead of the Planetary Ruling Cards themselves. Just remember to use the first two connections when doing any comparison and you will retain a higher degree of accuracy.

I have created a Relationship Reading Worksheet to use when you do the Complete Relationship Reading that includes the Planetary Ruling Card. Copies are found on the following pages. I suggest that you use these to minimize the complications that may arise. You may wish to make many copies of these forms to use for the different readings you do. You will need one of these sheets filled out for each of the two people you are doing a reading for, since we do it from each person's point of view.

Because there are more cards to consider, this reading consists of six separate steps. If you are reading for a Scorpio person, it would be best here to choose one of their two Planetary Ruling Cards instead of doing them both. Doing both would require more steps in order to be complete.

The six steps to do a Planetary Ruling Card Reading are as follows:

1. Write in the Birth Card to Birth Card connections into the Reading Worksheet.

2. Look for Matches between the Planetary Ruling Cards and Birth Cards.

3. Find and read the first two connections between your Birth Card and your partner's Planetary Ruling Card.

4. Find and read the first two connections between your Planetary Ruling Card and your partner's Birth Card.

5. Find and read the first two connections between your Planetary Ruling Card and your partner's Planetary Ruling Card.

6. Synthesize it all together and combine what you have found with the Birth Card to Birth Card reading that you have already completed.

Step 1

For the first step, write in the 3-5 connections that you found between the Birth Cards in the first part of this chapter. The Relationship Reading Worksheet allows you to write in the abbreviation for each connection and the page number where the actual complete description of it is located. You can turn to the last page in the book to get those page numbers quickly, and then look them all up later once you have all the connections written in. I have included room for up to twelve total connections, which should be more than enough for most readings that you do.

Step 2

The second step is very important, especially in some cases. In many successful marriages, the Birth Card of one person is the same as the Planetary Ruling Card of the other. In other cases, both Planetary Ruling Cards are the same even though the Birth Cards are different. Both of these connections are important, but you must look for them on your own. If you find the first one, where one Birth Card matches the second's Planetary Ruling Card, read about it on page 324. It is called the Birth Card/Planetary Ruling Card match (MATCH). Then, if you find both Planetary Ruling Cards to be the same, read about it on page 325, the Same Planetary Ruling Card connection (SHARE).

Here's one more thing to consider about the Same Planetary Ruling Card connection. If two people are born on the very same day of the year, they will likely have the same Birth Card and Planetary Ruling Card. When this is the case, the SBC or Same Birth Card connection is really predominating over the Same Planetary Ruling Card connection. There is much more intensity in the SBC connection on account of its mirroring quality. This doesn't usually happen in the SHARE connection. When two people have the same birthday, I usually only read for the SBC connection and not both. There is a unique exception that you should also look for. It is possible to have the same Birth Cards and same Planetary Ruling Cards and not be born on the same day. Take, for instance, two people, one born on June 10th and the other on September 4th. Both of these people are 7♦ and both have the 5♠ as their Planetary Ruling Card. This is because one is a Gemini and the other is a Virgo, which are both ruled by Mercury. In these rare cases, read both the SBC and SHARE connection because they are different enough in light of the fact that they are different Sun signs.

Steps 2, 3, and 4 are best explained by doing an actual reading. Let's take an example to explain how this works. Follow this carefully and you will have no trouble doing these steps in the Planetary Ruling Card reading.

Example

Let's say that we are doing a reading for a woman who is born on May 30th and a man born on September 29th. We look them up and get the following information:

WHO	BIRTHDATE	BIRTH CARD	PLANETARY RULING CARD
MARILYN	MAY 30	2♣	K♣
JOSHUA	SEP 29	8♥	6♠

Taking it from Marilyn's point of view first, we will fill out the Relationship Reading Worksheet with the five connections between her 2♣ Birth Card and Joshua's 8♥ Birth Card. These are found on page 55. They are:

Con1	Con2	Con3	Con4	Con5
URF	NERS	PLFS	MOF	PLRS

We go ahead and write these into the Relationship Reading Worksheet, leaving us space for seven more connections if we need them (see completed worksheet on next page). Also we write in that these connections are between the Birth Cards (BC to BC if you prefer abbreviations).

Next, we make a quick check to see if these two have a Birth Card to Planetary Ruling Card Match (MATCH) or if they have the same Planetary Ruling Card (SHARE). We see that they do not, and we move to the next step. If they did have one of these connections, we would have written it in on the worksheet at Connection Number 6.

The next step involves taking Marilyn's Planetary Ruling Card and comparing it to Joshua's Birth Card. We turn to the page that has the Relationship connections for the K♣ card, her Planetary Ruling Card, and look up the first connection listed under the 8♥, his Birth Card. The first one listed is 'SAF,' which stands for 'They are Saturn to You in the Life Spread.' The second connection, just after that one is 'VER,' which is a reversed Venus Connection in the Life Spread. We would look up the meanings of these two connections to see how they fit into the dynamics of the relationship. Notice here that we do not read any of the other connections listed. For the reasons mentioned earlier, only the first two connections apply in this Planetary Ruling Card Reading.

For the next step we just reverse the previous step, taking Marilyn's Birth Card, the 2♣ and comparing it to the Joshua's Planetary Ruling Card, the 6♠. Turning to the Relationship Connections for the 2♣ (page 55), we locate the first connection between the 2♣ and the 6♠. We notice that it is called 'PLF.' Looking up this connection we see that it means 'They are Pluto to You in the Life Spread.' We read that meaning and proceed to the next connection, which is 'NEF'. This connection says 'They are Neptune to you in the Life Spread.' We would then go to the pages where the interpretations for these two connections are found. Once you have read these two interpretations you are ready to proceed to the next step.

To complete the fourth step, we look on the same K♣ page, her Planetary Ruling Card, for the first connection with the 6♠, his Planetary Ruling Card. There we notice that the first connection is listed as 'NEF'. We then look up the meaning of the 'NEF' connection and discover that it means 'They are Neptune to You in the Life Spread.' Again, the next connection is a 'PLR' which means 'You are Pluto to them in the Life Spread.' We read the meaning of that and we are now ready to complete with this reading by synthesizing it all together.

THE COMPLETE RELATIONSHIP WORKSHEET

From Person One's Point of View

Person One's Name: **Marilyn**   Card: **2♣**   Person Two's Name: **Joshua**   Card: **8♥**

Birthday: **5/30**   Planetary Ruling Card: **K♣**   Birthday: **9/29**   Planetary Ruling Card: **6♠**

#	Abbrev.	Page#	Using Which Cards	Notes:
1	URF	300	BC to BC	Joshua is Uranus to Marilyn Life Spread
2	NERS	307	BC to BC	Marilyn is Neptune to Joshua Spiritual Spread
3	PLFS	310	BC to BC	Joshua is Pluto to Marilyn Spiritual Spread
4	MOF	277	BC to BC	Joshua is the moon Card to Marilyn Life spread
5	PLRS	31	BC to BC	Marilyn is Pluto to Joshua Spiritual Spread
6	SAF	296	Marilyn's PR to Joshua's BC	Joshua is Saturn to Marilyn Life Spread
7	VER	282	(K♣ to 8♥)	Marilyn is Venus to Joshua Life Spread
8	PLF	309	Marilyn's BC to Joshua's PR	Joshua is Pluto to Marilyn Life Spread
9	NEF	306	(2♣ to 6♠)	Joshua is Neptune to Marilyn Life spread
10	NEF	306	Marilyn's PR to Joshua's PR	Joshua is Neptune to Marilyn Life Spread
11	PLR	30	(K♣ to 6♠)	Marilyn is Pluto to Joshua Life spread
12				

Relationship Index Worksheet

Which Cards being compared?	Attraction	Intensity	Compatibility
Birth Card (BC) to BC	4	2	0
One's BC to Two's Planetary Ruling Card (PR)	3	6	-4
One's PR to Two's BC	1	2	1
One's PR to Two's PR	5	3	2
Total	13	13	1
Average (Total divided by 4)	3.25	3.25	.25

THE COMPLETE RELATIONSHIP WORKSHEET

From Person One's Point of View

Person One's Name: _____ Card:_____ Person Two's Name: _____ Card:_____

Birthday: _____ Planetary Ruling Card: _____ Birthday:_____ Planetary Ruling _____

#	Abbrev.	Page#	Using Which Cards	Notes:
1				
2				
3				
4				
5				
6				
7				
8				
9				
10				
11				
12				

Relationship Index Worksheet

Which Cards being compared?	Attraction	Intensity	Compatibility
Birth Card (BC) to BC			
One's BC to Two's Planetary Ruling Card (PR)			
One's PR to Two's BC			
One's PR to Two's PR			
Total			
Average (Total divided by 4)			

To begin our synthesis, let's write in the Relationship Index Values from each of the comparisons we have done. We first take the BC to BC Indexes on the page with Marilyn's Birth Card (page 55). We get the Indexes for the 2♣ compared to the 8♥ and write them in on the worksheet where it says Birth Card (BC) to BC. They are: Attraction: 4, Intensity: 2, Compatibility: 0. Since we are already on the correct page, we can get the values for Marilyn's Birth Card (2♣) with Joshua's Planetary Ruling Card (6♠) and write them in on the worksheet where it says One's BC to Two's Planetary Ruling Card (PR). They are: Attraction: 3, Intensity: 6, Compatibility: -4.

Now turn to Marilyn's Planetary Ruling Card (K♣) page and get the Index Values for the K♣ compared with the 8♥. This is found on page 253 and the values are: Attraction: 1, Intensity: 2, Compatibility: 1. Finally, on the same page get the values for the K♣ and the 6♠, Joshua's PR Card. They are: Attraction: 5, Intensity: 3, Compatibility: 2.

Now we can add together the Index values from all four comparisons, getting a total of: Attraction: 13, Intensity: 13, Compatibility: -1. When we then divide these by four to get the average, we get: Attraction: 3.25, Intensity: 3.25, Compatibility: -.25. I recommend rounding these off to 3, 3, and 0, giving us a pretty good indication of this relationship using both the Birth Cards and the Planetary Ruling Cards of Marilyn and Joshua.

This concludes how we look them all up and write them down. Though not shown here, you can also do the connections from Joshua's point of view based upon what we have just done. Now let's take a closer look at this fictitious relationship to see what we can learn about it from the connections we have looked up.

Synthesizing Our Example Reading

First, we look at these two people's Birth Cards and see that Marilyn is the more marriageable of the two. Joshua's 8♥ Birth Card is known to play the field a lot. Once an 8♥ realizes the charm and magnetism they have with the opposite sex, they usually choose to use this to create a series of love affairs rather than waste it all on one person. This is more true of the men than the women. Then again the 6♠ Planetary Ruling Card can also have some intimacy problems, mostly due to the

3♥ in Saturn in the 6♠ Life Path. This creates a hidden fear of not getting enough love . So, I would say that as soon as this relationship gets beyond the honeymoon stage, which could last anywhere from 3 weeks to a year, that Joshua will be the one who leaves. The 6♠ is a card that usually refuses to work on emotional problems. Marilyn's cards, though not perfect, show much more marriage potential. But if she attracted someone who is as unmarriageable as Joshua, she is probably not ready for a long–term committed relationship either. So, just from their birthdays, we would predict a relationship with a short life span.

Next, we get into the reading by looking at the Indexes. In the case of our fictitious clients, Marilyn and Joshua, we have a lot of Attraction and Intensity, and slightly below average Compatibility. Just this alone indicates that this is probably a relationship that will be used by both partners mostly for spiritual growth. We might call this a 'working relationship,' in that both partners will have to put forth some effort to make it work. The high Intensity level shows that there is a lot for each partner to work on. Scanning down the list of connections, we see that there are four Pluto connections. This is probably where most of the high Intensity comes from. And if we look carefully, we see that these Pluto connections are evenly distributed—two are aimed at Marilyn (where Joshua is her Pluto Card) and two at Joshua. So, these two would share equal responsibility for having to undergo some personal transformation over the course of this relationship. So much Pluto energy could get these two into some real battles at times. Pluto often threatens our security as nothing else can. But before we draw any important conclusions, let's see what else these two are dealing with in the context of this relationship.

The next connection that stands out as being predominant is Neptune—we have three Neptune connections listed. And again these are somewhat equally distributed. Even though Marilyn receives two Neptune connections from Joshua, they are much farther down the list and probably combine together to equal the one in which she is Neptune to him. Neptune is all about hopes and dreams, and when we are with someone with whom we have strong Neptune connections, we feel a sense of destiny and timelessness about the love we have for them. These two probably feel psychically connected and probably imagine that this relationship is matching up with many of their dreams and hopes for true love. However, all of the Pluto connections suggest that many of these dreams will be tested and that some of them are bound to be destroyed in the process of transformation which is so strongly indicated between them. Pluto tells us that there will be a lot of change happening with each partner but doesn't tell us what this change will be about. The proliferation of Neptune connections suggests that some of this change will be about the validity of their love fantasies, which they stimulate in each other.

We have one Moon connection and one Venus connection. These connections are the best indicators of Compatibility, but two is not a lot. However, this does tells us that there are some good feelings between them (Venus) and the potential for intimacy (Moon). When we look at this Moon connection, we see that Joshua is Marilyn's Moon Card. This means that to achieve the potential of a deep intimacy and love bond, which is indicated by the Moon connection, Joshua will have to play the supportive role and allow Marilyn to be the real leader of this relationship. This may or may not work, especially when we see that Joshua is also Marilyn's Saturn Card. This tells us that he will also have some criticism to share with her, that he is her teacher in some way. Whether or not he would feel comfortable letting her lead the relationship, especially when he sees her faults so easily, would be a real determining factor in how well these two will be able to access the closeness that comes from this Moon connection.

The only connection we haven't mentioned is the first connection we found, the Uranus connection. Uranus connections may or may not be the deciding factor in a relationship. If there had been two or more Uranus connections, I would have thought this could be an issue that these two are working on. But since there is only one, this probably just means that both Marilyn and

Joshua appreciate a relationship that allows each of them some freedom. They would be friends first and lovers second, or this relationship would never materialize.

STEP FOUR—THE PERSONALITY CARD READING

The Planetary Ruling Card Reading is an essential step if we are doing as complete a Relationship Reading as possible, unless one or both of the people you are reading for are Leos. Leos, as you may recall from Chapter One, have no separate Planetary Ruling Card to read for. This last reading, the Personality Card Reading, is one you will use only at certain times. Every so often, you will come upon someone who is operating as one of their Planetary Ruling Cards more or less exclusively. Or, the person you are reading for is a Leo and you don't have as many connections as you would like for the reading. In either of these cases, make sure to check the connections for the Personality Cards as part of the reading.

What we basically want to do with this reading is find out how their Personality Cards affect each other. After having completed the previous kinds of readings, you probably have a good idea how to do this reading. To be sure, let's look at it step-by-step. As in the case of the Planetary Ruling Card readings, we will only be using the first two connections found between the two cards. All we want is the basic and foremost connections. That will be enough to give us a good idea of the connections.

When you want more connections to fill out the picture of someone's relationship, I suggest using the Jack for men and the Queen for women. These Personality Cards are the ones we use the most when we are romantically involved. So, for the purposes of learning this technique, we will use a set of example people, one male and one female, and use their Jack and Queen respectively. Let's use the birthdays below and take a look at how we would do this:

WHO	BIRTHDATE	BIRTH CARD	PR CARD	SEX	PERSONALITY CARD
Suzanne	7/30	J♥	none	F	Q♥
Harold	9/16	8♣	6♦	M	J♣

First of all, when using the Personality Cards, we don't have to use them for both people. We could just as easily use only the Personality Card of one of the people. You can decide if you want to use the Personality Cards

for one or both. With this couple we will first use a Personality Card for Suzanne, since she has no Planetary Ruling Card. If you look at the worksheet on the next page, you will see that by doing the Birth Card and

Planetary Ruling Card readings, we were able to obtain seven connections. That may be enough for some people, but let's try for ten or eleven. That would be closer to the number we get with most readings. If we take Suzanne's Queen (Q♥) and compare it with Harold's Birth Card and Planetary Ruling Card (8♣ and 6♦), that will give us four new connections, for a total of eleven. That will be enough for this reading.

So, here are the steps we will use to get all of the connections using Suzanne's Personality Card with Harold's Birth Card and Planetary Ruling Card.

1. Take the first two connections between Suzanne's Personality Card (Q♥) and Harold's Birth Card (8♣).

2. Take the first two connections between Suzanne's Personality Card (Q♥) and Harold's Planetary Ruling Card (6♦).

The connections for both of these steps are found on the connections page for the Q♥, page 231. And as you can see on the worksheet, I have filled in the extra connections by comparing the Q♥ with both the 8♣ and the 6♦. Remember to only use the first two connections listed.

At the bottom of the worksheet, I have summed up the Indexes as well, using the separate Indexes from each comparison we used. This worksheet is the relationship from Suzanne's point of view only, but it illustrates how you would add Personality Cards to any reading you are doing.

Using More Than One Personality Card

If we were using one Personality Card for each person, the process would become much longer. But remember that you only need ten or eleven connections. Once you have that many, you can stop the process. Here are some of the permutations that you should consider if using two Personality Cards (one for each person for whom you are reading):

1. Person One's Personality Card with Person Two's Birth Card (as above).

2. Person One's Personality Card with Person Two's Planetary Ruling Card (also, as above).

3. Person Two's Personality Card with Person One's Birth Card.

4. Person Two's Personality Card with Person One's Planetary Ruling Card.

5. Person One's Personality Card with Person Two's Personality Card.

THE COMPLETE RELATIONSHIP WORKSHEET

From Person One's Point of View

Person One's Name: __Suzanne__ Card: __J♥__ Person Two's Name: __Harold__ Card: __8♣__

Birthday: __7/30__ Planetary Ruling Card: __NONE__ Birthday: __4/16__ Planetary Ruling Card: __6♦__

#	Abbrev.	Page#	Using Which Cards	Notes:
1	KRMA	321	BC to BC	They are Karma Cards
2	POWR	323	BC to BC	They nave a Power Connection
3	CLF	316	BC to BC	Harold is Suzanne's Cosmic Lesson Card in the Life Spread
4	CLFS	316	BC to BC	Harold is Suzanne's Cosmic Lesson Card in the Spiritual Spread
5	PLF	309	BC to BC	Harold is Suzanne's Pluto Card in the Life Spread
6	MARS	287	Suzanne's BC to Harold's PR	Suzanne is Harold's Mars Card in the Spiritual Spread
7	MOFS	278	Suzanne's BC to Harold's PR	Harold is Suzanne's Moon Card in the Spiritual Spread
8	JUF	290	Suzanne's Personality Card to Harold's BC	Harold is Suzanne's Jupiter Card in the Life Spread
9	CRFS	314	Suzanne's Personality Card to Harold's BC	Harold is the Cosmic Reward to Suzanne in the Spiritual Spread
10	CLFS	316	Suzanne's Personality Card to Harold's PR	Harold is the Cosmic Lesson to Suzanne in the Spiritual Spread
11	MAM	288	Suzanne's Personality Card to Harold's PR	Mutual Mars in the Life Spread
12				

Relationship Index Worksheet

Which Cards being compared?	Attraction	Intensity	Compatibility
Birth Card (BC) to BC	6	8	2
One's BC to Two's Planetary Ruling Card (PR)	7	3	4
One's PR to Two's BC	6	1	5
One's PR to Two's PR	6	7	2
Total	25	19	5
Average (Total divided by 4)	6.25	4.75	1.25

PC

Chapter Three
The Descriptions of the Birth Cards and the Relationship Connections between Them

In this chapter, you will find a separate description for each of the 52 card personalities and the Joker (who is all cards and no card at once). This is where you will discover each of traits that make up each of the individual Birth Card personalities. This is also where you can look up the relationship connections between any card and all the other cards in the deck.

The Birth Card descriptions are all taken from the card's position in the Life and Spiritual Spreads, as well as from the Life Path Cards. The Life Path Cards are listed for each of the cards and these will give you some basis for a more in-depth study of card science. If you want to learn more about the Life Path Cards, read the section in Chapter Seven called *The Life Spread, Spiritual Spread & Our Life Path Cards*. There is some information that you can delve into once you know the relative significance of each of them.

Each Birth Card has a name or phrase that is used to make a quick identification of its common character traits. Some of these names are flattering and others are not. I have endeavored to use the more positive names for the cards while at the same time bringing out some of the more challenging natures of the cards in the descriptions. Some cards commonly have very difficult lives, as illustrated by the cards in their Life Path. But they also have a good side that can be accessed by its possessor. Even in the case of the most difficult of Life Paths, one always has the opportunity to turn it around and make it a shining success. Therefore, these descriptions present both the positive and negative sides of each of the cards, and have left it up to you to decide how the individual is accessing those potentials.

YOUR KARMA CARDS

The pages for each Birth Card list the Karma Cards for that person. In every case except for the Fixed and Semi-Fixed Cards (see Chapter One), the first Karma Card listed represents the person you owe something to and the second is the person who owes you something. Also, the first Karma Card is the one that represents past-life characteristics that you will be improving upon in this lifetime, while the second represents past-life gifts that you have. Read all about the Karma Card connection in Chapter Five to find out more about your relationships with Karma Card people.

YOUR KARMA COUSINS

Our Karma Cousins represent people with whom we share a common Karma Card. For example, if you are the 9♣, one of your Karma Cousins is the 10♠ because both of you have the Q♥ as a Karma Card. In Karma Cousin relationships, there is an exchange of energy (see the detailed description of the Karma Cousin connection in Chapter Five) but they are not your mirror as in Karma Card relationships. As in the Karma Cards, the first one listed is the one you are sending energy toward and the second is the one is giving something to you. It is nice to know who these people are so that when you meet them you know which way the basic energy of your relationship is flowing. The Fixed and Semi-Fixed Cards have no Karma Cousins.

YOUR PAST-LIFE CARDS

In truth, there are many cards with which each of us have past-life connections. Anyone with whom we have Spiritual Spread connections could technically be called a past-life card. However, the Past-Life Cards listed on your Birth Card page are some of the strongest ones. You will probably feel an immediate connection with anyone born under one of these Birth Cards. These people are also those with whom you have better than average compatibility and with whom you could probably forge a wonderful relationship, friendship, or marriage.

AN EXAMPLE WHERE A PERSONALITY CARD READING PROVED INSIGHTFUL

One of my students is an 8♥ who is married to a 7♣. She often complains about how she wishes he would grow up. He is always the life of the party, telling jokes, drinking a little too much, and entertaining others. He was operating almost exclusively out of his J♣ Personality Card and I wondered why this was so. When I studied their connections I noticed that the 8♥ is Saturn to his Personality Card, the K♣, which means that she would tend to be critical of him when he acts Kingly or mature. I also noticed that the Q♥, her Personality Card, is Pluto to his K♣ Personality Card. From these two difficult connections to his King, I could tell that whenever he chose to operate as the K♣, she would become very repressive and difficult for him. Unconsciously, he got the message and decided to operate almost exclusively as the J♣, which has a nice Venus connection to her 8♥. I asked her how she felt about giving him the responsibility and leadership of the family and relationship, thereby letting him be the King. She said that would make her very uncomfortable. She didn't trust his leadership or direction. This, in a nutshell, described their relationship and accounted for his almost peculiar behavior patterns. Because he did not receive any positive response or encouragement to be the head of the household (the King), he continually played out the Jack role, where he received her affections (Venus). Once she became aware of this in our conversation, she realized that she could change this by consciously giving him her trust and encouragement to help him become more responsible and to take a stronger leadership role in the marriage.

TIPS AND HINTS, QUESTIONS AND ANSWERS

Hint: Always check out the marriageability of the people for whom you are reading.

Chapter Seven has a section called *The Marriageability Factor*. Here you will find all of the cards in the deck ranked according to how, on average, they relate to commitment, along with the most likely reasons they have trouble with commitments. As you study any particular couple, it would be good to refer to this section to get an idea of who you are dealing with. If you have two people, for example, who both rank 5 or more on the unmarriageability factor, it would be safe to say that neither of these two are really looking for any serious kind of commitment or marriage. They may even tell you that they are, but usually the cards tell you the real story. Read the entire section on marriageability and you will fully understand how that dynamic works. After you understand it, you will be able to tell over 90% of the time if the people involved are just playing around or if they are truly interested in finding someone and settling down.

Hint: Look for multiple occurrences of the same kind of connection for themes in the relationship.

As illustrated in the sample reading in Chapter Two, when you see two, three or more of the same kind of connection, i.e., Mars, you know you have an important theme in that relationship. Once you see a lot of some connection, read the section entitled *What the Connections with Others Tell Us About Ourselves* in Chapter Seven to discover more about that theme and what it means to you and your partner. A dominant theme in a relationship will often reveal the underlying reasons why we are in that particular relationship. The importance of this cannot be stressed enough. In my work of doing readings, I endeavor to show people the real reasons for their actions so that they can make a choice to do something differently if they like. Until we understand why we make certain choices, we cannot just try to choose something else. I study people's existing and past relationships carefully because, by studying the dominant themes, they tell me just what they learned in those relationships and often what they were really seeking for themselves. This information is priceless.

Hint: Look at everyone's partner as a reflection of themselves.

This hint will give you so much information that you will become a master at reading people. Just ignore what they tell you about their life and look at how they feel and think about their partner. Bingo! You have an exact description of how they feel about themselves and how they see themselves. For example, if you hear someone say, 'My partner is just so afraid all the time. I can't stand putting up with his (or her) fear all day long.' Then you know that this person is very fearful themselves and that they don't like being reminded of this by their partner. This same person may appear to be fearless and very capable. They may tell you they are thinking of leaving a relationship because they feel that their partner is not on the same level. But in truth this person is very afraid and chose someone to reflect this to them to see if they could learn to love this part of themself. If they leave this relationship, they will attract another partner just like that one. Use this tool in your readings and it will reveal many important things to you.

Hint: How to tell if a relationship or marriage will last:

If the two people you are studying are very compatible, that is a good sign for a long–term relationship. But you must also check out their marriageability. If either one of the partners is unmarriageable, then you need to ask yourself, 'Is this person aware of their personal problems and making a sincere and determined effort to heal themself.' Most of the unmarriageables are that way because of emotional/intimacy problems of one kind or another. Very few of them truly choose a life without intimacy. So, most of those unmarriageables have problems that could be addressed and healed. If they do this, they can become marriageable. But don't be fooled. It takes a sincere and determined effort to heal ourselves of these kinds of problems. Few people are interested enough to make this effort. But some will. And if you find such a person in a relationship with someone who is more marriageable, and if the compatibility is good between them, you can predict long–term success and happiness.

Question: What if one person's Personality Card is the same as the other person's Birth Card?

Answer: This is an interesting situation that occurs when one person's Birth Card is a Jack, Queen or King—the same as the other person's Personality Card. The best answer is that the person who has the royal Birth Card will have an innate understanding of that aspect of the other person's personality. A Q♦ Birth Card, for example, feels a kinship with all Diamond females, a sort of understanding of life from their point of view. Does that help them get along with these women better? It can, but that really depends upon how much the Q♦ likes themself and the connections they share with each individual card.

Question: Which suits get along the best?

Answer: To be accurate, one should always look at the individual cards to assess this. But if I had to come up with a quick answer to this question, I would say that Clubs and Diamonds share the overall best compatibility as do Hearts and Spades. This can be observed by looking at the connections between the Personality Cards of the pairs of suits (J♣ with Q♦, J♠ with Q♥, etc). But never use this rule to make a positive determination. There are many Club cards that have particular difficulty with certain Diamond cards and the same applies to Hearts and Spades.

Question: What are the best connections for marriage?

Answer: The one connection found most among successfully married couples is the Moon connection. Venus is also a great blessing in relationships, but it seems to be the Moon connection that makes people feel as though they could bond in a more significant way. It doesn't always guarantee a successful marriage, but it does seem to compel us to at least make the attempt. When we look at the Moon connection, we see the Sun and Moon together, the essential archetypes for male and female, Adam and Eve and so forth. It is the strongest marriage connection that exists. There is an section about this in Chapter Seven if you want to learn more about it.

Question: Why am I attracted to people with whom I have such low compatibility?

Answer: Many of us will go through a phase of life where we learn a lot of lessons through the vehicle of challenging relationships. Saturn connections in particular can be quite difficult to deal with. If you find that you are attracted to these challenging relationships, you have to assume that there is something important for you to learn from them. What we are attracted to is exactly what we need in a spiritual sense, to get to the next point in our life. Our attractions may not make any sense from a practical point of view, but they are accurate reflections of our own process of self-understanding. Whether we are attracted to Saturn, Mars or whatever, it reveals something important about what we want to learn about ourselves.

The bottom line is that we will attract the same person that reflects how compatible we are with ourselves.

This is a golden rule. Our relationships are indeed a reflection of how we are inside and how we feel about ourselves. The very minute we begin to love ourselves more, we attract a more loving partner.

Question: What is a quick way to get an idea of how two people get along?

Answer: Just look at the Indexes on their Birth Card page. Take the first person, turn to the page that has the connections list for their Birth Card and look at the Index values for their Birth Card compared to the other person's Birth Card and Planetary Ruling Card. By just scanning down the list, you can tell, at a glance, how that person gets along with the other cards in the deck.

Question: Would it be okay to use more than eleven connections? I can see that my partner and I have a lot more than that.

Answer: You can do more if you like, but you will find it a bit redundant. As you get beyond the eleventh connection, the importance of the connections you find is fairly insignificant. The only exception to this would be when you find a Moon connection further down the list. Moon connections are very significant for relationships and if you see one beyond the seventh, it still could have an impact on the relationship. It would be a good idea, if you and your partner do not have any Moon connections within the first seven, to see if there are any Moon connections at all. If there are, I would include them in the reading because of their importance.

Question: What do you consider to be the ideal Index values for marriage?

Answer: In my studies, high Attraction, low Intensity, and high Compatibility are the ideal combination for marriage. Values such as a 5, 2, 6 would be good, or a 7, 1, 4. Again this is no guarantee but the high Attraction gives you the 'glue' that holds the partnership together. Without some attraction, you may find no reasons for being together. Low Intensity is good so that the relationship has some peace to it. High Intensity relationships always seem to be in turmoil, like a continual conflict. High compatibility means that the two of you have a lot in common. Common ground is the foundation of successful relationships. Anything above 1 on the Compatibility scale is enough for marriage.

The Aces

"In the beginning was the Word, and the Word was with God, and the Word was God."

In these words, from the beginning of the Book of John, we get the very essence of the Aces. Above all else, the Ace represents the most primary of the masculine, creative principal, the Word that calls forth things into being. In Genesis, we see God creating the heavens and the Earth, all by simply saying it was so ('and God said…and lo and behold…came into being'). The world we know is made up of a huge matrix of masculine and feminine energies, interacting and evolving and yet always staying in balance. All masculine energy is a part of God's creative force whereas feminine energy is the fertile, receptive force of God. We might say that all of our creating ultimately comes from the mind of God, and those of us who are creative are vessels for His ideas. Who else puts all these ideas into our minds? All Aces, regardless of their sex, will have a somewhat masculine nature, either physically or just as part of their personality, and will reflect this masculine, creative principle in their lives.

Aces know very well about creating and manifesting. Their lives are a constant chain of one creation after another. They exemplify the creative force and are conduits of many new ideas and projects. One might say that they are constantly receiving input from some higher force to go forth and create something new. They love new beginnings and they love to see their ideas come into materialization. Seeing, hearing, tasting, or touching something they have created brings them great pleasure. It is part of their birthright to bring many things into being which were not there before. This brings them the greatest satisfaction and the greatest challenge.

Aces are not usually known for their patience. With so much to accomplish in this lifetime and so little time to do it, they hardly have any time to waste standing in line or waiting for others to finish their sentences. They are bubbling over with the desire to make something happen. It is not in their nature to wait for something to happen. They often dislike waiting in lines, either of people or in traffic. If they seem a little short with you, it is because they have something important that they want to get done, not that they don't like you.

However, they can also be charming and caring. Three of the Aces, the A♦, A♣, and A♠, each have a Two as one of their Karma Cards. This hidden influence brings a certain amount of caring and consideration for others, mostly because, on some level, they need the presence of other people in order to feel complete. It is a paradox that the cards that often feel the need to be by themselves also have a great longing for the perfect mate or companion. They also excel at communications for the most part. Their lives are often an endless flow of phone calls, emails, and letters. They are surrounded by people most of the time. Don't be fooled by this appearance, however. Aces are individuals above all else. They need time to themselves to explore who they are on a basic level. Being an Ace means being self-absorbed to a certain degree and many of them can be categorized as loners. It is an Aries energy. Aries is the first sign in the zodiac and people of this sign are known to be self-engrossed. In spite of the Two influence, nothing means anything in their life if it is not contributing something to them in a tangible way. If their relationship with you has outlived its ability to give them something they want or need, you may be history.

The A♥ personifies the 'Search for Self' in more ways than the other Aces, though they all have undertaken this search in one way or another. Their suit tells us in which basic area of life they emphasize this search. A♥ people search for themselves in their relationships. This includes not only lovers and mates, but family and friends as well. The A♣ searches for his or her own meaning through the books they read and things they learn in other ways. Like the A♥, they too seek the perfect love relationship that will fulfill their deep yearnings for completion. The A♦ finds conflict between their driving ambition and the desire for companionship and marriage. They cannot seem to have both at the same time. Like all Diamonds, they tend to value themselves based upon what they have or how successful they are financially. They seek to acquire or attain something that is so valuable that it will make them the valuable person that they want to be. The A♠ person usually has difficulties in love that make finding happiness seem impossible. They often abandon the idea completely and let all of their passion express itself in their work and careers. Perfection in their work, either through quality or quantity, is their means of finding the love for themselves that they seek. They are considered one of the most ambitious cards in the entire deck.

In all cases, the hidden motive for the Aces is self-acceptance. However, since there is so much masculine energy being expressed as action and accomplishment, they seek to find themselves in the reflection of their accomplishments instead of just stopping and looking within. Hopefully they will love what they have created and complete the circle, discovering that what they were looking for is already within them. They are the prodigal sons and daughters seeking to come home.

The Desire for Love Card

THE DESCRIPTION OF THE A♥ PERSON:

The meaning of the A♥, the first card in the deck, is the 'desire for love.' However, the desire for money is also present because of the A♦ Karma Card. Being the first card in the deck, one may assume that like Aries, the first sign in the zodiac, these are young souls, apt to make a lot of mistakes and prone to selfishness. This is the case with some of them, but is by no means the majority. Many have great success in their life as writers or in other creative occupations. They have a double-ace influence which can make them impulsive. This is actually a symbol of courage, which is one of their primary traits. What is often missing is the wisdom that combines with this courage to direct their actions toward a successful outcome. The successful ones practice patience and learn to look before they leap.

People with this birth card have strong spiritual inclinations, but they are often 'tempted' off the path by indecision and hidden desires. In particular, the fear of not having enough money needs to be dealt with so that they can have more success and peace of mind. The A♦ Karma Card indicates the need to develop a sense of gratitude and prosperity. But with this same A♦ being their Mercury Card in their Life Path, the acquisition of money or things will be a prominent theme in life just the same. These people are achievers and often have great financial success.

They need to be careful to not let themselves get stretched too far or in too

many directions, which could cause great stress and physical problems. The 3♥ Karma Card along with the two Threes in their Life Path give them tremendous creative potential. But every gift can be a liability at times and the downside of the Three is indecision, worry, and stress. Quiet time away from their work is a healing remedy. These same Threes create the need for variety in work and A♥ are better off structuring their life and work so that they have some flexibility available at all times. All are Capricorns, so their work is important, as is the recognition it brings. The 3♠ Planetary Ruling Card tells us that many of them will have a reputation as an artist or creative person. Much difficulty in later life, both emotionally and mentally, can be avoided if they turn their interests toward metaphysics and self-understanding. If they do focus their attention on finding spiritual meaning, their last years will be the most satisfying of their entire life.

They are often restless souls whose changing values will be one of the greatest crosses they bear. They should avoid a tendency toward fickleness and promiscuity if they are ever to find the peace of mind and heart they seek. Finding an outlet for selfless giving brings them the highest rewards.

SOME OF THE A♥ ISSUES CONCERNING RELATIONSHIPS:

The A♥ is embarking on a new adventure and seeking out love experiences at every turn. They are sometimes emotionally restless and can have changing values that cause consequential changes in their romantic lives. They usually enjoy the company of 'women of means' and are generally well-liked by all. If one is considering a relationship with an A♥, it would be wise to realize that unless the A♥ is aware of their tendency toward indecision and restlessness in love, it is

---

KARMA CARDS:

A♦   3♥

KARMA COUSINS:

2♦   Q♣

PAST-LIFE CARDS:

K♠   2♥

likely that they will not be around for long. A♥ can also be very selfish and concerned only with their own needs. Fears about not having enough money and 'things' can interfere with their love life. To be happy, an A♥ would probably need a relationship that had some variety of shared experiences, good communications, and opportunities to travel. These would help satisfy all of the creative and restless urges that are part of the A♥ pattern.

A♥ males get along well with all Diamond females. The A♥ females get along well with Club males in general, and Spade males find them enchanting and hard to resist.

PROFILE

The Ace of Hearts and the Search of Self

The A♥ card is the first card in the deck, if we count from the Natural or Spiritual Spread. More than any other card, it represents the coming out into the world of our soul and personality. As a one, it is a masculine and creative force. It represents the first stepping out from the unmanifested potential of the 0 (zero). As such it represents the word (one) of God being made manifest, sort of like an instruction to go forth and create something.

As in all the odd numbered cards, those who are the Ace of Hearts are never truly at rest. They are always seeking, inventing or creating something new. However, the A♥ is more concerned with a discovery of their self-identity than anything else. The A♥ is somewhat synonymous with the first house of the zodiac which is ruled by Aries. A♥ people can be very self-centered and in many cases, selfish. There is only one birth date that corresponds to the A♥ and that is December 30th. Sitting so close to the Joker and the K♠ makes these people somewhat independent and materialistic. But these are the children of the deck and their actions are more attributed to their quest for self-identity than to the accumulation of possessions or power. Though on the outside they may appear to be very ambitious and materialistic, the cards tell us that inwardly this is just their way of searching for who they are.

Since the A♥ can be defined as 'the desire for affection,' we find that many A♥ people have an inner conflict between their need to love themselves and their need to be acknowledged by others. Because of their 3♥ Karma Card, they could be worried about not getting enough affection from others. This same card could also account for a promiscuous nature or a certain amount of restlessness in their love life. They tend to have a somewhat intellectual approach to love—many concepts and ideas that need real experience to validate. They will try on certain beliefs about love and see if they work and then try something else, evaluating, comparing and trying to figure it all out with their mind. They will spend this life gaining experience and usually through trial and error they will gradually come into the wisdom about love that they seek. When it is all said and done, their wisdom tells them that the answers to their questions and problems lie within themselves—their feelings and beliefs. On the highest level, the A♥ means 'love of the self.' If we first can love ourselves, we can then find love everywhere we go. For the A♥ it often takes a long time for them to turn their attention within, but ultimately this is where they find what they are looking for.

We must remember that Aces are always loners to some extent. They need time to be alone and ask the question, 'What will make me happy?' It is love of self that brings the truest satisfaction, but how can love of self and love of another coexist in a human relationship? Who comes first, our partner or ourself? First of all we can realize that the love we feel for another person and the wonderful qualities that we see in them are actually within our self. They may have been the catalyst that helped us to see those parts of ourselves, but in truth these qualities and feelings belong to us alone. This is an important part of the A♥ lesson. In truth, our partner may or may not share the wonderful feelings or qualities that we are experiencing. Our feelings are just that, our feelings. When we come to that realization, we begin to see that all of our relationships are just mirrors of ourselves. We can transfer love we feel back to ourselves and really see just how special we are. Then we can love our partners without being afraid that they will run away and take all this love we feel with them.

LIFE SPREAD CARDS

PLANETARY CARD	SYMBOL	CARD
MOON	☽	8♠
SUN (BIRTH CARD)	✳	A♥
MERCURY	☿	A♦
VENUS	♀	Q♦
MARS	♂	5♥
JUPITER	♃	3♣
SATURN	♄	3♠
URANUS	♅	9♥
NEPTUNE	♆	7♣
PLUTO	⯗	5♦
RESULT (COSMIC REWARD)	♃+	Q♠
COSMIC LESSON	♄+	J♣

PLANETARY RULING CARDS

BIRTH DATE	ASTROLOGICAL RULING SIGN	PLANETARY RULING CARD
DEC 30	CAPRICORN	3♠

Who A♥ with	The Connections Between Partners					Overall Index Ratings		
	Con1	Con2	Con3	Con4	Con5	Attraction	Intensity	Compatibility
A♥	SBC	MOR	VEFS	MOF	VERS	7	0	5
2♥	MORS	JUMS	VEF	MOFS	PLF	6	-3	7
3♥	KRMA	VEFS	NEF	NEFS	MAM	7	3	3
4♥	MAFS	JUR	CLRS	URRS	JURS	3	2	3
5♥	MAF	JUFS	VEF	VEFS	MAFS	6	1	5
6♥	CLR	SAFS	CRR	VEMS	MAF	2	4	-1
7♥	URFS	NEFS	PLRS	NEF	PLR	4	2	2
8♥	NEFS	PLRS	NERS	VEM	URFS	6	2	3
9♥	URF	PLFS	JUMS	SAF	URFS	2	3	-2
10♥	MAR	CRFS	CLF	CRRS	JUR	6	6	0
J♥	CLFS	VEM	MOFS	URR	VEMS	6	0	4
Q♥	JURS	URMS	MARS	MAR	JUR	3	2	4
K♥	VERS	VEF	SARS	VEFS	VER	5	-1	1
A♣	MORS	JUMS	MOR	VEF	PLF	6	-3	6
2♣	VERS	VEM	VEMS	MAF	URF	7	-2	3
3♣	JUF	PLF	MAF	NEF	PLR	6	4	2
4♣	CRR	VEMS	CLR	SAFS	CLRS	3	2	1
5♣	MAF	JUFS	CRR	VEMS	CRRS	6	2	3
6♣	MOF	URRS	PLR	PLRS	URR	4	0	2
7♣	NEF	PLR	NER	PLF	MARS	6	4	3
8♣	URR	CLFS	VEM	MOFS	NER	4	1	2
9♣	MARS	SAR	SARS	VEM	MAR	3	5	2
10♣	NER	PLF	MARS	JUR	CLRS	6	4	3
J♣	CLF	MAR	CRFS	CRF	MARS	7	7	-1
Q♣	MAM	MAMS	KRMC	VEFS	VER	7	5	3
K♣	VER	MAM	SAMS	MOF	URRS	5	3	-1
A♦	KRMA	MOR	PLR	NEF	NEFS	7	3	2
2♦	PLR	MOR	KRMC	MORS	CRR	6	1	1
3♦	MAF	JURS	CLR	SAFS	VEF	3	3	3
4♦	CRRS	MAF	JUFS	MAFS	CRR	6	4	2
5♦	PLF	JUF	NEF	PLR	JUFS	5	3	1
6♦	SAR	MARS	SAF	URR	SAFS	0	6	0
7♦	JUMS	URF	PLFS	URFS	PLF	2	1	0
8♦	CRF	VERS	NEF	PLR	NEFS	7	2	3
9♦	VEF	PLF	CLF	PLFS	JUMS	7	4	3
10♦	VER	SARS	MAM	MAMS	CRF	5	4	5
J♦	SAF	CLF	VER	CLFS	JUF	2	5	-2
Q♦	VEF	MAF	JURS	MOR	JUR	6	0	5
K♦	JUF	NERS	VEM	VEMS	MAF	6	-1	7
A♠	URFS	VERS	MAF	URF	NEF	4	1	0
2♠	MAM	SAMS	MAR	PLRS	VER	5	8	-1
3♠	SAF	SAR	JUF	URR	SAFS	-2	4	-3
4♠	JUR	CLRS	URRS	MAFS	SAR	1	1	4
5♠	CRRS	MAR	CRFS	CRF	JUR	6	5	1
6♠	MAR	PLRS	VEF	SARS	MAM	5	5	3
7♠	NERS	VEM	NEFS	PLRS	CRRS	6	1	4
8♠	MOF	URRS	VER	PLRS	SAM	4	-1	2
9♠	VEF	SARS	MAR	PLRS	MARS	4	3	3
10♠	JURS	URMS	MAFS	MAM	MAF	3	2	2
J♠	NER	PLF	MARS	NEF	PLR	7	5	2
Q♠	CRF	VERS	VER	SARS	PLF	6	2	6
K♠	MOFS	URR	CLFS	VEM	MOF	5	-1	4

Desire for Knowledge

DESCRIPTION OF THE A♣ PERSON:

The desire for knowledge, accompanied by the desire for love (2♥ Karma Card), is the main influence for this card. Combine these and you have a person who is a student of love as much as one who would truly like to find their ideal mate. This card has been known for promiscuity, but this is only true until they find the person of their dreams. They would rather be with anyone than be alone, but they will not give themselves fully until the right person comes along. Like all Aces, they are impatient and restless. Their curiosity leads them to be avid students, often with immense libraries and a collection of learning material of all kinds. This same curiosity usually keeps them youthful, even into the last years of their life. They are always interested in new things, ideas, and topics of discussion.

They are very smart and can use their brains and creativity to generate ample funds. They can make money in things associated with the arts or groups of women, anywhere creativity and quick thinking can be utilized for profit. They are very congenial and considerate and this helps them make friends at work and gives them good communication skills. Most people feel very comfortable around them because of their ability to make others feel special and included. They have very quick, sharp minds, and they are witty and avid talkers.

Their mothers are usually an especially important figure in their lives. She is usually a very powerful woman with a sharp mind and a great deal of intuition. Like the A♦, who also has a Queen as their Mercury Card, the relationship with their mother formed lasting impressions upon them that often affects their love life and relationships with women in general throughout their life.

Their later years will not be satisfactory unless they turn to spirituality for guidance. The two Sevens in Uranus and Neptune, which represent the last part of their life, can either bring material problems or spiritual success. The happiest ones are those whose eternal quest for knowledge extends to self-knowledge as well. They are often the 'divine discontents' needing travel and changes in their life and in their work to satisfy both their desire for knowledge and their inner restlessness.

SOME OF THE A♣ ISSUES CONCERNING RELATIONSHIPS:

This is one of the four special cards we call the Semi-Fixed Cards. The A♣ has a unique connection with the 2♥, its Karmic Soul Twin, which only two other cards in the deck share (the 7♦ and 9♥). Though you see seven Karma Cards listed, only the 2♥ is close to them. The A♣ and 2♥ are nearly exact mirrors of each other, sharing each other's personality traits and characteristics. Because the 2♥ is the card of the 'lovers,' the A♣ has a lifetime ambition to find the perfect love. This doesn't necessarily mean the perfect marriage. We can marry our perfect lover, but marriage is not necessarily a requirement when the 2♥ is concerned. What the A♣ is looking for is the love relationship—the love affair that is timeless and eternal, perhaps out of this world.

Like the 2♥, many A♣ have the reputation of being promiscuous. However, this only occurs among those who have not yet found the true love they are searching for. If and when they find the person of their dreams they are devoted

---

KARMA CARDS:

2♥   7♦   9♥   J♥   8♣   K♠

KARMA COUSINS:

NONE

PAST-LIFE CARDS:

K♥   2♣

---

and monogamous. They have that romantic glow in their eyes because they know there is a special relationship out there for them somewhere. They never let go of the dream of true and lasting love. Consider yourself lucky if they have chosen you as this special person in their life.

Like some other cards, the A♣ has very high ideals about love. Because of this, they can crash very hard when their dreams are not met. They tend to go into a relationship with great expectations and enthusiasm, especially when they think they have found 'the one.' If they place too many expectations on the relationship and the relationship fails, they may close up and vow to never trust or open up again. Their dreams are never quite lost, but they may never take the chance again in order to protect themselves. The ones who have been hurt in this way need to see their relationships in a more realistic light. The best relationships are created by working on their personal and emotional issues in an open and loving way, not just by finding the right person to be with, which can be the illusion created by their 2♥ Karma Card.

GENERALITIES BETWEEN THE PERSONALITY CARD CONNECTIONS

Female A♣ are often found with other Club males with whom they generally have congenial connections for friendship or love. Diamond males usually bring problems for them, especially the Jack and King. Spade men love the A♣ woman. Heart women have difficulty with the A♣ males. Male A♣ always have other Club females as friends and, in some cases, lovers.

The Lonely Ace of Clubs

A♣ people seem to come in two varieties. There are very gregarious ones who go from love affair to love affair, and there are those who seem to go through long dry spells in their love life. Believe it or not, these two types are both displaying the A♣ pickiness about their lovers. Why? Well, even the A♣ who are outgoing and gregarious are not really letting any of their lovers get too close to them. They, like the ones who have long dry spells, are waiting for that perfect person to come along, the person they can trust with their heart and soul. For this reason, A♣ are often lonely people. They are waiting for someone who is truly special to them and they just will not accept anything less. Ah, but when they do find that person, watch out! Few cards in the deck can fall in love as deeply or, for that matter, be as deeply hurt.

We have to keep in mind that the A♣ most important Karma Card is the 2♥. The 2♥, besides being the love affair card, sits in the Neptune/Venus position in the Grand Solar Spread. This combination of Neptune (fantasies, dreams, and mysticism) and Venus (love, relationships, and pleasures) is *the* most romantic and addicting of all the relationship cards in the deck. But these very same high ideals about love can make the A♣ very lonely. They may never meet someone who can match up to their fantasy or their long list of requirements. This can make for a lot of lonely A♣ people.

The other danger with the 2♥ is that it creates such a fantasy of love and such a dream of the perfect companion that when the A♣ finally finds someone who seems to be this perfect person, they literally take off on a romantic flight that most of us couldn't even imagine. As we know, those that fly the highest, fall the farthest. And so it is with the A♣ person. If the partner they have chosen is not really all that they imagine them to be, the conflicts that ensue can be very painful.

Some A♣ are of the type who simply use other people in a variety of ways. They are often good looking and have a bit of sexual charisma. Sometimes they will use others for sex or use them for money and security. But you can always bet that an A♣ person is either in love or they're not. There is no middle ground for these people. If you are dating or married to one of them, you would do well to ask yourself if you are 'the one' they have been waiting for. If not, it is likely that you are just being used for some other purpose. However, if you *are* the one, then you have someone who would trade the whole world just to be with you.

ACE OF CLUBS

LIFE SPREAD CARDS

PLANETARY CARD	SYMBOL	CARD
MOON	☽	3♥
SUN (BIRTH CARD)	✳	A♣
MERCURY	☿	Q♣
VENUS	♀	10♠
MARS	♂	5♣
JUPITER	♃	3♦
SATURN	♄	A♠
URANUS	♅	7♥
NEPTUNE	♆	7♦
PLUTO	♇	5♠
RESULT (COSMIC REWARD)	♃+	J♥
COSMIC LESSON	♄+	9♣

PLANETARY RULING CARDS

BIRTH DATE	ASTROLOGICAL RULING SIGN	PLANETARY RULING CARD
MAY 31	GEMINI	Q♣
JUN 29	CANCER	3♥
JUL 27	LEO	A♣
AUG 25	VIRGO	Q♣
SEP 23	VIRGO OR LIBRA	Q♣ OR 10♠
OCT 21	LIBRA	10♠
NOV 19	SCORPIO	5♣ & 5♠
DEC 17	SAGITTARIUS	3♦

Who A♣ with	Con1	Con2	Con3	Con4	Con5	Attraction	Intensity	Compatibility
A♥	MOF	MOFS	JUMS	VER	URRS	6	-3	8
2♥	KRMA	NEF	NEFS	PLR	SAF	6	5	1
3♥	MOF	MOR	MORS	PLR	JUMS	7	-3	8
4♥	CLRS	MAR	VEF	SARS	VEFS	4	3	2
5♥	JUR	CRRS	CLR	URR	MAF	2	1	2
6♥	PLRS	MAFS	VEM	JUF	MAF	6	3	2
7♥	URF	NERS	PLFS	PLR	URRS	4	3	-1
8♥	PLR	URRS	URF	NERS	PLFS	2	3	-1
9♥	KRMA	SARS	NEF	PLR	NEFS	4	6	0
10♥	JURS	SAR	CLFS	PLF	SAMS	1	4	-1
J♥	KRMA	CRF	MARS	VER	VEMS	7	6	2
Q♥	SAR	VERS	VEF	SARS	CLF	3	1	2
K♥	MOFS	MORS	MOR	URF	JUF	7	-3	9
A♣	SBC	NEF	PLR	NER	PLF	6	5	0
2♣	MORS	SAF	MOFS	NER	PLF	4	1	3
3♣	VEFS	VER	VERS	MAR	NEF	7	-1	7
4♣	MAFS	VEM	MAF	JUFS	PLRS	7	3	4
5♣	MAF	JUFS	JUR	CRRS	MAFS	5	2	4
6♣	NER	SAFS	MAM	VERS	VEFS	4	4	0
7♣	URFS	JUM	MAR	JUMS	CLR	2	1	2
8♣	KRMA	NEFS	PLRS	CRF	MARS	7	6	0
9♣	CLF	PLFS	SAR	VERS	MAMS	5	6	-3
10♣	JUR	CRFS	MAR	MARS	CLRS	5	4	2
J♣	SAR	CLFS	SAM	JURS	JUR	0	5	-2
Q♣	MOR	MOF	URR	PLRS	PLR	5	-1	5
K♣	VEMS	CRR	MAM	MAMS	NERS	7	2	4
A♦	VERS	VER	URRS	SAF	CLF	4	0	3
2♦	VERS	NER	SAFS	SAF	CLF	3	3	0
3♦	JUF	PLRS	JUMS	PLR	MAR	3	1	2
4♦	CLR	URR	PLF	SAMS	JUR	2	4	-2
5♦	MARS	VEFS	MAR	VERS	JUM	7	3	4
6♦	MAMS	CLF	PLFS	JURS	PLF	6	7	-2
7♦	KRMA	NEF	PLR	SARS	NEFS	5	5	0
8♦	MAR	URFS	JUM	JUMS	MORS	4	2	2
9♦	MARS	JUMS	JUM	VEFS	SAFS	4	1	3
10♦	MOR	MAFS	VEM	URR	PLRS	7	1	5
J♦	SAM	JURS	SAR	CLFS	JUR	-1	4	-1
Q♦	JUMS	JUF	MARS	SAFS	PLR	2	1	2
K♦	VER	VEFS	VEF	NEF	PLR	7	-2	8
A♠	SAF	URF	NERS	PLFS	MORS	1	4	-3
2♠	CRR	URR	VEMS	PLFS	CRRS	5	2	1
3♠	JURS	MAMS	SAM	MAM	SAMS	3	5	1
4♠	MAR	JUR	CRFS	CLRS	CRF	5	4	2
5♠	PLF	SAMS	JURS	CLR	URR	2	5	-3
6♠	URR	CRR	CRRS	VEMS	URRS	3	1	2
7♠	VER	PLR	URRS	PLRS	VEF	4	1	2
8♠	MAM	VEMS	NER	SAFS	NERS	6	3	2
9♠	MOFS	URR	MOF	URRS	JUF	4	-2	6
10♠	VEF	SARS	CLRS	SAR	VERS	2	1	2
J♠	URFS	JUM	JUR	CRFS	URF	1	-1	3
Q♠	MAR	MARS	MAFS	VEM	CLR	8	6	1
K♠	KRMA	VER	VEMS	NEFS	PLRS	7	2	4

Desire for Love & Money

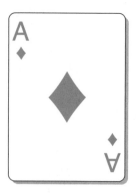

DESCRIPTION OF THE A♦ PERSON:
The inherent passion in this card can be expressed in a variety of ways, but it always seems difficult for them to have both money (or career) and love at the same time. Perhaps this is because their nature is to focus all of themselves in one particular direction to the exclusion of all others. In any case, this theme is prominent with both male and female A♦.

They can be impatient, selfish, and mercenary, or they can be the greatest of givers. They are the Jupiter/Neptune card in the Life Spread, and Jupiter tends to expand the Neptunian ideals and charitability to great extremes at times. They are all kindhearted on one level and will go out of their way to help those less fortunate. They are kind to animals and hate to see others suffer. The strong Neptune influence can make them aspire to high ideals and many make great contributions to a worthy cause. Most A♦ people fancy themselves as saviors of one kind or another, saving their friends, family, business associates, lovers, or married partners. But Neptune can be an illusion that leads us on a path of great deception and misplaced ideals. It all depends upon the individual's ability to discriminate. Paul Newman is an A♦ who has done much for charities. Adolph Hitler, an infamous A♦, thought he was doing a good thing for the world and found a way to feel good about the slaughter of millions of innocent people. These two represent the opposite extremes of Neptune's

idealism. We find a great diversity in just how this dreamy, optimistic nature is expressed by A♦ people, but it is always there.

These people are creative and capable of working two jobs at once. They meet new people every day and much of their good fortune comes from these meetings. They are ambitious and most have some artistic ability. Their work usually involves travel, which they love. Their life is a series of phone calls and communications of all sorts and usually a flurry of activity. Regardless of what they do, they believe they are here to help the world and make an important contribution in the process. All of them are inclined to be psychic and many are naturally attracted to the metaphysical side of life. If money or power does not take top priority in their values, they can have lives of great satisfaction and accomplishment.

SOME OF THE A♦ ISSUES CONCERNING RELATIONSHIPS:
As mentioned earlier, the main challenge for the A♦ in love is whether they will have to give up their careers to have the love they want. They often have a distant relationship where they see their partner every so often. This allows them to have ample time for their work, which is usually of primary importance. In other cases, they and their partner spend a lot of time traveling. At least once in their life, many A♦ experience a lesson about the importance of having a partner with them as opposed to being separated by miles and miles.

There is a strong Neptune/Pisces element in the A♦ life which spills over into their personal relationships. Though they see the highest in their partners and are natural caretakers of them, sometimes the partners don't live up to their end of the bargain and the A♦ becomes disappointed or angry. They need to learn how to speak

---

KARMA CARDS:

2♦   A♥

KARMA COUSINS:

6♣   3♥

PAST-LIFE CARDS:

K♣   2♦

up about their own needs and learn how to see others for who they really are. With communication, all things are possible.

Many have said that A♦ men should never marry. Their restless nature seems better suited to love affairs than to long–term commitment. However, if they come to terms with this restlessness, they may find the perfect partner who will travel with them, which can satisfy the same energy that usually results in love affairs.

A♦ females always do better with Clubs men, especially those who act more on the mature side of their personality. All A♦ have many Diamond females as friends, but Diamonds are not generally recommended for marriage. An A♦ male might do better with a Heart female. However, with an A♦, one should look at the specific cards on an individual basis to get the whole story.

PROFILE

The Ace of Diamonds's Love Life

It is interesting how often the A♦ creates distance between themselves and their mates. Their 5♥ in Venus has a lot to do with why their love life turns out in this way. All Fives have a Sagittarian quality about them. Sagittarius is the sign of the adventurer, the person who loves travel and wants to see the world. The 5♥ in Venus can be compared to having Venus in Sagittarius, Venus in the 9th house, or Venus aspected by the Planet Jupiter, since it rules both the 9th house and Sagittarius. You will find that most A♦ have one of these astrological connections found in their natal chart.

At any rate, the A♦ person almost always seems to have some element of travel or distance in their personal relationships. They will often fall in love with someone who travels a lot and is frequently away from home. In other cases, they are the ones who do the traveling while their partners remain at home. At the extremes, they will travel together or even allow their partners the freedom to date other people. In all cases, there is some sort of distance between them and their closest relationship. Sometimes

this distance is a good thing if both partners like it and accept it as part of their relationship. In other cases, the distance is a real problem. Much of this can be traced to the karmic implications of having Venus in Sagittarius.

In his book, *Astrology Plus*, Hilarion tells us that those with Venus in Sagittarius are here to learn about the value of having their mates and lovers with them. He says that in their lifetime there will be one or many relationships that are 'at a distance' and that this distance will create a longing in them to have their partners with them. This longing serves to balance out a past-life pattern of always being away from their partners. This seems to be very true of A♦ people. Eventually they learn that it is important not only to have a partner in love, but also that this partner be with them physically, sexually, and emotionally. To learn this lesson, the A♦ starts out creating these long-distance relationships but sooner or later changes their value system in this area and creates a healthier, more balanced pattern.

LIFE SPREAD CARDS

PLANETARY CARD	SYMBOL	CARD
MOON	☽	A♥
SUN (BIRTH CARD)	☀	A♦
MERCURY	☿	Q♦
VENUS	♀	5♥
MARS	♂	3♣
JUPITER	♃	3♠
SATURN	♄	9♥
URANUS	♅	7♣
NEPTUNE	♆	5♦
PLUTO	♇	Q♠
RESULT (COSMIC REWARD)	♃+	J♣
COSMIC LESSON	♄+	9♦

PLANETARY RULING CARDS

BIRTH DATE	ASTROLOGICAL RULING SIGN	PLANETARY RULING CARD
JAN 26	AQUARIUS	7♣
FEB 24	PISCES	5♦
MAR 22	ARIES	3♣
APR 20	ARIES OR TAURUS	3♣ OR 5♥
MAY 18	TAURUS	5♥
JUN 16	GEMINI	Q♦
JUL 14	CANCER	A♥
AUG 12	LEO	A♦
SEP 10	VIRGO	Q♦
OCT 8	LIBRA	5♥
NOV 6	SCORPIO	3♣ & Q♠
DEC 4	SAGITTARIUS	3♠

| Who | The Connections Between Partners | | | | | Overall Index Ratings | | |
A♦ with	Con1	Con2	Con3	Con4	Con5	Attraction	Intensity	Compatibility
A♥	KRMA	MOF	NEF	NEFS	MAMS	8	3	4
2♥	VEF	URFS	SAR	MORS	VEFS	3	-1	5
3♥	MAMS	MOF	KRMC	VERS	VEFS	8	2	5
4♥	SAR	MAM	JUM	MAMS	MAFS	3	5	0
5♥	VEF	MAFS	CRRS	MAF	JUFS	7	3	4
6♥	MAFS	CLR	CLRS	VEFS	VER	5	3	1
7♥	MAM	MAF	MAFS	URFS	NEFS	7	7	0
8♥	MAM	NEFS	PLRS	MAMS	NERS	7	6	1
9♥	SAF	URFS	VER	URF	PLFS	0	3	-2
10♥	JUR	CRF	MARS	SAF	MAR	3	4	1
J♥	VEMS	NER	PLF	URRS	PLR	6	1	2
Q♥	MAR	MAM	SARS	VEM	VEMS	6	5	1
K♥	VEFS	VEM	MARS	JUR	MAR	7	0	7
A♣	VEF	URFS	VEFS	SAR	JUMS	4	-1	5
2♣	VEM	MAF	VEFS	MAR	VERS	8	2	6
3♣	MAF	NEF	PLR	JUFS	VEMS	7	4	2
4♣	CLR	CLRS	CRRS	MAFS	MOF	3	3	0
5♣	CRRS	VEF	CLR	CLRS	MAF	4	1	3
6♣	PLRS	VER	KRMC	MORS	CRR	5	2	3
7♣	URF	NERS	PLFS	NEFS	PLRS	4	3	-1
8♣	NER	PLF	URRS	VEMS	VEF	6	2	1
9♣	SARS	VEM	MAR	URR	SAFS	3	3	1
10♣	JURS	JUM	PLR	SAR	SARS	0	0	2
J♣	CRF	MARS	VER	CLFS	JUR	7	4	2
Q♣	VERS	MAMS	MAR	CRFS	MARS	8	5	3
K♣	MOFS	VERS	VER	MAM	SAMS	7	-1	7
A♦	SBC	MORS	CRR	MOF	MOFS	6	1	5
2♦	KRMA	MORS	CRR	PLRS	NEF	6	3	3
3♦	VEFS	MAFS	MOR	MORS	MAF	8	0	7
4♦	MAFS	VEF	VEFS	CRR	CRRS	7	2	5
5♦	NEF	PLR	JUFS	CLF	PLFS	5	3	1
6♦	URR	SAFS	SARS	VEM	JUF	-1	3	-1
7♦	URFS	SAF	CLR	SAFS	JUMS	-2	4	-3
8♦	NEFS	PLRS	PLF	URF	NERS	5	4	-1
9♦	CLF	PLFS	MOR	NEF	PLR	7	5	-1
10♦	MAR	CRFS	VERS	PLF	URF	7	5	1
J♦	VER	CLFS	JUF	CRF	MARS	6	2	3
Q♦	MOR	VEFS	CLF	PLFS	CLFS	7	1	4
K♦	VEMS	MAF	MAR	VEM	JUF	8	2	5
A♠	MAF	VEM	VEMS	MAFS	URFS	8	2	5
2♠	VERS	MAMS	MOFS	MAM	SAMS	7	2	4
3♠	JUF	URR	SAFS	VER	CLFS	1	1	2
4♠	SAR	JURS	JUM	JUF	JUR	0	0	3
5♠	JUR	MAFS	CRR	CRRS	SAF	4	3	2
6♠	MAMS	MARS	VERS	JUF	MAR	7	5	3
7♠	VEMS	MAM	MAMS	NERS	VEM	8	3	4
8♠	VER	MOFS	PLRS	NEF	MOF	7	-1	6
9♠	MARS	VEFS	MAMS	URR	VEF	7	3	3
10♠	MAM	MAR	MARS	JURS	URMS	6	6	1
J♠	PLR	URF	NERS	PLFS	JURS	3	3	-1
Q♠	PLF	MAR	CRFS	NEFS	PLRS	7	7	-2
K♠	NER	PLF	URRS	VEMS	MAF	6	3	0

The Card of Ambition & Secrets

DESCRIPTION OF THE A♠ PERSON:

The A♠ is the ancient symbol of the secret mysteries, the most spiritual card in the deck, and yet, also the most ambitious and material-oriented in many cases. It has also been known as the Magi Card because the A♠ was, and still is, the symbol used by many of the esoteric schools of knowledge. Among them is The Order of the Magi, whose members are responsible for the preservation and dissemination of this very card system.

The A♠ person usually has a life-long conflict between their material, worldly urges and their deep, past-life spiritual heritage. This card has a Life Path with two Sevens and Two Nines, both spiritual numbers that represent trials and tribulations on the material plane. What these four spiritual cards are really telling the A♠ person is that happiness for them is only going to be found by adopting a spiritual viewpoint about their life and seeking satisfaction on that level. In fact, they have more ability and resources in the spiritual realms than most any other card in the deck, and once they begin to look in that direction, many doors that are unavailable to most open up. It is the realization of this that is the challenge.

The A♠ person seems to be a card of extremes—either highly materialistic and driven by his or her work and career or very spiritual with an esoteric mind. Even the materialistic ones have places and ways where they give to others. Giving is a part of their life that comes naturally to them all. Their Karma Card, the 7♥, suggests

---

KARMA CARDS:

7♥   2♣

KARMA COUSINS:

8♥   K♥

PAST-LIFE CARDS:

K♦   2♠

---

that some of their most challenging trials lie in the realm of relationships, family, and friendships. It also gives them a gift of being able to counsel their friends and others who are in need. Some even make a career of it. They are learning to let others be themselves and to love them unconditionally. Sometimes the lessons are very painful. In the end, these people become very loving and considerate of others. Their mission is to find the inner peace that comes through a life of service and dedication to higher principles. As their karma from previous births is discharged, they come to realize this and learn to follow the unwritten law that we reap what we sow. In many ways they have put themselves upon the cross. Whenever they deviate from the law or disregard their spiritual nature they seem to be unjustly punished.

Those A♠ who are mostly materialistic seem to have one problem after another. However, when they do follow higher principals and listen to their inner voice, they are guided and protected, finding the inner peace they seek through awareness of their wealth of spirit.

SOME OF THE A♠ ISSUES CONCERNING RELATIONSHIPS:

The success or failure of the A♠ relationships depends mostly upon whether or not they are taking a more spiritual approach to their life in general. Those who are more materialistically minded find themselves challenged again and again in the areas of love. For these people, emotional attachment brings continual pain. There can be betrayal by loved ones and family and disillusionment again and again until they realize that it is their own subtle attachments that lie at the root of these problems. Another element that is prominent for them is that they hold true love in such a high, idealistic place. Like the A♣ and others, the A♠ seeks a perfect union with another, one that is either spiritual or at least eternal in nature. They sense the possibilities of a divine union in love and often bring great expectations into their relationships. Once they set this dream aside for a while and begin working on their emotions and communication of feelings, their relationships improve, along with their chances of finding their soul mate. Their path in relationships is a difficult one, but not impossible.

At heart an A♠ is very loving and giving, with precious dreams of love that await fulfillment. This ideal relationship is not beyond their capability, but it usually comes later in life.

GENERALITIES BETWEEN THE PERSONALITY CARD CONNECTIONS

A♠ women always benefit from Heart males and they are usually bringing good things to Club females. Spade males tend to go for A♠ females and A♠ females like Diamond males, though it is not so easy for the Diamond male to be with them.

Princess Diana—The Ace of Spades

Princess Diana is a great example of the A♠ love life. Here we have a princess who married her prince, what appeared to be a story from a fairy tale. Most thought it would be a fairy-tale ending where the princess and prince got married and lived happily ever after. After all, they had everything going for them, didn't they? Even their astrological Sun signs (Cancer and Scorpio) are considered by many to be the most compatible signs in the zodiac. But her life turned out to be more like the classic A♠ person, which has some pretty difficult challenges in the area of love.

The A♠ is called the 'Magi Card,' as it has always been one of the most important ancient symbols for the secret mysteries of life. It is probably the most spiritual of all the cards in the deck and anyone who has this for their Birth Card is going to have to live a spiritual life or they will suffer enormously. Spiritual in this sense means Princess Diana is no more evolved than you or I. Her destiny put her in front of us to witness what happened in her life and through that perhaps all of us learned something about fame and royalty—namely that these things alone cannot make us happy. The A♠ person often has deep emotional scars and wounds to heal. Look at the cards in their Life Path: two Sevens and two Nines. One of the Nines is in Saturn. This is a very difficult combination. It doesn't matter who they marry or how much money or fame they have, these fears and emotional habits will come to play in the relationship of the A♠ and need to be dealt with. Every personal account of Princess Diana's life reveals emotional problems and challenges that contributed to their eventual separation.

The A♠ has a 2♥ in Neptune. More than anything, they yearn for the perfect love. They tend to be much too idealistic and fragile about love and set their sights way too high for anyone to meet. However, it is they who must fall when these ideals are crushed by cold hard facts. In Princess Di's case, she married Prince Charles, a Scorpio 6♣. They share many connections, most of which are good. However, the Neptune connection is there too. She must have thought she had the perfect marriage in the beginning. Actually, there were enough good connections between them that this could have been a perfect marriage. There are many great marriages with fewer good connections than they had. And though she is not necessarily to blame for the divorce, this does illustrate how one person's karma can affect the relationship.

A♠ people often have tragic emotional lives. They only find solace in giving of themselves to others. In this case Princess Diana was known to have taken up the cause of many charities and she used her position to help many. In this area she had all the success she could have wanted, a testament to the spiritual power of her Birth Card.

Princess Diana suffered a tragic life in many ways and a tragic death as well. She is living proof that our exterior circumstances are not the cause of our happiness or unhappiness. If those whose lives she touched can learn this one important lesson from her, then her life has fulfilled a wonderful purpose.

ACE OF SPADES

LIFE SPREAD CARDS

PLANETARY CARD	SYMBOL	CARD
MOON	☽	3♦
SUN (BIRTH CARD)	✳	A♠
MERCURY	☿	7♥
VENUS	♀	7♦
MARS	♂	5♠
JUPITER	♃	J♥
SATURN	♄	9♣
URANUS	♅	9♠
NEPTUNE	♆	2♥
PLUTO	♇	K♥
RESULT (COSMIC REWARD)	♃+	K♦
COSMIC LESSON	♄+	6♥

PLANETARY RULING CARDS

BIRTH DATE	ASTROLOGICAL RULING SIGN	PLANETARY RULING CARD
JAN 13	CAPRICORN	9♣
FEB 11	AQUARIUS	9♠
MAR 9	PISCES	2♥
APR 7	ARIES	5♠
MAY 5	TAURUS	7♦
JUN 3	GEMINI	7♥
JUL 1	CANCER	3♦

Celebrity Birthdays

BURT REYNOLDS
2/11/36 • *Actor*
JENNIFER ANISTON
2/11/69 • *Actress*
PRINCESS DIANA
7/1/61 • *Princess of Wales*
DAN AYKROYD
7/1/52 • *Actor*
EMMANUEL LEWIS
3/9/71 • *Actor*
JAMES GARNER
4/7/28 • *Actor*
RUSSELL CROWE
4/7/64 • *Actor*
ORLANDO BLOOM
1/13/77 • *Actor*
MATTHEW LAWRENCE
2/11/80 • *Actor*
WAYNE ROGERS
4/7/33 • *Actor*
LESLIE NIELSEN
2/11/22 • *Actor*
JACKIE CHAN
4/7/54 • *Actor*
LIL' BOW BOW
3/9/87 • *Rapper/Actor*
LIV TYLER
7/1/77 • *Actress*
HORATIO ALGER
1/13/1834 • *Author*
PAMELA ANDERSON
7/1/67 • *Actress*
SIDNEY SHELDON
2/11/17 • *Author*
TONY DORSETT
4/7/54 • *Football Star*
FRANCIS FORD COPPOLA
4/7/39 • *Movie Director*
BILLIE HOLIDAY
4/7/15 • *Singer*
KELLY ROWLAND
2/11/81 • *Singer*
BRANDY NORWOOD
2/11/79 • *Singer*
TAMMY WYNETTE
5/5/42 • *Singer*
THOMAS EDISON
2/11/1847 • *Inventor*
ALLEN GINSBERG
6/3/26 • *Poet*

Who	The Connections Between Partners					Overall Index Ratings		
A♠ with	Con1	Con2	Con3	Con4	Con5	Attraction	Intensity	Compatibility
A♥	URRS	VEFS	SARS	JUF	MAR	1	2	3
2♥	NEF	URF	SARS	SAR	VEF	1	3	0
3♥	URR	NER	JURS	VEFS	JUR	3	0	4
4♥	URF	MARS	VEF	SAR	MAF	3	4	1
5♥	SAFS	MARS	VERS	CLR	CLRS	3	7	-1
6♥	CLF	MOFS	CRF	CRRS	MOF	6	4	1
7♥	KRMA	MOR	PLRS	JUF	JUFS	6	5	3
8♥	JUFS	MORS	KRMC	URF	NERS	4	1	6
9♥	VEFS	NER	URRS	VEF	NERS	6	0	5
10♥	MAFS	VEF	SARS	SAF	VEFS	4	6	1
J♥	JUF	MAF	JUFS	JURS	NER	3	2	5
Q♥	CLR	URR	JUFS	JURS	SAFS	1	3	2
K♥	PLF	NEF	KRMC	URFS	URF	6	4	-1
A♣	SAR	URR	NEFS	URFS	MOFS	0	3	0
2♣	KRMA	PLFS	JUF	PLF	MOF	6	6	-1
3♣	JUF	MAFS	CRFS	MORS	CRR	5	3	4
4♣	CLF	CLFS	VEFS	VER	MAR	6	5	1
5♣	VER	MAR	MAFS	SAF	SAFS	5	6	2
6♣	MAFS	SARS	VEFS	NEF	JUFS	4	5	2
7♣	URR	SAFS	PLR	URRS	CLFS	1	5	-3
8♣	SAF	VER	SAFS	VERS	URFS	0	4	-1
9♣	SAF	JUF	NEFS	JUR	URFS	0	3	1
10♣	CRR	CLR	VEF	CLF	PLFS	6	5	1
J♣	SAF	VEFS	MAR	CRFS	MARS	3	6	0
Q♣	JUR	SAR	MAFS	CLFS	URR	1	5	1
K♣	VEFS	URRS	MOR	MORS	NEFS	6	0	6
A♦	JUF	MAR	VEF	VEFS	JUFS	4	2	7
2♦	VEF	VEFS	JUFS	MARS	MAF	6	2	8
3♦	MOF	VER	SAFS	VERS	CLF	5	2	5
4♦	CLRS	JUF	MAF	JUFS	SAFS	3	5	3
5♦	CRRS	MAF	JUR	JUFS	SAR	4	4	2
6♦	PLRS	SAF	VER	VEFS	JUF	3	5	0
7♦	VEF	NERS	MOR	SAR	NEF	6	1	5
8♦	PLR	URRS	CRR	PLRS	MAF	5	6	-2
9♦	SARS	MAFS	JURS	VER	VERS	2	5	2
10♦	JURS	MAF	JUFS	MARS	JUR	3	3	4
J♦	MARS	VEF	SAR	SAFS	VEFS	3	6	1
Q♦	VERS	JUF	MAR	MOF	SARS	5	2	6
K♦	MOFS	CRF	PLF	MAF	MAFS	7	5	2
A♠	SBC	MOF	MOR	PLRS	JUF	6	4	4
2♠	MORS	SAF	SAFS	VEFS	URRS	1	4	0
3♠	VEFS	SARS	MAF	PLR	PLRS	4	6	1
4♠	MAFS	URFS	JURS	CRR	URF	4	3	1
5♠	MAF	JUFS	VEF	CLRS	MAFS	6	4	4
6♠	SAFS	SAF	PLF	URF	PLFS	-1	7	-7
7♠	URFS	MOF	MOFS	CRF	JUFS	4	1	5
8♠	NEFS	CRRS	VEF	URR	JUFS	6	1	3
9♠	URF	PLFS	SAF	PLF	SAFS	1	6	-5
10♠	MAR	CRFS	JUR	CLRS	URRS	5	5	2
J♠	CLFS	CRRS	CRR	URR	SAFS	5	5	-2
Q♠	PLRS	MAF	JUR	MAFS	JURS	6	6	1
K♠	NER	URFS	VERS	PLR	NERS	6	1	2

The Twos

In the number Two, the drive and passion of the Ace finds its complement and balance. Sexual energy in males and females finds balance in being with someone who is a complement to themselves. It is this balance, achieved by finding our counterpart, that Twos are all about. Our world is a play of duality far more than most of us realize. Everything in our life is really nothing more than a mishmash of opposites blended together in different amounts to create all the textures of color, feeling, sounds, and ideas that we call our living universe. Twos have a natural understanding of the laws of balance and harmony. They seek to create balance in their own lives and in the lives of those around them. They are forever seeking their complement as much as the Ace is seeking to create something new. It is as a part of a successful relationship that Twos find satisfaction. If their relationships suffer, they usually suffer as well. They have a hard time separating themselves from their relationships.

Many Twos are accused of being afraid of being alone, but this is just one way of looking at it. We could just as easily say that the Aces are afraid of balance and stasis, or that they are afraid that they will not create anything new. Twos create relationships with others. They bond with us and make us feel part of their lives. In the process, we feel accepted and wanted. We find we have a place in their life, a home of sorts. Twos can be the very best at making us feel at ease and cared for.

The Two might make us feel smothered and manipulated as well. If a Two person is not aware of their deep drive for completion with others, they may try to tell themselves the opposite and execute most of their actions subconsciously. On the surface they may pretend to be aloof and uncaring. They may act as though they don't need anyone and that they would be just as happy alone as with a partner. Nothing could be further from the truth. No matter what they say or how they act, one of their primary motives is to find this completion. If it is not acknowledged openly and honestly, it can deviate into unhealthy emotional patterns and all sorts of undesirable behavior. All Twos are smart and they can create elaborate intellectual defenses against anyone trying to find out their true needs and motives. They can be the best and worst arguers. They are the best arguers in that their explanations and conclusions seem impenetrable. You may never win an argument with one of them. They are the worst arguers in that they deprive themselves of so much by building strong walls around themselves and alienating those around them.

Many of them go to extremes in love, often alternating between long periods of having no one and then falling head over heels in love. When they do fall in love in this manner, it is usually with someone who does not deserve such love or someone who cannot return it. Their zeal and enthusiasm tries to make up for what their partner is lacking. Unfortunately, who their partner really is wins out in the end and their high hopes fall far and fast. The pain of such lessons explains why many Twos avoid love for such long time periods. Humans will usually do more to avoid pain than we will to pursue pleasure.

Intelligent and often physically beautiful, Twos seem to have everything that one would want for happiness. But until they reach inside themselves to see and accept who they really are, their patterns of unhappiness will continue. Their eternal tug of war between being in a relationship and out of a relationship will continue. Their desperate needs for friendship and affection, love and touching, will go unfulfilled. The happy Two is the one who accepts his or her needs for a complementary relationship and goes about creating it. Why not just admit how important people and love are up front? Then they can accept this part of themselves and stop pretending to be something they are not, along with all the deviant behaviors that go along with it. In accepting, there comes a sort of freedom and peace. And as a special bonus, when they accept themselves just the way they are, they are no longer bound to be or act in that certain way. They are now free to choose to be one way or the other. The conscious Two understands and accepts their Two-ness in a way that allows them the freedom to manifest it the way they like instead of being compelled into addictive behavior patterns. They find union in a loving and conscious way.

The Love Affair Card

DESCRIPTION OF THE 2♥ PERSON:

As one of the special family of Semi-Fixed Cards, the 2♥ has a Karmic Soul Twin in the A♣ and shares many of that card's characteristics. Being Semi-Fixed also brings a strong will—they are certain about their direction and will accept it from no one else. They have marvelous minds and a natural, insatiable curiosity that leads to great mental development. However, they never stray far from the basic meaning of their card, that of the 'lovers.' They need other people and have very high, sometimes unrealistic, ideals about love and marriage. They always prefer being with someone to being alone, and will wait as long as necessary for the right person to come along to whom they can give their total and dedicated love. However, in some cases, they can shy away from the very thing they want so much when their delicate ideals about relationships come crashing against the rocks of reality. They must find a way to strike a balance between wanting a high, spiritual love and the realities of our world, which often conflict the tender dreams of love that the 2♥ holds. Developing a more practical approach to love can bring real benefits.

The 2♥ has a rather fortunate life path, especially in the areas of money and business. However, they should be careful in all of their business deals. Financial agreements should be clearly spelled out and defined to avoid problems. Like it or not, they almost always end up doing business in partnerships and this is where they need to exercise scrutiny. Care should be taken when mixing love and business, which is a strong possibility, because of a tendency for them to leave important expectations unspoken.

The 2♥ usually ends up associating with others of means and power and they prefer this kind of company. Financial fears crop up from time to time and must be handled carefully so that they do not affect their health and well-being. A study of metaphysics will always bring more positive guidance and fulfillment. Many have natural psychic abilities that can be used for fun or profit. But, as Capricorns, they all have a tendency to be too practical and hard on themselves and others.

SOME OF THE 2♥ ISSUES CONCERNING RELATIONSHIPS:

The 2♥ is a card that absolutely *must* have someone in their life. It is, after all, the card of the love affair. Like the A♣, they will usually choose to have 'anyone' in their life rather than no one. However, there are cases where they deny themselves love after they have been hurt or had their dreams destroyed. They have an intellectual approach to love and have to learn from experience to balance out all the concepts they hold with the truth they experience. They must also be careful about the way they express their passions, as they are required to pass through tests regarding the pursuit of personal pleasure, especially if it is at the expense of others.

GENERALITIES BETWEEN THE PERSONALITY CARD CONNECTIONS

2♥ women are often attracted to men of the Diamond suit, especially if they have some money or success. They also make good marriage partners to Heart males, who are very attracted to them. Also, they usually have some Spade males as friends. The male 2♥ often makes good friends with Club females.

KARMA CARDS:
A♣ 7♦ 9♥ J♥ 8♣ K♠

KARMA COUSINS:
NONE

PAST-LIFE CARDS:
A♥ 3♥

Karmic Soul Twins

The 2♥ is part of a special family of four cards that are usually referred to as the Semi-Fixed Cards. However, the Semi-Fixed title doesn't really tell the entire story of these special relationships among the cards. The Semi-Fixed Cards are two pairs of cards that move from one place in the Grand Solar Spread to one other place every other year of their life. The 2♥ and A♣ change places with each other each year as do the 7♦ and 9♥, the other pair. This is something that no other cards in the deck do. But what is most interesting is how these two pairs of cards are connected to each other. The 2♥ and A♣ are so much alike that it is difficult to distinguish their characteristics from each other. We can read either of their Life Path Cards for the other and it would be relevant. The same holds for the 7♦ and 9♥, the other pair of Karmic Soul Twins. From this point of view, it is almost as if they were soul mates. This doesn't mean, however, that you will find many 2♥ married to A♣. As a matter of fact you may find it difficult to even find a 2♥ since they are only born on December 29th and no other day. As rare as they are, it is amazing how often they have an A♣ as a parent, grandparent, brother, sister, lover or close friend.

A 2♥ meeting an A♣ would be like meeting someone else with your same Birth Card or birthday. The potential for feeling a sense of union and intimacy is enormous. If they did meet on a romantic level, their union could manifest itself as a dream-come-true relationship. But the Karmic Soul Twin relationship also implies some form of debt or unresolved business from a prior lifetime to be worked out. There is no way of determining what sort of debt this may be or who among the couple will be on the giving or receiving end of the bargain in this lifetime. But we do notice the preponderance of 2♥/A♣ relationships, one that is much greater than the law of averages. And we do know that these two cards displace each other in the Life and Spiritual Spreads. These facts alone tell us that there are important reasons for these two to be drawn together and that their relationship is one with special significance for both cards.

LIFE SPREAD CARDS		
PLANETARY CARD	**SYMBOL**	**CARD**
MOON	☽	9♠
SUN (BIRTH CARD)	☀	2♥
MERCURY	☿	K♥
VENUS	♀	K♦
MARS	♂	6♥
JUPITER	♃	4♣
SATURN	♄	2♦
URANUS	♅	J♠
NEPTUNE	♆	8♣
PLUTO	♇	6♦
RESULT (COSMIC REWARD)	♃+	4♠
COSMIC LESSON	♄+	10♥

Celebrity Birthdays

TED DANSON
12/29/47 • Actor
JON VOIGHT
12/29/38 • Actor
MARY TYLER MOORE
12/29/36 • Actress
ED FLANDERS
12/29/34 • Actor
JESSICA ANDREWS
12/29/83 • Singer

PLANETARY RULING CARDS		
BIRTH DATE	**ASTROLOGICAL RULING SIGN**	**PLANETARY RULING CARD**
DEC 29	CAPRICORN	2♦

Who 2♥ with	Con1	Con2	Con3	Con4	Con5	Attraction	Intensity	Compatibility
A♥	MOFS	VER	MORS	JUMS	URRS	6	-3	8
2♥	SBC	SAR	SAF	NEF	NEFS	2	6	-2
3♥	MORS	MOFS	MOF	PLR	JUMS	7	-3	8
4♥	VEFS	CRF	CLR	SARS	CLRS	4	2	3
5♥	MAFS	JURS	SAM	CRR	VEMS	3	4	1
6♥	MAF	JUFS	JUF	PLR	PLRS	5	2	3
7♥	URR	SAFS	URFS	NER	PLF	0	3	-3
8♥	URFS	PLRS	URR	SAFS	PLR	0	3	-2
9♥	KRMA	NEFS	PLRS	SAR	SARS	5	6	0
10♥	CLF	PLFS	JUR	CLRS	URRS	4	4	-2
J♥	KRMA	MAR	CRFS	VERS	VEM	7	6	2
Q♥	SAR	CLFS	CLR	SARS	VER	1	4	-3
K♥	MOR	MOF	URRS	MOFS	URF	6	-3	7
A♣	KRMA	NEF	NEFS	SAR	NER	6	5	1
2♣	NER	PLF	MOR	MORS	SAF	6	2	2
3♣	VERS	MAR	VEF	VEFS	NEF	7	1	6
4♣	JUF	CRR	VEMS	MAF	JUFS	5	0	5
5♣	CRR	VEMS	MAFS	JUF	MAF	6	2	4
6♣	NERS	VEM	SAF	NER	SAFS	4	2	1
7♣	JUMS	URF	JURS	URFS	JUM	0	-2	3
8♣	KRMA	NEF	PLR	MAR	CRFS	7	6	0
9♣	VER	SAR	CLFS	PLF	CLF	4	3	0
10♣	MARS	URF	JURS	CRF	JUR	4	3	2
J♣	JUR	SARS	CLF	PLFS	SAR	1	3	-1
Q♣	MORS	MOR	URR	PLRS	PLR	5	-1	5
K♣	MAMS	NERS	VEM	VEMS	JUM	7	2	4
A♦	VER	SAF	MOFS	URRS	VERS	3	0	3
2♦	SAF	VER	VERS	CLF	SARS	2	3	0
3♦	PLR	MAF	JUFS	JUF	MAR	5	3	2
4♦	JURS	SAM	JUR	CLRS	URRS	-1	1	2
5♦	MAR	JUM	VERS	MARS	VEFS	6	2	4
6♦	PLF	VER	MAM	SAMS	MAMS	6	6	-1
7♦	KRMA	SAR	NEFS	PLRS	NEF	4	6	0
8♦	JUMS	MARS	MAR	MORS	CLR	5	3	3
9♦	JUM	MAR	MARS	VEFS	JUMS	5	2	3
10♦	MARS	MAFS	VEM	URR	PLRS	7	5	2
J♦	JUR	SARS	MAM	SAMS	SAM	1	4	0
Q♦	PLR	JUM	JUMS	SAFS	JUF	1	1	1
K♦	VEF	VERS	PLRS	VER	NEF	6	-1	6
A♠	NER	PLF	URR	SAFS	SAF	3	5	-3
2♠	CRRS	MAMS	CRR	PLFS	URR	6	5	0
3♠	MAM	SAMS	PLF	JUR	SARS	4	7	-2
4♠	CRF	MARS	VEFS	MAR	VER	7	5	3
5♠	JUR	CLRS	URRS	CLF	PLFS	1	1	1
6♠	CRRS	MOF	URRS	URR	VEMS	4	0	4
7♠	PLRS	VEF	URFS	VER	NEF	4	1	3
8♠	NERS	VEM	MAMS	MAM	VERS	7	3	4
9♠	MOF	URRS	MOR	CRRS	JUF	5	-2	6
10♠	CLR	SARS	VEFS	SAR	CLFS	1	3	0
J♠	URF	JURS	MARS	URFS	JUM	2	1	2
Q♠	MARS	JUMS	MAFS	VEM	CLR	6	3	3
K♠	KRMA	VERS	VEM	NEF	PLR	7	2	4

2 ♣

The Conversation Card

2 ♣

DESCRIPTION OF THE 2♣ PERSON:

Among the people of this card you will note a wide variety of personalities. Some are fearful of nearly everything, especially of being alone, and will do everything in their power to make sure they are surrounded by people who admire them or are there to talk to. They are sociable and enjoy good stimulating conversations. Then there are those who are reclusive and appear to need no one. In truth they are just as afraid and always have one special person to whom they attach themselves. The A♠ Karma Card can mean an inner fear of death or change, which explains much of their behavior.

However, these people are endowed with many natural abilities and gifts. They can be exceptional in business and with people, preferring to work in partnership rather than alone. They actually have one of the more fortunate life paths. There is much protection surrounding this card and they all have much to be grateful for. If they simply recognize the abundance in their lives, they will help to dispel the underlying fear that can do so much damage.

The 2♣ loves to talk and share ideas. They have an incredible mind that can make the finest distinctions. They are witty and charming, unless they are caught up in fear, which makes them irritable and argumentative.

Much of their life is fated and part of their challenge is to simply accept things as they are, especially themselves and their closest relationships.

KARMA CARDS:

A♠   K♥

KARMA COUSINS:

7♥   9♠

PAST-LIFE CARDS:

A♣   3♣

SOME OF THE 2♣ ISSUES CONCERNING RELATIONSHIPS:

Some of the most physically beautiful, attractive, and intelligent people are 2♣ and one would usually look at them and think they could have almost anyone they desired. It is a mystery in some cases why they choose the people with whom they end up. This is more a trait in the female 2♣ than the males. Their love relationships are more a reflection of their state of inner wellness and self-love than of any other factor. If their inherent fear has not been recognized and confronted, they will often settle for anyone, just to avoid being alone, or for someone who is abusive, psychotic, or weird in some way. This can lead to codependent and other undesirable relationships.

Their 6♠ Pluto and Q♥ Result Cards are often the indicators of one or more fated relationships that are meant to help them learn the meaning of responsibility in their affections. The meaning of the 6♠ Pluto Card should be studied carefully, as it is often associated with the hurdle that stands between them and satisfaction in love. The 4♥ in Mars tells us that they often choose a mate who is very sexual, argumentative, or aggressive, and that the 2♣ themselves can be the instigator of the arguments that come up from time to time. The 2♣ has the kind of mind that can pick others apart and find all of their mistakes and shortcomings, but it doesn't seem to help them in the actual choices they make in their relationships. Many have been known to choose a mate who is less than ideal in many respects. Then, once they are with that person, their critical nature surfaces and they can spend a lot of time and energy focusing on the negative traits of their partner. A successful relationship often requires them to moderate this critical tendency to bring out the best in their mates, while at the same time not allowing their own idealism to turn a completely blind eye to glaring deficiencies in their partner's character.

Discrimination in their choice of partners will bring them great rewards. This is one of those cards that can usually have anyone they want for a partner. They have more freedom of choice in this area because they themselves have a lot to offer. If they take some time to understand their impulses, needs, desires, and feelings, they will attract a partner who is more loving and considerate, one who satisfies that 2♣ urge for the perfect companion with whom they may share everything.

2♣ women get along well with both male Clubs and Diamonds. If they are willing to be a more at-home, child-raising wife, the Club would probably make the best choice for a husband, especially the K♣. With Diamond men, there is a strong romantic connection which brings pleasure, but probably not anything lasting. 2♣ men should take care around Heart women, with whom they share a challenging connection.

PROFILE

The Fearful Two of Clubs

Florence Campbell is pretty hard on the 2♣ in her book, *Sacred Symbols of the Ancients*. According to her, the 2♣ is one of the most fearful and psychologically challenging cards in the deck. In my experience this does prove true for many of its natives. It is the A♠, their first Karma Card, that must be the culprit in all of this. Being a powerful symbol for death and transformation, the A♠ can bring a deep neurosis rooted in the basic fear of death. If one has a strong fear of death, it can cause fearful reactions in almost any area of their life. The 2♣ is not alone in this regard, but it is in their card that we find the most consistent displays of this principle.

Many 2♣ have imaginary, or psycho-somatic illnesses. They can become hypochondriacs to one degree or another and spend a lot of time and energy on the continuing saga of their health. Other 2♣ have specific phobias that are difficult for them, such as fear of flying, of being in enclosed spaces, or of being in tall buildings.

Not every 2♣ will admit to these fears, but most will. Their A♠ Karma Card represents the vast unknown that lies beyond our logical minds. For the 2♣ that unknown quality can bring up some of the most horrid fears. High among those fears is that of being alone. For example, a friend of mine is a 2♣. When his first wife left him, he became so afraid that he curled up into a ball in his bed and stayed there for 6 weeks! But overall, this man is a very sociable and successful person. He also has many, many friends and he arranges his life so

that he never has to spend any time all by himself. It seems true that the 2♣ would rather be with anybody than all alone. This is true for all Twos to some extent, but the 2♣ stands out in this regard.

When we make decisions from fear, the results are always a bigger problem than the original problem. When we are fearful, we are out of touch with our natural intuition. We are in a state of emergency, grasping for something that will quickly remedy our situation. Oftentimes the choices we make in this state satisfy our immediate need but are not good for the long–term. Fear is something all of us have to some extent. It is a natural part of life that has a good purpose in many situations, preventing us from doing things that may hurt us or others. But when it becomes excessive, it creates undesirable results, as occurs with some 2♣ people. They just keep making those decisions based on their fears, which perpetuates their problems.

The remedy for the 2♣ is to face that deep fear that is often haunting them. 'We have nothing to fear but fear itself,' said Winston Churchill and this is an applicable saying for the 2♣. For many of them, they first need to admit it to themselves. They have to turn the lights on in that darkened room of their mind and face the monsters that lie hidden there. Those who do face it discover a new power within them, the power of the mystic that is revealed by the A♠, the ancient symbol for secret knowledge and The Order of the Magi.

LIFE SPREAD CARDS

PLANETARY CARD	SYMBOL	CARD
MOON	☽	7♠
SUN (BIRTH CARD)	☀	2♣
MERCURY	☿	K♣
VENUS	♀	J♦
MARS	♂	4♥
JUPITER	♃	4♦
SATURN	♄	2♠
URANUS	♅	8♥
NEPTUNE	♆	6♣
PLUTO	♇	6♠
RESULT (COSMIC REWARD)	♃+	Q♥
COSMIC LESSON	♄+	10♣

PLANETARY RULING CARDS

BIRTH DATE	ASTROLOGICAL RULING SIGN	PLANETARY RULING CARD
MAY 30	GEMINI	K♣
JUN 28	CANCER	7♠
JUL 26	LEO	2♣
AUG 24	VIRGO	K♣
SEP 22	VIRGO OR LIBRA	K♣ OR J♦
OCT 20	LIBRA	J♦
NOV 18	SCORPIO	4♥ & 6♠
DEC 16	SAGITTARIUS	4♦

Who	The Connections Between Partners					Overall Index Ratings		
2♣ with	Con1	Con2	Con3	Con4	Con5	Attraction	Intensity	Compatibility
A♥	VEFS	VEM	VEMS	MAR	VERS	8	-2	9
2♥	HMOFS	NEF	PLR	MOF	SAR	6	0	5
3♥	VEMS	VEFS	CLFS	URR	VEF	6	-1	6
4♥	MAF	JURS	URM	JUR	CRRS	3	2	3
5♥	CLR	CLRS	JUF	SAF	MAFS	1	2	0
6♥	CRRS	VEFS	VERS	CLF	VEF	6	0	5
7♥	PLRS	JUM	KRMC	JUMS	URF	2	1	2
8♥	URF	NERS	PLFS	MOF	PLRS	4	2	0
9♥	NER	URRS	MOFS	JURS	VEF	4	-1	4
10♥	SARS	VEM	VEMS	MAR	CRFS	5	2	3
J♥	JURS	URF	URFS	JUF	JUR	0	-2	4
Q♥	CRF	MARS	JUF	NEFS	PLRS	6	4	2
K♥	KRMA	VERS	PLF	NEFS	NEF	7	4	2
A♣	MOFS	SAR	MORS	NEF	PLR	5	0	5
2♣	SBC	VERS	VEFS	NEF	PLFS	7	2	4
3♣	MORS	CRR	SAR	VEMS	MAM	5	0	4
4♣	VEFS	SAF	MAFS	CRRS	MAF	4	4	1
5♣	SAF	MAFS	CLR	CLRS	VEFS	2	5	-3
6♣	NEF	JUFS	VEF	JUMS	MAF	5	-1	6
7♣	URR	SAFS	NEFS	PLRS	PLR	1	4	-2
8♣	URFS	JURS	URF	VER	PLFS	1	-1	2
9♣	JUF	NEFS	PLRS	CRF	MARS	5	2	3
10♣	CLF	PLFS	JURS	CRR	CLFS	5	5	-2
J♣	MAR	CRFS	VEF	SARS	VEM	6	4	2
Q♣	CLFS	VEMS	MARS	JUR	VEM	6	2	3
K♣	MOR	SAF	VEF	JUMS	VEFS	3	0	4
A♦	VEM	MAF	VEFS	MAR	VERS	8	2	6
2♦	MAF	NEF	JUFS	VEM	VEMS	7	2	5
3♦	VERS	CRRS	MOF	CRR	CLF	6	0	5
4♦	JUF	CLR	CLRS	MAF	JUFS	2	1	3
5♦	SAR	VEMS	VER	MORS	CRR	4	0	4
6♦	JUF	NEFS	PLRS	PLR	NEF	4	1	3
7♦	NER	URRS	MOFS	VEF	NERS	5	0	4
8♦	JUR	MAMS	URR	SAFS	PLR	2	3	1
9♦	VER	SAR	VEMS	SARS	VERS	4	0	4
10♦	MARS	CLFS	JUR	MAMS	JURS	5	5	1
J♦	VEF	PLR	MAR	CRFS	SAR	6	3	2
Q♦	VERS	VER	CRR			7	-1	6
K♦	MAM	MAMS	MORS	CRR	MOF	8	4	3
A♠	KRMA	PLRS	JUM	JUMS	PLF	4	4	0
2♠	SAF	PLF	NEF	MOR	MORS	4	5	-2
3♠	PLR	VEF	VEFS	PLRS	NEF	5	1	4
4♠	JURS	CLF	PLFS	MAF	MAFS	5	4	0
5♠	SARS	VEM	VEMS	JUF	MAF	4	0	4
6♠	PLF	NEF	SAF	SAFS	URF	3	6	-4
7♠	MOF	MAM	MAMS	URF	NERS	7	3	3
8♠	VEF	JUMS	MOR	NEF	JUFS	5	-3	8
9♠	VERS	PLF	KRMC	NEF	URF	7	3	2
10♠	MAF	CRF	MARS	MAR	CRFS	8	7	0
J♠	URR	SAFS	CLF	PLFS	CLFS	1	5	-4
Q♠	JUR	MAMS	MARS	MAR	VEMS	6	4	3
K♠	URF	URFS	JURS	NER	VER	1	-1	2

The Wheeler Dealer Card

DESCRIPTION OF THE 2♦ PERSON:
The 2♦ has an innate intuition that, if followed, will always lead them to success and show them the right path to follow. Inherent in this intuition is a high set of values and often a mission in life that always involves partners and others. There is a certain amount of ambition, usually for money, that keeps them motivated. This ambition is good because they can get into ruts at times—especially in their closest relationships. If they tap into their inner guidance, they will find a path awaiting them that is fascinating and rewarding. They do best by establishing themselves in one business and sticking with it. This is one of the most successful cards in the deck, and they have only themselves to blame if they are not happy and productive. They are called the Wheeler Dealer Card because they love to be involved in business and finance, especially with their friends and associates. This is a partnership card which usually chooses to work with others rather than alone.

Two is the number of logic, and 2♦ have a mind that is quick at making distinctions and evaluations. They are often attracted to and good at working with computers for the same reason. It is only when the 2♦ is emotionally unfulfilled that their capable mind becomes pessimistic and argumentative.

Financially, this is one of the most fortunate cards in the deck. Most of them make considerable sums of money, especially after the age of 35. They have a lot to be grateful for.

KARMA CARDS:

6♣   A♦

KARMA COUSINS:

8♠   A♥

PAST-LIFE CARDS:

A♦   3♦

They should be careful that their social obligations do not tax their health and well-being. Sometimes they get so caught up in their and work that they forget to take care of themselves. They can make large sums of money in real estate, especially in their later years, and maintain good health throughout their lives. This is one of the cards that is likely to live to the age of 100. These people love to mix and mingle and arrange 'deals' with others.

For some 2♦, their life holds a special purpose, a mission that involves bringing higher knowledge of some kind to the world and those they love. These people are the messengers of light.

SOME OF THE 2♦ ISSUES CONCERNING RELATIONSHIPS:
Romantically, the 2♦ has strong and fixed attitudes, ideas, and principles about love that are admirable on one hand. On the other, they are their greatest hurdle to their romantic and emotional happiness. Many of them must learn that love and marriage are more than their fixed ideas about them. Once they are in a relationship, whether good or bad, they are usually stuck there by these fixed principles. This can cause them to linger where happiness is not. When this happens they become bitter and inclined to negativity, manifesting the argumentative side of this card. A male 2♦ in a marriage that is over emotionally will often have affairs, even multiple affairs, but will shun divorce at all costs. 'People should stay married forever' is a belief that all of them should examine for its validity before entering into marriage.

Their A♥ Pluto Card indicates a strong, but often hidden, need for affection which can go unnoticed or unacknowledged because they get so involved in the mental side of life and their work or business. This inner need for affection and self-respect is at the heart of most of their relationship issues and problems.

The 2♦ is usually a very intellectual person. This powerful mind, which serves them so well in their careers, can be a stumbling block to success in personal relationships, because it inhibits their ability to feel. With work, this inhibition can be overcome and they can learn to communicate the intimate feelings that are necessary for a healthy relationship.

2♦ females can make a good marriage to a Spade male. 2♦ men may do better with women from the Hearts suit. Both sexes have many Diamond women friends.

PROFILE

For Love and Money

The 2♦ and A♦ share some interesting patterns that have a lot to do with their love life. In both cases, this pattern stems from the two Aces that stand right next to each other in the Life Spread, the A♥ and A♦. If you look at the Life Spreads of both the 2♦ person and the A♦ person, you will see that these two Aces are prominent, not to mention the fact that the A♥ is the Karma Card to the A♦ and the A♦ is the Karma Card to the 2♦. We see that there is a lot of emphasis on these two Aces and this has a lot to do with how 2♦ and A♦ people are—both cards seem to have a hard time being successful in both work and love at the same time.

The 2♦ has the A♥ as their Pluto Card with the A♦ as the Result. Often, the Pluto and Result Cards act as sort of a choice that we must make. Do I want love (A♥) or do I want success in my career (A♦)? This is the question that faces both the 2♦ and A♦. In the case of the 2♦, their A♥ Pluto Card reveals a very deep need for affection that is a life-long challenge for them. The 2♦ has fine intellects and is usually very successful in their work. But in their love life, that A♥ is one of their biggest weaknesses. It is in this area that their fine intellects cannot help them.

When 2♦ people fall in love, they are overwhelmed in the relationship. The experience of having their need for affection fulfilled can be wonderful and powerful. When this happens they often think that the relationship is all that they need. It is like a person who is dying of thirst finding an oasis in the desert. Their work and careers often become secondary to their relationship. It is not balanced, but the A♥ need for affection is being met, so they go along with it. Later, though, as their relationship progresses beyond the honeymoon stage, problems begin to surface in the relationship. When this happens, the 2♦ person gets somewhat panicked. They try to figure out their love life and keep trying to apply their intellect to this emotional area to come up with a solution. When they do, they usually fail. All they have to work with is their fixed ideas about love and marriage. They keep thinking, 'I must stay married. I should stay married. It is better to be married than to be divorced,' and other such thoughts. They stay in a bad situation, constantly complain about it, but do nothing about it. Some 2♦ people actually go on to live with another lover for years and years, never divorcing their spouse. If their relationship does fail, they give up on love and go back to their jobs to regain their feelings of satisfaction. Thus, the cycle completes itself and starts all over again.

This cycle is not a hard and fast rule, though we can see it at work in many 2♦ people and their love lives. Those who are willing to face their deep needs for affection can overcome this pattern and do things differently. Overall, the 2♦ has more to be thankful for than any other card in the deck. They can be happy and productive and feel loved all at the same time.

TWO OF DIAMONDS

LIFE SPREAD CARDS

PLANETARY CARD	SYMBOL	CARD
MOON	☽	4♣
SUN (BIRTH CARD)	☀	2♦
MERCURY	☿	J♠
VENUS	♀	8♣
MARS	♂	6♦
JUPITER	♃	4♠
SATURN	♄	10♥
URANUS	♅	10♦
NEPTUNE	♆	8♠
PLUTO	♇	A♥
RESULT (COSMIC REWARD)	♃+	A♦
COSMIC LESSON	♄+	Q♦

PLANETARY RULING CARDS

BIRTH DATE	ASTROLOGICAL RULING SIGN	PLANETARY RULING CARD
JAN 25	AQUARIUS	10♦
FEB 23	PISCES	8♠
MAR 21	PISCES OR ARIES	8♠ OR 6♦
APR 19	ARIES	6♦
MAY 17	TAURUS	8♣
JUN 15	GEMINI	J♠
JUL 13	CANCER	4♣
AUG 11	LEO	2♦
SEP 9	VIRGO	J♠
OCT 7	LIBRA	8♣
NOV 5	SCORPIO	6♦ & A♥
DEC 3	SAGITTARIUS	4♠

Celebrity Birthdays

DENNIS HOPPER
5/17/36 • *Actor*
DUDLEY MOORE
4/19/35 • *Actor*
HUGH GRANT
9/9/60 • *Actor*
KATE HUDSON
4/19/79 • *Actress*
MATTHEW BRODERICK
3/21/62 • *Actor*
PETER FONDA
2/23/39 • *Actor*
SAM SHEPARD
11/5/43 • *Actor*
ELIZABETH ALLAN
1/25/34 • *Actress*
JAYNE MANSFIELD
4/19/33 • *Actress*
COURTNEY COX ARQUETTE
6/15/64 • *Actress*
ROSIE O'DONNELL
3/21/62 • *Actress/ Comedienne/Talk Show Host*
CHEECH MARIN
7/13/46 • *Comedian*
ADAM SANDLER
9/9/66 • *Comedian*
EDWIN NEWMAN
1/25/19 • *Journalist/ Author*
JOHANN S. BACH
3/21/1685 • *Musician*
TONI BRAXTON
10/7/67 • *Singer*
OZZY OSBOURNE
12/3/48 • *Singer*
TIMOTHY DALTON
3/21/46 • *Actor*
SUGAR RAY LEONARD
5/17/56 • *Boxer*
HARRISON FORD
7/13/42 • *Actor*
MICHAEL KEATON
9/9/51 • *Actor*
HELEN HUNT
6/15/63 • *Actress*
JIM BELUSHI
6/15/54 • *Actor*
ENYA
5/17/61 • *Singer*
ALEX HALEY
8/11/21 • *Writer*
HULK HOGAN
8/11/53 • *Wrestler*
SIMON COWELL
10/7/59 • *TV Personality*

Who	The Connections Between Partners					Overall Index Ratings		
2♦ with	Con1	Con2	Con3	Con4	Con5	Attraction	Intensity	Compatibility
A♥	PLF	MOFS	KRMC	CRF	MOF	7	3	2
2♥	SAR	VEFS	CLR	SAFS	VEF	1	2	1
3♥	PLF	MARS	VEM	URF	VEMS	7	4	0
4♥	JUM	MAMS	JUF	MARS	JUR	4	2	4
5♥	VEFS	VEF	CLRS	MAR	MAFS	6	0	6
6♥	VER	MOF	MORS	MAFS	VERS	8	-2	8
7♥	MAFS	VEM	VEMS	MAM	MAF	8	3	5
8♥	MAMS	MAFS	MOF	MAM	PLR	8	6	2
9♥	VER	CLR	SAFS	VEFS	VEF	3	1	3
10♥	SAF	JURS	MAM	CRR	CRRS	1	4	-1
J♥	PLR	MAF	VEF	NERS	PLFS	6	4	1
Q♥	VEMS	MARS	NER	URRS	VEF	6	1	4
K♥	JUR	MAR	URR	URRS	JUM	2	1	3
A♣	VEFS	SAR	CLR	SAFS	NEF	2	2	1
2♣	MAR	VEM	VEMS	JUR	NER	7	1	6
3♣	VEM	MAFS	MAR	MARS	MAF	8	5	3
4♣	MOF	VEF	CLRS	VER	VERS	6	-2	7
5♣	VEF	CLRS	MOF	MOFS	CLF	6	-1	6
6♣	KRMA	JUR	CRRS	NEF	PLF	5	4	2
7♣	PLRS	URFS	MOR	JUMS	MORS	3	0	2
8♣	VEF	NERS	PLFS	PLR	MAF	7	3	2
9♣	NER	URRS	VEMS	MAF	JUFS	5	1	3
10♣	SARS	MOR	JUMS	JUF	MAF	3	0	3
J♣	JURS	MAM	CRFS	SAF	CLR	3	4	1
Q♣	MARS	VEM	URF	PLFS	PLF	6	4	1
K♣	VERS	NEF	URR	NEFS	MOFS	6	0	5
A♦	KRMA	MOFS	CRF	PLF	NEFS	7	4	2
2♦	SBC	JUR	CRRS	MOFS	CRF	4	2	3
3♦	MORS	VER	CLF	CLFS	VEFS	7	0	5
4♦	VEFS	CRR	MAR	MAFS	VEF	7	2	4
5♦	MAFS	VEM	NEFS	PLRS	VEMS	8	3	4
6♦	MAF	JUFS	NER	URRS	VERS	5	2	3
7♦	CLR	SAFS	VER	VEFS	VERS	2	2	1
8♦	URFS	PLRS	JUF	NEFS	PLF	3	2	1
9♦	NEFS	PLRS	CLF	CLFS	MAFS	6	5	-1
10♦	URF	PLFS	MARS	VEM	MAR	5	4	-1
J♦	CRFS	VERS	JURS	MAM	SAR	5	2	3
Q♦	CLF	CLFS	MORS	NEFS	PLRS	6	4	0
K♦	MAR	VEM	MAMS	VEMS	MARS	8	4	4
A♠	VEM	VEMS	MAFS	MAR	MARS	8	1	6
2♠	JUF	VERS	VER	PLF	MAMS	6	-1	5
3♠	VERS	MAF	JUFS	CRFS	JUF	6	1	5
4♠	JUF	SARS	JUM	MAMS	MAM	2	1	3
5♠	CRR	SAF	VEFS	CRRS	JUR	2	3	1
6♠	JUF	URR	MOR	PLF	MAMS	4	0	4
7♠	MAMS	MAR	PLR	VEMS	MAM	7	6	1
8♠	NEF	VERS	KRMC	JUR	CRRS	6	1	5
9♠	URR	JUR	JUF	MARS	URRS	1	0	3
10♠	MARS	JUM	MAMS	VEMS	CRF	6	4	3
J♠	MOR	JUMS	PLRS	SARS	PLR	3	0	3
Q♠	URF	PLFS	URFS	PLF	MAR	4	4	-3
K♠	MAF	VEF	NERS	PLFS	PLR	7	4	2

The Friendship Card

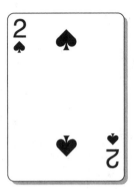

DESCRIPTION OF THE 2♠ PERSON:
The 2♠ is the card of work partnership and friendship. Twos are also known as fear cards, and usually it is the fear of being alone. The 2♠ is no exception. Many of them will go out of their way to keep themselves in the company of others and all are personally hurt when others betray their friendship or trust. The Karma Card of the 2♠, the 6♠, is one of the more potent of all the Karma Cards and tells us that the life of the 2♠ has a more fated quality to it than other cards. This same card can cause their lives to get in a rut from time to time and accounts for some challenges in their health. Positive health habits are essential for most of them.

The 2♠ location in the Uranus/Uranus position of the Spiritual Spread tells us that they all have strong intuitional gifts. However, to access this, they must develop a sincere interest in their spiritual side, something that most Spades tend to neglect in favor of their strong work and career interests.

They have strong, logical minds with which they can make a good living, but this same logic doesn't help them much in personal relationships. Many are so involved in their work and the power of their logic that they completely avoid their feelings and situations that test them in this area. This can include avoiding marriage and commitments in relationships. They are very congenial and have success in social situations but their 3♥ Pluto Card speaks of some doubts and

indecision both romantically and in general that can plague them throughout their life. Overall they have an easier life path than most and should not allow themselves to become self-indulgent or lazy. Often they marry into money.

Many 2♠ are destined for recognition or fame. The men especially excel at what they do and usually get promoted to positions of leadership. Their K♣ second Karma Card tells us that leadership abilities are found in all of them and come easily and naturally when the opportunity arrives.

If the 2♠ turns to spirituality, they can be very progressive, dynamic, and instrumental in shaping the world into one of harmony and cooperation. This is the Card of the New Age of Cooperation and Brotherly Love—the Age of Aquarius which our world is entering into at this very moment. In this way, the 2♠ can be role models of the friendship quality that we can expect to be a dominant theme for the next 2,000 years or so.

SOME OF THE 2♠ ISSUES CONCERNING RELATIONSHIPS:
The 2♠ person has some of the better marriage karma of all the cards in the deck. However, this good marriage usually comes later in life after they have resolved some of the indecision and fears related to being with someone else. They often have push-pull relationships. They first want their partner to get closer and then they push them away, afraid of what more intimacy might bring them. This card is highly logical and their approach to love often reflects this. They will analyze the concepts of marriage and of being together and try to come up with truths or conclusions about love and relationships so that they can have some kind of handle on them. But for the most part, these areas are of the emotional realm, an area that is often neglected by the 2♠.

KARMA CARDS:

6♠ K♣

KARMA COUSINS:

9♠ 8♠

PAST-LIFE CARDS:

A♠ 3♠

2♠ do have good karma from past lives of having given much in a marriage and will receive due payment at some point in their life. They are excellent husbands and wives—the kind that are steady and true. There can be long periods of inactivity in their love life and they have only themselves to blame for this. It is often their own fears or doubts that stop them from initiating new partnerships or commitments on a romantic level. Any work done on the emotional side is extremely helpful in this area.

Their 3♥ Pluto Card is the major culprit in their uncertainty about love and marriage. They often try to figure out love and marriage with their minds and go around in circles not realizing that it is their internal fears about what might happen that is causing their distress. In other cases, this 3♥ acts like a repelling magnet that keeps love away from them. Again, they are usually not conscious of its effect because most of their energy is centered in their logical, left brain.

GENERALITIES BETWEEN THE PERSONALITY CARD CONNECTIONS

2♠ men receive blessings from Heart females. Both sexes have Club females as friends and companions. Female 2♠ have strong fantasies about other Spade males, but Diamond males find them particularly attractive. Club males find them challenging.

Paul, a Classic Two of Spades

Paul is what we might call the classic 2♠. His birthday is May 4th and he fits the description of a hard-working, logical kind of guy that many 2♠ are. He is a computer programmer and very successful at what he does, working for one of the hottest computer game companies in Silicon Valley. Florence Campbell talks about the 2♠ in *Sacred Symbols of the Ancients*. She says that most Twos have a fear of being alone. Our Birth Card, like our sun sign, is an energy we tend to identify with so closely that we literally think we are that energy. For Twos, they tend to see themselves as being half of a partnership, as opposed to Aces who see themselves as individuals and loners to some degree.

Paul values his friendships with both men and women as one of the most important things in his life. He prefers to do most things with others rather than alone. Even when he is alone, he is usually on the phone with one of his buddies. He usually has one or more of his friends at his house or he will be out doing something with them. He puts a lot of energy into keeping his schedule full of things to do with others. Several times he has had one of his friends move into his apartment for a while. This is not so unusual in itself, but taken in the context of the rest of his life, we see a pattern emerging. When one of his best friends left the area and moved to another state, he broke down emotionally and was ill for a week or so. Friendships are more important to him than they are to the average person. Being a Spade, friendships involve doing things together rather than just talking or making money, as with the 2♣ or 2♦. He likes to ride bikes, go bowling, go cross-country skiing, play video games, and have group events at his house.

In the area of relationships, the story is a bit different. Paul has come close to marriage, but never gone all the way to the altar. He seems to attract those who cannot make a commitment, or he himself puts it off. His powerful and logical mind hasn't yet been able to come up with a definite solution or direction in the area of love and marriage.

The strong side of a Two is that they can be the best of friends. Paul has been a consistently good friend to all of his friends, even to his love partners from the past. The 2♠'s only challenge is the pain they feel when their friends leave them.

LIFE SPREAD CARDS

PLANETARY CARD	SYMBOL	CARD
MOON	☽	4♦
SUN (BIRTH CARD)	✳	2♠
MERCURY	☿	8♥
VENUS	♀	6♣
MARS	♂	6♠
JUPITER	♃	Q♥
SATURN	♄	10♣
URANUS	♅	8♦
NEPTUNE	♆	K♠
PLUTO	♇	3♥
RESULT (COSMIC REWARD)	♃+	A♣
COSMIC LESSON	♄+	Q♣

PLANETARY RULING CARDS

BIRTH DATE	ASTROLOGICAL RULING SIGN	PLANETARY RULING CARD
JAN 12	CAPRICORN	10♣
FEB 10	AQUARIUS	8♦
MAR 8	PISCES	K♠
APR 6	ARIES	6♠
MAY 4	TAURUS	6♣
JUN 2	GEMINI	8♥

Celebrity Birthdays

BILLY DEE WILLIAMS
4/6/37 • Actor
ROBERT WAGNER
2/10/30 • Actor
LAURA DERN
2/10/67 • Actress
AUDREY HEPBURN
5/4/29 • Actress
KIRSTIE ALLEY
1/12/55 • Actress
HOWARD STERN
1/12/54 • Radio Shock
Jock
RUSH LIMBAUGH
1/12/51 • Talk Show Host
RANDY TRAVIS
5/4/59 • Singer
JERRY MATHERS
6/2/48 • Actor
TAMMY WYNETTE
5/4/42 • Singer
DONOVAN
2/10/46 • Singer
GREG NORMAN
2/10/55 • Golfer
MARK SPITZ
2/10/50 • Swimmer
GORDY SINGLETON
3/8/37 • Co-Founder of
Motown
DOMINIQUE WILKINS
1/12/60 • Basketball
Player
JIM RICE
3/8/53 • Baseball Player
PRINCE WILLIAM
6/2/82 • Prince of Wales

Who	The Connections Between Partners					Overall Index Ratings		
2♠ with	Con1	Con2	Con3	Con4	Con5	Attraction	Intensity	Compatibility
A♥	MAM	SAMS	VEFS	PLF	MAF	5	6	-1
2♥	CRF	PLRS	CRFS	MAMS	URF	6	6	-1
3♥	PLF	MAM	SAMS	CLF	URF	5	8	-4
4♥	VER	VEFS	PLFS	SAR	VEF	6	0	4
5♥	MOF	MAFS	JUR	MAF	JUFS	6	1	5
6♥	JUF	SAFS	MAMS	MAM	JUFS	2	4	1
7♥	MOR	MOFS	SAM	SAMS	VER	4	1	5
8♥	MOR	URR	SAFS	VER	SAF	2	1	2
9♥	VEM	JUMS	PLRS	CRF	URR	4	0	4
10♥	MAF	PLR	SAF	MAFS	SAFS	4	7	-3
J♥	NEF	JUM	JUF	NEFS	JUFS	5	-1	5
Q♥	JUF	PLFS	MOR	PLF	VEFS	6	2	3
K♥	JUFS	SAR	NEFS	PLRS	PLR	2	2	2
A♣	CRF	PLRS	URF	VEMS	CRFS	5	3	1
2♣	SAR	MOFS	JUFS	PLR	NER	3	1	3
3♣	VEF	CLR	CLRS	VERS	VEFS	4	-1	5
4♣	MAMS	JUF	SAFS	JUFS	CRRS	3	4	1
5♣	MAMS	CRF	VER	PLRS	MAFS	7	5	1
6♣	VEF	URFS	MOF	PLR	URF	4	-1	5
7♣	MAFS	URF	NERS	PLFS	CRFS	6	5	-1
8♣	JUM	NEF	JUMS	SARS	JUFS	3	-1	4
9♣	JUF	CRRS	MAR	JURS	PLF	4	2	3
10♣	SAF	NEF	CRFS	VEFS	VEF	3	4	0
J♣	PLR	MAR	JURS	MAF	MAFS	5	5	0
Q♣	CLF	URF	VEMS	PLF	SARS	4	3	-1
K♣	KRMA	JUR	PLF	NEFS	URFS	5	4	1
A♦	VEFS	MAM	SAMS	MAMS	MORS	6	4	3
2♦	VEF	VEFS	JUR	PLR	URF	5	-2	7
3♦	JUF	SAFS	MARS	VEM	CLF	2	3	1
4♦	MOF	SAF	MAFS	JUR	MAF	4	3	2
5♦	CLR	CLRS	NER	URRS	VEF	2	1	0
6♦	CRRS	MORS	URFS	MAR	JURS	5	1	3
7♦	PLRS	VEM	JUMS	CRF	VEMS	5	1	3
8♦	URF	NERS	PLFS	CRR	CLFS	4	3	-1
9♦	NER	URRS	MARS	VEM	CLR	5	2	2
10♦	SARS	CLF	URF	VEMS	CRR	2	3	-1
J♦	MAR	JURS	MORS	PLR	URR	5	2	3
Q♦	MARS	VEM	NER	URRS	NERS	6	2	3
K♦	VERS	VEF	URR	SAFS	URRS	4	-1	4
A♠	MOFS	SAR	SARS	VERS	SAM	2	1	2
2♠	SBC	MAF	JUFS	JUR	MAR	5	4	3
3♠	MORS	CRRS	MAR	JURS	MARS	6	1	5
4♠	VEFS	SAF	NEF	VER	VERS	4	1	3
5♠	SAF	MAFS	MAF	MOF	MOFS	4	6	-1
6♠	KRMA	MAF	JUFS	NEFS	PLRS	6	5	2
7♠	URR	SAFS	VERS	MOR	MORS	2	1	1
8♠	URFS	JUR	KRMC	VEF	SAR	2	0	4
9♠	NEFS	PLRS	KRMC	JUFS	MAF	5	3	2
10♠	PLFS	VER	JUF	PLF	JUFS	6	3	1
J♠	CRFS	MAFS	SAF	NEF	JUF	5	6	-1
Q♠	CRR	CLFS	SARS	URF	NERS	3	4	-1
K♠	NEF	JUM	JUF	NEFS	JUFS	5	-1	5

The Threes

To fully understand the nature of Threes, and of all the odd-numbered cards in the deck, one must look back at the Ace and see it as an evolutionary step out of the Zero. The Ace is the most primary of all the odd-numbered cards and all of them reflect some of its qualities in some way. All odd-numbered cards represent a departure from the stability and evenness of the number preceding them. For the Three, this is a departure from the completion of the Two. Because the Three is the 'leaving' from the Two, many of them are never satisfied with what they have, and this is especially true in their personal relationships. It is not a quality to be faulted or looked upon as a bad thing. It is just the way it is. All of us at one time or another will experience what it is like to be a Three person by having those cards show up in one of our Yearly Spreads. We may have a 3♥ Long Range Card in one particular year and experience a great deal of variety or indecision about our romantic life. We may have a 3♦ Pluto Card another year and be challenged to transform our worries about money into positive, money-making ideas that we can implement for greater financial success. But for the Three person, this quality of leaving is basically a way of life that they must come to terms with at some point during their life if they are to have peace and contentment.

Peace and contentment are challenges for all the odd-numbered Birth Cards. The odd numbers always represent an imbalance which is seeking balance through the creation of something else. These odd numbers are essentially masculine in nature—creative and always in motion. Whether a Three person is male or female, they will exhibit this creative drive that seeks expression. Their peace will only come through some form of action or accomplishment on the material level which will ultimately lead them back to themselves. For the Three, the urge is for self-expression and variety. They are generators of ideas, thoughts, and feelings and must find a suitable outlet lest they suffer the consequence of worry and indecision.

Like Gemini sun sign people, Threes are versatile and often quite talkative. They can relate to many different kinds of people, cultures, and concepts because they are flexible. They are also quite resourceful and can come up with solutions to almost any problem that confronts them. If you need a good idea, talk to a Three. They usually have drawers full of ideas, some of which they are working on, but a multitude which they will never have the time or energy to start working on, much less complete. Art, music, and writing are excellent outlets

for a Three's abundant creativity. Many of them become successful in one or more of these fields and all of them need at least one of these outlets if they are to realize their birthright and achieve inner satisfaction. Many of them have several projects or jobs going at the same time. This gives them the variety they crave. When they start to get bored with one of the projects they are working on, they can switch to a second or third and keep going. This happens to be one of the successful strategies for Threes. Otherwise, many of them go from one job to another and never complete anything, which ultimately makes them depressed and miserable. They need to see at least some of their ideas come to fruition.

Threes love romance. Astrologically, the 5th house energy is related to both creativity and self-expression, along with love affairs and romance. Three people seem to have a strong connection to this 5th house in the ways they find fulfillment. It stands to reason that those with the greatest creative gifts would also have the strongest needs for romantic involvement and sexual pleasure. Add to this the Three's natural curiosity and desire for new experiences and variety and you can see why many Threes make great lovers but not-so-great marriage partners. They are just as likely to get bored in their relationships as they are with one of their current creative projects. They may feel like having a new affair to remedy the situation, and then jump back into your arms again when that gets boring. Though this may be a slight exaggeration, this is a common concern for Three people.

Another thing that can contribute to Threes' infidelity is their worrisome nature. Most of them, but especially the 3♣ and 3♦, are worried about not having enough (love, money, good health, etc.). Though this usually manifests as worry about finances, it can spill over into their romantic lives too. The Three person might reason that if they have two or three lovers available to them, they will have less chance of running out of love when they need it. This can also explain why they might shy away from commitment and long–term relationships.

If you put all of these ingredients together, you can see why Threes can be very complicated people with a great potential for either happiness or unhappiness. The happiest are those who have found a place where they can express their creativity and get well paid for it. They are recognized for their ideas and ability to communicate them. Many of them will make a real impact on the world with their creative gifts and we will admire them for their contributions.

Variety in Love

The 3♥ is the first card in the Life Spread of cards and represents the departure of Man and Woman from the Garden of Eden. Temptation was the reason for their departure and the 3♥ can indicate this temptation on many levels. Also, since it is the first card in the Life Spread, we might consider this card as the stepping out place into a world of duality and confusion. The 3♥ experience may be like your arriving on some alien planet for the first time and having to figure everything out for yourself.

In this regard, 3♥ people are eternally inquisitive and mentally well-equipped to evaluate and analyze the things they observe. Both sexes have particular success working with men and the females fare better than most women when working in male-ruled companies and associations. They are progressive in their work and usually improve their life or finances through travel or making changes. They are hard workers and have success whenever they apply themselves. They need a certain amount of change or travel in their vocation to be happy. 3♥ have tremendous artistic and creative potential. Expression is one of their strongest soul qualities.

Two of their most important lessons in life are overcoming their fear of poverty and learning to translate value-based indecision into creativity in their work or business. They are learning to develop faith that the necessary resources will always be there for them when needed. Much of their own financial lack, whether real or imagined, stems from unclarity about what is most important to them in life. In this case, their own natural creativity becomes a burden of indecision. They can come up with so many ideas of what to do and what they might want that they never finish what they start or accumulate enough to feel financially secure. This same indecision can be at the root of some very challenging and karmic relationships in which they meet someone who shares these same qualities and leaves them in doubt about whether or not they are loved.

Once the 3♥ has learned the value of foundation and stability, their creativity becomes a great talent that leads them toward their goals. Once they learn that it is as good to give as to receive, they find great fulfillment in giving love and truth to others in their life. Those who spend their later years pursuing metaphysical or religious subjects have more satisfaction and peace.

SOME OF THE 3♥ ISSUES CONCERNING RELATIONSHIPS:

Of the Threes, all of whom demand the freedom to explore possibilities, the 3♥ can become the most confused mentally and emotionally. In search of what and whom they love, they can often become uncertain or dissatisfied, even when they find the perfect love standing in front of them. On a deeper level, the 3♥ can represent emotional uncertainty. "Will I be loved?" and "Will I be happy in love?" are questions that are often foremost in their minds. This uncertainty can often be traced to emotionally challenging experiences in childhood. Sometimes the 3♥ energy results in sexual uncertainty and experimentation. Bisexuality and homosexuality are concepts that many 3♥ choose to explore in their quest for wisdom.

The A♥ first Karma Card tells us that what is most needed by the 3♥ person is to spend some time with themselves so that they can learn to be more emotionally self-reliant and self-sustaining. When the 3♥ learns to give some of their abundant energy to themselves, they feel

---

KARMA CARDS:

A♥ Q♣

KARMA COUSINS:

A♦ 10♦

PAST-LIFE CARDS:

2♥ 4♥

---

less needy and less frantic about getting love from others. Then, their love life becomes much more fun and enjoyable, which is how they would want it to be. These people love to be light and cheerful.

They are very charming and attractive people and have no trouble attracting others to love. The challenge comes once they find someone. They generally are attracted to those of wit and high intelligence, but often someone who is just as indecisive as themselves. The 3♥ can be one of the most fickle in the deck, but this same energy can be expressed as a profound ability to speak and express themselves. If there is the fickleness, one can find its roots in emotional conflicts and fear of commitment. One might say that the 3♥ is here to learn about love through experimenting with all sorts of relationship variations and ideas. Through these experiences, they obtain the wisdom that brings sureness to their decisions and more success in love and romance.

GENERALITIES BETWEEN THE PERSONALITY CARD CONNECTIONS

3♥ men have natural affections for most Club females. They also have a lot of attraction for Diamond females. The 3♥ female will have problems with many of the Club and Heart males. Spade males find the 3♥ female very attractive, but difficult in other ways.

The Threes' Creativity and Indecision

All of the Three Birth Cards strongly identify with their creative side. The 3♥, being the first of the Threes, is the most likely to make the mistakes associated with youthfulness (Hearts) and to have to learn from the school of hard knocks. To understand them a little better, it would be good to delve into the meaning of the number Three a little deeper. When we look at a Three, we see a Two and a One. The Two represents union and completion, balance and stability—the symbol of the happy, united couple. This is an inherent part of the Three person just as much as their other parts. This Two energy tells us that the Three person does value having a partner or complement in their life. This is a feminine principle and gives them satisfaction with what they already have, whether it is a person, a job, an idea, or whatever. The added One is the masculine principle that is always urging the Three person to go forth and try new things, relationships, and experiences of all kinds. However, the Three doesn't want to let go of the Two that they already have in order to get the new thing, person, or experience. It's like they want what they have and they want what they don't have, and they want them both at the same time. Other odd numbered cards share this quality of wanting new things, relationships, and experiences, but it is the Three that holds the distinction of also wanting to keep what they already have in the process.

This can create a problem for the 3♥, especially in personal relationships. First of all, there are few partners who will want to be one of many in the life of a Three person. Often, a person whose Birth Card is a Three, but especially the 3♥, has to lie to their partners in order to sustain the multiple relationships they seek. This lying takes up a lot of energy and causes stress, but because of their creative ability, it is something that they can pull off effectively if they want to. Next, because they go back and forth with their affections, they often feel insecure and worried about not getting enough love. This worry, in turn, motivates them to try even more relationships, and thus the cycle repeats itself, in some cases, indefinitely. It becomes a merry-go-round of love that brings little depth and satisfaction, but a lot of variety. Threes find this stimulating and fun, but also nerve-wracking and heart wrenching at times.

A major lesson for most Threes is that intimacy needs some form of commitment. Intimacy is what we all want on some level. We want to get so close to another person that we can feel and enjoy the depths of their love and our love for them. However, when we start to feel this tremendous love, we also become aware of other feelings that have been hidden from our conscious minds, feelings like fear of abandonment or our own rejection of ourselves. Thus, our search for love scares us more than anything. It takes a commitment with another person to give us the courage to hang in there and face these fears while we are enjoying the love we share with our partners. This is something that many Threes learn the hard way.

It is not that all Threes are such tortured souls. It is possible for any Three to face these inner fears and live a wonderful life with true love and intimacy for another person. Our Birth Cards merely reflect patterns of behavior. When these patterns are negative, they can be recognized, dealt with, and accepted to the extent that we are no longer affected by them. When we meet a 3♥ or any other Three, we can quickly see how they are doing in this process of acceptance and consciousness. Just ask them about their love life!

THREE OF HEARTS

LIFE SPREAD CARDS

PLANETARY CARD	SYMBOL	CARD
MOON	☽	K♠
SUN (BIRTH CARD)	✳	3♥
MERCURY	☿	A♣
VENUS	♀	Q♣
MARS	♂	10♠
JUPITER	♃	5♣
SATURN	♄	3♦
URANUS	♅	A♠
NEPTUNE	♆	7♥
PLUTO	♇	7♦
RESULT (COSMIC REWARD)	♃+	5♠
COSMIC LESSON	♄+	J♥

PLANETARY RULING CARDS

BIRTH DATE	ASTROLOGICAL RULING SIGN	PLANETARY RULING CARD
NOV 30	SAGITTARIUS	5♣
DEC 28	CAPRICORN	3♦

Who	The Connections Between Partners					Overall Index Ratings		
3♥ with	Con1	Con2	Con3	Con4	Con5	Attraction	Intensity	Compatibility
A♥	KRMA	VERS	MAMS	NEF	PLFS	8	5	2
2♥	MOFS	MOR	PLF	MORS	URF	7	-1	6
3♥	SBC	VERS	VEF	VEFS	VER	6	1	6
4♥	MORS	CLR	URR	MAF	URRS	4	0	3
5♥	VEFS	CRR	JUF	MAF	JUFS	5	0	6
6♥	MAFS	VEM	VERS	SAF	CLR	6	2	3
7♥	NEF	PLR	JUFS	NER	SAFS	4	2	2
8♥	NER	SAFS	CRRS	NEF	PLR	3	4	-1
9♥	URFS	JUM	PLF	MOR	URF	3	0	1
10♥	NEFS	MARS	CRF	MAR	CRFS	8	6	1
J♥	CLF	PLFS	MOF	MARS	CLFS	7	5	-1
Q♥	JUR	CRFS	URM	MAF	URRS	3	2	2
K♥	VER	CLFS	VEMS	NERS	VEM	7	0	5
A♣	MOR	MOFS	PLF	MOF	URF	7	-1	6
2♣	VEMS	URF	VER	CLFS	VERS	5	-1	5
3♣	JURS	JUF	JUR	CRRS	PLF	2	-1	6
4♣	VERS	JUF	MAFS	VEM	CRR	6	0	6
5♣	JUF	VEFS	VERS	VEF	NERS	5	-3	8
6♣	URR	VEMS	PLRS	PLR	URRS	3	1	2
7♣	VER	SARS	NEF	PLR	JUR	4	1	2
8♣	CLF	PLFS	MOF	MARS	URR	6	5	-1
9♣	JUR	CRFS	URM	MAR	MARS	3	2	2
10♣	MAR	SARS	SAR	VERS	NER	3	5	-1
J♣	MARS	NEFS	CLF	MOFS	VEMS	7	4	2
Q♣	KRMA	VEF	NEF	PLFS	MAM	7	4	3
K♣	SAM	PLR	PLRS	VER	MORS	2	5	-2
A♦	MAMS	VERS	KRMC	MOR	VEFS	7	2	5
2♦	URR	VEMS	MAMS	PLR	MAFS	5	2	2
3♦	SAF	MAFS	VEM	JUR	SARS	2	4	0
4♦	CRR	CRF	VEFS	SAFS	CRRS	5	3	1
5♦	JURS	JUMS	PLF	URFS	JUM	2	0	3
6♦	MAR	SAR	NEFS	MARS	CRF	5	6	0
7♦	PLF	URFS	JUM	MOR	JUMS	4	2	0
8♦	VER	SAR	JURS	JUR	CRFS	2	0	4
9♦	JUMS	JUR	SARS	JURS	SAR	0	-1	3
10♦	MAM	VEF	KRMC	SAR	JURS	5	3	3
J♦	MARS	VEMS	SAF			5	4	1
Q♦	JUR	SARS	SAF	JUMS	VEF	-1	1	1
K♦	CRRS	VERS	JUF	JUR	MARS	4	0	5
A♠	URF	NEF	PLR	JUFS	VEMS	4	1	2
2♠	PLR	SAR	CLRS	URRS	SAM	0	4	-3
3♠	MAR	SAF	SAR	NEFS	VEMS	3	6	-2
4♠	MAR	MORS	CLR	URR	JUR	5	2	3
5♠	CRF	NEFS	CRR	CRRS	NEF	7	4	2
6♠	SAR	CLRS	URRS	NERS	PLR	1	3	-2
7♠	CRRS	NER	SAFS	NERS	VEM	4	3	0
8♠	PLRS	SAM	URR	VEMS	MOF	2	4	-1
9♠	NERS	VER	CLFS	SAR	CLRS	5	2	1
10♠	MAF	URRS	MORS	CLR	URR	5	2	2
J♠	SARS	MAR	NER	PLF	MARS	4	6	-2
Q♠	SAR	JURS	MAM	VER	CRF	2	2	2
K♠	MOF	MARS	CLF	PLFS	MOFS	7	3	2

The Writer's Card

DESCRIPTION OF THE 3♣ PERSON:
The creativity in this card can manifest in many ways. On the high side, these people can be very successful writers, teachers or performers. On the low side, they can worry, become indecisive and spend their time on frivolous activities. Even among the most successful 3♣ we find worry and indecision as more-or-less constant themes in their life.

Success in life always depends upon the individual and how they use their God-given gifts and abilities. 3♣ are gifted, but their fear of poverty may entice them into using their creativity in questionable ways. If this happens, they seldom get away with it. They make great salespeople and propagandists, but they are ineffective until they decide upon one philosophy and stand behind it.

This is one of the strongest business cards. Their K♦ second Karma Card gifts them with natural business ability. They gravitate toward big money and big business and can easily position themselves in leadership wherever they work. The 5♦ first Karma Card, however, causes them to choose occupations where their freedom is not hampered too much. Thus, they will often choose to work for themselves or to freelance. Their natural gifts are creative and many become prominent authors, speakers, or producers in the entertainment industry.

They are sure to have some emotional losses—relationships that they think should last forever but don't, many of which are destined and karmic in nature. If they see them as 'completions' and graduations to a higher level, they can avoid disappointment. Their love has the potential to be realized on a more universal level.

If they utilize their inheritance of spiritual knowledge, much success can be realized. They are here to be transformers of energy—worry into creativity and fear into faith. In this manner they serve as powerful examples for us all.

SOME OF THE 3♣ ISSUES CONCERNING RELATIONSHIPS:
Here is a person who is basically indecisive—uncertain about making a commitment one way or the other. Then again, they love to try different things and to experience all that life has to offer. So, we note a lot of going back and forth in their choice of relationships. On the other hand, they may repeatedly attract those who reflect these qualities—afraid or unwilling to make a commitment. The happiest 3♣ seem to be those who accept their need for variety and simply date people for the pleasure it brings, foregoing the married life for satisfying love affairs.

Those who are married will often find a way to have someone on the side. Though there will be some losses in life, they can have love and happiness whenever they make a firm decision and refuse to accept less than what they truly want. These people have hearts of gold and will do almost anything for those they love. It is simply that they usually have much to come to terms with on a personal level before a long–term relationship can be successful.

GENERALITIES BETWEEN THE PERSONALITY CARD CONNECTIONS
Male 3♣ have a weakness for Diamond females, who also share a nice love connection with them. For this reason, this could be a good choice for long–

KARMA CARDS:

5♦ K♦

KARMA COUSINS:

9♦ 7♠

PAST-LIFE CARDS:

2♣ 4♣

---

term relationships. Likewise, the female 3♣ has some fantasies around Diamond males, who hold some sort of mystique for them. Male Clubs make good friends for both 3♣ sexes, but perhaps not the best marriage partners unless they can give them complete freedom. Both sexes are better off avoiding female Spades, who seem to bring more problems than good.

The Three of Clubs Panic Attack

Anyone who has had a relationship with a Three of Clubs will probably know what the title of this little article is all about. 3♣ people are usually happy, talkative, and generally fun to be with. But every so often they become distressed, confused, and may question everything. All Threes like to have some variety in their life and often keep their options open in case they get the desire to move in a different direction. However, keeping all those options open can sometimes become a burden. Too many choices can be as much a curse as they are a source of fun and excitement. No one knows this better than the 3♣.

Many 3♣ have these 'panic attacks' every so often. One moment they were feeling fine about everything and then something happens to scare them. Sometimes the catalyst is a mere thought or something they watch on television. When this occurs, their versatile minds kick in and begin sorting through every conceivable subject in their life that remains undecided. Then they begin questioning everything, including their own commitments, as they search for the answers to their fears.

For example, the 3♣ panic attack may begin with your 3♣ friend calling you or coming over to talk. They ask you a question about something that is bothering them and you give them a calm and reassuring answer. They appear to be satisfied with the answer, but a few minutes later, they will ask you the very same question again as though you hadn't answered it at all. Everything will seem hopeless and doubtful to them at that moment. Unfortunately, if you try to persuade them out of their doubt, it will just aggravate their condition.

Take, for example, the case of a man I know who is dating a 3♣. About every two weeks or so he will call me to say that his girlfriend is having second thoughts about their relationship. The truth is that she is having second thoughts about everything in her life. After this occurred several times, he discovered that the best thing to do is just relax and wait. He stopped trying to give her answers to all of her questions. He stopped trying to show her all the reasons why their relationship was just fine. He takes her out for a walk in the woods or a bike ride and all of her fears seem to vanish within minutes. These little panic attacks always pass.

The biggest mistake that a 3♣ person could make, or their partners could make for that matter, is to make important decisions while in the middle of one of these panic attacks. Because there is so much emotional energy stirred up at that time, it is impossible to see things clearly or to make an objective evaluation of the issues at hand. During these little attacks every choice seems wrong. The tendency of the 3♣ person is to pull back from everything, even the things that bring good energy into their lives.

This is a lesson for all of us, because the 3♣ person exemplifies our own minds. Many of us have our own little panic attacks or periods where we seem confused and doubtful about many things in our life. We can learn that all we have to do is relax and wait and the clouds that are fogging up our decision-making process will clear. The expression 'don't worry, be happy' strongly applies here. Like most of us, 3♣ people love to be happy. If we can remind them, and ourselves, of this when in the middle of one of these attacks, we can usually connect back with our joy and happiness and let go of all the mental stress and indecision.

LIFE SPREAD CARDS

PLANETARY CARD	SYMBOL	CARD
MOON	☽	5♥
SUN (BIRTH CARD)	✳	3♣
MERCURY	☿	3♠
VENUS	♀	9♥
MARS	♂	7♣
JUPITER	♃	5♦
SATURN	♄	Q♠
URANUS	♅	J♣
NEPTUNE	♆	9♦
PLUTO	♇	7♠
RESULT (COSMIC REWARD)	♃+	2♣
COSMIC LESSON	♄+	K♣

PLANETARY RULING CARDS

BIRTH DATE	ASTROLOGICAL RULING SIGN	PLANETARY RULING CARD
MAY 29	GEMINI	3♠
JUN 27	CANCER	5♥
JUL 25	LEO	3♣
AUG 23	LEO OR VIRGO	3♣ OR 3♠
SEP 21	VIRGO	3♠
OCT 19	LIBRA	9♥
NOV 17	SCORPIO	7♣ & 7♠
DEC 15	SAGITTARIUS	5♦

Celebrity Birthdays

BILL MURRAY
9/21/50 • *Actor*
DANNY DEVITO
11/17/44 • *Actor*
JOHN LITHGOW
10/19/45 • *Actor*
MATT LEBLANC
7/25/67 • *Actor*
TOBEY MAGUIRE
6/27/75 • *Actor*
SHELLEY LONG
8/23/49 • *Actress*
HELEN KELLER
6/27/1880 • *Handicapped Activist*
TIM CONWAY
12/15/33 • *Comedian*
JOHN F. KENNEDY
5/29/17 • *Former President*
BOB HOPE
5/29/03 • *Comedian*
ROSS PEROT
6/27/30 • *Businessman*
GENE KELLY
8/23/12 • *Actor/Dancer*
STEPHEN KING
9/21/47 • *Writer*
WALTER PAYTON
7/25/54 • *Football Player*
JULIA DUFFY
6/27/51 • *Actress*
ROB MORROW
9/21/62 • *Actor*
CECIL FIELDER
9/21/63 • *Baseball Player*

Who	The Connections Between Partners					Overall Index Ratings		
3♣ with	Con1	Con2	Con3	Con4	Con5	Attraction	Intensity	Compatibility
A♥	JUR	MAR	PLR	NER	PLF	4	3	2
2♥	VEFS	VERS	MAF	VER	VEF	7	-1	7
3♥	JUR	JUF	CRFS	JUFS	PLR	2	-1	5
4♥	VEM	VEMS	PLR	PLF	SAFS	6	1	4
5♥	MOF	VERS	VEFS	SAR	VER	6	-2	7
6♥	VEF	CLRS	MORS	MOR	VEFS	6	-2	7
7♥	CRRS	PLRS	JUM	MAMS	JUMS	4	3	1
8♥	PLRS	PLF	CRRS	JUF	NEFS	5	4	-1
9♥	VEF	NERS	PLFS	VERS	VER	7	1	4
10♥	NER	URRS	URF	PLFS	MAF	4	2	0
J♥	SARS	MAMS	CLR	SAFS	MAM	2	6	-3
Q♥	JURS	URFS	VER	CLFS	VEM	3	-1	4
K♥	MARS	VEM	MOFS	CRF	MAM	8	2	5
A♣	VERS	VEFS	VEF	MAF	VER	7	-2	8
2♣	MOFS	CRF	JUM	MAMS	MARS	6	1	4
3♣	SBC	JUF	JUR	NEF	PLFS	4	2	4
4♣	MORS	VEFS	VEF	CLRS	MAFS	7	-2	8
5♣	VEFS	MOF	MORS	MAFS	SAR	7	-1	8
6♣	MAFS	VEM	SAR	VEMS	CRR	6	3	3
7♣	MAF	JUFS	MOF	MAFS	SARS	6	2	4
8♣	CLR	SAFS	SARS	MAMS	VEF	0	5	-3
9♣	URFS	JURS	CRR	VEMS	CRRS	2	-1	3
10♣	SAF	NEFS	PLRS	PLR	VEMS	2	5	-2
J♣	URF	PLFS	MARS	NER	URRS	5	4	-2
Q♣	JUF	CRFS	URR	URRS	JUM	3	0	3
K♣	CLF	CLFS	VER	SAR	URF	4	4	-1
A♦	MAR	VEM	JUR	NER	PLF	6	2	4
2♦	VEM	MAFS	MAR	MARS	MAF	8	5	3
3♦	VEF	CLRS	VER	VERS	CLR	5	-1	6
4♦	VERS	MAF	JURS	MOF	MOFS	6	0	6
5♦	KRMA	JUF	NEF	PLF	NEFS	6	4	2
6♦	CRR	VEMS	URFS	MOR	MORS	5	-1	5
7♦	VEF	NERS	PLFS	VERS	VEFS	7	1	4
8♦	SAF	MAF	JUFS	MAFS	SARS	2	6	-2
9♦	NEF	VER	KRMC	JUF	MAF	6	1	5
10♦	URR	JUF	CRFS	SAF	CLR	1	2	1
J♦	MARS	MOR	URF	PLFS	NEF	6	3	2
Q♦	VER	NEF	URR	NEFS	MOFS	6	0	5
K♦	KRMA	PLF	NEFS	PLFS	NEF	8	7	-2
A♠	JUM	MAMS	CRRS	MOFS	CRF	5	2	3
2♠	VER	CLF	CLFS	VEFS	VERS	6	2	3
3♠	MOR	CRR	VEMS	MARS	MAR	7	0	6
4♠	PLR	SAF	NEFS	PLRS	VEM	2	5	-2
5♠	MAF	JURS	NER	URRS	VERS	5	2	3
6♠	MAM	JUMS	VER	VERS	URFS	5	1	4
7♠	PLF	PLRS	KRMC	JUF	NEFS	5	5	-1
8♠	SAR	CLF	CLFS	MAFS	VEM	3	6	-3
9♠	MAM	JUMS	MARS	VEM	MAR	6	4	3
10♠	VEM	VEMS	JURS	CLFS	PLF	6	-1	6
J♠	MAF	JUFS	SAF	NEFS	PLRS	4	4	1
Q♠	SAF	URR	MOR	URFS	CLR	0	2	-1
K♠	MAMS	CLR	SAFS	SARS	MAM	3	7	-3

Financial Creativity

DESCRIPTION OF THE 3♦ PERSON:
The 3♦ is considered one of the most difficult life paths of all the cards, especially when the 3♦ is a woman, because the Q♦, her Personality and Karma Card, is the other most difficult card in the deck. Indecision in values along with past-life relationship karma (6♥ Karma Card) can result in many challenges with their affections. They also can be some of the biggest worriers about their finances. All Threes are guilty of worry and indecision and must find constructive outlets for their overactive minds. The best remedy is to find some expression of their creativity. They must express themselves.

A natural interest in metaphysics should be cultivated if they are to know more peace in their lives and overcome the many hurdles and temptations. These people have a mind that can penetrate the secrets of the universe. Among these secrets lies the understanding about their lives and the personal karma they are here to deal with. This understanding brings much peace into their lives.

They always know right from wrong, though sometimes they try to ignore what they know. Not all 3♦ have these problems. Operating out of the high side of this card, they are extremely creative and productive, expressing themselves in a multitude of productive ways. They can be the greatest entertainers or public speakers.

They also have very powerful mind and usually a powerful voice to match. With this voice and the mental resources to back it up, they can be the most effective promoters once they have found something they believe in. Consider yourself lucky if you have a 3♦ promoting your products or services.

They have more satisfaction in business where they can travel or do various different things. There is usually someone younger for whom they must make sacrifices, often one or more of their own children. With two Nines in their Life Path, their later life can be disappointing, *unless* they have developed their spiritual side, which will give them peace and wisdom. These people are here to try many ideas on for size and then to settle on the truth. They always benefit from changes and travel and are advised to pursue a career that gives them some freedom in this area.

SOME OF THE 3♦ ISSUES CONCERNING RELATIONSHIPS:
The 3♦ card runs neck and neck with the Q♦ as being the most difficult in the deck in this area. There is such great creativity in this card that they come into this life feeling like there are boundless realms to explore and experience. At some point they realize that they also have tremendous fears of abandonment and betrayal that must be dealt with along the way. This usually manifests as multiple relationships or chronic indecision regarding matters of love and marriage. If they cannot deal with their own inner insecurities, they will usually choose to have transitory relationships. Multiple marriages are common with this card, as with the Q♦. The 7♥ in Venus tells us that they are learning to let others be as they are and to heal their own fears of betrayal or abandonment.

Their 6♥ first Karma Card tells us that they arrive in this life with the tendency to be somewhat thoughtless about other people's feelings, along with a carefree nature that can leave others feeling uncertain

---

KARMA CARDS:

6♥   Q♦

KARMA COUSINS:

4♣   9♦

PAST-LIFE CARDS:

2♦   4♦

---

about their affections. In this lifetime they will learn the value of being consistent with their love and affections. This usually takes time, so we naturally expect most of their romantic happiness to come later in life. That can be okay for a 3♦ since the romantic drives and desire for relationship in this card will usually sustain itself well into the last years of their life.

Female 3♦ are often attracted to Hearts and Spades males, though they mix well with Clubs as well. There are no definite suit connections of great strength. The men have a special feeling for Spade females, and Club females are very attracted to male 3♦.

PROFILE

How the Hardest Card in the Deck Finds Happiness and Love

The 3♦ Life Path presents many obstacles. When we consider the fact that Sevens and Nines are always considered to be the most challenging cards to have in one's Life Path and then notice that the 3♦ has two Sevens and two Nines in theirs, we get a sense for what their life must be like. Sevens and Nines are spiritual numbers and, as Olney Richmond says, spiritual numbers bring success on the spiritual levels and problems, challenges, and defeats on the mundane levels. The strong mundane cards are the Fours, Eights, and Tens. The two Sevens fall in the Venus and Mars positions. This indicates a lot of past-life karma in sex and relationships, such as a person who in a prior life abused their sexuality and partners in relationships and now has to meet with some of that karma in return. The two Nines fall in Uranus and Neptune. These relate to lessons about choosing the right occupation and overcoming a fear of loss, both physically and financially. So, we can see why Florence Campbell and Edith Randall considered this Birth Card as one of the most difficult, if not *the* most difficult card to be.

While many 3♦ are worried and have problems in their love life, there are also those that are beautiful examples of people accessing the highest potential in their Birth Cards. The 3♦ path is a hard one on the material level, but it is full of success and accomplishment on the spiritual level. This means that once the 3♦ person delves into the study of the self, they have a better chance than most to achieve a happiness that is not dependent on things in the world going their way. True happiness is that which does not depend upon external situations or circumstances to sustain it. It is the 3♦ that has the greatest chance of realizing this cherished goal. Cultivating their natural interest in mystical subjects always benefits the 3♦ life enormously. This includes the many religions, astrology, numerology, the Science of the Cards, and others. Consistent study eventually answers all of their questions and brings peace of mind and heart.

One of the happiest 3♦ I have ever met was a woman who worked as a cake decorator. She also held a position of responsibility and leadership in her church. She was a highly spiritual woman who lived her life by the principles she had learned from experience. She was always giving of herself to others, baking amazing desserts and bringing them with her to church each Sunday. She was always happy and productive and seemed very healthy, alive, and youthful well into her seventies.

THREE OF DIAMONDS

LIFE SPREAD CARDS

PLANETARY CARD	SYMBOL	CARD
MOON	☽	5♣
SUN (BIRTH CARD)	✳	3♦
MERCURY	☿	A♠
VENUS	♀	7♥
MARS	♂	7♦
JUPITER	♃	5♠
SATURN	♄	J♥
URANUS	♅	9♣
NEPTUNE	♆	9♠
PLUTO	♇	2♥
RESULT (COSMIC REWARD)	♃ +	K♥
COSMIC LESSON	♄ +	K♦

PLANETARY RULING CARDS

BIRTH DATE	ASTROLOGICAL RULING SIGN	PLANETARY RULING CARD
JAN 24	AQUARIUS	9♣
FEB 22	PISCES	9♠
MAR 20	PISCES OR ARIES	9♠ OR 7♦
APR 18	ARIES	7♦
MAY 16	TAURUS	7♥
JUN 14	GEMINI	A♠
JUL 12	CANCER	5♣
AUG 10	LEO	3♦
SEP 8	VIRGO	A♠
OCT 6	LIBRA	7♥
NOV 4	SCORPIO	7♦ & 2♥
DEC 2	SAGITTARIUS	5♠

Who	The Connections Between Partners					Overall Index Ratings		
3♦ with	Con1	Con2	Con3	Con4	Con5	Attraction	Intensity	Compatibility
A♥	MAR	JUFS	VERS	SAR	CLF	5	3	3
2♥	PLF	JUR	MAF	JUFS	MAR	5	4	1
3♥	SAR	MAR	JUFS	JURS	MARS	2	4	1
4♥	VERS	VER	URF	URR	SAFS	4	-1	4
5♥	JUM	JUMS	MORS	MOF	MOFS	4	-3	7
6♥	KRMA	VEM	VEMS	NEF	NEFS	8	2	5
7♥	VEF	MAFS	MOR	MORS	CRR	8	0	7
8♥	MAFS	VEF	VEFS	CLF	PLFS	7	3	4
9♥	MAF	JUFS	JUR	MAFS	VEM	5	2	4
10♥	MAM	SARS	JUF	NEF	JUFS	4	3	2
J♥	SAF	MAMS	URR	PLRS	SAFS	1	6	-4
Q♥	CRR	VER	URF	NERS	PLFS	5	1	2
K♥	CRF	VEFS	NEF	PLR	VER	7	2	4
A♣	JUR	PLF	MAF	JUFS	PLFS	5	3	1
2♣	VEFS	MOR	CRF	CRFS	CLR	7	0	6
3♣	VEFS	CLF	CLFS	VER	VEF	6	2	3
4♣	VEM	VEMS	KRMC	MOF	MOR	7	-2	9
5♣	MOF	JUM	JUMS	VEM	VEMS	5	-3	8
6♣	CLRS	MOFS	CRF	MAR	CRFS	5	2	2
7♣	JUR	CRRS	NER	SAFS	VER	2	1	2
8♣	PLRS	SAF	MAMS	URR	JUF	2	5	-3
9♣	URF	NERS	PLFS	CRR	MAFS	4	3	-1
10♣	PLR	URRS	VER	VERS	MAF	4	1	2
J♣	SARS	PLFS	MAM	MAMS	PLF	5	7	-4
Q♣	MAR	JURS	SAR	NEFS	PLRS	4	4	1
K♣	SAR	MARS	MAM	VEMS	JUR	4	5	0
A♦	VERS	MOFS	MAR	JUFS	MARS	7	0	6
2♦	MOFS	CLRS	VERS	VEF	CLR	5	-2	6
3♦	SBC	CRFS	CRRS	PLF	NEFS	6	6	0
4♦	MORS	JUF	JUM	JUMS	PLRS	4	-3	7
5♦	VEFS	URFS	URF	NERS	MAR	4	0	4
6♦	MAFS	URF	NERS	PLFS	SAF	5	5	-1
7♦	MAF	JUFS	JUR	PLR	SARS	4	2	3
8♦	NER	SAFS	SAM	JUR	CRRS	0	5	-2
9♦	URFS	CRFS	KRMC	VEFS	MAR	4	3	2
10♦	NEFS	PLRS	MAR	JURS	SAM	5	4	1
J♦	PLFS	SARS	MOFS	MAF	JUFS	5	4	-1
Q♦	KRMA	CRFS	NEF	NEFS	URFS	7	5	1
K♦	CLF	CLFS	MOF	MORS	VER	6	3	1
A♠	MOR	VEF	VEFS	CLR	CRR	6	-2	8
2♠	CLR	URR	VEMS	SAR	MARS	2	1	1
3♠	MAFS	PLFS	MAF	JUFS	SAF	7	7	-1
4♠	VERS	PLR	URRS	URF	URR	3	0	2
5♠	JUF	MAM	MORS	NER	URFS	5	1	5
6♠	CLR	URR	VEMS	NEF	PLR	3	0	2
7♠	CLF	CLFS	MAFS	PLFS		6	8	-4
8♠	SAR	MARS	CLRS	CRF	MAR	3	6	-2
9♠	NEF	PLR	CRF	CLR	URR	5	3	0
10♠	VER	CRR	CRRS	VERS		6	0	5
J♠	VER	JUR	CRRS	PLR	URRS	4	-1	4
Q♠	SAM	NEFS	PLRS	NER	SAFS	2	6	-2
K♠	URR	PLRS	SAF	MAMS	URRS	1	4	-3

The Artist's Card

DESCRIPTION OF THE 3♠ PERSON:

The 3♠ have the opportunity for great success in their life if they are willing to work for it. They have a heavier load than most, indicated by their position in the Saturn line. But if they work hard, they will receive the blessing of being in the Jupiter column (as seen in the Life Spread). Their 6♦ Karma Card tells us that there is a karmic debt to pay on a financial or 'value' basis. They are often associated with 6♦ persons, who are the collectors of these debts. The main lesson is to learn responsibility and fairness with financial dealings and money in general. The 3♠ person will often have to pass through some experiences where they feel they were treated unfairly on a financial level. The 6♦ tells us that most if not all of these are just the payments being made from lifetimes past.

The 3♠ can represent indecision about work or health and they should watch their health carefully. The more they worry about their health, the worse their condition may get, so they have a responsibility to watch their thoughts and feelings as they relate to health matters. In many cases, their health problems can be traced to emotional stress in their lives. Their strong work and career drives often interfere with their attention to their bodies and emotions. With such a strong creative urge, they can also spread themselves too thin and get stressed out at times.

Having the Q♠ in Jupiter (which has a 10♦ Karma Card) gives them the opportunity for great business success through mastery of their inner values. This can be one of their best avenues for satisfaction in life. These people are artistically gifted and can produce some of the most profound and inspiring expressions in the medium of their choice. If they just get clear about what is most important to them in life, everything they need and want will come to them. They can also excel at sales and promotion, though this avenue isn't as satisfying on the creative level as artistic pursuits. They are well-suited for having multiple occupations and usually choose this, but must be careful not to take on too much.

Being a Three brings a huge amount of creativity and this can also bring the temptation to tell half-truths or stories to make their lives easier. This is especially true because of their J♦ Karma Card. They can easily tell stories that are believed by others and never run out of marketable ideas. However, with the J♣ in their Saturn position, they will always meet with some disappointment or problems if they stray from strict honesty. Only the path of highest integrity and the willingness to put forth an honest work effort will bring them the success they want. Among them are some of the most successful artists in the world.

SOME OF THE 3♠ ISSUES CONCERNING RELATIONSHIPS:

The 3♠ is a highly creative and romantic person and needs a partner with whom they may share these interests. There are hurdles in love based upon inner fears of abandonment or rejection that must be dealt with, but overall they have good marriage potential. They need an outlet for their creativity, because their extra-marital affairs are usually the result of not giving themselves a positive creative outlet.

They will often attract a mate who is of a critical nature, one with a pessimistic attitude. But even so, this same mate usually

---

KARMA CARDS:

6♦   J♦

KARMA COUSINS:

9♣   J♣

PAST-LIFE CARDS:

2♠   4♠

makes good money and they enjoy that aspect of the relationship. There is a good deal of idealism in this card that can spill into their romantic involvements. Love can be a very spiritual thing for them and they often have lofty goals for their marriage, but this same idealism tends to blind them to the negative qualities of those they attract in love and they end up with those who don't really match up with their dreams.

There are often emotional challenges that began in childhood that must be dealt with before the 3♠ can have a happy married or romantic life. They also need to develop positive mental habits and affirmations about love if they are to overcome some of the challenges in this area. They are restless, a quality which may extend to their romantic lives. Finding the combination of qualities in someone else that matches their own diversity may take some time, but is entirely possible.

GENERALITIES BETWEEN THE PERSONALITY CARD CONNECTIONS

3♠ males are sought after by Diamond females who find them very attractive in general. Both sexes of 3♠ are often better off with a Club male in their lives, though they are a mixed blessing at best. Even Diamond males can be somewhat difficult at times. 3♠ females are attracted to Heart males.

The Actor and the Artist

It is interesting to note how much the Threes of the deck compare with the Jacks of their same suit. Even though the Jack seems to be such a different number (11), they exhibit many of the same qualities of the Three of their suit. The 3♠ and J♠ are a good example of this. One is known as the Artist's Card (3♠), and the other, the Actor (J♠). Yet many 3♠ are great actors and many J♠ are great artists. Spades are the strongest suit. Hearts represent feelings, Clubs represent thoughts, Diamonds represent values or what we want, but Spades represent what we actually do. The creative Spade is much more interested in the perfection of their doing than the feeling, idea, or cost of what they create. The Spade artist is a master of his or her craft, and both the 3♠ and J♠ take this approach. Since acting involves stepping into the life of some character and doing what he or she does, it becomes more apparent that the 3♠ could just as easily become an actor or actress as an artist, musician, or performer in other areas.

Like the Jacks, too, the Threes have a strong romantic streak in them. As mentioned before in this book, the astrological house that governs creative expression, the 5th house, also governs romance and sexual pleasure. Both the J♠ and 3♠ have gifts in the areas of romance. Anyone who has dated or married one will tell you that these cards excel in the romantic and sexual areas. They make some of the best lovers.

This does not mean they will make the best marriage partners, though. It is common knowledge that most actors, artists, and musicians usually have a love life that consists of a continuous stream of romantic involvements. Even when they marry, it is often of short duration or marked by one or more secret liaisons. The commitment ability or desire is simply not there. If you or I were to go to a bank and apply for a loan, the bank would deduct points from our credit worthiness if it was discovered that our occupation was actor or artist. Credit worthiness is associated with the ability to stay with one thing and see it through. Those who are the most romantic and creative are often lacking in this area. It is of little interest to them. The notable exceptions to this rule are those 3♠ and J♠ who have truly found themselves in their work. All of their creative and romantic drive is used up in their work, or at least enough of it that they don't need to seek new relationships in order to find that fulfillment.

LIFE SPREAD CARDS

PLANETARY CARD	SYMBOL	CARD
MOON	☽	3♣
SUN (BIRTH CARD)	✴	3♠
MERCURY	☿	9♥
VENUS	♀	7♣
MARS	♂	5♦
JUPITER	♃	Q♠
SATURN	♄	J♣
URANUS	♅	9♦
NEPTUNE	♆	7♠
PLUTO	♇	2♣
RESULT (COSMIC REWARD)	♃ +	K♣
COSMIC LESSON	♄ +	J♦

PLANETARY RULING CARDS

BIRTH DATE	ASTROLOGICAL RULING SIGN	PLANETARY RULING CARD
JAN 11	CAPRICORN	J♣
FEB 9	AQUARIUS	9♦
MAR 7	PISCES	7♠
APR 5	ARIES	5♦
MAY 3	TAURUS	7♣
JUN 1	GEMINI	9♥

Celebrity Birthdays

IVAN LENDL
3/7/60 • Tennis Player

DANIEL TRAVANTI
3/7/40 • Actor

GREGORY PECK
4/5/16 • Actor

JOE PESCI
2/9/43 • Actor

SPENCER TRACY
4/5/1900 • Actor

BETTE DAVIS
4/5/08 • Actress

GALE STORM
4/5/22 • Actress

MARILYN MONROE
6/1/26 • Actress

MIA FARROW
2/9/45 • Actress

GENERAL COLIN POWELL
4/5/37 • Chief of Staff

NAOMI JUDD
1/11/46 • Singer

DOUG HENNING
5/3/47 • Magician

ARTHUR HAILEY
4/5/20 • Novelist

PETER WOLF
3/7/46 • Rock Singer

CAROLE KING
2/9/42 • Singer

FRANKIE VALLI
5/3/37 • Singer

JAMES BROWN
5/3/33 • Singer

ALEXANDER HAMILTON
1/11/1755 • Statesman

WILLARD SCOTT
3/7/34 • Television Personality

ANDY GRIFFITH
6/1/26 • Actor

MORGAN FREEMAN
6/1/37 • Actor

HEIDI KLUM
6/1/73 • Model

Who 3♠ with	Con1	Con2	Con3	Con4	Con5	Attraction	Intensity	Compatibility
A♥	SAR	JUR	SAF	URF	SARS	-2	3	-2
2♥	MAM	SAMS	JUFS	CRRS	PLR	3	5	0
3♥	SAR	MAF	SAF	VEMS		2	5	-2
4♥	MORS	CRR	JUF	NEFS	PLRS	6	-1	6
5♥	VER	VEM	MAMS	PLF	VERS	8	1	5
6♥	VEF	SAR	JUR	MAM	PLRS	3	1	3
7♥	SAFS	MAM	MAMS	VER	VERS	4	6	-1
8♥	VER	NEF	JUFS	SAFS	MAM	5	1	4
9♥	MOR	CRRS	JUFS	CRR	JURS	5	-1	6
10♥	PLR	JUMS	SAF	VEFS	VEF	2	2	1
J♥	MAF	CLFS	MAFS	JUM	CLF	7	6	-1
Q♥	JUF	NEFS	PLRS	NEF	PLR	5	1	3
K♥	PLF	URFS	NER	JUMS	VER	4	3	-1
A♣	JUFS	MAM	SAMS	CRRS	MAMS	4	4	2
2♣	PLF	VERS	VER	PLFS	SAF	7	3	0
3♣	MOF	MAF	MARS	VEM	VEMS	8	2	5
4♣	VEF	MAMS	JUR	MAM	VEFS	6	2	5
5♣	MAMS	VER	VEF	VEFS	PLF	8	2	5
6♣	URR	SAFS	VEFS	SAF	MAMS	0	3	-2
7♣	VEF	SAF	PLRS	PLFS	VEM	3	3	0
8♣	MAFS	MAF	CLFS	MOF	CLF	8	6	0
9♣	CLR	CLRS	KRMC	NEF	PLR	3	3	0
10♣	PLFS	VEM	MORS	CRR	CRRS	7	2	3
J♣	SAF	CLF	KRMC	SARS	PLR	1	7	-4
Q♣	NER	URRS	NERS	VEMS	MAF	5	1	2
K♣	CRF	VEMS	MOFS	URR	SAFS	6	1	4
A♦	JUR	VEFS	SAR	URF	SARS	1	0	4
2♦	VEFS	JUR	MAR	JURS	CRRS	4	0	6
3♦	MAR	JURS	MARS	PLRS	SAR	5	5	1
4♦	VEM	VEFS	VER	VERS	VEF	7	-3	9
5♦	MAF	URF	NERS	PLFS	MOF	6	4	0
6♦	KRMA	CLR	CLRS	PLF	NEFS	4	5	-1
7♦	CRRS	MOR	JUFS	MORS	JURS	5	-1	6
8♦	SAF	PLRS	JUF	CRFS	VEF	1	4	-2
9♦	URF	NERS	PLFS	MAR	JURS	4	3	0
10♦	NER	URRS	JUF	CRFS	MAF	4	1	2
J♦	KRMA	CLF	SARS	PLF	NEFS	5	7	-3
Q♦	MAR	JURS	URF	NERS	PLFS	4	3	2
K♦	MARS	VEM	VEMS	MOF	NEF	8	1	6
A♠	VERS	SAFS	MAM	MAMS	PLF	4	5	0
2♠	MOFS	MAFS	VEM	VEMS	CRF	8	0	7
3♠	SBC	CLR	CLRS	CLF	SARS	3	5	-1
4♠	MORS	CRR	MOR	URFS	CRRS	6	-1	6
5♠	VEFS	PLR	JUMS	VEM	VEMS	5	-1	6
6♠	MAFS	VEM	VEMS	URFS	MOFS	7	1	5
7♠	NEF	JUFS	MARS	VEM	VEMS	6	1	5
8♠	URR	SAFS	CRF	VEMS	JUF	1	3	-1
9♠	URFS	MAFS	VEM	VEMS	CRR	5	1	3
10♠	JUF	NEFS	PLRS	MAM	MAR	5	2	3
J♠	PLFS	VEM	VEF	VER	VEMS	8	1	4
Q♠	JUF	CRFS	NER	URRS	SAF	3	2	2
K♠	CLFS	MAFS	MAF	JUM	CLF	6	6	-1

Home, family, stability, security, contentment, foundation, good supply of things needed for life—these are the keywords of the number Four and the people who bear this number on their Birth Card. Four people often look rounded or squarish in physical appearance. This applies both to Four Birth Cards as well as those with a Four as their Planetary Ruling Card. They look and seem like solid, grounded people. It inspires one with a sense of safety and security to be with them. It is no accident that the fourth house in astrology represents many of the same things. The sign of Cancer, which rules the fourth house, represents nurturing and security. All Fours, but certainly some more than others, are interested in security and stability in their lives. In whatever they are doing, we can see them creating this order and stability in their lives and in the lives of those they have chosen to protect.

Protection is another keyword for the number Four. And protection is their birthright. However, this protection only manifests itself to the Four person who is willing to work for things in their life. Through work all of their dreams are realized. Avoidance or ignorance of this single principle is probably the biggest cause of unhappiness in the life of a Four. Without this willingness to put in the effort, everything turns against them to varying degrees. With the application of commitment and effort, they can accomplish most anything they desire. The unhappy Four person is invariably the one who either avoids or resents how much work they must do.

Many Fours are also overly security conscious. It is the Four person who is not meeting up to their own inner requirements of work and commitment that becomes the controller who tries to keep everyone from doing anything that might upset their little box of a world they have created. The mother or father who controls their children and keeps them sheltered at home, not allowing them to develop any responsibility of their own, is often a Four. They will tell their friends and themselves that they are doing it to help their children, but in truth, it is stunting their development. They usually don't realize that their true motivations are the fears of losing their children, which represent a large part of their security system.

The boss who micro-manages his or her business may also be a Four. He may get so overly concerned with organization and details that he fails to see the big picture and actually does things that are counterproductive to the company's goals of serving its customers. He also may be blind to the possibilities that present themselves for expansion and growth. To a Four, too much growth can represent a threat to their security system. And no one can fight harder to keep things the way they are than a Four. In their eyes, if things are working well enough the way they are, why change them?

This does not mean that Fours dislike change for change's sake. No, they only fight against it if it seems to threaten their security system. As a matter of fact, the 4♦ and 4♣ are fairly progressive in many ways. They also like to travel a lot, which is typical of a Five. Perhaps this is because both of them have Fives as their first Karma Cards. These Five connections also account for why these two Fours have the most difficulty just doing their work and being happy about it. The 4♦ and 4♣ seem to have the most conflict between the happiness their work brings and the desire to just take off.

A Four person is someone who is good at organization, setting boundaries, establishing foundations, and managing and working. They are usually not found in positions of leadership, but tend to gravitate toward finding a suitable job where they can make their contribution without too much hassle from others. They are usually not the most creative people, nor are they the most far-sighted or broad-minded. But they personify an important and necessary element in our lives—the importance of security, stability, and hard work.

They will have to work hard during the course of their lives, but as they get into their later years, they find themselves with more money and freedom to travel and enjoy their life without so much hard work. If they can let go of their 'struggle mentality,' they will see that sometimes good things just flow to us without so much effort.

In relationships, their fate is mixed overall. They tend to want to settle down, but some of them, especially the 4♦, have difficult relationship issues to deal with and there can be no escaping the challenges in their romantic life.

Many of them are able to master certain skills and techniques in a way that is truly amazing. They rise to the top of their professions through the application of their organization and hard work. We can truly admire them for their accomplishments and we can trust them to deliver good products, ideas and services to us when we employ or hire them. 'Good' is a Four word and describes the qualities that they put forth most of the time in everything that they do.

The Marriage & Family Card

DESCRIPTION OF THE 4♥ PERSON:

Here we have the first Four in the deck, the first to seek stability and foundation. The 4♥ seeks this in relationships, either intimate or friendship and family related. These people have high ideals about love and family and when these ideals are not reached, the pain can be so great that they need some form of escape to soothe themselves. If their ideals are combined with truth and objectivity, these people can have wonderful lives of fulfillment in family and other love areas. They hear the inner call to help others and lay aside some of their personal considerations. If they do so, they have more satisfaction and fewer dreams that become nightmares.

Many 4♥ are healers and protectors. Others come to them for love and support in times of need. Satisfaction comes in giving of themselves and caring for others. They all have a need for self-expression and do well with groups and organizations as teachers and event organizers. Some have great scientific minds as well. They are very good with money and have no one but themselves to blame if their lives are not happy and productive. They must maintain good health habits, as this card, more than others, never gets away with indulgence, either physical or emotional.

All Fours can be controlling and the 4♥ will often try to control their family members in order to sustain what they consider to be the most important thing in their life—their family unit. If overdone, they will suffer when it comes time to let their children live their own lives. Even among friends, they will often try to keep a certain number of people in their lives for their own personal security. They need to watch out for codependent behavior. Not everyone in the world needs to be saved or nurtured, as much as the 4♥ may like to think.

The 4♥ has a strong, psychic side which, if developed, can bring them much success in the world. They all use it in their work, whether they are aware of it or not. They are usually most successful developing one thing and sticking with it.

Many 4♥ are destined to become important leaders in their chosen field, and part of the path to that high success causes them to face issues around money and power. Finding their own power while maintaining their foundation of love and support is an important step in this process.

SOME OF THE 4♥ ISSUES CONCERNING RELATIONSHIPS:

The 4♥ has high ideals in the areas of love and family, often too high for reality to match. These tender fantasies of love can often come crashing against the reality of the world and cause them considerable pain and despair. They are, however, very loving and devoted to their family and loved ones. There are bound to be some challenges in love along with the call to let others be as they are. Their high ideals can be reached when they find a more 'spiritual' way of looking at their love life. They are generally well-liked by men and have a certain power and charm when they apply themselves.

GENERALITIES BETWEEN THE PERSONALITY CARD CONNECTIONS

4♥ males have a way of stealing the hearts of Spade females, but usually can make better relationships with Diamond females. 4♥ females make good partners with Club males and good friends with Diamond males and Heart females.

KARMA CARDS:

4♠   10♠

KARMA COUSINS:

10♣   Q♥

PAST-LIFE CARDS:

3♥   5♥

The Cancer Card

The 4♥, more than any other Four, represents the home and family, subjects that are associated with the astrological sign of Cancer. The sign of Cancer governs the 4th house. Here we have issues concerning, home, family, the mother, nurturing, and security. All of these are prominent in the make-up of the 4♥ person. We can expect to always find strong Cancer, Moon, or 4th house aspects in the natal astrological charts of 4♥ people.

They are the protectors of the home and family unit, those that nurture their children, regardless of who their children may be. If you are a close friend or even a coworker of 4♥, they will treat you as they would their child and will take good care of you, regardless of whether that person is a male or female. This 4♥ nurturing is a very feminine trait, making 4♥ a lot like a Queen, which are also known for their nurturing traits.

But being so nurturing can also be a challenge at times. The 4♥ will usually seek to maintain the small circle of Hearts (people) that is represented by their card. The people in their life are their main security system. When one or more of these key people have to go elsewhere for some reason, the unaware 4♥ person may try to keep them, not realizing their fear of losing security is motivating them. The 4♥ only has three birthdays. One is a Capricorn, one a Sagittarius, and the last a Scorpio, the day of Halloween. It is the Scorpio birthday that will be the most controlling, because Scorpio is a controlling Sun sign to begin with. Add to that the fact that both of the Planetary Ruling Cards for the Scorpio 4♥ are Eights, which are also both power/control cards, and we can see that the Scorpio 4♥ would be the most likely to use control tactics to preserve their security systems. The Scorpio 4♥ is the one with the most power, whether it is used for good or it is abused. This gives them the great responsibility of being aware of themselves and not letting their fears dictate their decisions.

But, for the most part, the 4♥ are the ideal parents. Their children grow up strong and healthy because of the loving care they have received in their childhood. 4♥ people are reminders to us all of the importance of security, especially in the developing years of our childhood.

FOUR OF HEARTS

LIFE SPREAD CARDS

PLANETARY CARD	SYMBOL	CARD
MOON	☽	J♦
SUN (BIRTH CARD)	☀	4♥
MERCURY	☿	4♦
VENUS	♀	2♠
MARS	♂	8♥
JUPITER	♃	6♣
SATURN	♄	6♠
URANUS	♅	Q♥
NEPTUNE	♆	10♣
PLUTO	♇	8♦
RESULT (COSMIC REWARD)	♃ +	K♠
COSMIC LESSON	♄ +	3♥

PLANETARY RULING CARDS

BIRTH DATE	ASTROLOGICAL RULING SIGN	PLANETARY RULING CARD
OCT 31	SCORPIO	8♥ & 8♦
NOV 29	SAGITTARIUS	6♣
DEC 27	CAPRICORN	6♠

Who 4♥ with	Con1	Con2	Con3	Con4	Con5	Attraction	Intensity	Compatibility
A♥	MARS	MOFS	CLF	URF	JUF	6	3	2
2♥	VERS	CLFS	CRR	CLF	SAFS	5	3	1
3♥	MOFS	CLF	URF	MARS	MAR	6	2	2
4♥	SBC	NERS	NEFS	NEF	URRS	6	4	2
5♥	MORS	MOR	VERS	NEF	PLR	7	-2	8
6♥	VEFS	URR	CRFS	SAR	VER	4	1	3
7♥	SAF	MAFS	MAF	JUFS	URM	3	6	-2
8♥	MAF	JUFS	JUR	CLRS	URRS	4	2	3
9♥	CLR	SAFS	CLFS	CLF	SAMS	1	6	-4
10♥	URFS	URR	MOR	VER	URF	3	-1	3
J♥	NEFS	CRF	JURS	VEM	NEF	6	1	4
Q♥	URF	PLFS	KRMC	NERS	MAMS	5	4	-1
K♥	JUF	CRFS	MAR	PLRS	SAM	4	4	2
A♣	CLFS	VERS	MAF	VER	SAFS	6	3	1
2♣	MAR	URM	JUF	CRFS	JUFS	4	3	2
3♣	VEM	VEMS	PLR	SARS	PLF	6	0	4
4♣	VERS	VEFS	SAR	VER	JUMS	5	-1	6
5♣	VERS	MORS	MAM	MOR	NEF	8	-1	7
6♣	JUF	CRRS	JUM	MAMS	MAM	4	1	4
7♣	CRR	VEMS	PLF	URRS	CRRS	6	2	2
8♣	NEFS	CRF	JURS	VER	JUFS	6	1	4
9♣	MAMS	URF	PLFS	MAF	JURS	6	6	-1
10♣	NEF	URRS	KRMC	URR	MAR	4	2	2
J♣	URR	MOF	URFS	VER	URRS	3	-1	4
Q♣	MARS	MOFS	CLF	URF	MAM	6	4	2
K♣	VER	VEF	CRRS	VERS	PLRS	6	-1	6
A♦	JUM	MAMS	MARS	SAF	MAM	4	5	0
2♦	JUM	MAMS	JUF	JUR	MAFS	4	1	4
3♦	VEFS	VEF	URR	CRFS		6	-1	6
4♦	MOR	MORS	MAR	URF	SARS	6	0	6
5♦	PLR	SAR	VEM	VEMS	PLRS	3	2	1
6♦	MAF	JURS	MAMS	MOF	MAM	6	4	3
7♦	CLR	SAFS	CLFS	VEF	CLRS	1	4	-2
8♦	PLF	NER	SARS	CRR	VEMS	5	5	-2
9♦	SAR	VEF	PLR	PLRS	VEFS	3	2	1
10♦	MAM	MARS	NER	PLF	SARS	7	7	-1
J♦	MOF	URR	URRS	CRF	JUR	4	-1	4
Q♦	VEF	SAR	URF	SARS	VEFS	2	1	2
K♦	SARS	VEM	VEMS	JUR	CLRS	3	0	4
A♠	URM	SAF	MAFS	MAR	MARS	2	5	-2
2♠	VEF	SAF	VER	VERS	PLRS	4	0	3
3♠	MAF	JURS	MOF	MOFS	CRF	6	1	5
4♠	KRMA	NEF	PLFS	NEFS	URRS	7	6	0
5♠	URFS	MOR	MORS	URF	SARS	4	-2	4
6♠	SAF	PLRS	SAM	VEF	VEFS	0	5	-3
7♠	JUR	CLRS	URRS	SARS	MAF	1	1	2
8♠	CRRS	VER	JUF	MAF	JUFS	5	0	5
9♠	PLRS	SAM	JUF	CRFS	SAF	1	5	-2
10♠	KRMA	NERS	NEF	PLFS	URF	7	5	0
J♠	URRS	CRR	VEMS	NEF	MAR	5	1	3
Q♠	NER	PLF	SARS	MAM	PLFS	5	6	-2
K♠	CRF	JURS	NEFS	CRFS	JUR	5	2	3

Note: The header spans "The Connections Between Partners" over Con1–Con5 and "Overall Index Ratings" over Attraction, Intensity, Compatibility.

4 ♣

Mental Satisfaction

DESCRIPTION OF THE 4♣ PERSON:
Though this is a card of stability, the underlying 5♣ also indicates a hidden restlessness that can manifest in several ways. These people are progressive and can utilize this to create new ideas in their chosen line of work, rather than let the restlessness keep them from achieving any success. These people know what they know and are not likely to change their minds on your behalf unless they see the value of change for themselves. 'Stubborn' may describe them better in many cases. They are fond of argument, since they usually win, and usually do well in legal matters.

They have a good constitution and are not afraid of hard work. This is a successful card. They are good at sales work and enjoy talking about what they believe in. They are popular and do well in groups. As long as they don't let their love of debate get out of hand, they will keep a fine reputation in their work. However, they also want a successful love life and this is their major life challenge.

Often the drive and determination of the 4♣ masks a desire to be accepted by others, the same acceptance that they find difficulty in giving themselves. In other cases, their desire for work success competes with their desire for love and affection. Their last years of life are often the most successful and they usually end up with much financial opulence or protection. The 4♣ collectively are the 'keepers of knowledge.' They show us that information has a practical value and that we can be happy and successful by applying what we already have.

SOME OF THE 4♣ ISSUES CONCERNING RELATIONSHIPS:
Though it can manifest in many ways, the 4♣ need for affection is a major issue in their life. Combined with a certain restlessness and fear of commitment it can, in some cases, be the cause for untold painful relationships. This is not true for all of them though. Their basic karma in love is good. If they can find a partner who also appreciates a little space, they will be happier.

Their J♠ in Venus tells us that they must also watch for a tendency to be attracted to those of low reputation and morality. If they are choosing to operate on the lower side, they can be some of the most romantic but dishonest lovers in the deck, or they will attract others with these characteristics. Many are drawn to artists or others in the creative fields, but these are often the ones with questionable characteristics. This same J♠ can be expressed on a higher level as an attraction to those with a more spiritual perspective on life, and these relationships generally fare better.

GENERALITIES BETWEEN THE PERSONALITY CARD CONNECTIONS
Female 4♣ make easy friends and companions with Spade males, but Diamond and Heart males find the 4♣ women especially appealing. Other Club males will usually be a big challenge. Male 4♣ have a weakness for other Club women, but also Spade women, especially if they themselves are under 24 years old (acting as the J♣).

KARMA CARDS:

5♣   6♥

KARMA COUSINS:

5♥   3♦

PAST-LIFE CARDS:

3♣   5♣

The Four of Clubs's Love Life

Because the 4♣ has the J♠ in their Venus position, they are very predisposed to having relationships with those who are dishonest or of lower morals. The J♠ is the card of the actor and the thief. So, 4♣ are often found with musicians, artists, actors, or those of questionable motives or values. Even when happily married, the 4♣ should be somewhat wary of their mates. For example, one 4♣ woman was happily married for 30 years. Then her husband died. After his death, she found out that for over 20 years, he had been having affairs with other women. However, he had so cleverly disguised it that she never once suspected it. The J♠ card aptly describes the way he behaved in their relationship.

The J♠ card is the strongest of the Jacks, all of whom have the potential to be liars when their creative energy is expressed in a negative manner. Since he is the strongest of these Jacks, the J♠ is usually associated with more dramatic examples of both the positive and negative sides of the Jack. For the 4♣, this J♠ tells us either that they can be very dishonest in their own love life or that they attract others who are. This can include lying about their true intentions; using others for sex, emotional security, or money; never meaning what they say; and being completely unable to trust anyone else. It is true that a liar cannot believe anyone else.

Take the case of the following 4♣ woman who exemplifies one of these patterns in her relationships. She basically goes through a lot of relationships, often with musician and dead-beat types. These relationships always have the theme of somebody using somebody else. Usually it is her that is getting used, since she has more money than most of them. Once, she revealed that she used her money to attract them and keep them, because secretly she didn't think that she was enough all by herself. This was interesting since she seemed to be an attractive and successful woman who would not need any help attracting a mate. However, each time she let the money issue come up in her relationships, it ended shortly thereafter with her feeling used and, in some cases, robbed.

The other side of the J♠ is a signpost to happiness for the 4♣, whether they be male or female. This powerful Jack, which can represent dishonesty and deception, can also represent spiritual initiation. In this context, spiritual initiation means realizing that a better life is available to us and then making the change to a more positive expression, one guided by higher principles and truth. 4♣ who are happily married are usually those who have decided on a philosophy of life that is important to them and then made the commitment to that philosophy. Truthfulness is a common example of a philosophy that could change one's life if practiced every day. The 4♣ first has to be honest with himself (or herself) about the fears that tempt them into making choices that result in such negative results. With self-honesty and, later, honesty with those around them, they will discover the truth about themselves and their romantic attachments. This can lead them to a high spiritual state in their love life that few other cards will have the opportunity to experience. To have a relationship guided by a philosophy of truth can bring incredible intimacy and profound love experiences. Inwardly this is what all 4♣ are longing for and what is available to them once they make the change.

FOUR OF CLUBS

LIFE SPREAD CARDS

PLANETARY CARD	SYMBOL	CARD
MOON	☽	6♥
SUN (BIRTH CARD)	✳	4♣
MERCURY	☿	2♦
VENUS	♀	J♠
MARS	♂	8♣
JUPITER	♃	6♦
SATURN	♄	4♠
URANUS	♅	10♥
NEPTUNE	♆	10♦
PLUTO	♇	8♠
RESULT (COSMIC REWARD)	♃ +	A♠
COSMIC LESSON	♄ +	A♦

PLANETARY RULING CARDS

BIRTH DATE	ASTROLOGICAL RULING SIGN	PLANETARY RULING CARD
APR 30	TAURUS	J♠
MAY 28	GEMINI	2♦
JUN 26	CANCER	6♥
JUL 24	LEO	4♣
AUG 22	LEO OR VIRGO	4♣ OR 2♦
SEP 20	VIRGO	2♦
OCT 18	LIBRA	J♠
NOV 16	SCORPIO	8♣ & 8♠
DEC 14	SAGITTARIUS	6♦

Who 4♣ with	Con1	Con2	Con3	Con4	Con5	Attraction	Intensity	Compatibility
A♥	CRF	VEMS	CLF	CLFS	VEFS	7	3	2
2♥	JUR	MARS	VEM	CRR	VEMS	5	1	5
3♥	VEFS	CRF	VEMS	PLFS	JUR	7	1	5
4♥	SAF	VEF	JUMS	VEFS	VERS	2	1	3
5♥	VEM	VEMS	KRMC	MORS	MOFS	7	-2	9
6♥	KRMA	MOF	PLF	PLFS	VEM	8	5	1
7♥	CLR	CLRS	JUR	CRRS	MAF	2	2	1
8♥	JUR	CRRS	MAR	CLR	CLRS	3	2	2
9♥	PLRS	CRR	VEMS	MARS	VEM	6	3	2
10♥	URF	NERS	NEFS	PLR	PLRS	4	2	1
J♥	NER	URRS	MAF	JUFS	URF	4	2	2
Q♥	SARS	VEF	JUMS	URR	SAFS	1	1	2
K♥	MAR	JURS	VERS	SAR	CLF	4	3	3
A♣	MARS	VEM	JUR	CRR	VEMS	6	1	5
2♣	VERS	MAR	JURS	SAR	MARS	5	2	4
3♣	MOFS	VERS	VER	CLFS		7	-2	7
4♣	SBC	MORS	MOF	MOFS	MOR	7	0	7
5♣	KRMA	MORS	VEM	VEMS	PLF	8	1	6
6♣	VEFS	PLF	MOR	MORS	CLR	7	0	5
7♣	MAFS	VEM	MAF	VEF	VEFS	8	3	5
8♣	MAF	JUFS	NER	URRS	MAFS	5	3	3
9♣	URR	SAFS	SARS	JUF	NEF	-1	3	-2
10♣	URFS	VEF	MAFS	SAF	NER	3	2	2
J♣	NEFS	MAM	URF	NERS	URFS	6	3	2
Q♣	PLFS	VEFS	NEF	VER	NEFS	8	2	2
K♣	CRFS	MAMS	PLF	PLFS	MAM	8	8	-2
A♦	CLF	CLFS	MOR	CRF	VEMS	6	4	0
2♦	MOR	VEFS	CLF	CLFS	VER	7	0	5
3♦	VEM	VEMS	KRMC	MOF	MARS	7	-1	8
4♦	PLR	VEM	VEMS	JUMS	SAF	5	0	4
5♦	VERS	MOFS	MAR	VER	CLFS	7	0	6
6♦	JUF	URR	SAFS	VER	VERS	1	0	2
7♦	CRR	VEMS	PLRS	MARS	VEM	6	2	3
8♦	MAF	MAM	MAFS	VEM	URR	8	6	1
9♦	MARS	VERS	MAR	JUM	VEM	7	3	3
10♦	NEF	PLFS	MAM	MAMS	PLF	8	6	-1
J♦	MAM	VER	NEFS	MAMS		8	4	3
Q♦	MARS	VEM	VEMS	JUM	MAR	7	1	5
K♦	VER	MOFS	MAR	MARS	MOF	8	1	6
A♠	CLR	CLRS	VERS	VEF	MAF	4	1	2
2♠	MAMS	JURS	CRFS	JUR	SARS	4	3	3
3♠	VER	JUF	MAM	MAMS	VERS	6	1	5
4♠	SAF	URFS	MAM	URF	NER	0	4	-3
5♠	PLR	URF	NERS	SAF	NER	2	3	-2
6♠	JURS	SAR	MAMS	CRR	VEF	2	2	2
7♠	MAR	VER	JUR	CRRS	JURS	5	2	4
8♠	PLF	CRFS	VEFS	MAR	CRF	7	6	0
9♠	SAR	MAR	JURS	PLF	JUR	3	4	0
10♠	VEF	JUMS	SARS	MOF	CRRS	4	-1	5
J♠	VEF	MAFS	VEM	URFS	MAF	7	1	5
Q♠	MAM	NEF	MAF	MAFS	NERS	8	6	1
K♠	MAF	JUFS	NER	URRS	SAR	5	3	2

Stability in Values

DESCRIPTION OF THE 4♦ PERSON:

The 4♦ is a card of protection in finances. However, that protection is only accessed through hard work. This card, above most others, must put forth the effort to reap the rewards, but the rewards are surely there. If they try to get something for nothing, failure and frustration will be the result. Any money they have or receive will always entail some responsibilities.

They have very good business sense and the ability to manage and organize a business successfully. Though others may see them as stubborn, they know that maintaining order and structure in their life and being clear about what is most important to them will always bring success and satisfaction. They are not going to change anything in their life that is working well for them, no matter what others think or say. Even as children, most of them know what is important to them and what is not.

To achieve success, they often have to come to terms with their own inner restlessness (5♠ Karma Card) and dissatisfaction which tends to lead them away from establishing themselves in one area and making true progress. The work they must do often involves their marriage or their closest relationships. These people are very sociable, meet many people, and usually have many friends. There are difficulties to be dealt with in their life and they must watch a tendency to get into a rut and get stuck there. However, all they need to do to have more happiness is to *work*. Once they get into action, everything smooths out and their fears are laid to rest.

The last years of their life often have the most freedom, happiness, and financial blessings. They are usually long-lived and enjoy traveling the world in their later years, experiencing the things they longed for in their youth.

SOME OF THE 4♦ ISSUES CONCERNING RELATIONSHIPS:

4♦ men and women have high ideals concerning love and these ideals can cause confusion in real-life romantic situations. Though stable and tough on the outside, inwardly the 4♦ is a very restless person. Some of this restlessness applies to their romantic lives, so it is not surprising that some of them are challenged to settle down with one person. In addition, they have a karmic pattern that invariably creates one or more difficult marriages, usually ending in divorce. Add all this together and you have people who truly want a good relationship, but must pass some tests to acquire it.

For 4♦ people, male or female, relationships are work and more work. They are often deprived of the life of ease and luxury until later in their life. Problems always ensue if they look upon their relationships as a means of escape from the harshness of life.

They have more than their share of charm and can usually get what they want in a romantic situation. They must be careful not to abuse this power. When they do, the payback is swift and painful, sometimes affecting their health. They must practice high integrity in relationships to avoid some very challenging karmic involvements.

KARMA CARDS:

5♠   5♥

KARMA COUSINS:

10♥   5♣

PAST-LIFE CARDS:

3♦   5♦

4♦ men would be wise to avoid all females of the Heart suit, with whom they have unusually difficult karmic ties.

The 4♦ woman can make a good marriage with a Spade man, especially the 2♠. Club males hold a certain fascination for 4♦ women and Diamond men love to romance them.

The Working Life

People who are Fours are like Ford pickups, generally built tough and able to withstand a lot of punishment. It is not surprising then that many of them have difficult situations to contend with in their life. Roseanne Barr, formerly Roseanne Arnold, has had such a life, as she described in her autobiography. She is a Scorpio 4♦, which seem able to take even more abuse than the other 4♦ people. Nothing ever comes to them without a lot of work and many of them resent having to work so hard during their life. Even the things most would consider blessings will always have some strings attached in the case of the 4♦, which makes their life experience a little more embittered than the rest of us.

Many fours, and 4♦ especially, have a strong 'struggle' ethic. The key to their happiness is to recognize this aspect of themselves and to re-evaluate it. Though they seem to attract tough situations and these seem to be their lot in life, it is actually their inward belief about life that is the cause of these experiences. If it is a deep-seated belief of mine that I

have to work hard for everything in my life and few things will come easily to me, then I will tend to see the world in that way and attract those sorts of experiences to me. This is exactly what happens to many 4♦ people. They don't really like to get caught up in a life of struggle and drudgery. Their adventurous side would much rather be traveling and having new adventures. So, they have the motivation to put an end to this belief system that seems to sustain their hardships.

It is not an easy task to unravel one's core beliefs and examine them for their validity, but it can be done. The happy 4♦ person loves his or her work, but doesn't feel burdened by it. They have a keen sense of value that can benefit all they come in contact with—a practical approach to work, finances, and life that brings stability and protection. The happy 4♦ makes room in their consciousness for good things to come easily to them—and they do. Then their work ethic becomes their crown instead of the cross they must bear.

FOUR OF DIAMONDS

LIFE SPREAD CARDS

PLANETARY CARD	SYMBOL	CARD
MOON	☽	4♥
SUN (BIRTH CARD)	☀	4♦
MERCURY	☿	2♠
VENUS	♀	8♥
MARS	♂	6♣
JUPITER	♃	6♠
SATURN	♄	Q♥
URANUS	♅	10♣
NEPTUNE	♆	8♦
PLUTO	♇	K♠
RESULT (COSMIC REWARD)	♃+	3♥
COSMIC LESSON	♄+	A♣

PLANETARY RULING CARDS

BIRTH DATE	ASTROLOGICAL RULING SIGN	PLANETARY RULING CARD
JAN 23	AQUARIUS	10♣
FEB 21	PISCES	8♦
MAR 19	PISCES	8♦
APR 17	ARIES	6♣
MAY 15	TAURUS	8♥
JUN 13	GEMINI	2♠
JUL 11	CANCER	4♥
AUG 9	LEO	4♦
SEP 7	VIRGO	2♠
OCT 5	LIBRA	8♥
NOV 3	SCORPIO	6♣ & K♠
DEC 1	SAGITTARIUS	6♠

Who 4♦ with	The Connections Between Partners					Overall Index Ratings		
	Con1	Con2	Con3	Con4	Con5	Attraction	Intensity	Compatibility
A♥	MARS	CRF	CRFS	MAR	JURS	7	6	0
2♥	JUFS	SAM	CLF	URF	SAF	0	4	0
3♥	CRF	SARS	CRR	VERS	CRFS	4	4	0
4♥	MOF	MAF	MOFS	NER	PLF	8	1	5
5♥	KRMA	VEF	NEF	NEFS	VEMS	7	3	5
6♥	JUMS	MOFS	NEF	MORS	PLF	6	-2	6
7♥	VEF	CLFS	VER	VEFS	MAFS	7	0	5
8♥	VEF	SAR	VEMS	MAFS	VEM	5	0	5
9♥	MAFS	SAF	CLF	URF	SAFS	2	7	-4
10♥	NER	PLF	KRMC	URRS	VERS	6	4	0
J♥	PLF	CRRS	MOR	URFS	CLR	6	3	0
Q♥	SAF	MAMS	PLRS	NEFS	URR	2	6	-3
K♥	JUR	SAF	PLFS	CLF	CLFS	1	4	-2
A♣	CLF	URF	JUFS	SAM	SAF	1	4	-1
2♣	JUR	CLFS	CLF	MAR	JURS	3	3	1
3♣	VEFS	MORS	CRR	JUF	CRFS	6	-1	7
4♣	VEMS	JUMS	PLF	VEM	SAR	5	0	4
5♣	VEMS	VEF	KRMC	SAR	NEF	6	0	6
6♣	MAF	MAM	VERS	MAFS	VEM	8	5	2
7♣	CLR	CLRS	NEF	JUFS	JUM	3	1	2
8♣	CRRS	PLF	CRR	VEMS	URFS	6	3	0
9♣	PLRS	SAF	MAMS	VEFS	VEF	3	5	-1
10♣	URF	NERS	PLFS	JUM	MAF	4	2	0
J♣	NER	PLF	URRS	VER	NEFS	6	3	0
Q♣	SARS	CRF	URFS	NER	CRR	2	4	-1
K♣	MAR	JURS	MOR	MAM	MAMS	6	3	4
A♦	MARS	VERS	VER	CRF	MAR	7	3	4
2♦	VERS	MAF	MARS	CRF	VER	8	3	3
3♦	MOFS	JUMS	PLFS	JUR	JUM	5	-1	5
4♦	SBC	VERS	VEF	VEFS	VER	6	1	6
5♦	MORS	CRR	URR	SAFS	VEFS	4	0	3
6♦	VEFS	PLRS	VEM	VEMS	PLR	6	0	6
7♦	SAF	MAFS	CLF	URF	MOF	2	6	-3
8♦	NEF	JUFS	PLR	CLR	CLRS	4	1	3
9♦	URR	SAFS	PLFS	MORS	CRR	2	4	-2
10♦	URFS	SARS	PLR	PLRS	SAR	0	3	-2
J♦	VER	NEFS	PLRS	VEM	NER	7	0	5
Q♦	PLFS	MOFS	URR	SAFS	URRS	4	3	-1
K♦	JUF	CRFS	VEFS	SAR	VEMS	4	0	5
A♠	CLFS	JUR	MAR	JURS	SARS	3	3	1
2♠	MOR	JUF	MAR	JURS	SAR	5	0	6
3♠	VEM	VEFS	VER	NEFS	PLRS	7	-2	8
4♠	MAF	URF	NERS	PLFS	MOF	6	4	0
5♠	KRMA	VERS	NEF	NEFS	PLF	7	3	3
6♠	JUF	MOR	MORS	MAF	JUFS	6	-2	8
7♠	SAR	VEMS	JUF	CRFS	VEF	3	1	4
8♠	MAM	MAR	JURS	MAF	MAFS	7	6	1
9♠	JUF	MAF	JUFS	CRRS	SAF	4	1	4
10♠	MOF	SAF	MAMS	URR	SAFS	3	3	0
J♠	JUM	CLR	CLRS	URF	NERS	1	0	1
Q♠	PLR	URFS	NEF	JUFS	NEFS	3	2	1
K♠	PLF	CRRS	CLR	PLFS	VEM	6	5	-3

4♠ Satisfaction in Work Card

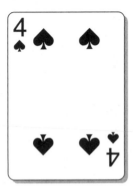

DESCRIPTION OF THE 4♠ PERSON:
The 4♠ is the card of satisfaction through work. This is one of the most 'solid' of all the cards in the deck. The people of this card often seem like a rock or square in some fashion. They are stable and hardworking and can be counted on when you need them. They have one of the most fortunate life paths in terms of money and success and usually enjoy the work they do. However, their Saturn card, the A♦, tells us that even though they are fortunate, they usually worry about money anyway, and this can interfere with their own success if not checked. The 10♥ in Mercury usually gets them instant acceptance at social occasions and they make good communicators or speakers. Some can be successful writers, advertising executives, or performers of the literary arts.

Fours can be very stubborn and the 4♠ has the right to be. With the 10♣ Karma Card, they know a lot and must live by their own truth. They are very intelligent and intuitive and dislike being restrained in any way. The 10♦ in Venus gives them wealthy friends, but they should not place too much emphasis on money with their choice of friends or lovers.

They usually have a good constitution, and their health is best cared for by natural methods. They are a worker card and it is in their work that they find true peace and satisfaction. They will often align themselves with a humanitarian mission and find great satisfaction.

The later years are often spent fulfilling their dreams of traveling the world, something they usually don't get enough of in their early years.

SOME OF THE 4♠ ISSUES CONCERNING RELATIONSHIPS:
These are very giving and loving people, and though they can be tough and stubborn, they will usually give you anything from the generosity of their heart. They are attracted to those of financial means and can get caught up in trying to 'look good' in their relationships and forget the real values that good relationships are based on. It is usually not wise for them to mix money and pleasure, or business and personal relationships. Their own fears about finances will usually cause too much stress and confusion in their love life. They would like someone they can travel with, and their karma for marriage is better than average.

GENERALITIES BETWEEN THE PERSONALITY CARD CONNECTIONS
4♠ often have Diamond females as friends and associates. 4♠ females hold a special fascination for Diamond males, and Spade males find them very physically attractive. Males of the Club suit are usually problematic for 4♠ of both sexes. A 4♠ female could make a good marriage with a Spade male, especially one who is more responsible and mature.

KARMA CARDS:
10♣ 4♥

KARMA COUSINS:
J♠ 10♠

PAST-LIFE CARDS:
3♠ 5♠

Survival or Happiness?

What lies behind that stern and sometimes smug exterior of the 4♠ person? Often, it is a strong drive for security and material comforts. Out of all the Fours, the 4♠ is perhaps the most security-driven. Just being a Four in itself implies a desire to create a situation where one has all their basic needs provided for. The 4♠ seeks security in their work. They are great workers and always feel better when they are working.

But another factor enters into the equation for the 4♠ person that makes them even more motivated than other cards in the deck. That factor is the A♦ in the Saturn position of their Life Path. The card we have in Saturn often points to an area where things in our life are difficult. In some cases it represents things that are almost impossible to fulfill. In the case of the 4♠, their desire for money, or the fear of going without, is an area of difficulty. In most cases, this is such a deep-seated fear that it is largely unconscious. But this fear can be one of the most important driving factors in their life and needs to be examined if they want to be free from a life of struggle. A common trait associated with 4♠ people is that of being workaholics. Other cards, such as the A♦, A♠, and 10♠, can manifest this quality as well, but for different reasons. For the 4♠ this overworking nature can often be traced to this eternal quest for material security. The A♦ in Saturn can produce a sort of nagging fear that the things and resources we need will not be there when we need them. If we are unaware of these feelings and unable to see them for what they are, we could spend our entire life trying to fill the void they create.

This underlying sense of lack puts many 4♠ into eternal survival mode, whether they realize it or not. In survival mode, we tend to think short-term and our decisions often create long–term problems. In many cases, our decisions tend to create the very thing we are trying to avoid. This tendency can be changed by 4♠ if they are willing to look at themselves and understand what motivates them.

Conscious awareness is the key that changes all of this. Just asking themselves if they are enjoying their work or not is a good first step. If we are not enjoying our work, then we are probably doing it out of some fear that we have. The more fear we have, the less we enjoy the work. Fours already have a natural capacity to enjoy work, so they must be ruthlessly honest when they ask this question. Then, if they discover that there are some negative factors that motivate them to work so hard, they can begin to reassemble their life with happier results.

FOUR OF SPADES

LIFE SPREAD CARDS

PLANETARY CARD	SYMBOL	CARD
MOON	☽	6♦
SUN (BIRTH CARD)	✳	4♠
MERCURY	☿	10♥
VENUS	♀	10♦
MARS	♂	8♠
JUPITER	♃	A♥
SATURN	♄	A♦
URANUS	♅	Q♦
NEPTUNE	♆	5♥
PLUTO	♇	3♣
RESULT (COSMIC REWARD)	♃+	3♠
COSMIC LESSON	♄+	9♥

PLANETARY RULING CARDS

BIRTH DATE	ASTROLOGICAL RULING SIGN	PLANETARY RULING CARD
JAN 10	CAPRICORN	A♦
FEB 8	AQUARIUS	Q♦
MAR 6	PISCES	5♥
APR 4	ARIES	8♠
MAY 2	TAURUS	10♦

Celebrity Birthdays

JACK LEMMON
2/8/25 • Actor
NICK NOLTE
2/8/40 • Actor
ROBERT DOWNEY, JR.
4/4/65 • Actor
ROB REINER
3/6/45 • Actor/Director
HEATH LEDGER
4/4/79 • Actor
LESLIE GORE
5/2/46 • Actress
NANCY MCKEON
4/4/66 • Actress
MAYA ANGELOU
4/4/28 • Author/Poet
JOHN GRISHAM
2/8/55 • Author
GEORGE FOREMAN
1/10/49 • Boxer
TOM ARNOLD
3/6/59 • Comedian
ALAN GREENSPAN
3/6/26 • Federal Reserve Chairman
TED KOPPEL
2/8/40 • Newscaster
ED MCMAHON
3/6/23 • Television Personality
ROD STEWART
1/10/45 • Singer
GARY COLEMAN
2/8/68 • Actor
BING CROSBY
5/2/04 • Singer/Actor
MICHELANGELO
3/6/1475 • Artist
GABRIEL GARCIA-MARQUEZ
3/6/28 • Author
ELIZABETH BARRETT BROWNING
3/6/1806 • Poet
DAVID BECKHAM
5/2/75 • Soccer Player

Who 4♠ with	Con1	Con2	Con3	Con4	Con5	Attraction	Intensity	Compatibility
A♥	JUF	CLFS	URFS	SAF	MARS	2	2	0
2♥	CRR	MAF	VEF	CLRS	MAFS	6	3	2
3♥	JUF	CLFS	URFS	MAMS	MAF	4	3	2
4♥	KRMA	NEF	NEFS	URFS	NER	6	4	2
5♥	NEF	PLR	MAR	MAM	MAMS	7	5	1
6♥	URR	SAR	VEFS	MAR	URRS	2	2	1
7♥	URMS	SAFS	MARS	CLF	VEM	1	5	-2
8♥	SAFS	MAFS	VEM	URMS	JUR	2	4	-1
9♥	CLF	VEF	CLRS	MAF	VEFS	5	3	2
10♥	MOR	VER	MORS	JUR	URFS	6	-3	8
J♥	VEM	CRFS	VER	VEMS	NEFS	8	0	7
Q♥	URFS	MAFS	MOF	URF	PLFS	5	2	2
K♥	PLR	SAMS	JUFS	CLR	SAFS	1	5	-2
A♣	MAF	CRR	VEF	CLRS	JUF	6	3	3
2♣	JUFS	MARS	PLR	SAMS	CLR	3	4	1
3♣	PLF	VEMS	NER	JURS	SAR	6	2	1
4♣	SAR	MAM	URR	URRS	NEF	2	4	-1
5♣	MAM	NEF	PLR	SAR	SARS	5	5	0
6♣	MAM	JUMS	MAF	JUFS	JUR	5	3	3
7♣	CRRS	MAR	NEFS	MARS	CRR	7	5	1
8♣	VER	VEM	CRFS	VERS	VEMS	7	-1	7
9♣	MAFS	MOF	MOFS	VEM	MAMS	8	1	6
10♣	KRMA	MAR	NEFS	NEF	PLF	8	7	1
J♣	VER	URRS	MOR	MORS	URR	5	-2	6
Q♣	MAMS	VEF	NERS	PLFS	SAF	7	4	2
K♣	VERS	MAF	JUFS	CRR	MAFS	6	1	4
A♦	SAF	JUR	JUF	CLFS	URFS	-1	2	0
2♦	JUR	MAM	JUMS	SAF	SAFS	1	2	2
3♦	VEFS	URR	URF	SARS	PLF	3	0	2
4♦	MAR	MORS	NEF	PLR	URR	7	3	3
5♦	VEMS	PLRS	PLF	PLFS	PLR	6	3	0
6♦	MOF	MAFS	MOFS	CRF	CRFS	8	1	5
7♦	VEF	CLRS	CLF	MAF	CLFS	5	2	2
8♦	CRRS	PLFS	MOR	PLF	NER	7	4	0
9♦	PLRS	URF	SARS	VEMS	URR	2	2	0
10♦	VEF	NERS	PLFS	MAMS	MAM	7	3	2
J♦	URRS	MOFS	CRF	VER	PLR	5	0	4
Q♦	URF	SARS	VEFS	PLRS	VEF	2	1	1
K♦	NER	PLF	JURS	MAFS	VEM	6	3	1
A♠	MARS	URMS	JUFS	CRF	URM	4	3	2
2♠	VERS	VEFS	SAR	NER	VEF	5	-1	5
3♠	MOFS	CRF	MOF	URRS	CRFS	7	0	5
4♠	SBC	PLF	NEFS	NEF	PLFS	7	6	-1
5♠	MORS	MOR	MAR	VER	MARS	8	0	7
6♠	VEFS	CLR	SAFS	VERS	VER	3	1	3
7♠	MAFS	VEM	NER	PLF	JURS	7	3	3
8♠	MAF	JUFS	MAM	JUMS	MAMS	6	4	3
9♠	CLR	SAFS	PLR	SAMS	VEFS	0	5	-3
10♠	URFS	URF	KRMC	NERS	NER	2	1	1
J♠	MAR	NEFS	KRMC	MAM	URRS	7	6	2
Q♠	PLFS	VEF	NERS	CRRS	NER	7	3	1
K♠	CRFS	VER	VEM	VEF	CRF	7	1	5

The Fives

Five is one of the most important of all the numbers because it is what many call 'the number of man.' Five, more than any other number, symbolizes our race and the characteristics of those of us living here on Earth. It is no accident that we have five fingers on each hand and that there are five visible (to the naked eye) planets in our sky at night. Even the Great Pyramid of Giza, which to this day is the only man-made object that is discernible from those orbiting our planet, has five points. Perhaps its creators intended it to be a sign to any galactic travelers that those living on this particular planet are a Five-like race.

Five is the number of adventure and of seeking new experiences in the realm of duality. The Five constantly seeks to expand itself and to discover what else lies beyond the security of home. We, as a race of beings, have a dominant theme of constantly exploring different experiences and forms of personal expression. We are constantly in motion. Each generation seeks to improve on their parents' generation. Improvement and progress are words dear to the heart of our planet, but especially to Five people. It is interesting to conceive of a planet of beings with a different number as their base. What about a planet of Fours, whose main concern was security? Though your Birth Card may be a Four or a Two, you exhibit many Five characteristics just by the virtue of being a human.

Since we are all Fives on one level already, what happens when you are also a Five Birth Card? Now, we have a more or less exaggerated version of the Five energy. In many cases, Five Birth Cards exhibit such an extreme example of the quest for new experiences that it is difficult for those around them to understand their motives. Fives will often take great risks and endure hardships, all in the name of adventure. Whatever they are doing in their life, regardless of what their motivations may seem to be, their true motivation is that of gathering new experiences, ideas, relationships, and value systems. They are explorers with an insatiable thirst to find out what lies beyond the horizon.

In general, Fives do better with occupations that afford travel and variety. Travel brings opportunities to meet new people and be exposed to entirely new situations and customs, which all Fives love and appreciate. Even if they are in one job for a while, they will be progressive and try to take it into new directions. Sales in one form or another seems to be a common Five occupation. There is something about their desire to understand and experience everything that makes them great salespeople. They seem to be able to relate to almost everyone on their own level, making them feel at ease and understood. These are some of the most important ingredients of a successful salesperson. Sales also fits them because it usually affords them the freedom to create their own schedule.

Along with being a Five comes a great deal of discontentedness and restlessness. Unlike other cards, even the odd-numbered ones, these people will often just get up and leave or move to a new location when a restless urge overtakes them. Though they vary from person to person, many of them are like the proverbial Wandering Jew and often they feel as though they have no real home. Home is the domain of the Four, remember, and the Five is the number which evolved out of the Four. For them to seek security would be like going backward in one's evolution. The Five is the one always seeking to leave the comfort and security of the known. To a Five, settling down into a normal home life can seem like a prison. Freedom is the most important word in their vocabulary. If anything seems to hamper their freedom, they will usually rebel or simply leave. Commitments in personal relationships may also seem to hamper their freedom as well, and this is why Fives as a group are some of the least marriageable of all the cards. They may actually live with a person for a number of years without any formal commitments or contracts. Some of them do get married, of course, but the usual expression of the Five always leaves some options open. The people that they are most attracted to are usually the other cards that dislike commitments as well, such as Threes, the Q♣, and Q♦, for example. The question for a Five in relationship may be, 'Can one person truly satisfy my need for a well-rounded experience in the love department?' More often than not the answer is no.

For a Five to be happy, they must fully accept who they are. To go from one job, relationship, or living situation to another, over and over again, is not what our society considers especially honorable. It often leaves one feeling insecure as well, because no one thing was pursued long enough to make a success of it. This can create an inner conflict with the Five person, many of whom also have urges for financial or romantic security. These urges conflict directly with Five energy and thus we find that many of them are constantly in conflict within. The happiest Fives are those who claim their birthright and understand that this world is nothing more than something for them to explore. Nothing is as important as what they are learning and getting from their experiences. Five in its highest expression is the number of wisdom. Wisdom only comes through direct experience and if we talk to a Five, we are talking to someone who has 'been there, done that.'

The Emotional Adventurer

DESCRIPTION OF THE 5♥ PERSON:

All Fives need to settle down a bit if they ever want to achieve any long–term success in their life, and the 5♥ is no exception. Their 4♦ Karma Card tells us that these people have an issue around security that will be an ongoing theme in their life until they come to terms with it. Their security fear is primarily financial in nature. Hard work and sticking with one thing will always bring success. The question is if they be able to stay in one place long enough to reap the rewards. Many of them do, but it is often not easy for them, nor does it seem to come naturally. The 5♥ wants to experience all that love and money has to offer. But how can this experience be accomplished if one is stuck in the same place and same job for extended periods of time? The answer often is an occupation that requires travel. Extensive travel is just fine with them. They are usually ready and able to go almost anywhere.

The 5♥ is on a quest of sorts, being seekers of new and different relationship experiences. Usually, their current relationship is just another experience to them. Those that do stay married for a long time are there because of something important they want to feel and experience. Once they have gotten their fill of a certain thing, whether it be a person or the feelings they have for them, they may just move on without hesitation. Some 5♥ are promiscuous and unable to make commitments at all. But sometimes their quest for experiences will be satisfied by traveling and visiting foreign countries. In this way, they gather the new experiences they seek. In addition to representing our

relationships, the suit of Hearts is also connected to our home and family. The 5♥ may make new homes and circles of friends in foreign countries to satisfy their quest for the new.

The 5♥ has the 5♣ as their second Karma Card and the 5♦ as their Saturn card in their Life Path. This makes them more restless in many ways than some of the other Fives. There are few even-numbered cards in their Life Path at all. This tells us that the 5♥ is creative and usually on the move. Many have an artistic talent, one that is either expressed professionally or in the things they do around the home and with loved ones. They also have a gift for the comprehension of spiritual ideas and principles and some have a unique gift or ability mind-wise, like a photographic memory or being a math-whiz.

Overall, the large amount of odd-numbered cards represents challenges and problems that must be resolved by spiritual approaches. For example, the two Nines in Mars and Pluto show that these people must often relinquish their personal desires and wishes in order to get what they want. When they try to make things work out their way, they often meet with disappointment. But when they let go, everything comes their way. This backward approach to life is typical of cards that have a lot of odd-numbered cards in their Life Path, and it is a challenge to learn and understand. Ultimately the 5♥ person learns to walk the path of faith, symbolized by their 7♠ Cosmic Reward card. They realize that by following one's personal path and being true to oneself, everything always turns out for the best. Once the 5♥ begins to learn from their many experiences, they acquire the wisdom they seek and with that wisdom often comes a responsibility to share it with others. Many become the best teachers. What they impart comes from the wisdom of their direct experience.

SOME OF THE 5♥ ISSUES CONCERNING RELATIONSHIPS:

The 5♥ by nature is somewhat restless in

KARMA CARDS:

4♦   5♣

KARMA COUSINS:

5♠   4♣

PAST-LIFE CARDS:

4♥   6♥

matters of love and at some point in their life realize that they need some freedom in their love life. A successful relationship can be had with other cards that enjoy the same freedom and individual expression that they do. Like other Fives, the 5♥ often have an inner fear of commitment, seeing it as something that will deprive them of seeing the world. Though they can be happily married, most would be happiest as a single person, or at least in a relationship that gives them lots of space and freedom to move.

The 5♥ also has a strong 3♠ as the Venus card in their Life Path. This brings a love of creativity and artistic expression, plus an attraction to those types of people, but they also like variety in personal relationships. For some, the grass will always seem greener elsewhere or they will feel a need for more than one partner.

Endings of relationships for the 5♥, if they come, will usually be bitter and difficult, often marred by anger and resentment. Symbolized by the 9♥ in Mars, they rarely come out on top in divorce proceedings unless they relinquish all of their personal desires. Those that experience one of these difficult separations may decide to never take that chance again and remain single for the duration of their life. Their path in relationships is spiritual. That means that success will only be found through developing faith and trust and letting go of personal attachments that are rooted in fear or anger. The Nine symbolizes victory on the spiritual level and a sense of divine love. They are one of the few cards with the capacity to experience this.

GENERALITIES BETWEEN THE PERSONALITY CARD CONNECTIONS
A 5♥ male could make a good marriage with a Diamond female and often have Spade females as friends. The 5♥ female is captivated by younger Club males but can probably have a better relationship with a Diamond male.

Five of Hearts's Restless Heart

We always have more than one way to manifest the energies of our Birth Cards and of the cards found in our Yearly Spreads. The 5♥ person is no exception and any student of the cards can imagine what some of those manifestations can be. The 5♥ in a Yearly Spread can be an indicator of divorce. Does this mean that the 5♥ person is always destined for divorce? Not necessarily. However, there are many 5♥ people who do go from one relationship to another. And why shouldn't they? It is often their mission in life to experience just what different kinds of relationships are like. Any Five is a gatherer of experience. Since experience is what brings us wisdom, most Fives end up as very wise people and perhaps the soul of a Five person has directed them into a Five incarnation for the express purpose of developing and acquiring this wisdom that comes only from experience.

The 5♥ person is seeking experience on the level of relationships, friendships, marriages, love affairs, divorce, and other love-related happenings. There are some 5♥ who get married once, stay married for about 20 years, then get divorced and never marry again. It is as if they try out marriage and commitment and really get into it to get the complete experience of it. But then, when they are done, they just discard it and never do it again. It is interesting to note that most Fives are never remorseful about their past or present. They seem to have some presence of mind about their decisions even though many of them seem to defy normal social logic.

There are many 5♥, especially those born before 1946 or so, who got married and stay married. They have found a different way to manifest the 5♥ energy, which is to have a constant turnover of new friends and acquaintances in their social life. These people are constantly meeting new people. They are very gregarious and outgoing and are usually the life of the party wherever they go.

Those born after 1960 tend to be a new breed. Now that we, as a culture, more or less accept non-marriage relationships, most 5♥ of the newer generation are travelers who change relationships frequently. They often go from one love affair or marriage to the next. This might be considered a more progressive form of the 5♥ energy since it is less traditional than the form expressed by those born before 1946. Still, there are examples of other forms of this Five expression around today, even with the younger generation and this will continue to evolve. There are many more ways this could be expressed that are not mentioned here, and I hope you take note of the different ones that you encounter. What we must always keep in mind as we observe any Five person is this: whatever they are doing, one of the main reasons for doing it is simply for the experience. They just want to know what it feels like. Once they have satisfied that need, they will invariably move on to a new experience. If it takes a 30-year marriage to get the full experience, then that is what they will do. If it only takes a one-night stand, then they will create that. If we look carefully at what they are creating, we will know which experiences they need in order to satisfy their restless heart.

FIVE OF HEARTS

LIFE SPREAD CARDS

PLANETARY CARD	SYMBOL	CARD
MOON	☽	Q ♦
SUN (BIRTH CARD)	✳	5 ♥
MERCURY	☿	3 ♣
VENUS	♀	3 ♠
MARS	♂	9 ♥
JUPITER	♃	7 ♣
SATURN	♄	5 ♦
URANUS	♅	Q ♠
NEPTUNE	♆	J ♣
PLUTO	♇	9 ♦
RESULT (COSMIC REWARD)	♃ +	7 ♠
COSMIC LESSON	♄ +	2 ♣

PLANETARY RULING CARDS

BIRTH DATE	ASTROLOGICAL RULING SIGN	PLANETARY RULING CARD
OCT 30	SCORPIO	9 ♥ & 9 ♦
NOV 28	SAGITTARIUS	7 ♣
DEC 26	CAPRICORN	5 ♦

Who 5♥ with	Con1	Con2	Con3	Con4	Con5	Attraction	Intensity	Compatibility
A♥	MAR	JURS	VER	VERS	MARS	6	2	5
2♥	MARS	JUF	CRFS	MAF	JURS	6	4	3
3♥	VERS	MAR	JURS	CRF	JUR	5	1	5
4♥	MOFS	NER	PLF	PLRS	MOF	7	1	3
5♥	SBC	VER	VEF	NEF	NEFS	7	2	5
6♥	MORS	VEM	VEMS	JUM	JUMS	7	-4	9
7♥	VEFS	MAFS	VEM	SARS	MAF	7	2	5
8♥	MAFS	VEM	CRF	VEFS	VEF	8	2	5
9♥	MAF	JUFS	JURS	JUF	CRFS	4	1	5
10♥	URR	SAFS	NEF	PLR	PLRS	1	4	-2
J♥	URFS	SARS	CRR	VEMS	URF	2	1	0
Q♥	NEFS	PLRS	MAM	SAF	MAMS	5	5	-1
K♥	PLFS	CLF	CLFS	CRRS	SARS	6	7	-4
A♣	JUF	CRFS	MARS	MAF	JURS	5	3	3
2♣	CLF	CLFS	SARS	PLFS	JUR	4	6	-4
3♣	MOR	SAF	VEF	VEFS	VERS	4	0	5
4♣	VEM	VEMS	KRMC	MORS	MOFS	7	-2	9
5♣	KRMA	NEF	PLFS	VEM	VEMS	8	5	2
6♣	VERS	JUR	CLRS	URRS	MAF	3	-1	4
7♣	JUF	CLR	NERS	CLRS	VEFS	3	0	3
8♣	CRR	VEMS	URFS	SARS	CRRS	4	1	3
9♣	MAM	NEFS	PLR	PLRS	NEF	6	5	0
10♣	MAMS	CLR	NERS	NER	PLF	6	5	0
J♣	NEF	PLR	URR	SAFS	NER	3	3	-1
Q♣	VERS	SAR	SARS	VER	NEFS	3	1	2
K♣	MARS	JUR	CLRS	URRS	MAR	3	3	2
A♦	VER	MAR	JURS	MARS	CRFS	6	2	4
2♦	VERS	VER	CLFS	MAF	CLR	6	1	4
3♦	JUM	JUMS	MORS	MOF	MOFS	4	-3	7
4♦	KRMA	VER	NEF	PLFS	NEFS	7	4	2
5♦	SAF	PLF	MOR	MORS	CRR	3	4	-1
6♦	PLR	MAM	VEF	VEFS	VERS	6	3	3
7♦	MAF	JURS	JUFS	JUF	CRFS	4	1	5
8♦	URF	URRS	JUF	NEF	JUFS	2	-1	3
9♦	PLF	MOF	SAF	URR	SAFS	3	4	-2
10♦	SAR	URF	URRS	URFS	MAMS	0	2	-1
J♦	VEF	NEF	PLR	VER	NEFS	7	0	5
Q♦	MOF	JUM	JUMS	PLF	PLFS	5	-1	4
K♦	VEF	MOR	CRF	JUF	CRFS	7	-1	7
A♠	SARS	VEFS	CLF	CLFS	VEF	3	3	1
2♠	MARS	MOR	JUF	CRR	VEF	6	1	5
3♠	VEF	PLR	VEM	MAMS	VEFS	6	1	5
4♠	NER	PLF	MAMS	MOFS	MAF	8	5	0
5♠	URR	SAFS	KRMC	VER	VERS	1	3	0
6♠	CRRS	JUF	CRR	VEF	PLF	5	1	4
7♠	CRF	VEF	MAFS	VEM	SAR	7	3	4
8♠	JUR	CLRS	URRS	MARS	VERS	2	0	3
9♠	CRRS	PLFS	PLF	CLF	SARS	6	6	-4
10♠	PLRS	MOFS	NEFS	MOF	VEFS	6	0	4
J♠	CLR	NERS	JUF	MAMS	JUM	4	2	2
Q♠	URF	URRS	SAR	PLR	MAFS	1	2	-1
K♠	SARS	CRR	VEMS	URFS	PLF	3	2	0

The Quest for Truth

DESCRIPTION OF THE 5♣ PERSON:
The 5♣ means changes and restlessness of the mind. We find these people have a lot of curiosity that keeps them almost constantly on the move. The 5♥ Karma Card tells us that they also have many changes in their romantic life as well, and for this reason they are not usually well-suited for marriage. These people are basically adventurous and want to do some exploring and research. For this same reason, things and people associated with commitment are usually avoided like the plague. This makes them nomadic and changeable to the extreme in some cases. The 5♣ is *the* most restless card of all. Though they are very flexible, moves to new homes or change of lifestyles usually do entail many responsibilities and challenges, as symbolized by the 5♠ in Saturn.

The A♠ in Venus speaks of secret love affairs and indecision about which to choose. This same Ace also gives many of them a very sexy and rich voice. The 7♦ in Jupiter is a millionaire's card and many 5♣ have lots of money, though they often spend it or lose it as fast as they get it. Speculation and gambling should be avoided. Though they are luckier than most, their tendency to spend it makes them bad at what gamblers call 'money management,' which is essentially knowing when to quit. They are wonderful in sales and promotion because they can relate to so many people on their own level. The Virgo and Gemini birthdays often have an especially powerful voice

or way of expressing themselves that can bring great success in sales or promotions.

Their natural curiosity brings them much knowledge, but they do not apply it often or they stick to one train of thought. This tends to make them skeptics, not even getting satisfaction from their own self-created belief structures. Often a 5♣ will take the opposite side of an argument, just so they are not tied down to one concept. An interest in spiritual studies brings more satisfaction in their later years and provides answers that bring more peace into their lives. A spiritual teacher would be helpful in this regard.

SOME OF THE 5♣ ISSUES CONCERNING RELATIONSHIPS:
Depending upon the individual, being a 5♣ can be a blessing or a curse in the realm of relationships. On the high side, they are progressive and can relate to anyone on their level. This makes them well-liked and sociable. On the other hand, the fear of commitment can be so great that they attract the most unusual situations and may never have the peace of a deep connection. There will be emotional losses in their life regardless of avoidance, but their attitudes and values tell the real story.

The 5♣ is considered to be one of the most unmarriageable cards in the deck because of their restless nature. One way or another, most of them avoid commitment as much as possible. If they are cunning as well, they will make it appear as though the reason they are not making a commitment is their partner's faults. In truth, they are deeply afraid that any relationship may deprive them of their freedom.

Because of their avoidance of commitment and their A♠ in Venus, they are often attracted to married people or have secret affairs. They also like to keep their private lives to themselves. The single

---

KARMA CARDS:

5♥   4♣

KARMA COUSINS:

4♦   6♥

PAST-LIFE CARDS:

4♣   6♣

---

life is the way for most 5♣, but there are those exceptional ones who settle down and make great contributions in love and work.

GENERALITIES BETWEEN THE PERSONALITY CARD CONNECTIONS

5♣ of both sexes often make friends with Heart males, who have a fondness for them. However, there is also a karmic bond between them that can be difficult at times. Club females also enjoy the company of 5♣ of both sexes. 5♣ women can make a good marriage with certain Diamond males and are usually attracted to certain Spade males.

Bruce, the Happy Five of Clubs

Bruce is a 5♣ who exemplifies many of the positive 5♣ traits. Many 5♣ are not very happy with themselves. They complain about never having accomplished something of merit in their lives, or are constantly worried about money. But Bruce is a person who appears to have fully accepted his restless and inquisitive nature and has integrated that into his life in a positive way. At 41 years old, he has never been married and he travels a great deal. He has had some financial success in his life and for years he didn't need to work. Remember that 7♦ in Jupiter in the Life Path of the 5♣? It often brings in a great deal of money in the life of the 5♣, and in Bruce's case, it gives him a natural sense of abundance and prosperity that seems to follow him wherever he goes.

Bruce has gone through periods in his life where he actually moved to a new house two or three times a year. He seems to be constantly on the move and appears to have many places he calls home. He knows a lot about many subjects and makes many friends wherever he goes. He doesn't mind not having a committed relationship in his life and he is okay with casual relationships, which is unusual since most people cannot emotionally handle that kind of relationship.

Bruce takes great pride in his car. It would make sense that his car would be so prominent in his value system since it represents his freedom on the earthly plane. This is a trait in many 5♣. He takes tremendous care of his car, worries about it, and sometimes talks about it as if it were a real person.

Bruce represents the happy side of the 5♣. He is someone who has accepted his nature and made the best of it. You won't find many 5♣ who are this happy, but they are out there. Most of them are dissatisfied with their life and cannot seem to resolve the conflict between their freedom and having some sort of foundation in their life. The happiest 5♣ are those who realize they are here to collect experiences and ideas and allow themselves the freedom to do just that. At the same time, they have faith that their needs will be provided as is necessary. The ones who do this usually get more than just their basic needs. Their 7♦ in Jupiter is a card of true spiritual and material abundance and this is the birthright of the 5♣.

LIFE SPREAD CARDS

PLANETARY CARD	SYMBOL	CARD
MOON	☽	10♠
SUN (BIRTH CARD)	✳	5♣
MERCURY	☿	3♦
VENUS	♀	A♠
MARS	♂	7♥
JUPITER	♃	7♦
SATURN	♄	5♠
URANUS	♅	J♥
NEPTUNE	♆	9♣
PLUTO	♇	9♠
RESULT (COSMIC REWARD)	♃ +	2♥
COSMIC LESSON	♄ +	K♥

PLANETARY RULING CARDS

BIRTH DATE	ASTROLOGICAL RULING SIGN	PLANETARY RULING CARD
MAR 31	ARIES	7♥
APR 29	TAURUS	A♠
MAY 27	GEMINI	3♦
JUN 25	CANCER	10♠
JUL 23	CANCER OR LEO	10♠ OR 5♣
AUG 21	LEO	5♣
SEP 19	VIRGO	3♦
OCT 17	LIBRA	A♠
NOV 15	SCORPIO	7♥ & 9♠
DEC 13	SAGITTARIUS	7♦

Who 5♣ with	Con1	Con2	Con3	Con4	Con5	Attraction	Intensity	Compatibility
A♥	CRFS	JUR	MAR	JURS	CRF	4	3	3
2♥	CRF	VEMS	MAR	JURS	JUF	6	2	4
3♥	JUR	VER	NEFS	VERS	VEFS	5	-2	7
4♥	VEFS	MAM	MOF	MOFS	NER	8	0	7
5♥	KRMA	VEMS	PLF	PLFS	NEF	8	5	1
6♥	VEM	VEMS	KRMC	MOFS	MOR	7	-2	9
7♥	MAF	CLRS	VEF	VEFS	CLR	6	2	3
8♥	CLRS	JURS	MAF	MAFS	VEM	4	2	2
9♥	JUR	CRRS	JUF	MAR	JURS	3	0	5
10♥	PLRS	URFS	SAF	URR	SAFS	0	4	-3
J♥	URF	NERS	SAR	MAFS	VEM	3	2	0
Q♥	PLR	URRS	MOF	NEF	JUFS	4	1	2
K♥	CLF	SARS	SAR	MARS	PLF	2	6	-4
A♣	MAR	JURS	CRF	VEMS	JUF	5	3	4
2♣	SAR	MARS	VEF	CLF	SARS	3	4	0
3♣	VERS	MARS	MOR	MOFS	SAF	7	0	5
4♣	KRMA	MOFS	PLF	PLFS	VEM	8	5	1
5♣	SBC	MOFS	MORS	NEF	PLFS	7	2	5
6♣	MORS	CLR	URR	MAR	VER	4	0	4
7♣	VEFS	URR	VEMS	JUF	MAFS	5	-2	6
8♣	MAFS	VEM	URF	NERS	SAR	6	2	3
9♣	NEF	JUFS	PLR	URRS	VERS	4	1	3
10♣	NER	SAFS	MAM	MAMS	URFS	3	6	-2
J♣	URFS	PLRS	NEF	PLR	NEFS	3	3	0
Q♣	VER	NEFS	JUR	MAMS	PLFS	6	1	5
K♣	PLFS	MAR	MARS	CRFS	MAMS	8	8	-2
A♦	CRFS	VER	CLFS	CLF	CRF	6	4	1
2♦	VER	CLFS	MORS	CLR	URR	5	0	3
3♦	MOR	VEM	VEMS	JUM	JUMS	7	-4	9
4♦	VEMS	SAF	KRMC	VER	PLR	3	2	2
5♦	VERS	SAF	PLF			3	4	-1
6♦	VERS	NEF	JUFS	MAMS	PLR	6	0	5
7♦	JUF	JUR	CRRS	MAR	JURS	3	0	5
8♦	URR	VEMS	MAFS	VEFS	MAF	5	1	4
9♦	JUM	PLF	MARS	VERS		5	3	1
10♦	MAMS	VER	NEFS	MAFS	SAR	8	4	3
J♦	MAMS	URFS	MAM	VEF	VER	6	4	2
Q♦	JUM	MOR	MOF	MARS	JUMS	5	-2	7
K♦	MARS	VERS	JURS	VEF	VER	6	1	5
A♠	VEF	MAF	SAR	MARS	SARS	5	4	2
2♠	CRR	VEF	PLFS	MAMS	JURS	6	3	2
3♠	MAMS	VERS	VEF	VER	PLR	7	2	5
4♠	MAM	NER	SAFS	VEFS	PLF	5	5	0
5♠	SAF	PLRS	VEMS	PLR	URR	1	4	-2
6♠	CRR	VEF	PLF	JURS	CRRS	5	2	3
7♠	JURS	MARS	CLRS	CRF	MAR	4	3	2
8♠	MAR	PLFS	MORS	CLR	URR	7	5	0
9♠	PLF	CLF	SARS	CRR	VEF	5	6	-3
10♠	MOF	VEFS	PLR	URRS	PLRS	5	-1	5
J♠	VEFS	NER	SAFS	CLR	NERS	3	2	2
Q♠	MAFS	MAMS	URR	VEMS	URF	6	5	1
K♠	SAR	MAFS	VEM	URF	NERS	4	3	1

The Seeker of Worth

DESCRIPTION OF THE 5♦ PERSON:

This card has its share of challenges and its share of gifts. Like all Fives, 5♦ dislike routine and abhor anything that pretends to limit their freedom or put them in a box. They can be perpetual wanderers, never settling down for anything long enough to make it pay off. But others find value in a relationship or job and stay with it, creating some security in an otherwise insecure life. The main areas of restlessness include work and relationships. All 5♦ have an inner sense of dissatisfaction, but they also want to accomplish something of value and gain stability in their lives. These two ideals often conflict and it is a trick for them to find a career that gives them both. For many, sales is the work of choice. They can relate to people on all levels and this gives them great success in this area.

There are likely to be financial losses in their life and situations where their kind-hearted nature costs them a great deal. Being closely associated with the 9♦ card makes them very giving people and tells us that there are outstanding debts to be paid in this life from the past. These people are givers who love to share their resources with their family and close friends, though at times they seem to be taken advantage of by others and may resent it. For them, giving is both a gift and a lesson.

They are inherently spiritual, being situated in the Neptune column, and know what is of true value. Their knowledge extends to the psychic realms—

many 5♦ have great ability in this area. The challenge comes in practicing what they know. They come into this life with a certain amount of karma which often takes considerable hard work to discharge. If they are lazy, there will be many problems. They must practice what they know and do what it takes to get the job done without shirking responsibility. Such a strong Neptune influence creates a desire to help others as part of their life's work. If they align themselves with a higher purpose or ideal, they can become the creators of their destiny and have much more success and fulfillment

The first 45 years of life are the most challenging. Their life improves considerably as they get older. They often come to a crossroads at mid-life when they must face their fears once and for all. This is the time that many of them get interested in self-help subjects or spirituality. A transformation occurs and their life begins anew in many respects. Many become an authority in some area, either as an author or teacher, and are looked up to for leadership and guidance.

SOME OF THE 5♦ ISSUES CONCERNING RELATIONSHIPS:

5♦ are restless and changeable romantically. They are often averse to commitment. For these reasons, many of them have difficulty making a relationship work for an extended period of time. They are very romantic and many have a lot of charm and sexual prowess, as symbolized by their J♣ in Venus, which has another Jack, the J♦, as its Karma Card. For this reason, they are considered to be some of the best lovers.

They are attracted to those of wit and creativity, and they themselves can be quite charming, but also calculating and crafty, when it comes to love. In many cases, love is a mental game to them and many of them lose sight of their feelings

---

KARMA CARDS:

9♦   3♣

KARMA COUSINS:

Q♦   K♦

PAST-LIFE CARDS:

4♦   6♦

---

as they get wrapped up in their analysis of all the concepts of love. They can be very sneaky and dishonest in this area if they so choose. At the same time, contact with books and other educational material about love and relationships always has a tremendous impact on them and brings them up to a higher level and more happiness.

The whole concept of marriage and the yearning for intimacy that love requires is a major challenge for them, one that they are sure to deal with often during the course of their life. Being a Five, they often will not want to return to the confinement of the 'box' that marriage can represent. They want to explore and undertake new adventures.

GENERALITIES BETWEEN THE PERSONALITY CARD CONNECTIONS

5♦ males have strong connections with Spade females. Female 5♦ are attracted to male Clubs and hold a certain fascination for Diamond males. They need a relationship that doesn't cramp their lifestyle too much.

Freedom Versus Security & Accomplishment

My best friend Mark is a classic 5♦ who demonstrates how many Fives have an inner conflict between their freedom and their desire to achieve security and make a mark for themselves in the world. Mark and I grew up together and have shared many wonderful adventures. When we were 18, we just took off and went traveling across the U.S. This is the kind of relationship that we have always enjoyed. I could just call him and say, 'Mark, let's take off and go across the country,' and he would usually be ready to go. This is a classic 5♦ trait. If you suggest a trip for any reason, they are usually inclined to drop everything and go with you.

When I was around age 36 or so, my life began to settle into one line of work and my life had more of a plan to it. I became less changeable and, in the process, became more successful, while Mark still traveled and moved fairly frequently. After a while my success became a reminder to Mark of how he had not accomplished anything substantial with his 5♦ lifestyle of change and adventure. This caused some tension between us as I began to personify the part of Mark that wanted success but which conflicted with his freedom-loving part.

This is not to say that all 5♦ have such a strong struggle, but it is a common trait. The question for any Five is: Should I spend my entire life pursuing new adventures and exploring new and uncharted realms, or should I establish some security and foundation from which I can launch my adventures? It is interesting that most people equate money with freedom. They tell you that money does not buy happiness, but it does give you the freedom to do what you want, when you want, and opens many doors of possibility that were once closed. If this is true, then it is sort of a cosmic joke that the 5♦ person who wants freedom so much will have to settle down for a while and focus themselves on one occupation long enough to make the money that will allow them to have more adventures. Perhaps this is the lesson for the 5♦: I can earn even more freedom and have even more and better adventures if I set aside some time in my life to create the financial prosperity that will give me this freedom. But for many 5♦, this is one of the most difficult things to do. This is why many of them gravitate toward work as salespeople. Many sales jobs allow the individual freedom to travel as part of their work. This often kills two birds with one stone by allowing the 5♦ to create some financial independence and not feeling caged in while doing it. It is these sorts of success formulas that separate the happy 5♦ from the others.

LIFE SPREAD CARDS

PLANETARY CARD	SYMBOL	CARD
MOON	☽	7♣
SUN (BIRTH CARD)	✳	5♦
MERCURY	☿	Q♠
VENUS	♀	J♣
MARS	♂	9♦
JUPITER	♃	7♠
SATURN	♄	2♣
URANUS	♅	K♣
NEPTUNE	♆	J♦
PLUTO	♇	4♥
RESULT (COSMIC REWARD)	♃+	4♦
COSMIC LESSON	♄+	2♠

PLANETARY RULING CARDS

BIRTH DATE	ASTROLOGICAL RULING SIGN	PLANETARY RULING CARD
JAN 22	AQUARIUS	K♣
FEB 20	AQUARIUS OR PISCES	K♣ OR J♦
MAR 18	PISCES	J♦
APR 16	ARIES	9♦
MAY 14	TAURUS	J♣
JUN 12	GEMINI	Q♠
JUL 10	CANCER	7♣
AUG 8	LEO	5♦
SEP 6	VIRGO	Q♠
OCT 4	LIBRA	J♣
NOV 2	SCORPIO	9♦ & 4♥

Who 5♦ with	The Connections Between Partners Con1	Con2	Con3	Con4	Con5	Overall Index Ratings Attraction	Intensity	Compatibility
A♥	PLR	NER	PLF	JURS	JUFS	4	3	0
2♥	MAF	VEFS	JUM	MAFS	VERS	7	2	4
3♥	JUFS	PLR	URRS	JUM	JUMS	2	0	3
4♥	PLF	VEMS	SAF	VEM	PLFS	5	4	-1
5♥	SAR	MOFS	CRF	PLR	MOF	4	2	2
6♥	VEFS	VERS	MAF	VEF	CLRS	7	0	7
7♥	JUMS	JUF	CRFS	JUFS	CRRS	3	-1	5
8♥	JUF	JUMS	PLF	PLRS	CRRS	3	1	2
9♥	VER	VEFS	SAR	VEF	NERS	5	-1	6
10♥	MAFS	VEF	NERS	NER	URRS	7	3	3
J♥	MAM	VEF	CLRS	MAMS	SARS	6	4	2
Q♥	VER	CRRS	JURS	VERS	URFS	5	-1	5
K♥	MAMS	SAF	VEMS	MARS	VEM	5	5	0
A♣	MAF	VEFS	MAFS	VERS	JUM	8	3	4
2♣	SAF	VEMS	JUF	CRFS	MAMS	2	2	1
3♣	KRMA	JUR	NEF	PLFS	NER	5	4	2
4♣	VEFS	MORS	VEF	CLRS		6	-3	8
5♣	SAR	VEFS	PLR			2	2	1
6♣	VEM	VEMS	CRR	MARS	CRF	7	0	6
7♣	MOF	MAFS	SAFS	JUR	MAF	5	3	2
8♣	VEF	CLRS	MAM	VEFS	CLR	5	1	4
9♣	CRRS	VER	MORS	URFS	JURS	5	-1	5
10♣	PLRS	SAFS	VEMS	URF	SAF	1	4	-2
J♣	VEF	NERS	NEF	PLR	URFS	6	1	4
Q♣	URRS	JUM	JUFS	CLR	SAFS	0	-1	2
K♣	URF	SARS	CLF	CLFS	CRR	1	4	-2
A♦	NER	PLF	JURS	MARS	VEM	6	3	1
2♦	MARS	VEM	VEMS	NER	PLF	8	2	4
3♦	VERS	URR	NEFS	URRS	MAF	5	0	3
4♦	MOFS	CRF	SAR	URF	SARS	4	2	2
5♦	SBC	MAF	JUFS	JUR	MAR	5	4	3
6♦	MORS	CRRS	MAR	MARS	VEM	7	2	4
7♦	VEFS	VER	VERS	SAR	VEF	6	-2	7
8♦	MAFS	MOR	MOF	MOFS	VER	8	0	7
9♦	KRMA	MAF	JUFS	URR	NEFS	6	5	2
10♦	CLR	SAFS	URRS	JUM	MOR	0	2	-1
J♦	NEF	PLR	URFS	MAR	VEF	5	3	1
Q♦	URR	NEFS	KRMC	VERS	MAF	5	2	3
K♦	PLFS	JUR	KRMC	JUF	JUFS	4	3	2
A♠	JUF	CRFS	JUMS	SAF	VEMS	3	1	3
2♠	CLF	CLFS	VERS	URF	SARS	4	4	-1
3♠	MAR	MORS	NEF	PLR	URFS	7	3	3
4♠	VEMS	PLRS	PLF	PLFS	PLR	6	3	0
5♠	MAFS	MOFS	CRF	JUF	CRFS	7	3	4
6♠	VERS	CLF	CLFS	MAM	JUMS	6	3	1
7♠	JUF	PLFS	MOR	PLF	JUFS	6	2	2
8♠	CRR	VEMS	URF	SARS	VEM	4	0	3
9♠	MAMS	VERS	MAM	JUMS	MARS	7	4	3
10♠	PLF	VER	VERS	SAF	VEM	6	2	1
J♠	SAFS	MOF	PLRS	MAM	JUR	2	4	0
Q♠	MOR	CLR	SAFS	MAFS	VER	4	2	2
K♠	VEF	CLRS	MAM	MAMS	VEFS	6	2	4

The Wanderer

DESCRIPTION OF THE 5♠ PERSON:

The 5♠ is the card of changes and travel. These people have a certain amount of restlessness that manifests itself in interesting ways. Most of them dislike routine and find occupations that afford some variety. Many of them are avid travelers or move to a new home on a frequent basis. However, their restlessness often applies to their spiritual quest, their quest for truth, and the development of their inner self. With the J♥ in Mercury there is a certain amount of sacrifice made for loved ones in their lives, or for an education. This is especially true in their early life. Their Karma Card, the 10♥, gives them much social success, but sometimes their social life can seem to be a burden, or is overdone in some ways. The 9♣ in Venus speaks of a giving love nature that others may take advantage of. The many disappointments on a personal level, especially with friends and loved ones, comes from this spiritual Nine in their relationship position. Therefore, they usually have more success with groups than on a one-to-one basis. They have strong spiritual inclinations and must learn to express unconditional love in their closest relationships in order to access the high side of the spiritual cards (9♣ and 9♠) that are found in the personal positions (Venus and Mars) of their Life Path. Most of the cards in their Life Path are successful ones so we tend to see the 5♠ as one of the more fortunate cards in the deck, materially speaking.

They have a sound sense of values and good organizational ability. Many of them are very successful salespeople or financial counselors. Their life improves with age, especially after age 39, when they go through a shift for the better. Happiness in love and financial success usually come after this time and their need for travel gradually dissipates as they find more contentment in the enjoyment of their home and family life.

SOME OF THE 5♠ ISSUES CONCERNING RELATIONSHIPS:

These people are popular and well-liked. They enjoy love, romance, and travel. There are sure to be some disappointments in love from time to time, because they are here to 'complete' some relationships they began in past lives and let them go. The two Nines in Venus and Mars tell us that there will be some key relationships in their life that to them may seem to be just what they want, but will not work out as planned. With the right attitude, these endings can be translated as graduations, crowning achievements in completing certain chapters of soul development as it pertains to their personal relationships. The 5♠ person needs to realize that those relationships that seem to be taken from them are probably not good for them and are best left alone.

These two Nines are strong and evident in their personal lives. With Venus and Mars, we expect to find cards of our own personal and romantic fulfillment. But these are cards that entail giving up what we want. For some 5♠ this can be a great challenge, while for others it causes the development of a great spiritual love nature. They are capable of making sacrifices for those they love and of generally allowing their partners the freedom to be their best.

There is also the 2♥ in Jupiter to consider, and this card at the very least will bring a lifelong friendship that is

---

> **KARMA CARDS:**
> 10♥ 4♦
>
> **KARMA COUSINS:**
> J♣ 5♥
>
> **PAST-LIFE CARDS:**
> 4♠ 6♠

uniquely rewarding. But it can also bring a great love into their life, once they have learned the lessons of the two Nines. For this reason, their greatest experience of love often comes later in their lives.

GENERALITIES BETWEEN THE PERSONALITY CARD CONNECTIONS

5♠ women make good wives with Heart males, though it will not be without some challenges and difficulties. Diamond males make good friends. Club females have a certain weakness for 5♠ males. 5♠ females can get along with other Spade males, though there are bound to be some lessons learned in the relationship.

The Five of Spades's Thirst for Experience

Being the strongest of the Fives, the 5♠ is most known for the extent of what they will do in order to have new experiences in their life. This is true of all the Fives, but the Spade card in any suit is always the strongest, so in the 5♠ we can see more dramatic examples of this. Five, being the 'number of the race of man,' represents people who are here to taste what life is about. They want to know what it is like in different kinds of situations and environments and experience what the world has to offer.

Take, for example, the 5♠ person who, without fail, moves to a new house or apartment every six months. More importantly, to him, this is a normal mode of living for everyone. He could not imagine living in one place longer than that. This is one way of being a 5♠. He is just trying out new living situations.

Another 5♠ man is a 'Jack of all Trades.' In this particular 5♠ quest, he has tried more kinds of work and creative enterprises than most people. In his office are the books, machines, accessories, and other necessary items for over 20 different businesses. He excelled as a salesman, as many Fives do, but even the success of that career did not satisfy his desire to gather new experiences. Today, he is still trying out new jobs and exploring new areas and ways to make money.

Finally, another 5♠, this time a woman, has two homes (and offices) about 300 miles apart. She has arranged her life so that she has to travel back and forth from one place to the other every two weeks or so. Her work mainly involves promoting large events such as concerts and art shows (all the domain of the 10♥ Karma Card). At one point in her life she met a man and began dating him. They began living together, even though she was usually away every couple of weeks doing business in her other location. Once, while she was away, her boyfriend befriended another woman who was down and out and invited this other woman to come and live in an apartment adjoining his house. When the 5♠ returned, there was another woman on the property having breakfast each morning with her boyfriend. It all looked very suspicious. The 5♠ did what all of her friends thought was unexpected and unusual: she tolerated this other woman's presence. As it turned out, this other woman ended up staying for months and the 5♠'s boyfriend helped the other woman start a new business and did a lot of good things for her. All of the 5♠'s closest friends told her she was crazy to put up with this other woman in her life.

Finally, after about a year, things came to a head and the other woman left. The 5♠ confided that the real reason she put up with this situation for so long was that she had never in her life felt jealousy in a relationship. Her boyfriend was the first man she had ever met who made her feel possessive and jealous. She wanted to know what that really felt like, so she endured that situation for a year. When she had felt jealous enough, she decided that she was satisfied with her experience and quickly ended the situation.

This is an example of how a Five can make a decision that others may find hard to understand, but from their point of view it makes perfect sense. Their quest for new experiences, and the basic desire to experience almost everything they can, is the underlying motivator that sets them apart from every other number in the deck.

FIVE OF SPADES

LIFE SPREAD CARDS		
PLANETARY CARD	SYMBOL	CARD
MOON	☽	7♦
SUN (BIRTH CARD)	☀	5♠
MERCURY	☿	J♥
VENUS	♀	9♣
MARS	♂	9♠
JUPITER	♃	2♥
SATURN	♄	K♥
URANUS	♅	K♦
NEPTUNE	♆	6♥
PLUTO	♇	4♣
RESULT (COSMIC REWARD)	♃ +	2♦
COSMIC LESSON	♄ +	J♠

PLANETARY RULING CARDS		
BIRTH DATE	**ASTROLOGICAL RULING SIGN**	**PLANETARY RULING CARD**
JAN 9	CAPRICORN	K♥
FEB 7	AQUARIUS	K♦
MAR 5	PISCES	6♥
APR 3	ARIES	9♠
MAY 1	TAURUS	9♣

Who	The Connections Between Partners					Overall Index Ratings		
5♠ with	Con1	Con2	Con3	Con4	Con5	Attraction	Intensity	Compatibility
A♥	CRFS	CRR	MAF	CRRS	JUF	6	5	1
2♥	JUF	CLFS	URFS	PLR	SAMS	2	2	1
3♥	CRR	CRFS	NER	NERS	CRF	6	4	1
4♥	MOFS	URR	SAFS	URRS	MOF	2	0	2
5♥	VEFS	SAR	KRMC	URF	SARS	3	2	3
6♥	NEF	PLF	JUR	NER	JURS	6	3	2
7♥	VER	MAR	JURS	MARS	VEM	6	2	5
8♥	VEFS	VER	VERS	VEF	SAR	6	-2	8
9♥	SAFS	MOF	PLR	SAMS	MOFS	1	4	-1
10♥	KRMA	VER	PLF	NEFS	PLFS	7	5	1
J♥	MOR	CLR	PLFS	VEM	MORS	6	0	4
Q♥	URR	SAFS	VEF	VEFS	SAF	1	2	0
K♥	SAF	MAF	JUFS	CRR	MAFS	2	5	-1
A♣	PLR	SAMS	JUF	CLFS	URFS	2	5	-2
2♣	MAR	JURS	SAF	SAFS	VEM	2	5	0
3♣	MAR	JUFS	URF	SARS	NEF	3	3	2
4♣	PLF	SAR	NEF	URR	NEFS	4	5	-2
5♣	SAR	PLF	PLFS	VEMS	URF	4	5	-3
6♣	MAFS	VEM	CRF	CRFS	MAF	8	4	3
7♣	MAM	JUMS	CLRS	CLF	URFS	4	3	1
8♣	MOR	CLR	PLFS	VEM	MAR	6	1	3
9♣	VEF	VEM	VEMS	PLRS	VEFS	7	-2	8
10♣	VEF	MAFS	CLF	URFS	MOFS	6	2	3
J♣	NERS	PLFS	KRMC	JUM	VER	6	3	1
Q♣	NER	CRR	PLRS	MAF	SARS	5	4	0
K♣	MAMS	SAR	MARS	MAFS	VEM	6	7	0
A♦	CRF	CRFS	JUF	MARS	SAR	6	4	1
2♦	CRF	SAR	VERS	CRFS	MAF	5	4	1
3♦	JUR	NEF	URRS	MAM	MOFS	4	0	4
4♦	KRMA	VEFS	PLF	NEFS	NEF	7	4	2
5♦	JUR	CRRS	MAR	JUFS	MARS	4	2	4
6♦	VEM	VEMS	VEF	VERS	VER	8	-3	10
7♦	MOF	SAFS	PLR	SAMS	SAF	1	4	-1
8♦	CLRS	NEFS	MAM	JUMS	MAMS	5	3	1
9♦	JUR	CRRS	URRS	VER	URR	2	-1	4
10♦	PLRS	NER	NEFS	MOR	URFS	5	2	2
J♦	NERS	PLFS	JUM	VERS	VER	6	2	1
Q♦	URRS	JUR	CRRS	SAF	JURS	0	1	1
K♦	URF	SARS	MAR	JUFS	VEFS	2	3	1
A♠	MAR	JURS	VER	CLFS	MARS	5	3	3
2♠	SAR	MARS	MORS	MAMS	MAR	5	5	1
3♠	VERS	VEM	VEMS	NERS	PLFS	7	-2	7
4♠	MOFS	VEF	MAFS	MOF	MAF	8	-1	7
5♠	SBC	VER	VEFS	VEF	VERS	6	1	6
6♠	MORS	MAF	JUFS	SAR	MARS	6	1	4
7♠	VEFS	URF	SARS	SAR	VEMS	2	0	3
8♠	MAFS	VEM	MAMS	VEF	MAM	8	4	4
9♠	MAF	JUFS	SAF	MORS	CRR	4	3	2
10♠	URR	SAFS	URRS	SAF	MAMS	-1	4	-4
J♠	CLF	URFS	MAM	JUMS	VEF	4	3	0
Q♠	NEFS	PLRS	CLRS	VEM	PLR	5	2	1
K♠	CLR	PLFS	VEM	MOR	CLRS	5	2	1

The Sixes

One of the symbols for the sign of Libra is the Scales of Justice, symbolizing that all things must ultimately be brought into balance. This symbol is another way of representing the ageless Law of Karma, the law of cause and effect that governs everything that happens in this world that we know. It is karma and the law that all Sixes are very familiar with. They are all aware of this law on some level and find various ways to integrate it within the fabric of their lives. Some are excessively aware of it, being overly cautious never to do or say anything that will upset the karmic balance in their lives. Many of them are concerned about ever having any debts to anyone that must later be repaid. They will go out of their way to avoid incurring any debts for just this reason. Others are aware of the law, but feel hampered and constricted by it to the point that they try and slip through life without having to pay their way. These are the ones who are irresponsible and continually meet up with problems when they try to get something for nothing, or when they expect others to take care of them. But in both extremes, and in all the various stages in between, all Six people are conscious on some level of the Law of Karma. That is their birth number and it will remain with them until they pass from this life to the next.

Sixes know about destiny and fate. Theirs is the number of fate. They sense that much of their life is destined because of their actions from lives past. They often wonder about what sorts of things, both good and bad, will come to them through the inevitable Law of Karma. They can be guilty of just waiting around for things to happen and it is known that all of them get into a rut every now and again. Some of them sense that terrible things may be in store for them in the future and they dread the prospect. Others sense that something good is coming, such as a windfall of money, for some good deeds they performed in past lives. It is surprising how many 6♦ play the lottery, for example. Fate does come to the Six, but often after long periods of waiting. Their lives seem to go a certain way for a long time and then finally change to a new condition. This long time can be up or down, financially, relationship-wise, or otherwise. In many cases, they must prod themselves out of their complacency to get themselves motivated to make the next step. Attempts to change them usually meet with failure. A Six person will budge only when they are ready.

Even though Libra represents the 7th house astrologically, it is the sign most closely associated with the number Six. Six is symbolized by the Star of David, the two, interlocking triangles, one pointing up, the other down. This symbolizes balance and peace. Like Librans, Sixes are definitely peacemakers of a sort. They love peace and harmony and will go out of their way to promote it. But also like Librans, Sixes can be guilty of not accepting the aggressiveness and other emotional qualities that life often contains. They may try to avoid their own feelings and situations of conflict because that would upset their peace and balance. When this drive for peace becomes an escape from reality, it inevitably backfires and their own naturally aggressive side comes out for all to see. The Six person can be the one who ignores their own anger until it builds up and blows off like a volcano.

At heart, Sixes are fairly competitive, which seems like a paradox because of how much they like peace. It is interesting to note how many successful athletes are Sixes. Because of their balanced nature, when their competitors press on them, they press back with equal force. This is a key to their success in sports and in business, where they often excel. They have a sense of fairness and competition that can bring them success in the eyes of the world. It is interesting that the 6♥ card falls in the Mars row and column of the Life Spread, giving it a double Mars connotation. Though we may think of the Sixes as being the most docile and quiet, they can be the most aggressive and competitive when they are stirred up.

Sixes are known to be some of the most psychic cards in the deck. Perhaps this is because they achieve enough peace in their life that they are in a better position to hear 'the voice within.' Many Six people become professional psychics, and all will admit to receiving impressions from time to time. Many people who are Sixes have come to fulfill a special and unique purpose during the course of their life that will involve becoming a signpost to others of a better way of life. John the Baptist is a classic example. Though he himself was not Jesus, the son of God, he cleared the way for the coming of Jesus and led people to him. So it is with many of the Sixes. Some will become famous spiritual leaders and teachers, while others will practice their uplifting of souls among the members of their family or coworkers. It is those Sixes that listen to their inner voice who realize that they are here to bring others to the light. They find that their life has much more meaning than just getting by day-to-day and fulfilling their personal desires and ambitions.

The Peacemaker Card

DESCRIPTION OF THE 6♥ PERSON:

This is a card of peace, harmony, and stability in love and family. The 6♥ person is aware of the 'law of love' and strives to maintain stability in relationships. This stability can make for a satisfying life or one of monotony and boredom. It all depends on how it is handled by the individual. They are somewhat fixed and dislike changes and upsets. Sometimes this can keep them in a relationship longer than necessary as they sort out their intentions and motives.

They are usually successful and can apply their great mental power to most any area with success, in spite of occasional fears about not having enough. Success lies in knowledge and communications fields, and they usually do better by developing one area and sticking to it. They have the power to learn practically anything.

This card has an inherited creative gift. Many of them find success as designers, artists, or even as creative financial planners. They can be very entrepreneurial and are never at a loss for good ideas on how to generate income.

They are here to settle karmic love debts, to forgive and forget, and they can rise to the heights of spiritual awareness through their actions. They never get away with injuries to others and are well aware of this fact. Being the same card as that which governs Christmas day, their lives are intended to be that of plenty and giving, sharing their wealth of love

with those around them. It is interesting to note how often a 6♥ has either six children, which Hearts often represent, or when the number of people in their closest circle are six. This occurs with other Heart cards as well.

When a 6♥ feels that they have been wronged, or that someone in their care has been treated unjustly, we see the power of their competitive side emerge. They can become very forceful when provoked in this manner. This competitive nature can extend into their business dealings as well, or in sports. They can keep a cool exterior while engaged in heated battles.

Some 6♥ will experience the discovery of a special 'mission' in life, one that involves bringing love into the lives of others in a special way. It is here that they find their highest fulfillment and happiness.

SOME OF THE 6♥ ISSUES CONCERNING RELATIONSHIPS:

In the process of learning the responsibility of love, some 6♥ will have personal relationships to deal with that come from a past life. These can be of a positive or negative nature, depending upon their unique karma, but these relationships always seem fated. For this same reason, many 6♥ feel that there is a special love for them somewhere out there. They sense and believe that someday some special person will magically show up in their life to make everything better for them. This may or may not happen, but many of them carry this dream throughout their life.

Their basic love karma is good and they can have an ideal marriage. They prefer to be with those they can do business with and expect those they marry to hold up their end of the bargain. They are usually able to get what they want in matters of love as long as they maintain the attitude of being responsible and

---

KARMA CARDS:

4♣   3♦

KARMA COUSINS:

5♣   Q♦

PAST-LIFE CARDS:

5♥   7♥

listening to the call of the higher love nature within them.

GENERALITIES BETWEEN THE PERSONALITY CARD CONNECTIONS

6♥ women are often attracted to men of the Spade suit, and among those they attract, there will likely be one or more that will be of the irresponsible or dishonest side of the J♠, their Mars card. Both sexes will enjoy the company of Club women, especially the 4♣, 8♣, and 10♣. The 4♣ man is a strong marriage card for a 6♥ women, with whom they share a karmic bond. Men of the Heart suit should usually be avoided by 6♥ women.

The Law of Love

The Law of Karma extends into every important area of our life, but it seems that in today's age relationships take on a more pronounced importance. We learn so much about ourselves from our personal relationships that it is no wonder that it has become the number one vehicle for personal development. Until we have mastered a loving relationship, we really are not ready to proceed in any sense with our personal or spiritual development. Personal relationships are the 'final frontier' of personal growth. The 6♥ card implies so much that is important for each of us. 6♥ people, as the carriers of this message, also play a role in teaching us the true meaning of love.

As in all of the Sixes, we find two distinct types of 6♥, those that are very responsible about their love involvements and those that are very irresponsible. Even those that appear responsible often carry on negative relationship practices that eventually catch up with them. The Law of Love, to which they are intimately tied, guarantees that none of them will get away with any misconduct in the area of relationships in this lifetime. They must abide by what is true and fair or they will suffer the consequences. When we look at a Six, we see the six-pointed Star of David. This star, having two triangles, interlocked in a perfect balance, symbolizes the Law of Karma. What we sow, we shall reap. What we take

shall be taken from us and what we give will be given to us in return. This is the unchanging law that our universe is bound by. The Six person is here to embody that law for us, either by being a faithful practitioner or by being an example of one who abused it and paid the price.

6♥ are the peacemakers of the deck. They know that peace only happens when everything is in perfect balance and harmony. They desire this balance and the peace that goes with it. Often, though, they tend to avoid situations that are unpleasant and not peaceful. They tend to be put off by ugliness and unruly emotional conduct. However, these are a part of life. If they avoid these things, their peace is a sham, an escape from what life is really about. The peace they seek only comes by acknowledging the polarities of life. It is only in embracing our most unpleasant thoughts and actions that we find true acceptance, which is the mother of all peace. The 6♥ must learn to embrace the less attractive qualities in themselves and others in order to find that perfect love.

The 6♥ has often been referred to as the 'perfect love of Christ.' It is akin to a love that surpasses all materiality and embraces the polarities of life. Every 6♥ person can become aligned with this love when they accept themselves and their loved ones with all their imperfections.

SIX OF HEARTS

LIFE SPREAD CARDS

PLANETARY CARD	SYMBOL	CARD
MOON	☽	K♦
SUN (BIRTH CARD)	✳	6♥
MERCURY	☿	4♣
VENUS	♀	2♦
MARS	♂	J♠
JUPITER	♃	8♣
SATURN	♄	6♦
URANUS	♅	4♠
NEPTUNE	♆	10♥
PLUTO	♇	10♦
RESULT (COSMIC REWARD)	♃+	8♠
COSMIC LESSON	♄+	A♥

PLANETARY RULING CARDS

BIRTH DATE	ASTROLOGICAL RULING SIGN	PLANETARY RULING CARD
OCT 29	SCORPIO	J♠ & 10♦
NOV 27	SAGITTARIUS	8♣
DEC 25	CAPRICORN	6♦

Who 6♥ with	Con1	Con2	Con3	Con4	Con5	Attraction	Intensity	Compatibility
A♥	CLF	SARS	MARS	VEM	CRF	4	5	-1
2♥	MAR	JURS	PLFS	PLR	JUR	5	4	1
3♥	MARS	VEM	CLF	SARS	VEF	6	4	2
4♥	VERS	URF	CRRS	SAF	VER	3	0	2
5♥	MOFS	JUMS	VEM	VEMS	JUM	6	-3	8
6♥	SBC	MOR	MOF	PLF	PLFS	7	3	3
7♥	MORS	CRR	VEFS	CLR	CLRS	6	-1	5
8♥	VEFS	MORS	CRR	JUR	CRRS	6	-2	7
9♥	MAFS	VEM	PLR	PLFS	PLRS	7	4	1
10♥	NEF	JUFS	MAMS	NER	URF	6	2	4
J♥	URR	SAFS	URRS	JUF	NER	-1	2	-1
Q♥	URFS	JUM	CRRS	SAR	SARS	1	1	1
K♥	VER	NEFS	PLRS	CRFS	JUR	6	1	4
A♣	PLFS	MAR	JURS	PLR	MARS	6	6	-1
2♣	CRFS	CLR	VER	NEFS	PLRS	5	3	2
3♣	VER	CLFS	MOF	MOFS	VERS	7	-1	5
4♣	KRMA	MOR	VEM	VEMS	PLF	8	1	6
5♣	VEM	VEMS	KRMC	MOFS	MOR	7	-2	9
6♣	CRF	VEF	VEFS	CLRS	PLF	6	1	4
7♣	VERS	JURS	MAF	PLRS	MAFS	5	1	4
8♣	JUF	URR	SAFS	URRS	MAF	0	1	1
9♣	SAR	URFS	JUM	SAF	URR	-1	2	-2
10♣	MAF	PLRS	URF	URFS	PLR	4	4	-1
J♣	MAMS	NEF	JUFS	NEFS	SARS	6	4	3
Q♣	VEF	MARS	VEM	PLF	SAMS	7	2	4
K♣	MAM	JUR	SARS	CRF	CRFS	4	4	1
A♦	MARS	VEF	CLF	SARS	CLFS	6	4	1
2♦	VEF	MARS	MOR	MOFS	VEFS	8	0	7
3♦	KRMA	PLF	NEFS	VEM	VEMS	8	5	1
4♦	JUMS	NER	MOFS	MORS	PLR	5	-1	5
5♦	MAR	VER	CLFS	VERS	VEFS	7	3	3
6♦	SAF	SAR	JUF	MAFS	URR	-1	4	-2
7♦	PLR	MAFS	VEM	PLFS	CRR	6	5	0
8♦	JURS	NERS	VERS	MAF	NER	5	0	5
9♦	MAR	VEM	URFS	MARS	CRFS	6	4	3
10♦	PLF	SAMS	VEF	NERS	NEF	5	5	-1
J♦	MAMS	MAM	PLFS	VER	SARS	8	7	-1
Q♦	VEM	MAR	KRMC	MARS	CRFS	7	4	4
K♦	MOF	VER	CLFS	CLF		7	0	4
A♠	CLR	MORS	CRR	CRFS	MOR	5	1	3
2♠	JUR	SARS	MAM	MAMS	JURS	2	3	2
3♠	SAF	VER	JUF	MAFS	PLFS	2	3	0
4♠	URF	MAF	VERS	SAF	URFS	3	3	0
5♠	NER	NEF	JUFS	JUMS	PLR	5	1	4
6♠	JUR	CLRS	URRS	SARS	JURS	0	0	2
7♠	MOF	VEFS	MAR	VER	CLF	7	0	7
8♠	CRF	MAM	PLF	CRFS	SAR	7	7	-2
9♠	JUR	CLRS	URRS	VER	NEFS	2	-1	3
10♠	CRRS	VERS	URFS	JUM	VEF	4	0	4
J♠	MAF	PLRS	VERS	VEF	MAFS	7	4	2
Q♠	NERS	PLF	SAMS	JURS	MAM	4	5	-1
K♠	URRS	JUF	URR	SAFS	MAF	0	1	1

The Missionary Card

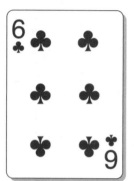

DESCRIPTION OF THE 6♣ PERSON:

This card is also known as the psychic card and it is surprising to see how few of the people of these birth dates are aware of their gift. The 6♣ also means responsibility to truth. These people must learn to find a system of truth they can believe in and by which they can live their life. Once attained, there is no limit to how much good these people can do in the world.

Those who have not yet found their path can be the biggest worriers and procrastinators of all the cards in the deck. They have a responsibility to maintain inner balance and peaceful communications with those in their lives. They often attain financial affluence and have an inherent protection over their lives. This is one of the cards that can attain the highest degree of material or spiritual success. On the other hand, they can get caught up in their complacency and never amount to anything.

As the card of 'responsibility of the spoken word,' the 6♣ always has issues about what they say and what they do as a result. Some will profess their truthfulness for years while secretly keeping their own lies. In all such cases, their lies catch up with them sooner or later with dire consequences. People who represent the high side of the 6♣ always practice what they preach and are careful about what they say.

The 6♣ has special karma with the abuse of power that they usually have to deal with at some point in their life.

They will either be given some position of power and learn about it through how they deal with it, or they will attract another powerful person who perpetrates some power struggles in their life. Either way, they learn the true meaning of power and how its tendency is to corrupt the holder.

Some 6♣ have a special mission in their life, one that involves bringing others to the threshold of some ancient and powerful truth. These are the bringers of light. Once they tap into their hidden reserves and their natural intuition is recognized, they find their lives guided and protected from the highest sources possible.

SOME OF THE 6♣ ISSUES CONCERNING RELATIONSHIPS:

6♣ love to be in love, but often there are some childhood issues that impinge on their ability to choose wisely. The tendency of a Six is to avoid their feelings and emotions, which make them appear emotional or upset. But these feelings are essential if the Six person is to truly understand their self and get to the bottom of the issues that influence them in their choice of relationships.

The women make good wives and mothers, while the men are often dominated by certain women in their life. This is connected to their 8♠ Karma Card. The 6♣ is gifted with many pleasurable experiences. They will experience more than the average amount of romantic and sexual enjoyment over the course of their life due to the Q♥ in their Venus position. They only have to watch out for the tendency to overindulge in the sensual side of life. This same Q♥ gives good marriage karma, and they usually have at least one very good marriage in their life.

Their notions about love and marriage tend toward the idealistic and romantic sides. They need to take care in their choices, because sometimes their ideal

---

KARMA CARDS:

8 ♠   2 ♦

KARMA COUSINS:

K ♣   A ♦

PAST-LIFE CARDS:

5 ♣   7 ♣

---

mate may not turn out to be what they imagined them to be.

GENERALITIES BETWEEN THE PERSONALITY CARD CONNECTIONS

6♣ males are often found with Heart females, for whom they hold a lot of affection. Both sexes have difficulty with Spade males, especially the Spade over 36 years old. Diamond males have difficulty with the 6♣ females, although the attraction is there. All 6♣ have other Club males as friends.

Our Life's Purpose

Every card in the deck has some highest form of expression that lies inherent in its suit, number, and position in the Life Spread. If each of us just understood what that highest expression is, we could accelerate our journey toward fulfillment and peace of mind. When we find our purpose, we are given a tremendous boost of energy and enthusiasm for our work. It ceases to become a job and becomes a mission because we lose our petty self-oriented identity and unite with a cause much greater than ourselves. This gives us powers and abilities we never thought possible. The 6♣ is a perfect example of how we can truly benefit from knowing what our highest expression or purpose is. The suit of Clubs pertains to knowledge and communications. All Clubs people are, on some level, seeking the perfect information that will change their life, just as Diamonds are seeking the perfect thing to own or have that will bring them fulfillment. The Six of Clubs can be the one who leads others to a higher form of knowledge, a form that can better their lives in many ways.

Many 6♣ are great teachers, bookstore owners, counselors, and publishers. Some of the world's greatest spiritual teachers have been and are 6♣. When they are in their own groove, they are acting as a catalyst in people's lives, initiating them into a new way of thinking, just as John the Baptist baptized people and led them to Jesus. The 6♣ person can be instrumental in leading others to their own higher self. They can also be successful in more mundane kinds of work. However, without the depth that comes from being an instrument in the transformation of others, the 6♣ does not really fully express his or her fullest potential.

Six is a static number and for this reason any of the Sixes can get into ruts at times. Their lives can seem very boring and without much purpose or direction to it. However, within the silence created by the unchanging energy of the Six, they achieve a sort of balance in which a silent voice speaks to them and them alone. If they listen to this inner voice, they are given the keys to the kingdom, and to their own path. Their natural intuition and ability to see things from both sides gives a great deal of intuition to all Sixes. Whether or not the Six person listens to this inner voice determines if they are fulfilled. The 6♣ is not going to be truly happy unless he or she is a conduit for information of a constructive or even spiritual nature. It just goes with the territory and the decision to be born under the rulership of that card.

We do not know the intimate details or the mechanics of why one soul would choose what card to be in each lifetime. All we know is that once a particular card has been chosen, by the day of our birth, we are then working under a definite structure of life experiences that has within it a personal plan for highest fulfillment and expression. By accessing this structure we can actually experience the cosmic flow of the universe.

LIFE SPREAD CARDS

PLANETARY CARD	SYMBOL	CARD
MOON	☽	8♥
SUN (BIRTH CARD)	✳	6♣
MERCURY	☿	6♠
VENUS	♀	Q♥
MARS	♂	10♣
JUPITER	♃	8♦
SATURN	♄	K♠
URANUS	♅	3♥
NEPTUNE	♆	A♣
PLUTO	♇	Q♣
RESULT (COSMIC REWARD)	♃+	10♠
COSMIC LESSON	♄+	5♣

PLANETARY RULING CARDS

BIRTH DATE	ASTROLOGICAL RULING SIGN	PLANETARY RULING CARD
MAR 30	ARIES	10♣
APR 28	TAURUS	Q♥
MAY 26	GEMINI	6♠
JUN 24	CANCER	8♥
JUL 22	CANCER	8♥
AUG 20	LEO	6♣
SEP 18	VIRGO	6♠
OCT 16	LIBRA	Q♥
NOV 14	SCORPIO	10♣ & Q♣
DEC 12	SAGITTARIUS	8♦

| Who | The Connections Between Partners | | | | | Overall Index Ratings | | |
6♣ with	Con1	Con2	Con3	Con4	Con5	Attraction	Intensity	Compatibility
A♥	PLFS	URF	VEMS	MOR	URFS	5	2	1
2♥	NEF	SARS	VERS	NEFS	VEM	5	1	3
3♥	URF	VEMS	PLF	URFS	PLFS	4	1	1
4♥	JUR	MAM	JUMS	CRF	CRFS	4	2	3
5♥	VEFS	MAR	MOFS	CLF	URF	7	2	5
6♥	VERS	CLFS	CRR	VER	PLR	6	1	3
7♥	VEMS	MOF	MARS	MAFS	VEM	8	0	7
8♥	MOF	PLR	VEMS	MAMS	MAFS	7	1	5
9♥	VEF	CLRS	VERS	NEF	SARS	5	0	5
10♥	CRRS	CLR	SAFS	VER	SAF	2	3	-1
J♥	PLRS	SAF	NEF	MAFS	VEFS	3	5	-2
Q♥	VEF	NERS	CRF	SAF	MAFS	5	2	3
K♥	URRS	JUM	NER	JURS	JUR	1	-1	3
A♣	NEF	SARS	VERS	MAM	VEFS	5	2	3
2♣	NER	JURS	MARS	URRS	JUM	4	1	3
3♣	MARS	VEM	VEMS	SAF	CRF	6	3	3
4♣	VERS	MOFS	CLF	URF	PLR	6	0	4
5♣	MOFS	CLF	URF	VEFS	VERS	5	0	4
6♣	SBC	MAF	JURS	JUF	CRFS	5	4	2
7♣	MORS	JUF	PLF	PLRS	URFS	5	0	4
8♣	VEFS	PLRS	SAF	NEF	MAFS	4	3	1
9♣	SAF	MAFS	VEF	NERS	NER	3	5	-1
10♣	MAF	JUFS	MAM	JUMS	MAMS	6	4	3
J♣	CLR	SAFS	SAR	MAMS	CRRS	0	5	-3
Q♣	PLF	URFS	URF	VEMS	MARS	4	3	-1
K♣	URR	NEFS	KRMC	VER	MAF	5	2	3
A♦	PLFS	JUF	KRMC	CRFS	VEF	6	4	1
2♦	KRMA	JUF	CRFS	PLFS	NER	6	5	1
3♦	CLFS	MORS	CRR	VER	CLF	6	2	2
4♦	MAR	VEFS	MAM	MARS	VEM	8	5	3
5♦	VEM	VEMS	CRR	MARS	CRF	7	0	6
6♦	SAF	MAFS	JUR	MAF	JUFS	2	5	-1
7♦	VERS	VEF	CLRS	NEF	SARS	5	-1	5
8♦	JUF	MORS	URFS	CLF	JUFS	4	-1	5
9♦	CRR	VEMS	VEM	NEFS	PLRS	7	0	5
10♦	PLF	URFS	MOF	URF	PLFS	5	3	-1
J♦	SAR	MAMS	CLR	SAFS	CLRS	1	6	-3
Q♦	CLFS	CRR	VEMS	MAF	CRRS	6	4	1
K♦	MARS	VEM	PLR	CLR	PLRS	6	3	2
A♠	MARS	VEMS	NER	JURS	NERS	6	2	4
2♠	VER	MOR	PLF	URR	NEFS	7	0	4
3♠	SAR	MAMS	URF	SARS	VERS	2	5	-1
4♠	MAM	JUMS	MAF	JUFS	JUR	5	3	3
5♠	CRRS	MAR	MARS	VEM	CRR	7	5	2
6♠	MOR	PLF	VER	SAF	VERS	6	1	2
7♠	PLR	MOF	MOFS	MAMS	CLR	6	1	4
8♠	KRMA	MAF	JURS	URR	NEFS	5	5	2
9♠	URRS	JUM	MOR	PLF	MORS	3	-1	3
10♠	CRF	JUR	VEF	NERS	VEFS	5	1	5
J♠	MORS	MAF	JUFS	URR	MAFS	6	1	5
Q♠	JUF	CLF	JUFS	URF	PLFS	3	1	3
K♠	SAF	NEF	MAFS	VEFS	PLRS	3	5	-1

Financial Responsibility

DESCRIPTION OF THE 6♦ PERSON:
The number Six implies responsibility and karma. The suit of Diamonds relates to finances. 6♦ people are keenly aware of financial debts and their repayment. This peculiar trait often manifests as a sort of paranoia about having outstanding debts. For example, a 6♦ might pay their phone and utility bills ahead of time, just so they won't have to think about what they might owe in the future. This is a common trait in 6♦ men and women.

Like all Sixes, they receive exactly what they give to others. There can be both huge financial losses and gains as their past-life accounts are settled. As individuals, they seem to fall into two categories—those who go out of their way to repay their debts, and those who are irresponsible when it comes to finances and need to learn to stand on their own two feet. Sometimes debts might be owed to them. Regardless of the situation, we can be sure that the 6♦ is getting exactly what he or she deserves.

They may fall into slumps as a result of their inertia, so they need to prod themselves into action every once in a while. Once they get going, they can attain most anything they desire. There is protection for them in work and action, not in waiting for the lottery.

On a deeper level, the 6♦ person may be here to help others come to a greater understanding of values. If they accept what they receive inwardly through their natural intuition, they will always be happy, regardless of the circumstances in their life. If they have discovered their special mission in life, they will not worry about how much money they have. These people make great teachers. They are givers and can be entrusted with great responsibility. What they have to give is a clear knowledge of higher values and the discrimination to make better personal choices. They are the keepers of the law.

SOME OF THE 6♦ ISSUES CONCERNING RELATIONSHIPS:
Underneath the tough exterior of the 6♦ lies a person who is having a difficult time meeting their needs for affection. There are often deep fears of abandonment that underlie much of what they do in their personal relationships. Until those fears are dealt with directly, they can have a hard time understanding the repeated failures that make up their love life.

They also have a highly mental approach to love that can lead them to think they can set up their love life as one would a college curriculum. When their brilliant romantic schemes are being subtly driven by fears, they backfire. They must learn to first give themselves the affection they seek from others. Honesty about their own feelings and emotions can bring them the information they need to make better assessments of their relationship problems. They must also practice being honest with themselves and others and not fall into creatively talking themselves into and out of situations while avoiding their true feelings. The 6♦ karmic pattern usually involves one breakup of a major relationship which transforms their life and teaches them about themselves.

GENERALITIES BETWEEN THE PERSONALITY CARD CONNECTIONS
Both sexes have an affinity for others of the Diamond suit, though the women can also be attracted to Heart males. Spade males are a big challenge and problem for most 6♦ females.

KARMA CARDS:
9♣ 3♠

KARMA COUSINS:
Q♥ J♦

PAST-LIFE CARDS:
5♦ 7♦

The Six of Diamonds Sports Figure

Many successful sports competitors are Sixes and the 6♦ is no exception. OJ Simpson, Joe Montana, Joe Louis, Jack Nicklaus, and Fred Couples are all 6♦ who have achieved a measure of fame because of their natural sports ability. These people are known to have a tremendous drive for success and the ability to operate like magic under the intense pressure of professional competition. What is it about the 6♦ that can manifest this way? What are the hidden elements that go into creating such a successful competitor?

6♦ people often have deep emotional wounds that are hidden from the view of the world by their friendly exterior. This can be recognized in their Life Spread as the A♥ in the Saturn position. These emotions can be the catalyst for a very intense drive for success. The A♥ in Saturn creates a desire to be liked and accepted that is nearly impossible to fulfill. Thus, the 6♦ person is often extremely sensitive and introverted on a personal level. However, on the exterior they seem happy and well-adjusted. Sixes dislike appearing emotional or even the least bit affected by things. They are known to have a cool exterior.

This may or may not be the main factor in a 6♦'s success as a competitor. The other quality of the 6♦ that comes into play is what we might call the 'get even' quality that all Sixes have to some degree. The Six is a number of fairness. If the Six feels they have been attacked, they will respond in kind equal to the amount of force that they perceive was sent to them. Many sporting events consist of attacks, defense, and counterattacks, and this is where Six energy can work like magic. Not only that, but the Six is already able to act and appear unworried about whatever is going on in their life. 6♦ competitors often have the reputation for keeping calm under intense pressure, a quality that scares competitors and encourages those on their own teams. All of these qualities combine together to create a very successful sports figure, and some of the best we know are the 6♦.

SIX OF DIAMONDS

LIFE SPREAD CARDS

PLANETARY CARD	SYMBOL	CARD
MOON	☽	8♣
SUN (BIRTH CARD)	✴	6♦
MERCURY	☿	4♠
VENUS	♀	10♥
MARS	♂	10♦
JUPITER	♃	8♠
SATURN	♄	A♥
URANUS	♅	A♦
NEPTUNE	♆	Q♦
PLUTO	♇	5♥
RESULT (COSMIC REWARD)	♃+	3♣
COSMIC LESSON	♄+	3♠

PLANETARY RULING CARDS

BIRTH DATE	ASTROLOGICAL RULING SIGN	PLANETARY RULING CARD
JAN 21	CAPRIC. OR AQUARIUS	A♥ OR A♦
FEB 19	AQUARIUS	A♦
MAR 17	PISCES	Q♦
APR 15	ARIES	10♦
MAY 13	TAURUS	10♥
JUN 11	GEMINI	4♠
JUL 9	CANCER	8♣
AUG 7	LEO	6♦
SEP 5	VIRGO	4♠
OCT 3	LIBRA	10♥
NOV 1	SCORPIO	10♦ & 5♥

| Who 6♦ with | The Connections Between Partners | | | | | Overall Index Ratings | | |
	Con1	Con2	Con3	Con4	Con5	Attraction	Intensity	Compatibility
A♥	SAF	URF	SARS	MAF	MAFS	0	5	-4
2♥	PLR	MAMS	MORS	VEF	MAM	6	3	2
3♥	MAF	SAF	NERS	MAFS	SAR	4	7	-2
4♥	MAR	JUFS	MOR	MAM	MAMS	6	3	4
5♥	PLF	VERS	VEFS	MAM	VER	7	2	2
6♥	SAR	JUR	MARS	SAF	URF	0	4	-1
7♥	VEF	MAM	MAMS	PLFS	JUR	7	4	3
8♥	MAM	MAMS	VERS	VEF	VEFS	8	4	4
9♥	MORS	MAMS	MAR	MOR	CRRS	8	3	5
10♥	VEF	PLRS	VEM	VEMS	PLR	6	0	6
J♥	MAFS	JUM	MOF	MOF	MAF	7	1	5
Q♥	MAM	CLR	KRMC	CLRS	PLR	4	5	0
K♥	NER	PLF	CRR	VEMS	MAF	7	4	0
A♣	MAMS	PLR	MORS	CLR	PLRS	6	4	1
2♣	PLFS	NER	PLF	JUR	NERS	6	5	-2
3♣	CRF	VEMS	MOFS	URR	NEFS	7	0	5
4♣	JUR	VEFS	SAR	URF	SARS	1	0	4
5♣	VEFS	PLF	JUR	NER	JURS	5	1	4
6♣	JUF	MAR	JURS	SAR	MARS	3	2	4
7♣	VEMS	VEFS	VER	VERS	VEF	7	-3	9
8♣	MOF	MAFS	JUM	MOFS	CRF	7	0	6
9♣	KRMA	CLR	CLRS	NEF	PLFS	4	5	0
10♣	CRRS	VER	MOR	MORS	VEM	7	-1	6
J♣	PLRS	SAFS	VEF	VEFS	SAF	2	4	-1
Q♣	NERS	MAF	JUFS	CRR	MAFS	6	3	2
K♣	URRS	CRFS	JUF	JUFS	CRF	3	1	3
A♦	URF	SARS	MAR	JURS	SAF	1	3	-1
2♦	MAR	JURS	URF	SARS	NEF	3	3	2
3♦	MARS	SAR	NEF	PLR	URFS	4	5	-1
4♦	VERS	VEM	VEMS	PLF	PLFS	8	-1	6
5♦	MOFS	MAFS	VEM	CRF	VEMS	8	1	6
6♦	SBC	CLR	CLRS	CLF	CLFS	3	5	-1
7♦	MORS	MAMS	MAR	CRRS	JUFS	7	3	4
8♦	VEFS	VER	SAFS	VEMS	SAF	4	0	4
9♦	MAFS	VEM	NEF	PLR	URFS	7	3	3
10♦	MAF	JUFS	NERS	VER	SAFS	5	2	3
J♦	SAFS	CLF	KRMC	CLFS	PLRS	2	7	-4
Q♦	NEF	PLR	URFS	MARS	MAFS	5	4	1
K♦	URR	NEFS	CRF	VEMS	VERS	5	1	3
A♠	PLFS	VEF	SAR	VERS	JUR	5	3	1
2♠	CRFS	URRS	MOFS	MAF	MAFS	6	3	2
3♠	KRMA	CLF	CLFS	NEF	PLFS	6	7	-2
4♠	MOR	CRRS	MAR	JUFS	MARS	6	1	5
5♠	VEM	VEMS	VEF	VERS	VER	8	-3	10
6♠	CRR	VEMS	CRFS	MAF	MAFS	7	3	3
7♠	VERS	URR	NEFS	MAM	MAMS	6	1	3
8♠	JUF	URRS	VER	URR	SAFS	2	-1	4
9♠	CRR	VEMS	NER	PLF	MOR	7	1	3
10♠	MAM	MAR	JUFS	PLR	JUF	6	5	2
J♠	VER	VEMS	CRRS	PLF	PLFS	7	0	4
Q♠	VER	SAFS	MAF	JUFS	VEFS	4	2	2
K♠	JUM	MOF	MAFS	VEF	JUMS	5	-1	6

6♠ The Card of Fate

DESCRIPTION OF THE 6♠ PERSON:

The 6♠ is called the card of Fate because it is the strongest symbols of the Law of Cause and Effect. What we sow, we shall reap, for good or ill. When our Birth Card is a Six, we can expect there to be 'fated' events at different times in our lives. These are events that were set into motion by our actions or words in previous lifetimes whose effects were set aside to be experienced later, when conditions are right to create an equalizing of those events. Some of these events can be positive and helpful, while others may show us what it is like to be on the receiving end of some negative occurrence. For the most powerful of the Sixes, the 6♠, life just seems to have more of these fated events than most, so much so that many 6♠ begin to view life as a place where they have few choices and little power to change its outcome. It is true that we cannot change events once they are set into motion, but there are still many events in life over which we have tremendous responsibility, and our choices in this life are always important in this regard. This is one of the major lessons for the 6♠.

This is a powerful card, and the card of a person who is here to learn the responsibility of such power. These people either align themselves to a higher purpose and vision and achieve great success, or have their power turned against them for their own downfall. As a rule, these people are very responsible for their actions, but a strong Neptune influence can lead many of them down the road of escapism and time lost in fantasy and illusion. They are dreamers to be sure, and as such they must be careful to keep their dreams aligned with high ideals and principles if they wish to prevent them from becoming nightmares. They must latch on to the highest dream they can and use their power to attain it. Nothing can stop them once this vision is clear. Fulfillment on every level is guaranteed.

This card has some of the greatest potential for success and recognition of any card in the deck and many of them are slated for great achievement. The 8♦ in Mars and K♠ in Jupiter hint of the huge potential for financial gain. Of course, for this to be realized, they must take action and be willing to bear great responsibility.

They must watch a tendency to fall into a comfortable or uncomfortable rut. They can also be very stubborn. Through the acquisition of knowledge, they find great fulfillment, life purpose, direction, and many good friends. Some of their greatest challenges come in the area of love and romance. Their own indecision works against them.

Having the 9♠ as their first Karma Card, there are sure to be losses in their life, tragic in some cases. However, the 9♠ also guarantees great success when they are focused on a vision of helping the world with their many gifts. They can be the greatest givers of the deck, expressing themselves in a more universal manner. Many rise to great heights in their work.

SOME OF THE 6♠ ISSUES CONCERNING RELATIONSHIPS:

The 6♠ cannot stop thinking about love and romance. At the same time, they tend to have a somewhat mental approach to the whole situation that causes them to

---

KARMA CARDS:

9♠   2♠

KARMA COUSINS:

K♥   K♣

PAST-LIFE CARDS:

5♠   7♠

---

undergo many experiences, both up and down, while they gather experience to back up their concepts and ideas. They can tend to be drawn into multiple relationships and this usually has negative consequences for them. The desire for multiple relationships is usually rooted in their hidden fear of not getting enough affection that underlies these attempts. This fear, symbolized by the 3♥ in Saturn, can make it very difficult to have true intimacy with another until it is recognized and acknowledged.

Both sexes are attracted to those of intelligence and wit. The women like men of wealth, authority, or prominence. They can be crafty or dishonest in love matters, much like the 5♦ and 6♦, and must avoid trapping themselves in their own stories and beliefs.

GENERALITIES BETWEEN THE PERSONALITY CARD CONNECTIONS

6♠ men have great connections with Heart women, but would have to assume a back seat in the relationship for it to really work. Club males find 6♠ females quite alluring and Diamond males like them as friends. 6♠ females benefit from other Spade males in many ways.

Fate Versus Free Will

According to many published stories and interviews in the 1890s, Olney Richmond had proof that life is completely fated and destined. There are several accounts of his ability to predict without fail what cards would be drawn from a deck by any individual once he knew the time of day and the date of birth of that person. Olney stated over and over again that everything in this world that we know operates on strict and fixed mathematical principles and laws, and that not even one small bird falls from the sky except under the direction of these laws and principles. Hindu astrologers share this same belief. Those who have mastered that art can, only knowing your date, time, and place of birth, tell you when you will marry, how many children you will have, what kind of work you will do and the exact date of your death.

This is a hard concept for most of us to accept. We like to believe that we have some choice about what happens to us. Let's face it. There are thousands of books, many of which you and I have read, that teach us how to change our destiny and be the 'captain of our fate.' These books have helped many people to a certain extent. And yet, how is it that Olney and these astrologers can make such accurate predictions? They can do this without even meeting you or knowing your name.

The Hindu priests and wise men, though fatalistic in this regard, still tell us that in order to actualize our destinies, we have to follow our Dharma. Dharma defined briefly means 'right action.' They say that we still have to do the right thing and persevere in our lives, even though we are already fated to be a certain way and to have things turn out the way they do. Whether our lives are completed fated or not, a lot of how we, as individuals, approach this subject can be seen in our Birth Cards.

The odd-numbered cards, such as the Threes and Aces, are always 'creating' stuff in their lives. For this reason, they tend to believe that they create their own destiny. The even-numbered cards, and especially the Sixes, tend to let things come to them. Sixes are very fixed people and resistant to change in general. You will find this out if you spend some time with one of them. They will not budge until they want to. As a matter of fact, they can get stuck in a rut and seem unable to give themselves the push they need to get started. Perhaps this is why their lives seem more fated than other cards. They never seem to be the cause of anything in their life since they did not start it by their own efforts. It seems to just come to them while they sit there staring into space. The 6♠, being the strongest of the Sixes, is the most likely to act in this manner and to have these beliefs about fate and destiny.

Florence Campbell, in her book, *Sacred Symbols of the Ancients*, seems to imply that Six people have the ability to tune into the actual workings of fate itself through their intuitive gifts. Even though their life may seem to be in a rut at times, in the peace of that stillness, they can tune into the inner voice that is only heard when our minds are relatively silent. Because of this, they are privy to information that is rarely noticed by the other cards in the deck. Part of this information is their own destiny and their role in helping the world. If any 6♠ listens to their inner voice, they will discover that fate has a special mission for them and that they can be of great help to humankind in some way.

LIFE SPREAD CARDS		
PLANETARY CARD	**SYMBOL**	**CARD**
MOON	☽	6♣
SUN (BIRTH CARD)	☀	6♠
MERCURY	☿	Q♥
VENUS	♀	10♣
MARS	♂	8♦
JUPITER	♃	K♠
SATURN	♄	3♥
URANUS	♅	A♣
NEPTUNE	♆	Q♣
PLUTO	♇	10♠
RESULT (COSMIC REWARD)	♃+	5♣
COSMIC LESSON	♄+	3♦

PLANETARY RULING CARDS		
BIRTH DATE	**ASTROLOGICAL RULING SIGN**	**PLANETARY RULING CARD**
JAN 8	CAPRICORN	3♥
FEB 6	AQUARIUS	A♣
MAR 4	PISCES	Q♣
APR 2	ARIES	8♦

Who 6♠ with	Con1	Con2	Con3	Con4	Con5	Attraction	Intensity	Compatibility
		The Connections Between Partners				Overall Index Ratings		
A♥	MAF	PLFS	MAMS	SAF	CLFS	7	8	-3
2♥	CRFS	URF	VEMS	MOR	URFS	5	1	3
3♥	SAF	CLFS	URFS	MAF	PLFS	1	6	-5
4♥	SAR	VERS	PLF	JUFS	PLFS	4	3	0
5♥	JUR	CRF	VER	CRFS		5	1	4
6♥	JUFS	CLF	URF	VEMS	JUF	3	0	3
7♥	SAM	SAMS	VER	SARS	SAR	-1	6	-3
8♥	VER	MORS	CRR	SAM	SAMS	5	1	4
9♥	URR	VEMS	URF	VEM	JUMS	3	-2	4
10♥	SAFS	MAM	MAMS	MAFS	MOFS	4	8	-2
J♥	JUF	NEFS	JUMS	VER	JUFS	4	-2	6
Q♥	MOR	PLF	JUFS	MAR	JUF	6	1	4
K♥	PLR	NER	KRMC	SAF	MAFS	4	5	-1
A♣	URF	CRFS	VEMS	CRF	URFS	4	2	2
2♣	PLR	NER	SARS	SAR	URR	2	4	-2
3♣	VEFS	URRS	JUM	JUMS	MAM	3	-1	5
4♣	JUFS	CRF	VER	SAF	MAMS	4	2	3
5♣	CRF	VER	JUFS	PLR	CRFS	5	2	3
6♣	MOF	PLR	SAR	VEFS	JUR	4	0	4
7♣	VEF	MAF	JUF	SAFS	NEFS	5	2	4
8♣	JUMS	JUF	NEFS	PLF	JUM	4	0	4
9♣	MAR	MOR	MOF	JUF	CRRS	7	1	6
10♣	VEF	JUF	SAFS	NEFS	VERS	3	0	5
J♣	MAFS	URR	PLRS	SAFS	MAM	3	5	-2
Q♣	NEF	SAF	CLFS	URFS	CRRS	3	4	-2
K♣	NER	PLF	KRMC	MAR	JURS	6	5	0
A♦	MAMS	JUR	MAF	PLFS	MAFS	6	6	1
2♦	JUR	MOF	PLR	MAMS	URF	4	0	4
3♦	CLF	URF	VEMS	NERS	NER	4	2	1
4♦	JUR	MOFS	MOF	MAR	JURS	5	-2	7
5♦	VEFS	CLR	CLRS	NER	URRS	4	0	3
6♦	MAR	MARS	VEM	VEMS	CRF	8	4	3
7♦	VEMS	URR	URF	JUR	PLRS	3	-1	4
8♦	MAF	URFS	VEF	VEFS	VEM	6	1	4
9♦	CLR	CLRS	NERS	VEFS	NER	3	1	1
10♦	CRRS	NEF	URFS	VEM	SARS	5	1	2
J♦	URR	PLRS	MARS	VEM	VEMS	4	2	1
Q♦	NERS	CLF	URF	VEMS	CLR	4	2	1
K♦	URRS	JUM	JUMS	MORS	CRR	2	-2	4
A♠	SARS	SAM	SAMS	PLR	NER	-1	7	-4
2♠	KRMA	MAR	JURS	NEF	PLFS	6	6	1
3♠	MARS	VEM	VEMS	URR	PLRS	7	1	4
4♠	VERS	VEF	SAR	CLF	SARS	4	0	4
5♠	MOFS	SAFS	MAM	MAMS	JUR	4	4	1
6♠	SBC	SAF	MAFS	MAR	JURS	3	7	-2
7♠	MORS	CRR	URRS	JUM	JUMS	4	-1	5
8♠	SAR	VEFS	NER	PLF	MOF	4	2	1
9♠	KRMA	SAF	MAFS	NEF	PLFS	4	8	-2
10♠	PLF	JUFS	SAR	MOR	MORS	4	2	1
J♠	JUF	SAFS	NEFS	VEF	NEF	2	2	3
Q♠	URFS	CRRS	MAF	MAFS	CRR	5	4	0
K♠	JUF	NEFS	JUMS	JUFS	NEF	4	-1	6

The Sevens

Seven is the first of what I call the spiritual numbers, Nine being the other. Seven in some ways is the most significant. If we take all the cards from one suit of the deck and lay them out from the Ace to the King from left to right, the Seven will fall in the exact center. There are seven visible planets, seven days of the week, seven chakras in the body, and seven seals mentioned in the Book of Revelations in the Bible. The number Seven has great significance in the calculations used to create the Yearly Spreads and in other calculations involving esoteric mathematics and geometry. It has always been regarded as an important spiritual symbol and is used in many religions and cultures.

As another of the odd numbers, Seven represents a state of imbalance and a movement away from stasis and balance. In this case, the movement is away from the stability of the Six. Because the Six can represent that state of receiving instructions and directions from a higher source, the Seven represents a stepping off from that place into what could be a scary place where nothing is known for sure. In the Seven, we step away from the security that comes from organization and harmony in the external world and are asked to find peace and contentment within ourselves in spite of external circumstances. To do this represents a high spiritual state of being, and one that is not easily obtained. Even Jesus said that it is more difficult for a man to enter into the Kingdom of Heaven than it is for a camel to pass through the eye of a needle. The Seven is the gateway to the Kingdom of Heaven. At its very essence, the Seven represents faith.

People with Seven Birth Cards walk the line between the mundane and the spiritual and they get the chance to experience both during the course of their life. However, being a Seven, they are not truly content and happy unless they are in the spiritual side of life. When they are carefree and full of appreciation for the wonder and splendor of their life, they are happy and content. They are carefree because they live knowing that all of their needs are being provided for. They have a direct connection to a higher source that guarantees that they will be taken care of. They have no worries in the world and are actually experiencing higher states of consciousness: spiritual consciousness.

When the Seven person falls back into the material world, they meet with untold problems and concerns. They are afraid of not having enough. They feel insecure and unloved. They worry, and this worry tortures them. They try to manipulate others and their environment to protect themselves, but it just makes matters worse. They can become morose and depressed and, in some cases, develop very negative attitudes about life that seem to perpetuate their misery. Miserable or miserly is a good description of the Seven person who is operating on the mundane side of their personalities. They live in a world where there just isn't enough.

Having been born a Seven actually means that this life will be sort of a do-or-die crash course in spiritual lifestyle. The Seven person, probably more than any other card in the deck, will not be able to get away with any behavior that is less than 'living in the truth.' The ultimate truth is that we are all loved and cared for by God, the Universe, or whatever you want to call it. The Seven person will have to walk and live in this truth or suffer greatly as a consequence. As a result, we find that Sevens often come in two varieties—those who are very happy and unattached about things in their life, and those who are unhappy and worried all the time. The ones that are unattached seem to live magical lives, where things just come to them when they need it. They are giving and understanding and, for the most part, carefree about their needs being met. They are often engaged in service to others and are capable of great deeds for the cause of humanity. The other Sevens are living in a world of lack and poverty, trickery, and manipulation. They are rarely happy with their life.

It is interesting to note that most of the Sevens have power cards that are their first Karma Card. The 7♥ has the 8♥, the 7♣ has the 8♦, and the 7♠ has the K♦. All of these connections indicate the misuse of power in a former incarnation. Many people of these cards come into this life with a tendency to force things to get their way, along with a habit of avoiding responsibility for their own fears and insecurities. Now, in this lifetime, each time they assert their power from the wrong place, they run into innumerable obstacles and suffer as a result. It is only when they learn the use of power to help others that they find that things work out in their favor.

So, the Seven is constantly challenged and it is not an easy path for most. But the possibilities for experiencing higher states of consciousness and being are also present. Many Sevens accomplish what no other card in the deck can—spiritual enlightenment and freedom from the cares of the world.

The Spiritual Love Card

DESCRIPTION OF THE 7♥ PERSON:
The 7♥ has a quest for the truth about love and relationships. They are old souls who have come here to reach the highest in these areas, 'or else.' With two Nines in their Life Path, they have come to complete a grand cycle in their soul's work and to let go of many things so that they may progress to the next level. These people must learn to let go of personal attachments and give to others without expectation of return or reward. On the low side, these people can be preoccupied with many suspicions and jealousies, which is merely a reflection of their own insecurities. On the high side, we find counselors and those who make great personal sacrifices for others and who give much to the world. You can always go to a 7♥ for an understanding and sympathetic ear. All must find some way to give to the world to attain peace and satisfaction. This usually manifests as teaching, counseling, or consulting.

Their health should be watched carefully as these people bring into this life some past life karma that could manifest as health challenges. Whenever there is a problem, it either calls for a change of lifestyle or a need to let go of some part of it. For example, they might have to quit a certain job because it is just too stressful. They often come into this life with certain physical habits, brought over from previous lives, that are hard to stop. Even smoking can be one of these. Some of these unhealthy patterns will be difficult to let go of, but it is their destiny to do just that.

It is interesting how many 7♥ men get involved in the financial world. Some of the most successful financial managers and business owners have this card. Both male and female 7♥ have a certain amount of ambition and drive and know how to be successful in the world.

Part of their challenge is to balance out their desire for material success with inclinations toward fairness in all their friendships and relationships. There can be strong ambitions that conflict with the desire to maintain harmonious relationships at times.

Anyone born as a Seven or Nine must learn to give and let go or suffer great pain and disappointment. The 7♥ are the givers of knowledge and love and can experience the highest degree of unconditional love.

SOME OF THE 7♥ ISSUES CONCERNING RELATIONSHIPS:
Being a Heart, you would be correct in assuming that 7♥ relationships are the biggest area for personal growth and development. And so they are. The 7♥ will often try to dominate or control their loved one and this usually will not work out well for them. The other possibility is that they attract a partner who is dominating. Powerful is the word that almost always describes their mates. Being such a powerful spiritual number, anything less than the truth and nonattachment will always cause more suffering than it is worth. They enjoy traveling with the person they love and can be somewhat restless emotionally. Love affairs can often start suddenly and end just as suddenly. In the end they will find the best companion in someone that they have a 'friends first' relationship with. In their heart of hearts, this is what will give them the most satisfaction. It is just that they have to get over their habitual control impulses to realize this.

KARMA CARDS:

8 ♥   A ♠

KARMA COUSINS:

7 ♠   2 ♣

PAST-LIFE CARDS:

6 ♥   8 ♥

They are quite sociable and charming. It is only in their closest relationships that they meet with the challenges. The male 7♥ is aggressive in meeting new friends and lovers.

When a 7♥ of either sex meets a K♥, they know they have met their match, someone who can handle them and not restrict them. Diamond females tend to bring good things into the lives of both sexes. Diamond males are a challenge in many ways to all 7♥.

Seven of Hearts—Unconditional Love

The 7♥ is, in his or her essence, a very loving person who yearns for a life free of fears about love and affection. They want to just love everyone for who they are and be a sort of lighthouse of unconditional love. However, many of them also have a deep inner conflict with this that comes from a previous incarnation. Their 8♥ Karma Card tells us that they have had a previous life where they had, and often abused, a great emotional power. In that former existence, they got used to having their own way and allowed themselves a lot of leeway in the expression of their sexuality or just their personality. It is likely that they abused others by making them feel unworthy of their love, or unworthy of love in general. This past-life influence surfaces in the life of the 7♥ person in many ways. It is very often represented in their natal chart by poorly aspected planets in Scorpio or the 8th house, the positions of power and control. You see, it is one of the missions of the 7♥ to let go of this control aspect. They must do this if they are to ever experience their destiny of unconditional love.

Each of us is born with certain 'soul patterns.' They essentially are patterned ways of responding to given situations. For example, 'When someone says something in a certain way, I believe that they don't love me,' is a typical soul pattern. It's like we believe in something already, even though our rational minds know that it is not true. Most phobias are soul patterns, but each of us have other patterns that affect us in more important areas.

For the 7♥, there is a soul pattern of feeling and believing that others are out to control them. This is usually more apparent in their love relationships than in business or casual relationships. Therefore, many of them put a lot of effort into making sure that they maintain control in their relationships and do not let anyone else get the upper hand. This goes directly against their unconditional love nature and thus the conflict. Soul patterns are not forever. They can be changed by addressing the feelings that lie at their source. The 7♥ has no choice but to deal with them. Gradually they become more powerful in their unconditional love nature than they were with their controlling 8♥ nature. They find the beauty in actually allowing everyone in their life to just be themselves. When they allow others the freedom to be who they are, they discover the most priceless gift—their own true loving self.

SEVEN OF HEARTS

LIFE SPREAD CARDS

PLANETARY CARD	SYMBOL	CARD
MOON	☽	A♠
SUN (BIRTH CARD)	☀	7♥
MERCURY	☿	7♦
VENUS	♀	5♠
MARS	♂	J♥
JUPITER	♃	9♣
SATURN	♄	9♠
URANUS	♅	2♥
NEPTUNE	♆	K♥
PLUTO	♇	K♦
RESULT (COSMIC REWARD)	♃+	6♥
COSMIC LESSON	♄+	4♣

Celebrity Birthdays

ANGIE DICKINSON
9/30/31 • *Actress*
JANE ALEXANDER
10/28/39 • *Actress*
CHARLES M. SCHULZ
11/26/22 • *Cartoonist*
RICH LITTLE
11/26/38 • *Comedian*
BRUCE JENNER
10/28/49 • *Olympic Athlete*
TINA TURNER
11/26/38 • *Singer*
JOHNNY MATHIS
9/30/35 • *Singer*
CHARLIE DANIELS
10/28/36 • *Singer*
DENNIS FRANZ
10/28/44 • *Actor*
JOAQUIN PHOENIX
10/28/74 • *Actor*
JAMI GERTZ
10/28/65 • *Actress*
JULIA ROBERTS
10/28/67 • *Actress*
BILL GATES
10/28/55 • *Founder of Microsoft*

PLANETARY RULING CARDS

BIRTH DATE	ASTROLOGICAL RULING SIGN	PLANETARY RULING CARD
SEP 30	LIBRA	5♠
OCT 28	SCORPIO	J♥ & K♦
NOV 26	SAGITTARIUS	9♣
DEC 24	CAPRICORN	9♠

Who 7♥ with	Con1	Con2	Con3	Con4	Con5	Attraction	Intensity	Compatibility
		The Connections Between Partners					Overall Index Ratings	
A♥	URRS	NER	PLF	JURS	NERS	4	2	0
2♥	URF	SARS	URR	NEFS	PLRS	1	2	-1
3♥	NER	PLF	JURS	URRS	SAR	4	3	0
4♥	SAR	MARS	URMS	JUR	CLRS	2	4	0
5♥	VERS	MAR	MARS	VEM	SAFS	7	3	3
6♥	MOFS	CRF	CLF	CLFS	VER	7	2	3
7♥	SBC	MORS	MOF	MOFS	MOR	7	0	7
8♥	KRMA	MORS	NEF	NEFS	PLF	8	3	4
9♥	VEFS	MOR	URR	NEFS	PLRS	6	-1	6
10♥	MAFS	VEM	VEMS	VEF	VEFS	8	0	7
J♥	MAF	JUFS	PLR	NERS	VERS	5	3	2
Q♥	SAFS	JUR	CLRS	URRS	JUF	-1	2	-1
K♥	NEF	PLR	URFS	PLFS	JUM	5	3	0
A♣	URR	NEFS	PLRS	URF	SARS	3	2	0
2♣	PLFS	JUM	KRMC	JUMS	MOF	5	3	1
3♣	CRFS	JUMS	PLF	PLFS	JUM	5	4	-1
4♣	CLF	CLFS	MAR	MOFS	CRF	6	6	-1
5♣	MAR	VERS	CLF	CLFS	VER	7	4	1
6♣	VEMS	MARS	MOR	MAFS	NEFS	8	1	6
7♣	CRR	CRRS	VEM	SAF	NEF	4	2	2
8♣	VERS	MAF	JUFS	PLR	NERS	6	1	4
9♣	JUF	SAFS	VER	VERS	SAF	1	1	2
10♣	CLR	VEM	CRRS	URMS	JUF	4	0	3
J♣	SAMS	MAFS	VEM	VEMS	CRR	5	5	1
Q♣	SAR	MAMS	NER	PLF	JURS	4	5	-1
K♣	SAR	VEFS	NEFS			4	2	3
A♦	MARS	URRS	MAM	MAR	VEM	6	5	1
2♦	MARS	VEMS	VEM	MAFS	MAR	8	3	5
3♦	VER	MOFS	CRF	MAR	MARS	7	1	5
4♦	VEF	VERS	VER	CLRS	MAF	6	-2	7
5♦	JUMS	JURS	CRFS	JUR	CRRS	2	-1	5
6♦	VER	JUF	SARS	MAM	MAMS	4	1	4
7♦	MOR	VEFS	URR	NEFS	PLRS	6	-2	6
8♦	CRR	JUR	PLRS	SAF	NEF	2	2	1
9♦	JURS	MAR	JUMS	PLR	SARS	3	2	3
10♦	SAR	MAMS	JUR	PLRS	MAF	3	5	0
J♦	SAMS	SARS	MAM	MAMS	JUR	2	7	-3
Q♦	MAR	VER	JURS	VERS	MARS	6	2	5
K♦	PLF	CRFS	MOFS	CRF	PLFS	8	5	-1
A♠	KRMA	MOF	NEF	NEFS	PLFS	8	3	4
2♠	SAM	SAMS	MOF	MORS	VEF	1	4	0
3♠	SARS	MAM	MAMS	VER	SAMS	4	6	-1
4♠	URMS	CLR	VEM	SAR	MARS	2	1	1
5♠	VEF	MAFS	VEM	VEMS	MAF	8	1	7
6♠	SAM	SAMS	SAF	VEF	SAFS	-2	8	-5
7♠	PLF	MORS	KRMC	NER	URFS	7	3	1
8♠	VEMS	NEFS	SAR	VEFS	MAFS	6	0	5
9♠	SAF	NEF	PLR	URFS	SAM	1	5	-3
10♠	JUR	CLRS	URRS	SAR	MARS	1	1	2
J♠	CRRS	CLR	VEM	CLRS	VEMS	4	1	3
Q♠	JUR	PLRS	CRR	CLR	CRRS	2	1	2
K♠	PLR	NERS	VERS	MAF	JUFS	5	2	2

The Sevens ♥ 141

Spiritual Knowledge

All Sevens are highly spiritual cards, but it is up to the individual to manifest this spirituality and to turn negativity into accomplishment and personal freedom. Until they do this, the Seven influence causes one trouble after another in their life. The 7♣ challenge rests in the negative aspects of the mind, which are worry, doubt, and pessimism. They have much inherent inspiration and insight, but when they don't follow it, Saturn's influence brings much despair and sometimes depression. They have the power to overcome their problems and to attain the fame and recognition they secretly desire, but they must apply themselves diligently.

They are likely to have large sums of money at different times in their life, but often they spend it as fast as they get it. They are not the best money managers. The 8♦ Karma Card not only gives them the desire for recognition, but also can make them into just as much of a power shopper as the 8♦. Money can be spent faster than it is made, though they can drive a hard bargain. All their difficulties in life can be traced directly to their thoughts. So the 7♣, more than any other card, has a great responsibility to maintain positive, healthy thoughts. Any contact with spiritual thoughts or ideals is sure to have a positive effect on them.

Developing honesty and integrity is part of the 7♣ challenge, due to the J♠ Karma Card, often called 'The Thief.' If they let their desire for success override their integrity they will suffer, especially in the areas of love and family.

SOME OF THE 7♣ ISSUES CONCERNING RELATIONSHIPS:

The 7♣ person has neither bad nor good karma in the area of love. The true story of their love life comes as a result of how they handle the other areas of their life. The good news is that if they apply themselves, they have more chances than any other card in the deck to attain mastery of their emotions and romantic involvements.

They have some karma to be sure, and sometimes this karma may be reflected in learning to let go of personal attachments to others or in creating a positive attitude about their partner as well as the rest of their life. They always operate better if they are married, having more success financially and otherwise, and will sooner or later make that commitment.

The men have the J♠ Karma Card to add to their relationship issues. Many of them see themselves like a romantic, famous actor. For this reason they can be promiscuous and deceiving. This can include extramarital affairs, or whatever will help them feel 'special,' which is what many 7♣ want most.

If they do attain the fame they seek, they are more tempted with indecision in their personal life and in the choice of a mate. This can often result in remarriage.

GENERALITIES BETWEEN THE PERSONALITY CARD CONNECTIONS

The 7♣ has a special connection with Spade women or women who are hard working and determined, regardless of suit. Female 7♣ tend to hold fantasies about other Club men and are greatly challenged by Diamond males, represented by their J♦ Pluto card. A male Spade might be the perfect match for a female 7♣.

KARMA CARDS:
8♦   J♠

KARMA COUSINS:
Q♠   10♣

PAST-LIFE CARDS:
6♣   8♣

Bill 7♣ and Hillary 9♥ Clinton

In many ways, Bill and Hillary are the ideal couple. The 7♣ and 9♥ sit right next to each other in the Mundane Spread. This alone is a great connection for marriage. But there is more. The 7♣ sits in 'front' of the 9♥. This means that the 7♣ is the Mercury Card to the 9♥ and that the 9♥ is the Moon Card to the 7♣. This is a good combination when the person in the rear is willing to allow the person in the front to be the leader of the relationship. In this case, Hillary seems fairly content with being Bill's support person and allowing him, at least by appearances, to take the role of leader. The support person can be instrumental in giving the front person the things that they need to do their jobs. Hillary, being the Semi-Fixed Scorpio that she is, undoubtedly is a great support to Bill, giving him a sense of structure and security. Bill, being a Leo 7♣, is bound to go through the ups and downs of feeling confident and then not. 7♣ people are known to have some extremes of mood to their personality, first happy-go-lucky and then worried and pessimistic. Hillary's fixed nature certainly must provide Bill with a sense of stability and help to smooth out the swings in his state of mind that so many 7♣ go through.

Bill's first Karma Card is the 8♦, the Sun Card, which sits at the exact top center of the Mundane Spread. For this reason, we note that most 7♣ have a strong, but outwardly hidden, desire for fame and power. It is especially powerful when someone who is Sun-ruled (Leo) by birth is also associated with the Sun Card. This tends to amplify or even exaggerate the leadership urges and the desire for fame and power and authority. On the exterior, Bill presents us with a philosophy that appears spiritually based (7♣ being the Spiritual Knowledge Card). Underneath, however, the cards reveal that his true motives may be simply to achieve as much recognition and adoration as he can. This explains why he appears to base his policy upon public approval ratings instead of any personal conviction to a philosophy or ideology.

Hillary has similar motives, all her own. Being a Scorpio she has two planetary ruling cards, the Q♠ and the K♣, both signs of authority and leadership. It is interesting to note that the Q♠ is the first Karma Card to the 8♦ and that it is the Sun Card in the Spiritual or Natural Spread. So we see that she, too, has great leadership ability and desire to control and gain power. With such a dynamite combination of energies, it is not surprising just how successful they have been. 9♥ are the saviors of the deck. It is not surprising to see Hillary putting so much energy behind providing health care to the entire country. This alone would represent great fulfillment of the 9♥ 'Universal Love' card. In many ways, she is a more effective leader than her husband because she truly believes in her causes and is less prone to deviate from them to win public approval.

LIFE SPREAD CARDS

PLANETARY CARD	SYMBOL	CARD
MOON	☽	9♥
SUN (BIRTH CARD)	☀	7♣
MERCURY	☿	5♦
VENUS	♀	Q♠
MARS	♂	J♣
JUPITER	♃	9♦
SATURN	♄	7♠
URANUS	♅	2♣
NEPTUNE	♆	K♣
PLUTO	♇	J♦
RESULT (COSMIC REWARD)	♃+	4♥
COSMIC LESSON	♄+	4♦

PLANETARY RULING CARDS

BIRTH DATE	ASTROLOGICAL RULING SIGN	PLANETARY RULING CARD
MAR 29	ARIES	J♣
APR 27	TAURUS	Q♠
MAY 25	GEMINI	5♦
JUN 23	CANCER	9♥
JUL 21	CANCER	9♥
AUG 19	LEO	7♣
SEP 17	VIRGO	5♦
OCT 15	LIBRA	Q♠
NOV 13	SCORPIO	J♣ & J♦
DEC 11	SAGITTARIUS	9♦

Celebrity Birthdays

ROBIN WILLIAMS
7/21/52 • *Actor/Comedian*
IAN MCKELLAN
5/25/39 • *Actor*
ANNE BANCROFT
9/17/31 • *Actress*
JOSH HARTNETT
7/21/78 • *Actor*
DONNA MILLS
12/11/43 • *Actress*
PENNY MARSHALL
10/15/42 • *Actress*
RITA MORENO
12/11/31 • *Actress*
MATTHEW PERRY
8/19/69 • *Actor*
ERNEST HEMINGWAY
7/21/1899 • *Author*
MIKE MYERS
5/25/63 • *Actor/Comedian*
SUSAN SEIDELMAN
12/11/52 • *Director*
MILES DAVIS
5/25/26 • *Jazz Musician*
WILMA RUDOLPH
6/23/40 • *Olympic Athlete*
BILL CLINTON
8/19/46 • *President*
LEE ANN WOMACK
8/19/66 • *Singer*
JERMAINE JACKSON
12/11/54 • *Singer*
ISAAC STERN
7/21/20 • *Violinist*
DON KNOTTS
7/21/24 • *Actor*
JOHN STAMOS
8/19/63 • *Actor*
JON LOVITZ
7/21/57 • *Comedian*
CONNIE SELLECCA
5/25/55 • *Actress*
CAT STEVENS
7/21/48 • *Singer*

Who 7♣ with	Con1	Con2	Con3	Con4	Con5	Attraction	Intensity	Compatibility
A♥	NER	PLF	URR	NEFS	PLRS	5	4	-1
2♥	URRS	JUM	JUMS	URR	JUFS	1	-2	3
3♥	NER	PLF	SAFS	VEF	NEF	5	5	-1
4♥	CRF	VEMS	PLR	URFS	CRFS	6	2	2
5♥	JUR	CLF	CLFS	VERS	NEFS	4	2	2
6♥	VEFS	MARS	VEM	JUF	CRFS	7	1	6
7♥	VEM	CRF	CRFS	SAR	NER	6	3	3
8♥	VEM	SAF	SAR	NER	CLFS	2	3	0
9♥	MOF	URRS	JUM	CLF	VEM	4	-1	4
10♥	CLR	CLRS	MAF	JUFS	MAM	3	3	0
J♥	CRRS	MORS	VER	CRR	VEFS	6	0	5
Q♥	PLRS	VEFS	VER	VEMS	SAF	5	0	4
K♥	NERS	PLFS	URF	SARS	MAF	4	4	-2
A♣	URRS	JUM	MAF	JUMS	URR	2	0	2
2♣	URF	SARS	NERS	PLFS	PLF	2	4	-2
3♣	MAR	JURS	MOR	MARS	SARS	5	3	4
4♣	MARS	VEM	VERS	VEFS	MAR	8	1	6
5♣	VERS	JUR	MARS	VEM	URF	5	-1	6
6♣	MOFS	PLR	PLFS	JUR	URF	5	1	2
7♣	SBC	VERS	VEF	MAMS	VEFS	7	2	5
8♣	MORS	CRRS	MAM	MOR	VER	7	0	5
9♣	VEFS	PLRS	VEMS	PLR	VER	6	0	5
10♣	MAFS	VEF	KRMC	MAMS	MOF	8	4	4
J♣	MAF	JUFS	PLF	CLR	CLRS	5	4	1
Q♣	SAFS	CRR	JUF	CRRS	VEF	1	3	0
K♣	NEF	PLR	URFS	MARS	CLR	5	3	0
A♦	URR	NEFS	PLRS	PLFS	NER	4	3	0
2♦	PLFS	MOFS	URR	NEFS	PLRS	6	3	1
3♦	JUF	CRFS	VEFS	SAR	MAMS	4	1	4
4♦	CLF	CLFS	MAM	JUMS	JUR	5	5	-1
5♦	MOR	JUF	MAR	JURS	MARS	5	0	6
6♦	VEMS	VEFS	VER	VERS	VEF	7	-3	9
7♦	MOF	URRS	JUM	MOFS	CLF	4	-2	5
8♦	KRMA	VERS	VEF	NEF	NEFS	7	2	5
9♦	JUF	SAR	MAMS	MOR	MORS	4	1	4
10♦	CRR	SAFS	VEF	JUR	VEFS	2	2	2
J♦	PLF	VER	MAF	JUFS	CRR	7	4	1
Q♦	SAR	MAMS	JUF	CRFS	JUFS	3	4	1
K♦	MAR	JURS	SAF	SAFS	JUR	1	5	-1
A♠	URF	SARS	PLF	URFS	CLRS	1	3	-3
2♠	MARS	VER	NEF	PLR	URFS	7	3	3
3♠	VER	VEMS	PLF	SAR	PLFS	6	1	3
4♠	MAFS	CRF	VEMS	CRFS	MAF	8	5	2
5♠	MAM	JUMS	CLR	CLRS	CLF	4	3	1
6♠	VER	MAF	JURS	MARS	MAR	6	2	4
7♠	SAF	VEM	URR	VEMS	JURS	2	1	1
8♠	PLR	NEF	URFS	MOFS	URF	4	2	1
9♠	MAF	JURS	NERS	PLFS	VER	6	3	2
10♠	CRF	VEMS	PLRS	SAF	MOFS	5	3	2
J♠	KRMA	VEF	MAMS	NEF	NEFS	8	4	3
Q♠	VEF	CRR	KRMC	VERS	MORS	6	0	6
K♠	MORS	CRRS	MOR	VEFS	MAM	7	-1	7

The Card of Spiritual Values

DESCRIPTION OF THE 7♦ PERSON:
The 7♦ is one of those unique cards called a Semi-Fixed Card. As part of a special family of seven uniquely different cards, these people fall into a different category and have a special mark on their lives. They are very stubborn, but they are also extremely creative and some are destined to become millionaires in this life by accessing the high side of this spiritual money card. By suit, they are always connected with money. As a spiritual number, they must maintain a non-attached attitude about money or they will experience continual problems in this area. They are either worrying about it all the time or not worrying and having as much as they like. Regardless, many of their life lessons will come through this avenue.

The other avenue is their close relationships. Family, lovers, and friends are all very important to the 7♦ person. They have close ties, for better or worse, with their family and share in their trials. They have a high, spiritual love nature that often entails making personal sacrifices for their family and other close relationships. There is little they wouldn't do on behalf of their parents or family. This is one of the most spiritual cards in the deck and, as such, their success comes from approaching life in ways other than traditional or materialistic. The most successful among them are the ones who live in the faith that all their needs will always be provided.

They are usually restless, making frequent changes in either occupation or location.

Their love life usually entails sacrifice and disappointment until they learn to let others go and be as they are. In their spiritual studies they find inner satisfaction and validation for their own intuition. Once on the spiritual path, everything in their life is put into proper perspective and they can excel in any chosen field.

SOME OF THE 7♦ ISSUES CONCERNING RELATIONSHIPS:
For such a spiritual card as the 7♦, issues in relationships revolve around letting go of personal attachments and developing a more spiritual approach to love. They are, by nature, very loving people and are willing to make sacrifices on behalf of those they love. They are bound to have one or more karmic love involvements that challenge them to raise their level of love to more spiritual and responsible heights. Like other cards, they have high ideals associated with love and partnership. But these people are more or less destined to have these ideals tested every step along the way. Their stubbornness and independence attracts powerful relationships into their life, ones that teach them important lessons.

GENERALITIES BETWEEN THE PERSONALITY CARD CONNECTIONS
Most 7♦ females are attracted to, and often marry, men of the Heart suit. They also hold some fantasies about Diamond men. The male 7♦ is attracted to Spade females and usually has many Club females as friends and associates. Club males challenge the 7♦ female.

KARMA CARDS:
9♥ A♣ 2♥ J♥ 8♣ K♠

KARMA COUSINS:
NONE

PAST-LIFE CARDS:
6♦ 8♦

Seven of Diamonds Are from Some Other Planet

7♦ people are different from the rest of us. They are different in some sort of undefinable way that can only be detected by getting to know one of them. Just look at the list of some of its natives and I think you will see what I mean. Andy Warhol, David Lynch, George Carlin, and Federico Fellini are just a few 7♦ that most of us have heard about. They just don't seem to operate under the normal rules of life, that the rest of us do. Their ideas, viewpoints on life and priorities often seem at odds with the social norms of our society and culture. As a matter of fact, it seems like all the Fixed and Semi-Fixed Cards are from some other planet. These cards, the 8♣, K♠, J♥, A♣, 2♥, 7♦, and 9♥, seem to share the quality of being different from the rest of the 45 cards in the deck. We usually find people of these cards hanging out with each other. Most 8♣ will have a close friend or relative that is a 7♦ or J♥. The cards in this special Family of Seven seem to understand each other while the rest of us just stare and wonder what's going on.

All of these cards are somewhat strong-willed and fixed in their natures. Once they have made up their minds, it is next to impossible to dissuade them from their course. They are all hard workers and can be counted on in emergencies or to keep their word. They give many of us the feeling of safety and sureness with their strength of will. However, that same fixed nature can make them very difficult and unable to see others' points of view.

Still, we owe them much. 7♦, especially, are so creative and come up with some of the most outrageous and greatest ideas. They have the ability to tap into the spiritual money realms where the very best sales and promotional ideas come from. These ideas are usually progressive and different, and yet highly effective. Those of us who have a 7♦ doing either creative or sales work for us are highly fortunate.

SEVEN OF DIAMONDS

LIFE SPREAD CARDS

PLANETARY CARD	SYMBOL	CARD
MOON	☽	7 ♥
SUN (BIRTH CARD)	✳	7 ♦
MERCURY	☿	5 ♠
VENUS	♀	J ♥
MARS	♂	9 ♣
JUPITER	♃	9 ♠
SATURN	♄	2 ♥
URANUS	♅	K ♥
NEPTUNE	♆	K ♦
PLUTO	♇	6 ♥
RESULT (COSMIC REWARD)	♃ +	4 ♣
COSMIC LESSON	♄ +	2 ♦

PLANETARY RULING CARDS

BIRTH DATE	ASTROLOGICAL RULING SIGN	PLANETARY RULING CARD
JAN 20	CAPRICORN	2 ♥
FEB 18	AQUARIUS	K ♥
MAR 16	PISCES	K ♦
APR 14	ARIES	9 ♣
MAY 12	TAURUS	J ♥
JUN 10	GEMINI	5 ♠
JUL 8	CANCER	7 ♥
AUG 6	LEO	7 ♦
SEP 4	VIRGO	5 ♠
OCT 2	LIBRA	J ♥

Who 7♦ with	The Connections Between Partners					Overall Index Ratings		
	Con1	Con2	Con3	Con4	Con5	Attraction	Intensity	Compatibility
A♥	JUMS	URRS	PLR	URR	PLRS	1	0	1
2♥	KRMA	SAF	NER	PLF	NEF	4	7	-3
3♥	PLR	JUMS	URR	PLRS	URRS	2	2	0
4♥	VER	CLFS	SAR	VEMS	CLF	5	2	2
5♥	MAR	JUFS	SAR	MARS	JUR	4	4	2
6♥	PLF	CRF	VEMS	MAR	JURS	7	5	0
7♥	MOF	VER	NEFS	VERS	URF	7	-2	7
8♥	MOF	MOFS	PLR	URRS	URF	5	-1	5
9♥	KRMA	MAM	MAMS	NEF	PLFS	8	8	0
10♥	JUR	CRRS	MOR	MORS	CRR	4	-1	6
J♥	KRMA	VEF	CRR	SAFS	VEMS	5	4	2
Q♥	MAFS	SAM	SAR	VEMS	MAF	3	6	-1
K♥	URF	JUF	JUFS	MOFS	NEF	3	-2	5
A♣	KRMA	NER	PLF	SAF	NEF	5	7	-2
2♣	VER	NEFS	URF	NEF	URFS	6	0	4
3♣	VERS	NEF	PLR	URFS	VER	6	0	4
4♣	CRF	VEMS	JUR	PLF	PLFS	6	2	3
5♣	JUR	MAR	JUFS	CRF	VEMS	4	1	5
6♣	VEFS	VERS	CLF	SARS	VER	5	0	5
7♣	MORS	CLR	VEM	MOR	URFS	6	-2	6
8♣	KRMA	VEMS	VEF	CRR	SAFS	6	2	4
9♣	MAF	MAFS	SAM	MOFS	CLF	6	7	0
10♣	CLRS	VER	CLFS	VERS	JUR	4	1	3
J♣	JUR	CRRS	JUFS	JUF	SAR	2	-1	5
Q♣	URR	PLRS	PLR	MAFS	VEM	3	3	-1
K♣	NERS	JUM	PLFS	VERS	PLF	5	2	1
A♦	URRS	CLF	SARS	JUMS	SAR	1	3	-1
2♦	CLF	SARS	VEFS	URRS	VEF	3	3	0
3♦	MAR	JURS	PLF	SAFS	JUF	4	5	0
4♦	SAR	MARS	MOR	MAR	JUFS	4	4	1
5♦	VERS	VEFS	VEF	SAF	MARS	5	-1	6
6♦	MOFS	MAF	CRFS	MAMS	CLF	8	4	3
7♦	SBC	MAM	MAMS	NER	PLF	7	7	0
8♦	MORS	CLR	VEM	MAR	MAF	6	0	5
9♦	VEFS	SAFS	VERS	SAF	MARS	2	2	1
10♦	MAFS	VEM	URR	PLRS	PLR	6	3	2
J♦	JUFS	CRFS	JUR	CRRS	CRF	4	1	4
Q♦	SAFS	MAR	JURS	VEFS	JUR	1	4	0
K♦	NEF	PLR	URFS	VER	NEFS	5	2	2
A♠	VER	NEFS	MOF	SAF	VERS	6	0	5
2♠	PLFS	VEMS	NERS	JUM	VEM	7	2	2
3♠	CRFS	MOFS	JUFS	MOF	JURS	6	0	6
4♠	VER	CLFS	CLRS	CLR	MAR	5	2	1
5♠	MOR	SAR	MARS	SARS	PLF	4	3	1
6♠	VEMS	JUF	PLFS	URF	URR	5	0	4
7♠	NEF	PLR	URFS	URF	VER	4	2	1
8♠	VERS	NERS	JUM	VEFS	NER	5	-1	6
9♠	JUF	URF	VEMS	JUFS	URR	3	-2	6
10♠	SAR	VEMS	MAFS	SAM	SAMS	3	4	0
J♠	CLRS	URFS	JUM	JUR	CRFS	1	0	2
Q♠	MAFS	VEM	MORS	CLR	MAF	7	2	5
K♠	KRMA	CRR	SAFS	VEMS	VEF	4	5	0

The Faith Card

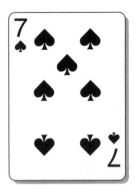

DESCRIPTION OF THE 7♠ PERSON:

This card is regarded as one of the most spiritual in the deck and these people can have great success in life as long as they do not disregard the wisdom that is intended to guide them through life. These people are here to learn to trust and keep their faith in spite of circumstances. Their main challenges will come in the areas of work and health. Maintaining a positive attitude about life is probably one of the hardest challenges when your physical body is having afflictions of one sort or another. But that is exactly what many 7♠ must do.

The underlying K♦ mandates that they must live the higher values they know if they are to have the blessings and power that is inherently available to them. That same K♦ gives them a lot of inner strength and the tendency to push things at times. It is the only one-eyed King in the deck. For that reason, the 7♠ must watch out for a tendency to be one-sided and subjective in their communications with others. Being the 7♠ puts them on the line. They must think, speak and act from a higher perspective or suffer innumerable ills, often physically oriented. Most of their problems translate as ailments, accidents, or other physical afflictions.

Their Life Path is one of the better ones in the deck. The fact that their Birth Card sits in the Jupiter column of the Life Spread indicates that they will get many of their personal wishes fulfilled in this lifetime. They have many talents they can utilize for success and satisfaction in

their lives and many become prominent and successful. Even their Saturn card, the 4♦, is a symbol of protection and security. Nothing can truly hurt them but their own fears or doubts.

They are protected by a high, spiritual force, but this must be actualized by aligning their actions with their highest truth and motives. Once they do, their lives assume a magical quality. Many take on a special mission to help the world and are unlimited in the good they can do. Those who are stuck on self-centered thoughts and motives are destined to suffer to some extent. They must live what they know and follow their intuitive guidance. Many marry into money or receive support from romantic associations. They can always do well if they work hard and maintain honesty. Nothing can stop them but themselves.

SOME OF THE 7♠ ISSUES CONCERNING RELATIONSHIPS:

These people have some of the better marriage karma of the cards in the deck, and the benefits of marriage can extend into both the financial and spiritual realms. They are attracted to those of financial means and mental power and must watch a tendency to give too much importance to the financial aspects, in which case their lack of higher values will bring them more problems than good.

7♠ women are generally strong-willed, much like the K♦, their Karma Card. For this reason, they often have trouble resigning to a role of a passive, retiring female. They can stand up to any man, and he had better be confident in himself if he is to get along with her.

In spite of their good marriage karma, they still cannot escape from the challenges of their Birth Card, which impinge on all areas of their life, including their love relationships. They may be overcome by fear or a negative take on life even when

---

KARMA CARDS:

K♦   8♥

KARMA COUSINS:

3♣   7♥

PAST-LIFE CARDS:

6♠   8♠

they have all the things they wanted. They must learn to keep the faith and stay positive to keep positive energy flowing with their partner.

GENERALITIES BETWEEN THE PERSONALITY CARD CONNECTIONS

7♠ women are attracted to both Diamond and Club males. Club males also have much affection for them. Spade females are attracted to 7♠ males. Diamond females find them difficult. 7♠ males have some challenges with Hearts females.

The Accident-Prone 7♠

When you meet a 7♠ person, before they tell you anything about their life, ask them this question: "Have you ever been in a serious car accident?" You will be surprised at how many times you discover they have had a significant accident in their life, often recently. Many of them seem to have lives that are a series of auto accidents. Not that the only accidents they have are auto accidents, but they do seem to be a common theme.

In a workshop I taught in Michigan, a woman came into the class on crutches. You guessed it, she was a 7♠. I couldn't tell if she had been involved in an accident or if she had a crippling disease. When I asked her about it, she revealed that she had indeed been in a motorcycle accident. She was a very petite woman who didn't seem like the motorcycle type, but indeed she was.

Another example is the 7♠ waitress, who appeared to be in her early twenties. I asked her the big question, this time expecting her to say that she hadn't had any car accidents, because she looked too young. However, a surprised look came over her face and she told us about a car accident she was involved in a year before. She wasn't badly hurt, but it was a fairly big accident.

Whether or not all 7♠ people have car accidents, there is no doubt that they work out most of their personal karma through the vehicle of their bodies. This process often involves afflictions and diseases, sometimes sexually transmitted, which more or less become the dominant theme in their relationships, marriages, and life as a whole. This struggle often lasts for many years.

I have yet to meet a 7♠ that hasn't had some sort of physical challenge in their life. This is represented by their Birth Card, the card of challenges on the bodily or physical level. It is not the ailment or affliction itself that is the point. It is the fact that whatever is going on with them on the physical side becomes one of the most dominant themes in their life. For the 7♠, the stage where they meet with the most challenges is that of their health and the relationship with their body.

Keep in mind, though, that the 7♠ is not a card of defeat. All Sevens represent challenges that can be turned into victory with the proper attitude and application of spiritual principles. The high side of the 7♠ is that it is the strongest card of Spiritual Victory and the overcoming of all mundane problems through faith. All physical afflictions, or at least their effect on us, can be eliminated through the application of positive thoughts and attitudes of gratefulness. The 7♠ has the ability to do this more than any other card in the deck.

SEVEN OF SPADES

LIFE SPREAD CARDS		
PLANETARY CARD	**SYMBOL**	**CARD**
MOON	☽	9♦
SUN (BIRTH CARD)	✳	7♠
MERCURY	☿	2♣
VENUS	♀	K♣
MARS	♂	J♦
JUPITER	♃	4♥
SATURN	♄	4♦
URANUS	♅	2♠
NEPTUNE	♆	8♥
PLUTO	♇	6♣
RESULT (COSMIC REWARD)	♃+	6♠
COSMIC LESSON	♄+	Q♥

PLANETARY RULING CARDS		
BIRTH DATE	**ASTROLOGICAL RULING SIGN**	**PLANETARY RULING CARD**
JAN 7	CAPRICORN	4♦
FEB 5	AQUARIUS	2♠
MAR 3	PISCES	8♥
APR 1	ARIES	J♦

Who	The Connections Between Partners					Overall Index Ratings		
7♠ with	Con1	Con2	Con3	Con4	Con5	Attraction	Intensity	Compatibility
A♥	NEFS	VEM	CRFS	NERS	PLFS	8	2	4
2♥	PLFS	VER	URRS	VEF	PLF	6	2	1
3♥	CRFS	NEFS	VEM	MAFS	NEF	8	3	3
4♥	JUF	CLFS	URFS	MARS	VEM	4	2	2
5♥	CRR	SAF	VEMS	JUFS	VER	3	2	2
6♥	MAF	MOR	VERS	VEF	JUF	8	0	6
7♥	NEF	URRS	KRMC	PLR	MOFS	5	2	2
8♥	KRMA	NEF	PLF	PLFS	NEFS	8	7	-1
9♥	URR	MORS	NER	PLF	URRS	4	1	2
10♥	VER	VERS	PLF	VEFS	MAR	7	0	5
J♥	JUF	SAFS	URFS	MAM	SAR	0	3	0
Q♥	CLF	SAF	MAFS	MAMS	MAF	4	8	-4
K♥	MAM	MOR	VEFS	MOF	SAFS	7	1	5
A♣	PLFS	VEF	PLF	URFS	VER	7	4	-1
2♣	MOR	URRS	MAM	MAMS	URR	5	1	3
3♣	PLR	JUR	KRMC	NERS	PLFS	3	3	1
4♣	MAF	JUFS	VEF	JUF	CRFS	6	1	5
5♣	JUFS	CRR	MAF	MAFS	CLFS	5	3	3
6♣	PLF	MORS	MAMS	MOR	CLF	8	4	1
7♣	SAR	URF	VEMS	JUFS	VEM	2	0	2
8♣	MAM	JUF	SAFS	URFS	SAF	2	4	0
9♣	MAMS	CLF	VEFS	JUR	VERS	6	4	2
10♣	JUFS	MARS	VEM	VEMS	JUF	6	0	7
J♣	VER	MAF	CRRS	MAR	CRR	7	3	3
Q♣	MAFS	CRFS	VEF	CLRS	VEFS	7	4	3
K♣	VEF	URF	SARS	MORS	SAR	3	0	4
A♦	MAMS	NEFS	VEM	VEMS	MAM	8	3	4
2♦	MAMS	PLF	MAF	MAM		9	9	-2
3♦	CLR	PLRS	CLRS	MARS	VERS	3	3	-1
4♦	SAF	VEMS	VERS	CRR	JUR	3	1	2
5♦	JUR	MOF	PLR	PLRS	JURS	3	-1	4
6♦	VEFS	MAMS	NER	JURS	URF	6	1	5
7♦	URR	NER	PLF	URRS	URFS	3	2	-1
8♦	URF	VEMS	MAR	SAFS	NEFS	4	2	2
9♦	MOF	CLR	PLRS	JUR	JURS	4	0	4
10♦	VEF	CLRS	MAFS	MAR	SAFS	5	3	2
J♦	MAF	CRRS	NER	JURS	VER	6	3	2
Q♦	CLR	PLRS	MOF	MOFS	CLRS	4	1	2
K♦	KRMA	NERS	PLR	PLF	PLFS	6	6	-1
A♠	URRS	MOR	MORS	CRR	JUMS	4	-2	5
2♠	URF	SARS	MOFS	CRF	VEF	2	1	2
3♠	NER	JURS	VEFS	MAF	CRRS	5	1	5
4♠	MARS	VEM	JUF	CLFS	URFS	6	2	4
5♠	VERS	SAF	VEMS	URR	SAFS	2	1	2
6♠	MOFS	CRF	VEFS	URF	SARS	6	0	5
7♠	SBC	NERS	NEF	NEFS	NER	6	4	2
8♠	MORS	VEF	PLF	CLF	PLFS	7	1	4
9♠	VEFS	MAM	MOFS	CRF	MAR	8	2	5
10♠	SAF	MAFS	JUF	CLFS	URFS	2	5	-2
J♠	JUFS	SAR	JUF	CLRS	VEMS	1	0	4
Q♠	MAR	SAFS	NEFS	VEF	CLRS	4	6	0
K♠	URFS	MAM	JUF	SAFS	URF	2	3	0

The Eights

"Power corrupts, absolute power corrupts absolutely."
—Adlai Stevenson

Having passed through the challenge imposed by the Seven, the Eight represents a multiplication of energy, twice that of the Four. Where the Four represents good supply, security, and foundation, the Eight symbolizes all that plus more. This translates as power—the ability to effect change in whatever direction they choose by focusing their energies. The number eight, in the cycle from one to ten, represents the point of fullness and the time of harvest. With Eights we see one of the strongest manifestations of their suit, shining examples of what that suit can produce or create. Most Eights are producers and hard workers. They enjoy watching their power manifest things so well and so quickly. But like any of the other gifts represented by our Birth Card, power can be used or abused. Eights are faced with this choice throughout their life, and it is a dominant theme that many of them are here to get clear about. Power can be used to help others and to create more goodwill and prosperity, or it can become an addiction and a means to escape from inner fears and insecurities.

Power stems from the highest power, and the highest power is that of God or the Creator. If it is true that all things happen only by the will of God, then when we are given some power to play with, we tend to feel as though we have a divine right to its use. However, just because we have been given the commission of power doesn't mean that we have become perfect and incapable of making mistakes. This is the misconception that people in positions of power sometimes have. Instead of seeing themselves as vessels of God's will, they begin to see themselves in distorted ways. They begin to think that they are perfect and infallible. They begin to imagine they are God-like or, in some cases, immortal. This is when power becomes dangerous, like giving a real gun to a child. If an Eight person is not aware enough to realize that they are only vessels of God's power, they will make the mistakes associated with the misuse of it.

In the astrological natal charts of most, if not all, Eights, you will find a strong element of Scorpio, Pluto, or Eight House energy. All Eights will behave a little like Scorpios, regardless of their sun sign. Pluto is the overall ruler of this element. He is the planet of death and destruction, and this Pluto influence has profound meanings to the Eight person. The essential meaning of Pluto and Scorpio is self-transformation. When the Pluto or Scorpio influence is strong within a person's makeup, as it is with Eights, there will inevitably be some major changes in the person's life from time to time. These changes can range from the way they approach relationships to the way they think or deal with money. We might say that all Eights will pass through several 'personal deaths' during the course of their life. Some part of their personality will die, making way for the new. Like the Phoenix, the Eight person will arise from the ashes of their own burial to fly again with new wings. The eagle is the symbol for Scorpio, but it only represents the Scorpio that has undergone this essential transformation. This will be the same for the Eight.

They usually attract powerful people into their lives that match their own power. There will be some degree of power struggles or attempts to control or manipulate until the Eight person learns that the change that is really needed is within themselves. When the Eight turns their tremendous power back onto themselves in an effort to make internal changes, they access some of their highest power. Most of the Eights have powerful, spiritual cards as their Karma Cards. These represent the presence of potent spiritual energy. When the 'little deaths' occur for the Eight person, they are assisted by these spiritual energies and are reborn with even more power than before. The new person they become often bears little resemblance to the person they were before. Some people may even have difficulty recognizing them. It is much like the snake shedding its skin.

Eights all share this scorpionic legacy to some extent. They are the people that shine forth with all the brilliance of their suit to exemplify the best of what that suit can manifest.

Because the 8th house and Scorpio deal with the goods and possessions of others, by necessity Eights get involved with the finances of others at certain points in their life, often inheriting the responsibility of handling the estates of their parents and others. As a rule, they do well with this and can be trusted to fairly and honestly manage funds. Whether it involves the care of the family estate or managing the finances of a family-run business, they perform their duty in a way that is to be admired. The enlightened Eight person stands as an example of someone who has passed through the fires of self-transformation. The power that at one time was turned upon the world outside of them has been turned within and has effected a truly inspired change in them. They become reminders to us of our own divinity.

The Emotional Power Card

DESCRIPTION OF THE 8♥ PERSON:
The 8♥ has 'power in love' and all Eights have to exercise discrimination and responsibility in its use. They are unsurpassed in charm and magnetism, but some can become addicted to the power they wield and use it unwisely at the expense of others. Both Karma Cards of the 8♥ are Sevens. This tells us that they will see almost immediate results when they misuse their power with others, but it also gives them a great deal of spiritual wisdom that helps guide their actions. By following the truth, they know inside they can rise to great heights in sharing their love and healing power with others. This is a healer's card, one who can truly give others the love they need to heal themselves.

The 8♥ has one of the most fortunate Life Paths and many are destined to become well-known teachers, artists, statesmen, and performers. Their Life Path Cards include the 10♣, 8♦, and K♠, all of which reside in the Crown Line of the Life Spread. The top three cards that make up the Crown Line give great potential for recognition and success. Even the lowliest 8♥ will gain some recognition among their friends and family.

Health is an area where there will be challenges unless the 8♥ pays close attention to it. Many get so involved in their work and families that they neglect their bodies to the point of breakdown. The 7♠ first Karma Card will demand full payment for neglect in this area. With so much going for them, you would think

they could just relax and enjoy life, but they often set such a fast pace for themselves that it becomes detrimental.

It is interesting how often the 8♥ person has an immediate family or circle of friends that consists of exactly eight people. Eight hearts means eight people that they love. Many have eight children, eight wives, etc.

They have great minds, which excel as teachers or in any occupation where a good mind will make a difference. They have to work hard for the money they make, but it can be made and they need not worry about it. Many 8♥ achieve some measure of prominence in their lifetime, especially after the age of 36 when there can be a rising up in power and accomplishment. With all the power at their command, there is little they cannot do so long as it is not motivated by fear.

SOME OF THE 8♥ ISSUES CONCERNING RELATIONSHIPS:
Similar to the 7♥, these people have power, for better or worse, that they must learn to administer with wisdom. These are the 'Playboys' and 'Playgirls' of the deck. They have the charm and magnetism to get what they want and they are the ones who go after who they want. They know how to love others and make them feel very special. They are less needy than most cards and thus they usually retain the upper hand in all of their relationships. For this reason, they will often go from one relationship to the next, leaving if and when the relationship starts to make them uncomfortable.

In marriage they can be somewhat aggressive. 8♥ women are often so aggressive that it scares some of their suitors away. Some men would prefer a woman who was less forceful.

In the areas of love, the 8♥ must be aware of what they do and to whom they do it. Out of all the cards in the deck they

---

KARMA CARDS:

7♠   7♥

KARMA COUSINS:

K♦   A♠

PAST-LIFE CARDS:

7♥   9♥

---

will have the swiftest karmic paybacks for wrong actions. Their power must be harnessed and used with maturity and wisdom if they are to attain true happiness.

GENERALITIES BETWEEN THE PERSONALITY CARD CONNECTIONS

Club males find 8♥ very difficult, especially the female 8♥. Diamond males like them. Male 8♥ have strong attractions to women of the Heart suit and are usually compatible with them, except for the J♥, who is a sort of a nemesis to them.

Eight of Hearts—The Playboy/Playgirl Card

Being an 8♥ gives one a great deal of power in the emotional arena. With such power, an 8♥ can easily get what they want from most people in their life. This power is actually the power to really 'nuke' someone with attention and admiration. When an 8♥ person wants to, they can make you feel like the most adored and desirable person in the world. This is a powerful tool and they can use it in any way they choose. Richard Gere, John F. Kennedy Jr., and Joe DiMaggio are all 8♥. There are many more, of course, but one quick look at the men of this card and you can see certain things they have in common. These three, for example, are what we might consider 'ladies men.' On some level, all Eights are here to learn about the use or abuse of power. Actually, all of our Birth Cards have some sort of power associated with them. It is just that in the case of the Eights, this power is much more dramatic.

The 8♥ person discovers this power early in life. They realize that they can use it to get their emotional needs met or for other ends. Men of this card could easily become professional gigolos. They could use it to seduce women. They could also use it to become a professional healer or counselor. It all depends upon the self-awareness and values of the individual.

Those that are not yet aware of how their actions affect others and the law of karma will most likely abuse this power. However, the 8♥ has two Sevens as Karma Cards, the 7♠ and 7♥. Seven cards are the most spiritual in the deck and always create problems if we are doing things without being conscious of them. These two cards tell us that even though the 8♥ may abuse his or her power, they will not get away with it in this lifetime. Difficulties will arise every time they abuse their God-given gifts.

The power of the 8♥ person is limited to the arena of relationships. Hearts are the very first suit in the deck, and have no jurisdiction over the other suits. However, the other suits have jurisdiction over the hearts. The 8♥ person's power can only affect the 'inner child' within us. Their manipulations may be characterized by actions such as withholding affection, shaming, or making others feel unworthy of love itself. Many 8♥ choose to work with or associate with children because that is where they have the most power. The adults they manipulate are usually those with poor self-images, who depend on them for their feelings of well-being. A person with a well-developed inner child will be unaffected by the 8♥'s manipulation. And a person who is clear about what is true in their life can rise above any problems presented by an 8♥ person.

The 8♥ will live and die by the decisions they make regarding their power. They each have a wonderful gift that could be used to help and to heal. If guided by wisdom, it will bring wonderful results in their own lives and the lives of all they touch.

EIGHT OF HEARTS

LIFE SPREAD CARDS

PLANETARY CARD	SYMBOL	CARD
MOON	☽	2♠
SUN (BIRTH CARD)	✳	8♥
MERCURY	☿	6♣
VENUS	♀	6♠
MARS	♂	Q♥
JUPITER	♃	10♣
SATURN	♄	8♦
URANUS	♅	K♠
NEPTUNE	♆	3♥
PLUTO	♇	A♣
RESULT (COSMIC REWARD)	♃+	Q♣
COSMIC LESSON	♄+	10♠

PLANETARY RULING CARDS

BIRTH DATE	ASTROLOGICAL RULING SIGN	PLANETARY RULING CARD
AUG 31	VIRGO	6♣
SEP 29	LIBRA	6♠
OCT 27	SCORPIO	Q♥ & A♣
NOV 25	SAGITTARIUS	10♣
DEC 23	CAPRICORN	8♦

Who	The Connections Between Partners					Overall Index Ratings		
8♥ with	Con1	Con2	Con3	Con4	Con5	Attraction	Intensity	Compatibility
A♥	NERS	PLFS	MAM	NEF	SARS	7	5	-1
2♥	URRS	PLF	URFS	PLFS	URF	3	4	-3
3♥	NEF	SARS	NERS	PLFS	CRF	5	4	0
4♥	MAR	JURS	SARS	CLF	URF	3	4	1
5♥	MARS	VEM	VER	CLFS	CRR	7	2	4
6♥	VERS	JUF	CRFS	MARS	MOFS	6	0	5
7♥	KRMA	MOFS	PLF	NEFS	JUMS	7	4	2
8♥	SBC	NER	MOFS	NEF	MORS	6	2	4
9♥	MORS	PLF	URFS	URR	VEFS	5	1	2
10♥	VEFS	CRR	VEMS	MAFS	VEM	7	0	6
J♥	SAF	MAFS	URF	PLRS	JUF	1	5	-3
Q♥	MAF	JUFS	CLF	URF	VERS	5	3	2
K♥	SAFS	URR	NEFS	PLRS	SAMS	0	5	-3
A♣	PLF	URFS	URRS	URR	NEFS	3	3	-2
2♣	URR	NEFS	PLRS	JUMS	SAFS	3	2	1
3♣	PLFS	PLR	CRFS	JUR	JUMS	5	5	-2
4♣	JUF	CRFS	CLFS	VERS	MAF	5	2	3
5♣	CLFS	MARS	VEM	JUF	CRFS	6	4	2
6♣	MOR	PLF	VEMS	MARS		8	1	4
7♣	VEM	SAF	NEF	CLRS	VEMS	4	2	2
8♣	SAF	MAFS	URF	PLRS	MAM	2	6	-3
9♣	VERS	MAF	JUFS	MAM	MAMS	7	2	4
10♣	JUF	CLRS	VEMS	SARS	CLR	2	0	4
J♣	CRR	VEMS	JUR	VEFS	VER	5	-1	6
Q♣	CRF	NEF	SARS	MAF	JURS	5	4	1
K♣	SAR	MOF	VEF	URF	SARS	3	0	3
A♦	MAM	NERS	PLFS	MAMS	MARS	8	7	-1
2♦	MOR	MAM	MAMS	MARS	PLF	8	4	3
3♦	MARS	VERS	VER	CRF	MAR	7	3	4
4♦	VER	MARS	VEM	SAF	VEMS	6	1	4
5♦	PLR	PLFS	JUR	JUMS	JURS	3	3	0
6♦	MAM	MAMS	VERS	VEF	VEFS	8	4	4
7♦	MORS	PLF	URFS	MOR	URR	6	1	3
8♦	SAF	NEF	CLR	CRRS	VEM	2	4	-1
9♦	PLR	MOF	JURS	CLR	PLRS	3	1	3
10♦	MAF	JURS	CRF	CLR	CRRS	5	4	2
J♦	JUR	VEF	CRR	VEMS	MAF	5	-1	7
Q♦	MARS	PLR	CLR	PLRS	MAR	5	6	-1
K♦	PLFS	NER	KRMC	NERS	PLF	7	5	-1
A♠	JUMS	MOFS	KRMC	URR	NEFS	4	-1	5
2♠	MOF	VEF	SAR	URF	SARS	4	-1	5
3♠	VEF	MAM	MAMS	JUR	NER	7	3	4
4♠	SARS	JUF	MAR	JURS	MARS	2	3	2
5♠	VEFS	VER	VERS	VEF	MAFS	7	-2	8
6♠	VEF	SAMS	MOF	MOFS	CRF	5	1	5
7♠	KRMA	NER	PLF	NEFS	PLFS	7	6	-1
8♠	SAR	MOR	MORS	VEF	VEMS	5	-1	5
9♠	SAMS	SAFS	VEF	VEFS	SAF	0	5	-2
10♠	CLF	URF	MAR	JURS	MAF	4	4	0
J♠	CLRS	VEMS	VEM	JUF	JUFS	4	-2	6
Q♠	CLR	CRRS	MAF	JURS	SAF	3	3	0
K♠	URF	PLRS	SAF	MAFS	URFS	1	4	-3

The Mental Power Card

DESCRIPTION OF THE 8♣ PERSON:

The 8♣ is one of the three Fixed Cards. With their strong mental power, they are not easily swayed by others' views and opinions. Many successful attorneys are 8♣. However, their power can be applied to any of the mental fields with great success. For example, many chemists, rocket scientists, and nuclear physicists are also 8♣. They really can learn anything.

Their life path is one of the most successful in the deck. They can achieve almost anything they set their mind to and most attain wealth and prominence, but they must make sure their life is kept in balance. Mental and emotional peace is essential to maintaining success. They have much psychic power and can be great healers. All of their gifts can be applied to great success and they only need to become aware of their true goals to have a life of success and accomplishment.

Being so fixed has its own drawbacks, mainly that it is difficult for them to deal with changes. It is their mind—their concepts, ideas, and principles—that is the most fixed. They are often born with a certain set of principles they will live their life by and refuse to change. However, there will inevitably be certain periods of their life where changes of their mental structures must and will come. These periods are difficult, but a part of the 8♣ karmic path. They are always healthier and more alive after the changes, which come as a sort of death and rebirth.

KARMA CARDS:

J♥ K♠ A♣ 2♥ 7♦ 9♥

KARMA COUSINS:

NONE

PAST-LIFE CARDS:

7♣ 9♣

Working with a J♥ or K♠ will bring far-reaching success if together they are committed to doing some great work for humanity. For best results, they should let their work come before their personal lives and keep them separate.

SOME OF THE 8♣ ISSUES CONCERNING RELATIONSHIPS:

The 8♣ essentially has good marriage karma. First of all, being a Fixed Card, they are less prone to the emotional changes other cards have. Their 4♠ in Venus is also a sign that they appreciate the stability of home and family enough to avoid the changes in love life that affect so many others. However, most 8♣ people will, at one point in their life, experience a difficult divorce or separation. This usually comes in association with someone of the Diamond suit.

For the 8♣, this destined romantic break-up is a karma that must be dealt with from the past, usually a past life. Because of their fixed nature, when these changes come, they are not easy to deal with. The women often end up in association with a younger, Diamond male who introduces them to a highly spiritual or romantic love. This usually occurs in their forties. When they discover that there is more to the world than just their fixed mental concepts, they come face to face with their desire for adventure and a variety of love experiences. So, it often takes this divorce or change to help them graduate to a new level in their life and to break out of their fixed pattern.

Sometimes there are secret affairs before, during, and after this change. Once this change happens, they are more free to pursue whatever kinds of relationships fit their needs. The female 8♣ should never allow her personal relationships to be more important than her life's work. When she does, she always loses most of her power and becomes entangled in emotional morass and confusion.

GENERALITIES BETWEEN THE PERSONALITY CARD CONNECTIONS

8♣ males are often attracted to Diamond females, who always brings challenges to their lives. A Diamond female is often the one they are destined to eventually become divorced from. The female 8♣ has better success with the Diamond males. The 8♣ male will have attraction for Heart females. Both sexes get along well with Club males.

Eight of Clubs Can Be Very Fixed

8♣ people, being one of the three Fixed Cards, are primarily fixed in their minds. Once they get something set in their minds, they are usually unable to change it or remove it. The following story illustrates that point.

During a recent workshop, one of the women shared a story about her 8♣ husband. He is a successful man by most standards, but has some quirky stubborn ways.

In the town where they lived, the town officials changed the direction of two main streets that had been running one-way in a certain direction for over 20 years. This change in direction was intolerable for the 8♣ man. As a result of this, he decided that he just would not drive on those streets anymore. This was all the more amazing, because in order to not drive on those streets, he had to travel over five miles out of his way each time he drove his car to or from his town. In his mind, however, this was the better of two choices. This is a case where an 8♣ concept was held fast, even though it may have been impractical by normal standards. To the 8♣, changing their own minds can seem an enormous task that they are unwilling to undertake.

Many 8♣ people go through most of their life being fixed with particular concepts, principles or beliefs. For the most part, they are successful with these and have a happy life. But inevitably, the call comes forth from within to move on, and to evolve into broader ways of looking at the world and their personal lives. The change that is required can take years to complete. Because of the Q♦ Pluto Card in their Life Path, this change is often catalyzed by some person of the Diamond suit, be it male or female.

As a matter of fact, most 8♣ women meet a man of the Diamond suit in their late forties or early fifties who acts as this catalyst for their personal transformation. Sometimes it can even occur earlier and, in some cases, it occurs more than once. It usually begins as a love affair or extreme infatuation with the Diamond man, who is often younger in age. This man awakens romantic and other feelings within them that they never experienced before. The 8♣ woman usually falls in love with the Diamond, in spite of the fact that the relationship is impractical or unworkable from many perspectives. And though these relationships rarely last long, they have a permanent effect on the life of the 8♣ woman—she is transformed into a world that has more possibilities for personal happiness and experiences.

For all their power, 8♣ people have their own crosses to bear. It usually takes a major crisis in their lives to change their minds or their habits. This is why there are often dramatic events that occur in the life of an 8♣ person. It takes more energy to get them to change or move. We might say that God wants us all to evolve and change to a certain extent. From one point of view, that is what life is all about. It is this evolution that meets head-on with the 8♣ fixed nature.

EIGHT OF CLUBS

LIFE SPREAD CARDS

PLANETARY CARD	SYMBOL	CARD
MOON	☽	J♠
SUN (BIRTH CARD)	✳	8♣
MERCURY	☿	6♦
VENUS	♀	4♠
MARS	♂	10♥
JUPITER	♃	10♦
SATURN	♄	8♠
URANUS	♅	A♥
NEPTUNE	♆	A♦
PLUTO	♇	Q♦
RESULT (COSMIC REWARD)	♃+	5♥
COSMIC LESSON	♄+	3♣

PLANETARY RULING CARDS

BIRTH DATE	ASTROLOGICAL RULING SIGN	PLANETARY RULING CARD
MAR 28	ARIES	10♥
APR 26	TAURUS	4♠
MAY 24	GEMINI	6♦
JUN 22	GEMINI OR CANCER	6♦ OR J♠
JUL 20	CANCER	J♠
AUG 18	LEO	8♣
SEP 16	VIRGO	6♦
OCT 14	LIBRA	4♠
NOV 12	SCORPIO	10♥ & Q♦
DEC 10	SAGITTARIUS	10♦

Who 8♣ with	Con1	Con2	Con3	Con4	Con5	Attraction	Intensity	Compatibility
A♥	URF	NEF	PLR	URFS	CLRS	3	2	0
2♥	KRMA	NER	PLF	NERS	PLFS	7	6	-1
3♥	URF	JUFS	CLR	PLRS	MOR	2	0	2
4♥	VEF	JURS	NERS	CRR	JUFS	4	-1	6
5♥	CRF	VEMS	CRFS	MARS	VEM	7	3	3
6♥	JUR	MAR	JURS	PLFS	URF	3	2	3
7♥	VEFS	VEF	MAR	JURS	PLF	6	0	6
8♥	MAM	VEFS	SAR	MARS	URR	5	4	2
9♥	KRMA	VEM	VEMS	NERS	PLFS	7	2	4
10♥	MAF	MAFS	MOFS	CLFS	VEMS	8	5	2
J♥	KRMA	POWR	CLR	CLRS	NEF	5	6	0
Q♥	JUR	CRRS	JURS	MORS	CRR	3	-1	5
K♥	URR	PLRS	URRS	PLR	JUF	1	2	-1
A♣	KRMA	NERS	PLFS	NER	PLF	7	6	-1
2♣	URRS	VEF	URR	PLRS	JUFS	2	0	3
3♣	CLF	SARS	VER	CLFS	SAR	3	4	-2
4♣	MAR	JURS	MARS	VEM	JUR	5	3	4
5♣	MARS	VEM	CRF	VEMS	MAR	8	3	4
6♣	VERS	SAF	VER	NEFS	PLRS	4	1	2
7♣	MOFS	MAM	MOF	CRFS	VEF	8	1	6
8♣	SBC	POWR	CLR	CLRS	CLF	4	6	-1
9♣	MORS	CRR	JUR	CRRS	MOR	5	-1	6
10♣	VEFS	MOF	VEF	VEMS	VER	7	-3	10
J♣	MAFS	MAR	MAF	CLR	CLFS	7	7	0
Q♣	JUFS	JUF	PLR	VERS	MAF	3	-1	5
K♣	SAFS	JUM	SAF	JURS	NER	-2	4	-2
A♦	NEF	PLR	URFS	VER	NEFS	5	2	2
2♦	VER	NEFS	PLRS	VERS	NEF	7	0	4
3♦	PLFS	JUR	PLF	SAR	MAMS	5	5	-2
4♦	CRFS	CRF	VEMS	PLR	CLF	7	4	1
5♦	VER	CLFS	VERS	CLF	SARS	6	2	2
6♦	MOR	MORS	CRR	MARS	JUM	7	-1	7
7♦	KRMA	VEMS	VEM	NERS	PLFS	7	2	4
8♦	MAM	MAMS	MOFS	VEF	MOF	8	4	4
9♦	VERS	PLF	VER	CLFS	MAMS	7	2	2
10♦	JUF	JUFS	MAMS	VER	PLR	4	0	6
J♦	MAR	MARS	MAFS	CLR	CLRS	7	7	0
Q♦	PLF	PLFS	VERS	MAM	SAR	7	6	-3
K♦	SAR	MAMS	CLF	SARS	MAM	3	7	-3
A♠	VEF	VEFS	URRS	JUR	NEF	5	-2	7
2♠	JUM	JUMS	SAFS	NER	JUR	0	0	2
3♠	MARS	MOR	MAR	CLRS	JUM	7	3	3
4♠	VEF	VEFS	VEM	CRRS	VEMS	7	-2	9
5♠	MAF	CRFS	MOF	CLF	PLRS	7	5	1
6♠	JUMS	PLR	JUM	JUR	NERS	2	-1	3
7♠	MAM	SAR	MAMS	JUR	SARS	4	6	0
8♠	SAF	SAFS	VERS	JUR	SARS	-2	4	-3
9♠	PLR	URR	PLRS	JUMS	VEF	2	2	0
10♠	JURS	JUR	CRRS	NER	JUF	2	-1	5
J♠	MOF	MOFS	VEFS	CRF	VERS	8	-2	9
Q♠	MAMS	JUF	MAM	VEFS	MOFS	7	3	4
K♠	KRMA	POWR	NEF	NEFS	CLR	7	6	1

The Sun Card

DESCRIPTION OF THE 8♦ PERSON:

As the Sun (✳) Card, the 8♦ has the opportunity to rise to great heights in this life. Regardless of whether they make the move for great fame, they are always respected and looked up to in their work. They love to 'shine' and be noticed by others, and they have a great deal of leadership ability. These people are powerful and can be dominating if their power becomes an addiction. Much of their karma is worked out through power and control struggles with others. They dislike being controlled and try to maintain power in their relationships.

Their Eight power and position in the Crown Line gives them an independent and sometimes 'pushy' nature. In any case, they know what everything is worth and can drive a hard bargain. To many 8♦, power means having and spending money. 8♦ often get such a rush from spending money that it can become something of an addiction. The male and female 8♦ are especially known to be able to spend huge sums of money quickly. These are the 'power shoppers' of the deck. The slogan, 'When the going gets tough, the tough go shopping,' was probably written by an 8♦.

They can achieve anything through hard work and the application of their inherent intuition. When they learn to direct their power back toward themselves and their personal transformation, and stop trying to change the world, they can attain the lasting peace of inner power and self-mastery, the keywords of their Q♠ Karma Card.

They have good minds and a keen desire to learn new things. If they are willing to work for it, there is little they cannot achieve and few problems they cannot overcome. They have the power to conquer and rule and, as long as it is not misused, it will bring them satisfaction. Some 8♦ are afraid or unwilling to take on the responsibility that comes with this power and thus forfeit much of their God-given talent and potential.

SOME OF THE 8♦ ISSUES CONCERNING RELATIONSHIPS:

In love they tend toward fickleness and indecision. The independent, changeable nature of the 8♦ may resist marriage, or, in other cases, they continually attract others who cannot make a commitment. Many 8♦ practice 'serial monogamy.' They have three, four, five, or more marriages. In truth, they have a need for variety in love that often cannot be satisfied by one person.

They must learn to give others freedom of expression without trying to change them. They also need to learn to accept themselves as they are and learn how to give themselves the love they seek from others. Their A♠/7♥ Pluto and Cosmic Reward cards tell us that it is in releasing their fears of abandonment, and by not using their abundance of power to bully their loved ones that they have some of the greatest challenges.

As a rule they know what they want and are willing to go after it. What they want will, unfortunately, eventually change.

In most cases it is wise for them to always place their careers in front of relationships. They usually lose some of their power when they try to make a relationship more important than their work. Both sexes fare better with those of the Club suit. Adopting a less attached view of love brings them many blessings.

KARMA CARDS:

Q♠ 7♣

KARMA COUSINS:

10♦ J♠

PAST-LIFE CARDS:

7♦ 9♦

8♦ women are best suited for marriage to a Spade male, especially if he is accomplished and powerful. Heart males provide a lifetime friendship. The 8♦ male is often sought by Heart females and he receives blessings from Club females. He may find greatest compatibility with Spade females, though it is important to examine the Birth Card connections on an individual basis before drawing any conclusions.

Eight of Diamonds Women

What do Loni Anderson, Dolly Parton, and Tammy Faye Bakker all have in common? They are all 8♦ women. These three women all share some physical attributes that are common for 8♦ women. These three even look a lot alike. When we remember that the 8♦ is the Sun Card, it may help us understand why these women share essentially the same look. Most 8♦ people you meet will have that huge, sunny face. It is their entire countenance, in fact, that bestows that sunny appearance. Usually they are smiling, and their smiles are often very exaggerated, having a larger than average mouth and lots of beautiful teeth. The 8♦ is very much a Leo card, regardless of the sun sign of the person who has it. We will almost certainly find an important Leo aspect in their astrological charts. The Leo quality is often associated with a Lion—there is usually a mane of hair, or hair that stands out in some way. Of course, not all 8♦ women are of this particular physical type, but it is surprising to note how many of them are.

Another 8♦ characteristic is the raw power they have when it comes to money, especially when it comes to money and business. Never make the mistake of thinking any of them are pushovers. If anything, they will attempt to force you to do things that you wouldn't ordinarily do. Regardless of their appearance, these women know exactly what everything is worth and can drive a hard bargain. When it comes to money, or anything valued, the 8♦ can be very strong-willed, even ruthless in some cases. Look further and you will always find either a strong Pluto, Scorpio, or 8th house influence in each of their astrological natal charts.

EIGHT OF DIAMONDS

LIFE SPREAD CARDS

PLANETARY CARD	SYMBOL	CARD
MOON	☽	10♣
SUN (BIRTH CARD)	☀	8♦
MERCURY	☿	K♠
VENUS	♀	3♥
MARS	♂	A♣
JUPITER	♃	Q♣
SATURN	♄	10♠
URANUS	♅	5♣
NEPTUNE	♆	3♦
PLUTO	♇	A♠
RESULT (COSMIC REWARD)	♃+	7♥
COSMIC LESSON	♄+	7♦

PLANETARY RULING CARDS

BIRTH DATE	ASTROLOGICAL RULING SIGN	PLANETARY RULING CARD
JAN 19	CAPRICORN	10♠
FEB 17	AQUARIUS	5♣
MAR 15	PISCES	3♦
APR 13	ARIES	A♣
MAY 11	TAURUS	3♥
JUN 9	GEMINI	K♠
JUL 7	CANCER	10♣
AUG 5	LEO	8♦
SEP 3	VIRGO	K♠
OCT 1	LIBRA	3♥

Who 8♦ with	Con1	Con2	Con3	Con4	Con5	Attraction	Intensity	Compatibility
A♥	NERS	PLFS	VEF	CRR	VEFS	7	3	2
2♥	JUMS	MAF	MOFS	CLF	VEM	6	1	4
3♥	VEF	JUF	CRRS	SAF	JUFS	3	0	5
4♥	PLR	CRFS	SAF	NEF	SAFS	3	6	-3
5♥	NER	JURS	URF	VEMS	URR	3	-1	4
6♥	JUFS	MAR	NEF	SARS	NEFS	5	3	3
7♥	CRF	SAR	NER	PLF	URFS	4	5	-2
8♥	SAR	NER	URR	VEMS	CRF	2	2	1
9♥	MOFS	CLF	VEM	MAF	MAR	7	2	4
10♥	MAMS	CLRS	CLFS	VEM	CLR	5	5	0
J♥	VER	MOR	MAM	VERS	CRRS	7	-1	6
Q♥	VER	SAF	PLRS	VERS	VEFS	3	2	1
K♥	MAFS	MAM	VERS	VEM	MAF	8	4	3
A♣	MAF	JUMS	MOFS	CLF	VEM	6	2	3
2♣	PLF	URFS	MAFS	MAM	JUF	6	5	-2
3♣	MARS	SAFS	SAR	MAR	JURS	2	7	-3
4♣	MAR	URF	VEMS	JUFS	MAM	5	2	3
5♣	URF	VEMS	MAR	MARS	VERS	5	2	3
6♣	JUR	URRS	MOFS	CLR	JURS	2	-2	5
7♣	KRMA	VEFS	PLF	NEFS	VER	7	4	2
8♣	MAM	VER	MOR	MAMS	MORS	8	2	5
9♣	VER	VERS	JUM	VEFS	PLRS	6	-2	7
10♣	MOF	CRFS	MAFS	VEF	MAMS	8	2	5
J♣	CLRS	CRR	MAFS	MAMS	MOR	5	4	1
Q♣	JUF	CRRS	VEF	JUR	VEFS	4	-1	7
K♣	CLR	PLRS	URR	NEFS	SAF	2	3	-1
A♦	NERS	PLFS	URRS	PLR	URR	5	4	-2
2♦	URRS	JUR	NERS	PLFS	URR	2	1	1
3♦	NEF	SARS	JUFS	SAM	JUF	2	3	2
4♦	NER	JURS	CLFS	PLF	CLF	4	3	1
5♦	MARS	MORS	MOF	MOR	VEF	8	0	7
6♦	VERS	SAR	PLFS	VEF	SARS	4	2	1
7♦	MOFS	CLF	VEM	MAF	MAR	7	2	4
8♦	SBC	VEFS	VERS	NEF	PLFS	7	2	4
9♦	MORS	JUFS	MARS	VEF	JUF	6	-1	7
10♦	JUR	VEFS	KRMC	JUF	CRRS	3	-1	7
J♦	CRR	MAFS	SAR	PLFS	CLRS	5	5	-1
Q♦	JUFS	NEF	SARS	MORS	NER	4	0	4
K♦	SAFS	URR	VEMS	URRS	SAR	0	3	-1
A♠	PLF	URFS	CRF	JUF	PLFS	5	4	-2
2♠	URR	NEFS	PLRS	MAR	CLR	4	3	0
3♠	SAR	PLFS	VERS	CRR	MAFS	4	4	-1
4♠	CRFS	MOF	PLR	PLRS	MAFS	6	3	2
5♠	CLFS	MAMS	NER	JURS	NERS	6	5	0
6♠	MAR	VERS	VEM	URR	NEFS	7	2	4
7♠	URR	VEMS	SAFS	SAR	NER	1	2	0
8♠	CLR	PLRS	JUR	JURS	PLR	1	1	1
9♠	VERS	VEM	MAFS	MAM	MAR	8	1	5
10♠	SAF	PLR	VER	VERS	NEF	2	3	-1
J♠	VEFS	MOF	KRMC	MOFS	VEF	7	-2	9
Q♠	KRMA	JUR	VEFS	PLF	NEFS	5	3	3
K♠	MOR	MAM	VER	MORS	MAMS	8	0	6

The Power in Work Card

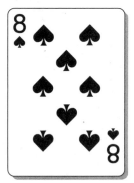

DESCRIPTION OF THE 8♠ PERSON:

As the 'Eight of Eights,' the power card of power cards, the 8♠ has the heaviest burden and obligation to use his or her power for good. All of them are tempted to take this power and use it to escape from their fears and avoid facing themselves from time to time. They are here to work and make a contribution, and ultimately this must take priority over their romantic life. These are the workers and the workaholics of the deck. Their power is expressed through action and the force of their indomitable will.

It would seem natural that those with the greatest power at their disposal would be most likely to abuse it. Merely having the gift of such power could be the justification to use it any way we choose. One might think, 'If I am given such power, it must mean that I am to use it and that I am right.'. Nothing could be further from the truth, and the 8♠, and all the other Eights for that matter, suffer from the results of actions based on that misconception.

Spades take us into the spiritual realms, though most Spade people cannot unrivet their attention from material gain and mastery. Success is almost easy for them, as long as they are willing to work for it. They know that they possess great power. The test comes in how they choose to use it. When they work from a lower sense of values, or when operating from their 'fear pattern,' they can use this power to avoid the truth and destroy themselves.

They need to be admired and will work hard for admiration and respect. They make good providers and will often try to marry those who are also of means. They are one of the few cards that always seem to come out on top financially when their marriages end. They can handle obstacles, which often serve as a measure of their true abilities. They have a profound healing power, and, if directed, can transform the lives of those they meet. Part of their life challenge involves developing a more positive attitude about life amid the changes that life is sure to bring their way. Study of spiritual subjects always brings healing and more personal freedom.

SOME OF THE 8♠ ISSUES CONCERNING RELATIONSHIPS:

The 8♠ is one of the more emotionally grounded cards in the deck and they usually do not have the indecision or restlessness that affects so many of the other cards in the deck. This gives them better than average chances of success in marriage or committed relationships. However, they are usually somewhat immature emotionally and it often takes some time for them to understand the workings of love as well as they do their work. They tend to take an intellectual or concept-based approach to love, romance, and marriage and learn by trial and experimentation. Though their work is usually a major theme in their life, they also seem to have love on their mind more than others would suspect.

They are attracted to those with whom they have great communication, and respect those who are of higher intelligence. They often find the person they are looking for while on the job. Many of them form working or financial partnerships with their mates. Finances seem to be an important issue in their choice of mates. Their practical side tells them that being with someone who has more money is

---

KARMA CARDS:

K♣   6♣

KARMA COUSINS:

2♠   2♦

PAST-LIFE CARDS:

7♠   9♠

better and they often follow this rule in their choices.

With so much power at their disposal, the 8♠ usually finds out that this same power can ruin the delicate balance that is required in a loving relationship. Those who are aware of their own personal fears have more success in relationships.

GENERALITIES BETWEEN THE PERSONALITY CARD CONNECTIONS

8♠ men are very attracted to Diamond females, but they can also fight with them a lot. Both sexes enjoy the friendship of other Spades, both male and female. Diamond males find the 8♠ of both sexes very challenging and difficult.

8♠ is a power card and will have control issues with anyone born as a Jack or higher of any suit.

The Eight of Spades that Stopped the Class

The 8♠ seems to surpass the other Eights in their ability to make things happen by sheer sense of will and determination. A few specific cases will illustrate this.

A couple of years ago I was teaching a class in Concord. Everyone had name tags on with their Birth Cards written them. One of the ladies was an 8♠. I happen to know that I am the Mars Card in the Life Path to the 8♠ person. So, I was wondering if I would inadvertently do something that would make her angry with me. About two-thirds of the way through the class she stood up with a major complaint about how I was teaching the class. The entire class literally sat still for a minute or so, breathlessly waiting to see what would happen. She had directly challenged me, and for a moment it looked like the class would just end right there. I thought for a moment and then composed an answer that seemed to address her concerns. But I was impressed at how easily she had stopped our class and forced me to come up with an answer for her question. Not many people can shut me up, especially when I am in the middle of teaching a class, but she did. A powerful lady indeed!

Another example occurred when I was working in a business of about 300 people managing a construction department

doing renovations on houses. We had strict guidelines about the work we were doing and for years I never saw anyone stray outside those boundaries. Then I began supervising an 8♠ man who came to work for our department. Though he performed his job more than adequately, he also had some personal projects that he wanted to accomplish which were very important to him. He started a huge gardening project and began involving some of our materials, and lots of his time, for his community gardening effort. In spite of everything that I and others in the company did or said to dissuade him, he succeeded in creating this huge garden project. He was always butting heads with those in authority or those he worked with in order to do what he wanted, but he did accomplish what he set out to do. So we can see this one 8♠ literally fighting against a company of 300 people and getting away with it.

This demonstrates the indomitable will that many 8♠ possess. They don't always create a feeling of cooperation and mutual support in those around them, but they do get things done. Not all of them have to fight the establishment to get what they want, but when they do, they often have enough power to pull it off. This exemplifies power and what it really means.

EIGHT OF SPADES

LIFE SPREAD CARDS

PLANETARY CARD	SYMBOL	CARD
MOON	☽	10♦
SUN (BIRTH CARD)	☀	8♠
MERCURY	☿	A♥
VENUS	♀	A♦
MARS	♂	Q♦
JUPITER	♃	5♥
SATURN	♄	3♣
URANUS	♅	3♠
NEPTUNE	♆	9♥
PLUTO	♇	7♣
RESULT (COSMIC REWARD)	♃+	5♦
COSMIC LESSON	♄+	Q♠

PLANETARY RULING CARDS

BIRTH DATE	ASTROLOGICAL RULING SIGN	PLANETARY RULING CARD
JAN 6	CAPRICORN	3♣
FEB 4	AQUARIUS	3♠
MAR 2	PISCES	9♥

Who	The Connections Between Partners					Overall Index Ratings		
8♠ with	Con1	Con2	Con3	Con4	Con5	Attraction	Intensity	Compatibility
A♥	MOR	URFS	VEF	PLFS	URF	5	-1	4
2♥	NEFS	VEM	MAM	VEFS	MAMS	8	2	5
3♥	PLFS	MOR	URFS	SAM	URF	4	3	0
4♥	CRFS	MAR	JURS	VEFS	VEF	6	3	3
5♥	JUF	CLFS	URFS	MAM	MAF	4	2	2
6♥	CRR	PLR	MAM	CRRS	VERS	5	4	0
7♥	NERS	VEMS	SAF	MARS		5	2	2
8♥	MOFS	SAF	MOF	VER	PLR	4	0	4
9♥	NEF	VEFS	MAM	PLR	VEF	7	2	4
10♥	VER	MARS	VEM	VEMS	CRRS	7	0	6
J♥	JUF	SAFS	NEFS	SAR	PLRS	1	3	0
Q♥	SAFS	VEFS	VEF	PLF	NERS	3	3	1
K♥	VER	JUMS	MORS	URRS	JUM	4	-3	6
A♣	MAM	NEFS	VEM	VEFS	VEMS	8	2	5
2♣	VER	JUMS	NERS	MOF	NER	5	-2	6
3♣	SAF	CRF	VEMS	CLR	PLRS	2	4	-1
4♣	PLR	MAF	CRR	CRRS	VERS	6	5	0
5♣	MAF	JUF	CLFS	URFS	PLR	5	4	1
6♣	KRMA	MAR	JUFS	PLF	PLFS	6	7	0
7♣	PLF	URR	MAFS	NER	URRS	5	5	-2
8♣	SAR	JUF	SAFS	NEFS	SARS	0	3	-1
9♣	VEF	SAFS	JUR	JURS	SAF	1	1	3
10♣	MAMS	URR	MAFS	MAR	JURS	6	6	0
J♣	CLRS	VEM	VER	JUR	VERS	4	-1	5
Q♣	PLFS	MOF	MOFS	PLF	URFS	7	2	1
K♣	KRMA	MAFS	URRS	PLF	PLFS	6	7	-1
A♦	VEF	NER	MOR	URFS	MORS	6	-2	7
2♦	NER	MAR	KRMC	JUFS	VEF	6	3	3
3♦	CRR	MAF	CRRS	SAF	MAFS	5	5	-1
4♦	MAM	MARS	VEM	JUF	CLFS	7	4	3
5♦	CRF	VEMS	VEM	SAF	URR	5	1	3
6♦	JUR	VEF	URF	SARS	URFS	2	-1	4
7♦	VEFS	NEF	MAM	NEFS	JUM	7	1	5
8♦	CLF	JUFS	PLF	PLFS	JUF	5	4	-1
9♦	VEM	VEMS	MAF	CRRS	CRF	8	0	6
10♦	MOF	CLF	JUFS	CLFS	VEM	6	1	4
J♦	CLRS	VEM	URF	SARS	MOR	3	0	2
Q♦	MAF	CRRS	VEM	VEMS	SAF	7	3	3
K♦	CLR	PLRS	SAF	MOFS	CLRS	1	3	-2
A♠	NERS	VER	JUMS	VERS	MARS	6	-1	5
2♠	URRS	SAF	KRMC	VERS	MAFS	1	3	-1
3♠	URF	SARS	JUR	CLRS	VEM	0	1	1
4♠	MAR	JURS	MAMS	CRFS	MAM	6	5	2
5♠	MARS	VEM	VER	MAM	MAMS	8	3	4
6♠	SAF	VERS	MORS	URRS	NEF	2	1	1
7♠	MOFS	CLR	PLRS	VER	PLR	5	0	3
8♠	SBC	MAFS	MAR	JUFS	MARS	6	7	1
9♠	MORS	SAF	VERS	JUF	URRS	3	0	4
10♠	VEFS	CRFS	SAFS	CRF	VEF	5	3	2
J♠	URR	MAFS	PLF	MAMS	MAF	6	6	-1
Q♠	CLF	JUFS	MOF	SAR	CLFS	4	2	2
K♠	JUF	SAFS	NEFS	SAR	JUFS	1	2	1

The Nines

"All good things must to come to an end."

In the natural course of the cycle of all things, both living and inanimate, there comes the time of dissolution, of ending. In the course of a lifetime, we will pass through many such cycles with things such as relationships, ideas, jobs, living locations, and personal possessions. In all these things will be a beginning, represented by an Ace, and an ending, represented by the Nine. Nine represents that stage of experience where that which was is now ending. It is much like our graduation year in high school. During that year, we are still in school but there is a knowledge that everything that has been will be gone after that year is up. It is as much a year of farewells as it is a year to celebrate our accomplishments. Graduation can be cause for celebration or for sadness and concern for our future. As with all things, our personal attitude determines how it will be experienced by each of us.

Being born a Nine is like having an entire lifetime that is like your senior year in high school. The lifetime of a Nine marks the ending of a great cycle in the person's evolution, one in which much was learned and gained by the individual, but also one which is now complete and must be allowed to fade out in preparation for a new cycle to begin. During their lifetime, Nines will inevitably have to say good-bye to people, things, ideas, lifestyles, and ways of communicating that have reached the end of their usefulness in their lives. But whether this lifetime is looked upon with joy and celebration, or with sadness and feelings of loss and trepidation about the future, will again depend upon the individual.

Nine follows the eight numerologically. Eight represents the point of fullness, the harvest season in the cycle from one to nine. Once we have tasted the fullness of the eight and harvested it for all its value to us, we enter the nine stage of death and decay. Being a Nine is sort of like the field of wheat that has already been harvested. There is nothing there but the remains of a bountiful crop.

The suit of the Nine person will give us insight into the area in which they have reached a point of fulfillment. For the 9♥, there is completion with key relationships and ways of loving others. The 9♣ will let go of beliefs, ideas about life and themselves, and ways of communicating with others. The 9♦ will find that things and people they value will be taken away or at least need to be released. The 9♠ in many ways has the strongest burden. They need to sublimate their will to the will of God. They will have to let go of power struggles with others as well as things related to their lifestyle, health, and occupation.

Like a person who is moving to a new house and holding a garage or yard sale where they sell their possessions at a fraction of what they are worth, the Nine person will be seen giving things away throughout their life. Indeed, a Nine is never truly fulfilled unless they find ways to give of themselves to others. Many of them take this to the highest level and become saviors of humanity. Many great spiritual leaders and teachers have Nines as their Birth Cards. Often it is the utter frustration with all the disappointments in their personal lives that motivates Nines to take on such cosmic or universal work. In many ways, the Nine is the opposite of the Ace. Whereas the Ace actually needs to be selfish and self-centered, the Nine cannot. Each time the Nine tries to do things just for themselves, they reap untold misery and pain. It simply goes against the grain of their soul's essence. Nine

is the second and last of the spiritual numbers, Seven being the first. Like the Seven, the Nine must follow a higher path to be completely fulfilled. And often this path is the exact opposite of what is believed and taught in our society. Thus, early life can be very confusing for the Nine person, who tries to approach life in the traditional manner and meets up with repeated failure. The conscious ones catch on quickly and realize that they are different and need different motivations in order to have a successful life.

Nines can develop strong victim-savior complexes and all of them exhibit this to some degree. Nine represents the letting go of our personal desires and identity and merging ourselves into the universal consciousness. In this regard, the Nine person often identifies themselves with a great purpose—that of saving the world in some way. Instead of just thinking of themselves and their own personal needs, the Nine person now identifies with the world at large. In their 'nine-ness' Piscean manner, they go about trying to save people in their world. They are softhearted and gentle and are there for you if you need a shoulder to cry on or someone to sympathize with your problems. They will nurse you back to health and will accept you when no one else will.

However, there are two big problems with the savior complex that many Nines exhibit. First of all, it represents a complete denial of our personal power. If a Nine person is out to save you, they are, in effect, telling you that you are incapable of taking care of yourself. Whether those words are actually used or not, that is the underlying message of saviors of all kinds. Secondly, in most of the cases, the Nine person has not yet resolved their internal conflict about their own personal needs and the needs of the world that they feel compelled to resolve as part of their life's work. A lot of confusion can occur for the Nine person because they have a hard time separating their personal motives from their universal motives. This often creates a scenario where the Nine person professes to be motivated from the purest of intentions, such as saving the world or saving individuals, when in truth they are often selfishly motivated. Just like the rest of us, Nines get afraid, and some of them thirst for power or fame or wealth. Ultimately their true motivations are revealed, or the person they are trying to save resents being labeled a failure and rebels against them. There have been some Nines who genuinely make a selfless contribution to the lives of others, and all of them experience truly selfless acts at times during their life. It is the Nine's personal challenge to make the clear distinction between their selfish and selfless actions, thoughts, and words. This is especially true right now, as we see the end of the Age of Pisces and the beginning of the Age of Aquarius. The Nine energy and the Pisces energy are one in the same. The clarity of the Aquarian energy will help all Nines make these important distinctions in their life.

Nines that are accessing the power of letting go that is inherent in their Birth Card are happy and somewhat carefree. They are giving and less attached to people and things in their life. They have a look of wisdom on their face. They understand life as no others can because they can see well beyond their personal identity to the broad picture of the universe. The compassion they exude is real and comes from having consciously passed through many endings. Their happiness is real because it is not based on the acquisition of any thing or person. It is based on the knowledge that they are in tune with the will of God and the cosmic flow.

The Universal Love Card

DESCRIPTION OF THE 9♥ PERSON:
The 9♥ is a card of great fulfillment, great loss, or both. This card, and its displacement, the 7♦, are both spiritual numbers and the fulfillment that comes is rarely personal until all personal desires are set aside and put in their proper place. This is the double Saturn card—these people cannot deviate from what is true and 'right' without swift, and sometimes bitter, rebuke. All Nines have come to settle affairs and debts from the past, to pay what they owe and move on. For the 9♥, there will be some completions or endings of key relationships that represent their completion of certain 'soul chapters.' If these endings are resisted, they will be interpreted as disappointment and loss instead of the graduations that they truly represent. Their life path is full of spiritual lessons. Those who heed the call and adhere to higher values will have seemingly blessed lives, while those who give in to their fears and escapist tendencies will suffer greatly. There are likely to be financial losses during certain periods of their life and these can be interpreted as payment of past obligations, which is what they truly are.

They are givers, endowed with great minds and hearts to share with the world. Many are found in the counseling fields out of their natural desire to give to others. They must be careful not to play the martyr and to keep it on a business basis. Their intellectual creativity is unsurpassed and can be applied to any field of science or business with great success. Part of their challenge is to use this creativity maturely and not to travel the lower path of dishonesty or cheating. The 9♥ is either a very happy, giving person or one who has suffered many disappointments in life. It is always up to the individual to manifest his or her higher side, even when working with such a spiritually challenging soul pattern.

SOME OF THE 9♥ ISSUES CONCERNING RELATIONSHIPS:
Unless operating on the higher and universal side of the nine, the people of this card can have some of the most difficult personal relationships of any card in the deck. There is bound to be loss, and it is only their attitude that can turn these losses into completions or fulfillment. They are somewhat restless emotionally and are likely to either change their minds about what kind of relationship they want or attract those who cannot make the commitment that love demands.

The 9♥ can be a very codependent card. Many of them adopt a victim-savior attitude in their personal relationships, creating a multitude of problems and making it harder to sort through the challenges when they appear. If they stop telling themselves that they are doing everything to help their partners, they can get to the truth faster and find the satisfaction they seek.

GENERALITIES BETWEEN THE PERSONALITY CARD CONNECTIONS
9♥ men are often attracted to women of the Spade suit and the 5♠ would make for a good marriage. 9♥ women are often found with other Heart males, though a Club male may also prove interesting and fruitful.

KARMA CARDS:
7♦   A♣   2♥   J♥   8♣   K♠

KARMA COUSINS:
NONE

PAST-LIFE CARDS:
8♥   10♥

The Nine of Hearts and Seven of Diamonds—Karmic Soul Twins

The 9♥ is one of four 'special' Birth Cards we call the Semi-Fixed Cards. There are two pairs of cards in this four, and each pair shares a special relationship with their other half. The 9♥ and 7♦ are one of these magical pairs and they have their own unique place among the cards. They are almost opposites in some ways and yet they are nearly identical at the same time. The 7♦ sits in the Venus/Venus position in the Life Spread, which represents pleasantness, beauty, abundance of material comforts, and pleasure. When we double this pleasure aspect, we can imagine a life that is the height of pleasure and ease, but perhaps too much so. The 9♥ sits in the Saturn/Saturn position, which is nearly the opposite of the 7♦ position. Saturn represents limitations, karmic debts, and difficult lessons to learn in life. When doubled in this manner, we can only imagine how challenging the life may be.

So we can see these two cards at nearly opposite ends of the spectrum as indicated by their position in the Life Spread. However what is unique about these cards is that each new year, their Birth Card moves to the opposite spot in the Life Spread. So, though at birth they are situated as described, in the very next year of life they switch places. The 9♥ moves to the Venus/Venus position and the 7♦ moves to the Saturn/Saturn position. This continues throughout their entire life, a phenomenon that is unique to these two cards alone and that sets them apart from the rest of the deck.

Because these two cards switch places each year, their life experiences are often very much the same. Though they experience the heights of pleasure and good fortune at times, they also experience the opposite extreme of painful lessons and challenges. There are dramatic emotional losses (9♥) just as often as there are huge financial gains (7♦). Both cards are highly spiritual, being both spiritual numbers, and their success in life depends a great deal on how much they have integrated a spiritual philosophy into their lifestyle.

When a 9♥ meets a 7♦ person, they have the potential for a very uniquely intimate relationship. Because they are so uniquely connected and share so many of the same qualities, they have the possibility to connect as few other Birth Cards can. The union of these two cards could be one of great depth and intimacy. But by the same token, because they are so much alike, the mirroring principle will be a major factor in the relationship. If they haven't yet learned to accept the various parts of their own personality, great friction could result that could keep them apart. If they have learned to love themselves, this could be a match made in heaven, one that few other cards are capable of experiencing.

LIFE SPREAD CARDS

PLANETARY CARD	SYMBOL	CARD
MOON	☽	3♠
SUN (BIRTH CARD)	☀	9♥
MERCURY	☿	7♣
VENUS	♀	5♦
MARS	♂	Q♠
JUPITER	♃	J♣
SATURN	♄	9♦
URANUS	♅	7♠
NEPTUNE	♆	2♣
PLUTO	♇	K♣
RESULT (COSMIC REWARD)	♃+	J♦
COSMIC LESSON	♄+	4♥

PLANETARY RULING CARDS

BIRTH DATE	ASTROLOGICAL RULING SIGN	PLANETARY RULING CARD
AUG 30	VIRGO	7♣
SEP 28	LIBRA	5♦
OCT 26	SCORPIO	Q♠ & K♣
NOV 24	SAGITTARIUS	J♣
DEC 22	SAG. OR CAPRICORN	J♣ OR 9♦

Celebrity Birthdays

BRIGITTE BARDOT
9/28/34 • *Actress*
ELIZABETH ASHLEY
8/30/41 • *Actress*
JACLYN SMITH
10/26/47 • *Actress*
GWYNETH PALTROW
9/28/72 • *Actress*
WILLIAM F. BUCKLEY
11/24/25 • *Author*
ED SULLIVAN
9/28/02 • *Entertainer*
HILLARY CLINTON
10/26/46 • *Senator/ Former First Lady*
FRED MACMURRAY
8/30/08 • *Actor*
BOB HOSKINS
10/26/42 • *Actor*
STANLEY LIVINGSTON
11/24/50 • *Actor*
BARBARA BILLINGSLEY
12/22/22 • *Actress*
IVAN REITMAN
10/26/46 • *Filmmaker*
LADY BIRD JOHNSON
12/22/12 • *Former First Lady*
DIANE SAWYER
12/22/46 • *Journalist*
ROBERT PARISH
8/30/53 • *Basketball Player*
TIMOTHY BOTTOMS
8/30/51 • *Actor*
KITTY WELLS
8/30/19 • *Singer*
MARCELLO MASTROIANNI
9/28/24 • *Actor*

Who	The Connections Between Partners					Overall Index Ratings		
9♥ with	Con1	Con2	Con3	Con4	Con5	Attraction	Intensity	Compatibility
A♥	URR	PLRS	SAR	URRS	JUM	0	2	-1
2♥	KRMA	NERS	PLFS	SAFS	MAM	5	7	-2
3♥	URRS	JUM	URR	PLRS	VEMS	1	0	2
4♥	CLF	SARS	CLR	SAMS	CLRS	1	6	-3
5♥	MAR	JURS	MARS	JUF	CRFS	5	4	3
6♥	MARS	VEM	PLFS	PLF	PLRS	8	5	0
7♥	VERS	MOFS	MOF	URF	NERS	6	-3	7
8♥	MOFS	URF	VERS	PLR	URRS	4	-1	5
9♥	SBC	MAM	MAMS	SAFS	SARS	5	8	-1
10♥	MORS	CRR	JUF	SARS	JURS	4	-1	5
J♥	KRMA	VEFS	SAF	CRRS	VEM	4	4	2
Q♥	MAFS	VEM	SAMS	MAF	SAM	6	6	1
K♥	JUFS	NEF	URFS	URF	MOFS	3	-1	4
A♣	KRMA	SAFS	NERS	PLFS	MAM	4	8	-3
2♣	NEF	URFS	JUFS	MORS	VER	5	-1	5
3♣	VER	NEFS	PLRS	VEF	VEFS	6	0	5
4♣	PLFS	JUF	CRFS	MARS	VEM	6	4	0
5♣	JUF	CRFS	MAR	JURS	PLFS	5	3	3
6♣	VER	CLFS	NER	VEF	VEFS	6	1	4
7♣	MOR	URFS	JUM	CLR	VEM	4	-2	5
8♣	KRMA	VEM	VEFS	SAF	CRRS	6	3	4
9♣	MAF	MAFS	VEM	CLF	PLFS	8	6	1
10♣	VERS	CLR	CLRS	JUR	CRFS	3	0	3
J♣	JUF	CRF	JURS	MORS	CRR	4	0	5
Q♣	VEMS	URRS	JUM	PLR	URR	3	-1	4
K♣	PLF	VEM	JUMS	NER	NERS	6	2	2
A♦	SAR	VEF	URR	PLRS	URRS	2	2	1
2♦	VEF	VER	CLFS	SAR	CLF	5	1	4
3♦	MARS	VEM	JUR	MAR	JURS	6	2	5
4♦	MARS	SARS	MAR	JURS	SAR	4	6	0
5♦	VEF	SAF	VER	NEFS	PLRS	4	1	3
6♦	MAF	MOF	MOFS	MAMS	CLF	8	2	4
7♦	KRMA	MAM	MAMS	PLF	NEFS	8	8	-1
8♦	MAF	CLRS	VEMS	MOR	MORS	6	2	4
9♦	SAF	JUR	VEF	VEFS	MARS	1	1	2
10♦	PLR	VEMS	MAF	CLRS	MAFS	6	3	2
J♦	CRF	JURS	MOF	JUF	JUFS	4	0	5
Q♦	JUR	SAF	SAFS	JUMS	MAR	-2	3	-1
K♦	VER	NEFS	PLRS	URF	NEF	6	1	3
A♠	VERS	NEF	URFS	VER	NEFS	6	-1	5
2♠	VEM	JUMS	URF	PLF	PLFS	5	0	3
3♠	MOF	CRF	JURS	CRFS	MAMS	6	1	5
4♠	CLR	VERS	CLF	SARS	VER	3	2	1
5♠	SARS	MORS	CRR	MARS	MOR	4	2	2
6♠	URF	VEM	JUMS	VEMS	URR	3	-2	5
7♠	URF	MOFS	NEF	PLR	URFS	4	0	3
8♠	NER	PLF	VER	CLFS	VERS	7	3	0
9♠	JUFS	URF	JUF	URR		1	-2	5
10♠	SAMS	CLF	SARS	MAFS	VEM	2	7	-3
J♠	MOR	VERS	URFS	JUM	JUR	5	-3	7
Q♠	MAF	CLRS	VEMS	PLR	MAFS	6	4	1
K♠	KRMA	SAF	CRRS	VEM	VEFS	4	5	0

9 ♣

The Universal Knowledge Card

DESCRIPTION OF THE 9♣ PERSON: This is a card of expanded consciousness. Those who have this Birth Card experience revelations about life and the truth behind what is going on here on Earth that few other cards do. These revelations come from time to time when the 9♣ person releases his or her attachment to some of their preconceived ideas and notions. It is also a card of negative thinking and any individual of this Birth Card must let go of many negative mental patterns accumulated from past lives if they are to access the inherent power in this card. There are many who succeed in letting go and many who reach the very heights of recognition through their work of giving knowledge to the world.

This is also a card of sexual enjoyment. The Q♥ Karma Card and 2♥ in Venus creates a highly sensuous side with strong romantic drives. If their sensuous side is allowed to dominate, much time and energy is wasted that could otherwise elevate them to great accomplishment.

The 9♣ is here to end a major cycle in their soul's development, a completion that should see them giving their wealth of knowledge to the world. There are some debts to be paid, especially to those of the Q♥ card and to their own families, but once these debts are paid, they can proceed with their cosmic task of enlightening the world. Financially, they do well in their own business if they don't let the pursuit of money spoil their spiritual values. They are often assisted in their

business and financial goals by successful Diamond-suited businesspeople.

Some of their life challenges revolve around honesty and integrity. They are often involved with others who are not so high in these areas, which can pull them down. They are here to learn to focus their mental power and stick to a philosophy that will guide them through the ups and downs of life.

SOME OF THE 9♣ ISSUES CONCERNING RELATIONSHIPS: The 9♣ is a loving and highly sexed individual. They actually love romance more than marriage. The 2♥ in Venus tells us that it is the love affair that they are most attracted to. Marriage is seen as more of a responsibility and duty than a goal pursued for its inherent pleasure. This may explain why so many of them have extramarital affairs or choose to just be single so that they may pursue their love interests freely. They are also very devoted to their children. They are destined to have one or more very challenging relationships in their life as they grow and learn about the responsibilities involved in a true partnership. It is also likely that they will experience one major love separation or divorce that will alter their life course.

9♣ women have a particular karma that usually results in a husband of the Diamond suit who often provides them lots of money. Their K♦ in Jupiter is the symbol for this man that most of them marry at some point in their life. The 6♦ Birth Card in particular is one that many 9♣, both male and female, are destined to be with.

The 9♣ has high love ideals and can be romantic to the extreme. Often, this fragile dream of love and their misplaced hopes and dreams come crashing against the rocks of reality, and they suffer as a result.

KARMA CARDS:

Q♥ 6♦

KARMA COUSINS:

10♠ 3♠

PAST-LIFE CARDS:

8♣ 10♣

9♣ women frequently end up with Diamond and Spade men. Diamond males usually have something to give them, while the Spade males are a constant challenge. The male 9♣ has close ties with and lots of attraction for Heart females.

The Sexy Nine of Clubs

A quick look down the list of 9♣ celebrities reveals that many of our sexiest actors and actresses possess this Birth Card. Jack Nicholson, Demi Moore, Al Pacino, and others have this unique card. Nothing about the 9♣ card itself reveals this secret about them, but the cards in their Life Path and their Karma Cards do. The foremost indicator of this is the 2♥ in Venus. First of all, we need to understand how significant the 2♥ card itself is. It is the Venus/Neptune card in the Life Spread, which is extremely significant. Venus, representing love, marriage, and sensual pleasures, finds its highest expression in the sign of Pisces, where it is considered to be 'exalted' astrologically. This tells us that the highest expression of love is the Piscean love, which is selfless and universal. The 2♥, being the Neptune/Venus card, inherently has this selfless and timeless love quality. It is the most romantic card in the deck, representing the eternal lovers and the archetypes of them. When we think of great love affairs such as Romeo and Juliet we can see them symbolized in the 2♥, the card of the lovers. This relationship has nothing to do with marriage and it is important to see this distinction. The marriage cards are typically the 4♥ and Q♥. The 9♣ person has the unique quality of being the only card in the deck who has the 2♥ in Venus. This puts the most romantic card in the position of love and romance—a powerful combination.

The second element in the 9♣ makeup is the Q♥ first Karma Card. The Q♥, besides representing marriage, is the card of sexual enjoyment and sensual pleasures. As the first Karma Card, we know that 9♣ people have challenges in this area. Many of them have a highly sensual side they might have difficulty controlling. This can also make them a bit lazy at times, as the Q♥ can mean overindulgence in sensual pleasures and an easy-going nature that dominates the personality.

When we combine these two powerful influences together, the result is often a highly sensual individual with a strong propensity for romance and sexual involvements. They tend to see relationships as vehicles for the fulfillment of these drives more than anything else. And most people who have either dated or married one of these cards will tell you that they are unusually gifted as lovers.

LIFE SPREAD CARDS

PLANETARY CARD	SYMBOL	CARD
MOON	☽	J♥
SUN (BIRTH CARD)	☀	9♣
MERCURY	☿	9♠
VENUS	♀	2♥
MARS	♂	K♥
JUPITER	♃	K♦
SATURN	♄	6♥
URANUS	♅	4♣
NEPTUNE	♆	2♦
PLUTO	♇	J♠
RESULT (COSMIC REWARD)	♃+	8♣
COSMIC LESSON	♄+	6♦

PLANETARY RULING CARDS

BIRTH DATE	ASTROLOGICAL RULING SIGN	PLANETARY RULING CARD
JAN 31	AQUARIUS	4♣
FEB 29	PISCES	2♦
MAR 27	ARIES	K♥
APR 25	TAURUS	2♥
MAY 23	GEMINI	9♠
JUN 21	GEMINI	9♠
JUL 19	CANCER	J♥
AUG 17	LEO	9♣
SEP 15	VIRGO	9♠
OCT 13	LIBRA	2♥
NOV 11	SCORPIO	K♥ & J♠
DEC 9	SAGITTARIUS	K♦

Who 9♣ with	Con1	Con2	Con3	Con4	Con5	Attraction	Intensity	Compatibility
A♥	MAFS	SAFS	VEM	SAF	MAF	3	6	-2
2♥	VEF	CLR	PLRS	MAR	SAF	4	2	2
3♥	MAFS	CRR	JUF	CRRS	URM	5	3	2
4♥	MAMS	MARS	PLR	URR	PLRS	6	6	-1
5♥	MAM	PLFS	NER	JURS	NERS	6	5	0
6♥	SAF	URF	SARS	URR	NEFS	-2	4	-4
7♥	JUR	VEFS	SAR	SARS	VEF	2	0	4
8♥	VEFS	MAMS	JUR	MAR	JURS	6	2	5
9♥	MAR	CLR	PLRS	MARS	VEM	5	5	0
10♥	VEM	VEMS	VEFS	VER	VERS	8	-3	10
J♥	MOF	VEF	JUMS	MOFS	CRF	6	-3	8
Q♥	KRMA	CLRS	PLR	PLF	NEFS	5	6	-2
K♥	MAF	CRRS	JUR	NERS	PLFS	6	4	1
A♣	CLR	PLRS	VEF	MAR	SAF	3	3	0
2♣	JUR	NERS	PLFS	SAR	MAF	4	3	1
3♣	URRS	CRFS	JUF	JUFS	CRF	3	1	3
4♣	URF	SARS	NER	JURS	SAF	0	2	0
5♣	NER	JURS	MAM	URF	SARS	3	2	2
6♣	SAR	MARS	VER	NEF	URFS	4	3	1
7♣	VERS	PLF	PLFS	VEMS	VEF	8	2	1
8♣	MOFS	CRF	MOF	VEF	JUMS	7	-1	7
9♣	SBC	CLRS	CLF	CLFS	CLR	4	6	-2
10♣	MORS	VEM	PLF	MARS	MOR	8	0	5
J♣	VEFS	VEM	VEMS	PLRS	NER	7	-2	8
Q♣	CRR	MAFS	VERS	URF	NERS	6	3	2
K♣	JUFS	VER	PLR	VERS	URRS	4	-1	5
A♦	SAFS	VEM	NEF	URFS	MAFS	3	3	0
2♦	NEF	URFS	SAR	MARS	SAFS	3	3	0
3♦	URR	NEFS	PLRS	SAF	VEMS	3	2	0
4♦	PLFS	VER	MAM	SAR	MAMS	6	5	-1
5♦	CRFS	URRS	VEF	MOFS	MAFS	5	1	3
6♦	KRMA	CLF	CLFS	PLF	NEFS	6	8	-3
7♦	MAR	CLR	PLRS	MARS	SAM	4	6	-1
8♦	JUM	VERS	VEF	VEFS	VER	5	-3	8
9♦	VEMS	CRFS	MAFS	VEM	NEF	8	2	5
10♦	VERS	CRR	MAFS	JUM	MAM	6	2	4
J♦	VEFS	NER	PLF	SAFS	CLF	5	3	1
Q♦	VEMS	URR	NEFS	PLRS	NEF	5	0	4
K♦	JUF	URRS	MAMS	URR	NEFS	3	1	3
A♠	SAR	JUR	NERS	PLFS	CLF	2	3	0
2♠	MAF	JUFS	JUR	CRFS	URRS	4	2	4
3♠	CLF	CLFS	KRMC	NEF	PLFS	6	6	-2
4♠	MARS	MORS	VEM	MAMS	MOR	8	2	5
5♠	VER	VEM	VEMS	PLFS	VERS	8	-2	7
6♠	MAF	MOR	MOF	CRR	VEMS	8	1	5
7♠	MAMS	JUF	VEFS	CLR	VERS	6	2	5
8♠	VER	JUFS	SAR	MARS	SARS	3	1	4
9♠	MOR	MAF	CRRS	CRR	VEMS	7	2	4
10♠	PLR	MAMS	KRMC	CLRS	NEF	5	5	0
J♠	PLF	VERS	MORS	VEM	VEMS	8	1	4
Q♠	JUM	VERS	VER	SAFS	MAM	3	-1	4
K♠	VEF	JUMS	MOFS	CRF	MOF	6	-2	7

Universal Values—The Giver

DESCRIPTION OF THE 9♦ PERSON:

People who are 9♦ are here to 'let go' and complete a major chapter in the evolution of their soul and personality. This entails a lot of giving to others and a willingness to release both people and material things from their life when the time comes. If they have not heeded the call to give and let go of others, money, relationships, and love, their life can be filled with disappointment and remorse. Those on the positive side are philanthropic, generous, happy, and productive. All have the opportunity to experience firsthand the heightened consciousness that comes from living a 'universal' life.

Despite losses from time to time, these people can do very well in business, especially when it involves selling or other creative enterprises. They are great at promoting things they believe in. They are great talkers and communicators. Many become counselors, if not professionally, then at least with their friends and family. If they keep their values in proper perspective, they may even attain affluence. A disregard for the higher laws, e.g., we must give in order to receive, will inevitably result in misfortune and misery. They should be careful while driving and when taking any kind of risks. They can be reckless or accident-prone on the road.

They also have great minds and many are attracted to professional work that allows them to use their intellectual abilities. Many become successful attorneys or excel in any of the communications fields due to the powerful K♣ in their Mars position. This card also gives them more success than most other Birth Cards when it comes to legal matters and disputes. The 9♦ also is unusually gifted when it comes to doing sales and promotional work. They can make more money doing sales than most anything else, though most of them choose a line of work intellectually stimulating to them.

One of the challenges of the 9♦ is to develop and use their charm and power to do good work. Many of them are destined to make great contributions to the world, often by leading others to a higher form of knowledge or understanding.

SOME OF THE 9♦ ISSUES CONCERNING RELATIONSHIPS:

9♦ like to have someone to talk to and prefer relationships with those who are witty and smart. Most of them have at least one challenging marriage of a karmic nature and there are usually responsibilities associated with family, spouses, or children. Marriage is usually karmic, or destined, and often long-lasting. They tend to have traditional values about marriage, are very giving people, and are typically easy to get along with.

The 9♦ usually sees marriage as a 'job' entailing many responsibilities, and their families are often the major source of the work they do in this lifetime.

GENERALITIES BETWEEN THE PERSONALITY CARD CONNECTIONS

Female 9♦ are often attracted to Club males, which can make for good marriage or business partners. Spade women love 9♦ men, but Diamond women find them very challenging. The female 9♦ does well with other Diamond men. The male 9♦ should always beware of female Club cards, except the J♣, who might make a good marriage partner. Both sexes should be careful around anyone possessing a Q♦ birth date, their first Karma Card. They often have unexpected and unusually challenging karmic debts with these people.

KARMA CARDS:

Q♦   5♦

KARMA COUSINS:

3♦   3♣

PAST-LIFE CARDS:

8♦   10♦

Money, 'Things,' and the Nine of Diamonds

Many 9♦ people feel as though they get the short end of the stick when it comes to money in their life. Usually, when they lend money, it is never repaid. When they go into financial partnerships, their partners seem to end up with the lion's share of the profits, or the partnership goes sour and they end up losing their investment. There can also be losses during their life because of theft or other illegal activities perpetrated on them by other people. They also never seem to win at gambling. They seem to be the ones who are always giving while others take advantage of them. This card seems to have a much higher incident of these sorts of events than the average person and often it leads the 9♦ person into believing they are cursed in some way. They feel especially singled out for financial loss and begin to believe that they are the victims of some cosmic joke.

These are all the manifestations of the Nine energy when applied to the suit of money and values. The underlying message for the 9♦ person is that they arrive on the planet with a host of value-related beliefs, ideas, concepts, needs, and personal attachments that must be let go of. Diamonds represent whatever we value in our life, or the priority of what is important to us. For the 9♦, there are things in their value system that will be realigned over the course of their life. Much of this realignment will occur through apparent losses with respect to specific things or people.

The 9♦ must develop an awareness of the universal laws being manifested in their life. Those who take a thoughtful approach to the events of their life will realize that for each thing they supposedly lose, new avenues are opening and they are getting more in touch with the cosmic flow. When they truly release their attachments, spiritual gifts are showered down upon them. They realize the beauty in releasing things in their life that are holding them back from a new and more beautiful life that is just now emerging. They begin to identify with a much larger image of themselves, one that includes the needs of others as well as their own. The result is that they are happy and enlightened, having made the transition to a more universal approach to life. This universal, rather than personal, point of view is the ultimate destination for all 9♦.

NINE OF DIAMONDS

LIFE SPREAD CARDS

PLANETARY CARD	SYMBOL	CARD
MOON	☽	J♣
SUN (BIRTH CARD)	✳	9♦
MERCURY	☿	7♠
VENUS	♀	2♣
MARS	♂	K♣
JUPITER	♃	J♦
SATURN	♄	4♥
URANUS	♅	4♦
NEPTUNE	♆	2♠
PLUTO	♇	8♥
RESULT (COSMIC REWARD)	♃+	6♣
COSMIC LESSON	♄+	6♠

PLANETARY RULING CARDS

BIRTH DATE	ASTROLOGICAL RULING SIGN	PLANETARY RULING CARD
JAN 18	CAPRICORN	4♥
FEB 16	AQUARIUS	4♦
MAR 14	PISCES	2♠
APR 12	ARIES	K♣
MAY 10	TAURUS	2♣
JUN 8	GEMINI	7♠
JUL 6	CANCER	J♣
AUG 4	LEO	9♦
SEP 2	VIRGO	7♠

Who 9♦ with	The Connections Between Partners					Overall Index Ratings		
	Con1	Con2	Con3	Con4	Con5	Attraction	Intensity	Compatibility
A♥	CLR	PLRS	JUMS	VER	PLR	2	1	1
2♥	JUM	MAFS	VERS	MAF	JUMS	5	1	4
3♥	JUMS	SAF	CLRS	JUF	SAFS	-1	2	0
4♥	SAF	PLFS	VERS	VER	PLF	3	5	-3
5♥	PLR	URF	SARS	MOR	SAR	2	2	-1
6♥	MAF	URRS	VEM	MAFS	VEFS	6	3	3
7♥	JUFS	PLF	SAFS	MAF	JUMS	3	4	-1
8♥	PLF	MOR	JUFS	CLF	PLFS	6	3	1
9♥	SAR	VERS	MAFS	JUF	VER	4	2	2
10♥	VEF	MOF	JUF	CRFS	SAR	6	-2	7
J♥	MAMS	VEFS	MAM	VEF	CLRS	7	4	4
Q♥	VERS	VER	CRRS			7	-1	6
K♥	VEF	MAMS	SAF	VEMS		5	3	3
A♣	MAFS	JUM	VERS	JUMS	MAF	5	1	4
2♣	VEF	SAFS	SAF	VEMS	VEFS	2	2	1
3♣	NER	MAR	KRMC	JURS	JUFS	5	3	3
4♣	MAF	MAFS	VEFS	JUM		7	4	3
5♣	PLR	JUM	SAR	VEFS		2	2	1
6♣	CRF	VEMS	VEM	NERS	PLFS	7	1	4
7♣	JUR	MOFS	MAM	SAF	MAMS	4	1	4
8♣	VEFS	MAMS	PLR	VEF	CLRS	6	2	4
9♣	MARS	VEM	VEMS	CRRS	VER	8	1	5
10♣	URF	MAM	PLFS	PLRS	CRR	4	5	-2
J♣	MOF	JUF	VEFS	VEF	PLF	6	-3	8
Q♣	SAF	CLRS	JUMS	MORS	URRS	0	2	-1
K♣	MAF	CRRS	NEF	URFS	VEM	6	4	2
A♦	CLR	PLRS	NERS	PLFS	MOF	4	3	-1
2♦	NERS	PLFS	CRF	VEMS	CLR	7	4	0
3♦	URRS	MAF	KRMC	CRR	MAFS	5	4	1
4♦	URF	SARS	JUF	CRFS	PLR	1	2	0
5♦	KRMA	MAR	JURS	PLF	NEFS	6	6	1
6♦	MARS	VEM	URR	NEFS	PLRS	6	2	3
7♦	VERS	SAR	MAFS	SARS	VEFS	4	2	2
8♦	MOFS	VER	JUR	JURS	MAFS	5	-3	8
9♦	SBC	CRR	MAFS	MAR	JURS	6	6	1
10♦	MORS	SAF	CLRS	VER	JUR	2	1	2
J♦	JUF	VEFS	URR	NEFS	PLRS	4	-1	6
Q♦	KRMA	CRR	MAFS	URRS	PLF	6	6	0
K♦	JUFS	NER	MOR	MORS	PLFS	5	-1	6
A♠	SAFS	JUFS	VEF	VEFS	JUF	1	1	3
2♠	NEF	URFS	CLF	CLFS	MAF	5	4	0
3♠	URR	NEFS	PLRS	MARS	VEM	4	2	1
4♠	PLFS	URF	SAF	URR	SAFS	1	5	-5
5♠	JUF	CRFS	VEF	URF	SARS	4	0	4
6♠	CLF	CLFS	NEF	URFS	NEFS	5	5	-1
7♠	MOR	JUFS	PLF	CLF	PLFS	6	1	3
8♠	VEM	VEMS	MAF	CRRS	CRF	8	0	6
9♠	CLF	CLFS	VEF	MAMS	VERS	6	5	0
10♠	VERS	SAF	VER	PLF		4	2	1
J♠	MAM	JUR	URF	CRR	URFS	3	2	2
Q♠	VER	MORS	MOFS	NEF	PLR	7	-2	8
K♠	VEFS	MAMS	PLR	VEF	CLRS	6	2	4

The Universal Life Card

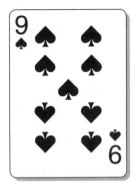

DESCRIPTION OF THE 9♠ PERSON:
This is the most potent of the universal cards, with the strongest internal urges to let go of negative patterns in their personality and lifestyle. Among these people you will find those whose lives are filled with losses, and others whose lives are filled with giving and fulfillment. All of the qualities of the other three Nines are found in this 'Nine of Nines' Birth Card. On some level, there is a very important release that must occur for them, some key aspect of their personality that must be allowed to die so that they may be reborn anew. This may be as simple as a personal health habit or work routine, or it may involve the ways they deal with relationships or finances. In some cases, it can involve all of these at the same time. These people can never completely ignore their inherent spirituality or psychic side. Those that acknowledge this important part of themselves are guided to a life of universal giving and letting go of that which no longer serves their higher interests. In this regard, some of them can make the greatest contributions to the world. This is the 'Giver of Givers' card.

Many are successful artists, teachers, or performers. The K♥ Karma and Venus Card gives them strong emotional and love power, charm, and wisdom that can bring much success with the public. Many are gifted with artistic or musical ability. This same K♥ card helps them through some of the emotional endings they are sure to encounter, giving them the wisdom to conquer their emotions and fears.

These people also have a good deal of business ability which can bring financial success if applied. However, their greatest fulfillment will come on a 'mission of love.' The broader the scope of their work, and the more they focus on giving to larger groups, the more their inherent power shines and the farther they rise to prominence on their path to the divine.

SOME OF THE 9♠ ISSUES CONCERNING RELATIONSHIPS:
The 9♠ has all the charm and emotional power to attract a mate when they want one. However, being the 'Nine of Nines,' there are bound to be losses in their life, and there can be a subtle fear that if they open up and love someone, they will lose them. Also, many 9♠ have emotional trauma early in life that leaves scars that interfere in personal relationships. However, with all the charm they possess, if a 9♠ is without a partner, know that they are keeping others away with all their might. Otherwise, they can have anything they want romantically.

The 9♠ woman is fairly strong-willed and independent, due to the K♥ Karma Card. This can make for challenges in their personal relationships. Not all men can handle such power from a female. They can easily be single parents for the same reason—any woman who is a King can be both father and mother to her children. At any rate, the 9♠ woman is not going to take too much grief from any one man, unless she is mired in codependent behavior and trying to 'save' her partner.

They are truly giving and wonderful people and their love is for groups as much as it is for the individuals in their hearts. There will be emotional endings and completions with key people in their life. However, these do not need to be translated as losses.

> **KARMA CARDS:**
> K♥ 6♠
>
> **KARMA COUSINS:**
> 2♣ 2♠
>
> **PAST-LIFE CARDS:**
> 8♠ 10♠

9♠ men have a special affinity for Heart females, a friendship that can extend to marriage. 9♠ females will meet other Spade males, with whom they share this same connection. Heart males also have a great love connection with 9♠ females. 9♠ females have strong physical attractions for Diamond males.

This Is My Last Lifetime

Have you ever met someone who told you that this is their last incarnation? I have and I have to stop myself from laughing when I do. I may not be right about this, but it would seem to me that anyone who is in their last incarnation would be a very happy person who has seen all of their dreams, desires, and wishes fulfilled. Since I haven't met anyone like that yet, I don't believe I have met anyone who is experiencing their last lifetime.

One of the first people to tell me this was a Pisces 9♠ woman. She is a book editor and organizer. She wasn't very happy, but she shared with me that she had a strong sense that this lifetime was her last here on the planet. At the time, I just sort of laughed to myself, thinking, 'sure lady, it's my last lifetime too,' but I later realized that there was some truth to what she said. Every 9♠, and even the other Nines for that matter, are here to complete a major cycle in the evolution of their soul. The 9♠ is the most potent of these Nines because Spades are the last suit. So the 9♠ has to be someone who, in this lifetime, will be making a major completion of great importance on the spiritual level. By the way, this 9♠ woman exemplified many of the positive 9♠ traits. The work she did was solely done for the benefit it would bring others. She received absolutely none of the recognition for her valuable contributions and instead chose for it all to go to the authors for whom she worked.

This means on the practical level that this will be the last lifetime for the 9♠ person to be doing certain kinds of work and to be living a certain kind of lifestyle. Remember that spades are associated with our work, health, and lifestyle—the things that we do each day and each year. In terms of doing, each 9♠ person will be making numerous completions of some of these things as their life progresses. So, in effect, this is their last lifetime for certain parts of their life, and I now believe that this woman was intuiting this but misinterpreting what she perceived.

The 9♥ is here to complete and let go of certain relationships and ways of being in relationships that are no longer appropriate for their evolution. The 9♣ is here to complete and let go of certain ways of thinking and communicating that are no longer helpful to them. The 9♦ is here to let go of certain desires and values and ways of making money that have outlived their usefulness. The 9♠ can encompass all of these and more. Spades have always been the strongest suit. When we get Spades in our life path, they will affect our lifestyle and the things we do. Therefore, the 9♠ person has much more to let go of and complete than the other Spades. To them, it could seem like their entire existence is coming to an end. But we must remember that every ending is a graduation. The 9♠ is preparing for a new life that is much healthier and happier. It only seems sad when they focus their attention on all the things in their life that seem to end.

LIFE SPREAD CARDS

PLANETARY CARD	SYMBOL	CARD
MOON	☽	9♣
SUN (BIRTH CARD)	☀	9♠
MERCURY	☿	2♥
VENUS	♀	K♥
MARS	♂	K♦
JUPITER	♃	6♥
SATURN	♄	4♣
URANUS	♅	2♦
NEPTUNE	♆	J♠
PLUTO	♇	8♣
RESULT (COSMIC REWARD)	♃+	6♦
COSMIC LESSON	♄+	4♠

PLANETARY RULING CARDS

BIRTH DATE	ASTROLOGICAL RULING SIGN	PLANETARY RULING CARD
JAN 5	CAPRICORN	4♣
FEB 3	AQUARIUS	2♦
MAR 1	PISCES	J♠

Who 9♠ with	Con1	Con2	Con3	Con4	Con5	Attraction	Intensity	Compatibility
A♥	VER	SAFS	MAFS	NEFS	MAF	4	4	1
2♥	MOR	URFS	JUR	MOF	CRFS	4	-2	6
3♥	NEFS	VER	SAFS	CLR	VEF	4	2	2
4♥	PLFS	SAM	CLF	SARS	MORS	3	7	-5
5♥	CRFS	PLR	PLRS	JUR	CRF	4	4	0
6♥	JUF	CLFS	URFS	SAF	NER	2	2	1
7♥	SAR	SAMS	URR	PLRS	NER	0	5	-3
8♥	SAMS	VERS	SAR	SARS	VER	1	4	-1
9♥	JUR	JURS	URR	VEMS	URF	1	-2	6
10♥	JUM	MAMS	MAR	JURS	CRF	5	3	3
J♥	VER	JUFS	PLF	JUR	VERS	5	-1	5
Q♥	MORS	CRR	MOF	MOFS	MOR	7	-2	8
K♥	KRMA	VEF	SAFS	NEF	NEFS	5	4	2
A♣	MOR	URFS	JUR	MORS	URF	4	-2	6
2♣	URR	PLRS	KRMC	VEF	SAFS	2	3	1
3♣	MAM	JUMS	MAF	CRRS	MAFS	6	4	1
4♣	SAF	PLR	JUF	CLFS	URFS	0	4	-3
5♣	PLR	CRFS	SAF	CLR	SAFS	2	6	-4
6♣	MOFS	URF	URFS	JUM	MOF	3	-2	5
7♣	MAR	JUFS	VEFS	VEM	NEF	6	1	6
8♣	PLF	VER	JUFS	URF	PLFS	5	2	1
9♣	MOF	CRF	VEMS	MAR	CRFS	8	1	5
10♣	NEF	PLR	VEFS	CLF	SARS	5	3	2
J♣	JUM	MAMS	MAFS	JUMS	URR	5	3	2
Q♣	CLR	NEFS	VEM	VEMS	NEF	6	0	4
K♣	JUR	NERS	PLFS	MOFS	NER	5	1	3
A♦	MAFS	URF	VER	SAFS	VERS	4	3	1
2♦	URF	MAFS	JUF	JUR	URFS	3	1	3
3♦	NER	PLF	JUF	CLFS	URFS	5	3	0
4♦	MAR	JURS	CRFS	JUR	SAR	4	3	3
5♦	MAM	JUMS	MAMS	VEFS	CLR	6	3	3
6♦	CRF	VEMS	MOF	URRS	NEF	7	0	5
7♦	JUR	URR	VEMS	JURS	URF	2	-2	5
8♦	VEFS	VEM	MAFS	MAR	JUFS	7	1	7
9♦	CLRS	CLR	VER	NERS	VEFS	3	1	2
10♦	VEM	CLR	MAFS	CLF	CRRS	6	2	3
J♦	URRS	JUM	MAMS	JUMS	URR	2	1	2
Q♦	CLRS	NER	PLF	VER	NERS	5	3	0
K♦	MAF	CRRS	MAM	JUMS	VERS	7	4	1
A♠	URR	PLRS	SAR	PLR	SARS	1	3	-2
2♠	NERS	PLFS	KRMC	SAR	MARS	5	5	-1
3♠	URRS	CRF	VEMS	MARS	VEM	5	2	3
4♠	CLF	SARS	PLFS	SAM	PLF	3	7	-5
5♠	MAR	JURS	SAR	MOFS	CRF	4	3	2
6♠	KRMA	SAR	MARS	NEF	NEFS	5	6	0
7♠	VERS	MAF	CRRS	SAMS	MAM	6	4	2
8♠	MOFS	JUR	SAR	VEFS	NER	4	-1	6
9♠	SBC	VEF	SAFS	SAR	MARS	3	5	0
10♠	MORS	CRR	PLFS	SAM	PLF	6	3	1
J♠	NEF	PLR	VEFS	MAR	JUFS	6	2	3
Q♠	MAFS	VEM	VEFS	MAR	VEMS	8	2	5
K♠	JUFS	PLF	VER	JUF	NEFS	5	1	4

The Tens

To truly understand the Tens, we must also be familiar with the Aces, because these two cards are very much alike and share important qualities. The Ten even has the familiar One in the front of its name. This alone should be a clue to the student of the cards as to the nature of the people of these cards. Like the Aces, Tens possess a lot of drive and ambition. Also like the Aces, Tens can be very self-centered or selfish. This can be evidenced further by the realization that all of the Tens have at least one Ace in a prominent position in their Life Spread. The 10♥ and 10♦ both have the A♥ and A♦ in their Life Spread. The 10♣ has the A♣ and the 10♠ has the A♠. These Aces cause the Tens to be on a soul search over the course of their life. They turn their attention upon themselves to find answers and reasons for the value of their life. To others, this can show up as selfishness. While they are focused upon their own feelings, thoughts, needs, and desires, the Ten may not pay much attention to others in their environment. Indeed, many Tens look upon themselves as selfish, and it is an important personal issue that they must come to terms with during the course of their lifetime. Are they truly selfish? Is being selfish really a bad thing? Is there such a thing as good selfishness? Is there a way to balance out the needs of others with their own? These are all questions they must answer for themselves.

The main difference between Tens and Aces is the Zero after the One and what that represents. Just as an Eight is two Fours, the Ten can be looked upon as two Fives. Five being the number of experience, the Ten person has a great deal of experience they can draw upon for success. This Zero represents the experience of completing a major cycle of evolution, going all the way from the Ace through the Nine and now to the Ten, where a new cycle begins. However, in this new cycle, the Ten will carry with it all of the wisdom that was acquired in the previous cycle. This explains why the Tens have such a capacity for success in their life. All Tens have great success potential and many rise to prominence if that is what they desire. Their suit will tell us the main area of their wisdom and success in this lifetime. The 10♥ has a command over people or children. The 10♣ arrived here with a head full of knowledge to share with the world. The 10♦ can handle a business with ease, the larger the better, and the 10♠ has the drive to accomplish anything they set their minds to. They are unparalleled workers and achievers. Unlike the Aces, the Tens don't have to learn very much to achieve success. They do like to learn new things, but they already possess a great deal of experience which they discover as they apply themselves to their careers.

The Zero is also the number we associate with the Joker. The Joker is the only card in the deck which has no personal identity of its own. Instead, the Joker borrows identities from other cards and can essentially become that card for whatever length of time he or she chooses. The Ten person also has this capacity to some extent. They have all the numbers from Ace through Nine already under their belt. They understand all the principles and abilities of these numbers and can implement their qualities at will. It is interesting to note that two of the Tens, the 10♣ and 10♥, have Jacks as their first Karma Cards. These Jacks act much like the Joker, the Joker being the Jack of all Jacks in the deck, or the 'super Jack.' With Jacks as Karma Cards, and with the other Tens having Jacks in their Life Path, we see that Tens and Jacks have some strong connection that may further connect them to the Joker and its propensity for multiple personalities.

The downside of being a Ten is that they can become obsessive with respect to something about their suit. The 10♥ can be obsessed with their families, or with their audiences if they are performers. 10♣ have difficulty sleeping at night because their heads are so full of thoughts and ideas. The 10♦ can make money the most important thing in their life and the 10♠ can be the world's worst workaholic and Type A personality. This obsession can become destructive in some cases. Tens can be very 'all or nothing' kinds of people. When they pursue something, they go full tilt. Then they crash as they go to the opposite extreme. They can get hooked on harmful things because 'all or nothing' is an addictive-prone personality type.

We can relate Tens to the 10th house of the Astrological chart. The 10th house is governed by Saturn and is concerned with reputation and career. Many Tens, it will be noted, have either strong 10th house planets or planets in Capricorn, or they are aspected by Saturn in their natal charts. This creates a drive for prominence and achievement, and in some cases an emotional need for attention and recognition. It is part of the Ten's life work to understand this drive and to come to terms with it. Yes, Tens can achieve great things, things that we may applaud them for, but the real question they must answer is whether they did it for the right reasons. Only they know the answer to this. If approached consciously, their work will bring additional happiness to them and those around them. If not, it will cause one problem after another and deprive them of the real goal for which they were working. Tens, like the rest of us, are seeking inner contentment and peace. In their case, this seems to come through the avenue of achievement, success, recognition, and respect. Over the course of their life they will learn that even these qualities must come from within.

Success with Groups

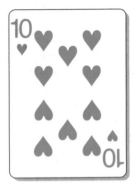

DESCRIPTION OF THE 10♥ PERSON:

Like the A♥, these people have much ambition in their life and could stray off the path of truth as a result. However, they have already experienced the truth and they have this knowledge as their birthright to guide them each step of the way. They are creative and usually artistic. They are leaders, not followers. They love children and groups of people, who they may regard as their children or audience. They are either in a field where they can perform in front of others or are surrounded by many family and social concerns. In either case, they are surrounded by the ten hearts signified by their birth card.

The 10♥, having two Aces in their Life Path and being part Ace themselves (1 + 0 = 10), have a strong need to explore themselves to determine what is most important to them personally in life. Because many of them are so self-engrossed in this process, others may see them as selfish or self-centered. However, only those who make acquisition of money and things their primary goal manifest this selfishness to the exclusion of other's needs. For the most part, 10♥ value their relationships higher than most other things on their list and are considerate and kind.

Honesty is an important issue with this card, whether it is just to be more honest to themselves or to develop a philosophy that overrides all the ups and downs that tempt them to be less than forthright in their communications with others. Until they make this commitment to personal truth, their life can be a complex mire of stories upon stories. In this case, much energy is expended to maintain the illusions they create. This energy could be better spent in productive forms of self-expression and leadership.

They are innovators and they can make a great contribution in their chosen field as long as they exercise clarity in their judgment. Their motives can either be humanitarian or selfish, and this usually has a lot to do with their ultimate destination. They are independent and often impulsive, but this is usually kept in balance by their wisdom. They can make a unique mark on the world through the application of their inherent gifts. They are usually gentle and wise people, or at least the wisdom will be there. Their wisdom is their protector and guiding light.

SOME OF THE 10♥ ISSUES CONCERNING RELATIONSHIPS:

10♥ have 'power in love' and are attracted to those of power. They are also not afraid to work for the love they want in their personal relationships. They are charming and well-liked. They will make the first move to start a relationship and then are willing to work for it. This can be just the winning formula for success in love or marriage. These people have basically good karma in love, but there can be some indecisiveness that may lead to problems. Relationships with Diamond women are often karmic and difficult, as these women remind them of some of this indecision and fickleness.

10♥ are very smart people, and when they apply their mental power and creative energy to the area of love, it can get them into trouble when they try too hard to make things turn out as they plan. Love cannot be planned and manipulated in the same way that we plan out our daily schedule. Often there is the need to

---

KARMA CARDS:

J♣   5♠

KARMA COUSINS:

J♦   4♦

PAST-LIFE CARDS:

9♥   J♥

---

learn to feel things in matters of love instead of thinking them out.

GENERALITIES BETWEEN THE PERSONALITY CARD CONNECTIONS

10♥ males are often attracted to Club women and both sexes would do better to avoid Diamond women. Try this out for a motto: 'Just say no to Q♦ women.' The 10♥ woman is a great challenge for most Diamond males as well. Spade males benefit from associations with 10♥ people of both sexes. A 10♥ male and certain Spade females could make a good marriage.

Wesley Snipes—The Ten of Hearts

The 10♥ has a lot of traits from its first Karma Card, the J♣. Wesley Snipes is a good example of this—you must take a closer look at the J♣ to fully appreciate it. Keep in mind that usually our first Karma Card represents qualities we possess that tend to be expressed negatively. However, positive aspects are expressed as well. Snipes gets his boyish masculinity and good looks from his J♣ first Karma Card. The most masculine cards in the deck are the Aces, Tens, Jacks, and Kings. Having both a Ten and Jack for two of the significators guarantees a strong, masculine personality and physique, which serves Snipes very well as a hero in movies such as *The Art of War* (2000), *Passenger 57* (1992), and *Blade* (1998), and he is also a very likable ladies' man.

One outstanding trait of the J♣ is their strong mentality and often argumentative nature. This is a card of genius and often a photographic memory. The negative side is a tendency toward very fixed ideas. Many J♣ men have very fixed ideas about love and marriage. They will have huge expectations for the women in their life to live up to, most of all after they are married. In 1997, Snipes was quoted as saying, "I don't understand the mandate of being together forever. The idea that you should do that is wrong. It makes us slaves to a societal mandate. You can still love, but it doesn't mean you have to be tethered to the flesh." This is a very J♣, conceptual attitude toward marriage. He also has a progressive nature, which is very J♣-like. He insisted that the role of Mimi (played by Ming-Na), his character's wife in the film *One Night Stand* (1997), be played by an Asian woman in order to "push the boundaries of racial-sexual taboos." In 2003, Wesley married Nikki Park, the mother of his second child, who is Asian. So it seems that Wesley often tries to push what are considered to be social norms. This is a very Aquarian trait, which we commonly associate again with the J♣.

Another trait of the J♣ is their argumentative nature. J♣ actually enjoy debates and are often seen as those who initiate arguments of all kinds. Taken to extremes, these can become rivalries and conflicts. For his part, Wesley Snipes has been involved in more than his share of legal battles, likely because of this very trait.

But above all else, 10♥ love having an audience and the presence of groups around them. Being an actor is a perfect place to have this desire fulfilled. And this is where they differ from those of the J♣ Birth Card. Though sociable, the J♣ does not make this area as high of a priority in their life. 10♥ people will always make sure they have a crowd surrounding them.

LIFE SPREAD CARDS

PLANETARY CARD	SYMBOL	CARD
MOON	☽	4♠
SUN (BIRTH CARD)	☀	10♥
MERCURY	☿	10♦
VENUS	♀	8♠
MARS	♂	A♥
JUPITER	♃	A♦
SATURN	♄	Q♦
URANUS	♅	5♥
NEPTUNE	♆	3♣
PLUTO	♇	3♠
RESULT (COSMIC REWARD)	♃+	9♥
COSMIC LESSON	♄+	7♣

PLANETARY RULING CARDS

BIRTH DATE	ASTROLOGICAL RULING SIGN	PLANETARY RULING CARD
JUL 31	LEO	10♥
AUG 29	VIRGO	10♦
SEP 27	LIBRA	8♠
OCT 25	SCORPIO	A♥ & 3♠
NOV 23	SAGITTARIUS	A♦
DEC 21	SAG. OR CAPRICORN	A♦ OR Q♦

Celebrity Birthdays

SAMUEL L. JACKSON
12/21/48 • Actor
INGRID BERGMAN
8/29/15 • Actress
GERALDINE CHAPLIN
7/31/44 • Charlie's Daughter
ANDY DICK
12/21/65 • Comedian/ Actor
HARPO MARX
11/23/1893 • Comedian
CHARLIE PARKER
8/29/20 • Jazz Musician
HELEN REDDY
10/25/42 • Singer
MICHAEL JACKSON
8/29/58 • Singer
CHRIS EVERT
12/21/54 • Tennis Player
CARL BANKS
8/29/62 • Football Player
SHAUN CASSIDY
9/27/59 • Singer
MEATLOAF
9/27/47 • Singer
MARION ROSS
10/25/36 • Actress
JANE FONDA
12/21/37 • Actress
STEVE KERR
9/27/65 • Basketball Player
ANNE TYLER
10/25/41 • Author
J. K. ROWLING
7/31/65 • Author
BOB KNIGHT
10/25/40 • Basketball Coach
PHIL DONAHUE
12/21/35 • Talk Show Host
FLORENCE GRIFFITH-JOYNER
12/21/59 • Athlete
WILL PERDUE
8/29/65 • Basketball Player

Who 10♥ with	Con1	Con2	Con3	Con4	Con5	Attraction	Intensity	Compatibility
A♥	MAF	CRRS	JUF	NERS	CLR	6	3	2
2♥	CLR	PLRS	JUFS	JUF	CLFS	2	1	1
3♥	NERS	MAF	CRRS	MAFS	CRR	7	5	1
4♥	URRS	MOF	URF	VEF	URR	3	-1	4
5♥	URF	SARS	PLFS	NER	PLF	2	4	-3
6♥	NER	JURS	URR	NEFS	MAM	4	1	3
7♥	MARS	VEM	VEMS	VERS	VER	8	0	6
8♥	VERS	MARS	VEM	VEMS	CRF	8	0	6
9♥	MOFS	CRF	JUFS	JUR	SAFS	5	0	5
10♥	SBC	VERS	VEF	VEFS	VER	6	1	6
J♥	MORS	CLRS	VEMS	MAR	MOR	6	-1	6
Q♥	VEFS	VEM	VEMS	URR	SAFS	6	-2	7
K♥	CRR	MAFS	SAFS	VEM	VEMS	5	4	1
A♣	JUFS	CLR	PLRS	SAF	CLRS	1	2	1
2♣	SAFS	VEM	VEMS	CRR	MAFS	3	2	2
3♣	NEF	URFS	MARS	PLR	URR	5	3	1
4♣	URR	NEFS	PLFS	NER	JURS	5	2	0
5♣	PLFS	URF	SARS	URR	NEFS	3	4	-3
6♣	CRFS	VEF	SAR	CLF	SARS	4	3	1
7♣	CLF	CLFS	MAMS	JUR	VEFS	5	5	-1
8♣	MAR	MORS	CLRS	VEMS	MARS	7	2	4
9♣	VEM	VEMS	VEFS	VER	VERS	8	-3	10
10♣	JUF	JUR	VEFS	MOF	MOFS	4	-3	9
J♣	KRMA	VERS	PLF	PLFS	NEF	7	5	0
Q♣	MAF	NERS	MOR	MORS	NER	8	2	4
K♣	VEMS	MAR	VEF	JUF	VEFS	7	0	7
A♦	JUF	SAR	MAF	CRRS	CRR	3	3	2
2♦	SAR	CRFS	JUF	JUFS	MAM	2	3	1
3♦	MAM	NER	JURS	SAF	SAFS	3	4	0
4♦	VEF	URF	KRMC	SARS	NEF	4	1	4
5♦	MARS	VER	NEF	URFS	NEFS	7	2	3
6♦	VER	VEM	VEMS	PLF	JUMS	7	-2	7
7♦	MOFS	CRF	JUFS	JUF	CRFS	6	0	6
8♦	MAMS	VEM	CLF	CLFS	CLRS	7	5	1
9♦	VER	SAF	JURS	MARS	MOR	3	1	2
10♦	MOR	MAF	VEM	VEMS	PLRS	8	0	6
J♦	PLF	JUMS	KRMC	VERS	SAF	5	3	0
Q♦	SAF	JURS	MAM	VER	PLR	1	3	0
K♦	PLR	NEF	URFS	MAF	URF	4	3	0
A♠	MARS	VEM	VEMS	SAFS	SAM	5	3	3
2♠	MAR	SARS	MAM	MAMS	VEMS	5	7	0
3♠	PLF	JUMS	VER	SAR	VERS	5	2	1
4♠	MOF	JUF	URRS	VEF	MOFS	5	-3	7
5♠	KRMA	VEF	PLF	PLFS	NEFS	7	5	1
6♠	SARS	MAM	MAMS	MAR	MARS	5	7	-1
7♠	PLR	VERS	VEF	VEFS	MAF	6	0	4
8♠	VEF	VEMS	CRFS	MAFS	VEM	8	0	7
9♠	CRR	MAFS	SARS	MAM	MAMS	5	6	0
10♠	URRS	VEFS	URR	SAFS	URF	1	0	1
J♠	JUR	VEFS	CLF	CLFS	JUF	4	0	4
Q♠	VEM	MOR	MAMS	MOF	NEFS	8	-1	8
K♠	CLRS	VEMS	MAR	MORS	CLR	5	1	4

10 ♣

Mental Accomplishment

DESCRIPTION OF THE 10♣ PERSON:

The 10♣ is a very independent person. Regardless of sex, they will act as though they are a King or a Queen. The females have masculine minds and natures, and all want complete and unrestrained freedom to do what they choose, when they choose it. The 10♣ have come full circle in their quest for knowledge. They have a powerful mind and a consuming desire for more knowledge that makes them progressive and usually very successful. In this life, they must learn to regain the control over their mind, which has developed somewhat of a life of its own. Many 10♣ complain of having trouble sleeping because of the endless chatter of their marvelous mental equipment. The best path back to self-mastery is to direct the mind into right motives, higher principles, and hard work. They need to work hard and keep busy to be happy.

The 3♥ in Mars makes for emotional restlessness and undecidedness about their choice of occupation, which can be a strain on relationships and hold them back from achieving their highest ambitions. The 3♦ challenge card also bears this out and tells us that they will be doing much experimenting as they work to find out what really satisfies them.

The J♠ Karma Card can be a blessing or a curse, depending upon how it is manifested by the 10♣ person. It is the card of the 'Actor,' but also of the 'Thief' and the 'Spiritual Initiate.' The potential is there for great success in the arts, involvement with spiritual subjects and study, but also for using their gifts in a less than honest way.

The strong desire for spiritual wisdom and study of spiritual philosophies will bring contact with many uplifting groups and will increase their enjoyment of life. Their greatest fulfillment will come through work that allows them some freedom and expression of their creativity. Their greatest challenge lies in making up their mind about which way to go or what it is that will truly satisfy them.

SOME OF THE 10♣ ISSUES CONCERNING RELATIONSHIPS:

Being so independent, powerful, and creative, the 10♣ usually has some difficulty in establishing a long–term relationship. Look at Madonna, Barbra Streisand, and Shirley MacLaine as perfect examples of this. The ones who realize the success potential of their card may just be better off being single and admitting that right up front. However, there is an undeniable thirst for love, and love has its own truth with which they must contend. Love always wants more of itself, and it wants more intimacy, which brings greater pleasure and feelings of union. For most people, this requires making a commitment, and this is where the 10♣ has the challenge. It is either them or their partner who cannot make a choice to have just one person.

10♣, regardless of their sex, have such strong career and work drive that few if any would sacrifice this for the sake of a personal relationship. The ones that do find satisfaction in marriage manage to maintain their careers while their husbands or wives take care of the domestic responsibilities. The female 10♣, because the Q♣ in their Saturn position of their Life Path, have some emotional issues that make it difficult to achieve any depth of intimacy with their partners. That,

---

KARMA CARDS:

J♠   4♠

KARMA COUSINS:

7♣   4♥

PAST-LIFE CARDS:

9♣   J♣

combined with their highly independent and willful natures often precludes marriage and long-term relationships.

Usually the 10♣ has a short attention span when it comes to personal relationships. The Threes in Mars and Pluto make them variety-prone and likely to change frequently. They have the desire to experience many different relationships or multiple relationships at the same time.

It is important to realize that the 10♣ can have whatever they want in personal relationships. The K♠ in their Venus position tells us that they, more than any other card in the deck, can become the master of their emotions and basically choose whatever they want in romance and marriage. It is mostly a matter of

interest and personal commitment that separates those who have successful marriages from those who don't. For the most part, the world is theirs for the taking.

GENERALITIES BETWEEN THE PERSONALITY CARD CONNECTIONS

10♣ women are usually attracted to men of power or high standing, especially males of the Spade suit. The men should avoid women of their own suit, as it is likely to be a heavy karmic relationship with a great price or burden. 10♣ females don't get along with other Club females. 10♣ females are very difficult for most Heart males, though Diamond males receive some blessings from them.

The Ten of Clubs's Quest for the Right Occupation

Most 10♣ people are somewhat restless in both their love life and their career ambitions. Remember that Tens are much like Aces, the Ace is a One and the Ten is a One with a Zero. But the 10♣ has some additional factors that make them even more restless, such as the 3♥ in Mars and the 3♦ Pluto Card. Not only that, but their card sits in the Crown Line of the Grand Solar Spread alongside the 8♦ and K♠. All the cards there are very independent by nature, but the 10♣ is the most restless of them all.

The Threes in their Life Spreads make them inquisitive. They want to try out different sorts of things. This same Three energy can bring great indecision over their choice of occupation and romantic partners. Florence Campbell, coauthor of *Sacred Symbols of the Ancients*, says that more than any other card in the deck, the 10♣ has a need to establish what is their choice of occupation if they are ever to know any success or satisfaction in their lives. Being such an independent and powerful person can actually be a handicap in this area. It is kind of like being a kid in a candy store. There are so many options that it becomes overwhelming.

There are many successful 10♣ people in the world, and among them we find one common thread—they all know what their life's work is and are committed to doing it. Of all the cards in the deck, the 10♣ has some of the greatest potential for success. Barbara Streisand, Diana Ross, Madonna, Kim Basinger, Luciano Pavarotti, and Shirley MacLaine are all 10♣, just to

mention a few. All it takes is a commitment to one path for this success to materialize. I have been asked many times by 10♣ people the same question: 'What sort of work should I do?' So many of them have this eternal question that seems to plague them and is the one insurmountable block that keeps them from the success that they know is their birthright. It almost appears that there are two kinds of 10♣ people—the successful ones who have made a commitment to some direction in their work and the unsuccessful ones who haven't. The solution for the ones who are still asking the eternal question is to just get started doing something and make a success of it. The question of what should we do in our work can often become an excuse to not do anything. If the 10♣ just gets started being a success at what they are already doing, chances are that it will lead them to the realization of what sort of work would be most fulfilling for them. Usually this work will involve a lot of creative expression and the dissemination of knowledge to others. It also usually involves them becoming a leader in some way, because these are the natural traits of the 10♣.

This is one of the most creative cards in the deck. Creative people need outlets for personal expression as well as some variety. They detest monotony and boredom. An occupation that has many dimensions to it and allows for a lot of creativity or expression is the one best suited to 10♣. They also have a thirst for knowledge that often leads them to a love for books.

LIFE SPREAD CARDS

PLANETARY CARD	SYMBOL	CARD
MOON	☽	Q♥
SUN (BIRTH CARD)	✳	10♣
MERCURY	☿	8♦
VENUS	♀	K♠
MARS	♂	3♥
JUPITER	♃	A♣
SATURN	♄	Q♣
URANUS	♅	10♠
NEPTUNE	♆	5♣
PLUTO	♇	3♦
RESULT (COSMIC REWARD)	♃+	A♠
COSMIC LESSON	♄+	7♥

PLANETARY RULING CARDS

BIRTH DATE	ASTROLOGICAL RULING SIGN	PLANETARY RULING CARD
JAN 30	AQUARIUS	10♠
FEB 28	PISCES	5♣
MAR 26	ARIES	3♥
APR 24	TAURUS	K♠
MAY 22	TAURUS OR GEMINI	K♠ OR 8♦
JUN 20	GEMINI	8♦
JUL 18	CANCER	Q♥
AUG 16	LEO	10♣
SEP 14	VIRGO	8♦
OCT 12	LIBRA	K♠
NOV 10	SCORPIO	3♥ & 3♦
DEC 8	SAGITTARIUS	A♣

Celebrity Birthdays

ALAN ARKIN
3/26/34 • Actor
CHET ATKINS
6/20/24 • Actor
GENE HACKMAN
1/30/30 • Actor
JAMES CAAN
3/26/39 • Actor
LAURENCE OLIVIER
5/22/07 • Actor
HUGH JACKMAN
10/12/68 • Actor
TIMOTHY HUTTON
8/16/60 • Actor
LEONARD NIMOY
3/26/31 • Actor/Director
JAMES CAMERON
8/16/54 • Filmmaker
FAITH FORD
9/14/64 • Actress
JENNIFER GREY
3/26/60 • Actress
KIM BASINGER
12/08/53 • Actress
SHIRLEY MACLAINE
4/24/34 • Actress
BARBRA STREISAND
4/24/42 • Actress/Singer
NICOLE KIDMAN
6/20/67 • Actress
JOHN GLENN
7/18/21 • Astronaut
TENNESSEE WILLIAMS
3/26/11 • Author
SAMMY DAVIS, JR.
12/8/25 • Entertainer
NAOMI CAMPBELL
5/22/70 • Actress
STEVE TYLER
3/26/48 • Lead Singer–Aerosmith
JIM MORRISON
12/8/43 • Musician
LUCIANO PAVAROTTI
10/12/35 • Opera Singer
DIANA ROSS
3/26/44 • Singer/Actress
MADONNA
8/16/58 • Singer

Who 10♣ with	The Connections Between Partners					Overall Index Ratings		
	Con1	Con2	Con3	Con4	Con5	Attraction	Intensity	Compatibility
A♥	JUFS	JUM	MAF	NEF	PLR	4	0	4
2♥	MAFS	JUF	CRRS	CLFS	URR	5	3	2
3♥	MAF	SAF	VEFS	SAFS	NEF	3	6	-1
4♥	NER	URF	KRMC	URFS	MAF	4	2	1
5♥	MAMS	URR	NEFS	PLRS	NEF	6	4	1
6♥	MAR	URRS	PLF	URFS	PLFS	5	5	-2
7♥	CLF	VEM	JUR	CRF	CRFS	5	2	3
8♥	JUR	CLF	VEM	CLFS	VEMS	4	1	3
9♥	VEFS	CLFS	JUF	CRRS	CLF	5	1	4
10♥	JUR	MORS	VER	MARS	JUF	5	-2	7
J♥	VEMS	VEF	VERS	CRR	VEM	7	-3	8
Q♥	MOF	URF	MOFS	VEM	VEMS	6	-3	7
K♥	CLRS	CLR	PLRS	SAR	PLR	1	3	-2
A♣	JUF	CRRS	MAFS	CLFS	MAF	5	3	2
2♣	CLR	PLRS	CRF	CLRS	JUFS	3	3	-1
3♣	SAR	NERS	PLFS	VEMS	PLF	4	4	-1
4♣	URRS	NEF	SARS	MAR	VER	3	3	1
5♣	NEF	SARS	MAMS	URRS	MAM	4	4	0
6♣	MAR	JURS	MAMS	SAFS	MAM	4	6	1
7♣	MARS	MOR	KRMC	MAM	VER	7	3	4
8♣	VERS	VEMS	VEF	MOR	VER	7	-3	9
9♣	MOFS	VEM	MOF	CRFS	PLR	8	-2	8
10♣	SBC	MAM	NEF	PLFS	MAR	7	7	0
J♣	MORS	PLR	VERS	JUR	JURS	5	-1	6
Q♣	SAF	VEFS	MAF	MAMS	SAFS	3	5	-1
K♣	CRR	MAFS	SAR	NER	MAMS	5	5	0
A♦	JUFS	JUM	SAFS	PLF	SAF	1	2	1
2♦	SAFS	MAR	JURS	JUFS	JUM	1	4	0
3♦	PLF	URFS	MAR	VEF	VEFS	6	4	0
4♦	URR	NEFS	PLRS	VER	MARS	4	2	2
5♦	PLFS	URR	SAR	NERS	SARS	3	5	-3
6♦	CRFS	MOFS	VEM	VEF	MOF	8	0	7
7♦	CLFS	VEFS	JUF	CRRS	VEF	5	1	4
8♦	MOR	MARS	CRRS	PLFS		7	3	3
9♦	URR	PLFS	MAM	PLRS	CRF	5	5	-2
10♦	SAF	VEFS	VEF	NERS	PLFS	3	2	1
J♦	PLR	VERS	MORS	URRS	PLRS	5	0	3
Q♦	PLF	URFS	URR	CRF	URRS	4	4	-2
K♦	VEMS	SAR	NERS	PLFS	JUR	4	1	2
A♠	CRF	CLF	VEM	CLR	PLRS	6	4	1
2♠	SAR	NER	VER	CRR	MAFS	4	3	1
3♠	CRFS	PLR	VERS	PLRS	VEM	5	3	1
4♠	KRMA	PLF	NEFS	NER	MAF	7	7	-1
5♠	VER	MARS	JUR	URR	NEFS	5	1	4
6♠	VER	SAR	NER	JUR	SARS	3	1	3
7♠	VEMS	JUR	JURS	MAFS	VEM	4	-2	7
8♠	MAMS	CRR	MAFS	MAR	JURS	7	6	1
9♠	CLRS	VER	NER	PLF	VERS	5	1	2
10♠	URF	NER	MOF	MOFS	VEM	5	-1	5
J♠	KRMA	MAM	MARS	PLF	NEFS	8	8	-1
Q♠	MOR	MORS	PLFS	SAF	VEF	6	0	4
K♠	VEF	VERS	VEMS	VEFS	CRFS	7	-3	9

The Blessed Card

DESCRIPTION OF THE 10♦ PERSON:
This card sits in the very center of the Life Spread, protected on all sides by Jupiter's blessings. It is *the* card of material opulence, though few of them actually achieve this reality. However, all 10♦ are protected financially and will always have a certain amount of good luck. To achieve their highest potential, they need to be involved in a business, preferably their own. They have the know-how to manage and run a business of any size. Many of them inherit or marry into wealth. They love to be the center of attention, which is in direct correlation to their card sitting in the very center of the Life Spread.

With so many blessings, you might expect them to be generous souls, but that is not always the case. Many of them simply direct these blessings to the acquisition of more money, and some even become ruthless in this regard. Others, however, pay heed to their Q♣ Karma Card, the card of intuition and service through knowledge, and devote their talents and resources to helping the world. All Tens are in danger of becoming overly fixated on accumulation of things related to their suit. For the 10♦, this would manifest as a money fixation. Some 10♦ can be very selfish.

With their creativity and intelligence, they are always successful in whatever they undertake. Usually this power is directed toward business and financial gain and there is no size business or financial enterprise they cannot handle. If they develop their spiritual awareness, their later years will be filled with the expansion of their mind and soul instead of doubt and indecision. Many find an artistic avenue of expression in their later years, which brings many rewards.

SOME OF THE 10♦ ISSUES CONCERNING RELATIONSHIPS:
10♦ have a strong desire for love and relationships. They also have karma from past lives that must be discharged through one or more difficult divorces or separations. The karma they bring into this life is that of having been the one who left another unfairly and unlovingly. In this life, they are likely to receive the same treatment from another, often the same person they were with before.

They want love and are usually the ones who initiate new relationships. Their own emotionally restless nature must be dealt with before they can have a successful marriage. They often find themselves in situations where they must sacrifice their own need for affection for higher reasons or to help others in need. They are learning to love themselves and the child within. Finding that relationship within brings them more fortune in other relationships as well.

The female 10♦ should not let relationships come before her work and career, except in a few cases where there is great compatibility. There always seem to be great burdens associated with romance and marriage because of the 5♥ in Saturn and the fact that their Personality Card for the female side is the notorious Q♦, who has so much indecision romantically.

GENERALITIES BETWEEN THE PERSONALITY CARD CONNECTIONS
They find pleasant relations with male Hearts, though some will be challenging. Male and female 10♦ receive blessings from other Diamond women, especially those involved in business. Female 10♦ are very compatible with most Club males.

KARMA CARDS:

Q♣   Q♠

KARMA COUSINS:

3♥   8♦

PAST-LIFE CARDS:

9♦   J♦

The Ten of Diamonds and the Search for Love

The 10♦ can be humanitarian and giving or very selfish and self-centered. Sitting in the exact center of the Life Spread can make them feel that the entire world revolves around them and that they deserve the constant attention of everyone. They may also believe they are the most truly blessed card and don't really have to worry so much about being taken care of. In any case they like to think they are very important and special. The A♥ is their Venus card in their Life Spread, and it is displaced by another Ace, the A♦. This card represents the search for self. As much as they may want to be loved by others, there is invariably a conflict between giving to themselves and giving to others. Relationships often require compromises and adjustments. The 10♦ may see these compromises as taking away from what they want for themselves, so for them they can be seen as sacrifices. Many 10♦ reach a point in their lives where they must choose between loving themselves and loving their mate or partner. The 5♥ in Saturn is almost a guarantee that when that time comes, it will be a challenging choice for them. They often have a karmic separation, and though the actions of their partner seem cruel and unjust to the eyes of many, a deeper analysis of the relationship and the events around it can reveal the responsibility of the 10♦ person in this situation. The 5♥ represents personal freedom on one level. The price for that freedom is high for the 10♦, because that card falls in Saturn, the position of karmic debts. Once the 10♦ has passed through this test, they rarely compromise this freedom again, usually leaving their options open.

The 10♦ also has another Ace in Mars, the A♦. These two Aces can make them appear totally self-centered, mercenary, and egotistical. But what is really going on here is the search for self. By necessity, the 10♦ must focus their attention within to find the meaning of life. Others may interpret this as selfish, but the 10♦ sees this as the way life is for them. They receive the highest blessings when they truly look within themselves for the meaning of life.

The Q♣, as their first Karma Card, tells us that many of them have a higher purpose in this life other than amassing money and possessions. This purpose will involve a mission of love, one that will somehow nurture others with knowledge and truth. Those who have found this hidden side of their personality can achieve the extraordinary and reach new heights of personal and professional achievement and satisfaction.

LIFE SPREAD CARDS

PLANETARY CARD	SYMBOL	CARD
MOON	☽	10♥
SUN (BIRTH CARD)	✳	10♦
MERCURY	☿	8♠
VENUS	♀	A♥
MARS	♂	A♦
JUPITER	♃	Q♦
SATURN	♄	5♥
URANUS	♅	3♣
NEPTUNE	♆	3♠
PLUTO	♇	9♥
RESULT (COSMIC REWARD)	♃+	7♣
COSMIC LESSON	♄+	5♦

PLANETARY RULING CARDS

BIRTH DATE	ASTROLOGICAL RULING SIGN	PLANETARY RULING CARD
JAN 17	CAPRICORN	5♥
FEB 15	AQUARIUS	3♣
MAR 13	PISCES	3♠
APR 11	ARIES	A♦
MAY 9	TAURUS	A♥
JUN 7	GEMINI	8♠
JUL 5	CANCER	10♥
AUG 3	LEO	10♦
SEP 1	VIRGO	8♠

Celebrity Birthdays

JAMES EARL JONES
1/17/31 • Actor
MARTIN SHEEN
8/3/40 • Actor
CHRIS FARLEY
2/15/65 • Actor
CANDICE BERGEN
5/9/46 • Actress
JESSICA TANDY
6/07/09 • Actress
MUHAMMAD ALI
1/17/42 • Boxer
LILY TOMLIN
9/1/39 • Comedienne
JOEL GREY
4/11/32 • Entertainer
TOM JONES
6/7/40 • Entertainer
SUSAN B. ANTHONY
2/15/1820 • Historical Figure
ETHEL KENNEDY
4/11/28 • Robert's Wife
NEIL SEDAKA
3/13/39 • Singer
TONY BENNETT
8/3/26 • Singer
BILLY JOEL
5/9/49 • Musician
MIKE WALLACE
5/9/18 • Television Journalist
OLEG CASSINI
4/11/13 • Designer
GWENDOLYN BROOKS
6/7/40 • Poet
PRINCE
6/7/58 • Singer
HUEY LEWIS
7/5/51 • Singer
ANNA KOURNIKOVA
6/7/81 • Tennis Player
DR. PHIL MCGRAW
9/1/50 • Psychologist/ Talk Show Host

Who 10♦ with	Con1	Con2	Con3	Con4	Con5	Attraction	Intensity	Compatibility
A♥	VEF	SAFS	MAF	CRRS	MAM	4	4	1
2♥	MARS	VEM	MAFS			8	4	3
3♥	MAM	VEF	KRMC	SAFS	VER	5	4	3
4♥	MAM	VER	NEFS	PLRS	MAF	7	3	3
5♥	SAF	URRS	MAMS	URR	URFS	0	4	-3
6♥	PLR	SAMS	NER	NERS	PLFS	3	6	-2
7♥	MAR	JUFS	MAM	SAF	MAMS	5	5	1
8♥	MAR	JUFS	VER	CLFS	CRR	6	3	3
9♥	PLF	MARS	VEM	VEMS	MAR	8	5	1
10♥	MOF	VEM	VEMS	PLFS	MAR	8	-1	7
J♥	VEF	JUR	PLF	VEFS	VERS	5	-1	6
Q♥	MAM	JUMS	MAF	VEFS	URR	6	3	3
K♥	CLR	MAFS	VEM	VEMS	MAF	6	2	3
A♣	MARS	VEM	MOF	MAFS		8	2	5
2♣	MAFS	JUFS	MAM	CLR	CLRS	5	4	2
3♣	URF	CLF	SARS	CRR	MAFS	2	4	-2
4♣	NER	MAMS	PLR	SAMS	PLRS	5	6	-1
5♣	MAMS	SAF	NER	VEF	NERS	4	5	-1
6♣	MOR	URR	PLRS	PLR	URRS	4	0	2
7♣	CRF	JUF	VERS	SAR	SARS	4	2	3
8♣	JUR	VEF	JURS	MAMS	PLF	4	-1	6
9♣	VEFS	MAM	JUMS	MAR	JURS	6	2	5
10♣	SAR	VER	NEFS	PLRS	VERS	4	2	2
J♣	VEM	VEMS	MORS	MOF	MOFS	8	-4	10
Q♣	KRMA	MAM	PLF	NEFS	PLFS	8	8	-1
K♣	CLRS	VEM	SAFS	MOR	MORS	3	1	3
A♦	MAF	CRRS	URR	PLRS	VEF	5	4	1
2♦	URR	PLRS	MAF	CRRS	MAFS	4	4	-1
3♦	NERS	PLFS	PLR	SAMS	JUF	5	5	-2
4♦	URRS	PLFS	SAF	SAFS	PLF	1	6	-5
5♦	CLF	SARS	MOFS	URF	URFS	3	3	0
6♦	MAR	JURS	VEFS	NEF	URFS	5	2	4
7♦	MARS	VEM	PLF	URF	PLFS	7	4	1
8♦	JUF	VERS	KRMC	CRF	JUR	4	0	6
9♦	MOFS	JUF	VEFS	CLF	SARS	5	-1	7
10♦	SBC	PLF	PLFS	JURS	NEF	6	7	-2
J♦	MORS	NEF	URFS	VEM	VEMS	6	-1	6
Q♦	JUF	VEFS	NERS	PLFS	MOFS	5	0	5
K♦	CRR	MAFS	URF	VER	CLFS	5	3	1
A♠	JUFS	MAM	MAFS	JUF	SAF	5	3	3
2♠	SAFS	CRFS	CLRS	VEM	CLR	2	5	-2
3♠	NEF	URFS	MAR	JURS	MORS	5	2	3
4♠	VER	NEFS	PLRS	MAM	MAMS	7	2	3
5♠	PLFS	MOF	URRS	NEF	NERS	6	2	1
6♠	CRFS	VEM	SAFS	NER	URRS	4	3	1
7♠	VER	CLFS	CRR	MAFS	MAR	6	3	2
8♠	MOR	CLRS	VEM	CLR	JURS	5	-1	5
9♠	VEM	CLR	CRFS	CLF	MARS	6	2	3
10♠	MAF	MAM	JUMS	MOR	MAMS	7	4	2
J♠	SAR	CRF	MOFS	SARS	VER	3	3	1
Q♠	KRMA	PLF	NEFS	JUF	VERS	7	5	1
K♠	JUR	VEF	MAR	MORS	JURS	5	-1	7

The Work Success Card

DESCRIPTION OF THE 10♠ PERSON:

The 10♠ can be very materialistic and workaholic types. When they are, their home life always suffers, and they suffer with it. Home and family are very important to them as well. What their main focus in life is depends upon the individual, but many of them will have a conflict between these two basic desires. The women, especially, have trouble keeping a satisfying family life while pursuing a career at the same. There are many spiritual influences present in their life path that can make these people the masters of their destiny and lead them to great heights in helping others. However, there is also a pull toward material accomplishment that can blind them to their possibilities and limit their growth potential. As Spades, they have the opportunity to transcend the material through spiritual awareness.

There can be indecision about love and problems in marriage revolving around a fear of poverty. If they misuse the power given to them, they can cause many difficulties in their personal lives. And yet, these people are capable of great, unattached spiritual love. They can have everything they want if they look to their higher sides for direction and guidance.

Having both Karma Cards that reside in the Neptune line of the Life Spread can create a tendency toward addictive behavior. Combine that with their drive and the tendency to do everything 'all the way,' and you find a personality that often goes to extremes, in both good things

and bad. They learn through experience, and they do experience life to its fullest. Their ups and downs can be dramatic in some cases.

The 10♠ will meet with endings in this life designed to teach them the value of letting go of personal attachments to ideas and lifestyles. Meeting this challenge, they can live to experience the heights of spiritual awareness and understanding, which is a part of their destiny.

SOME OF THE 10♠ ISSUES CONCERNING RELATIONSHIPS:

Those with this card often have an inner conflict between their work and their families, to which they are both strongly devoted. Highly ambitious and creative, they can become indecisive in love which can lead to problems. They are often unsure of what they truly want in love matters, or they continually attract romantic partners who cannot make the commitment. In either case the outcome is the same—changes and fluctuations in the romantic life. Financial issues are usually connected to separations, and they usually don't get the good end of the bargain.

There is also a bit of uncertainty about love and romance, indicated by their 3♦ in Venus, that they must contend with before a successful, long–term relationship is achieved. This uncertainty usually delays the fulfillment until later in life. Much like the 2♠ and 8♦, who have the 3♥ to contend with, the 10♠ must get answers for a lot of questions before they can proceed ahead with such an important commitment.

Their basic love karma is good and there is no reason they cannot have a good marriage. They are very giving and loving, and only need to find a way to balance their desire for a family life with their naturally intense, ambitious nature.

KARMA CARDS:

4♥   Q♥

KARMA COUSINS:

4♠   9♣

PAST-LIFE CARDS:

9♠   J♠

In general, 10♠ males can make good marriages with many of the female Club cards. The 10♠ females have a weakness for Heart males and have good love connections with Diamond males. Other Spade males are also good for them on the romantic level.

The All or Nothing Ten of Spades

The 10♠ is usually a person with big career ambitions. As the 'Ten of Tens,' they personify the Capricorn, 10th house drive for success and recognition. They can be very practical and determined about their drive for success and many of them achieve their goals. The only thing that interferes with this determined drive for recognition is their desire for love, home, and family. It is interesting how the cards with such extreme opposite tendencies are found within the personality of one person. The 10♠, who is all work- and success-oriented, has two Heart cards for their Karma Cards, the 4♥ and Q♥. Both of these cards are sort of the opposite of the 10♠, being closely connected to home and family. In astrology, the 10th house (10♠) sits directly opposite the 4th house (4♥, Q♥) of home, security, feelings, and nurturing. It is peculiar that the 10♠ has such strong inner connections with the two main cards for marriage and family life. In my experience, these opposing influences can manifest in their lives in different ways, but all within the realm of their meanings.

Look at Christie Brinkley as an example. She is a 10♠ who was married to Billy Joel (10♦) for awhile. In her case, she was completely devoted to her career for a long time and, as we know, was very successful. Then, the longing for the home and family life caught up with her and she got married and had a child. Her marriage to Billy Joel lasted about nine years. It is likely that one of the reasons for their breakup is she missed being her career self. At any rate, she got back into her career and we began to see her appearing in magazines again. At the time of this writing, she is remarried and we'll just have to see what happens next. Many 10♠ will have a repeating cycle like this throughout their life as they shift from one side of their personality to the other.

A 10♠ client of mine had similar experiences. She was very successful before she got married. However, she married in her late twenties and spent 15 years raising her kids and being the mother (Q♥). When she came to me for a reading, she was in such an inner conflict about wanting to go back to work. 'If I go back to work, I will be abandoning my husband and family. How do I resolve this conflict?' It was clear that there was no middle ground between work and love life or family life for her. Both urges seem equally strong and in direct conflict with each other.

Another example is a 10♠ man who hasn't been in a relationship for six years as of this date. When asked about it, he says, 'I don't have time for a relationship right now.' He is going to school to be a doctor and working at night to pay for it. But it is also obvious he feels pretty lonely. He finds time to go skiing and to do things with friends, but he seems to avoid intimate relationships. Once, he admitted that his last experience in a relationship caused him a lot of problems. It seems that for him, the hassle that goes with being in relationship is a price too high to pay right now. Whatever the reason, though, we can see that he is acting like his Birth Card. He is in the work phase now, but any day he could fall in love and be back into the love, family, and home life phase of his karmic pattern.

TEN OF SPADES

LIFE SPREAD CARDS

PLANETARY CARD	SYMBOL	CARD
MOON	☽	Q♣
SUN (BIRTH CARD)	✴	10♠
MERCURY	☿	5♣
VENUS	♀	3♦
MARS	♂	A♠
JUPITER	♃	7♥
SATURN	♄	7♦
URANUS	♅	5♠
NEPTUNE	♆	J♥
PLUTO	♇	9♣
RESULT (COSMIC REWARD)	♃+	9♠
COSMIC LESSON	♄+	2♥

PLANETARY RULING CARDS

BIRTH DATE	ASTROLOGICAL RULING SIGN	PLANETARY RULING CARD
JAN 4	CAPRICORN	7♦
FEB 2	AQUARIUS	5♠

Who	The Connections Between Partners					Overall Index Ratings		
10♠ with	Con1	Con2	Con3	Con4	Con5	Attraction	Intensity	Compatibility
A♥	JUFS	URMS	MAM	MAR	URFS	3	2	3
2♥	CLF	SAFS	VER	SAF	VEMS	2	5	-3
3♥	MAR	URFS	JUFS	URMS	MOF	4	2	2
4♥	KRMA	NEFS	URRS	PLF	NEF	6	5	0
5♥	PLFS	MOR	MORS	NERS	SAR	7	2	2
6♥	CRFS	VER	JUMS	VEF	VEFS	6	0	5
7♥	JUF	CLFS	URFS	CLR	URR	2	1	1
8♥	CLR	URR	SAR	MARS	JUF	1	3	-1
9♥	SAMS	SAF	VEMS	VER	SAFS	0	5	-2
10♥	URF	SARS	URFS	VERS	URR	0	1	0
J♥	NEF	JUR	MAFS	JUFS	NEFS	5	1	5
Q♥	KRMA	NER	PLF	NEFS	URF	7	6	0
K♥	MOFS	CRF	JUF	CRFS	MORS	6	0	6
A♣	VER	SAFS	CLF	SAF	VEMS	2	4	-1
2♣	MAF	CRRS	MAR	CRR	MAFS	7	6	0
3♣	CLRS	VEM	VEMS	JUFS	PLR	5	-1	5
4♣	VER	JUMS	MOR	CRFS	SAFS	5	-1	5
5♣	MOR	PLFS	VER	JUMS	VERS	7	0	4
6♣	CRR	VERS	MAFS	JUF	VER	6	1	4
7♣	SAR	MORS	VEM	CRR	VEMS	4	0	4
8♣	JUFS	NEF	JUR	MAFS	JUF	4	0	6
9♣	PLF	NER	KRMC	MAM	MAMS	7	6	-1
10♣	URR	MORS	VEM	URRS	NEF	4	-2	5
J♣	URR	VEMS	NER	PLF	VERS	5	0	3
Q♣	MOF	MAMS	MAR	URFS	MARS	7	3	3
K♣	PLRS	VERS	VER	PLR	VEF	5	1	3
A♦	MAM	MAFS	JUFS	URMS	MAF	6	5	2
2♦	MAFS	CRR	MAM	JUM	MAMS	7	5	1
3♦	VEF	CRFS	CRF	VEFS	URRS	7	1	5
4♦	URF	SARS	PLFS	MOR	SAR	2	3	-1
5♦	VEFS	PLR	VEF	SAR	JUFS	4	0	5
6♦	MAM	PLF	JUR	NERS	PLFS	6	5	-1
7♦	SAF	VEMS	SAMS	VER	SAFS	1	4	-1
8♦	SAR	VEFS	PLF	VEF	NER	4	2	1
9♦	VEFS	SAR	VEF			4	0	5
10♦	MAR	MOF	MAMS	VEFS	MAM	8	4	4
J♦	JUR	NERS	PLFS	MOF	NER	5	1	3
Q♦	VEF	VEFS	CRF			7	-1	8
K♦	CLRS	VEM	SAR	MARS	SARS	3	2	1
A♠	MAF	CRRS	JUF	CLFS	URFS	5	4	1
2♠	PLRS	PLR	JURS	VEF	JUR	3	2	1
3♠	JUR	NERS	PLFS	MAM	MAF	5	3	1
4♠	URRS	URR	KRMC	NEFS	NEF	3	1	1
5♠	URF	SARS	URFS	VERS	SAR	0	1	0
6♠	PLR	JURS	MOFS	CRF	PLRS	4	1	3
7♠	SAR	MARS	CLRS	VEM	CLR	3	4	0
8♠	VERS	CRR	CRRS	SARS	VER	5	1	3
9♠	MOFS	CRF	PLR	JURS	PLRS	5	1	3
10♠	SBC	NEFS	NER	NERS	NEF	6	4	2
J♠	MORS	VEM	URR	URRS	VEMS	5	-2	7
Q♠	VEFS	MAR	SAR	NER	PLF	5	3	2
K♠	JUR	MAFS	JUFS	NEF	CRF	4	1	4

The Jacks

"I won't grow up!"
—*Peter Pan*

The Jack is the youngest member of the royal family. He can be looked upon in several ways, all of them meaningful. First, he can be seen as the Prince who will someday become the King. As the Prince, he is youthful, romantic, creative, witty, and charming. However, he has not yet been given the responsibility and power that comes from being the King. Nor does he want so much responsibility. Jacks just want to have fun and play. At the same time, they want to be treated with respect and some measure of admiration. Someday, perhaps, they will become Kings. The transformation from youthfulness to responsibility is one of the most important life-long themes for the Jack person.

Another way to see a Jack is as the counsel to the King. He has influence with the King, but has his own interests at heart. He sits in the royal court, but assumes none of the overall responsibility for what happens. He can be bribed if you want him to act on your behalf in influencing the King in a certain way. Overall, he is somewhat dishonest but very creative and resourceful in keeping all of his affairs in balance without getting caught. He is a master of deception and stealth and can never truly be trusted.

These two pictures just about sum up the usual qualities of Jack Birth Cards. The youthful creativity is there in overwhelming abundance. Along with that is the temptation to misuse that creative energy for fun or profit, or simply to avoid unpleasant situations that one may have to face as a result of being 100 percent honest. The J♥ stands out as the only exception to this, but in truth many of these people also succumb to the misuse of their creative forces. However, overall, the J♥ has such a spiritual connection that they tend to focus more of their energy on being the martyr or savior and don't have much time for the craftiness of the other Jacks. Still, they are Jacks, and every once in awhile even they get that mischievous gleam in their eyes that tells you they are up to something.

But Jacks are also deemed the initiates of the deck. Initiation implies rising to a new, usually higher level. It is this new beginning that implies ending of some past ways of being. For the Jack, many of them are here to show that they can rise above their material nature to one that is more spiritual and less attached to worldly goods and matters. For a Jack to be truly self-realized, they will have to access the higher qualities of their suit in some fashion. This would mean the J♥ becoming a vessel for spiritual love, the J♣ for spiritual knowledge, the J♦ a representative of higher values, and the J♠ an example of one whose life is lived on higher, spiritual principles. Many Jacks achieve this and many do not. In their highest expression, they represent that person who has lifted him or herself up to a higher level of self expression. This also implies letting go of their lower natures, which in many cases are quite strong and difficult to renounce.

Jacks are always tempted to misuse their tremendous gifts and many of them will never rise up to anything but a thief. They have such a creative mind that they can tell lies that anyone would believe without question. This mind represents a great gift, but it is up to them to put it to a positive use. Those who do can achieve much.

Their naturally mental nature also makes it more difficult for them to know their own feelings. When they have so much success using their minds, their hearts are rarely used in getting what they want. All of these qualities combine in the Jack person to give them their life's biggest challenge—to seek the solutions to their problems by looking within, instead of using their wits and craftiness to get by. This turning within is the initiation that all Jacks represent.

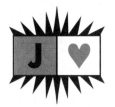

Sacrifice through Love

DESCRIPTION OF THE J♥ PERSON:

As one of the three Fixed Cards, the J♥ is strong about their version of love. They are surrounded by the Christ spirit of sacrifice through love. Even though they are a Jack, and they are sometimes immature and crafty, the J♥ is influenced by the wisdom of the Christ spirit, which gives them higher guidance and higher motives in general. They must watch, however, that their martyrdom does not get out of hand. They can also become escapists and misguided, but this is the exception rather than the rule.

Love is their power and birthright. They have come to love others and to show them the way by their example. They know how to love with the big-heartedness of a King, and once they decide that theirs is the mission of love, they do take on the yoke of responsibility admirably. They often make sacrifices in their life, and their personal fulfillment may be given up for some higher cause or philosophy. As born leaders, they must be successful in their own profession. These people are fixed and guided by a strong sense of justice and duty. They can be depended on for following through on promises, unless they get caught up in the lower side of the 'crafty Jack.'

They all carry the Christ spirit within them and everyone they associate with is in some way uplifted by their presence. They find their greatest fulfillment on a spiritual path or by bringing the higher energies to their work and lives.

SOME OF THE J♥ ISSUES CONCERNING RELATIONSHIPS:

Just because the J♥ is a spiritual card does not mean they don't exhibit any of the Jack characteristics. They too can get caught up in the youthful, playful, playboy or playgirl aspects of this card. They too can be tempted into affairs and romantic encounters, for the Jack is the most romantic card in the deck.

The sacrificial nature of the J♥ can work for good or ill in relationships, depending upon the person. These people have power and strength in their love natures, but a certain degree of immaturity may prove to be their undoing at times. They are usually devoted to higher ideals in love and have their own philosophy about it that no one can change. They will make sacrifices for you if they love you and you may be part of their plan to save the world.

However, in the same vein, the J♥ can use this 'savior complex' to do silly things in love—things like choosing a mate that is totally unworthy or broken in order to see their love heal someone. This can result in victim/savior or codependent relationships that have ill consequences.

After a few losses in love, the J♥ becomes sensitized to the pain the love can cause and becomes an understanding and loving mate. When they are devoted to a higher purpose, which many of them are, they are be the most devoted and trustworthy companions in the deck. They exemplify the love that is fixed and unwavering, and ready to make sacrifices on behalf of their loved ones if need be.

GENERALITIES BETWEEN THE PERSONALITY CARD CONNECTIONS

Diamond men are usually an unwise choice for love or marriage but other Heart men are great. Intensely strong karmic bonds are found with the K♠ and 8♣. However, the power generated can be too strong. J♥ usually prove a great challenge for any Club female.

KARMA CARDS:
K♠ 8♣ A♣ 2♥ 7♦ 9♥

KARMA COUSINS:
NONE

PAST-LIFE CARDS:
10♥ Q♥

Jack of Hearts—Savior or Martyr?

For better or worse, the J♥ is often associated with Jesus Christ, the savior and spiritual leader of the Age of Pisces, which is now coming to an end. He taught and exemplified a kind of love that transcends the normal human experience. His love through sacrifice is considered to be the highest form of love as symbolized by Venus in Pisces. This Neptunian quality has a great potential for either good or bad, depending upon how it is used. As we enter the Age of Aquarius, much of what this sacrificial love embodied is now considered to be codependent and addictive. We have seen countless examples of people and organizations abusing their spiritual power, as well as other powers, all in the name of giving to others. Many J♥ people become absolutely worn out by all of the giving that they do. Without giving something back to themselves, they eventually become depleted and spent. When this occurs, they actually end up having less of themselves to give and are less able to do the giving they like so much.

In Aquarius, much of what Pisces teaches us becomes irrelevant and useless. From the Aquarian point of view, Jesus didn't do anyone a favor when he sacrificed himself. By sacrificing himself, he was no longer around to do anyone any good. From one point of view, we could say that his actions represented an escape instead of a wonderful thing he gave us. This was perhaps not his intention or what really happened, but it does illustrate how the Piscean or Neptunian energies can be confused and abused in the here and now. The Bible says that only by believing in Him (Jesus) can we be saved. The Aquarian philosophy says give up your beliefs, foolish and otherwise, and look at the facts. Stop trying to save everyone and save yourself. You don't need a savior because you are already saved; you are a perfect unique human being with the power to have your life any way you want it.

Maybe this is why some J♥ people seem out of place in today's society. Many of them are still out there trying to save everyone and it is not working. It often takes years and years of torturous relationships for them to learn the value of selfishness and establishing boundaries in their love life. They are still out there, having secret affairs while telling themselves that they are doing it to help their secret lovers. They still have some trouble knowing when to give of themselves selflessly and when they should just say 'no' to others.

They are not the only card guilty of these things. All of us have some Neptune energy in our Life Path, some more than others. There is a fine balance between giving to others while giving up personal desires and taking some of that time and energy back to love one's self. Collectively, we are all learning to clear up the hazy, misguided, illusory nature of some of our actions and to get real. In the process, we get back our power and our Godliness and we find our connection with the God within in a different way, a way that feels right in this New Age of Enlightenment.

LIFE SPREAD CARDS

PLANETARY CARD	SYMBOL	CARD
MOON	☽	5♠
SUN (BIRTH CARD)	☀	J♥
MERCURY	☿	9♣
VENUS	♀	9♠
MARS	♂	2♥
JUPITER	♃	K♥
SATURN	♄	K♦
URANUS	♅	6♥
NEPTUNE	♆	4♣
PLUTO	♇	2♦
RESULT (COSMIC REWARD)	♃+	J♠
COSMIC LESSON	♄+	8♣

PLANETARY RULING CARDS

BIRTH DATE	ASTROLOGICAL RULING SIGN	PLANETARY RULING CARD
JUL 30	LEO	J♥
AUG 28	VIRGO	9♣
SEP 26	LIBRA	9♠
OCT 24	LIBRA OR SCORPIO	9♠, OR 2♥ & 2♦
NOV 22	SCORPIO	2♥ & 2♦
DEC 20	SAGITTARIUS	K♥

Who J♥ with	Con1	Con2	Con3	Con4	Con5	Attraction	Intensity	Compatibility
A♥	CLRS	VEM	VEMS	CLR	PLRS	4	0	4
2♥	KRMA	MAF	CRRS	CRR	MAFS	7	7	0
3♥	CLR	PLRS	CLRS	VEM	PLR	3	2	0
4♥	NERS	VEM	NER	CRR	JUFS	6	0	4
5♥	URRS	URR	NEFS	SAFS	CRF	1	2	0
6♥	URF	SARS	NEF	URFS	SAR	1	2	-1
7♥	MAR	JURS	SAR	MARS	JUR	3	4	2
8♥	SAR	MARS	JUR	SARS	MAR	2	4	0
9♥	KRMA	VERS	VER	CRR	MAFS	7	3	4
10♥	MOFS	MOF	CLFS	VEMS	MAF	7	-1	7
J♥	SBC	POWR	CLF	CLFS	CLR	5	8	-1
Q♥	MORS	NER	MOR	MAR	VERS	7	-1	6
K♥	JUF	VEFS	JUFS	VEF	URR	4	-3	8
A♣	KRMA	CRR	MAFS	MAF	CRRS	7	7	0
2♣	JUFS	JUR	JUF	VEFS	URR	2	-3	7
3♣	SAFS	MAM	SAF	JURS	MAMS	0	7	-4
4♣	NEF	URFS	URR	NEFS	URF	4	1	2
5♣	URR	NEFS	URRS	NEF	URFS	3	1	2
6♣	PLFS	PLF	SAR	NER	MARS	6	7	-5
7♣	CRFS	VEF	CRF	MOFS	MAM	7	2	4
8♣	KRMA	POWR	CLF	CLFS	PLF	6	8	-2
9♣	MOR	MORS	MARS	VER	JUMS	7	-1	7
10♣	VEMS	CRF	VEM	VER	VEFS	8	-1	7
J♣	MOFS	MAFS	CLR	MAR	MAF	7	3	3
Q♣	PLR	VERS	CLR	PLRS	VER	4	2	1
K♣	JURS	SAFS	NER	JUM	SAF	0	2	0
A♦	VEMS	PLF	CLRS	VEM	NEF	7	1	3
2♦	PLF	PLFS	VEMS	MAR	VER	8	6	-2
3♦	SAR	MAMS	URF	SARS	MAM	2	5	-2
4♦	MOF	URRS	PLR	CRFS	CLF	5	1	2
5♦	MAM	MAMS	SAFS	VER	CLFS	5	7	-1
6♦	MARS	MOR	MAR	JUM	MOR	7	3	4
7♦	KRMA	VER	VERS	CRR	MAFS	7	3	4
8♦	VEF	VEFS	CRFS	MOF	MAM	7	-1	7
9♦	MAMS	MAM	VERS	PLF	VER	8	6	1
10♦	VER	PLR	VERS	VEFS	JUF	6	-1	5
J♦	MAR	CLR	CLRS	MARS	MAFS	5	6	0
Q♦	MAM	SAR	MAMS	PLF	URF	5	7	-2
K♦	SAF	JURS	SAFS	JUR	SARS	-3	4	-2
A♠	JUR	MAR	JURS	JUFS	NEF	3	1	5
2♠	NER	JUM	JUR	NERS	JUMS	3	-1	4
3♠	MAR	MARS	CLRS	JUM		6	6	1
4♠	VEM	VEMS	NERS	CRRS	VEF	7	-1	7
5♠	MOF	MOFS	CLF	PLRS	VEM	7	-1	5
6♠	VEF	JUR	NERS	JUMS	JURS	4	-2	7
7♠	JUR	SARS	SAF	JURS	SAR	-2	2	0
8♠	PLFS	JUR	SARS	NERS	SAF	3	4	-2
9♠	VEF	JUF	VEFS	JURS	PLR	4	-2	8
10♠	NER	NERS	MORS	JUF	MARS	6	1	4
J♠	CRF	CRFS	VEMS	VERS	MOF	7	2	4
Q♠	VEFS	VER	VEF	MOFS	MAMS	7	-2	9
K♠	KRMA	POWR	CLF	CLFS	PLF	6	8	-2

The connections between partners and overall index ratings are shown in the table above, with columns for Who J♥ with, Con1–Con5, Attraction, Intensity, and Compatibility.

The Mentally Creative

DESCRIPTION OF THE J♣ PERSON:
Creative, dishonest, or a mixture of both? As we can imagine, those who are the most creative can also be the most dishonest, and vice versa. The J♣ is a card of mental and financial creativity. These people are energetic and productive. Their brilliant minds are far ahead of the common person and society. They are the people of the Aquarian Age, being neither entirely male nor female. They are progressive and on the cutting edge of the evolution of our society and world.

They have one of the finest minds in the deck and can always make a good living with it. They usually get involved in something entrepreneurial, the men more often than the women. If their work allows them some creative expression, they can find their groove and really enjoy it, while making a great deal of money at the same time.

They are mentally brilliant, but often fixed and prone to arguments (represented by the 2♣ in Mars). They usually cannot see that it is their own love of debate that is the cause of many of their disagreements with others. So, they will debate you when they can, and they always enjoy the mental exercise. Their own fixed minds sometimes get in the way of their seeing the truth, but it also gives them the capacity to finish what they start and to stand up for what they believe in.

As members of the royal family, they dislike pettiness and tend to be somewhat impatient with the failings of others.

They need respect and a position that allows their brilliant minds free reign to create and explore. They are never at a loss for ideas, some of which will bring them huge financial returns. On the negative side, the J♣ can be irresponsible and, in some cases, dishonest. They can see things from so many levels that nothing is really right or wrong—it is just another way of looking at things. And they can make up a story so quickly and so believable that they can explain away practically anything. They don't get away with much in that regard though. Saturn's hand always reminds them of the boundaries that keep them balanced and fair. The trouble comes when they start believing their own stories, departing from reality a little too far and creating a lot of hardship before getting back on course.

They are essentially good and giving people. Even though they are argumentative at times, they are loving and friendly to all they meet.

SOME OF THE J♣ ISSUES CONCERNING RELATIONSHIPS:
Such a strong and fixed mental approach to life can have its share of challenges for the J♣. Mental approaches don't always work in the realms of love. However, these people do not have particularly bad karma in this area. They need someone who is their friend first, and who will allow them some freedom to be themselves. If they have this, they are faithful and devoted. The men are excellent lovers and the women are excellent companions.

They often have to contend with the ill health of a loved one, mate, or family member. Or, their own health problems will become a prominent theme in their relationships. In most cases, their health issues are related to some emotional cause, whether it be family- or lover-related.

KARMA CARDS:
J♦   10♥
KARMA COUSINS:
3♠   5♠
PAST-LIFE CARDS:
10♣   Q♣

Female J♣ have a karmic bond with all Diamond males, though some are easier than others. They could have it easier with men of the Club suit. The male J♣ has a weakness for Heart females. Diamond females always have trouble and challenges with the J♣ male.

The Jack of Clubs's Love Life

There is some unusual quality about J♣ that is evident in all of them, but hard to describe. The women seem to be very different from the men. The women have a very peaceful demeanor. There is a certain calmness in their face and a look of intelligence about them. They are usually outspoken and a mental match for anyone. They have a very intellectual point of view about everything, including their love life. Though they obviously have feelings for those they love, they still see their relationship as some sort of mental concept. It is as though they have the feelings but also must contend with their powerful mind which draws conclusions about love and their love life from experience. The following story illustrates how the mental aspects of the J♣ love life can cause confusion.

One of my clients, a female J♣, was ready to start a sexual relationship, either with one of her female friends or with a man working on her house. This occurred after she discovered that her husband, whom she loved very much, was no longer capable of having sex due to an illness. To her it didn't seem to matter so much who it was, she just wanted to have her sexual desires fulfilled. So, she started trying to arrange sexual encounters that would take care of her needs without causing any difficulties in her marriage. Of course, like most J♣, she was choosing to not tell her husband about her plans, or about her feelings of not being satisfied. This caused a lot of internal conflict within her, because she realized that she had to live this double life—one that she told her husband about, and the other that she didn't. It also made her feel less intimate with her husband and she didn't like this feeling of separation from him. But, in her mind, she had many convenient reasons for keeping it a secret from him.

A J♣ can come up with more plausible explanations than any other card in the deck. However, sometimes these explanations do not touch upon the real truth. The real truth was that she was afraid to tell her husband or even bring up the subject of his sexual dysfunction because of the possibility of being rejected or of losing him. After months of going back and forth about finding another lover, she realized her fear and decided to confront her husband with her true feelings. When she did, he loved her even more than before and their relationship grew much closer as a result. All the planning and scheming she had done for months was literally meaningless in the light of the one simple conversation she had with her husband. This is just one way the J♣ mind can literally take off on a flight of its own. And this occurs when there is some fear that they are not dealing with directly. They often become so wrapped up in these mental flights that they forget why they are doing what they are doing, or even begin to believe their own excuses.

It is interesting that the J♣ woman was just as open to making love with the same sex as she was with the opposite sex. This is a hidden J♣ quality that manifests more often in the females than the males. Instead of the peaceful demeanor of the females, the men are often hyperactive and always doing something. They are great talkers and usually end up in businesses where their creativity and fast talking can be put to good use. They are very boyish in their looks and actions. They have that eternal gleam in their eye that tells you that they are up to something. Don't expect them to tell you everything and to become totally intimate with their thoughts. They always have some little plan or scheme going on in the back of their mind. Most women who have dated or married a J♣ are more than satisfied with their sex life. They will tell you that their husbands or boyfriends are the best lovers they've ever had. It must be that creative energy that makes them such good lovers. They are probably always coming up with new things to do in bed.

JACK OF CLUBS

LIFE SPREAD CARDS

PLANETARY CARD	SYMBOL	CARD
MOON	☽	Q♠
SUN (BIRTH CARD)	✳	J♣
MERCURY	☿	9♦
VENUS	♀	7♠
MARS	♂	2♣
JUPITER	♃	K♣
SATURN	♄	J♦
URANUS	♅	4♥
NEPTUNE	♆	4♦
PLUTO	♇	2♠
RESULT (COSMIC REWARD)	♃+	8♥
COSMIC LESSON	♄+	6♣

PLANETARY RULING CARDS

BIRTH DATE	ASTROLOGICAL RULING SIGN	PLANETARY RULING CARD
JAN 29	AQUARIUS	4♥
FEB 27	PISCES	4♦
MAR 25	ARIES	2♣
APR 23	TAURUS	7♠
MAY 21	TAURUS OR GEMINI	7♠ OR 9♦
JUN 19	GEMINI	9♦
JUL 17	CANCER	Q♠
AUG 15	LEO	J♣
SEP 13	VIRGO	9♦
OCT 11	LIBRA	7♠
NOV 9	SCORPIO	2♣ & 2♠
DEC 7	SAGITTARIUS	K♣

Celebrity Birthdays

DONALD SUTHERLAND
7/17/34 • *Actor*
HOWARD HESSEMAN
2/27/40 • *Actor*
LEE MAJORS
4/23/40 • *Actor*
BEN AFFLECK
8/15/72 • *Actor*
TOM SELLECK
1/29/45 • *Actor*
ANN JILLIAN
1/29/50 • *Actress*
DIAHANN CARROLL
7/17/35 • *Actress*
ELLEN BURSTYN
12/7/32 • *Actress*
GENA ROWLANDS
6/19/46 • *Actress*
HEDY LAMARR
11/09/13 • *Actress*
SARAH JESSICA PARKER
3/25/65 • *Actress*
SHIRLEY TEMPLE-BLACK
4/23/28 • *Actress*
JOYCE DEWITT
4/23/49 • *Actress*
KATHERINE ROSS
1/29/42 • *Actress*
KATHLEEN TURNER
6/19/54 • *Actress*
VALERIE BERTINELLI
4/23/60 • *Actress*
JOAN CUSACK
10/11/62 • *Actress*
RALPH NADER
2/27/34 • *Consumer Advocate*
ARETHA FRANKLIN
3/25/42 • *Singer*
ELTON JOHN
3/25/47 • *Singer/Musician*
HOWARD COSELL
3/25/20 • *Sportscaster*
OPRAH WINFREY
1/29/54 • *Talk Show Host*
CHELSEA CLINTON
2/27/80 • *Former President's daughter*

Who J♣ with	The Connections Between Partners					Overall Index Ratings		
	Con1	Con2	Con3	Con4	Con5	Attraction	Intensity	Compatibility
A♥	CLR	CRR	MAFS	MAF	CRRS	5	4	0
2♥	SAF	CLRS	JUF	CRFS	SAFS	0	4	-2
3♥	MAFS	CLR	MORS	NERS	MAF	6	3	2
4♥	URF	VEF	MOR	URRS	URFS	3	-2	5
5♥	NER	PLF	NEF	PLR	URFS	6	4	-1
6♥	MAMS	NERS	SAFS	NER	JURS	4	5	-1
7♥	CRF	VEMS	SAM	SAMS	MARS	4	5	1
8♥	CRF	VEMS	VEF	JUF	VERS	7	0	6
9♥	JUR	JUF	CRFS	SAF	CLRS	1	1	3
10♥	KRMA	VEFS	NEF	PLFS	PLF	7	4	2
J♥	MARS	MORS	CLF	CLRS	VEMS	6	3	2
Q♥	VEMS	VERS	NEF	PLR	VEFS	7	-1	7
K♥	MAF	CRRS	JUM	MAMS	JUMS	6	4	2
A♣	SAF	CLRS	JUF	CRFS	SAM	0	4	-2
2♣	MAF	CRRS	SAM	VEMS	VER	5	5	1
3♣	URR	PLRS	VER	NEFS	MAF	4	2	1
4♣	NERS	URRS	MAMS	MAM	URR	5	4	1
5♣	URRS	NER	PLF	NERS	PLFS	5	3	-1
6♣	CLF	SARS	JUFS	MAM	SAF	2	5	-1
7♣	MAR	JURS	CLFS	JUFS	PLR	4	4	2
8♣	MARS	MAF	MAR	CLRS	VEMS	7	7	1
9♣	VERS	VEMS	PLFS	VEM	NEF	8	-1	6
10♣	MOFS	JUFS	VEF	PLF	VEFS	6	-2	7
J♣	SBC	SAF	VEFS	SAR	VERS	2	5	0
Q♣	MORS	MAFS	VEM	VEMS	MAF	8	0	7
K♣	JUF	VEFS	PLF	MOF	VEMS	6	-1	6
A♦	CRR	MAFS	JUFS	MAM	CLR	6	4	2
2♦	JUFS	MAM	CLF	SARS	CRR	4	3	1
3♦	SAFS	MAMS	PLR	VERS	PLRS	2	6	-3
4♦	NEF	PLR	URFS	NER	PLF	5	3	0
5♦	VER	NEFS	MOR	URR	PLRS	6	-1	6
6♦	PLFS	VERS	SAR	SARS	VER	4	4	-1
7♦	JUF	CRFS	JUR	SAF	CLRS	2	1	3
8♦	CLFS	MOF	MAR	JURS	CRF	6	3	2
9♦	MOR	PLR	VERS	VER	NEFS	6	-1	5
10♦	VEM	VEMS	MORS	MOF	MOFS	8	-4	10
J♦	KRMA	SAF	SAR	NEF	PLFS	2	7	-3
Q♦	PLR	VERS	SAFS	MOR	MORS	3	2	1
K♦	MAF	URR	PLRS	VEF	VEFS	5	3	1
A♠	SAM	VEMS	MAF	CRRS	SAF	3	5	0
2♠	PLF	MARS	JUF	VEFS	MAF	7	5	1
3♠	SAR	PLFS	KRMC	SAF	CLR	2	6	-4
4♠	VEF	MOFS	URF	URFS	MOF	5	-2	7
5♠	VEFS	NEF	KRMC	PLR	URFS	6	1	5
6♠	MARS	JUM	MAMS	PLF	URF	6	5	0
7♠	VEF	MAF	CRF	VEMS	MAR	8	2	5
8♠	JUF	VEFS	CLF	SARS	CLFS	4	1	4
9♠	JUM	MAMS	MARS	JUMS	CRR	5	3	2
10♠	URF	VEMS	URRS	VEFS		3	-2	4
J♠	JUFS	MAR	JURS	MOFS	JUR	4	0	6
Q♠	MOF	VEM	VEMS	CLFS	URR	7	-2	7
K♠	MARS	CLF	CLRS	VEMS	MAF	6	5	0

The Salesperson Card

DESCRIPTION OF THE J♦ PERSON:
The J♦ is the salesperson's card. These people are sharp, clever, and always able to make a good living using their wit and charm. They are very independent and creative, and operate as much from their instincts as they do from their quick and creative minds. They can always get along and do well in life by virtue of their inherited financial expertise. Few heed the call of their highest ideals and become the King that stands close to them. Their natural psychic ability can lead them to direct spiritual realization, but all Jacks are fixed in their minds, which often prevents them from exploring the intuition which is one of their greatest gifts. Some J♦ become professional psychics while others may fear their open channel. In any event, most of them come to use it later in life.

The J♦ has great power to persuade others. They are successful in work that brings them in front of groups or individuals. They can make a good living in the entertainment or healing professions. Many are artistically inclined and some are particularly gifted in the artistic fields. They often would like to do something good for the world. However, being a Jack, they may live out their entire life just playing around and having fun.

Being the Uranus/Neptune card, J♦ usually like to keep their options open in their work and in their life in general. Their freedom (Uranus) means a lot to them—they often look upon it as sacred (Neptune). They will usually gravitate toward self-employment or occupations that give them a lot of freedom in setting up their own work schedule. This may be one reason so many of them gravitate to selling and promoting as a career. They are unequalled in this field. The expression of the salesman who sold 'ice cubes to Eskimos' must have been written about a J♦ person.

All Jacks can be immature and crafty, due to their vast creativity, and they usually mean well even when they are not able to come through on their promises. They love to play and, even in old age, retain a certain youthful quality. They love to be social making them the best salespeople in the deck. They must find a career that gives them an outlet for their creativity and recognition for their superior talents.

SOME OF THE J♦ ISSUES CONCERNING RELATIONSHIPS:
J♦ have an idealized concept of their personal freedom and, in many cases, this concept keeps them from ever making a commitment in a relationship. They will give you good reasons for why they have never settled down, based on their high ideals of personal freedom, but the truth often is that they are truly afraid of what a real commitment may cost them. Freedom, as mentioned earlier, is also a special word to them, and whether they admit it or not, it is one of the issues that keeps them out of more permanent commitments.

Every card in the J♦ Life Path (from their Mercury to Neptune Card) is in the Neptune line. They have the Q♥, the most dreamy love card there is, as their Neptune Card. Having so much Neptune energy in their love life makes these people have very high ideals about love. They can be the perfect lover or mate. They can get very creative with their romantic fantasies or suffer a great deal when people fail to match up with the wonderful potential the J♦ sees in them.

KARMA CARDS:
3♠   J♣

KARMA COUSINS:
6♦   10♥

PAST-LIFE CARDS:
10♦   Q♦

They have the power to get their way with people, but their own indecisive nature and sense of independence often gets the better of them. They can have a good relationship once they decide it is what they really want and are ready to settle down. Being so creative can make a J♦ a playboy or playgirl.

Male J♦ fantasize about female Heart cards, and male Clubs find the female J♦ very appealing, though sometimes very difficult.

The United States of America—Jack of Diamonds

Most people don't think of their country as having a sun sign or Birth Card, but when we look at our country from this point of view, it reveals much about us both as a culture and as a governmental/political body. July 4th is a J♦, which is often referred to as the 'Salesperson's Card.' J♦ people are usually gifted in promoting what they believe in and many have had much success as salespeople. On the other hand, some of them are irresponsible and crafty. But when we look at our country, how can see some of the J♦ traits?

Let's first consider some of the J♦ traits. The J♦ represents, in its highest manifestation, an initiation into a higher value system. When we get a J♦ card in our Yearly Spread, it might mean that we have a sort of awakening about what is truly important to us in life. We might suddenly realize that the people or things we thought we really wanted are not so important to us. We might, for example, realize that money isn't everything and that it has a proper place a bit lower down our list of things most-valued. A J♦ person, or country for that matter, is here to make this transformation at some point in their life. During the course of their life, we will see them do the lowest and highest as they learn their lessons. This means that the J♦ can be the biggest thief and then turn around and renounce their material interests in favor of a spiritual belief or ideal. Often, other countries of the world will classify the United States as the thief country that will do anything for the almighty dollar. Any serious student of world affairs will tell you that most, if not all, of our wars have been fought for financial reasons and not for the reasons we read about in the press.

Because the J♦ sits in the Uranus/Neptune position of the Life Spread, we see a curious mixture of influences. As you may know, we are currently in the twilight zone between the Pisces and Aquarian Ages, which are ruled by Neptune and Uranus, respectively. This may be telling us that the U.S. was meant to be the country to help lead the world through this transition from the 'I believe' generation of Pisces to the 'I know' generation of Aquarius. Another interpretation of this Uranus/Neptune position is that the J♦ represents the ideal (Neptune) of personal freedom (Aquarius). The U.S. was founded by people who escaped the persecution and censorship found in Europe and other parts of the world to create a new country where we enjoy freedom of speech and religion. The U.S. pioneered this new type of society. And as we can see, this new concept of government and society has been successful. The U.S. is now among the most highly advanced civilizations on the planet. Much of our technology can be attributed to the Uranus influence of the J♦ Birth Card.

Because of its J♦ Birth Card, the U.S. will always have dealings with money, and some of them will be underhanded, just as it is in the life of any J♦ person. You can almost bet that all of its involvements with other countries, whether they are trading or wars, will always have financial considerations at the root. But we can also feel certain that the U.S. will always stand for the freedom to be who we are. The ideal of religious and personal freedom upon which the U.S. was created will always be cherished and maintained through whatever episodes may occur in the national or international theatre.

JACK OF DIAMONDS

LIFE SPREAD CARDS

PLANETARY CARD	SYMBOL	CARD
MOON	☽	K♣
SUN (BIRTH CARD)	☀	J♦
MERCURY	☿	4♥
VENUS	♀	4♦
MARS	♂	2♠
JUPITER	♃	8♥
SATURN	♄	6♣
URANUS	♅	6♠
NEPTUNE	♆	Q♥
PLUTO	♇	10♣
RESULT (COSMIC REWARD)	♃+	8♦
COSMIC LESSON	♄+	K♠

PLANETARY RULING CARDS

BIRTH DATE	ASTROLOGICAL RULING SIGN	PLANETARY RULING CARD
JAN 16	CAPRICORN	6♣
FEB 14	AQUARIUS	6♠
MAR 12	PISCES	Q♥
APR 10	ARIES	2♠
MAY 8	TAURUS	4♦
JUN 6	GEMINI	4♥
JUL 4	CANCER	K♣
AUG 2	LEO	J♦

Who	The Connections Between Partners					Overall Index Ratings		
J♦ with	Con1	Con2	Con3	Con4	Con5	Attraction	Intensity	Compatibility
A♥	VEF	CLRS	SAR	CLR	JUR	2	1	3
2♥	JUF	SAFS	SAM	JURS	MAM	-1	4	0
3♥	VEMS	MAFS	SAR	CLR		5	2	3
4♥	MOR	URFS	URF	CRR	VEF	4	-1	4
5♥	VEF	NERS	PLFS	VER	NER	7	1	4
6♥	MAM	PLRS	MAMS	VEF	NERS	7	6	1
7♥	SAMS	JUF	SAF	MAFS	SAFS	0	6	-2
8♥	JUF	MAR	CRFS	SAMS	VER	4	4	2
9♥	CRR	JUFS	JURS	SAM	MOR	2	1	4
10♥	SAR	NEFS	KRMC	PLRS	JUM	3	4	0
J♥	CLF	MAF	CLFS	MARS		7	7	-2
Q♥	NEF	PLR	VEMS	JUF	NEFS	6	1	4
K♥	JUMS	VER	PLF	MAF	CRRS	5	1	2
A♣	SAM	JUF	SAFS	JURS	JUFS	-2	4	0
2♣	VER	SAF	MAFS	JUMS	PLF	3	3	0
3♣	MAFS	NER	PLF	URRS	VEFS	7	5	0
4♣	MAM	VEF	NERS	MAMS	URRS	7	3	3
5♣	MAM	MAMS	URRS	VER	NER	6	5	1
6♣	SAF	MAMS	CLFS	VEM	CRRS	3	6	-2
7♣	PLR	CRF	MARS	VEF	MAR	6	5	0
8♣	MAF	CLF	MAFS	MARS		8	8	-1
9♣	NEF	PLR	SARS	VERS	VEMS	5	2	1
10♣	PLF	VEFS	URFS	MOFS	PLFS	6	2	1
J♣	KRMA	SAR	NEF	NEFS	SAF	4	6	0
Q♣	VEMS	MOFS	MORS	MAFS	VEM	8	-2	9
K♣	MOF	MAF	JUFS	CLFS	VEM	7	1	5
A♦	VEF	CLRS	CRRS	JUR	CRR	4	0	4
2♦	CRRS	SAF	MAMS	VEF	CLRS	3	5	-1
3♦	PLRS	MORS	SAFS	MAMS	PLR	4	4	0
4♦	VEF	NERS	PLFS	NEFS	PLRS	7	2	3
5♦	NER	PLF	URRS	JUR	VERS	5	2	0
6♦	SARS	CLR	KRMC	SAFS	CLRS	0	5	-2
7♦	JURS	CRR	JUFS	SAM	CRRS	2	1	3
8♦	CRF	MARS	URR	PLR	SAF	5	5	-1
9♦	JUR	VERS	MORS	NER	PLF	5	-2	6
10♦	MOFS	VEMS	URR	NER	URRS	6	-2	6
J♦	SBC	CLR	SAFS	SAR	CLF	1	6	-3
Q♦	MORS	PLRS	JUR	VERS	MAR	5	0	5
K♦	VEFS	MAFS	MAR	CRFS	MARS	8	4	3
A♠	SAF	MAFS	SAMS	VER	VERS	2	6	-3
2♠	MAF	JUFS	URF	VEMS	MOR	6	2	4
3♠	KRMA	CLR	SAFS	SARS	NEF	2	6	-2
4♠	URFS	PLF	VEFS	MOR	MORS	5	1	2
5♠	NEFS	PLRS	JUM	VEF	NERS	5	1	3
6♠	URF	PLFS	MAF	JUFS	MAFS	5	4	-1
7♠	MAR	CRFS	VEFS	JUF	NEF	7	4	3
8♠	CLFS	VEM	MOF	SAF	MAMS	5	2	2
9♠	JUMS	URF	PLFS	URFS	JUM	2	1	1
10♠	MOR	NEF	PLR	JUF	NEFS	6	0	5
J♠	PLR	PLF	VEFS	PLFS	VEM	6	4	-1
Q♠	URR	MOFS	CRF	MARS	JUF	5	1	3
K♠	CLF	MAF	CLFS	MAFS	MARS	7	7	-2

The Actor Card

DESCRIPTION OF THE J♠ PERSON:
Through an excess of mental power and creativity, the J♠ can either become a visionary, a spiritual leader, or a thief. This card represents the 'spiritual initiate' but has also been called the 'Rip-off Card.' Most J♠ will have a little of both of these qualities present and it is up to the individual to direct their highly creative minds with truth and wisdom. Otherwise, they can become lost, believing the stories they concocted to avoid unpleasant life situations.

There is no doubt about their creative power and their ability to do anything with their minds. The question is whether they will direct this energy with wisdom and patience or whether they are lured by the 'easy wins' they can extract out of many situations and move toward the low side of their card. They sit in a powerful place, and this power can either take them to the highest or tempt them to the lowest.

Materially, this card has one of the easiest Life Paths of the entire deck. Much comes easily to them, but this can be the root of many of their problems. When life is too easy, people tend to not appreciate the value of what they have or are given and are more prone to abuse or ignore the good things they have. For the J♠ that take the route of the thief, this is usually part of the reason. They want to push life to the limits to experience some sort of challenge. Winding up in jail can be the challenge and remedy they seek. It is when they get caught and have to face themselves that many J♠ experience the spiritual initiation inherent in their card. Those that play with fire get burned sooner or later. And it is the fire that purifies them.

These people always do well with the public and can become successful artists or actors and actresses. They often inherit money even though they can make enough on their own. They are usually ambitious and can expect a successful life in most cases. It is their basic value system, learned in their childhood, that is most responsible for their direction and ultimate success.

SOME OF THE J♠ ISSUES CONCERNING RELATIONSHIPS:
The J♠ has some love karma to dispel in this lifetime. There are bound to be relationships that come into their lives to show them the value of truth, commitment, and the proper use of their strong sexual drive. They are very creative, romantic, and independent, and these qualities combined can get them into trouble if not coupled with wisdom and integrity. More than most cards, they dream of an ideal lover or partner and it is this dream that often keeps them searching. It may also be responsible for the high turnover rate in many of their love lives. It may be that no one person could ever match up to the high ideal of love they hold. Their success in love is always in their hands, so there is no one but themselves to blame if they are not satisfied in this area.

GENERALITIES BETWEEN THE PERSONALITY CARD CONNECTIONS
The J♠ female is trouble for the Heart male, usually too much for him to handle. Remember that Jacks, Queens, and Kings don't bow down to others and that J♠ women are as strong-willed as the men. Diamonds of both sexes usually do great with J♠ folks. The J♠ female usually has a high attraction to Club males, especially those who are more mature and powerful.

KARMA CARDS:
7♣   10♣

KARMA COUSINS:
8♦   4♠

PAST-LIFE CARDS:
10♠   Q♠

Jack of Spades—Spiritual Initiation

All Jacks represent initiations of one form or another. However, it is the J♠ who is the strongest symbol of initiation, the spiritual initiation. When someone is born as the J♠, we can bet that one of the themes in this person's lifetime will be the transition from the lower nature of the Jacks to the higher. The J♠ personifies both of these qualities in the extreme. In his or her lowest nature, the J♠ is someone who cannot be trusted and who is always up to no good. This person would be using their God-given creative gifts to fool others and take advantage of them, with no regard for how their actions are affecting those they are stealing from. Many J♠ people are operating primarily from this side of their card, and to be truthful, all of them have this side within them, whether they are currently choosing to express it or not. Perhaps it is because the J♠ can get so involved with the negative side of their card's expression that they can make the biggest turnarounds in their life. Out of all the Jacks, they seem to have the most interest in spiritual subjects. On some level they know that it is within them to make a great transformation in this lifetime. Many of them dive headlong into it at an early age, while others dabble in it but never get their feet wet. As in all things, each individual guides the course of his or her destiny and those decisions will tell, for better or worse, what the outcome of their life will be.

Spiritual initiation means renouncing the lower path for one that is higher and more in line with higher principles and beliefs. These beliefs may include the philosophies of honesty and integrity or of always being considerate of how our actions affect those around us. But it doesn't really mean much to just profess spiritual philosophy if your actions are just the opposite. The true spiritual initiation will cause a change in our *doing*, one of the keywords for the Spade suit. An example of a J♠ experience would be giving up smoking or doing yoga every day. The smokeless life or yoga has become a part of our *lifestyle*, another key word for Spades. I use the example of yoga because it is one of the many things that we can *do* that is spiritual in nature. By simply doing yoga, our inner awareness is heightened, even if we are only doing it to lose weight.

So, the J♠ will at some point begin to include spiritual 'doing' in their life if they are to rise to their fullest potential in this lifetime. It doesn't have to happen right away. There is no time limit. The mere fact that they are a J♠ tells us that they will experience all the levels of this card during their life. They may spend fifty years as a thief and a liar before they make the transformation, or they may follow those instincts in childhood and live a spiritually-based life from the beginning. They may fluctuate back and forth for fifty years too, or any number of other variations on the theme. They may even do a little of both at the same time.

I met a J♠ woman in Florida who was a professional astrologer and counselor. She was gifted at her profession, one of the best I have met, and she obviously was helping a lot of people. However, I also saw her cheat a couple of people in a business deal with no feelings of responsibility for her obvious actions. This illustrates how both qualities can exist in a person at the same time. This is how it is for all of us. We are each displaying some of the highest and lowest of our Birth Cards all the time. The extreme nature of the J♠ can serve to remind us of this and also to remind us of how each of us must go through spiritual transformation and initiation in this lifetime.

JACK OF SPADES

LIFE SPREAD CARDS		
PLANETARY CARD	**SYMBOL**	**CARD**
MOON	☽	2♦
SUN (BIRTH CARD)	✳	J♠
MERCURY	☿	8♣
VENUS	♀	6♦
MARS	♂	4♠
JUPITER	♃	10♥
SATURN	♄	10♦
URANUS	♅	8♠
NEPTUNE	♆	A♥
PLUTO	♇	A♦
RESULT (COSMIC REWARD)	♃ +	Q♦
COSMIC LESSON	♄ +	5♥

PLANETARY RULING CARDS		
BIRTH DATE	**ASTROLOGICAL RULING SIGN**	**PLANETARY RULING CARD**
JAN 3	CAPRICORN	10♦
FEB 1	AQUARIUS	8♠

Who J♠ with	Con1	Con2	Con3	Con4	Con5	Attraction	Intensity	Compatibility
A♥	NEF	PLR	MAFS	PLF	SAFS	6	5	-1
2♥	URR	JUFS	MAFS	URRS	JUM	2	1	2
3♥	SAFS	NEF	PLR	MAFS	MAF	3	6	-3
4♥	URFS	MAF	NERS	MOFS	VEM	5	2	2
5♥	CLF	NEFS	JUM	JUR	MAMS	5	2	2
6♥	MAR	PLFS	VER	MARS	VEF	8	6	0
7♥	CRFS	CLFS	VEMS	CLRS	CLF	6	4	1
8♥	CLFS	VEMS	JURS	CRFS	VEM	5	1	3
9♥	MOF	VEFS	CLFS	JUF	CRRS	6	-1	6
10♥	JUF	VERS	JURS	CLR	URRS	3	-2	6
J♥	CRR	VEFS	MOR	CRRS	VEMS	6	0	6
Q♥	VEMS	MOFS	VEM	PLR	PLRS	7	-2	7
K♥	SAR	NER	PLF	VERS	NERS	4	4	-1
A♣	URR	JUFS	URRS	JUM	JUF	1	-1	3
2♣	CLRS	SAR	URF	SARS	CLR	0	3	-2
3♣	SARS	JUR	MAR	JURS	SAR	1	3	1
4♣	VER	MARS	MAR	PLFS	VEM	8	4	2
5♣	CLF	NEFS	VER	MARS	VERS	7	3	2
6♣	URF	MARS	MOF	JUMS	MOFS	4	1	3
7♣	KRMA	VER	MAMS	NEF	PLFS	8	5	2
8♣	MOR	CRR	VEFS	MORS	VERS	7	-2	7
9♣	PLR	VEMS	VEF	VEFS	MOFS	6	-1	6
10♣	KRMA	MAM	NEF	PLFS	MAF	8	7	0
J♣	JURS	JUF	VERS	MAF	JUFS	3	-2	7
Q♣	SAFS	SAF	VEFS	MAF		0	6	-4
K♣	MAR	CRRS	URF	MARS	NEF	6	5	1
A♦	PLF	MOF	JUMS	NEF	PLR	6	2	2
2♦	MOF	JUMS	PLF	PLFS	SAFS	5	1	2
3♦	VEF	MAR	PLFS	CRF	URRS	7	4	2
4♦	JUM	CLR	URRS	CLF	NEFS	2	1	1
5♦	SARS	MAM	MOR	PLFS	JUF	4	4	0
6♦	VEF	PLR	PLRS	VEM	VEMS	5	1	4
7♦	CLFS	VEFS	JUF	CRRS		5	1	3
8♦	MORS	VER	KRMC	MAMS	VERS	7	0	7
9♦	MAM	CRF	URRS	SARS	JUF	4	5	0
10♦	SAF	MORS	CRR	SAFS	VEFS	1	3	-1
J♦	PLRS	VEM	JURS	PLF	PLR	4	2	2
Q♦	CRF	URRS	VEF	MAM	SAR	5	3	2
K♦	JUR	JURS	VEMS	MAR	SAR	3	-1	6
A♠	CLRS	CRFS	CRF	CLF	VEM	5	4	0
2♠	CRRS	JUR	SARS	NERS	MAR	3	2	2
3♠	PLRS	VEM	VEF	VER	VEMS	6	0	5
4♠	MAF	NERS	KRMC	MAM	URFS	7	5	1
5♠	CLR	URRS	JUF	VERS	JUM	2	-1	3
6♠	JUR	SARS	NERS	NER	PLF	2	2	1
7♠	JURS	JUR	CLFS	VEMS	SAF	2	0	4
8♠	URF	MARS	MAR	PLR	MAMS	5	5	0
9♠	NER	PLF	VERS	SAR	JUR	5	3	0
10♠	MOFS	VEM	URFS	VEMS	URF	6	-3	7
J♠	SBC	VER	MAMS	MAM	VEF	7	5	3
Q♠	MORS	SAF	VEF	CRR		4	1	3
K♠	VEFS	MOR	CRR	VEF	VERS	7	-2	8

The Queens

The Queen is a very powerful card. She is second in authority only to the King and in many ways is just as powerful, if not more powerful, than he. For this reason, a Queen person, regardless of sex, is aware of a certain power and responsibility they have in their life, one that can be used in positive ways or abused. The Queen is quite capable of ruling the kingdom, but would do it differently than the King. Her rulership would be more service-oriented and she would display more compassion as a rule. All Queens possess wisdom from having experienced so much in past lives. There are always some areas in life they will master with little effort. But those areas will usually not be personal relationships and marriage. Collectively, the Queens possess some of the most difficult love karma of any of the cards in the deck, especially the Q♦ and Q♣.

Queens are motherly by nature. Regardless of their occupation, they are mothering people through their work. They excel in helping others nurture and develop themselves. They have a natural desire to reach out to those in need of direction and support at certain stages in their evolution. They take great pleasure in knowing that they have contributed something to another's sense of well-being. They will feed you and offer you protection. The men and women of this card usually get along famously with children, whether or not they themselves have any.

But one of their faults is that they often hold on to those they love and actually prevent them from leaving the nest when they are ready. This habit comes from their strong identity as mothers. If there is no one to mother, they feel as though their life has no purpose. After all, what is a mother if there are no children to raise? So, when their fears of losing their identity become stronger than their love for their children, they hold back the growth of their children and do exactly the opposite of what they intend.

One challenge of the Queen is to translate this maternal desire to a broader level, away from their own families and onto the world at large. Queens can make excellent counselors, teachers, and promoters of good. They can play an instrumental part in helping large groups of people better their lives. They have a lot of natural leadership ability and are able to gather people together for a good purpose. The ones who direct their loving energies toward those outside of their immediate family find much success and satisfaction from their interactions.

This same desire to mother others can cause innumerable problems in their intimate relationships. If they are looking for someone to mother or someone who could mother them, they set themselves up for a very difficult relationship. A codependent mire of unclarity and unrealized dreams and needs is often the result of such a union. They invariably attract those who will take advantage of their need to be needed, or they themselves will be uncertain about where their true happiness lies. The Queen is a Twelve, which reduces numerologically to a Three. The Q♣ and Q♦ have Threes as their first Karma Card and Threes in Mars. All this 'Three energy' promotes indecision and insecurity in personal relationships, but the Q♣ and Q♦ have the worst time of it. At least the Q♠ and Q♥ have even-numbered Karma Cards, which gives them much more stability and peace. But even so, all of them have that creative Three urge that can lead to doubtful associations and indecision in their personal choices. Either that, or they attract others who display these characteristics. The Queen would sooner or later want to use some of her power to have romantic fun and adventure. In doing so, she will often create much uncertainty in her life.

The Queens represent some of the essential feminine archetypes. Whether a Queen is male or female, they will exhibit many of these basic feminine qualities. The Q♥ is the dreamy Aphrodite, the goddess of love and pleasure, who has a love for humanity that is very spiritual in nature. She is the woman all men dream of. The Q♣ is very much a businesswoman and organizer. She is highly intuitive, quick-tempered, and usually industrious. But she is also Mary, mother of Jesus, who makes great sacrifices on behalf of her children. She also possesses the highest spiritual gift—intuition. The Q♦ is the collector of things—usually money and relationships. She enjoys the things of the earth, much like the Q♥, but she is also very much involved in earning this wealth. She shares a higher sense of values with her children, who are not necessarily her biological children. These 'children' may be people that she works with. The Q♠ is Martha of the Bible, the tireless worker who knows the value of service and work. She is an organizer supreme and makes a tough boss. But inside she possesses the potential for the highest of spiritual accomplishments—mastery of the self.

The Loving Mother Card

DESCRIPTION OF THE Q♥ PERSON:

As the 'double Neptune' card, the Q♥ has its share of idealism. All of these people possess a certain charm and magnetism that attracts others. They are the 'mothers of love' and share this love with all they meet. They either get married and devote themselves to family or get involved in some professional career. They have more than average ability to be successful in many professions and, regardless of their sex, have especially good luck in professions where men predominate. This is represented by their K♠ in Mars, which is a very powerful card that will bring many of them great success throughout their life.

Both sexes take their role as mother or father very seriously. If they do become parents, there is little that can come between them and their children. They are very much like the K♥, who is usually more devoted to his or her children than to their spouse.

These people are very sweet, attractive, sociable, and loving. They can be very successful artists or performers and all have an appreciation for art and beauty. Many are aware of and make use of their abundance of psychic or musical ability. As long as their idealism is guided by truth, they can live the life of love and nurturing that is their birthright. This is the 'Loving Mother' card. Their calling in life has to include sharing their love with others, and the more, the better.

When operating on the lower levels, they can be overly self-indulgent, lazy, frivolous, and into the 'good life.' This is a card of enjoyment of the sensual pursuits and experiences. There are many codependents, escapists, and alcoholics among the Q♥. Once they set their sights in line with their high ideals and are ready to renounce laziness and complacency, there is no limit to how high they can climb in their work and career.

SOME OF THE Q♥ ISSUES CONCERNING RELATIONSHIPS:

The people of this card are usually attracted to those of power and financial strength. These are the 'darlings' of the deck. A female Q♥ represents Aphrodite, 'the woman all men dream of.' She is naturally blessed with all the feminine qualities that can make for a perfect wife or love partner. They are charming and devoted to their families and ideals of love. There is a certain gaiety and innocence about them and one would hesitate to ever criticize them for anything. Still, their ideals may be too high and sometimes they will attract a partner who will bring them back to earth. Hopefully, the fall will not be too high or too hard.

The males are likewise charming and graceful. They are more sensitive than most men and often become house-husbands who mind the children while their wives work as the bread winners. Both sexes are attracted to mates that are powerful and financially successful, and many of them marry into such a situation.

In some cases, the Q♥ charm turns to indecision and a certain disregard for the feelings of others. They can play the field with success, but will sometimes attract a partner who is unfaithful or indecisive.

GENERALITIES BETWEEN THE PERSONALITY CARD CONNECTIONS

The Q♥ female is strongly attracted to powerful men, especially of the Spade suit. Diamond males fall hard for Q♥ females and Club males find them very challenging. Both sexes of the Q♥ make good friends with Club females, but the male Q♥ finds these Club women somewhat unpredictable and hard to fathom.

KARMA CARDS:

10♠   9♣

KARMA COUSINS:

4♥   6♦

PAST-LIFE CARDS:

J♥   K♥

The Dreamy Queen of Hearts

The Q♥ is the Queen of sexual pleasure, romance, and child-rearing. However, she can be overly sensuous, too idealistic, and, in some cases, too laid back and lazy.

Once I was teaching a class of about eight women for a weekend-long Advanced Course. One of the ladies was a Q♥. Out of all the members of the class, she was the only one who laid down almost the entire time I was teaching. It was sort of comical really, the way she just lazed around and took it easy. Everyone in the class remarked about how she just propped herself up and lounged during the class. This would appear to be laziness to some people but I believe it was more of an enjoyment of the situation. Q♥ love their luxuries and comforts.

Q♥ of both sexes are often beautiful and charming, but they are just as often mired in codependent and victim-savior relationships where they are not getting their needs met. Keep in mind that this card is the only card in the deck with a double Neptune influence. While Neptune can inspire us to do great work to save the world, it can muddle up our personal lives to such an extent that happiness is impossible. For the Q♥, this codependent behavior occurs mostly with members of their family and their lovers/husbands/wives. When someone is so consumed with Neptune energy, they have great difficulty admitting that they have any needs of their own. Their entire life can be so filled with helping others and being there for everyone else that they become martyrs. This energy is good in their work, where many of them achieve great things. But this same influence always denies fulfillment in their personal relationships.

A classic Q♥ situation is as follows: A Q♥ woman is married to a successful, powerful man. The man has affair after affair, but the Q♥ stays in there hoping that someday he will change, or somehow telling herself that if she hangs in there and keeps giving to him, that he will someday see the light and begin loving her back. However, she never tells him what her needs are, or even that she has any needs at all.

The Q♥ person can improve their happiness level tremendously by practicing one simple thing—sharing their feelings and needs with their partner. It is simple, and yet scarier than most people could imagine. The truth is that the Q♥'s partner probably wants to give to them and take care of them, but the Q♥ must create a space for that to happen. He or she must be willing to take a risk and show their vulnerable sides to their partner. When this happens the possibility of true intimacy occurs with the one they love and they are able to share the joy for life that is the birthright of their uniquely beautiful card.

LIFE SPREAD CARDS

PLANETARY CARD	SYMBOL	CARD
MOON	☽	6♠
SUN (BIRTH CARD)	☀	Q♥
MERCURY	☿	10♣
VENUS	♀	8♦
MARS	♂	K♠
JUPITER	♃	3♥
SATURN	♄	A♣
URANUS	♅	Q♣
NEPTUNE	♆	10♠
PLUTO	♇	5♣
RESULT (COSMIC REWARD)	♃ +	3♦
COSMIC LESSON	♄ +	A♠

PLANETARY RULING CARDS

BIRTH DATE	ASTROLOGICAL RULING SIGN	PLANETARY RULING CARD
JUL 29	LEO	Q♥
AUG 27	VIRGO	10♣
SEP 25	LIBRA	8♦
OCT 23	LIBRA OR SCORPIO	8♦ OR K♠ & 5♣
NOV 21	SCORPIO	K♠ & 5♣
DEC 19	SAGITTARIUS	3♥

Who	The Connections Between Partners					Overall Index Ratings		
Q♥ with	Con1	Con2	Con3	Con4	Con5	Attraction	Intensity	Compatibility
A♥	MAF	JUF	CRRS	URM	JUFS	5	2	3
2♥	SAF	CLRS	VEFS	MARS	SAM	1	4	-2
3♥	JUF	CRRS	URM	URF	MAR	3	0	3
4♥	URR	PLRS	KRMC	NEF	NEFS	3	3	1
5♥	NERS	SAR	MAMS	PLF	URFS	4	5	-1
6♥	URRS	JUM	SAFS	CRF	CRFS	1	2	0
7♥	SARS	MAR	JURS	CLF	URF	2	4	0
8♥	MAR	JURS	CLR	SARS	URR	3	3	1
9♥	MARS	VEM	SAM	SAF	VEFS	4	5	1
10♥	VERS	VEMS	VEM	VEFS	VER	7	-3	9
J♥	MOFS	MAF	VEFS	JUF	CRFS	7	0	6
Q♥	SBC	NEF	CLFS	NER	CLRS	6	5	0
K♥	MORS	CRR	MAFS	MAF	CRRS	7	2	4
A♣	SAF	VEFS	CLRS	MARS	SAM	1	4	-1
2♣	CRR	MAFS	CLF	URF	JURS	5	4	0
3♣	JUFS	VEF	URRS	CRFS	JUF	4	-1	6
4♣	SAFS	PLF	URFS	URRS	JUM	1	5	-5
5♣	PLF	URFS	NERS	SAFS	MOR	4	4	-2
6♣	VER	NEFS	SARS	VEMS	CRR	5	0	4
7♣	PLFS	VEF	VEMS	VERS	SAR	7	1	3
8♣	JUF	CRFS	MOFS	MAF	VEFS	6	1	5
9♣	KRMA	CLFS	NEF	PLFS	PLF	7	7	-2
10♣	MOR	VEMS	URR	MORS	VEM	6	-3	8
J♣	VEMS	NER	PLF	VERS	VEFS	7	0	4
Q♣	URF	JUF	CRRS	URM	MAM	2	0	2
K♣	PLR	VERS	JUR	SARS	JUFS	3	1	3
A♦	MAF	VEMS	MAM	SAFS	VEM	7	4	2
2♦	VEMS	VER	NEFS	MAF	MAFS	8	0	6
3♦	CRF	URRS	JUM	VEF	URR	3	1	2
4♦	SAR	MAMS	NERS	PLFS	URF	4	6	-2
5♦	VEF	JUFS	CRFS	VEFS	URRS	5	-1	7
6♦	CLFS	MAM	KRMC	CLF	PLF	6	7	-2
7♦	MARS	SAM	VEM	SAF	VEFS	3	6	0
8♦	VEF	PLFS	SAR	VEFS	JUM	5	2	2
9♦	VEF	VEFS	VEMS	CRFS		7	-2	9
10♦	MAM	JUMS	URF	MAR	VERS	4	3	2
J♦	NER	PLF	VEMS	JUR	NERS	6	2	2
Q♦	CRF	VEMS	VEF	URR	NEFS	6	0	5
K♦	JUFS	CLR	CLRS	VEM	JUF	2	-1	4
A♠	CLF	URF	JURS	SARS	CRR	2	3	0
2♠	JUR	MOF	PLR	VERS	PLRS	4	-1	5
3♠	NER	PLF	JUR	NERS	PLFS	5	3	0
4♠	MOR	URR	PLRS	URRS	MARS	4	0	3
5♠	VERS	SAR	MAMS	URF	SARS	3	2	1
6♠	MOF	JUR	PLR	JURS	MAF	4	-1	6
7♠	CLR	MAR	JURS	SAR	MARS	3	4	1
8♠	SARS	PLR	VERS	VER	NEFS	3	2	1
9♠	MORS	MOF	MOFS	CRF	MOR	8	-3	9
10♠	KRMA	NEF	URR	PLRS	PLFS	5	5	0
J♠	VEMS	PLFS	MOR	MORS	VEM	8	0	5
Q♠	MAM	JUMS	VEF	VEFS	JUM	5	1	5
K♠	MAF	VEFS	JUF	CRFS	MOFS	7	2	5

The Mother of Intuition Card

DESCRIPTION OF THE Q♣ PERSON:

All Queens are service-oriented and receptive in nature. The mental nature of Clubs inclines the Q♣ to deal in the publishing trade, administrative work, or among the more aware ones, psychic work. Being Queens, they are always aware of their place in the royal court and resist anyone trying to mold them in any way. Their displaced card, the 3♥, as well as the 5♣ in their Venus position, tells us that uncertainty and indecision about love and friendship makes it hard for them to find lasting happiness in these areas. Their mental gifts are abundant, and whether they realize it or not, they are always receiving knowledge from their natural psychic gift. These people have incredible organizational minds, but live life at such a high pitch that they are often stressed out or overdoing it.

The A♠ in Jupiter promises many rewards if and when they follow spiritual or psychic lines of work or pursuits. They have a deep heritage of knowledge from past lives that is always available. The Q♣ is also known as the 'Mother Mary' card, and many of them have one or more 'children' for whom they must make sacrifices in their life, just as the Virgin Mary had to undergo the sacrifice of her son Jesus.

The Q♣ is very creative and resourceful, often having two or more jobs and many interests. They do best when there is some creative expression and freedom of movement in their careers. They are proud and do their jobs well. Some Q♣ are slated to make great contributions to our society. Their natural inclination to help and nurture others can be expressed in work that helps thousands of people or more.

SOME OF THE Q♣ ISSUES CONCERNING RELATIONSHIPS:

Though many Q♣ get married, not all are happy about it or make a success of it. These people have powerful minds and wills and not many partners can handle them and their willful ways. They also carry with them the karmic seeds for one or more difficult relationships that will be brought to fruition at some point in their life. For this reason, many of them try marriage once and then renounce it for the rest of their life. Some of them also change their mind a lot about what they want. This can make their partners feel very insecure about their love and cause a separation. They operate on higher frequencies, meaning their partner must have some mental ability and communication skills to make it work. There is also a certain amount of emotional indecision that adds to the challenges they have to deal with each time they fall in love.

Along with the Q♣, this card carries some of the most challenging emotional and relationship karma of all the cards in the deck. This is indicated by the 7♥ in Saturn and the 3♥ first Karma Card. Both of these cards indicate emotional needs that require care to deal with effectively. However, with a determined effort, any Q♣ can apply themselves in this area with great success.

The question is whether or not many of them will make the effort. Many Q♣ find a balance with a relationship that is long–term, but not exclusive or binding. Their work is often their first love and so relationships, and the work required to make true intimacy possible, are often put in a lower priority in their lives.

KARMA CARDS:

3♥   10♦

KARMA COUSINS:

A♥   Q♠

PAST-LIFE CARDS:

J♣   K♣

With all the love they have to give, they have some of the greatest potential for fulfillment in a relationship. They can be the Princess who marries the Prince and later becomes the Queen who lives happily ever after.

Spade males find the female Q♣ very attractive. Male Q♣ are attracted to Diamond females. The female Q♣ will usually have problems with most Heart males, though there are some exceptions.

PROFILE

The Impatient Queen of Clubs

The Q♣ is a very high-strung card. They are often impatient and intolerant of people they consider slow, dumb, or lazy. They themselves operate on a high pitch which most people would classify as stressful. There are so many Threes associated with their Birth Card and Life Path that the creative, resourceful, adaptable, but often quick-changing energy within them can make them appear like a normal person on some kind of 'speed drug.' This often manifests itself as people who think and drive very fast. The Mercury card in our Life Path often reveals something about our driving habits. The Q♣ has the 10♠ in Mercury, which is a powerful, 'got to get where I am going right now' kind of energy.

Take, for example, the Q♣ woman who was driving down the freeway one day when a man in a car cut her off as she was trying to exit. Whether he did it on purpose or not, she took it very personally. She became so angry with him that she ended up ramming her car into his. Later she regretted what she had done because it ended up costing her over $1,000. But during that moment, it seemed worth it to her. This particular woman is an exaggerated Q♣ in most every respect, but it does illustrate the high-strung nature that all of them possess. But most Q♣ wouldn't make the same choice she did in that situation.

Of the adults I personally have met who stutter, so far all of them have been Q♣. It seems like their mind is going so fast that their mouths just can't catch up with all they are thinking.

Q♣ are hard workers and you may be blessed to have one working for you. They like to get the job done and can tackle huge projects faster than most people. They are superb organizers and have a great deal of creative talent that can be employed in their work. And the ones that have slowed down a little have developed a little tolerance for the slowness of others. With this tolerance, they can enjoy the fruits of their own labors just that much more.

QUEEN OF CLUBS

LIFE SPREAD CARDS

PLANETARY CARD	SYMBOL	CARD
MOON	☽	A♣
SUN (BIRTH CARD)	✳	Q♣
MERCURY	☿	10♠
VENUS	♀	5♣
MARS	♂	3♦
JUPITER	♃	A♠
SATURN	♄	7♥
URANUS	♅	7♦
NEPTUNE	♆	5♠
PLUTO	♇	J♥
RESULT (COSMIC REWARD)	♃+	9♣
COSMIC LESSON	♄+	9♠

PLANETARY RULING CARDS

BIRTH DATE	ASTROLOGICAL RULING SIGN	PLANETARY RULING CARD
JAN 28	AQUARIUS	7♦
FEB 26	PISCES	5♠
MAR 24	ARIES	3♦
APR 22	TAURUS	5♣
MAY 20	TAURUS OR GEMINI	5♣ OR 10♠
JUN 18	GEMINI	10♠
JUL 16	CANCER	A♣
AUG 14	LEO	Q♣
SEP 12	VIRGO	10♠
OCT 10	LIBRA	5♣
NOV 8	SCORPIO	3♦ & J♥
DEC 6	SAGITTARIUS	A♠

Who Q♣ with	The Connections Between Partners					Overall Index Ratings		
	Con1	Con2	Con3	Con4	Con5	Attraction	Intensity	Compatibility
A♥	MAM	MAMS	KRMC	VEFS	VER	7	5	2
2♥	MOF	URF	PLFS	MOFS	MARS	6	0	3
3♥	KRMA	VER	MAM	MAMS	PLF	8	6	3
4♥	MAFS	MAMS	MOR	MORS	CLR	8	4	2
5♥	SAFS	VEF	NERS	VEFS	SAF	2	3	3
6♥	VER	PLRS	MAF	JUFS	MAFS	6	2	1
7♥	SAF	MAMS	CRR	JUF	NEF	3	5	3
8♥	CRR	MARS	SAF	MAMS	NER	4	6	-1
9♥	VEMS	URF	PLFS	MOF	URFS	5	0	-1
10♥	MAR	MOFS	NEF	NEFS	MOF	8	2	3
J♥	PLF	VEFS	MAR	JURS	CLF	6	4	5
Q♥	URR	MOR	MAMS	CRF	MARS	5	2	1
K♥	VEM	VEMS	CLRS	CLF	VER	6	-1	3
A♣	MOF	URF	PLFS	MOR	MARS	6	0	6
2♣	CLRS	JUF	VEM	VEMS	MAFS	4	-1	3
3♣	JUR	CRRS	URFS	JUM	VERS	2	-1	5
4♣	PLRS	VEF	NERS	VER	VERS	5	1	4
5♣	VEF	NERS	PLRS	JUF	MAMS	5	1	4
6♣	PLR	URRS	MAFS	VEM	URR	4	3	4
7♣	SARS	JUR	CRFS	CRF	VER	2	3	0
8♣	JURS	PLF	VEFS	MAR	JUR	5	2	1
9♣	CRF	MARS	URR	NEFS	VEFS	6	4	3
10♣	SAR	VERS	MAMS	MAR	SARS	4	4	1
J♣	MOFS	VEMS	MAR	MARS	VEM	8	0	1
Q♣	SBC	VER	VEF	NEF	PLFS	7	2	7
K♣	MORS	CLR	URR	VEMS	SAM	4	-1	4
A♦	VEFS	MAFS	VEM	MAM	MAMS	8	2	4
2♦	MAFS	VEM	PLR	URRS	VEFS	6	3	5
3♦	MAF	JUFS	VER	SAF	NERS	5	2	3
4♦	SAFS	NEF	CRR	URRS	CRF	2	5	3
5♦	URFS	JUM	SAR	CLFS	JUR	1	1	-2
6♦	NEFS	CRF	MARS	MAR	JURS	7	5	0
7♦	URF	PLFS	VEMS	MOF	PLF	5	2	2
8♦	JUR	CRFS	JUFS	SARS	VER	2	0	1
9♦	SAR	CLFS	URFS	JUM	JUMS	1	3	4
10♦	KRMA	PLF	PLFS	JUFS	MAM	7	7	-1
J♦	VEMS	MOFS	MORS	NEF	URFS	7	-3	-2
Q♦	MAF	JUFS	SAR	CLFS	JUR	4	4	9
K♦	VERS	JUR	CRRS	MARS	CRR	5	0	1
A♠	JUF	SAF	MAMS	CLRS	URF	1	3	5
2♠	CLR	URR	VEMS	NER	MORS	3	0	0
3♠	NEFS	VEMS	NEF	URFS	MAR	7	1	3
4♠	MAMS	SAR	VERS	MAFS	VER	6	5	5
5♠	NEF	MAR	SAFS	CRF	PLFS	5	6	1
6♠	NER	CLF	CLR	URR	VEMS	4	3	-1
7♠	MARS	VERS	CRR	CRRS	VER	7	3	0
8♠	MORS	PLR	URRS	PLRS	MOR	4	0	3
9♠	CLF	VEM	VEMS	NER	NERS	7	1	3
10♠	MOR	MAMS	MAFS	URR	MAF	7	3	4
J♠	SARS	SAR	VERS	CRF		1	3	3
Q♠	JUFS	JUR	KRMC	CRFS	SAR	2	0	-1
K♠	MAR	JURS	PLF	VEFS	MOF	6	3	5

The Philanthropist Card

DESCRIPTION OF THE Q♦ PERSON:

Like some other cards in the deck, the Q♦ has much indecision about values (3♦ Karma Card). This means they often have difficulty deciding what they want most. They love variety and are very creative and resourceful, unless they are worrying about money, which they often do. The Q♦ has expensive taste. When they get money, they like to spend it on items of high quality and usually high price. For this reason, they often spend beyond their means, which perpetuates their financial fears. Despite this, they are one of the most giving cards in the deck. The 9♥ in Jupiter and 9♦ second Karma Card give them a natural ability to let go and a natural desire to share their wealth with others. On one level, they represent the rich aunt or grandmother (or grandfather) who takes you out shopping for some new clothes or buys you an expensive birthday present.

Q♦ are known to be charming and enjoy the finer things in life. They are constantly seeking new adventures and sometimes relationships as well. The Q♦ has an innate good business sense and the talent of being able to promote their products or services. They can excel in many areas and have good leadership abilities. Regardless of what they do, they are Queens and therefore tend to 'mother' or 'nurture' others in their work and lives.

They have a naturally critical mind that is capable of doing intense analysis and planning. It also blesses them with the ability to see through the deceptions of others. However, this same mind can become negatively oriented when things don't turn out as they plan. They may then become very negative and critical of others. They all tend to have a somewhat pessimistic point of view at times, even though they are often unaware of it. They must practice a positive attitude to counterbalance this tendency.

If Q♦ people adopt a spiritual path in life, they can realize a special mission and achieve the heights of spiritual realization and self-mastery (Q♠ in Neptune). They also have a soul connection with many of the ancient sciences. A natural attraction to ancient mysteries and secret knowledge promotes the study of the eternal truths, which helps alleviate many of their mundane problems. If dedicated to a higher goal, there is no limit to how high they can climb in their lives. Some of the world's wealthiest people have been Q♦.

SOME OF THE Q♦ ISSUES CONCERNING RELATIONSHIPS:

As mentioned earlier, the Q♦ has some of the most difficult challenges that exist in the area of love. Being headstrong and proud, fond of variety, afraid of being abandoned, and having the power to get what they want when they want it can be a troublesome combination. Three or more marriages are common for this card, and even when they seem happily settled down, it is usually only temporary. They are quite charming and have a bit of charisma that makes it easy for them to start new relationships. The challenge for them is sustaining the relationship once it is started. They usually get their wishes, for better or worse, and must live with the consequences of their desires.

GENERALITIES BETWEEN THE PERSONALITY CARD CONNECTIONS

Q♦ males have fantasies about Spade females. Female Q♦ usually have a lot of passion for, and challenges with, Club males. They usually have great difficulty with most Heart males as well. Club women are both highly attracted to and irritated by the Q♦ male.

> **KARMA CARDS:**
> 3♦   9♦
> **KARMA COUSINS:**
> 6♥   5♦
> **PAST-LIFE CARDS:**
> J♦   K♦

The Queen of Diamonds's Love Life

The numbers of cards often have greater significance than we might first suspect. For example, many 8♥ people have eight children, or eight special people in their life that are part of their inner circle of loved ones. The Q♦ has a 3♣ in Venus, and perhaps this is why many Q♦ have three or more marriages. Of course, there are Q♦ who have only been married once, or those who never get married at all, but this is a curious pattern that is fairly common with this Birth Card.

If we look at the Q♦ Life Path, we note that there are actually three very important Threes there. The first is their 3♦ first Karma Card that signifies the basic uncertainty they have about what is most important to them in life. The second is their Venus Card, the 3♣, and the third is their Mars Card, the 3♠. Venus and Mars are often referred to as the 'personal planets,' because the cards found here, more than any others, reflect how we are in personal relationships, especially marriage, love, and sex. When someone has a Three or Five in even one of these positions, we can expect some variety and changes in their love life. With the two Threes, the Q♦ surpasses most other cards in the deck in the creation of new love relationships. Q♦ often can start relationships easier than they can stay with them. Three energy can become bored and restless if not allowed its expression. Three is the Two (two people together in this case) combined with the One (the desire for something new). Many Q♦ are never happy with what they have or they try to create multiple relationships at the same time.

Their 3♦ first Karma Card often creates an underlying fear of 'not getting enough' in the Q♦ personality makeup. It is usually this hidden fear that motivates many of them to create multiple relationships. Though on the surface they may profess that they are just bored with their current relationship or that they haven't found the right person, it could be that having one person is not enough to satisfy their need for security or variety. Many Q♦ men have what I call 'harem consciousness.' Though other cards have it too, this usually manifests in the Q♦ because of his inner insecurities that are often well-hidden from the view of those around them. If we see anyone going from one relationship to the next, we must look at this as being more significant than what they might tell us. Regardless of their reasons for this behavior, it is a definite sign that there is a deep inner conflict to be resolved.

When doing readings about choices in relationships, it is rare to recommend any Q♦ people for marriage. They are often highly unmarriageable, because of their relationship patterns. The truth is that this Q♦ pattern does not have to go on forever. The Q♦ that break this pattern are those who honestly confront themselves and put effort into unraveling their deepest fears. This is, at the very least, a gargantuan task. The Q♦ has always had the reputation of having some of the most difficult love karma of any card in the deck.

But those who have a personal commitment to finding the truth within them will make this journey. They can actually defy the normal Q♦ pattern and have a successful and long-lasting marriage or relationship. It is these examples, probably more than most other cards, that show us we are not limited by the expressed pattern of our Birth Card. The usual pattern of any Birth Card actually manifests as particular personal challenges for each person who has it. These are challenges, not fated curses. With conscious awareness and love, any negative pattern in any Birth Card can be transformed into a high expression of profound beauty.

QUEEN OF DIAMONDS

LIFE SPREAD CARDS

PLANETARY CARD	SYMBOL	CARD
MOON	☽	A ♦
SUN (BIRTH CARD)	✴	Q ♦
MERCURY	☿	5 ♥
VENUS	♀	3 ♣
MARS	♂	3 ♠
JUPITER	♃	9 ♥
SATURN	♄	7 ♣
URANUS	♅	5 ♦
NEPTUNE	♆	Q ♠
PLUTO	♇	J ♣
RESULT (COSMIC REWARD)	♃ +	9 ♦
COSMIC LESSON	♄ +	7 ♠

PLANETARY RULING CARDS

BIRTH DATE	ASTROLOGICAL RULING SIGN	PLANETARY RULING CARD
JAN 15	CAPRICORN	7 ♣
FEB 13	AQUARIUS	5 ♦
MAR 11	PISCES	Q ♠
APR 9	ARIES	3 ♠
MAY 7	TAURUS	3 ♣
JUN 5	GEMINI	5 ♥
JUL 3	CANCER	A ♦
AUG 1	LEO	Q ♦

| Who Q♦ with | The Connections Between Partners | | | | | Overall Index | | Ratings |
	Con1	Con2	Con3	Con4	Con5	Attraction	Intensity	Compatibility
A♥	VER	MOF	JUF	SAFS	MAR	5	-1	6
2♥	JUMS	SARS	PLF	JUM	JUR	2	2	0
3♥	JUF	SAFS	VER	SAR	JUMS	1	1	2
4♥	VER	URR	SAFS	SAF	VERS	1	2	0
5♥	MOR	PLRS	JUM	JUMS	PLR	4	-1	4
6♥	VEM	MAFS	KRMC	CRRS	MAF	7	3	4
7♥	MAF	VEFS	VEF	JUFS	MAFS	7	1	6
8♥	CLF	PLFS	MAF	MAFS	PLF	7	8	-4
9♥	JUF	SARS	JUMS	SAR	MAF	1	1	2
10♥	SAR	JUFS	PLF	VEFS	URFS	2	2	1
J♥	MAM	PLR	SAF	MAMS	URR	4	7	-3
Q♥	VEMS	CRR	VER	VERS		7	-2	7
K♥	VEF	CLFS	CRF	VEFS		6	2	4
A♣	JUMS	SARS	JUR	MAFS	PLF	2	1	2
2♣	VEFS	VEF	SAFS			4	0	5
3♣	VEF	URF	NERS	MORS	NER	5	-1	5
4♣	MAFS	JUM	VEM	VEMS	MAF	7	1	5
5♣	JUM	MOR	MAFS	MOF	JUMS	5	-1	6
6♣	MAR	CRFS	CLR	CLRS	CRF	5	6	0
7♣	SAF	MAMS	JURS	CRR	URFS	1	5	-1
8♣	PLR	MAM	PLRS	VEFS	SAF	4	5	-1
9♣	VEMS	NER	PLF	URRS	URF	6	1	2
10♣	CRR	URFS	URR	SAFS	PLR	1	3	-1
J♣	PLF	VEFS	MOFS	SAR	JUFS	6	2	2
Q♣	JUF	SAFS	JUR	VERS	MAR	1	1	3
K♣	VEMS	MAFS	VEM	MAR	CRFS	8	2	5
A♦	MOF	CLR	CLRS	VER	VERS	5	-1	4
2♦	CLR	CLRS	MOF	MOFS	NERS	4	0	3
3♦	KRMA	CRRS	VEM	NEF	PLFS	7	4	2
4♦	PLRS	URFS	MOR	MORS	URF	4	0	2
5♦	URF	NERS	KRMC	CRF	MARS	4	3	1
6♦	NER	PLF	URRS	VEMS	MAF	6	3	0
7♦	SARS	JUF	JUMS	MAF	JUFS	1	1	2
8♦	JURS	NEF	PLR	SAF	MAMS	3	2	2
9♦	KRMA	CRF	MARS	NEF	PLFS	7	7	0
10♦	JUR	VERS	NEF	PLR	NEFS	4	-1	5
J♦	MOFS	MAF	JUFS	PLF	VEFS	7	1	5
Q♦	SBC	CRRS	CRF	MARS	CRFS	6	6	0
K♦	MORS	VEF	CLF	PLFS	CLFS	7	1	4
A♠	VEFS	MAF	MOR	SAFS	VEF	6	1	5
2♠	MAFS	VEM	NEFS	VEMS	NEF	8	2	5
3♠	MAF	JUFS	NER	PLF	URRS	6	3	2
4♠	URR	SAFS	VER	VERS	PLFS	2	2	0
5♠	URFS	SAR	JUFS	PLRS	JUF	0	1	1
6♠	NEFS	CLFS	MAFS	VEM	CLR	7	4	2
7♠	CLF	PLFS	MORS	MOR	CLFS	7	4	0
8♠	MAR	CRFS	VEMS	VEM	SAR	7	4	3
9♠	CLFS	VEF	NEFS	NEF	PLR	6	3	2
10♠	VER	VERS	SAF			4	0	4
J♠	CRR	URFS	SAF	MAMS	VER	2	4	-1
Q♠	NEF	PLR	JUR	VERS	JURS	4	1	3
K♠	PLR	MAM	URR	PLRS	VEFS	4	4	-1

The Self-Mastery Card

DESCRIPTION OF THE Q♠ PERSON:

These people of much power and authority are, surprisingly, not always found in positions of authority or prominence. They often end up in menial positions where they bitterly complain about their position in life and never amount to much. They can become too ingrained in the struggle mentality and work ethic to see beyond it. However, this is the card of Self-Mastery that sits in the very crowning position in the Spiritual Spread. If these people recognize their powerful gifts and take responsibility for their life, they can rise to any heights they desire.

Among them we find some who are the most caustic and hard-driven and others who are the true mothers of the world who compassionately share and teach their wisdom. They are all born to rule, but they must actualize that destiny themselves. Their values play a key role in determining just how their lives turn out. If directed solely toward material gain, which is often the case, they lose most of their power and potential. They rise to their highest potential by following their intuition and inner guidance.

All Q♠ have the K♣ as their Planetary Ruling Card. This makes them highly intelligent, able leaders and brings them much success in education or writing. This also gives them a strong independent streak and a high degree of intuition. Accessing their highest potential often gets them involved as teachers and leaders.

They should avoid mixing love and money and there is always trouble when legal matters arise. They would do best to avoid arguments with men in powerful positions. They love to spend money and they hate getting the short end in legal affairs, but they usually do. They do best when they realize their place in the royal family and access the inner wisdom that is their birthright. They are exalted in the eyes of God. They have all the equipment necessary to do what they choose.

SOME OF THE Q♠ ISSUES CONCERNING RELATIONSHIPS:

The Q♠ has high ideals about love and marriage, so high that they could border on fantasy in some cases. They can be prone to affairs and these are likely to be more of a loss than a gain. There always seem to be large losses of money associated with love. They want to appear prosperous and have someone of means for a partner, but this usually doesn't happen. Later in life they find more success and fulfillment in love—that is, if they don't give up the dream of happiness before then. In some cases there is a strong independent nature that can make binding commitments, such as marriage, something to be avoided.

GENERALITIES BETWEEN THE PERSONALITY CARD CONNECTIONS

The Q♠ female is often married to a Club male, though the relationship is not always an easy one. Male Q♠ feel closest to Diamond females, for whom they hold a mystical fascination. Q♠ females are also very compatible with Diamond males, with whom they have a strong physical attraction and good communication.

KARMA CARDS:

10♦   8♦

KARMA COUSINS:

Q♣   7♣

PAST-LIFE CARDS:

J♠   K♠

The Queen of Spades—Self-Mastery

Our universe is composed of masculine and feminine energies and everything in it can be seen as a certain mixture of the two. Both masculine and feminine energy and their expressions are equally important. The universe would not exist without both of them in equal balance. The four Queens in the deck personify the feminine energy. They are the archetypes of femininity, and whether the person possessing a Queen Birth Card is masculine or feminine by birth, they will still embody many of the feminine, receptive principles.

The masculine energy is constantly in motion, never at rest, and always operating out of the creative urge, the Word. The feminine energy is receptive and passive. Instead of chasing down the things that they want, those with a strong feminine energy will attract things to them and become a receiver of energy. When we take this feminine Queen energy and combine it with the suit of Spades, we get the symbol for self-mastery. Spades refer to our spiritual development. Of course they are also strongly associated with work, labor, service, and health. But on their highest plane, the Spades suit is the suit of transformation of the soul.

When we meet a Q♠ person, we see someone who has the opportunity to embody the highest of spiritual principles. Not all of them do this though. Many of them get completely caught up in struggle and servitude. They become the laborers and drudges of the deck. Of course, all of the Spade cards can fall into this trap, but it is the Q♠ that loses the most when they disregard their gift. The Q♠ sits in the position of highest accomplishment in the Spiritual Spread, the Sun position. As such, they symbolize that which is the greatest goal on the spiritual level: self-mastery. And what is this self-mastery? What does it really mean?

Self-mastery is mastery of our world through self-awareness. We can struggle and struggle to make more money without success for a lifetime. Or, if we realize just how our inner fear of poverty is affecting us each day, we could completely remove the effects of this fear from our lives and become wealthy beyond imagination without any struggle or effort on our part. This is only one example of how self-mastery works. Instead of trying to change the circumstances of our life on an exterior level, such as who we are in relationship with, what kind of a job we do, or where we live, we go right to the source and magically change our lives without *doing* anything. The Q♠ teaches us that we only need to stay aware of ourselves in order to master the universe.

Jesus and other spiritual masters have taught us that 'the Kingdom of Heaven is within' and to 'lay up our treasures in heaven' where they will not be corrupted or lost. If we seek this kingdom inside of ourselves by developing our self-awareness, we can attain the heaven that everyone wants. When we are in touch with what is real and what we are feeling and thinking, we begin to see clearly how our thoughts, beliefs, attitudes, and feelings, not our actions, create our world. By merely being aware, our lives can be changed forever and we can reach that position of highest personal attainment.

QUEEN OF SPADES

LIFE SPREAD CARDS		
PLANETARY CARD	**SYMBOL**	**CARD**
MOON	☽	5♦
SUN (BIRTH CARD)	✳	Q♠
MERCURY	☿	J♣
VENUS	♀	9♦
MARS	♂	7♠
JUPITER	♃	2♣
SATURN	♄	K♣
URANUS	♅	J♦
NEPTUNE	♆	4♥
PLUTO	♇	4♦
RESULT (COSMIC REWARD)	♃ +	2♠
COSMIC LESSON	♄ +	8♥

PLANETARY RULING CARDS		
BIRTH DATE	**ASTROLOGICAL RULING SIGN**	**PLANETARY RULING CARD**
JAN 2	CAPRICORN	K♣

Who Q♠ with	The Connections Between Partners					Overall Index Ratings		
	Con1	Con2	Con3	Con4	Con5	Attraction	Intensity	Compatibility
A♥	CRR	VEFS	PLR	SAF	JUFS	4	2	2
2♥	MAFS	JUMS	MAF	CLF	VEM	6	4	1
3♥	SAF	JUFS	CRR	VEFS	JURS	1	2	1
4♥	NEF	PLR	SAFS	PLRS	VERS	3	4	-1
5♥	URR	URFS	PLF	MARS	SAF	2	3	-2
6♥	NEFS	MAM	SAM	PLR	SAMS	4	6	-1
7♥	JUF	PLFS	CLF	CRFS	CRF	5	4	0
8♥	CLF	CRFS	MAF	SARS	NERS	5	6	-2
9♥	MAR	CLFS	VEMS	PLF	MARS	7	6	0
10♥	VEM	MOR	NERS	MOF	MAMS	8	-2	8
J♥	VERS	MORS	MAMS	VEF	VER	8	-1	7
Q♥	VERS	JUM	MAM	JUMS	VER	5	-1	5
K♥	MAF	VEMS	JUF	MAMS	MARS	7	3	4
A♣	MAFS	MAF	JUMS	CLF	VEM	7	5	1
2♣	JUF	MAMS	MAF	VEMS	MAFS	7	3	4
3♣	SAR	MOF	URRS	URF	CLF	2	1	1
4♣	MAM	MARS	NEFS	NER	MAR	8	6	1
5♣	MARS	URR	URFS	MAM	MAMS	4	4	0
6♣	CLR	JURS	JUR	URRS		0	-1	3
7♣	VER	MOFS	KRMC	CRF	VEFS	7	0	7
8♣	MAMS	VERS	MORS	JUR	MAM	7	2	5
9♣	JUM	VEF	SARS	VEFS	MAM	3	-1	5
10♣	MOFS	PLRS	MOF	SAR	CRFS	5	0	4
J♣	MOR	URF	VEM	VEMS	CLRS	5	-2	7
Q♣	JURS	SAF	KRMC	JUFS	JUF	0	2	2
K♣	SAF	CRF	CLRS	CLR	JURS	1	5	-3
A♦	PLR	CRR	VEFS	MAF	CRRS	5	3	1
2♦	PLR	URR	PLRS	URRS	JUR	2	2	-1
3♦	SAM	NEFS	NER	PLF	NERS	3	6	-1
4♦	PLF	NERS	URR	URFS	URRS	4	4	-2
5♦	MOF	VEF	SAR	CLF	SARS	5	0	4
6♦	VEF	SARS	JUM	JUR	CRRS	2	0	4
7♦	MAR	CLFS	VEMS	MARS	VEM	7	5	2
8♦	KRMA	NEF	PLFS	VER	JUF	7	5	1
9♦	VEF	NER	PLF	MOF	MOFS	7	1	4
10♦	KRMA	JURS	NEF	PLFS	PLF	6	4	1
J♦	URF	JUR	CRRS	MOR	MORS	3	-1	4
Q♦	NER	PLF	SAM	VEF	JUF	4	4	-1
K♦	URRS	SAR	MAF	SARS	NERS	1	4	-1
A♠	JUF	PLFS	MAMS	JUFS	MAM	5	3	2
2♠	CRF	CLRS	URRS	SAF	SAFS	2	4	-2
3♠	JUR	CRRS	VEF	SARS	URF	2	0	4
4♠	PLRS	NEF	PLR	SAFS	VER	4	4	-1
5♠	NERS	VEM	PLF	PLFS	CLFS	7	3	1
6♠	URRS	MARS	CRF	CLRS	CRFS	4	4	0
7♠	MAF	SARS	NERS	URRS	CLF	4	5	-1
8♠	CLR	JURS	SAF	MOR	CLRS	0	1	1
9♠	MARS	MAF	VEMS	URRS	VEM	7	4	3
10♠	VERS	NEF	PLR	SAFS	MAF	5	2	2
J♠	MOFS	VER	SAR	CRF	VEFS	6	-1	5
Q♠	SBC	PLF	NEFS	JUR	VEFS	6	5	1
K♠	MORS	MAMS	VERS	MOR	JUR	8	0	7

The Kings

The King is the last card in each suit, representing the last stage of development. Within the King is the wisdom of having passed through every number below him in his evolution to the pinnacle of power. The King is the masculine archetype of leadership and power, accompanied by the wisdom of experience. All Kings know the right thing to do. However, they do not always act upon that wisdom, which is how we account for those Kings who are a discredit to their symbol. The problem lies primarily in the misuse of power, which is a very alluring and easily misused thing for all of us. You should also read about the Eights as you study the Kings because they share this power. Hopefully, the King has already learned about the misuse of power during his or her evolution and will not abuse it again. But there are always enough variations that we will eventually run across a King who personifies all that is bad and undesirable in a powerful person.

All Kings have a certain amount of pride. Because they are natural born leaders, they tend to set themselves apart from the world at large and see themselves as part of a special group of leaders. Even those who do not directly recognize this quality within themselves will exhibit some pride or aversion to being given direction by others in spite of themselves. Many Kings do not recognize the power they already have and are using in their life. Some actually believe they are somewhat powerless in their world, but a close examination of their life always reveals that they are stubbornly persistent in doing things their own way. Usually others respect them or fear them, even if they themselves are unaware of it because of their damaged self-image. For many Kings, all they need to know is that they are a King, one who is meant to lead. Often, this by itself is all they need to get their minds in sync with who they really are.

Any King's power is defined primarily by their birth suit. The K♥ has power with people and personal relationships. They are charming and very intelligent. The K♣ has mental power that can be applied in a multitude of professions or situations. They make the fine distinctions that separate truth from untruth. The K♦ is the powerful and often ruthless business person. When they decide to take over, there isn't much they cannot accomplish on the material level, though their personal happiness may be lost in the process. The K♠ has the power of the will backed by a deep wisdom. Their mind will never be swayed by others since their own wisdom is constantly telling them the truth.

Female Kings are an interesting quirk in the cosmic plan. Here is a soul in a woman's body that has definite leadership ability, decisiveness, and usually a bit of aggressiveness to match. Women like Sharon Stone, Faye Dunaway, Jacqueline Kennedy Onassis, Janet Jackson, Queen Elizabeth II, and Bridget Fonda all personify women who are strong leaders of men. A King is not an easy card to be for anyone because of the tremendous responsibility implied. The women have the added burden of balancing their male and female sides in personal relationships. This hurdle alone can take most of a lifetime to conquer.

Being a King implies responsibility, and perhaps this is another of the real reasons that some Kings never achieve their potential. Responsibility can be either distasteful or fearful for some Kings and they may make a decision early on to avoid this part of their life at all costs. When they do, they take off their crown and become either the Jack or Queen of their suit, throwing away most of their power and potential. Few K♠ are ready to wear their crowns. Since they are literally the King of Kings, their crown holds the most power, but also the most burden. Most K♠ feel more comfortable as a Jack or Queen. They make great artists, musicians, and actors, but few achieve the full potential of the most powerful card in the entire deck. However, the other Kings are also guilty of this same choice. Though it doesn't happen as often, other Kings will shy away from the responsibility of living up to their birthright. They just decide to have fun instead. In doing so, they throw away their power and then wonder why their life doesn't seem to make them happy. All Kings have an inner voice that tells them they are fit to be leaders. Until they fulfill this aspect of their destiny, they cannot truly be at peace with themselves.

Other Kings will abuse their power, forsaking their inherent wisdom and giving in to their fears. They will bully, dominate, and use others, but often claim that it is they who are being abused. These are the Kings who have lost their authority. However, this is not a common occurrence. Though we will find those who use their power unwisely, this is not the rule. Most Kings are aware of their power and have the wisdom and patience to know that it must be used with care and responsibility if it is to do any good to them or in the world. We can usually trust them to lead us to things that better our lives in many ways.

The Loving Father Card

DESCRIPTION OF THE K♥ PERSON:

Standing at the top of the suit of love, the K♥ recognizes that love is the highest power of all. These people make devoted parents, but not always the best spouses. Their devotion to their children and profession often displaces the love they would give their spouse. They do love everyone, forever, it's true, but sometimes the wrong associations bring problems. They should be careful of mixing with people with lower motives and lifestyles in this regard.

These people can be overbearing, as all Kings can, but this is only the case when they have been betrayed by those they hold closest to their hearts. From past lives, they bring with them the knowledge of mastery of their emotions and of their family life. Consider yourself blessed if they consider you to be one of their 'family.'

The K♥ can excel in business, especially as a dealer or advisor in the finances of others. They have more success in association with others or partnerships than they do alone. They have better than average luck in legal matters as well. It is not wise to argue with them. Their keen minds can always find a suitable response.

There are inevitable losses of loved ones in their lives, but they know the truth and can let go, though they still feel the pain. Many of them are mentally gifted and sometimes psychic. Much knowledge just flows to them and they use this to rise to the top in their careers.

SOME OF THE K♥ ISSUES CONCERNING RELATIONSHIPS:

Many say that the K♥ makes a great lover and father, but a lousy husband. As with all the Kings, the power can be used or abused. They are the 'Kings of Charm.' So, we find as many 'playboys' among them as we do with 8♥. The archetype of the K♥ is something like the sultan with his harem, and it is interesting how many male K♥ go unmarried, but manage to have a circle of women around them most of the time. These women may or may not be their lovers—they may be students, family members, or casual associates. Whatever the case, we often find some kind of group of admirers surrounding them.

Women K♥ have a problem in that they are so powerful and headstrong. They can usually stand up to any man and they usually insist on being the head of their household. This can be difficult for some male partners to deal with. Also, all K♥ have a very argumentative nature that can be difficult for anyone to deal with.

K♥ have a unusually strong sense of justice when it comes to love and relationships. They will often stand up for others who have been wronged and may step into the role of peacemaker in their work or family life. They likewise will seek some form of retribution if they feel they have been treated unfairly by others.

Their pattern indicates that there will be some fated relationships that occur, which will reflect back to them their own indecisive nature and the consequences of it.

GENERALITIES BETWEEN THE PERSONALITY CARD CONNECTIONS

Female K♥ would be wise to avoid men of the Spade suit. Male K♥ should be careful of Diamond females, though the latter find them very appealing. K♥ females make good marriages with Diamond males, especially if they are more on the mature and responsible side.

KARMA CARDS:

2♣ 9♠

KARMA COUSINS:

A♠ 6♠

PAST-LIFE CARDS:

Q♥ A♣

Jacqueline Kennedy Onassis, K♥

Jackie Kennedy passed away at age 64. She was a grand lady who distinguished herself by her manner and the way she handled her life. She captured our hearts with her charm and artistic bearing. We were fascinated with the way she dressed and decorated the White House, and especially the way she handled all of us in her King of Hearts way. Remember that the K♥ is the master of relationships, artistic pursuits, and style, among other things.

John Kennedy was a 3♣. With the K♥ having a Karma Card of the 2♣, this was an ideal pairing in many ways. The 2♣ is the Moon Card to the 3♣, which is often perfect for marriage. 3♣ have much uncertainty in the romantic area though, and it was probably inevitable that he would have affairs. Marilyn Monroe, a 3♠, must have been a huge attraction for him since she was his Mercury Card. Though Marilyn looked to John for support, because he is her Moon Card, he was unable to give that to her with his role as President. All in all it was a fated love triangle that has many connections for us to look at and learn from.

After John was assassinated, Jackie stepped into her K♥ power. The K♥ is the 'father card,' after all. She immediately made the welfare of her children her highest priority. Others were amazed at her power to take such good care of them in a time of great crisis. Later, she married Aristotle Onassis, a Q♦. The K♥ and Q♦ have a very good Venus connection in the Life Spread and there was certainly a genuine love between them.

After Aristotle's death, Jackie returned to New York and got involved in the publishing field. Remember that the 2♣ Karma Card makes the K♥ gravitate toward the communications fields. They are very smart and can stand on their own in any of these areas. They also bring their artistic talents to bear in their work.

The year before she died, Jackie had a K♣ Long Range, which was also associated with the 6♠ and 7♠. This is when her illness came to the forefront. The year she passed away, she had an A♦/9♦ Long Range, which sat on top of the A♠ and 2♣. All of these health and death cards were present around the time of her departure. It is interesting to note that at the time of her death she was in her Uranus period with a 3♣. Perhaps death, to her, meant returning to John F. Kennedy, her 3♣ husband.

LIFE SPREAD CARDS

PLANETARY CARD	SYMBOL	CARD
MOON	☽	2 ♥
SUN (BIRTH CARD)	✳	K ♥
MERCURY	☿	K ♦
VENUS	♀	6 ♥
MARS	♂	4 ♣
JUPITER	♃	2 ♦
SATURN	♄	J ♠
URANUS	♅	8 ♣
NEPTUNE	♆	6 ♦
PLUTO	♇	4 ♠
RESULT (COSMIC REWARD)	♃ +	10 ♠
COSMIC LESSON	♄ +	10 ♦

PLANETARY RULING CARDS

BIRTH DATE	ASTROLOGICAL RULING SIGN	PLANETARY RULING CARD
JUN 30	CANCER	2 ♥
JUL 28	LEO	K ♥
AUG 26	VIRGO	K ♦
SEP 24	LIBRA	6 ♥
OCT 22	LIBRA	6 ♥
NOV 20	SCORPIO	4 ♣ & 4 ♠
DEC 18	SAGITTARIUS	2 ♦

Who	The Connections Between Partners					Overall Index Ratings		
K♥ with	Con1	Con2	Con3	Con4	Con5	Attraction	Intensity	Compatibility
A♥	VERS	VEF	CLRS	VEFS	VER	6	-2	7
2♥	MOF	MORS	URR	MOR	URFS	6	-3	7
3♥	VEF	CLRS	VEM	VEMS	NEFS	6	-1	7
4♥	JUR	CRRS	PLF	SAMS	MAF	3	3	0
5♥	PLRS	CLR	SAFS	CLRS	CRFS	1	5	-3
6♥	VEF	NERS	PLFS	MAF	JUFS	7	2	3
7♥	NER	PLF	URRS	SARS	PLR	4	4	-2
8♥	SARS	MAM	NER	PLF	URRS	4	5	-2
9♥	JURS	URR	MORS	NER	URRS	2	-2	5
10♥	CRF	MARS	SAR	SARS	VEM	4	6	-1
J♥	JUR	VERS	URF	PLFS	JURS	3	-1	4
Q♥	MOFS	MAR	CRFS	CRF	MARS	8	4	3
K♥	SBC	VEFS	VER	SARS	VERS	5	2	4
A♣	MORS	MOF	URR	MOFS	URFS	6	-3	7
2♣	KRMA	VEFS	PLR	NEF	NEFS	6	4	3
3♣	MAFS	VEM	MAMS	MOR	MORS	9	3	5
4♣	MAF	JUFS	CLR	SAFS	VEF	4	3	1
5♣	CLR	SAFS	PLRS	MAF	JUFS	1	5	-3
6♣	URFS	JUM	JUF	NEF	JUFS	2	-1	4
7♣	NEFS	PLRS	MARS	MAM	SAF	6	5	0
8♣	URF	PLFS	JUR	VERS	URFS	3	1	1
9♣	MAR	CRFS	MOFS	NEF	PLR	7	4	2
10♣	CLFS	SAF	PLF	SAMS	CLF	2	8	-6
J♣	JUMS	CRF	MARS	MAR	CRFS	5	4	2
Q♣	VEM	VEMS	VEF	CLRS	CLF	7	-2	8
K♣	JURS	MOR	JUR	SAF	NERS	2	-1	5
A♦	VERS	JUF	VEM	MAFS	MAF	6	-1	7
2♦	JUF	URFS	JUM	VERS	MAF	2	-1	5
3♦	CRR	VEF	NERS	PLFS	VER	6	2	3
4♦	SAR	PLRS	JUF	MAR	JURS	2	3	0
5♦	MAMS	MAFS	VEM	SAR	VEMS	7	5	2
6♦	NEF	PLR	MAR	CRFS	CRF	6	5	1
7♦	URR	JURS	MORS	JUR	NER	2	-2	5
8♦	MARS	MAM	MAR	VEMS	NEFS	8	6	2
9♦	VER	MAMS	CLRS			6	2	3
10♦	CLF	VEM	VEMS	MAR	MARS	7	2	3
J♦	JUMS	VEF	PLR	URRS	JUM	3	-1	4
Q♦	VER	CRR	CLRS	VERS	NER	5	0	4
K♦	MOR	MAFS	VEM	MAM	MAMS	8	2	5
A♠	PLR	NER	KRMC	PLF	URRS	5	4	-1
2♠	JURS	SAF	NERS	PLFS	PLF	1	3	-1
3♠	NEF	PLR	JUMS	URRS	CRF	4	2	2
4♠	PLF	SAMS	CLFS	JUR	CRRS	3	7	-4
5♠	SAR	CRF	MARS	MAR	JURS	4	6	-1
6♠	VER	SARS	KRMC	JURS	PLF	3	2	3
7♠	MAM	MOR	SARS	MOF	VERS	6	2	4
8♠	URFS	JUM	VEF	JUMS	MOFS	2	-2	5
9♠	KRMA	VER	SARS	NEF	NEFS	5	4	2
10♠	JUR	CRRS	MOFS	MORS	CRR	4	-1	6
J♠	SAF	NEFS	PLRS	CLFS	NEF	2	5	-3
Q♠	MAR	VEMS	CLF	MARS	MAM	7	5	2
K♠	URF	PLFS	JUR	VERS	JUFS	3	1	1

The Master of Knowledge

DESCRIPTION OF THE K♣ PERSON:

Sitting atop the suit of knowledge and communication, the K♣ holds everything needed to be an authority in any area they choose. These people have a direct line to knowledge accumulated from many past lives. Rarely do they live their life by any doctrine or philosophy other than their own. The well that feeds their minds is inexhaustible and comes from a high source. These are the people who live by their own truth.

They can be found in all types of professions, usually in positions of responsibility. They are always respected in whatever capacity they are engaged. Among their numbers are some of the most successful artists, statesmen, and musicians in the world. One of their greatest assets is the ability to make fine distinctions and a witty and personable nature that usually makes them popular and well-liked. They seem to do their best work with a partner, and most K♣ are destined to be in partnerships.

For many K♣, challenges in life will revolve around abuses in drugs, alcohol, or some other form of escapism. These people are often very emotionally sensitive and have strong ties to a childhood that had its share of challenges. In a quest to understand and resolve those inner conflicts, the K♣ can go through all sorts of chapters in life, some of which seem the opposite of their highest potential. But their makeup is such that they usually wake up in their thirties and move into the recognition of the power and responsibility that is their birthright.

This is the most psychic card in the deck—so much so that their intuitive approach to life is second nature. Their greatest challenges lie in the concept of marriage and the occasional habit of getting into a comfortable rut and not pushing themselves to their highest potential. They have a lot to give to the world, which can lead to regret later in life if it is not fully expressed.

SOME OF THE K♣ ISSUES CONCERNING RELATIONSHIPS:

The K♣ has basically good marriage karma and they love the feeling of being in a close relationship. However, there are aspects of marriage that are very challenging for them. One of the major challenges is the part that tells them they will lose their personal freedom in a marriage. Freedom is an important word for the K♣, something to be treasured above all else, including a happy relationship in some cases. You might say that the K♣ has a problem around freedom, though it doesn't prevent all from getting married or settling down.

The female K♣ often has some major challenges associated with either marriage, sex, or children. The Q♥ Pluto Card can manifest in many different ways, but we always find some challenge connected to it in the lives of the female K♣. They would benefit from learning more about this card, which represents life-long transformation issues for them.

The male K♣ usually attracts women who personify some of the negative traits of the Q♥, the escapist or lazy and self-indulgent types. With both male and female K♣, there is a need to make fine distinctions between their inner truth and the dreams of romantic or marital happiness.

These strong-willed and powerful people make fine distinctions with their minds. Anyone who is involved with them has to

---

KARMA CARDS:

2♠   8♠

KARMA COUSINS:

6♠   6♣

PAST-LIFE CARDS:

Q♣   A♦

be able to handle this power and intensity without getting defensive, which is challenging in many cases. For this reason, the women are more masculine-oriented and in some cases domineering. It is sometimes difficult for them to find a partner with whom they can be themselves.

Both male and female K♣ get along best with Diamonds and have challenges with Hearts, except for the K♥, which is always a good connection. Their friends are usually Clubs to whom they often end up as mentors on one level or another.

PROFILE

The Highest Truth

K♣ make distinctions in their life about everything and are very sensitive to things that other people care little about. If something is not right with them, if some detail is missing, some 'T' uncrossed or some 'I' undotted, they will not feel at ease until the situation is remedied. They can be a stickler for details and, in their mind, there has to be a reason for everything. So, the K♣ is always searching for these reasons and is never truly satisfied until they have found the ones that resonate within them as the truth. Once they have found a truth about something that resonates in this manner, they will stick by it with all their heart and soul.

In their quest for higher and higher truths, they undergo many powerful transformations. They end up burning in the fires they create. So, if a K♣ is challenging you to face the truth they see in you, remember that their truth is a double-edged sword that cuts them just as deeply. Most of them seem to understand this, and when they give out criticism or suggestions, they do it with compassionate understanding of what they are saying.

At heart, the K♣ is very progressive and many people will consider their viewpoint to be somewhat unorthodox or even weird. But it is this same Aquarian quality that brings so many of them the ideas that will shape the future of our world. The fact that so many of them end up in positions of leadership and responsibility, and that they are among the four most common Birth Cards in the deck, tells us that they are a major force in the direction of our society and culture. A quick glance down the list of K♣ celebrities reveals just how many of them have made significant contributions to our world. If they have it their way, our world will be based upon clarity of thought and truth that can be understood and proven.

K♣ are always known for what they said or wrote. This is what the element of Clubs is all about. Communications, thoughts, words, ideas, beliefs, and mental distinctions are the realm of the Club suit. The most fulfilled among the Kings of this suit are those who stand and proclaim their highest truth to the world, and help others in the process.

LIFE SPREAD CARDS

PLANETARY CARD	SYMBOL	CARD
MOON	☽	2♣
SUN (BIRTH CARD)	☀	K♣
MERCURY	☿	J♦
VENUS	♀	4♥
MARS	♂	4♦
JUPITER	♃	2♠
SATURN	♄	8♥
URANUS	♅	6♣
NEPTUNE	♆	6♠
PLUTO	♇	Q♥
RESULT (COSMIC REWARD)	♃+	10♣
COSMIC LESSON	♄+	8♦

PLANETARY RULING CARDS

BIRTH DATE	ASTROLOGICAL RULING SIGN	PLANETARY RULING CARD
JAN 27	AQUARIUS	6♣
FEB 25	PISCES	6♠
MAR 23	ARIES	4♦
APR 21	ARIES OR TAURUS	4♦ OR 4♥
MAY 19	TAURUS	4♥
JUN 17	GEMINI	J♦
JUL 15	CANCER	2♣
AUG 13	LEO	K♣
SEP 11	VIRGO	J♦
OCT 9	LIBRA	4♥
NOV 7	SCORPIO	4♦ & Q♥
DEC 5	SAGITTARIUS	2♠

Celebrity Birthdays

DEAN MARTIN
6/17/17 • Actor
TONY DANZA
4/21/51 • Actor
TROY DONAHUE
1/27/36 • Actor
SEAN ASTIN
2/25/71 • Actor
ANDIE MACDOWELL
4/21/58 • Actress
BRIDGET FONDA
1/27/64 • Actress
DONNA REED
1/27/21 • Actress
JOAN CRAWFORD
3/23/08 • Actress
ZEPPO MARX
2/25/01 • Comedian
WOLFGANG AMADEUS MOZART
1/27/1756 • Composer
FIDEL CASTRO
8/13/27 • Dictator
ALFRED HITCHCOCK
8/13/1899 • Director
WALT DISNEY
12/5/01 • Entertainment Mogul
BILLY GRAHAM
11/7/18 • Evangelist
AKIRA KUROSAWA
3/23/10 • Movie Director
GEORGE HARRISON
2/25/43 • Musician
JOHN LENNON
10/9/40 • Musician
IGGY POP
4/21/47 • Rock Singer
QUEEN ELIZABETH II
4/21/26 • Queen
JONI MITCHELL
11/7/43 • Singer
BARRY MANILOW
6/17/46 • Singer
ANNIKA SORENSTAM
10/9/70 • Golfer
VENUS WILLIAMS
6/17/80 • Tennis Player

Who K♣ with	Con1	Con2	Con3	Con4	Con5	Attraction	Intensity	Compatibility
A♥	VEF	MORS	SAM	MAM	SAMS	5	2	4
2♥	MAMS	VEMS	NEFS	JUM	VEM	7	2	5
3♥	SAM	VEF	MOFS	PLF	PLFS	4	4	1
4♥	VEF	VER	CRFS	VEFS	MAR	7	0	7
5♥	MAFS	MAF	JUFS	PLRS	JUF	6	5	2
6♥	MAM	CRRS	SAF	MAFS	JUF	4	6	-1
7♥	SAF	VERS	NERS			2	3	-1
8♥	SAF	VER	MOR	URR	SAFS	1	2	1
9♥	PLR	NEFS	JUM	VEMS	VEM	5	1	3
10♥	VEMS	JUR	VERS	MAMS	MAF	6	-1	7
J♥	JUFS	SARS	NEF	JUF	SAFS	2	1	3
Q♥	PLF	VEFS	JURS	JUF	SAFS	4	2	2
K♥	MOF	JUF	JUFS	SAR	VER	4	-2	7
A♣	VEMS	MAMS	NEFS	JUM	CRF	7	1	5
2♣	MOF	VERS	SAR	VER	JUMS	5	-2	6
3♣	CLR	CLRS	URR	SAFS	VEF	0	2	-1
4♣	CRRS	PLRS	MAM	MAMS	PLR	5	5	-1
5♣	PLRS	MAFS	CRRS	MAF	JUF	6	5	0
6♣	URF	NERS	KRMC	MARS	VEFS	4	2	2
7♣	NER	PLF	URRS	CLF	PLFS	5	5	-2
8♣	SARS	JUFS	JUM	SAR	JUF	0	1	2
9♣	JURS	PLF	VEFS	URFS	VEF	4	1	3
10♣	CRF	MARS	MAF	SAF	NEF	6	7	-1
J♣	JUR	VERS	MOR	VEMS	PLR	5	-3	8
Q♣	MOFS	SAM	CLFS	VEM	CLF	4	3	2
K♣	SBC	JUF	MARS	JUR	MAFS	4	4	3
A♦	MORS	VEFS	VEF	NER	URFS	7	-2	8
2♦	VEFS	URF	NERS	MORS	NER	5	-1	5
3♦	SAF	MAFS	MAM	VEMS	JUF	4	6	-1
4♦	MAF	JUFS	MAMS	MAFS	MOF	7	4	3
5♦	URR	SAFS	MAR	CRFS	CLR	1	5	-2
6♦	URFS	JURS	CRR	VEMS	CRRS	2	-1	3
7♦	NEFS	JUM	PLR	VEMS	PLRS	5	1	3
8♦	CLF	PLFS	SAR	NER	PLF	5	7	-4
9♦	MAR	CRFS	VEMS	URR	SAFS	6	4	1
10♦	CLFS	VEM	MOFS	SAR	SARS	5	2	3
J♦	MOR	CRR	VEMS	JUR	VERS	6	-2	7
Q♦	VEMS	SAF	MAFS	MAR	CRFS	5	4	1
K♦	CLR	CLRS	VER	VERS	PLRS	3	1	2
A♠	VERS	MOF	MOFS	NERS	VER	7	-3	8
2♠	KRMA	JUF	NEF	PLR	PLFS	5	4	2
3♠	CRR	VEMS	URFS	MOR	MORS	5	-1	5
4♠	CRF	MARS	VEF	VEFS	MAR	7	4	3
5♠	MAMS	VEMS	MAF	JUFS	SAF	7	4	3
6♠	NEF	PLR	KRMC	JUF	MAF	5	3	2
7♠	VER	SAF	URR	SAFS	MOFS	1	2	0
8♠	KRMA	MARS	NEF	PLFS	URF	7	7	0
9♠	JUF	NEF	PLR	NEFS	PLRS	5	1	3
10♠	VEF	PLF	VEFS	PLFS	VER	7	2	3
J♠	MAF	NER	PLF	URRS	CRF	7	5	-1
Q♠	SAR	CLFS	VEM	CLF	PLFS	3	4	-1
K♠	JUFS	SARS	NEF	JUF	SAFS	2	1	3

The Kings ♥ 253

The Successful Businessperson

DESCRIPTION OF THE K♦ PERSON:

The K♦ is the master of values, finances, and business. In this regard, he or she can do very well in any business pursuit, applying their inherited knowledge to their work with much success. These people are always more successful as heads of their own business rather than working for others. They can be very mercenary when it comes to money and business, but they don't have to be.

This is the only 'one-eyed' King in the deck, which tends to blind them to certain aspects of life and situations. This can also make them very stubborn, seeing things from only their side of the issue. K♦ are known to make enemies for this very reason. Perhaps the upraised battle-ax on their card represents a fondness for competition. However, all of them know what is of real value and, if they follow their knowledge instead of their fears, they can be the most respectable people in the business world. They must always guard against using their power to get things to go their way at the expense of others. With so much inherent power, the K♦ can avoid dealing with their feelings, and this is where many problems are created. There are often emotional issues from childhood that must be dealt with before the higher side of this card can be manifested. Until then, they can appear cold and ruthless.

They are very creative and can make huge amounts of money by using this gift. The K♦ are powerful people who can do much good in the world. They can be examples of those who are 'in the world, but not of it.'

SOME OF THE K♦ ISSUES CONCERNING RELATIONSHIPS:

The K♦ is one of those cards that doesn't have any particular good or bad relationship karma. However, being Kings, they are quite powerful and unwilling to compromise, which can cause problems on the personal level. The women, especially, have to find a way to balance their strong masculine side in the context of a relationship where the accepted norm is the 'retiring female.' They tend to want to dominate, or at least be an equal to their mates, and some men are not able to deal with such power in a woman. Some of the women give up trying after a few unsuccessful attempts. Some of the men do likewise. Both sexes can be guilty of looking at love and marriage strictly from a financial point of view. It is always best for them to keep their business and love life separate until they find the right match.

Both sexes should learn to express their fears and emotions to have better luck in romance or marriage. Honest communication bridges the gap and brings more intimacy. They are attracted to those of wit and good education and are often found working with their spouse in a business.

GENERALITIES BETWEEN THE PERSONALITY CARD CONNECTIONS

K♦ females have strong ties with Heart males. This is a powerful combination, but not always an easy one. Diamond females are very fond of K♦ males and could make a good marriage with one. K♦ males often have great difficulty with Spade females and should avoid them for marriage.

KARMA CARDS:

3♣ 7♠

KARMA COUSINS:

5♦ 8♥

PAST-LIFE CARDS:

Q♦ A♠

How We Make Enemies

The K♦ has a standing reputation among card readers for having more enemy relationships than other cards in the deck. Arsenio Hall, a well-known K♦, has had more than one book written about his life and the enemies he has made in his rise to the top. Florence Campbell and Edith Randall call the K♦ the most materialistic and ruthless card in the deck. Among those who operate on the lower levels of their Birth Card, they say the K♦ will stop at nothing in order to gain the things they want or to have the upper hand. What could it be about them that gives them this reputation?

Did you ever notice that the K♦ is the only King with only one eye showing? This is also true of the J♥ and the J♠. These cards with only one eye showing tend to see the world one way and one way only. This trait is manifested differently in the three cards. In the J♠, which can manifest as the thief card, we often see an ongoing deception being played out in their life based upon their personal definition of what it is all about. In the J♥, the card of sacrifice, we see this blind-sightedness manifesting in their love life. They are often blind to the faults of others and tend to be used by them. But in the K♦, this one-sightedness happens in many of their professional affairs where they seem to have a hard time seeing beyond their own ideas, beliefs, and value systems to get the big picture.

Many K♦ have a Mercury/Moon aspect that is difficult. When Mercury and the Moon combine in our natal chart, we tend to think through our emotions. Technically, it is called subjective thinking. Subjective thinking tends to blind us to other points of view while causing us to attach ourselves to ideas and beliefs that are simply untrue. Give this subjective reasoning to someone who has a lot of pride and who is used to getting their way (because they are a King), and you may end up with a tyrant at times. Many people would agree that 'tyrant' exactly describes some of their K♦ associates.

Any Jack, Queen, or King person is used to having power over people in their life and each has their own way of using this power to get what they want. The temptation is always there to use and often to abuse this power. It is often more expedient for any of us to use whatever power we have to resolve a situation rather than face our own fears or feelings. If this happens repeatedly, we will gradually lose touch with our feelings, which are what we use to tell us what is real and unreal. We can get 'way out there,' so to speak.

In the case of the K♦, they also have a subjective mentality that can make them believe they are always right, when, in fact, their conclusions are based upon unfulfilled emotional needs that go unrecognized. They also seem to be less afraid to be confrontational with others than other cards. Creating a conflict with someone else doesn't seem to be a big problem to many K♦, and perhaps this is why some of them attract situations where others feel embattled by their presence.

The K♦ are essentially peace-loving individuals who have a strong sense of fairness in personal relationships that makes their lives easygoing and carefree most of the time. But, as with any other card, when they become afraid or emotional, they have a unique pattern of how they deal with the situation at hand. As with other Kings, the unaware K♦ is probably going to use their great power to make others change, and this is often where enemy relationships are born.

LIFE SPREAD CARDS

PLANETARY CARD	SYMBOL	CARD
MOON	☽	K♥
SUN (BIRTH CARD)	☀	K♦
MERCURY	☿	6♥
VENUS	♀	4♣
MARS	♂	2♦
JUPITER	♃	J♠
SATURN	♄	8♣
URANUS	♅	6♦
NEPTUNE	♆	4♠
PLUTO	♇	10♥
RESULT (COSMIC REWARD)	♃+	10♦
COSMIC LESSON	♄+	8♠

PLANETARY RULING CARDS

BIRTH DATE	ASTROLOGICAL RULING SIGN	PLANETARY RULING CARD
JAN 14	CAPRICORN	8♣
FEB 12	AQUARIUS	6♦
MAR 10	PISCES	4♠
APR 8	ARIES	2♦
MAY 6	TAURUS	4♣
JUN 4	GEMINI	6♥
JUL 2	CANCER	K♥

Celebrity Birthdays

CHUCK NORRIS
3/10/40 • Actor
JOHN SCHNEIDER
4/8/54 • Actor
GEORGE CLOONEY
5/6/61 • Actor
FAYE DUNAWAY
1/14/41 • Actress
SHARON STONE
3/10/58 • Actress
ANGELINA JOLIE
6/4/75 • Actress
WILLIE MAYS
5/6/31 • Baseball Star
ROBERT MERRILL
6/4/19 • Opera Singer
ABRAHAM LINCOLN
2/12/1809 • President
PRINCE EDWARD
3/10/64 • Prince
BOB SEGER
5/6/45 • Singer
ARSENIO HALL
2/12/55 • Talk Show Host
ANDY ROONEY
1/14/19 • Writer
JUDY BLUME
2/21/38 • Writer
FRANCO ZEFFIRELLI
2/12/23 • Director
BETTY FORD
4/8/18 • Former First Lady
DAVE THOMAS
7/2/32 • Wendy's Founder
DENNIS WEAVER
6/4/24 • Actor
MICHELLE PHILLIPS
6/4/45 • Singer
RICHARD HATCH
4/8/61 • "Survivor" Winner

| Who | The Connections Between Partners | | | | | Overall Index Ratings | | |
K♦ with	Con1	Con2	Con3	Con4	Con5	Attraction	Intensity	Compatibility
A♥	VEMS	JUR	NEFS	VEM	MAR	6	-2	7
2♥	VER	VEF	NER	PLF	URRS	6	0	5
3♥	VEFS	CRFS	JUR	NEFS	VEM	6	0	6
4♥	SAFS	NEF	PLR	JUFS	CLFS	2	5	-2
5♥	VER	JUR	CRRS	MAFS	MOF	5	0	5
6♥	MOR	VEF	CLR	CLRS	MAF	5	-1	6
7♥	PLR	MORS	CRR	CRRS	PLRS	5	2	2
8♥	NEFS	PLR	KRMC	PLRS	NEF	5	4	1
9♥	NER	PLF	URRS	VEF	NERS	5	3	0
10♥	PLF	MAR	URR	SAFS	NER	5	7	-3
J♥	SAR	JUFS	MAM	SAF	MAMS	1	4	0
Q♥	CLFS	VEM	JUR	JURS	CLF	4	1	3
K♥	MOF	MAM	MAMS	MAR	CRFS	8	4	3
A♣	VEF	VER	NER	PLF	URRS	6	0	5
2♣	MAM	MAMS	MORS	CRR	MOF	8	4	3
3♣	KRMA	PLRS	NEF	PLFS	PLF	6	7	-1
4♣	VEF	MAFS	MOR	MORS	MAF	8	0	7
5♣	MAFS	VER	VEF	VEFS	JUFS	7	1	6
6♣	CLF	PLFS	MAF	MAFS	VEM	7	7	-3
7♣	SARS	JUF	MAF	JUFS	SAR	2	2	2
8♣	SAF	MAMS	SAR	JUFS	MAM	1	6	-3
9♣	JUR	URF	NERS	URFS	MAMS	2	0	3
10♣	VEMS	JUF	NEF	PLR	JUFS	5	-1	6
J♣	MAR	VERS	PLF	URF	PLFS	7	5	0
Q♣	VEFS	CRF	MARS	JUF	CRFS	7	2	4
K♣	VEFS	CLF	PLFS	CLFS	VEF	6	3	1
A♦	VEMS	MAF	MAR	VEM	MAMS	8	3	5
2♦	MAF	VEMS	VEM	MAMS	MAFS	9	3	5
3♦	CLR	CLRS	MOR	MOFS	VEF	4	0	3
4♦	JUR	CRRS	URR	SAFS	VER	1	1	2
5♦	PLRS	JURS	KRMC	JUF	JUR	2	1	3
6♦	URF	NERS	JUR	MAFS	VEM	3	1	3
7♦	NER	PLF	URRS	VEF	NERS	5	3	0
8♦	SARS	URFS	URF	VEMS	SAF	0	2	-1
9♦	JURS	MOFS	PLRS	NEF	MOF	4	-1	6
10♦	CRF	MARS	VEFS	URFS	URR	6	4	2
J♦	VERS	MAFS	VEM	VEMS	MAR	8	1	6
Q♦	MOFS	CLR	CLRS	JURS	VER	4	-1	4
K♦	SBC	NEFS	NERS	PLF	PLR	6	5	0
A♠	MORS	CRR	PLR	MAM	MAMS	6	2	3
2♠	VEFS	URFS	JUM	JUMS	VER	3	-2	6
3♠	MAFS	VEM	VEMS	URF	NERS	7	1	5
4♠	NEF	PLR	JUFS	VEMS	SAFS	5	1	3
5♠	URR	SAFS	PLF	JUR	CRRS	1	4	-3
6♠	URFS	JUM	JUMS	MAR	CRFS	2	0	2
7♠	KRMA	NEFS	NEF	PLFS	PLF	8	6	0
8♠	CLF	PLFS	SAR	MORS	CLFS	5	6	-3
9♠	MAR	CRFS	MOF	URFS	JUM	6	4	2
10♠	CLFS	VEM	SAFS	SAF	MAFS	3	5	-2
J♠	JUF	VEMS	JUFS	MAF	SAR	4	-1	7
Q♠	URFS	CRF	MARS	SARS	SAF	3	4	-1
K♠	MAM	SAF	MAMS	SAR	JUFS	3	7	-2

The Master Card

DESCRIPTION OF THE K♠ PERSON:
The people of this card are masters of anything they decide to do. Unless the men decide to stay as Jacks, they always rise to the top of their chosen profession. However, it is interesting to note how many of the men get involved in the arts and entertainment fields and forego most of the power at their disposal. The female K♠ generally acts more as the Q♠ card. If they are not careful, they can become mired in mediocrity, just as many Q♠ can. But neither of these outcomes represents the highest potential that is available to all K♠. As the most powerful of the Kings, the K♠ is equipped to handle enormous responsibilities and many have become some of our greatest leaders. To access this great power, the K♠ individual must be ready and willing to accept great responsibility and take a position of leadership. They must set aside some of their restlessness in order to make a mark in one chosen field and then set the example for the rest of us to see.

In any case, the K♠ is the last card in the deck and the most wise and powerful. They have a high regard for wisdom, a love of learning, and are willing to do whatever it takes to achieve success and recognition to the extent that they desire. They are capable of managing the largest organizations, but don't always make that their chosen line of work. These people are completely 'fixed.' They will not budge or change for anyone and have tremendous inner strength and resolve. However, these same qualities make most life changes very difficult for them to deal with.

They have indecision about love and close relationships and often forego marriage for a single life. They are always enterprising and ambitious, rarely lazy or of a lower persuasion. Even though they don't all reach a high place, all of them have wisdom and rarely sink down to lowly acts. With all their abilities, they are often discontent. This can be interpreted as progressiveness or dissatisfaction. When they go within, to the spiritual realms, they are able to penetrate the deepest secrets with ease. These are the Masters of our physical and spiritual universes. When they accept the yoke of responsibility and the crown of authority that is their birthright, we all benefit from the contributions they make.

SOME OF THE K♠ ISSUES CONCERNING RELATIONSHIPS:
Love is one area where the K♠ has the most challenges. They tend to take a very mental approach to the subject and, because of this, changes and indecision are sure to result, which also leaves them feeling insecure and uncertain. This uncertainty can extend even into their sexual roles. Their karmic pattern also tells us that there will be betrayals at certain times in their life. Some of their greatest life lessons involve learning to let others be who they are and releasing emotional attachments to those they love. Combine all this together with their powerful will and we find that many of them rarely allow anyone get very close to them.

Their 7♥ Pluto Card tells us that the K♠ has a life-long goal to overcome fears of abandonment and betrayal. There will be episodes of both at different times in their life which will either serve to reinforce their negative beliefs about love or inspire them to take up the challenge of self-transformation in this important area.

KARMA CARDS:
8♣ J♥ A♣ 2♥ 7♦ 9♥

KARMA COUSINS:
NONE

PAST-LIFE CARDS:
Q♠ A♥

When they do mate, K♠ males often choose a Club or Heart female, with whom they share much physical attraction.

Heart males pose a problem for the K♠ female, as do Club females in a general way. Diamond males often have trouble with K♠ females, though they do share a lot of attraction between them.

The Heavy Crown of the King of Spades

Being the most powerful card in the deck, one might expect that every K♠ would be very successful and in a powerful position in their work and life. This is not so. Most of the K♠ don't seem to live up to that expectation. When we study the lives of K♠ people, we note definite patterns that reveal something about what it must be like to have such great power and responsibility.

Many K♠ are involved as salespeople, artists, musicians, gamblers, and other creative pursuits. In essence, they often prefer doing work that would be commonly associated with the J♠, the 'Actor's Card.' This is a playboy type, one who dabbles in many things but often refuses to make a firm commitment to any one profession or occupation. It is also playful and romantic. However, in making the decision to pursue the role of the Jack instead of the King, the K♠ loses much of the inherent power that is his or her birthright. Florence Campbell states, in *Sacred Symbols of the Ancients*, that in many cases it is disempowering for people to operate out of one of their personality cards. Since the K♠ is inherently more powerful and successful than the J♠, this illustrates one example of such a disempowerment.

The question remains as to why someone would who has such a high potential decide to 'throw it away' by operating out of their lesser Jack. There are several answers to this question. First, there is a timing to things. Some K♠ undoubtedly will become great later in their life. Perhaps there is some sort of incubation period or maturing process that they must undergo

before they make that big step into King-hood. Maybe they need to find something in their life that will call forth that inherent potential, a grand cause so to speak. One thing is certain: when the K♠ does assume his or her Kingship, they immediately fall into a position of responsibility and leadership. But for many of them, that responsibility is seen as more of a burden and restriction to their freedom than as a crown.

All K♠ have a 5♣ as their Planetary Ruling Card. The 5♣ is a Birth Card that is notorious for keeping options open and not making strong commitments, whether those be in work or love. All K♠ share some of this adventurous spirit and freedom-loving nature. To any Five, the notion of responsibility often seems to conflict with their personal freedom, so it is something that is frequently avoided. This also can contribute to a K♠ not taking up their crown in any given job or position.

When a K♠ does make a decision to commit, they usually rise to the top of their field. They are not that interested in the money they make, but in the mastery they can exhibit in their work and leadership. It is the doing of their work that is important, as opposed to the Diamonds, who are more concerned with what they are getting from the work than doing it. K♠ become masters of their chosen occupation and, in many cases, assume a position of leadership. They make the best teachers, and the weight of the crown they bear only makes them shine that much brighter.

LIFE SPREAD CARDS

PLANETARY CARD	SYMBOL	CARD
MOON	☽	8♦
SUN (BIRTH CARD)	✳	K♠
MERCURY	☿	3♥
VENUS	♀	A♣
MARS	♂	Q♣
JUPITER	♃	10♠
SATURN	♄	5♣
URANUS	♅	3♦
NEPTUNE	♆	A♠
PLUTO	♇	7♥
RESULT (COSMIC REWARD)	♃+	7♦
COSMIC LESSON	♄+	5♠

PLANETARY RULING CARDS

BIRTH DATE	ASTROLOGICAL RULING SIGN	PLANETARY RULING CARD
JAN 1	CAPRICORN	5♣

Who K♠ with	The Connections Between Partners					Overall Index Ratings		
	Con1	Con2	Con3	Con4	Con5	Attraction	Intensity	Compatibility
A♥	MORS	MOR	MAFS	URF	CLRS	7	-1	6
2♥	KRMA	VEFS	VEM	VEF	VEMS	7	1	7
3♥	MOR	MAFS	MORS	MAF	CLR	8	1	5
4♥	CRR	JUFS	CRRS	JUF	MARS	4	1	4
5♥	SAFS	PLR	SAF	CRF	VEMS	0	6	-5
6♥	URFS	URF	JUR	SARS	MAR	0	1	1
7♥	PLF	NEFS	URR	PLFS	NEF	6	5	-2
8♥	URR	PLFS	URRS	PLF	NEFS	4	4	-3
9♥	KRMA	SAR	CRFS	CRF	SARS	4	7	-1
10♥	CLFS	VEMS	CLF	PLRS	VEM	6	3	1
J♥	KRMA	POWR	PLF	PLFS	CLR	7	9	-2
Q♥	MAR	VERS	JUF	MARS	VER	6	2	4
K♥	URR	JURS	PLRS	JUF	VEFS	1	0	3
A♣	KRMA	VEF	VEMS	VEFS	VEM	7	1	7
2♣	URR	NEF	URRS	JUFS	VEF	3	0	3
3♣	MAMS	MAM	CLF	SARS	SAFS	6	8	-2
4♣	SAF	URFS	MAR	JURS	NEF	0	4	-2
5♣	SAF	SAFS	MARS	VEM	URR	0	6	-4
6♣	SAR	NER	MARS	JUR	SARS	2	4	0
7♣	MOF	VERS	MOFS	CRFS	MAM	8	-2	7
8♣	KRMA	POWR	PLF	PLFS	NEF	7	9	-2
9♣	VER	JUMS	MAR	VERS	JUM	5	-1	5
10♣	VER	VERS	CRRS	VEFS	VEMS	7	-2	7
J♣	CLR	CLFS	VEMS	MAFS	MAR	5	3	1
Q♣	MAF	MOR	MAFS	JUFS	PLR	7	3	4
K♣	JURS	NER	JUR	SARS	NERS	2	0	4
A♦	MAR	MORS	NEF	PLR	URFS	7	3	3
2♦	MAR	SAR	NER	MARS	VER	5	6	0
3♦	URF	URFS	PLFS	SAR	MAMS	2	3	-2
4♦	PLR	CLF	PLRS	VEM	SAFS	4	5	-2
5♦	MAMS	VER	CLFS	MAM	VERS	7	4	2
6♦	JUM	VER	JUMS	CLRS	MOR	3	-2	5
7♦	KRMA	CRF	SARS	SAR	CRFS	4	7	-1
8♦	MOF	MOFS	MAM	VEF	MAMS	8	-1	7
9♦	VERS	MAMS	PLF	MAM		8	5	1
10♦	MAF	MOFS	JUF	VER	JUFS	7	0	6
J♦	CLR	CLRS	MAR	MARS		4	4	-1
Q♦	URF	PLF	MAM	PLFS	SAR	5	6	-3
K♦	MAM	MAMS	URRS	SAR	SAF	4	6	-1
A♠	NEF	URRS	PLF	NEFS	URR	5	3	0
2♠	NER	JUR	NERS	JURS	JUM	3	0	4
3♠	CLRS	JUM	CLR	MARS	MAR	2	2	1
4♠	CRRS	VER	CRR	JUFS	VEF	5	0	4
5♠	CLF	PLRS	VEM	CLFS	VEMS	5	4	0
6♠	JUR	NERS	JURS	NER	JUMS	2	-1	5
7♠	URRS	MAM	URR	PLFS	JUR	3	3	0
8♠	JUR	SARS	NERS	JURS	SAR	1	1	2
9♠	JURS	JUR	NERS	PLR	VEF	2	-1	5
10♠	JUF	MARS	CRR	JUFS	MAR	5	2	4
J♠	VERS	VER	MOF	CRF	CRFS	7	-1	7
Q♠	MOFS	MOF	MAMS	VEFS	JUF	8	-1	8
K♠	SBC	POWR	NEF	NEFS	CLF	7	6	1

The Infamous Joker Card

As you may have gathered so far, there is little or no information in this book about those people born on the 31st of December. That is because this birthday corresponds to the Joker Card. Little is truly known about the Joker. He has no Life Path Cards or Yearly Spreads from which we can make any sort of predictions. In truth, the Joker can be any card in the deck that he or she chooses to be. The Joker was the Court Jester in days of old who ascended the throne on Fools' Day each year and impersonated the King, Queen, and all members of the kingdom. His day, December 31st, is the time of celebration of the New Year, which in ancient times was the day to make merry and folly of our serious natures. The Joker would make fun of everyone in the kingdom and, in doing so, show them how to lighten up a little. He could impersonate anyone with ease. The ability to take on a role at will is still part of the Joker's personality. Since we don't know which card they are being, it is difficult to make any definite statements about them.

A Joker might be considered to be the 'Jack of all Jacks.' This would tend to make them very creative, youthful acting and extremely independent. The Joker is part of the royal family and so we find that they are proud and not too fond of being told what to do, as is the case with most Jacks, Queens, and Kings. Because of the strong creative urges in the Joker, we find many are attracted to the stage or theater. This same creative energy can show up as a dishonest streak in some of them as well. Many are successful musicians or artists. Whatever type of profession they choose, they are independent and must maintain a certain amount of freedom if they are to be happy and satisfied.

They have the potential to be deeply spiritual, being the card that is often associated with God in the Tarot decks (The Fool Card, Number 0). Beyond this, there is little known about them. As Florence Campbell puts it, 'They are a mystery unto themselves.'

Chapter Four
Planetary Ruling Cards

Ace of Hearts as Your Planetary Ruler

This card tells us that you spend a lot of your time searching within yourself for the mysteries of life. You are somewhat of a loner, even though you value friendships a great deal as well. Ace of Hearts means desire for love so this will reflect itself in your life in a meaningful way, whether that means an eternal search for the right partner, or whether you seek the answer to your longings within yourself. The Ace of Hearts is also closely tied to the Ace of Diamonds, so you probably have a good amount of ambition as well. Your career or work is probably an area that you give a high priority to. Essentially, you are a passionate person who is seeking to understand your own heart.

Ace of Clubs as Your Planetary Ruler

This ruling card accentuates your curiosity about life and gives you a keen desire to learn new things. You may find yourself to be a collector of books, tapes, and other forms of information. This card also gives you a lot of passion for your work. You probably get lots of new ideas for things to do and learn. You are a vessel for good ideas and new projects to come through. You may find that you have a bit of impatience that goes along with your passionate approach to life. Personal relationships stand out as one of your most important life topics. You are on a quest for the perfect love. Until you find that special person, you may choose to be with many partners, since you don't like to be alone for too long. You have an interest in life that will keep you eternally youthful.

Ace of Diamonds as Your Planetary Ruler

This ruling card gives you a lot of passion for life, but especially for your job or for making money in general. As a matter of fact it may appear that your personal life is constantly competing with your work for your invaluable attention and time. It will be a trick to have both running successfully that the same time. You are basically a kindhearted person who cares a lot about other people. But your ambition and drive also keep your own goals in front of you, and others may see you as selfishly motivated because of this. You do have

much to accomplish in this lifetime, as if you have been given some special commission by the powers that be. Personal relationships will always be a bit of a challenge as you learn about love and personal integrity.

Ace of Spades as Your Planetary Ruler

This ruling card adds a lot of passion and ambition to your personality. It could even result in your becoming something of a workaholic. It will cause you to seek to find yourself in your work and in the things you create. You generate a lot of power and have a strong will. This will cause your life to be a series of chapters, and in each you have transformed into a new person. Inner transformation is a part of your life pattern and this may lead you to the study of metaphysics where you will find answers to the many questions about your life. You have a special inner power that can only be accessed by turning your attention within. Relationships will be a major challenge in your life until you face the truth about your own inner needs verses your external goals and dreams.

Two of Hearts as Your Planetary Ruler

This is a card of the heart, and it is called the 'Lovers Card'. Therefore, we know that relationships are extremely important to you, especially those of a more intimate nature. This card gives you a pleasing personality, one that others find soothing and attractive. It also makes you an eternally curious person who loves to learn new things and read new books. But more than anything else, you are on a search for the perfect love partner. You have high standards for love and are probably attracted to those with whom you have shared past lives. Only the highest form of love will truly satisfy you. It must be eternal and mystical. But, until you find that perfect love, you will usually make sure there is someone in your life that you can love. Love is very important to you.

Two of Clubs as Your Planetary Ruler

This card accentuates your mental abilities giving you a very logical and precise mind. For this reason, you can excel at many things that require clear thinking, analysis, and detail. This same mental quickness and precision can make you argumentative and when you are not feeling well, you could become a 'whiner'. You love to talk and will usually arrange your life in such a way as to have someone to share your thoughts with. Twos in general tend to shy away from being all alone. You may discover that you actually have fears of abandonment that could be worked on to improve your personal life. Workwise, this card is a blessing, promising success in any of the communications fields.

Two of Diamonds as Your Planetary Ruler

This ruling card gives you a lot of success with work and finances. You have an ability to find the right people to help you achieve your goals, and you are not lazy. You are bound to have some very prosperous cycles in your life, much more than the average person. You have a keen and logical mind that you depend upon for much of your success. But in personal relationships, your logic is more of a hindrance than a help. An inner desire for love and affection competes with your natural ambition in work matters and it seems difficult to have satisfaction in both areas at the same time. In general, you would tend to focus more on your work, where it is easier to manage. Emotionally you have a lot of work to do. You must also watch out for some fixed principles about love or marriage that cause you to stay in bad relationships much longer than need be.

Two of Spades as Your Planetary Ruler

This ruling card gives you a strong urge toward friendship and partnerships. You tend to create situations where you can work or play with those you call friends. You are a good friend yourself. It also gives you a very logical mind that can give you special abilities in the workplace. You may be drawn to computers or other areas where clarity of mind is a requirement. But the Two of Spades can also bring some uncertainties in the relationship department. There are probably some fears about love or marriage that must be faced and acknowledged before you will find happiness. Though your mind is well developed, you may have ignored your own needs and feelings, which are essential in developing harmonious intimate relationships.

Three of Hearts as Your Planetary Ruler

This is a card of uncertainty of the heart, but also one of creativity and variety. You probably have a good deal of artistic ability, whether or not you are currently expressing it. However, many people with this card are singers, musicians, or artists of other kinds. This card also inspires children, which are another form of creative expression. If children are important to you, this could be one of the reasons why. On other levels, the Three of Hearts means uncertainty of the heart. Your own emotional life could have some challenges as you probably try to use your mind to resolve your emotional problems without much success. You may be a 'love worrier'. There is a need to 'feel' and to let those feelings be expressed. That is the solution for the proper expression of this creative force that is a part of you. On the other hand, you may find more happiness in having multiple partners, which is another expression of this Three of Hearts energy.

Three of Clubs as Your Planetary Ruler

This ruling card bestows upon you more than average creativity and an urge to express the endless stream of good ideas that you get. You could find great success in writing, speaking, or some other form of creative expression. However, this same creativity can be the cause of great uncertainty at times. You may feel that having so many options and possibilities becomes as much as a curse as a blessing because there will be times when you can't make up your mind, or times that you worry excessively about inconsequential matters. The key is to get back into creative expression—it relieves the stress of the overactive mind signified by this card. This card may also make it difficult to make long–term commitments in personal relationships.

Three of Diamonds as Your Planetary Ruler

This ruling card gives you a lot of creative ability, which, if expressed, can bring you great success. However, an uncertainty about your line of work, or about what is most important to you in life may also cause a great deal of worry or stress from time to time. In particular, you may worry about money a lot, even when you are doing well financially. Creative expression is a healing balm for you. You may also find that you are drawn toward the study of mysteries, metaphysics, and other spiritual subjects. You have a natural gift of understanding and a keen mind that can penetrate the deepest subjects. Personally, you probably have many challenges in the relationship arena, also connected to your fluctuating values and abundant possibilities.

Three of Spades as Your Planetary Ruler

This ruling card gives you a lot of creative energy and it may result in your becoming an artist of some kind. You should know, however, that this is one of the cards in which success is only attained through hard work. Without it, your creativity will be wasted on stress, indecision, uncertainty, and worry. Unexplainable health concerns may dominate your attention from time to time, especially if you are very work oriented. Your work brings you peace, but don't ignore your health in the process. You have the capacity to work two jobs at the same time and you have a strong romantic streak and needs. If your romantic needs are not met in your current relationship you may be tempted to seek them elsewhere.

Four of Hearts as Your Planetary Ruler

This is called the family card and represents a foundation of love and all the good things associated with home and family. These things are very important to you and you probably go out of your way to make sure that you have a circle of close friends that you can count on, and that your home is comfortable and enjoyable. As a matter of fact, you may have special skills that relate to food, beauty, or home life in other areas. You are probably a good cook as well. In any case, you will find ways to create security among your inner circle of family and friends. You are a protector and helper to those you love and you hate to see any of them leave. Others feel nurtured in your presence though you must watch out to not smother them at times. Family life can bring you much joy, whether that comes by marriage, or just by creating your own family among those you love the most.

Four of Clubs as Your Planetary Ruler

This ruling card gives you a logical and fixed mind capable of learning things and becoming grounded in that knowledge. You will be 'good' at what you do, regardless of what that job or occupation is. You also have a good deal of promotional ability and get progressive ideas that can benefit your chosen line of work. An inner restlessness will cause some challenges for you. You may never feel satisfied with what you are doing, who you are with, where you are living, or otherwise. Travel heals your soul and brings fresh experiences that lighten your disposition. You benefit from staying with one thing for a long time and developing it to its fullest potential.

Four of Diamonds as Your Planetary Ruler

This ruling card gives you a lot of good organizational talent and the ability to manage money well. You are probably a good worker and may even enjoy kinds of work that others disdain. You can be stubborn about your likes and dislikes as well as your philosophies about money and life. You are fond of travel, but probably won't get to do a lot of it until you are older. To you, life is work, and you will always have to work in order to have any happiness. Even in your personal relationships, the work is a requirement. Nothing comes to you without a price. But the enjoyment of work can be part of the reward for doing it and will ultimately bring you everything that you desire.

Four of Spades as Your Planetary Ruler

This ruling card makes you more security oriented and encourages you to create a solid foundation in your life. It gives you good organizational skills and a logical mind that can keep your life peaceful. You tend toward family and home matters, making them extra important in your life. You are a hard worker and actually enjoy working, which also brings you peace. But keep in mind that others may not see value in the same things as you. They may think you are fairly stubborn and unwilling to see things from their point of view. You like to build a life on a firm foundation, one block at a time. You have fears about money that seem to come out of nowhere. You also tend to attract friends with money.

Five of Hearts as Your Planetary Ruler

Regardless of what your Birth Card is, you are a restless person who is seeking to learn about love through direct experience. For this reason, you may have many relationships over the span of your life. You may also seem to avoid commitments on an emotional level, as these may hamper your ability to get all of the experiences that you desire. Freedom is a very important word in your vocabulary. However, you may even get married, though few with this card do. If so, you are doing it for what you can learn from the experience more than anything else. You probably love to travel and have gravitated toward things and occupations that allow you the freedom to do so. You have some common sense about money and organizational ability that help you keep an ample supply of money on hand at all times. But essentially, you are a free spirit who loves to meet new people and have new experiences.

Five of Clubs as Your Planetary Ruler

This ruling card reflects a very restless side to your personality. Because of it, you are fond of travel, changes of residence, and meeting new people. This card also gives you more than average ability to sell or promote products and services. So, you would fit in the role of traveling salesperson quite readily, though this by no means is a sure indication of what you do for a living. The restlessness of this card extends to your romantic life as well. Whether you admit it or not, you probably have a problem with long–term commitments. This could be reflected as your choosing partners who cannot commit just as often as you not being willing to. You have a thirst for adventure that keeps you searching for what lies ahead, and perhaps often leaving the past behind.

Five of Diamonds as Your Planetary Ruler

The key words for fives are freedom and adventure. Because you have the Five of Diamonds as your ruling card, these two things are probably very important to you. You are fond of travel and of anything that will bring you fresh, new experiences. You have a natural way of dealing with people that makes them feel at ease. For this reason and others, you probably do very well in sales work. You are seeking to broaden your understanding of life by having as many new and different experiences as possible. You may have trouble with any sort of commitments, especially relationship and work, that may interfere with your ability to have these experiences.

Five of Spades as Your Planetary Ruler

This ruling card can cause you to do a lot of traveling or moving in your life. It basically adds a very adventurous side to your personality. You probably see life as an opportunity to experience many interesting things more than anything else. Even so called 'bad' experiences will have value to you, because of what you learn from them. You love to be with people and have some success in groups of all kinds. The larger, the better. You also have a fair amount of sales and promotion ability and could easily make a living doing this sort of work. You are amicable and can relate to most anyone on their level, making them feel comfortable with you. But your restlessness is the real heart of this card's meaning.

Six of Hearts as Your Planetary Ruler

This card makes you a peacemaker and you will find yourself in the position of mediator from time to time as a result. You have the ability to see both sides of any personal conflict between people. You enjoy seeing things turn out right and will often get involved if there is injustice being done. You will always want to see that what happens is fair and equitable. You really know what is fair and what is not. You can be very competitive. Though a peace-loving person, you will probably return 'an eye for an eye' when you are crossed. Many people with this card excel at sports or other competitive activities. You could even become a lawyer. You will feel often that your personal life gets into a rut. Once you get comfortable with a certain person, it is usually hard for you to change, even when you may want to. You will usually wait to see what will come your way instead of going out and making it happen as far as your love life is concerned. Indeed, most of your important personal relationships are 'destined'.

Six of Clubs as Your Planetary Ruler

This ruling card helps ground you and keep you on an even course. You tend to develop things and stay with them, which usually brings success, instead of leaving them half finished. You can be very stubborn at times and you have a competitive streak that takes others by surprise. Great success is a real possibility for you as long as you don't remain in a rut for too long. You must be true to your word or the karma of what you have said to others will come back in the same full force that you yourself avenge injustices. At heart you are a peacemaker and will go to great lengths to have a peaceful, calm environment. Be careful that you don't completely ignore your feelings. Though you may not always like your emotional side, or that of others, it is your direct connection to the truth that you hold so dear. You may have a special purpose to help others 'find the light'.

Six of Diamonds as Your Planetary Ruler

Because of this ruling card, you have a heightened sense of your own responsibility when it comes to financial matters. Either you go out of your way to pay off debts or you are keenly aware of what you owe and what others owe you. You have a competitive streak which can make you good in sports or other competitive activities. You are basically a person who appreciates peace and harmony. But sometimes you feel that your life is in a rut. You tend to let things come to you and once you are comfortable, you usually let them ride. Good things always come to you when you are working hard for them. But, you probably also feel sometimes that you may win the lottery or somehow come into some money in other ways.

Six of Spades as Your Planetary Ruler

This ruling card adds a strong, steadying influence to your personality, which can be good. You tend to create peace in your life and wait for things to come your way. Health matters will play an important role in your life as you are probably learning lessons about the results of whatever lifestyle you are leading. You don't get away with abuses in this area. You have great potential for success, but you must find ways to get yourself out of the ruts you get into at times in order to achieve it. You may find yourself waiting and waiting for something that never shows up because it wasn't pursued. Your life has a destined quality about it. When you least expect it, something dramatic happens to take you to the next chapter.

Seven of Hearts as Your Planetary Ruler

Your love life is very important to you and you have many challenges in this area that you are working on during the course of your life. You tend to attract powerful partners—those with a strong will. Once in a relationship, you get involved in power struggles with your mate. All of this is an attempt to learn unconditional love, which is something that you have a good

possibility of experiencing in your life. You know how to give to others without expectation and this makes you a good friend and effective counselor. When you apply this to your own love life, you experience great freedom and joy. You have a charming personality and the ability to heal others' emotional wounds.

Seven of Clubs as Your Planetary Ruler

This ruling card gives a spiritual or philosophical nature to your thinking and disposition. You may also be a skeptic or critic, but inwardly you hold onto some less practical ideas and beliefs. You have probably had many realizations about life as you experience mental 'awakenings' from time to time. You love to spend money and need to be careful in your management of it. You also secretly desire to be noticed or recognized by others and may gravitate toward a job that allows you this recognition or attention. You may find that you fluctuate between being very carefree and joyous and being quite worried and down about things. You may have some unusual mental gifts.

Seven of Diamonds as Your Planetary Ruler

This card can make you lucky with money, but it can also make you worry about money more than you should. It is a high spiritual influence that brings success by letting go of concerns. You have the potential to become a millionaire if you adopt a fearless attitude about your finances. This card also gives you a lot of creativity, especially when it comes to promoting and selling things. You probably have strong family values and feel that your family is one of the most important things in your life. You can be very stubborn, especially about what you want and don't want, and about the ways you handle your finances.

Seven of Spades as Your Planetary Ruler

This ruling card adds strength to your personality and gives you a certain amount of good fortune, especially in the areas of home and family. You may feel that you have a blessed marriage or relationship, or that many good things have come from your parents. Health concerns may play a major role in your life and you may be accident-prone. The Seven of Spades encourages us to have faith in life, in spite of whatever circumstances we may find ourselves in. In this regard, you may find yourself tested many times. You are probably attracted to those of intelligence and wit and with a bit of luck, you could marry one of them. Financial security is something that will only come through hard work.

Eight of Hearts as Your Planetary Ruler

You are a sociable person with a good deal of charm and magnetism. You enjoy having the attention of others and will find ways to insure that you get a certain amount of it most of the time. You have a lot of power with the charm you have and this can help you or get you into trouble. The Eight of Hearts is called the 'Playboy Card' and whether you realize it or not, you do have the ability to get what you want from others using the emotional power at your disposal. This is healing power as well. Most Eight of Hearts keep a circle of friends, family, or associates around them all the time. Their 'eight hearts' are an important part of their life, whether these are their friends, immediate family, students, employees, or lovers.

Eight of Clubs as Your Planetary Ruler

This ruling card gives you a great deal of mental power and adds a bearing of power to your entire personality. The mental aspects give you the ability to tackle enormous feats that require concentration and organization. Many with this card end up in professions where these traits are a requirement, such as law, writing, research, or management. You are probably good with people, especially in your work. You would tend to attract powerful partners on a personal level and may find that you get into power struggles with them. Your attitudes and principles of life are very fixed in some areas which gives blessings and problems. They make you dependable but hard to change.

Eight of Diamonds as Your Planetary Ruler

This card adds an element of power to your personality. It may also give you a desire and ability to become well known in some way. Your power is expressed through your values. You know what everything is worth to you and can drive a hard bargain. You are a powerful person and probably attract other powerful people with whom you must deal. You will probably be the one in your family to manage the estate and in that regard you are trustworthy and fair. You have some artistic ability that can bring you recognition, though you may just seek recognition through the acquisition of money and power. In love, you probably have some uncertainties

that must be dealt with before you can find true satisfaction.

Eight of Spades as Your Planetary Ruler

This ruling card adds a great deal of power to your personality, making you someone to be reckoned with on a personal level. It could also make you a workaholic. You probably attract others who are also powerful and in these relationships will resolve some of your power and control issues. You have a strong desire for work and to make money, but you must be careful not to abuse others to acquire your goals. Your power can be used for healing or to do many other good things. You probably have more energy than the average person and may seem to be somewhat of an extremist at times. But you learn by doing and trying things yourself. This card gives you the strength to overcome any obstacles and problems that come your way.

Nine of Hearts as Your Planetary Ruler

This ruling card adds a compassionate element to your nature, often inspiring you to do some good for the world. Others may call upon you to listen to their problems as you are a good listener and counselor. However, you are also very stubborn and fixed and others may find this annoying at times. This will be noticed more in your own personal relationships. You must not try to save your partner. This is one area where your compassion and universal love don't produce good results. This card also tells us that you may feel at times that you have lost many loves in your life. However, you also have the ability to feel connected on a universal level, free of all personal concerns and problems.

Nine of Clubs as Your Planetary Ruler

This ruling card adds a spiritual overtone to your personality, along with a desire to be of benefit to others, or the world at large. Many with this card dedicate themselves to some noble purpose. This is one of the sexiest cards in the deck, and you may find that romance is a very important area of your life. Mentally, you have probably suffered many setbacks and in some cases, this could affect your outlook on life. You are kindhearted and others may come to you for solace and a shoulder to cry on. You are very protective of children and want to see them receive the highest care. You may find you are drawn to spiritual studies, since they best explain some of your feelings about life and the occasional mental 'awakenings' that you experience.

Nine of Diamonds as Your Planetary Ruler

This card helps make you more of a giving person and you have probably noticed that others come to you for solace and advice. You will have to do a good amount of giving over the course of your lifetime. But this card also highlights your intellectual abilities as well as your ability to sell or promote what you believe in. You could make a lot of money in sales. But you may find yourself drawn toward a career that involves communications or using your well-equipped mind. Your mind is quick and makes fine distinctions. In love and marriage, there is always some work to do and you may find that you end up with your own family where you have to work a great deal to keep up. Either that, or your personal relationships will be challenging.

Nine of Spades as Your Planetary Ruler

This ruling card tends to make you a kindhearted and giving person, and one who understands the suffering that some people have to go through in this life. For this reason, others may come to you to talk about their problems and to be consoled. You are essentially a giver, and it seems that whenever you do things with selfish motivation, you have many problems instead of satisfaction. You may have experienced some personal losses in your life and your own health may be a concern from time to time. In this lifetime you are learning to disassociate yourself from your personal concerns and adopt a more universal view of life. You will have some profound spiritual awakenings that will open up new doors of understanding and experience.

Ten of Hearts as Your Planetary Ruler

This ruling card encourages you to be more of a social person. You are probably attracted to activities that involve groups of people and may even have a profession that puts you in front of groups of people or children in some way. You will usually be happiest when you have your 'ten hearts' around you. This card also accentuates your mental quickness and gives you a somewhat ambitious nature. Success with friends,

associations, and any work that puts you in front of the public eye is assured.

Ten of Clubs as Your Planetary Ruler

This ruling card adds an aura of specialness to your personality, drawing you toward a high position in your work or profession. Many people with this card become known in some way and others attain great fame. You have teaching ability and probably are a teacher, regardless of what kind of work you officially do. You excel in mental areas though all this power can also make you hyperactive mentally, creating stress or problems in sleeping. It's like your mind never stops. You may even be drawn toward a career as an artist, actor, or musician. You are personally an independent person and may have some trouble deciding which line of work to pursue.

Ten of Diamonds as Your Planetary Ruler

Be grateful that you have this card as a ruling card because it bestows some genuine good fortune on all who possess it. It is called the 'blessed card' and so many things in life will be just given to you. However, this does not guarantee your happiness. That will always depend upon your appreciation for what you have. This card also gives you an innate business ability. You could do very well in your own business, and the larger it is, the better. You probably enjoy being the center of attention and have some natural abilities, either artistic or otherwise, that can get you that attention. In relationships you are very self-centered and somewhat high strung. For these reasons, you may have some challenges in this area.

Ten of Spades as Your Planetary Ruler

This ruling card tends to make you a person who goes to extremes at times. When you get into something, you really get into it. You can be a workaholic and probably feel somewhat burdened by your work a lot of the time. You also have some desires for a settled and satisfying family life that may seem to compete with your ambitions at work. You do have the ability to take on enormous amounts of work and get it done and you can harness energy that few others could in the same situation. You desire to be known for something, for something you have done or created, and you will work like crazy until you achieve it. There are probably uncertainties surrounding your intimate relationships that could add to your inner conflict between love and work.

Jack of Hearts as Your Planetary Ruler

This ruling card accentuates the compassionate side of your personality, encouraging you to be selfless for those that you call friends and family. You may find that you go out of your way to help those in need. This card also brings a playful side to your personality. You probably like having fun at most of the things you do. However, the low side of the Jack of Hearts is that you can be stubborn at times and that you may exhibit some of the immature aspects of the Jack, such as acting immaturely or irresponsibly in certain areas of your life—particularly romantically. You are capable of making great sacrifices for those you love and of dedicating yourself to a higher cause. In doing so, you could make a profound mark on the world.

Jack of Clubs as Your Planetary Ruler

This ruling card gives you an eternally youthful quality. You love to have fun and have many creative ideas about how to do just that. Your creativity also extends into your work where you have entrepreneurial abilities. You have the ability to make a lot of money with your ideas, as long as you are willing to do the work. Your mind is quick and resourceful, but often stubborn and resistant to change. You may also be prone to make up stories to cover up what you are really doing. You are a great story teller. You may appear to be somewhat 'asexual' or might even be bisexual because this card is one of progressed attitudes about love and sex. Personal freedom is important to you, and for your relationships. You probably wouldn't enjoy being 'bound up' by someone.

Jack of Diamonds as Your Planetary Ruler

This ruling card gives you a lot of creative energy and makes you a playful person. Your creativity is especially good for coming up with good ways to make money and you have innate sales ability that could make you wealthy. You have a youthful countenance and will always enjoy having a good time. However, some may call you irresponsible if you let your good times become too important. You probably gravitate toward entrepreneurial work where you can put some of your ideas into action. You value your personal freedom above all else and for this

reason and others may find that long–term commitments have a hard time fitting into your plans. It would take a very particular kind of relationship to meet all your needs.

Jack of Spades as Your Planetary Ruler

This ruling card adds a strong, creative urge to your personality that could manifest in several ways. First of all, you may feel drawn toward acting or some form of artistic expression. Even if you are not, you have a lot of creativity that you do apply to whatever work you are doing. The Jack of Spades is also called the card of the 'thief' and because of the strong creative influence, people with this card often make few distinctions in the areas of honesty when it comes to getting what they want. This card is one of the 'one-eyed' Jacks. Therefore, others may see you as being one-sided in your opinions and attitudes. This is also the card of the spiritual initiate. You may feel drawn toward the study of spiritual subjects which can transform your life to a higher level.

Queen of Hearts as Your Planetary Ruler

This ruling card accentuates the motherly side of your personality, encouraging you to be a caretaker of others, especially anyone that you consider to be your 'children.' However, your children could be your friends or even those who work with you. You would make a wonderful parent in any case. This is also a card of appreciation for art and beauty and often bestows some artistic or musical ability upon its owner. One challenge associated with this card is to avoid getting into codependent relationships. The Queen of Hearts can get involved with saving others, which doesn't work well in personal relationships. This card increases your potential for great success in your life, especially if you have clear goals and directions. You could do some work that helps many people.

Queen of Clubs as Your Planetary Ruler

This ruling card gives you a strong motherly side, and regardless of what kind of work you do, you are probably nurturing others in some way. You have a quick mind that is attuned to high vibrations. You are smart and dislike others who are slow or lazy. However, it is your intuition that is your greatest potential gift. Spend some time developing it, and you will have a tool that will assist you for the rest of your life. In personal relationships you probably have trouble with commitment, or attract partners who do. You have so much creativity that indecision and uncertainty will be a problem from time to time. However, your work is important to you and in the course of your life you will help others find a better life for themselves by the invaluable information that you share with them.

Queen of Diamonds as Your Planetary Ruler

This ruling card gives you a certain pride in yourself that encourages you to maintain a sense of dignity in your affairs. You like your money and will usually purchase only those things of high quality, and usually high cost, when they might be a reflection on who you are. You have a lot of natural business skills that could bring you success in most any business, but there could be some uncertainty about which direction to go from time to time because you also have a great deal of creative energy. In personal relationships you have chosen to maintain a certain amount of personal freedom and this could preclude long–term commitments. You are an outgoing person and enjoy social events.

Queen of Spades as Your Planetary Ruler

This ruling card tends to make you a hard worker and a person who cares for others in a motherly sort of way. You probably get some very good organizational skills from this card and may be attracted to work that others would find distasteful. It does add a strong work-oriented nature to your personality and you may have to be careful that you do not find yourself in a position of drudgery and struggle. You can also be a very tough boss. On the spiritual side, this is the highest card of self-mastery, giving you a special opportunity to experience enlightenment and mastery of your life through self-reflection and understanding.

King of Hearts as Your Planetary Ruler

This ruling card accentuates the fatherly side of your personality, encouraging you to be a good parent. As a matter of fact, you probably take your parenting quite seriously, if you have children. Most people with this card do want children and have them sooner or later. This card gives you an authoritative bearing and leadership ability. You can stand up and claim your own space. If you are a woman, you have no trouble handling the men in your life. You are strong willed and have a quick mind that is capable of making fine distinctions. You probably did well in school. Finally, the King of Hearts bestows some romantic and charismatic power to you—the ability to use charm and persuasion to get what you want from others.

King of Clubs as Your Planetary Ruler

This ruling card adds a lot of power and maturity to your personality and gives you some mental gifts that many would be envious of. You have a strong intuition and a quick mind that is usually right. But you are also able to communicate your ideas and perceptions to others in a way that doesn't put them off. You have leadership abilities and probably assume some role of responsibility in your work. Either that, or you have your own business. You may have some challenges with commitments in personal relationships, or attract others who do. You are actually a good candidate for marriage, and once there, will find great satisfaction and peace of mind.

King of Diamonds as Your Planetary Ruler

This ruling card adds a lot of power to your personality making you someone to be reckoned with. Your power can be best expressed in a business enterprise where you have some natural abilities that make success almost certain. Be sure that you are the one in charge because this is where your real power comes through. This card gives you a lot of strength to overcome obstacles and to accomplish your goals. This same strength makes you stubborn at times. Because you are a self-made person, you tend to see things exclusively from your own point of view. You are powerful and others feel that power whether or not you are aware of it. You have leadership ability that magnifies when you are in positions of responsibility.

King of Spades as Your Planetary Ruler

This ruling card gives you a great deal of potential power, but along with that, a great deal of responsibility which few people choose to bear. You do have the ability to accomplish great feats in this lifetime, but you would have to abandon some of your creative and playful activities in order to attain this. You can be very bossy and stubborn, though you do have great wisdom to share with others. But will you follow your own wisdom? With this card you have absolutely no excuse for not having a very successful and satisfying life. But this again reflects how our choices in life are the true measure of who we are. Uncertainty and concerns around love, marriage, and romance are also there to deal with, whenever you decide to address them.

Chapter Five
Descriptions of the Relationship Connections

This is where you find out what the connections between you and your partner mean. They are listed in Planetary Order, beginning with the Moon and then progressing through Mercury, Venus, Mars, etc. through the Cosmic Lesson Connections. There are also the Karma Card, Karma Cousin, and Power Connections to consider which are very important. They fall into their own category, so to speak, as they are not calculated in the same way as the others. For the Planetary Connections, Moon through Cosmic Lesson, there are separate pages that will give you some general, but important information about those connections which may shed further light upon whatever relationship you are studying. I recommend that you read those pages as well, until you develop a full understanding of these connections. Those sections will also help you learn just how these connections were derived from the Life and Spiritual Spreads, for those interested in learning the mechanics of this system.

The Forward, Reverse, and Mutual Connections

How a certain Connection will affect the two partners in the relationship is often determined by the direction of the energy in that Connection. Most of the Connections have a flow of influence that is stronger from one partner's point of view than the other. As a Q♦ Birth Card, my Mars Card in my Life Path is the 3♠. When I meet someone who is a 3♠, the Mars energy is flowing from them to me and not mutually. I feel Mars energy as a result of their presence in my life and not vice versa. However, because I am experiencing this Mars energy from their presence, they, in turn, will see how I am affected by them and get sort of a reflection of that energy from me. For example, Mars energy can often cause feelings of passion. Though they would not feel the passion the way I would, they would see me having these feelings and be affected by the way I am reacting to them. This is why that

Mars Connection will show up in both of our lists of Connections, but with two different meanings. The meaning for the Mars Connection from one point of view, along with the Index values for that Connection, will be different than the point of view of the other partner who is only getting a reflection of that energy. In these Connections, it is easy to know which ones are Forward and which ones are Reverse. The Forward ones always have an "F" in the Code or abbreviation. For example, PLFS means that my partner is a Forward Pluto influence to me and that I experience Pluto energy the strongest in this Connection. In their list of Connections, it will be listed as PLRS, which is a Reverse Connection, and will have less impact in most ways.

There are, however, connections that are called Mutual. Because of the nature of how they were found, these connections are neither Forward nor Reverse and essentially affect both partners equally.

The Life and Spiritual Spread Connections

Most of the Connections also have an additional distinction relating to where they were found. This is whether they were found in the Life Spread or the Spiritual Spread. Spiritual Spread connections always have an "S" in their Code whereas the corresponding same Connection found in the Life Spread will not have that "S". In the previous example, the PLFS is a Spiritual Spread Connection, while the PLF is the same kind of Connection (a Pluto Forward Connection) but found in the Life Spread instead. You will learn more about the differences between these two as you study the meanings of the Connections themselves. The main distinction is that the Spiritual Spread Connections exist because of past-life involvement with the other person. They are the earned Connections, that is, earned by our deeds from the past, both positive and negative. The Life Spread Connections are just the result of how our personalities interact with each other.

THE MOON CONNECTIONS

A Moon connection occurs when two cards are sitting right next to each other in either the Life or Spiritual Spread. If we look at the Life Spread on page 343, we will see Moon connections between cards such as the 10♦ and 8♠, the 7♣ and 9♥, and the 8♥ and 2♠. Within any of these Sun-Moon pairs, the card on the right is the Moon Card to the card on the left, which is the Sun Card in these relative relationships. Thus, the 10♦ is the Moon Card to the 8♠ Sun Card, the 9♥ is the Moon Card to the 7♣, and the 2♠ is the Moon Card to the 8♥. As you can see, every card has two Moon Cards, one in the Life Spread and one in the Spiritual Spread.

Moon Relationships on the High Side

1. As soon as I met my partner, I knew that we had been together before and that we would be together in this lifetime.

2. We have a perfect male/female partnership. The things my partner likes to do, he or she does, and I enjoy doing the other things that he or she doesn't.

3. I have never felt this close to someone in my entire life.

4. We have excellent communication and are always able to talk things out. As a matter of fact, we can talk about anything.

There is a great deal of significance to the Moon Card connection. It is one of the closest of the connections that exist. What I mean by that is that people who share a Moon connection feel very comfortable and close to one another. There is often an immediate liking of each other when they first meet. This is especially true if the Moon connection is found in the Spiritual Spread. This implies a familiarity and recognition that could only have been created by having been together in a past life. There are many kinds of connections that stem from being together before. Some are not so good, as the connection in that lifetime was bad or worse. However, the Moon connection in the Spiritual Spread is one of the best for compatibility and it implies that the two of you were not only together, but that you were together in a very close and significant way. You created bonds in that lifetime that brought you very

close to one another, both mentally and emotionally. Now, when you meet, you feel this immediate flow of energy. The comfortable feeling you experience is one that has been earned by having been together before. This bond is so strong that people very often marry someone with whom they have this connection.

Even if the connection is found in the Life Spread, it is still very powerful. There is still the feeling of closeness and harmony between the partners. It is the Sun-Moon quality that often inspires us to marry someone with whom we have a Moon connection. The Sun and Moon are the essential symbols for the male and female energies. The Sun gives and the Moon receives. However, the Moon is responsible for nurturing and governing the cycles of growth. Our Moon governs the tides and is there at night when the Sun is not there to shine on us. In a Sun-Moon relationship, one of the partners is the Sun Card while the other is the Moon Card. To understand this dynamic of Sun and Moon is the key to understanding the many ways that Moon connections manifest themselves.

Moon Relationships on the Low Side

1. My partner and I are so close that sometimes we fight like brother and sister.

2. This relationship is just too easy.

The Sun person will provide the leadership and direction for the relationship. If you know any couple who shares a Moon connection, you can bet that the Sun person is the one that directs and often rules the relationship, regardless of their sex. A good friend of ours is a 10♣ woman who is married to her Moon Card in the Life Spread, the Q♥. She goes out and works and makes the money and he stays home and watches the children and takes care of the house. He loves playing this role and she enjoys being the breadwinner. But even beyond that, the Sun person provides the direction and leadership for the relationship. Whenever I meet a man who is married to someone who is his Sun Card (this means that he is her Moon Card), I just say, "She is the boss in this relationship. Right?" and he will always say something like "You got that right." For a Sun-Moon relationship to work, the Moon person must accept the Sun person as their leader or at least the direction-setter for the relationship.

The Moon person will provide nurturing and support to the Sun person. This can mean taking care of the house, cooking and cleaning, but it can also mean just being there emotionally or in some other significant way for them. The Moon person is there for the Sun person as support and help. They both get a lot from the relationship because both are receiving something they want. In many respects this Sun-Moon relationship is the ideal male-female bond. Male-female couples, where the male is the Sun person with the female being his Moon Card, form lasting bonds, often staying married for a long time. Even when the genders are different, as long as they play these gender-oriented roles within the boundaries of that relationship, it will be a successful bonding and stands the chance of lasting a long time. This means that regardless of sex, the Sun person must play the Sun, or leadership role, and the Moon person must play the Moon, or support role.

It does occur sometimes that a couple gets together who have this connection but for one reason or another, one or both of them cannot or will not play their gender role as defined by the connection. When this occurs, the rela-tionship is probably not going to work or last long, even though this is one of the best connections you can have.

Madonna and Sean Penn are a classic example. Sean Penn (9♣) is Madonna's (10♣) Moon Card in the Spiritual Spread. For that relationship to work, Sean would have had to play the support and nurturing role with Madonna. I am sure that this created a real conflict with him. For one, I am certain these two really loved each other and felt extremely close. I believe the problem was Sean's conflict with playing the nurturing role. He would have had to be the Moon person to make it work but that probably conflicted with his male-dominated personality. Madonna, of course, is very comfortable in the Sun role. Most 10♣ women are. But I know that even though she really wanted their relationship to work, it did not because of the incompatibility of their roles. And you will notice this too as you study the cards of your friends, family, and associates. The Moon connection always works great if the two individuals are willing to play their respective roles within the context of their being together. It is, after all, probably the best connection to have as far as marriage compatibility is concerned. And many successful marriages have it.

Code: **MOF** **Symbol:** ☽

Description: *They are Your Moon Card in the Life Spread*

Meaning of the Connection:

This is a strong connection for relationship and many with this connection get married or have strong bonds of friendship. There is something about this other person that makes you feel safe and grounded. You may even feel that this person brings out the 'nesting instinct' in you. If you are inclined toward marriage or long–term commitment, you have found someone with whom this has a great possibility of success. Though this person may tend to mother you at times, the connection between you gives you a strong feeling of protection and inner stability that allows you to feel that you have a strong foundation on which to build the rest of your life. In turn, your partner appreciates all the wonderful insight and information that you share with them. This connection works best when your partner is inclined to be in the role of a support person for you and when you have a clear direction of where you are going in your life. Otherwise, this beautiful connection, which is associated with so many successful relationships, could go to waste.

Affirmation for this Connection: *My partner and I get along very well and I feel safe, complete, and somehow nurtured when we are together.*

Attraction Index	Intensity Index	Compatibility Index
8	0	9

Code: MOFS **Symbol:** ☾

Description: *They are Your Moon Card in the Spiritual Spread*

Meaning of the Connection:

This person is one with whom you have a powerful connection that gives you a sense of safety and groundedness that encourages commitment and settling down. For this reason, many people with this connection get married and it is one of the best for long–term relationships of all kinds. There is an emotional and mental harmony between you that supports good communication—a vital ingredient to successful relationships. This same connection helps the two of you stay interested in each other and enjoy spending time together. When you met, there was probably an immediate feeling of recognition or familiarity that caused the two of you to hit it off right away. This is a very special connection that has its roots in a past life together of sharing and being close. Now you can benefit from that closeness that you helped create in that lifetime. This connection works best if your partner is willing to play a supportive role in your life and let you direct the action to a certain extent.

NOTES:

No better connection exists for marriage than this one. There is a closeness that is emotional as well as mental, and in some cases, psychic. But bear in mind the element of the gender roles as mentioned in the description of the Moon Connections on pages 276 and 277. Even this most wonderful connection does not guarantee success if the partners are not in line with those elemental energies.

Affirmation for this Connection: *My partner and I get along very well and I feel safe, complete, and somehow nurtured when we are together.*

Attraction Index	Intensity Index	Compatibility Index
8	0	8

Code: MOR **Symbol:** ☾

Description: *You are Their Moon Card in the Life Spread*

Meaning of the Connection:

This is an excellent connection for the two of you. It is one of the most common and most important in marriages and other intimate relationships. You have certain qualities that help your partner feel safe, protected, and firmly rooted in their life. You both enjoy conversation and exchange of ideas and thoughts. You communicate well with one another. When a person decides to get married, they look for these same qualities in making their choice. It is a 'good fit' and you may have many happy years together. This connection always works best when you are playing the supportive role with your partner. Otherwise, there can be conflicts of roles based upon gender.

Affirmation for this Connection: *I have a strong tie with my partner and I am able to provide him or her with a sense of foundation and support.*

Attraction Index	Intensity Index	Compatibility Index
8	0	9

Code: MORS   **Symbol:** ☾

Description: *You are Their Moon Card in the Spiritual Spread*

Meaning of the Connection:

This is a deep and powerful connection that has a strong magnetic pull which can often lead to marriage or a commitment of one kind or another. It is also one of the best connections for marriage, contributing a lot to your overall compatibility. There is both a past-life tie between you and a strong mental and emotional link that makes being together both easy and enjoyable for the two of you. In particular, you have a way of making your partner feel comfortable, safe, and protected. Unless other connections conflict with this one, your partner will want to be with you a lot and feel safe enough to explore deeper forms of commitment and intimacy. This connection also promotes good communications and the mutual expression of ideas and beliefs, which can be mutually enjoyable. You, as their Moon Card, will enjoy the new experiences that your partner brings into your life as you give him or her the support and feeling of groundedness that allows them to function better in the world.

Affirmation for this Connection: *My partner and I share a deep, past-life connection that makes us feel close. I am able to give him or her security.*

Attraction Index	Intensity Index	Compatibility Index
8	0	9

The Venus Connections

Venus, Goddess of Love, Ruler of the signs of Taurus and Libra and the 2nd and 7th houses of the astrology chart, is one of the most important planets in terms of personal relationships. Having a Venus connection insures a great degree of compatibility between the partners, even when other connections may paint a different picture. Cardwise, Venus represents things in the home, the family, and things of pleasure and beauty. A Venus connection implies that the two people involved share many of these things in a harmonious and compatible manner. There is ease and pleasure in being together. There are things and experiences of pleasure that can be shared. Sharing promotes the feeling that it is right to be together so it is no wonder that so many good relationships have one of these powerful connections.

Venus Relationships on the High Side

1. My partner and I have so much in common, it just feels right being together.

2. We have the greatest sex together. He or she seems to know exactly what I like.

3. We like the same art, home decorations, food, music, and other important things.

4. My partner reminds me that life can be enjoyable and pleasurable.

5. We are friends: first, foremost, and forever.

A Venus connection occurs when two cards are one space away from each other in either the Life or Spiritual Spread. If we look at the Life Spread on page 343, we will see Venus connections between cards such as the J♣ and 7♠, the K♣ and 4♥, and the A♠ and 7♦. When counting the two spaces, if we reach the end of a row, we go down to the next row and to the far right side. The card on the right is receiving the Venus energy from the card on the left and thus this connection is stronger from their point of view than the other. So, in our examples, the J♣ receives Venus energy from their Venus Card, the 7♠. The 4♥ is the Venus Card of the K♣, thus it receives Venus energy from the 4♥. The A♠ receives Venus energy from the 7♦. The card giving the Venus energy is also affected because they feel the way the energy is being so well received by their partner and thus they get a reflection of good energy back. The energy is always felt more strongly by the one receiving it, however.

There are also diagonal, or 'mutual,' Venus connections such as those between the J♠ and 3♠ or the Q♦ and 6♥ in the Life Spread. With these connections, the Venus energy flows in both directions so that no one card is doing all the receiving or giving. In some ways, these are the best because they represent sort of a 'doubled' Venus connection in which both people give and receive the wonderful energy of pleasure and harmony.

Venus Relationships on the Low Side

Note: There are no low sides to the Venus relationship, other than possibly overemphasizing the pleasure-seeking aspect of it.

A Venus connection in the Life Spread means that you just happen to have many things in common that you enjoy and take pleasure in. You probably have similar value systems as well, denoted by Venus's rulership of Taurus and the 2nd house. Having the same values is very important in love relationships. If partners disagree on what is most important in life, their chances of staying together are slim, even if the sex life is fantastic. Thus, this connection provides many of the essential pieces that are required for a successful relationship. It is not a guarantee, but it definitely points things in the right direction.

A Venus connection in the Spiritual Spread, however, has nothing to do with values or things of pleasure that we share. Here, a Venus connection implies that the two people already have a strong love bond created by having been together in a former lifetime. In that lifetime, they probably achieved a deep love and respect for each other as a result of having passed through many tests in their relationship. This connection is one of the most common for the 'love at first sight' experiences that we have. There is usually instant recognition of each other and instant good feelings for each other. You may have things in common or not, but the love between you is there and usually strongly felt by both partners. This connection gives your relationship a head start in many ways because you already have a foundation of love that will otherwise take years to establish. There is usually trust, respect, and appreciation for each other right away, for no apparent reason.

Venus energy is good for love, romance, sex, setting up a household, and most important, for helping to build a lasting friendship. You can consider your relationship blessed if you share one of these connections.

Code: VEF   **Symbol:** ♀

Description: *They are Venus to You in the Life Spread*

Meaning of the Connection:

You feel a lot of love and appreciation for your partner because you basically enjoy and like him or her the way he or she is. There is something about this person that makes them very enjoyable for you to be with. This is a great connection for marriage. The two of you like and enjoy many of the same things and feel that you have a lot in common. This can make it very easy to be together and increase the feeling of 'rightness' of being together. This connection is good for any kind of relationship. You two are very compatible and share pleasurable times together.

NOTES:

The planet Venus is associated with the pleasure principle. Having more pleasure in a relationship adds a lot to the ability to be together for extended periods of time and thus is, in itself, great for marriage. However, Venus alone may not be enough to warrant a long–term relationship. Oftentimes those who share a Venus relationship merely become best of friends. However, when two people who are married share this connection, it is a very good sign for the success of that marriage, unless other connections subtract from the compatibility of their being together.

Affirmation for this Connection: *I truly love and enjoy my partner. We have what it takes to get along very well and be lovers or friends.*

Attraction Index	Intensity Index	Compatibility Index
7	0	10

Code: VEFS   **Symbol:** ♀

Description: *They are Venus to You in the Spiritual Spread*

Meaning of the Connection:

There is a strong 'love bond' between you that is difficult to explain because it is love that was created in a past life. For this reason, you probably experienced what is called 'love at first sight' when you first met. The sense of familiarity that you feel for each other is also the result of a subconscious link—a link that was created by being together before and having worked on your relationship a great deal at that time. The two of you have a lot of appreciation for each other and thus are very compatible. You enjoy each other's company and find that you like many of the same things in life. You basically find pleasure in similar things and in being together. This is a very good connection for marriage or any kind of relationship. Even without doing anything, there is a strong love bond between you that could be the foundation for a successful relationship of any type in this lifetime. Given this good, solid foundation, you need only decide what to build on it!

Affirmation for this Connection: *My partner and I share a deep love connection that is hard to explain but very evident. Our love seems to be eternal.*

Attraction Index	Intensity Index	Compatibility Index
8	0	10

Code: VER   Symbol: ♀

Description: *You are Venus to Them in the Life Spread*

Meaning of the Connection:

Your partner just adores you and the two of you have quite a bit in common that makes you feel comfortable with one another and helps you enjoy your time spent together. This is a great connection for marriage or friendship. You find much pleasure in being together and have a good deal of mutual appreciation and enjoyment. For these reasons, you both have made a good choice in choosing this relationship.

Affirmation for this Connection: *There is a strong bond of love and friendship between my partner and I. We enjoy similar things and each other.*

Attraction Index	Intensity Index	Compatibility Index
7	0	10

Code: VERS   Symbol: ♀

Description: *You are Venus to Them in the Spiritual Spread*

Meaning of the Connection:

The two of you have been together before and there is much love flowing between you from that lifetime and perhaps others. You may have felt some of that 'love at first sight' energy when you first met. You can be friends or lovers. You also could get more serious and deeply involved. Just exactly what you do with this 'foundation of love' that exists between you is up to you but one thing that is for sure is that you have a great start for a meaningful and lasting relationship—a much better start than you'll have with just about anyone else that you may encounter.

NOTES:

One of the outstanding qualities of this wonderful connection is that it is an 'earned connection.' This means that the feelings you have for each other were created by a prior lifetime of being together. This connection is often responsible for 'love at first sight' and other such phenomena. Usually there is an instant recognition or acceptance of each other. This connection adds a tremendous boost to a relationship's compatibility and is common among successful marriages.

Affirmation for this Connection: *My partner and I share a deep love connection that is hard to explain. Our love is timeless and eternal.*

Attraction Index	Intensity Index	Compatibility Index
7	0	10

Code: VEM

Symbol: ♀

Description: *You are Venus to each other in the Life Spread*

Meaning of the Connection:

You have found someone with whom you have a lot in common. The two of you have very similar value systems and thus you are very compatible. You have found someone that you can enjoy life's pleasures with and there should be no reason why the two of you could not have a successful and happy relationship. You probably enjoy similar kinds of music and food and your sex together is probably very satisfying for both of you. This is an especially powerful connection because it is what I call a 'mutual connection.' This means that it works in both directions. It is the same for you as it is for your partner and this strengthens the connection quite a bit. Liking the same things is not everything that is needed, but it is something that gives you a head start and a great foundation for having a great relationship.

NOTES:

The Mutual Venus Connections are perhaps the best of all since the affectionate energies run in both directions at once. For this reason, the Intensity Index becomes a negative value. This sort of connection actually removes any negative intensity in the relationship that may be present from other connections, making compatibility much more likely. If you have one of these connections, consider your relationship to be somewhat blessed.

Affirmation for this Connection: *My partner and I really enjoy our time together. We fit together perfectly in many areas.*

Attraction Index	Intensity Index	Compatibility Index
7	-4	10

Code: VEMS

Symbol: ♀

Description: *You are Venus to each other in the Spiritual Spread*

Meaning of the Connection:

There is a strong 'love bond' between you that is difficult to explain because it is love that was created in a past life. The two of you have a lot of appreciation for each other and thus you are very compatible. Even when you first met, you recognized this love that you feel for each other. It is like it has always been there, or like you have been together before. This particular connection is very strong because it is a mutual connection in the Spiritual Spread. This means that it is more potent and that the feelings of love that you share run deeper than in other Venus connections. Of course, it is a very good connection for marriage or any kind of relationship. Even without doing anything, there is a strong love bond between you that could be the foundation for a successful relationship of any type in this lifetime. Given this good, solid foundation, you need only decide what to build on it!

Affirmation for this Connection: *My partner and I have a love that is timeless and eternal. This love can carry us through all of life's experiences, good and bad.*

Attraction Index	Intensity Index	Compatibility Index
9	-5	10

THE MARS CONNECTIONS

Mars is the God of War and Lust. The planet Mars is often called 'The Angry Red Planet.' It should come as no surprise then that Mars connections could make us angry at times. Essentially, though, Mars is energy, a lot of energy. It can be used or abused just like anything else in our life. But Mars cannot be ignored. If we have Mars connections, we will have to do something with this energy or it will tend to create conflict in our lives. Mars is like a magical, but angry, Genie in a bottle. He will do many things for us and fulfill our wishes as long as we keep him busy. The moment he is idle though, he will begin to turn on us, his anger needing an outlet in which to manifest itself. This Genie must be kept busy constantly. Mars relationships are like this.

Mars Relationships on the High Side

1. My partner excites me and helps get me moving.

2. We do lots of things together. We work out, go hiking, ride bikes, jog, and other fun things.

3. I am a lot more physically fit as a result of this relationship.

4. I have the greatest and most passionate sex in this relationship.

5. My partner and I work together in the same business, very successfully I might add.

6. Through this relationship I am getting more accomplished than ever before and as a result, I am realizing my dreams and ambitions.

A Mars connection occurs when two cards are sitting three spaces apart from each other in either the Life or Spiritual Spread. If we look at the Life Spread on page 343 we will see Mars connections between cards such as the 5♥ and 9♥, the 9♠ and K♦, and the 6♠ and 8♦. The latter two examples illustrate how we count the relative spaces between cards when they fall at the end of a row or at the bottom of the spread, as in the case of the 6♠. In the Life and Spiritual Spreads, the natural order is from right to left, just the opposite of how we read. In all of these examples, the first card listed is receiving Mars energy from the second card, because the second card is in front of them if we count from right to left. The card receiving the Mars energy is more affected by the connection than the one dishing it out. If I am a 9♠ person,

then a K♦ person is my Mars Card in my Life Spread. Their actions and speech will tend to stimulate me in a Martian sort of way. That is, they will either excite my passion or anger. They, in turn, will feel my passion or anger and be affected by me, but I am the one who is directly affected the most. Therefore, the connection is stronger from my point of view.

There are also diagonal, or 'Mutual' Mars connections that are very significant. Examples of this in the Life Spread would be the J♣ and 2♦, the 6♥ and K♣, and the 10♣ and J♠. These are stronger than the regular Mars connections because they run in both directions at once. Both of the partners are receiving and giving the Mars energy, so this tends to amplify the Mars energy.

Mars Relationships on the Low Side

1. My partner irritates me and gets on my nerves. Sometimes I want to slap him/her.

2. All we seem to do is fight and bicker about everything. I am getting tired of fighting all the time.

3. Once the sex wore off, all we have done is fought.

4. I know that my partner is trying to deliberately hurt me in any way they can.

5. I compete with my partner all the time, trying to show him/her that I am the better person in this relationship.

A Mars connection in the Life Spread is a personality connection. This means that characteristics of a person's personality stimulate us to feel passion or anger. Our Mars Card in our Life Spread can represent qualities of our own that we get angry with ourselves about. For example, my Mars Card is the 3♠. I can get mad at myself sometimes when I cannot make up my mind as to what to do or which way to go. If I meet a 3♠ person and see them being so indecisive, I could get mad at them because they are reminding me of how I am the same way. This is often the case in Life Spread Mars connections. The person receiving the Mars energy will be getting a reminder of qualities that they already are mad about within themselves. Thus, the Mars person in their life can stimulate their anger or aggression. However, Mars energy is also lustful. A person who is our Mars Card can be someone that we want passionately and sexually.

A Mars connection in the Spiritual Spread has different elements. Here, the Mars energy felt for another person is a function of the two having spent time together in a previous lifetime. As soon as they meet, they feel this passion or anger, and a sense of recognition as well. Often, the reason for the Mars connection is that the two were lovers in that lifetime, or perhaps competitors or fellow warriors of some kind. In some cases, there is unfinished business from that lifetime that needs to be rectified or completed. For example, I have seen many cases where the story goes something like this: Two people met in a former lifetime and felt a tremendous attraction for each other. Because of the circumstances in their lives at that time, they were unable to consummate the relationship. These sorts of Spiritual Spread Mars relationships are very satisfying in the beginning. There is such a great feeling of completion and fulfillment while making love. However, it is just as possible that a Spiritual Spread Mars connection stems from some unfinished anger or hatred from a previous lifetime. In this case, there can be attraction in the beginning, but soon after, the anger and hostility toward one another becomes apparent and later becomes the major focus of the relationship. In these situations, there can be destructive or abusive behavior as the two try to reconcile the intense anger that they left incomplete or unfinished from that previous time of being together.

Mars connections make for really good, and often, very successful, working relationships. To work together in a business endeavor is one of the best channels for Martian energy. Sex is also good, but can only go so far when two people are together for the long–term. Mars energy helps keep us active and alive. It stimulates us to work, be productive, be physically active and to stay healthy. Couples with Mars connections usually do more things together. They go hiking, ride bicycles, jog, go camping, dancing, bowling, and share in other physical activities. These activities bring joy and contentment into the relationship. The Martian God is pleased and ceases to annoy us.

Code: MAF   Symbol: ♂

Description: *They are Mars to You in the Life Spread*

Meaning of the Connection:

Your partner either turns you on, or makes you mad, or both. Your partner stimulates you and gets you going. The two of you need to do things together that are physical or work related or you will fight with one another. This is a great influence for passion and sex but it just as easily can turn into competition and anger. This is a great connection for working together as a couple, jogging, riding bikes, working out, and for sexual compatibility. It makes your relationship more intense and interesting but must be handled with awareness to keep the energy flowing in positive directions.

Affirmation for this Connection: *My partner excites me and stimulates me. I can use this energy constructively and passionately to better my life.*

Attraction Index	Intensity Index	Compatibility Index
9	8	0

Code: MAFS   **Symbol:** ♂

Description: *They are Mars to You in the Spiritual Spread*

Meaning of the Connection:

The two of you were probably brothers, lovers, or competitors in a past life, thus there is a lot of passionate Mars energy between you. This manifests as either a lot of lust, anger, or both. Do things together to channel this powerful physical energy and you will have less of the anger and competition part. This connection can produce either a powerful physical and sexual attraction or powerful competitive and hostile feelings. In some cases you will have both. Know that these feelings are the result of being together before in a similar role and that now you can channel the enormous energy stirred up by this relationship into positive channels for greater success and happiness.

NOTE:

In astrology there are aspects, such as Mars in the 11th house, that indicate people who were considered enemies in a former lifetime that we are drawn to be with again to work out our differences. Spiritual Spread Mars relationships can act in the same way. Anyone with whom you share this connection could be an enemy from a past life with whom you have unfinished business. However, when two lovers come together with this connection, there is usually some past life attraction that never had the opportunity to be fully expressed. This can create a powerful attraction between two people along with the unconscious desire to fulfill some desires that were left incomplete in a former life. In these cases, the relationship represents a fulfillment of passionate energies and can be quite enjoyable. There are cases, though, where two lovers are drawn together who were also enemies before. Though the passion is very much present, there can also be considerable resentment and competitive feelings that surface later in the relationship as the real reason for their being together becomes realized and manifested.

Affirmation for this Connection: *My partner excites me and stimulates me. I can use this energy constructively and passionately to better my life.*

Attraction Index	Intensity Index	Compatibility Index
9	8	0

Code: MAR   **Symbol:** ♂

Description: *You are Mars to Them in the Life Spread*

Meaning of the Connection:

You are the person that excites your partner, turns him or her on, makes them angry, or all of the above. This is an energetic connection that is great for sex and for doing other physical things together. Keep doing things together and find positive outlets for the energy that the two of you generate or you will find yourself getting angry and being competitive with each other. On the other hand, you will never be bored with one another, as you stimulate each other to get moving. On a deeper level, you remind your partner of things that they may not like about themselves. In this case, they have probably chosen you to help them learn to love themselves in these areas. Though the attraction is great don't be surprised if they are furious with you from time to time. On the other hand, if the two of you keep busy and do physical things together, this could be the relationship of your dreams.

NOTES:

Remember that you may remind your partner of one or more parts of themselves that they may not necessarily like. Anyone who is our Mars Card can represent our own qualities that cause us to get upset at ourselves. Thus, when one of these people shows up, there is always the possibility that we will get angry at them. This is because they so vividly exemplify those characteristics for us. This is how you may be showing up for your partner. Understanding this can help in many ways. Mars energy always needs a positive outlet or it will turn to anger and competition. Knowing this, you can always benefit from Mars relationships by simply doing things together. Make love, go outside and take walks together, work out at the spa, or try working together in a business or job. All of these provide a constructive outlet for this aggressive energy that will keep both of you happier and more content in being together.

Affirmation for this Connection: *I excite and sometimes aggravate my partner. We enjoy doing things together and use our intense energy constructively.*

Attraction Index	Intensity Index	Compatibility Index
8	9	0

Code: MARS   **Symbol:** ♂

Description: *You are Mars to Them in the Spiritual Spread*

Meaning of the Connection:

Your partner either has a strong sexual attraction for you or is highly irritated by you. You stimulate them in a strong way which can help them start things and engage in physical activities. This connection is great for sex, for exercise, or for working together but if the two of you just sit around the house you will likely get into disagreements and arguments. Keep moving and find positive expressions for the powerful energy that you stir up in each other and you will be making the most of this important connection. This is also a good connection for being in business as a partnership. This connection is a carry-over from a past life relationship in which the two of you were either lovers, brothers, competitors, or enemies.

NOTES:

Read the Notes under the "MAFS" connection to get more insight into this connection. Much of what was written there applies here except that the roles are reversed, in this case you are the one who is either a stimulation or irritation to your partner. However, all that is said about the past-life connections applies here.

Mars relationships neither add to nor subtract from the Compatibility of a relationship since the way it affects the relationship is so strongly dependent on how the energies of the relationship are used. If used constructively, this connection could actually add to the Compatibility. On the other hand, if used negatively and allowed to channel into anger and aggression, this connection could be the biggest problem that exists between two partners.

Affirmation for this Connection: *I excite and sometimes aggravate my partner. We enjoy doing things together and use our intense energy constructively.*

Attraction Index	Intensity Index	Compatibility Index
8	8	0

Code: MAM   **Symbol:**

Description: *You are Mars to each other in the Life Spread*

Meaning of the Connection:

You both find each other very stimulating. This encourages both of you to do things and it was probably the main cause of all the attraction you felt when you first met. Indeed, this is one of the better connections for sexual passion and pleasure. However, Mars energy can be too much at times. It's kind of like a monkey on your back in that it always needs something to do or else it will turn to competition and anger at times. If you find that the two of you are fighting or not getting along, it might just be because you aren't going out and doing things together. Sex is good, but you need more things to do besides sex because you can't do it all the time. You have more Mars energy together than most couples and you are going to have to find constructive channels for this energy if you don't want to fight all the time. Working together is also a great thing to do.

Having chosen this 'two-way' Mars connection has to mean that you both are either really wanting to get more active in your life or that you are wanting to deal with and work out all your issues around anger and competition. It could actually be a combination of both. Whatever the case, this double Mars connection creates a tremendous amount of energy that must constantly be channeled into positive directions if it is going to be a blessing in your relationship.

Affirmation for this Connection: *My partner and I channel our abundant energies into positive and constructive acts. We enjoy our active life together.*

Attraction Index	Intensity Index	Compatibility Index
8	8	0

Code: MAMS   **Symbol:** ♂

Description: *You are Mars to each other in the Spiritual Spread*

Meaning of the Connection:

The two of you were either lovers, brothers, or competitors in a past life, thus there is a lot of Mars energy between you. This manifests as a lot of passion, a lot of anger, or both. It is also very possible that the two of you had a great, but unfulfilled passion for each other in some previous lifetime. We often attract someone with this connection in order to work out either an unfulfilled desire with them or to resolve an unresolved conflict from a previous time of being together. This is why this connection has such a powerful attraction along with some feelings of familiarity when you first met. (Read the MAFS Notes for more about this past-life element.)

Do things together to channel this powerful physical energy and you will have less of the anger and competition part. This connection can produce either a powerful physical and sexual attraction or powerful competitive and hostile feelings. In some cases you will have both. Know that these feelings are the result of being together before in a similar role and that now you can channel this enormous energy stirred up by this relationship into positive channels for greater success and happiness.

Affirmation for this Connection: *My partner and I come together to resolve passion and anger from the past. We find constructive outlets for our energies.*

Attraction Index	Intensity Index	Compatibility Index
9	9	0

THE JUPITER CONNECTIONS

Jupiter is known as the 'Great Benefic.' The largest planet in our solar system, it is the only one that gives off more energy than it receives. Jupiter in the Astrological natal chart, as well as the Jupiter Card in our Life Spread, represents areas where we have an abundance of some quality, so much so that we actually enjoy giving it out to others. Jupiter is also called the 'Guru planet.' He is a spiritual teacher and the repository of integrity and higher knowledge. As Jupiter transits our natal chart, from house to house, he brings with him many blessings of different kinds. He is always giving us something, whether we are aware of him or not.

Jupiter Relationships on the High Side

1. I openly receive the many things that my partner brings into my life.
2. My partner reminds me that the universe is full of things to be grateful and happy about.
3. Together we share in the infinite abundance of the universe.
4. With my partner, I am learning how to receive blessings.

Jupiter connections are like this too. When we are someone's Jupiter Card, we just have a natural inclination to give to them and to share with them the abundance that we have in our life. There is nothing expected in return, it just feels natural to give. Often, what is given is financial support or blessings. Marriages with Jupiter connections are often prosperous and there is usually an abundant flow of money and property between the partners. Friendships with Jupiter connections are likewise abundant, though the abundance doesn't have to be expressed financially. There is often a good flow of information, guidance, inspiration, and sound advice. In all cases, the Jupiter connection inspires us to drop our fears and focus our attention on just how wonderful our lives really are. Just that attitude alone is priceless.

Jupiter Relationships on the Low Side

1. I take my partner for granted.
2. My relationship is somewhat boring and uneventful. Things are just too easy.
3. Love is more than money and things. I want real love in my marriage or relationship.

The Jupiter connection occurs when two cards are four spaces apart in either the Life or Spiritual Spread. This can be in any direction, left, right, up, down or on a diagonal. If we look at the Life Spread on page 343, we will see Jupiter connections between cards such as the 3♥ and 5♣, the 5♦ and A♠, the A♠ and 10♦, and the 8♠ and K♠. These examples illustrate the many different directions that a Jupiter connection can occur in. There is a definite direction to the connection when it occurs horizontally or vertically. For example, with the 3♥ and 5♣, the 3♥ receives Jupiterian energy from the 5♣, which is its Jupiter Card in its Life Spread. You can check this by looking at the Life Spread of the 3♥ on page 343. In this example, it is the 5♣ that has a strong desire to give to the 3♥. As the 3♥ person receives this energy and appreciates it, they will reflect back to the 5♣ this satisfaction and gratitude. Thus the 5♣ person receives a reflection of what they have given. So, the connection affects them too, but not as strongly as the 3♥. In all these horizontal cases, the energy is received by the card on the right.

Vertical connections works the same way in most cases except the energy is received by the bottom card. In the case of the 5♦ and A♠, it is the 5♦ who is receiving from the A♠. You will not find the A♠ listed as the Jupiter Card in the 5♦ Life Spread, but it still has a Jupiter influence on the 5♦. It is just that it is in a vertical direction. The case of the 8♠ and K♠ is a bit different. If we examine their relationship in the Life Spread on page 343, we will note that each of them is Jupiter to the other if we count in a vertical direction. Four spaces up from the 8♠ is the K♠. But also, if we count four spaces up from the K♠, having to start at the 6♣ at the bottom, we get the 8♠ as a Jupiter influence to it as well. Therefore, we note that when two cards fall in either of the three center columns they will share a Jupiter influence equally. It is, in essence, a doubled Jupiter influence.

The diagonal influences work in much the same way because they are felt by both partners. I call them a 'mutual' connection because there is no definite direction in diagonal connections. The A♠ and 10♦ are a good example of this. They are in a Jupiter (4 spaces apart) relationship to each other, but since diagonals have no direction, it is mutually shared and enjoyed. When we find mutual Jupiter connections or the vertical ones in the three center columns, as I mentioned earlier, we have a very powerful influence for prosperity and mutual appreciation. Relationships with these connections often enjoy a great deal of prosperity. This will also occur in any relationship that has two or more Jupiter connections.

As good as a Jupiter connection is, it is not enough in itself to keep a relationship together. It doesn't have much of an attraction to it and attraction is often the glue that binds people together. If the glue is already there, however, Jupiter connections will strengthen the bonds between the partners and increase the likelihood that the two will stay together.

Jupiter connections in the Spiritual Spread have a more philosophical and spiritual bent to them. Because these are past-life connections, they usually indicate that the two partners were together in a former lifetime in a way that caused them to share the same ideological or philosophical beliefs. They may have studied in the same religious order, for example. In any case, they find that they have much in common in this lifetime regarding their beliefs about religion, the law, or life in general. The propensity to give to one another is also there, though it is usually less financial than the Life Spread connections.

We are fortunate to have the planet Jupiter as part of our universe. It reminds us that there are some things in life that are given freely and that receiving is as joyous as giving.

Code: JUF **Symbol:** ♃

Description: *They are Jupiter to You in the Life Spread*

Meaning of the Connection:

Your partner usually has a desire to give things to you and basically is encouraged to help and protect you. This is a great connection for marriage or friendship as it promotes giving and receiving between the two of you. Allow yourself to receive to get the highest and most rewards from this relationship. Also remember to appreciate what you are receiving if you are to have this relationship continue to be a blessing in your life.

NOTES:

This connection adds a lot to the ability of two people to coexist in a harmonious fashion and thus I have given it a high rating in the compatibility area. However, it does nothing to attract two people together. Therefore, if your relationship connections are predominately Jupiterian, you probably won't have much of a desire to be together. Still, this connection is a blessing to any relationship and will help counteract other connections that may take away from the overall compatibility or harmony.

Affirmation for this Connection: *My partner is a blessing in my life and I can derive great joy by appreciating and paying attention to this blessing.*

Attraction Index	Intensity Index	Compatibility Index
0	0	8

Code: **JUFS**   **Symbol:**   ♃

Description: *They are Jupiter to You in the Spiritual Spread*

Meaning of the Connection:

This connection is a strong bond that adds many blessings to your relationship, whether it is marriage, friendship, or business. Though it is not strong on the attraction level, it will contribute a lot to your overall compatibility and joy in being together. Your partner likes to give to you and you probably share many of the same philosophical beliefs and ideas that make your being together enjoyable and harmonious. Their advice to you could be some of the most valuable of your entire life, so listen carefully. Keep your heart and mind open to receiving their gifts and you both will benefit greatly.

NOTES:

This connection stems from the Spiritual Spread which means that it has its roots in some past life when the two of you were together. It is likely that you gave much to your partner in that lifetime because in this lifetime you are basically meant to collect payment and receive the good they have to offer. This good may be on a material level or on a spiritual level but it is there for you if you are open to receiving.

Affirmation for this Connection: *My partner is a blessing in my life and I can derive great joy by appreciating and paying attention to this blessing.*

Attraction Index	Intensity Index	Compatibility Index
0	0	8

Code: **JUR**   **Symbol:**   ♃

Description: *You are Jupiter to Them in the Life Spread*

Meaning of the Connection:

You really like your partner and enjoy sharing your abundance with them. You like to give them financial assistance, gifts, and well-intentioned guidance and advice. This is a beneficial connection for marriage or business or both and promotes a relationship based upon higher values and spiritual truths or philosophy. This connection works best if your partner appreciates the things you are giving to them.

Affirmation for this Connection: *I am a blessing in the life of my partner and I love to share my abundance them and give to him/her freely.*

Attraction Index	Intensity Index	Compatibility Index
0	0	8

Code: JURS   **Symbol:**   ♃

Description: *You are Jupiter to Them in the Spiritual Spread*

Meaning of the Connection:

You have a good connection with your partner that encourages you to share your abundance and wealth with him or her. This can also be a spiritual connection and it is possible that the two of you have been together in a past life in a spiritual way. Your philosophies are likely to be similar and you have a mutual giving attitude toward each other. In particular, you will feel the urge to give to your partner and the giving you do is likely to be more significant than just money or gifts of the earth. This giving will be good for both of you and be a part of the blessing that this relationship represents to you both.

NOTES:

The urges you probably feel to help or give to your partner likely stem from a past life when your partner gave a lot to you in the same way. All the Spiritual Spread connections have their roots in a relationship that came before. Knowing that your partner gave much to you in a former lifetime can make your giving to him or her just that more fun and rewarding.

Affirmation for this Connection: *I am a blessing in the life of my partner and I love to share my abundance and give to him/her freely.*

Attraction Index	Intensity Index	Compatibility Index
0	0	7

Code: JUM   **Symbol:**   ♃

Description: *You are Jupiter to each other in the Life Spread*

Meaning of the Connection:

Both you and your partner enjoy sharing and giving to each other and this one aspect of your relationship is a major blessing to both of you. Because giving and receiving is such a vital part of successful relationships, this connection greatly increases your chances of long–term success. Another important aspect of this connection is that it will encourage financial prosperity in your relationship. Since financial considerations are among the most prominent issues for couples and since financial problems are at the top of the list of reasons for relationship break-ups, this connection greatly increases your prospects for continued success.

NOTES:

Jupiter has always been considered to be one of the most beneficial connections two people can have. It promotes ease and abundance. Jupiter always bestows blessings on anything he touches. Because this is a mutual connection, it is practically doubled for you and your partner. This occurred because you are Jupiter to each other in a 'diagonal' direction in the Life Spread. This sort of connection can actually make the difference between the success and failure of your relationship. All you need to do to access all of this abundance is to begin appreciating your partner and all of the things that he or she does for you.

Affirmation for this Connection: *My partner and I enjoy helping and giving to each other. We are a double blessing on many levels.*

Attraction Index	Intensity Index	Compatibility Index
1	-3	5

Code: JUMS   **Symbol:**   ♃

Description: *You are Jupiter to each other in the Spiritual Spread*

Meaning of the Connection:

This connection is a strong bond that adds many blessings to your relationship, whether it is marriage, friendship, or business. Though it is not strong on the attraction level, it will contribute a lot to your overall compatibility and joy in being together. You both enjoy giving to each other and you share many of the same philosophical beliefs and ideas. You tend to have the same opinions about what is important in life, especially on the spiritual level, or on the level of integrity and honesty. You are both there for each other when you are needed and you have good advice and other things of value to offer each other when needed. If you both keep your heart and mind open to giving and receiving the many gifts you share, you both will benefit greatly.

This connection springs from a past life in which the two of you shared some experiences in which you both developed some deep understanding about what is true and untrue in life. This could have been as fellow members of some religious order or in some other kind of institution where philosophy was one of the major focuses. Now, in this life, you tend to see things the same way in the areas of right and wrong.

NOTES:

This is one of the most beneficial of the 'spiritual' connections that two partners can have. First of all, it is a past-life earned connection. For this reason, the connection tends to run deeper and have more meaning than the same connection in the Life Spread. Secondly, it is a Jupiterian connection. Jupiter is one of the most important of the spiritual planets. It has been called the 'Guru Planet,' the Lord of Wisdom and Abundance. This connection guarantees that there is some sort of deep bond on the level of your beliefs and philosophies. If you access this and openly discuss your relationship in light of this, you could find that there is much more meaning for your being together than you first thought. This, of course, presupposes that these things, like life purpose and spirituality, are important to you.

Affirmation for this Connection: *My partner and I share a common philosophy and a natural desire to give to each other. We appreciate all that we share.*

Attraction Index	Intensity Index	Compatibility Index
1	-3	5

THE SATURN CONNECTIONS

Saturn is undoubtedly the most feared of all the planets in the zodiac. All of us have to contend with him over the course of our life, some more than others. Most of the suffering and hardship in our lives has been attributed to Saturn. He is called the Lord of Karma, the overseer of justice, the one who doles out punishment to those who have done harm to others in the past. But to look upon Saturn with fear and trepidation is to miss the true essence of this important planet in our lives. Saturn brings many blessings to those who heed his call. Only those people who are unaware of just how he works cower in fear at the mention of his name.

Saturn Relationships on the High Side

1. I openly receive the many suggestions that my partner gives me to improve my life.

2. My partner reminds me of how I can become more responsible and grown up. I appreciate this.

3. I feel this relationship is more mature and grounded than any I have ever had.

4. I can see major improvements in my relationships with others and my career as a result of this relationship.

5. This relationship has lifted me to a higher status level and to a place of more recognition.

Saturn is best symbolized by the scales of justice that are also associated with the sign of Libra. It is interesting to note that Saturn is in its highest, or exalted sign in Libra. Whether we like it or not, our universe operates on the basic principle of cause and effect. This alone guarantees that whatever we do, say, or think will ultimately return to us. Whatever we do to others will be done to us, merely to complete the circle of experience if for no other reason. It is not until we know what it is like to be the giver and receiver of our actions that we are ready to move on to the next step in our evolution. If I have hurt you by my actions and I am unaware of just how that feels, I will inevitably need to experience that same thing from your point of view in order to complete my experience of it. It will not be enough for me to just do it without knowing what it is like to

be on the receiving end as well. Ultimately Saturn represents the conscious awareness of how we are affecting those in our environment by our actions and deeds. If we are conscious of this, Saturn rewards us with a good reputation and recognition from others, all qualities of the 10th house, which Saturn rules.

A Saturn connection occurs when two cards are sitting five spaces apart from each other in either the Life or Spiritual Spread. This can occur from left to right, from down to up, or on a diagonal. If we look at the Life Spread on page 343, we will see Saturn connections between cards such as the Q♦ and 7♣, the 5♣ and 5♠, the J♥ and 3♠, and the 4♥ and 9♠. Study each of these examples carefully and you will learn how all the connections in this book are derived. When the connections are horizontal or vertical, as in the first three examples, one of the cards is receiving the Saturn energy while the other is giving it out. In our examples, the 7♣, 5♠, and 3♠ are each giving the Saturn energy to their partners. When this occurs, the card that is receiving the energy is affected more strongly by it. When the cards are diagonal to each other, as in the last example, the Saturn energy is mutually given or received. This has the effect of increasing the Saturn energy between them.

In relationships where there are Saturn connections, one or both of the partners will be a reminder to the other of how they could be doing things better in their life. A person who is Saturn to me would probably feel like telling me all the things that I should be doing in my life. Other connections, such as Venus, Moon, or Jupiter could cause them to tell me these shoulds in a loving manner that would be easier to digest. Still, just their presence in my life will, on some level, be a reminder to me of some of my shortcomings. In extreme cases, a Saturn person can be cruel, judgmental, harsh, cold, and even verbally and physically abusive. When I witness people who are in abusive Saturn relationships I often ask myself why would they put up with such treatment from their partner. This question has led me to understand that we attract what we are inside. If inside myself I already feel judgmental and harsh on myself, then I will attract someone who personifies this. So, I note that many people who are in Saturn relationships are those who are very hard on themselves already. Even though you may not notice this because their partners seem so hard on them, it is really they themselves that are the culprit. Why would anyone put up with constant criticism and abuse if they did not believe, on some level, that they deserved it?

The good thing about these kinds of relationships is that they usually do not last forever. The person who is hard on themselves and attracts a Saturn partner eventually becomes aware of their self-rejection and changes. Once they begin loving themselves, the Saturn partner is no longer relevant in their life. At that point, they usually leave the relationship, or their partner leaves them. The energy between them no longer supports the critical side of the Saturn connection and someone has to change.

Sometimes Saturn relationships happen in order to pay off a past-life debt. This is especially true when the partners share a Saturn connection in the Spiritual Spread. In these relationships, usually one of the partners had caused great pain or harm to be done to the other while they were together in a former lifetime. This could have been emotional pain caused by a separation or adultery or it could have been harm on some other level. In either case, one of the main purposes of this relationship will be to settle this debt between them.

Not all Saturn relationships are harsh and cruel. Many can be quite constructive and productive. Remember that Saturn is connected to the success and recognition of the 10th house. There are cases when the Saturn relationship provides just what is needed for an individual to achieve his or her goals and ambitions. It will require hard work on the part of the individual, but the guidance, direction, and support of the Saturn person

---

Saturn Relationships on the Low Side

1. My partner is constantly criticizing everything I do and say.

2. Our life is so hard together. I can never seem to do or say things right.

3. All we do is fight and bicker, and it always seems to be my fault.

4. There isn't much joy and kindness in our relationship, just work and more work. I feel like I am in boot camp.

5. I feel like I am being dominated by some slave driver.

6. My partner is abusive, both verbally and otherwise. They continually do unloving things to me.

7. I don't deserve the treatment I am receiving from my partner.

---

will have a very constructive and positive effect. They will have a sense for what their partner should do to realize their goals. All Saturn relationships have a positive effect ultimately. All of them teach us something about being fair, loving ourselves, becoming more responsible and adult-like, and self-disciplined. Because of this, we should not always frown when we see that we have a Saturn connection with another. There may be some very good things in store for us if we are willing to honestly look at ourselves and make improvements where they are indicated. Secretly, this may be the reason we feel such an attraction for them.

Code: SAF   **Symbol:** ♄

Description: *They are Saturn to You in the Life Spread*

Meaning of the Connection:

Your partner acts as a teacher to you in some ways and you may or may not like it. He or she is probably a source of limitation, burden, or other problems for you, being critical of you in some areas and telling you what you 'should' be doing to improve yourself. This can make you mad or feel limited by his or her presence in your life. Saturn relationships are usually difficult in one or more ways. However, for you, this could be a real opportunity to grow as an individual. If you can take their criticism impersonally and use it constructively, you could make huge strides in your personal or professional development. It all depends upon you and what you choose to do with it.

Affirmation for this Connection: *I chose my partner to help me grow and become more mature and responsible. I accept them as my teacher and guide.*

Attraction Index	Intensity Index	Compatibility Index
-5	8	-9

Code: SAFS   **Symbol:** ♄

Description: *They are Saturn to You in the Spiritual Spread*

Meaning of the Connection:

Your partner is in your life to settle a past life debt with you. In settling this debt they may do or say things that seem harsh, critical, and unloving to you and you may or may not resent this. In truth, he or she is a teacher for you with many valuable things to share that will help you become more mature, responsible, and ultimately, successful. However, this kind of relationship is very challenging and takes the utmost in patience and self-honesty to handle in a positive way. For you, this may often seem too difficult to accomplish and you may find that you succumb to looking upon it as being troublesome instead of the blessing that it has the potential to be.

This is one of the most potent of the karmic relationships. This means that it is highly likely that this relationship has a major impact on your life, that its importance cannot be underestimated in terms of how much of an ultimate blessing it can be for you. However, as in all Saturn relationships, a constructive attitude, one in which you are open to learning and seeing your faults, is a requirement to access these blessings.

NOTES:

When someone is Saturn to us, they are often found using the words "You should do this" or "You should do that." This is much the same as a father instructs his son or daughter. Indeed, Saturn is known as the 'great father.' However, the recipient of such admonishments isn't generally receptive to them.

Affirmation for this Connection: *I chose my partner to help me grow and become more mature and responsible. I accept them as my teacher and guide.*

Attraction Index	Intensity Index	Compatibility Index
-5	9	-9

Code: SAR   **Symbol:** ♄

Description: *You are Saturn to Them in the Life Spread*

Meaning of the Connection:

You are a challenging influence in your partner's life. It is likely that you are often judging him or her and pointing out areas where he or she needs improvement. He or she sees you as a restrictive and perhaps burdensome influence. You may find that you just naturally want to either criticize your partner or make suggestions about how he or she could improve their life or performance. If you become overly critical you will find them avoiding contact with you or opposing you, so your role as 'teacher' must be handled carefully. Just how this connection affects your relationship will depend on what other connections you share and the attitude of your partner. If he or she accepts your role as a teacher in his or her life, this relationship will go a lot smoother. Otherwise, all your efforts to teach or help your partner will only create more friction and animosity between you.

Affirmation for this Connection: *I am my partner's teacher and guide and I use this power with love and understanding.*

Attraction Index	Intensity Index	Compatibility Index
-2	9	-3

Code: SARS   **Symbol:** ♄

Description: *You are Saturn to Them in the Spiritual Spread*

Meaning of the Connection:

For whatever reason, you have been selected to play the role of a teacher to your partner and they may or may not appreciate the lessons that you have to share with them. Even if you don't realize it, you are somewhat hard on them, probably pointing out their weaknesses and showing them how they can do or be 'better' or how they can become more mature and responsible. This can cause them to see you as a problem and someone to be avoided because few people enjoy criticism.

It is quite likely that the two of you have been together before and that one of your roles in this lifetime is to return to them something that they have given to you in a former existence. However, the thing that is given is not always well received. In this case, especially, your suggestions for their improvement may not always be appreciated.

However, if your partner is able or willing to look at and accept their own shortcomings, you can be a blessing in their life, one that helps them to realize their highest dreams and ambitions.

Affirmation for this Connection: *I am my partner's teacher and guide and I use this power with love and understanding.*

Attraction Index	Intensity Index	Compatibility Index
-2	5	-4

Code: SAM   **Symbol:** ♄

Description: *You are Saturn to each other in the Life Spread*

Meaning of the Connection:

This is a rare connection and a powerful one. Most people will never have the opportunity to experience this double-Saturn connection that you two share. Saturn is about becoming more realistic, self-responsible, honest, and fair. These qualities are ultimately what make people successful in their life and careers. However, if we are really out of touch with these qualities a connection like this could be complete hell. So, this connection is a challenge, to both of you really. Both of you will be reminded of things that you can do to improve yourselves and many of the things that you think you 'should' do.

If you can handle the heat, this could be one of the most constructive and rewarding relationships of your life. If you have chosen this relationship, it is either because you want more concrete success in your life, you want to grow up and get real, or you want to be challenged so that you learn to really love yourself in spite of what others may say or think about you. In 90 percent of the cases, relationships with this connection are challenging. If you are up to the challenge get ready for work and later, great success.

NOTES:

This, and the next connection are probably the most challenging aspects a couple could share. It holds the possibility of two great extremes, both almost opposites of each other. Because Saturn has so much to do with karma, problems, and challenges, this double Saturn connection could result in one of the most unhappy experiences for both couples where they constantly are criticizing each other to the point that the love between them is lost. On the other hand, this connection could indicate that both partners chose this relationship to learn to take full responsibility for their lives and both had a desire to grow into more successful individuals. If they look at each other as their teacher in a positive way, this powerful connection could actually catapult them into more personal and professional growth than would be possible with any other connection.

Affirmation for this Connection: *My partner and I use this relationship to grow in our level of self-responsibility. We appreciate the lessons we learn.*

Attraction Index	Intensity Index	Compatibility Index
-4	10	-6

Code: SAMS   Symbol: ♄

Description: *You are Saturn to each other in the Spiritual Spread*

Meaning of the Connection:

Your partner is in your life to settle a past life debt with you. In settling this debt they may do or say things that seem harsh, critical and unloving to you and you may or may not resent this. You may act this way with him or her as well because this is a mutual connection with a very karmic overture. In truth, he or she is a teacher for you with many valuable things to share that will help you become more mature, responsible and ultimately, successful. However, this kind of relationship is very challenging and takes the utmost in patience and self honesty to handle it in a positive way. For you, this may often seem to be too difficult to accomplish and you may find that you succumb to looking upon it as being difficult and troublesome instead of the blessing that it has the potential to be.

This is one of the most potent of the karmic relationships. This means that it is highly likely that this relationship has a major impact on your life, that its importance cannot be underestimated in terms of how much of an ultimate blessing it can be for you. However, as in all Saturn relationships, a constructive attitude, one in which you are open to learning and seeing your faults, is a requirement to access these blessings. All of this applies to your partner as well. Being a double connection, the heat is definitely turned up to it's highest degree. You both must have wanted to grow or you wouldn't have been attracted to each other to begin with. Acknowledge your reasons for being together and you are well on your way to reaping the rewards of this powerful connection.

Affirmation for this Connection: *My partner and I are learning to become more adult and completely self-responsible. We are growing up together.*

Attraction Index	Intensity Index	Compatibility Index
-4	10	-6

THE URANUS CONNECTIONS

Uranus rules the sign of Aquarius and the 11th house astrologically. They are related to groups of people like associations, corporations, clubs, and fraternities. Aquarians themselves are the 'friends of man.' Typically they are friends with all, though they have few truly intimate relationships. Aquarians see themselves more as part of a group than as the other half of a couple. They promote equality and cooperation among the people in their life. They are known to place a high value on their personal freedom as well as their right to express their individuality. Often, they will go out of their way to do or say the unorthodox, in a proud proclamation of their uniqueness. This stark individuality and uniqueness are the hallmarks of the Aquarian/Uranian energy. It should come as no surprise then that when someone is Uranus in relation to us, that they would go to great lengths to protect and preserve these qualities for themselves, often to our own dismay.

Uranus Relationships on the High Side

1. Mutual respect and appreciation for each other.
2. Allowing the partner do the things they want to do without expectations or attachments.
3. Mutual friends. Usually the couple is part of a large circle of friends.
4. Friends for life, friends-first attitude.
5. Willingness to allow the relationship to end if that's what would be best for one or both of the partners.

The Uranus connection occurs when two cards are six spaces away from each other in either the Life or Spiritual Spread. This can happen from right to left as in the case of the J♥ and 6♥ in the Life Spread on page 343, or vertically, as in the case of the 10♥ and 9♦ in the same spread. In these cases one of the two cards is receiving the Uranian energies from the other. The J♥ receives Uranian energy from the 6♥ and the 10♥ receives Uranian energy from the 9♦. In your own Life Spread chart, you will see a card, your Uranus Card, that is one of the cards that you receive Uranian energy from. If you meet such a person you will be the one that needs to give them complete freedom if you want to

have a good relationship with them. There are probably many other cards that you have Uranus connections with, found in both the Life and Spiritual Spreads.

There are also diagonal or mutual connections such as between the A♠ and 4♥ and the 3♥ and Q♥, both in the Life Spread. But these are rare since only two are found in each of the Life and Spiritual Spreads. Because these connections have no implicit direction they are stronger than the direct or vertical connections listed previously. Both partners give and receive the Uranian energy, which strengthens the bonds.

Uranus Relationships on the Low Side

1. One partner trying to control and manipulate the other unsuccessfully.
2. Uncertainty about the affections of your partner.
3. Nothing in common, no shared experiences or points of view.
4. Rebelliousness and avoidance tactics by one or both of the partners.
5. Struggling to hang on to the partner.
6. Unwillingness to face one's fears of abandonment or rejection.

Uranus connections in the Spiritual Spread are usually easier to manifest on the higher levels. This is because the two of you have already been together before in an Aquarian type relationship and have already learned to be 'friends-first' and to give each other mutual respect and freedom. Though you probably will not know why, you will tend to warm up to this person when you first meet and have these mutual good feelings for them.

The Uranus connection represents, at its highest level, that state of relationship where there are no expectations and a complete recognition of a person's individuality. This means no personal attachments, addictions, or contracts that commit our partner to meeting our personal desires or needs. This kind of relationship is difficult for most people to achieve because it requires us to let go of our many fears of abandonment and betrayal. In a Uranian relationship, we will have to allow our partner to be themselves or we will end up struggling with them all the time and eventually drive them away from us.

I have often noted relationships between parent and child where the child was Uranus to the parent. This can be a very difficult connection because the parent's natural inclination is to direct and guide the life of the child. But when the Uranus connection is present, all attempts to direct the child will fail and cause the child to rebel against the authority the parent represents. The child sees his or her parent as trying to control or change them and the parent sees the child as a rebellious and uncontrollable problem child. If the parent is narrow-minded, they will make all sorts of attempts to 'help' their child. Some of these can be quite dramatic and harmful to the child. Ultimately the child will resent all such attempts and break away from the parent for good. In this kind of relationship, the burden of the responsibility lies with the parent. The parent should be the one to let go and allow the child the freedom to express themselves as they wish. It will actually help the child to be allowed complete freedom (and responsibility) for their life, even at an earlier age than one would normally give them this much freedom.

In personal, intimate relationships the Uranus energy can create either the greatest friendship, or great feelings of uncertainty between the partners. If the relationship is founded on the notion that both partners are 'friends-first' above all else, then it can become a beautiful expression of unconditional love and acceptance. I have witnessed some of these relationships and I have to admit that they are few and far between. When they work though, they are quite beautiful. Usually the partners have separate jobs but they share the same friends. They give each other the freedom to travel and they support their partner's need to find his or her highest expression. There is respect for each partner's differences as well as the things they have in common.

However, in other cases, the Uranus relationships can start out like this but later evolve into a relationship where the two partners have so little in common that they begin to question why they are together at all. They will say things like "We never do anything together" or "He (she) doesn't like any of the things that I like." At this stage, they are yearning for more of a feeling of closeness and companionship and perhaps are not appreciating the freedom that the Uranus connection brought into their relationship as much as they did in the beginning of the relationship.

Some people have the special karma of having a true and lasting life-long friend. This is someone who loves you whether you are here or there, no matter how much time has elapsed in your relationship, and it does not matter what you have done or where you live. When you get the chance to spend time together, you thoroughly enjoy it but you place no expectations upon each other as to how often you get together. I know about these special relationships because I have one with a friend I have known since childhood. And wouldn't you know it, he is my Uranus Card in my Life Spread!

Code: URF   **Symbol:** ♅

Description: *They are Uranus to You in the Life Spread*

Meaning of the Connection:

Your partner is always doing the unexpected and you can never seem to know whether or not he or she is coming or going. They can be a source of uncertainty in your life that you may or may not like. You are unable to control them in any way and you would be much better off if you let them live their life just as they please. If you do, you will find that you have a best friend for life. On the positive side it is likely that the two of you allow each other the space to do your own thing and to pursue your separate dreams and ambitions. It is especially important that you give this space to your partner.

Affirmation for this Connection: *My partner is my best friend and allows me to be myself without expectations or attachments. I return the favor.*

Attraction Index	Intensity Index	Compatibility Index
0	0	0

Code: URFS   **Symbol:**   ⯂

Description: *They are Uranus to You in the Spiritual Spread*

Meaning of the Connection:

It is likely that you and your partner shared a past life in which you were friends or members of a group or association with a specific cause. In that lifetime you learned to respect each other's individuality and personal freedom. In this lifetime you probably feel the same way and this connection gives you a certain amount of mutual respect for each other that is quite admirable. This connection may cause some uncertainty in you at times because someone who is Uranus to us will often do the unexpected from our point of view. On the positive side, these unexpected acts are helping you let go of seeing them or other things in old, traditional ways and helping you open up to new possibilities in your life. If you have a desire for a relationship with someone who will be a friend for life and who will never expect you to change or give up your individuality, this could be just the one for you. Otherwise the extreme individuality of this connection may be too much for you, not providing enough security or togetherness for your liking.

Affirmation for this Connection: *My partner is my best friend and allows me to be myself without expectations or attachments. I return the favor.*

Attraction Index	Intensity Index	Compatibility Index
0	0	0

Code: URR   **Symbol:**   ⯂

Description: *You are Uranus to Them in the Life Spread*

Meaning of the Connection:

As far as your partner is concerned, you want to have complete freedom to be yourself and you expect them to give this freedom to you. However, from their point of view they may experience this as your being unpredictable or unreliable, unless they are willing to let you come and go as you please. It is likely that you scare them or leave them feeling uncertain about your affections at times. However, this same influence could make you the very best of friends provided that both of you are willing to have this much freedom in your relationship. The other connections between you will help to tell the complete story of your being together and more fully explain how the two of you handle this connection.

Affirmation for this Connection: *My partner and I are friends in the truest sense of the word and allow each other the freedom to be ourselves.*

Attraction Index	Intensity Index	Compatibility Index
0	0	0

Code: URRS   **Symbol:** ⊞
                                                                                  ○

Description: *You are Uranus to Them in the Spiritual Spread*

Meaning of the Connection:

The two of you are friends from past lives and there is a certain amount of mutual respect and appreciation for your individuality that comes with this connection. This can be a great friendship as long as the two of you do not place expectations on each other. However, there may be times when it seems that the two of you have little in common. The truth is that you are friends and you will spend time together, though not always in any regularly scheduled way.

Affirmation for this Connection: *My partner and I are friends in the truest sense of the word and allow each other the freedom to be ourselves.*

Attraction Index	Intensity Index	Compatibility Index
0	0	0

Code: URM   **Symbol:** ⊞
                                                                                  ○

Description: *You are Uranus to each other in the Life Spread*

Meaning of the Connection:

You and your partner share a very unique and rare connection that is only possible with eight cards in the deck. This is a connection of mutual friendship and personal freedom of expression. Basically you are friends first, lovers and partners second. This is the connection of true unconditional love. You must both allow each other complete freedom to do and be who you will. Any attempt to control or change your partner will cause the space between you to expand rapidly, and in extremes, to break you apart. It is our fears that cause us to try to change or control our partners. Perhaps you have chosen this relationship in order to learn that true love does not require any control or power with our partners. Let the love between you flow, like a gentle breeze between you, so that there is enough space for the two of you to breath and retain your personal sense of individual self-expression.

Affirmation for this Connection: *My partner and I are friends first and always allow each other complete freedom of self-expression.*

Attraction Index	Intensity Index	Compatibility Index
0	0	0

Code: URMS   Symbol: H
                                                               H
                                                               O

Description: *You are Uranus to each other in the Spiritual Spread*

Meaning of the Connection:

You and your partner likely shared a past life in which you were friends or members of a group or association with a specific cause or philosophy. In that lifetime you learned to respect each other's individuality and personal freedom as you joined together for a common cause. From this past experience, the two of you have a deep respect for each other's space and allow each other to express your individual differences as a natural part of the relationship. It is likely that the two of you allow each other plenty of time to pursue your individual goals and aspirations. Sometimes you may feel as though you are leading somewhat separate lives. But you also must realize that you chose this relationship to be an example of true friendship in the fullest sense of the word. You are learning non-attachment and how to respect your own individual needs and expressions through the vehicle of this unique relationship.

NOTES:

This is one of the most powerful of the unconditional love connections, mostly because it is from a past-life, but also because it is one of the few 'mutual connections' that exist between the Birth Cards. In a way it is much better than the other mutual Uranus connection because the two of you have already learned how to let each other be without trying to change each other. Thus, this connection can be the foundation for a very happy life together. There are, of course, other connections between you and some of these may pose problems of one kind or another. Keep in mind, though, that this deep feeling of companionship between you is always there to set the stage for a mutual understanding. Remember that you only want the best for your partner and they feel the same way toward you.

This connection only occurs between cards that fall at the outer corners of the Life and Spiritual Spreads. If you look on pages 342 and 343 you will see that these cards—the 7♥ and 4♠ are in opposite corners in the Spiritual Spread along with the 10♠ and A♥. Moving to the Life Spread we have the A♠ and 4♥ in one set of diagonal corners and the Q♥ and 3♥ in the other. So, we note that this is a fairly rare connection, though it is powerful.

Affirmation for this Connection: *The friendship that we share is deep and real. It allows us to be completely ourselves with each other at all times.*

Attraction Index	Intensity Index	Compatibility Index
0	0	0

THE NEPTUNE CONNECTIONS

Neptune is probably one of the least understood of all the planets, simply because its basic nature is to obscure and confuse. If we consider that our movie industry is governed by this planet, it helps us to understand its true nature. Neptune delights us with visions and dreams of the way our lives can be. In many cases it inspires us to perform great deeds of heroism and sacrifice. But it also deceives us and leads us down the primrose path of illusion. Neptune also governs drugs, chemicals, spiritualism, psychic phenomena, and all forms of escapism. All of these things can lift us up to new heights or become a vehicle for our avoidance of the truth. When we go to a movie, we are transported into another world. For a couple of hours we are living in another reality where anything can come true. Actors in movies act with incredible confidence, skill, and power. Some of them appear to be infallible and perfect. They live the perfect life and overcome all the bad guys and demons in their life. To escape to a movie can be quite an enjoyable experience unless we allow ourselves to believe that what we experienced in the movie is real. If we walk out of the movie determined to be or do like the actors that we just perceived, we are probably setting ourselves up for a rude awakening. The sounds, lights, and fury of the movies are not the same as real life. People in real life are not perfect. Life itself is a continuous stream of challenges. Our own emotions are uncontrollable and our lives often seem to get worse each year instead of better. We long for that happy ending where we walk off into the sunset with the person of our dreams. Still, movies can inspire us to become something that we already are, if we remember to look within ourselves for those solutions. Going to a movie is much like taking a drug. We go inside, escape from our reality for a while, and return to the real world afterward.

Neptune Relationships on the High Side

1. My partner inspires me to expand my life on many levels.
2. I am psychically attuned to my partner. I can read their thoughts and feelings.
3. I am continually grateful for my partner's contributions to my life.
4. I can give up the search for the perfect mate—I have found them.

Relationships with Neptune connections are like going to a movie or taking a drug. In them we see endless possibilities for our own personal happiness in the eyes of our beloved. We often place them up on a pedestal and worship them. They become our savior. Finally, we think to ourselves, we are living the life of our dreams with the person that we have always longed for. Relationships with Neptune connections are often past-life relationships. Because we sense that we have been with our partner before, we sense the timeless and eternal quality of love. This reinforces our belief that this is our soul mate, the person of our dreams. These relationships often begin very mysteriously and magically. We seem to be destined to meet this person because when we do meet them, it seems to happen by such a fluke of fate or accident that is so unusual. Being with them helps us perceive ourselves in a different way, perhaps in a way that we have yearned for for a long time. It's no wonder that these relationships are often the most difficult to end. They become addictive because there is so much that we need and want from them.

A common problem with Neptune relationships is that we imagine that our partner can perceive and respond to our needs without us ever telling them what they are. In truth we find that in many cases, the partner who is doing the expecting is incapable or afraid of communicating just what their needs are. The problem is that even though they don't say anything, they still expect them to be fulfilled. When they are not, anger can be the result, as well as other behavior patterns of escapism and illusion.

People who are strongly Neptunian or have a lot of Pisces energy in their natal Astrological charts will tend to attract one Neptune type relationship after another. It can take as long as an entire lifetime for them to learn the lessons involved with these connections. This is because Neptune is such a hidden, unseen influence that it makes it very difficult to bring its influence into the realm of the conscious mind where it can be dealt with effectively.

The Neptune connection occurs when two cards are seven spaces away from each other in either the Life or Spiritual Spread. This only occurs in the direct and vertical directions. There are no diagonal or mutual Neptune connections. If we look at the diagram of the Life Spread on page 343, we see Neptune connections between the A♣ and 7♦, the A♥ and 7♣, and between the 8♥ and 3♥. I included that last one so you can see how to count when you get to the bottom left hand corner of the Life Spread. In all these examples, the second card is the Neptune Card of the first. When someone is our Neptune Card, we are the ones who are completely taken with them on some level. We are receiving this Neptune energy from them and thus are the most affected by it. For this reason, it is very easy for them to deceive us if they want to. They can use us to get the things they want and we would probably never know it. Neptune connections in the Life and Spiritual Spreads are pretty much equally strong. The main difference is that the Spiritual Spread Neptune connections also have the telepathic communication syndrome. Each partner often knows what the other is thinking even when separated by thousands of miles. This form of communication happens in many relationships. But in the Neptune relationship it usually happens sooner and is more pronounced.

The main lesson we learn in Neptune relationships is about our own dreams and desires. The Neptune person often represents to us qualities that we want but didn't know that we wanted until we fell in love with them. They serve to awaken in us some of our deepest urges and desires. The trouble is that these desires and dreams are so deep within us that we are not that conscious of them. This causes us to really believe that it is this other person who is responsible for the way we feel. We project all of our needs and desires onto this

---

Neptune Relationships on the Low Side

1. I am hopelessly addicted to my partner. Like a drug addict, I will do anything to be with them. I would even die to be with them.

2. I am refusing to see the faults in my partner.

3. I am selfishly expecting my partner to be everything that I want and not seeing them for who they are.

4. Confusion in communications. Unspoken expectations that create conflict and fear. I expect my partner to know my needs without my having to tell them.

---

person and in the process we may distance ourselves from our own personal power. These relationships often end badly. There is usually a rude awakening that is so shocking that we go from one extreme to the other. Just as much as we were enamored and attracted to the other person, we are now repulsed by them and cannot wait to distance ourselves from them. However, it is our dreams that we are distancing ourselves from. Ultimately we must acknowledge the things they awakened in us as our own and find ways to bring these dreams into fruition for ourselves. In this way, the Neptune people in our life perform a priceless service. They awaken us to important, often vital, parts of ourselves that were once hidden from our view.

Code: NEF   **Symbol:** ♆

Description: *They are Neptune to You in the Life Spread*

Meaning of the Connection:

Your partner is probably the man or woman of your dreams in one or more important ways. You have many fantasies about them and see them through 'rose-colored glasses.' They can do no wrong in your eyes, but are you seeing them for who they are or who you would like them to be? This can be very romantic or it can be a nightmare. It all depends on you. Oftentimes, people with this connection have a strong psychic link. In other cases there is a strong element of spirituality between them. In all cases, you should be advised that it would be very easy for your partner to deceive and take advantage of you. Because your fantasy about them is so strong, they could hold a certain 'spell' over you that could be dangerous. This connection is one of the most romantic and can inspire magical feelings in you and your partner. Taken to its highest form, this connection could inspire you and your partner to perform some great deed for the world.

    NOTES:

The Neptune connection is in essence a higher octave of the Venus Connection. Astrologically, the planet Venus is exalted in Pisces, the sign ruled by Neptune. Therefore, Neptune has the potential to bring out the highest form of love, the love that entails sacrifice and selflessly giving to another. However, in this the dawning of the Aquarian Age, much of Neptune's influence in our lives tends to go to the down side and we usually experience the more negative effects in Neptunian relationships. This means misplaced fantasies, dreams, and intentions. Many people who have strong Neptune influences in their love life end up in painful codependent and addictive relationships. Some can even be abusive. Neptune can be very deceptive and addicting and as in most of the connections listed here, how it manifests in your life will depend more upon you than the connection itself. To get the most benefit from this connection, set high ideals for your relationship in terms of what the two of you may contribute to the world. This will activate the highest vibrations of Neptune, the planet of Universal and Cosmic Love.

Affirmation for this Connection: *My partner is the person of my dreams. We share a strong psychic link and through them I experience my unlimitedness.*

Attraction Index	Intensity Index	Compatibility Index
8	0	3

Code: NEFS   **Symbol:** ♆

Description: *They are Neptune to You in the Spiritual Spread*

Meaning of the Connection:

You have a strong psychic link to your partner and there can be a lot of fantasy and idealism that you have about him or her. Though this can seem like the relationship of your dreams, it could also turn out to be a nightmare if you refuse to see them as they truly are. Try to see how strongly you project your fantasies on them and take a moment to separate what you want them to be from who they really are. In this manner your own projections will not block the truth and you will be able to have a relationship with a real person instead of a dream that is constantly threatening to become a nightmare. It is very likely that you and your partner were together before and in that former existence shared this same deep, psychic connection. You could have a very special purpose for being together, one that will make an important contribution to the world around you. This is the connection of 'Universal Love.'

Affirmation for this Connection: *My partner is the person of my dreams. We share a strong psychic link and through them I experience my unlimitedness.*

Attraction Index	Intensity Index	Compatibility Index
8	0	3

Code: NER **Symbol:** ⯓

Description: *You are Neptune to Them in the Life Spread*

Meaning of the Connection:

Your partner sees you as his or her 'dream come true' and it is likely that you cannot do any wrong in their eyes. However, you may feel at times that they don't really know the real you and you may get tired of playing some make-believe role for them. This is also a very romantic connection and keeps the romance going in a relationship for years and years. You have a power over your partner and with it you can deceive them if you want and they will never know that you are doing it. Though it is nice to have someone worship you, you want to be loved for who you are, which can be difficult sometimes with this connection. Still, you have a way of pleasing your partner and this creates a strong bond between you. It is also possible that you could use this connection to inspire your partner to work with you in fulfilling an important goal in terms of your life's work. This is the connection of 'Universal Love.'

Affirmation for this Connection: *My partner gives me the power to fulfill his or her dreams. I use this power to bring them truth and love.*

Attraction Index	Intensity Index	Compatibility Index
8	0	3

Code: NERS **Symbol:** ⯓

Description: *You are Neptune to Them in the Spiritual Spread*

Meaning of the Connection:

Your partner feels a deep, subconscious link with you and on many levels you represent a dream come true for him or her. This same connection makes them liable to see you through rose-colored glasses and to project their fantasies on you. While this can be very romantic and idealistic, you may get tired of playing out this fantasy role for them, which may not be the real you at all. It is also likely that the two of you share a deep spiritual connection and this can be good if it is not used to deceive or take advantage of one another. You, especially know that you hold a sort of mystical power over your partner and have more responsibility to be honest and truthful with them. This connection can provide the two of you with inspiration and direction to achieve some important and worthwhile goal connected with helping the world. Take this connection of 'Universal Love' and put it to good use.

Affirmation for this Connection: *My partner gives me the power to fulfill their dreams. I use this power to bring them truth and love.*

Attraction Index	Intensity Index	Compatibility Index
8	0	3

THE PLUTO CONNECTIONS

Pluto is the God of destruction and death. He rules over sex, death, rebirth, and the goods of the dead. Pluto and Mars are connected as they are co-rulers of the sign of Scorpio. And in many ways, the connections are similar. However, if Mars is anger, lust, and war, Pluto is Mars to a higher octave. It is anger that is taken so far that it becomes revenge. It is lust that is based on power, not just desire, and it is the war that cleanses the planet of the lower and darker elements. Pluto is about power—financial power, will power, sexual power, and the power that comes from position. Whoever has got the power wins the game. In Pluto relationships, there are often power struggles between the partners. When we realize that it is a struggle that is going on between the partners, we immediately know that there are probably some false conceptions at the root of it. If two people are attracted to a relationship with strong Pluto connections, it is certain that one or both of the partners has a preconceived notion that others are trying to control or manipulate them. Because they believe this, they eventually attract a partner who believes the same thing. Now, they are involved in a power struggle between them that could take a lifetime to understand and heal.

Pluto Relationships on the High Side

1. My partner reminds me of things I can achieve and become.
2. I am energized by my partner's presence in my life.
3. I am transformed by my partner's presence.
4. I let go of all the negative aspects of my past that have been holding me back.

Pluto connections occur when two cards are eight spaces apart from each other in a horizontal direction of either the Life or Spiritual Spread. This is always counted from right to left. For example, if my Birth Card is the 10♦, I count eight cards to the left beginning with the 8♠ and I arrive at the 9♥ as my Pluto Card. This is illustrated in the Life Spread on page 343. Other examples on the same page would be the 5♠ and 4♣, the 4♦ and K♠, and the 10♣ and 3♦. In each of these examples, the second card is Pluto to the first. The second two examples

illustrate where we go when we are counting and we reach the bottom, right hand corner. They also illustrate where we go when we reach the end of the Crown Line (the top three cards). There are no mutual (diagonal) or vertical Pluto connections.

Pluto Relationships on the Low Side

1. I fight with my partner all the time.
2. My partner is constantly in my face reminding me of my shortcomings.
3. My partner is trying to control and manipulate me through many kinds of persuasion.
4. We fight a lot about money and who is in control.
5. Sometimes I feel that I would like to kill my partner, they make me so angry.
6. I have never been so angry with someone in all my life.

When someone is my Pluto Card, they are the ones that are doing things in a way that is bringing Pluto energy into my life. They may or may not be aware of how they are affecting me because from their point of view the Pluto connection does not exist. They only experience my reactions and responses to their actions, which are stimulating me in a Pluto way. Therefore it is the person who is receiving the Pluto energy who is more affected by this connection, in this case me. And exactly how would I be affected?

Our Pluto Card in our Life Spread represents some area of our life in which we will undergo a major transformation over the course of our life. It is not the only area, but it is one of the most important. It could be about most any life topic. For example, the 10♣'s Pluto Card, the 3♦, tells us that the 10♣ is here to transform their indecision about what they want (3♦) into creative self expression. Now, if I begin a relationship with someone whose Birth Card is my Pluto Card in either the Life or Spiritual Spread, I am in essence saying that I want to be reminded of the changes that I must make so that I will get on with it. A Pluto person, even without their knowing it, acts as a reminders to us of what we need to change in ourselves. They challenge us to let go of all the personality traits, fears, beliefs, and attitudes that perpetuate the negative qualities that we want to change. As such they become the messengers of our death and transformation. Not in the literal sense, but death of the parts of ourselves that we secretly know are destined to pass away.

Often we are afraid to let go of the past and of qualities that we have known for so long, even though we know that they are not good for us. Therefore, we often fight with our Pluto partner as if our life depended on it. Interactions with them can dredge up some of our deepest and darkest secrets and we may be surprised at our own reactions to them. In some cases, Pluto relationships are out and out power struggles, sort of like *The War of the Roses* movie. There can be vindictiveness and the desire to get even. Of course this only occurs when one or both of the partners are failing to take any responsibility for the relationship.

Not all Pluto relationships are so dramatic. Taken with a positive attitude, a person who is our Pluto Card represents a goal that we have in mind for ourselves. Something about them is very attractive to us. I often speak about the Pluto connection as the moth that is being drawn into the flame. The moth is very attracted to the flame, which will ultimately send it along its way to its next state of being, whatever that is. But we don't have to look upon our Pluto person as someone who will kill us. There is something that we want to become that they reflect to us. We are challenged by their presence to make the changes in our life that will help us achieve our dreams and ambitions. This is the attitude that will bring us the most benefits from interactions with someone who is our Pluto Card.

Code: PLF   **Symbol:**

Description: *They are Pluto to You in the Life Spread*

Meaning of the Connection:

There is something very challenging for you about your partner. He or she causes you to make changes in your life and helps you to expand beyond your present capabilities or self-imposed limitations. It is likely that the two of you have 'battles of the will' at times. The two of you may be vying for control in the relationship and this can get intense. However, if handled with awareness, this could be one of the most valuable relationships of your life. It will transform you and help you reach your highest potential while encouraging you to let go of emotional attachments or negative habits that are holding you back. To get the most out of this connection, resist the temptation to try and change or control your partner and use this energy to change yourself. That is what this relationship is meant to be for you - a stimulus to change. While not an easy relationship by most standards, its value to you could be enormous. This connection is usually associated with strong sexual attraction.

NOTES:

The Pluto Connection is related to Mars, but it is Mars taken to a higher octave. Instead of the lust and anger of Mars, we get the control and power complexes of Pluto. As in the Mars Connection, Pluto has a high level of attraction and intensity. Ultimately, how this relationship is for you will depend on your relationship with yourself. The Pluto person reminds us of some qualities in ourselves that we have 'contracted' to change in this lifetime. If you are aware of your own faults and are able to accept them, this relationship will not seem too intense and challenging. On a spiritual and personal development level, this can be one of the most important and valuable relationships of your life. This connection has a negative 5 in Compatibility because few people can live with this kind of intensity for long periods of time. Of course, other more harmonious connections can help to offset this intensity and help the two coexist in agreement.

Affirmation for this Connection: *My partner's presence reminds me of those things that I most desire and want to change about myself..*

Attraction Index	Intensity Index	Compatibility Index
8	9	-5

Code: PLFS

Symbol: (ᴏ)

Description: *They are Pluto to You in the Spiritual Spread*

Meaning of the Connection:

Your partner challenges you to be more than you are and to grow in new areas. There can be 'battles of the will' or it can be challenging in many ways. You have chosen him or her to help you transform yourself and to grow and develop yourself in new ways as you let go of the past. On a personality level, this can often be difficult as your partner seems to be constantly confronting you with areas where you are not strong yet. In other cases, it could seem as though he or she is constantly trying to control you. This connection implies that the two of you have probably been together in a previous life and are here to complete some leftover business from that time. Some of this business can seem very challenging to you, especially if you attempt to change them or make them conform to how you think they should be. However, taken with the right attitude, this relationship can be a springboard to a new life where you are more powerful and free from self-limiting beliefs and attitudes. In that light, this person could be the most important one in your life.

Affirmation for this Connection: *My partner's presence reminds me of those things that I most desire, and want to change about myself.*

Attraction Index	Intensity Index	Compatibility Index
6	8	-5

Code: PLR

Symbol: (ᴏ)

Description: *You are Pluto to Them in the Life Spread*

Meaning of the Connection:

Whether you realize it or not, you represent a major challenge for your partner. You are someone who both challenges and transforms him or her. Even without you knowing it, you have a powerful effect on your partner causing intense feelings to come up. This may be the cause of the 'battle of wills' or power struggles that you experience at times in this relationship. On a deep level, you represent qualities or things that your partner wants for him or herself. To acquire these qualities, he or she must make large-scale changes within themselves. For this reason, they may not always enjoy your presence in their life though they may feel compelled to confront the issues that you bring up in them. There is an important reason for you to be in your partner's life. They have either consciously or unconsciously chosen you to help them grow as a person. For this reason, this may be the most important relationship of their life. However, this depends entirely on their level of self-acceptance and on how aware they are of the reasons for the intense feelings and experiences that you bring into their life.

Affirmation for this Connection: *My partner chose me to help develop important aspects of their personality. I understand the powerful effect I have on them.*

Attraction Index	Intensity Index	Compatibility Index
4	5	-3

Code: PLRS   **Symbol:** ʬ

Description: *You are Pluto to Them in the Spiritual Spread*

Meaning of the Connection:

You, as a person in the life of your partner, represent a part of his or her lifetime challenges and goals. For this reason, you may seem to be very challenging or even difficult for him or her at times. This connection brings out our deepest feelings and sometimes the urge to change or control our partner. This is likely what your partner is feeling about you. There exists with the connection the possibility that the two of you have been together before and that in that former existence, you left some aspects of your relationship incomplete. Know that you have a powerful effect on your partner, one that reminds them of things that they are working on changing in themselves at a deep level. If they are making good progress with those internal changes, the relationship with you will seem easier and more on the positive side, instilling them with more power to create things in their life.

Affirmation for this Connection: *My partner chose me to help develop important aspects of their personality. I understand the powerful effect I have on them.*

Attraction Index	Intensity Index	Compatibility Index
6	8	-5

The Cosmic Reward and Cosmic Lesson Connections

The Cosmic Reward position represents an undiscovered planet in our solar system, one that lies beyond Pluto. Even if such a planet is never discovered, there is much proof in the cards that there is at least an energy, associated with the planet Jupiter, that somehow governs or reflects aspects of our life and personality. To understand both this connection and the Cosmic Lesson connection, it is helpful to examine the following chart.

	1	2	3	4	5
Earth-Bound	Mercury	Venus	Mars	Jupiter	Saturn
Universal	Uranus	Neptune	Pluto	Cosmic Reward	Cosmic Lesson

As you look at this, remember the significance of the number Five, the number of man. Here we have two sets of five planetary connections. The connections in the bottom row are definitely related to their counterparts in the top row. Uranus governs the sign of Aquarius, in which Mercury is exalted. A planet is considered exalted when it is situated in its sign of highest expression. Mercury found in Gemini or Virgo represents a great, logical mind. But put Mercury in Aquarius and you have a genius. The same holds true for Venus, which is exalted in the sign of Pisces, which is ruled by Neptune. The Mars/Pluto connection is similar, though not exact. Mars is not traditionally known to be exalted in Scorpio, the sign ruled by Pluto, but I would suggest that in fact it is. Each of the planets listed in the 'Universal' line represent its corresponding planet in the 'Earth—Bound' line stepped up to a higher octave or level. For example, the Aquarian mind is connected to the higher intelligence or 'knowing' of the universe and not bound by the logic and careful plodding of the Gemini or Virgo mind. Similarly the Piscean love nature is love for humanity, not the love for one other person (Libra) or of earthly things (Taurus).

Cosmic Reward Relationships on the High Side

1. My partner is a continuous blessing in my life. The more I am with him/her, the more I appreciate what he/she is to me.

2. I am grateful for the many things they give me on so many levels.

3. My partner reminds me that the universe is full of things to be grateful and happy about.

4. I feel I was destined to be with my partner.

Since the Cosmic Reward and Cosmic Lesson Cards follow the Pluto Card in the Life Spread, their association with Jupiter and Saturn become clear. This gives us some hints about their meaning that ordinarily would remain a mystery since we have little experience with them and there is little research done on them. They are the 9th and 10th cards from our Birth Card in either the Life or Spiritual Spread (always counted from right to left). Therefore, if we look at the Life Spread chart on page 343, we see that the A♦ Birth Card would have the J♣ as its Cosmic Reward Card and the 9♦ as its Cosmic Lesson Card. To take another example, look at the 6♣ Birth Card. Counting right to left and then going up to the top (Crown Line) and then from the K♠ to the 3♥ position, we find its Cosmic Reward Card to be the 10♠ and the Cosmic Lesson Card to be the 5♣.

The Cosmic Reward Card, associated with Jupiter, brings us many blessings, just as our Jupiter Card does. However, these blessings may be more on the spiritual or universal level than on the financial levels generally associated with Jupiter. Also, I have noted that the blessings of the Cosmic Reward Card are generally not noticed very much by an individual until they have passed through and met the challenges and changes implied by their Pluto Card. Thus, in a Cosmic Reward relationship, the blessings of that relationship only become apparent after a period of time. Early in a relationship, the Cosmic Reward person will seem to be more of a challenge, much like the Pluto person. They act as another reminder of the work that we must do on ourselves to advance our sense of self-understanding. Therefore, a Cosmic Reward relationship can be very challenging to the person who is still mostly unaware of themselves and has not been engaged in self-analysis and discovery. However, to the person who has done this important self work, the Cosmic Reward relationship is a major blessing to be appreciated more and more. In a general sense, this implies that the Cosmic Reward relationship gets better with age, because our self understanding usually grows with age. However, I do not wish to imply that you have to be old to enjoy it. It all depends upon your level of commitment to personal growth. If we see a relationship where this connection is prominent, let's say the first or second connection of the five, and if the person receiving this energy is having a hard time, we can conclude that they still have a lot of work to do on understanding themselves. It is really as simple as that.

Cosmic Reward Relationships on the Low Side

1. I try to change and control my partner.
2. I want my partner so much and I can't seem to have them or make them love me.
3. I fight with my partner a lot and resent the things they say and do.
4. Sometimes I get so angry at my partner that I don't know what to do.

Cosmic Lesson Relationships on the High Side

1. My partner is helping me achieve my highest goals and ambitions.
2. I feel good knowing that they are there to guide me on the right path to my destiny.
3. My partner reminds me of my highest potential and points the way for me to get there.
4. My partner provides helpful suggestions and ideas to further my career ambitions.

One last important element to the Cosmic Reward Card is that of the 'destined love affair' or 'destined marriage.' It is fairly common for a person to marry their Cosmic Reward Card, often after having had many other relationships. This card is the same card as the 'Result Card' used in *Cards of Your Destiny* book. As our lifetime Result Card, the Cosmic Reward Card often represents a person that we are destined to end up with by the end of our lifetime. In many cases this means marriage.

The Cosmic Lesson Card is associated with Saturn. It represents a responsibility and lesson within a broader scope than our earthly affairs. With the Cosmic Lesson position, we turn our attention to more universal matters.

Our Saturn Card in our Life Spread can often signify the work that we do. It can be what we are known to do or be, or it can somehow describe our careers. Similarly, our Cosmic Lesson Card may signify the role we play in the more universal sense of the word. This may be our debt to society, for example, or that role that we must play in order to satisfy the powers that be, whether you call that power God or the universal life force. In any case, when we are in a relationship with a person who is our Cosmic Lesson Card, we are reminded in some way of the things that we 'should' do.

Cosmic Lesson Relationships on the Low Side

1. I resent my partner's attempts to help me.
2. My partner is constantly criticizing me and finding fault with the things I do and say.
3. I feel like my partner doesn't love or care for me because of the things he or she says and does.
4. My partner is abusive and cruel to me in one or more ways.
5. Nothing I do is ever enough for my partner.

'Should' is a big Saturn word. Keep that in mind when you think about Saturn or the Cosmic Lesson Card. So, someone who is our Cosmic Lesson Card may use that word a lot when talking to us, just as the Saturn person does. The Cosmic Lesson person will see the areas in which we can make changes in our life that will benefit us ultimately. Their influence could help us be more successful, even if that success is only a goal that we keep to ourselves. But the Cosmic Lesson relationship could also be as difficult as a Saturn relationship if we go into it completely unaware in certain areas of our life and have attracted this person to wake us up. As with Saturn, Cosmic Lesson relationships can happen because we secretly hate ourselves on some level. If this is the case, they will reflect that hate or rejection by acting it out in our presence. In other words, some of these relationships will have an element of cruelty or abuse to them. But this is only the case when the individual already hates the way they are and they are piling up abuses on themselves for something they did in the past. In its highest expression, the Cosmic Lesson relationship will act as a solidifier of our dreams and ambitions and will greatly aid us in achieving some great purpose in our life.

Code: CRF **Symbol:** ♃+

Description: *They are Your Lifetime Cosmic Reward Card*

Meaning of the Connection:

This person is someone who challenges you and yet somehow points the way to your own destiny and fulfillment. It is entirely possible that the two of you are destined to be together in a significant way, even married. On some level they represent a 'reward' for you, one that you earn from going through the transformation that is a part of your soul's destiny in this lifetime. In a sense, this relationship can feel like a true blessing, once the challenges associated with it are met and dealt with.

NOTES:

What I am calling the Lifetime Cosmic Reward Card is the same as the Pluto/Result Card in the Age 90 Spread in *Cards of Your Destiny*. This card is associated with Jupiter and thus acts as a beneficial influence. However, since it is so close to the Pluto Card, it can be very challenging as well. In relationships I have found that we only realize the blessings of this card if and when we have dealt with the challenges and lessons associated with our lifetime (Age 90) Pluto Card. Therefore, how you experience this person's influence in your life probably has more to do with whether or not you have faced the issues of your Pluto Card than with how they are. Anyone who is our Cosmic Reward Card can be one of the biggest blessings in our life when we are prepared to open up to that possibility.

Affirmation for this Connection: *My partner reminds me of wonderful things that are a part of me. They are a blessing to me if I am ready and willing to accept it.*

Attraction Index	Intensity Index	Compatibility Index
5	7	0

Code: CRFS **Symbol:** ♃+

Description: *They are Your Spiritual Cosmic Reward Card*

Meaning of the Connection:

This person represents part of your 'soul's development' and you could be greatly challenged by their presence in your life. They could be difficult to be with in some ways, but inwardly you sense that being with them is helping you transform yourself in some areas of your highest potential. This is a strong connection that could imply a destined relationship and once you have begun to meet your 'soul's challenges' in this lifetime, you will begin to see this person as one of your biggest blessings and rewards for work done on yourself.

NOTES:

This connection is just like the one before it except that it stems from a connection in the Spiritual Spread. Therefore the Jupiterian blessings that you are likely to receive from this person stem from a past-life association or from past-life good karma. However, just as in the previous connection the rewards associated with this connection are usually not experienced until we have conquered, or at least faced, the issues represented by the Pluto Card in our Life Spread. Until that time, those who are our Cosmic Reward Cards can seem to be challenging and difficult to the extreme, in much the same way as someone who is our Pluto Card.

Affirmation for this Connection: *My partner reminds me of wonderful things that are a part of me. They are a blessing to me if I am ready and willing to accept it.*

Attraction Index	Intensity Index	Compatibility Index
7	5	0

Code: CRR **Symbol:** $2\!\!\!+$

Description: *You are Their Lifetime Cosmic Reward Card*

Meaning of the Connection:

You, as an important person in the life of your friend, represent a part of his or her lifetime challenges and goals. Actually, you are the 'reward for changes made' in one or more important areas of their life. For this reason you may be viewed by him or her as challenging or difficult. However, once they have made the necessary changes and met their self-imposed challenges, your relationship will take on the feeling of gratitude and happiness. Often, couples with this connection are destined to be together to complete important lessons in life and love. Once your partner has met their lifetime challenges and changes, you will become the biggest blessing in their life.

NOTES:

As in the previous two connections, this one is associated with the planet Jupiter, but it is Jupiter taken to a higher octave. Jupiter on a mundane level relates to material blessings but on a higher octave it goes to the spiritual level and becomes 'cosmic blessings.' In truth you are a blessing to your partner, but he or she will not be able to realize the fullness of that blessing until he or she deals with the spiritual challenges of his or her lifetime Pluto Card. The Cosmic Reward or Blessing Card is closely related to the Pluto Card. As far as your relationship is concerned, you are either perceived as a great blessing or a great challenge, depending upon where your partner is with respect to his or her personal and spiritual development. In any case, it is very likely that he or she chose you to help them go through a large scale transformation of their personality or some other important aspect of their life.

Affirmation for this Connection: *I challenge my partner to open up and accept the blessings of the universe. I bring the highest blessings to them.*

Attraction Index	Intensity Index	Compatibility Index
7	5	0

Code: CRRS **Symbol:** $2\!\!\!+$

Description: *You are Their Spiritual Cosmic Reward Card*

Meaning of the Connection:

As a person in your partner's life, you represent a sort of 'cosmic reward' for spiritual or inner work that they are doing in this lifetime. In practical terms this connection often manifests as your being challenging and unreachable for them, but this is part of what they have chosen to do and you are playing a key role in their transformation. This key connection is often found among couples who are destined to be together for a significant amount of time.

NOTES:

This connection is very much like the one before it except that it is connected to a past life with your partner. Because this connection comes from the Spiritual or Natural Spread, it suggests that one of the reasons for you two being together is to either settle or continue some past-life association. In the case of this particular connection, the past-life association was likely very important in terms of your partner's growth as an individual. You are here in this life to give to them something of extreme value. However, until your partner has dealt with their lifetime Pluto Card (the one from the Age 90 Spread), you may seem to be more of a problem than a blessing to them.

Affirmation for this Connection: *I challenge my partner to open up and accept the blessings of the universe. I bring the highest blessings to them.*

Attraction Index	Intensity Index	Compatibility Index
7	5	0

Code: CLF
Symbol: ♄ +

Description: *They are Your Lifetime Cosmic Lesson Card*

Meaning of the Connection:

This person plays the role of 'teacher' for you in some fashion in your life. Whether he or she is aware of it or not, their presence in your life is a reminder of some great lesson that you must learn regarding your role here on the planet. For this reason, you may not always appreciate their presence in your life. They may remind you of some of your own shortcomings or they may play the role of the critic in some manner. On the positive side of things, this relationship has the potential to help you achieve much greater success in your work because your partner will somehow remind you of the things you need to do to access your highest potential. Taken with the right attitude, this relationship could lead to many and powerful realizations about yourself that have the highest value in your own path to fulfillment. Otherwise you may just see them as a 'thorn in your side.'

NOTES:

This connection is one of the more difficult to understand. It represents someone who is the 10th card in our direct Life Path. This 10th card is associated with Saturn but it is Saturn taken to a higher octave. Because it is connected to Saturn, these relationships can be difficult and heavy feeling. However, on the spiritual side, this connection is a reminder of our responsibility to the world in terms of our work or choice of career. For this reason, being with someone with whom you share this connection can be an important reminder of what your highest role may be in this life. If you find that somehow they remind you of parts of yourself where you feel you are lacking, then this can be instrumental in your finding the path to your highest potential. These reminders do not always come to us in a happy form, therefore, this connection does not bode well for long–term ease and compatibility unless you have other more harmonious connections to offset it. If you have chosen a relationship with someone with this connection, it could represent an unconscious desire to find the role that suits you best as it relates to your being a contribution to the world in a powerful and meaningful way. This is especially true if this is the first or second connection between you.

Affirmation for this Connection: *This person shows me my highest potential and points to my highest role in this lifetime in a way that inspires me to greater heights.*

Attraction Index	Intensity Index	Compatibility Index
5	7	-4

Code: CLFS
Symbol: ♄ +

Description: *They are Your Spiritual Cosmic Lesson Card*

Meaning of the Connection:

This connection is one that is on a deeper level and more difficult to perceive than most. The best way to describe it is that your partner represents a part of the lessons you are here to learn in this lifetime. Specifically they reflect the lessons you are learning involving your responsibilities in the larger scheme of things—to society, and to the race of man. In some way, this person reminds you of things you must do or become that will be a help to the world. If you are cosmically inclined, this relationship could lead you to your destiny. However, it also could simply serve to remind you of your shortcomings and the areas where you may need self-improvement.

NOTES:

Just as in the case of the CLF connection, this connection is related to Saturn taken to a higher octave. The difference here is that this is the 10th card of the Spread taken from the Age 89 or Spiritual Spread (see previous page) instead of the Age 90 or Mundane Spread. This brings in the possibility of a past-life connection in conjunction with the lessons being learned through this relationship. Therefore, the possibility is that the two of you have been together before and that the role this person is playing in your life stems from a prior association, perhaps one that was left incomplete in that earlier lifetime. Still, the connection remains the same as one that reminds you of a role you must play if you are to follow your destiny and attain your highest potential. If this connection is number one or two, it is very likely that this person is playing an instrumental role in helping you find your path to power. Though not an easy connection on the compatibility level, this could be one of the most powerful and important relationships of your life. Taken with the proper attitude, it could provide the catalyst for finding your life's work and purpose on a more universal level.

Affirmation for this Connection: *This person shows me my highest potential and points to my highest role in this lifetime in a way that inspires me to greater heights.*

Attraction Index	Intensity Index	Compatibility Index
5	7	-4

Code: CLR   **Symbol:** ♄ +

Description: *You are Their Lifetime Cosmic Lesson Card*

Meaning of the Connection:

This connection implies that your presence in the life of your partner is one that will teach him or her much that they need to learn in this lifetime. Whether you are critical of the way they do certain things or you play the role of teacher in their life, there is much of value that they can learn from you. However, don't expect them to always like these lessons or be anxious to hear about all the ways they can improve who they are or what they are doing. Even if you don't say anything, your presence in their life is teaching them invaluable lessons that they may someday express gratitude for. In the meantime there may be personality conflicts as these lessons are learned.

NOTES:

The way you affect your partner may not have much to do with what you consciously do or say. This is a connection that is not well understood and is more subtle than most. It has some Saturnian qualities to it because in essence, it represents a higher octave of Saturn, the great teacher. In some fashion you are a teacher to your partner. The way these Saturn connections typically operate in our relationships, it is not necessarily what we are consciously saying or doing that makes it challenging for our partner, but just our presence in his or her life that somehow reminds them of where they might be lacking. In the case of this connection, you remind your partner of where they could be in terms of their life's work. This can be disconcerting or extremely constructive, depending upon how they take it and respond to it. If this connection is number one or two, you are likely playing an extremely important role in the development of their character and destiny. This connection can be challenging on a compatibility level, especially from your partner's point of view and therefore it can work against long–term ease and peacefulness. However, handled in the right way by the right person, it could be the most important relationship of your lives.

Affirmation for this Connection: *I remind my partner of a significant aspect of their highest potential. I show them what they can do and become.*

Attraction Index	Intensity Index	Compatibility Index
5	7	0

Code: **CLRS**   **Symbol:**   ♄ $^+$

Description: *You are Their Spiritual Cosmic Lesson Card*

Meaning of the Connection:

Though difficult to describe, this connection is one that can be very important if either of you are seriously interested in self-development and personal transformation. This connection implies that you act as a 'teacher' to your partner—someone who leads him or her to a more mature and self-responsible way of looking at themselves and their role in the world. You represent part of their cosmic destiny or role and as such you have a profound effect on them. On a mundane level, you could find that you are often critical of them or even harsh. For this reason he or she may not always appreciate your contribution to their life or enjoy your company.

NOTES:

The only difference between this connection and the previous one is that this one stems from connections in the Spiritual Spread instead of the Life Spread. This means that this connection is likely to stem from a past-life association that left some unfinished business to be completed in this lifetime. In this example, it is likely that you are repaying your partner, being a teacher for them in some way that will help them to take more responsibility for their contribution to the world in this lifetime. How they handle your influence in their life is likely to reflect their own relationship with their inner sense of connectedness with their life's purpose. You could be just the person that helps them to crystallize their desire to do something meaningful in their life.

Affirmation for this Connection: *I remind my partner of a significant aspect of their highest potential. I show them what they can do and become.*

Attraction Index	Intensity Index	Compatibility Index
5	7	0

THE KARMA CARD, KARMA COUSIN, SAME BIRTH CARD, AND OTHER CONNECTIONS

From one point of view all relationships are karmic in nature. Karmic means that the bottom line reason for its existence is to balance out the scales of our debts and good deeds from the past. Karma is a deep subject and I do not intend to go into great detail in this book. But essentially, we create karma whenever we perform an action or deed without knowing or realizing how it will affect those around us. The planet Saturn is often called the 'Lord of Karma.' He is usually the one who makes sure that we find out, at some point in our evolution, what it is like to experience a certain situation from all sides. If, for example, I have made a commitment to one person and then I fall in love with someone else and leave the first person, there is a strong possibility that I will create some karma that will later have to be dealt with. This would be true if I ignored how much pain and suffering I caused the other person when I left so capriciously. They say that all is fair in love and war. I don't believe however, that we are relieved of our karma in those arenas. On the contrary, I think it is in those two areas that we accumulate the most karma and have some of the most difficult lessons to learn.

But we must keep in mind that there is good karma just as much as there is bad karma. Many of the gifts, abilities, and good fortune that we experience may be attributed to acts and deeds that helped others in a past life. And sometimes relationships come into our life for the express purpose of returning to us a wonderful gift that we gave with love in a former lifetime. In some cases, these relationships are Karma Card relationships.

In most Karma Card relationships there is a specific flow of energy. When I say most, I specifically refer to the 45 Birth Cards which have only two Karma Cards. On the list on the next page, you will see all the Birth Cards and their corresponding Karma Cards. Seven Birth Cards have six Karma Cards while the other 45 Birth Cards have two. Within the group of seven there is no way to know which way the payment of energy is flowing. We only know that there is an important reason for these two to be together and that some form of exchange will happen within the context of their relationship. Within that group of seven, the A♣ and

2♥ share the closest bonds with each other. The 9♥ and 7♦ also have a similar bond. If you look on the Life and Spiritual Spreads on pages 342 and 343, you will note that these four cards merely switch places with each other. This is a unique quality that no other cards have. These four cards are known as the 'Semi-Fixed' cards. The other three of the seven, the K♠, 8♣, and J♥ are equally unique in that these cards are found in the same exact place in both spreads. They are called the Fixed Cards and their personalities will reveal a strong fixed nature in some respect. When either two of these three interact, they share what I call the Power connection. These people, being so fixed and strong-willed, generate a tremendous amount of power when they get together. So much, in fact, that few of these relationships last very long.

But in the other 45 Birth Cards we always know who owes who. Looking at the list on the next page, the first card listed is the one we owe and the second card is the one that owes us. For example, if I am a 6♣ Birth Card, I owe a debt of some kind to the 8♠ person while the 2♦ person owes me something. You can use this formula to really penetrate to the heart of some Karma Card relationships. This flow is distinctive and accounts for the success or failure of these relationships to a large degree. For example, if I am in a relationship with someone that I owe a debt to, this relationship will need, among other things, two things to be successful. First of all, I must be willing to give whatever is asked of me from the partner that I owe. Secondly, my partner must be willing to receive what I give. These two requirements are an absolute necessity for the success of the relationship. Without it, these relationships can become very ugly, even abusive. The implied flow of energy will continuously seek to be fulfilled. When the partners resist it, there will be friction and problems. I have seen many examples of couples in a Karma Card relationship that just doesn't work. The partner who is meant to be the giver might say, "I am tired of giving. I want someone to give to me." Or, the other partner may not be willing or open to receive. Either way, it creates struggle, competition, and often resentment and animosity.

The other very important factor about Karma Card relationships is that you are mirrors of each other. In some way, the two of you are very much alike. However, just as in the Same Birth Card (SBC) connection,

Your Card	Your Karma Cards		Your Card	Your Karma Cards
A♥	A♦, 3♥		A♦	2♦, A♥
2♥ *	A♣, 9♥, 7♦, 8♣, J♥, K♠		2♦	6♣, A♦
3♥	A♥, Q♣		3♦	6♥, Q♦
4♥	4♠, 10♠		4♦	5♠, 5♥
5♥	4♦, 5♣		5♦	9♥, 3♣
6♥	4♣, 3♦		6♦	9♣, 3♠
7♥	8♥, A♠		7♦ *	9♥, A♣, 2♥, J♥, 8♣, K♠
8♥	7♠, 7♥		8♦	Q♠, 7♣
9♥ *	7♦, A♣, 2♥, 8♣, J♥, K♠		9♦	Q♦, 5♦
10♥	J♣, 5♠		10♦	Q♣, Q♠
J♥*	K♠, 8♣, A♣, 2♥, 7♦, 9♥		J♦	3♠, J♣
Q♥	10♠, 9♣		Q♦	3♦, 9♦
K♥	2♣, 9♠		K♦	3♣, 7♠
A♣*	2♥, 7♦, 9♥, 8♣, J♥, K♠		A♠	7♥, 2♣
2♣	A♠, K♥		2♠	6♠, K♣
3♣	5♦, K♦		3♠	6♦, J♦
4♣	5♣, 6♥		4♠	10♣, 4♥
5♣	5♥, 4♣		5♠	10♥, 4♦
6♣	8♠, 2♦		6♠	9♠, 2♠
7♣	8♦, J♠		7♠	K♦, 8♥
8♣*	J♥, K♠, A♣, 2♥, 7♦, 9♥		8♠	K♣, 6♣
9♣	Q♥, 6♦		9♠	K♥, 6♠
10♣	J♠, 4♠		10♠	4♥, Q♥
J♣	J♦, 10♥		J♠	7♣, 10♣
Q♣	3♥, 10♦		Q♠	10♦, 8♦
K♣	2♠, 8♠		K♠*	8♣, J♥, A♣, 2♥, 7♦, 9♥

*These cards are in a special family that is unique and different in their connections. All seven of these cards are connected but there is no indication of which direction the karmic energies are flowing.

the success of the relationship depends upon how much you are able to love yourself. A SBC or KRMA relationship will hold up a clear mirror in front of us. A small example may help clarify this point, which is so important. Let's say that you are someone who hates people who are inconsiderate and selfish. Let's say you are a 2♣ Birth Card, because this is a good example for this point. Then you meet an A♠ person who is fun, outgoing, aggressive, but also selfish and inconsiderate of others (Aces are often self-centered and engrossed). You feel a powerful attraction to this person, who is your first Karma Card and you get involved and now you are living together. Now you really begin to notice how selfish and inconsiderate your A♠ partner is. You get mad and

you quarrel with them. What you probably don't see is that you are just like this A♠ person. Because you are the 2♣, you have the same qualities of selfishness within you. However, you are probably suppressing them, perhaps because, as a child your parents admonished you every time you acted selfishly. Your parents' attempts to control your behavior created a conflict and separation within you. Your spontaneous part is aggressive and self-oriented (the A♠ part). Your parents may have made you feel guilty for being that way so you repressed it in order to get their approval. Now, as an adult, you are still repressing that part of yourself and you haven't had much fun in your life since you were 6 years old. Now, you attract a mate who exemplifies all those qualities that you have repressed and you are faced with the conflict within yourself that has been waiting to be resolved since childhood.

One of the most important laws of relationships is that everything we see in our partner is a reflection of who we are. This becomes especially important to remember in Karma Card or Same Birth Card relationships. On the one hand, because you are so much alike, you have the potential to experience a unique kind of closeness and intimacy that other relationships could never have. On the other hand, the mirroring quality of this relationship is highly pronounced and thus you are faced with yourself in a much more intense fashion.

Karma Cousin relationships are like the Karma Card relationship because they do have a flow of energy. However, they do not have the same mirroring quality that is so pronounced in Karma Card connections and that is the main distinction. Also, the debt is not so great or heavy in these relationships. With Karma Card connections, the intensity factor is very high. In Karma Cousin connections, it is a lot lower and less prone to be dramatic and challenging. Karma Cousin relationships can be very fun in many cases and usually we have to look at the other connections to determine the overall quality of the relationship.

Karma Card Relationships on the High Side

1. This feels like a destined relationship. I knew from the moment we met that we would be together.

2. I feel closer to my partner than I ever have with anyone in my life.

3. We are soul mates.

4. I enjoy giving to (receiving from) my partner. It is a natural part of the love we share for each other.

Karma Card Relationships on the Low Side

1. I feel like I have been drawn into a special hell that seems impossible to get out of.

2. All we do is fight about everything.

3. I hate the things my partner says and does. I don't know how I attracted someone who is so different from me.

4. I am tired of giving and doing things for my partner. It is time they did something for me.

Code: KRMA   **Symbol:** ✡

Description: *You are Karma Cards to Each Other*

Meaning of the Connection:

This is one of the most common and most powerful of the relationship connections. One of you owes a debt to the other from a past life and in this life the debt will be settled. You can get along very well as long as both of you are willing to give and receive. If not, this could be a difficult relationship. You are strong mirrors of each other and there may be times that you don't like what you see. If there is anything in your partner that you do not like, realize now that those are parts of yourself that you have either forbidden to express or have for some reason avoided up until now. In truth, you two are very much the same and in this regard this connection is a deep bond that can make you feel very close to one another. You have attracted this person in order to explore other facets of loving yourself and you have chosen a mirror to help you learn to love yourself. This is one of the more powerful and intense connections for relationship and it must be handled with awareness if this power is to be used in constructive and loving ways.

NOTES:

The six-pointed star was chosen for this connection because it is associated with the number six, the number of karma and fate. The two triangles, representing the polarities of male and female, fire and water, are perfectly interlocked and represent balance. The paying of karma is nothing more than the balancing of the scales.

In most Karma Card relationships there is a flow of energy from one person to the other. When this flow is allowed to happen, the relationship proceeds very well. When either one of the two disregard this basic flow or refuse to allow it to happen, pain and suffering are always the result. In the table on page 320, the first Karma Card listed is the one that you owe some debt to from a past life. The second card is the person that owes you something. When there are more than two cards listed, there is a special consideration described on page 319.

Affirmation for this Connection: *I was drawn to this person to settle an unfinished past life situation. We have a very close and special connection.*

Attraction Index	Intensity Index	Compatibility Index
7	9	0

Code: KRMC   **Symbol:** ✡+

Description: *You Two are "Karma Cousins" to Each Other*

Meaning of the Connection:

The two of you have a karmic relationship. This means that one or both of you have a debt to settle with the other. This debt can take many forms and should add depth and meaning to your relationship. This is a good connection for friends or married couples. You have been together before and feel a strong bond in this lifetime as well. To get the most out of this relationship, always look for ways that you can give to your partner and always express appreciation for their contribution in your life. This is a special relationship and it could have a major impact on your life.

NOTES:

The Karma Cousin relationship is formed when two cards share a common Karma Card. For example, the 10♦ is both a Karma Card to the Q♣ and the Q♠. Thus, the Q♣ and Q♠ are Karma Cousins. Just as in the case of the Karma Card relationship, there is likely to be a flow of energy between the two cards, from one to the other. However, I have noted that these relationships do not have as much intensity as the Karma Card relationships, and the flow of energy is generally in a more friendly manner. We might say that the Karma Cousin relationship is a less intense version of its counterpart, the Karma Card relationship. To determine the flow of energy and to see who is giving and who is receiving, use the Karma Card chart on the previous page. First look up the two Birth Cards on the chart and see which of you owes which other Karma Card that you share. For example, if you are a 5♦ and you have a friend who is a Q♦, you notice that you both share the 9♦ as a Karma Card. Because the 5♦ owes the 9♦, you would also be giving to the Q♦, your Karma Cousin.

Affirmation for this Connection: *There is a beneficial flow of energy between myself and my partner. This flow makes us feel good while being together.*

Attraction Index	Intensity Index	Compatibility Index
5	5	3

Code: POWR

Symbol: ✳

Description: *You Have a Strong Power Connection*

Meaning of the Connection:

The two of you share a unique connection called the Power Connection. Because of the special, fixed nature of your two cards, there is considerable power generated when you are together. This power, if channeled constructively, could truly be used to change the world. However, if the two of you do not have a strong purpose in being together, this same power will probably become destructive to your relationship and cause you to engage in control struggles with each other. In most cases, this results in the destruction of the relationship. The two of you are extremely 'fixed' in some ways and need a common purpose upon which to base your being together. Thus, the two of you have a bigger responsibility than most to find a suitable purpose for your relationship that will stimulate the two of you to achieve your highest potential.

NOTES:

This connection only appears between any two of the three 'fixed' cards and thus is not a very common connection. Florence Campbell said that if any two of the three fixed cards get together, they would have the power to change the world. In this connection we are talking about more power than is generated by any other connection in the cards. Thus, this power has more potential for good and potential for destruction as well. In my experience, two people who have this connection will not last long together unless they join forces in a common purpose that is bigger than the two of them. In this manner the power finds a constructive outlet and peace ensues.

Affirmation for this Connection: *My partner and I together generate a tremendous power that we can use to change the world and to accomplish great deeds.*

Attraction Index	Intensity Index	Compatibility Index
7	9	0

Code: SBC

Symbol: ♥ ♥

Description: *You Have the Same Birth Cards*

Meaning of the Connection:

The two of you share the same birth and destiny card. This makes you feel very close in many ways but also makes you strong mirrors of each other. If you are not getting along at any time, it is because one or both of you does not like what you see in the mirror—a reflection of yourself! You are together to learn how to love yourself and the relationship will reflect exactly how well you can do that. Look carefully at the things that you like and dislike about your partner and you will discover an enormous amount about yourself. If you have learned to love yourself, this relationship will seem to be like a 'soul-mate' connection to you. The closeness and harmony you feel is only limited by how you feel about all the aspects of your own personality—your own self acceptance.

NOTES:

Those that choose to be with someone who is their same birth card usually are doing it to develop more self-love. Most of us are composed of many facets, some of which we express and some of which we choose not to express. When we meet someone of our same birth card, they often are choosing to express parts of themselves that are the same as the parts of ourself that we choose not to express. This can result in our getting angry with them. For example, a person who is trying to stop smoking often begins by getting angry at others who smoke. Inside, this person still wants to smoke but has decided not to express that side of his or her personality any more. Those who are smoking remind this person of their own inner desire to smoke, the desire that he or she is suppressing. Thus they get angry, which is really fear underneath, in this case, fear that he or she will start smoking again.

Therefore, those who are our same birth card have the potential to show us parts of ourselves that we have suppressed or abandoned. These may be parts that we were not even aware of. If you are in one of these relationships and you see anything about your partner that you do not like, take a closer look at your feelings. You may discover something very important about yourself and how much you love certain aspects of your own personality.

Affirmation for this Connection: *I chose this relationship to be a mirror of myself so that I can learn to love myself completely.*

Attraction Index	Intensity Index	Compatibility Index
5	8	0

Code: MATCH or MTCHR **Symbol:**

Description: *You Have a Birth Card/Planetary Ruling Card Match*

Meaning of the Connection:

In this relationship, one of your Birth Cards matches the Planetary Ruling Card of the other. This is a powerful connection that is often found among the connections of successful married couples. This connection is one in which you are a lot alike in many important ways. This makes you feel very close and comfortable in being together. There is a certain 'rightness' about being together that can make you think this is a relationship that could last a long time. Also, the person who has the matching Birth Card will tend to encourage the Planetary Ruling Card person to express himself or herself. The Birth Card person will be very supportive, giving his or her partner a boost of self confidence. People often visualize a happy, successful relationship as one in which the partners are supportive and proud of each other's accomplishments. This connection lends itself to these qualities and in many cases manifests as mutual support for each other's careers and ambitions.

NOTES:

This connection is a lot like the SBC connection, but doesn't seem to manifest the same intensity. Where the SBC connection creates a strong mirroring effect that can often lead to a lot of conflict or issues, this connection is usually taken on a much more positive level.

Affirmation for this Connection: *My partner and I are each other's complements. We have much in common and support each other's goals and dreams.*

Attraction Index	Intensity Index	Compatibility Index
8	2	8

Code: SHARE Symbol: ♥ + ♥ +

Description: *You Have the Same Planetary Ruling Cards*

Meaning of the Connection:

In this relationship, you have the same Planetary Ruling Cards. This helps you feel strongly connected to each other and is another connection that is often found among successful marriages. There is a strong sense of unity between you. You have some important things in common and this can help you feel very close to each other. Intimacy is heightened and the two of you really could reach heights of intimacy that most couples will never experience. This connection is good for communications, for work, and for general compatibility. You can't help but appreciate each other since you are so much alike. Unless other connections between you contradict strongly, this is a great indicator of a potentially great relationship. Much like the previous connection (MATCH), you are supportive of each other in a real and positive way.

NOTES:

This connection would not be considered as significant for two people who are the exact same birthday. In that case, we must look at the SBC connection as being predominant. Though some of the qualities expressed here would be found, the intensity of the SBC connection would probably be more noticeable. Of course, we must keep in mind that even SBC connection relationships can be very positive and intimate. It is just that in most cases they have a higher intensity level because of the strong mirroring effect, which doesn't always manifest with the SHARE connection alone.

Affirmation for this Connection: *My partner and I are very much alike. We rejoice in our wonderful level of intimacy and support each other's goals and dreams.*

Attraction Index	Intensity Index	Compatibility Index
8	2	8

Chapter Six
The Meaning of the Indexes

When you are reading the connections between two cards and you see an Index Rating for that relationship, there is a brief meaning for that particular number that you can use to understand more about the Rating given. These meanings are used primarily for the Overall Index Rating, not the individual connection ratings. Remember that the Indexes extend from -10 to +10 in most cases. I will give the meaning that best represents the numbers of the Indexes. Keep in mind that these are generalities in most cases.

ATTRACTION INDEX MEANINGS

Index	Meaning
-4	You find it hard to be with this person on many levels. Why are you with them?
-3	There are things about this person that push you away from them.
-2	You will find things about this person that repel you at times.
-1	You don't have any attraction to this person in some important areas.
0	You have little attraction to this person. Are you sure you are interested at all?
1	You have some attraction for this person, but not much.
2	You have some attraction for this person and find them interesting in some ways.
3	You are interested in this person and attracted to them in some ways.
4	You are very attracted to this person and find them very stimulating and interesting.
5	You are strongly attracted to this person and enjoy being with them.
6	You have a very strong attraction to this person and want to be with them.
7	You have a powerful attraction to this other person. It could be fate!
8	You have an intense attraction to this person and cannot stay away from them.
9	You have a major attraction to this person. You are like magnets!

Note: None of the Relationships in this book have an Attraction Index lower than -4 or higher than 9

INTENSITY INDEX MEANINGS

Index	Meaning
0	This relationship runs very smoothly without major challenges or problems.
1	This is mostly a calm relationship. Not overly dramatic or problematic.
2	This relationship is mildly intense with very few challenges or problems as a whole.
3	This relationship has some intensity to it and can be challenging at times.
4	This relationship can be very intense and challenging sometimes. You can grow in it.
5	This person challenges you in many ways and you can learn a lot from this relationship.
6	This relationship is very intense and could teach you a lot about yourself and life.
7	This relationship is a real test of inner strength and ability to handle yourself.
8	This relationship is an intense learning experience for you. Could be very difficult!
9	This is one of the most intense and challenging people you have ever been with.

COMPATIBILITY INDEX MEANINGS

Index	Meaning
-9	This is an extremely difficult relationship for you. Only a saint would pursue it.
-8	You may want to seriously question yourself about why you are in this relationship.
-7	You two are not compatible at all. Why are you together? You must want to learn a lot.
-6	This relationship is not a happy, fun experience. There is much for you to learn.
-5	This relationship will have many problems for you to overcome. Is it worth it?
-4	The two of you don't see eye to eye on many things. It will be hard on you at times.
-3	There are times when you feel judged or criticized. Fortunately, this does not happen very often.
-2	Though you don't always get along, there are some reasons for being together.
-1	Overall, the two of you are okay. Some good things and some challenging.
0	You have some things in common with this person. That's a good start.
1	You two are compatible and it shows. You enjoy being together.
2	You two have a lot in common and like being together.
3	You two have reasons for being together and have enough compatibility to be married.
4	You are very compatible and could be married.
5	The two of you are very close and get along very well. Would you like to get married?
6	This is a very good relationship for you and one that you could live with long–term.
7	You two are very, very compatible and could get along in any situation you chose.
8	You two could be best friends for life or married for 40 years. It's up to you.
9	You two could be married for a lifetime. But is there a lot of attraction?

Note: None of the Relationships in this book have a Compatibility Index lower than -9 or higher than 9

Chapter Seven

More about the Cards and the Connections

THE MARRIAGEABILITY FACTOR

Many cards are what I term 'unmarriageable.' These cards represent people who, for one reason or another, have great difficulty with the concept of commitment. There are many cards that fall into this category and I will list them for you. Before I do however, I must say that even though these cards are typically unable or unwilling to make commitments, there are exceptions, even though in my own experience I have found few exceptions at most. The only exceptions I have found to these unmarriageable cards fall into two categories:

1. They are over 55 years of age and come from a tradition where you got married and stayed married. These exceptions are becoming fewer each year. These are the people who got married in the '30s, '40s, '50s. Not too many of them around these days.

2. They are keenly aware of their emotional problems and have made a personal commitment to work on them, using their relationships as a tool for their personal growth. Though this sounds like a goal that many would aspire to, in reality there are very few people who are doing this. Not many people have experienced enough pain to make their spiritual growth a full-time job. But there are a few. And these are the unmarriageables that become marriageable.

I will list each card in the deck, how unmarriageable it probably is, and then list the probable factors that there could be commitment problems. Check both Birth Cards and Planetary Ruling Cards in this list. It only takes one of them to account for a commitment problem, though the Birth Card factors will be slightly more significant than the Planetary Ruling Card factors.

Here are the cards listed along with their most common factors involved in their inability to make commitments. Next to the Birth Card is a number from one to ten. Ten represents the most unmarriageable influences possible and one the least. This means the people with the highest numbers are the ones least likely to make any sort of commitments in personal relationships. All the cards with Rankings above 5 are highly suspect.

Marriageability of the Cards (lower means more marriageable)
A higher ranking means less marriageable and more problems with commitment

Birth Card Ranking	Factors Involved	Birth Card Ranking	Factors Involved	Birth Card Ranking	Factors Involved	Birth Card Ranking	Factors Involved
A♥—5	1	A♣—5	1, 4	A♦—6-10*	1, 2	A♠—7	3, 4
2♥—5	4	2♣—2		2♦—2		2♠—4	1, 4
3♥—7	1	3♣—10	3, 4, 5	3♦—8	1, 3	3♠—6	1, 4
4♥—5	4	4♣—5	2	4♦—5	3	4♠—2	2
5♥—7	1, 2	5♣—10	2	5♦—8	2, 4	5♠—5	
6♥—2		6♣—2		6♦—5	3	6♠—5	3
7♥—5	3	7♣—4	1	7♦—5	3	7♠—4	5
8♥—7	6	8♣—4	3, 6	8♦—7	1, 3	8♠—6	1, 5
9♥—5	4	9♣—4	4	9♦—4	1	9♠—5	5
10♥—3	1	10♣—9	1, 5, 6	10♦—7	1, 2, 3	10♠—2	
J♥—3	4	J♣—4	2	J♦—7	2, 4, 5	J♠—6	6, 5
Q♥—3	4	Q♣—9	1, 2, 3, 5	Q♦—8	1, 2, 3, 5, 6	Q♠—2	
K♥—6	5, 6	K♣—5	4, 5	K♦—5	1, 5	K♠—5	2, 3, 5

- *A♦ men are the ones with the higher numbers. In general I would rank A♦ men at an 8 or 9 and the women at a 4 or 5.
- Rankings under 3 are people that typically have fairly good marriage karma and less difficulty with commitment.

When looking at this table, use both the Birth Card and Planetary Ruling Card(s). All of these cards are important enough to influence the overall marriage-ability of the person. For example, if the person's Birth Card is very unmarriageable but the Planetary Ruling Card is more marriageable, their chances of making a commitment are better. The Birth Card is the stronger of the two and should always be considered first.

Another interesting point is that people whose Sun Sign is a fixed sign, such as Taurus, Aquarius, and Scorpio, are generally better at commitment than the mutable signs (Gemini, Sagittarius, Virgo, and Pisces) and the cardinal signs (Cancer, Libra, Capricorn, and Aries). Leos are fixed but often they love romance so much that their lives become a string of new love affairs.

The most common factors associated with unmar-riageability are:

1. The Three-Energy influence—This makes a person become bored easily with one relationship while at the same time bringing a lot of uncertainty and fear about getting enough affection. This person may never make a commitment or may practice what they call 'serial monogamy.' In serial monogamy, the person makes commitments but they never last very long. Within a year or two they find reasons to break off their relationships and go on to someone new. These people have a lot of fear related to getting enough affection. Instead of facing that fear and dealing with it first-hand, they try to keep a steady supply of romantic partners on hand so that they never have to feel the abandonment that is within them. Many of them profess how much they want to get married and complain about how they always seem to attract men or women who are unable to make commitments. These people often fall in love with married people because with a married person they themselves will never have to make any sort of commitment. These people actually have some of the strongest fears about love. Their mind is usually quite well developed and it goes around and around trying to understand love without feeling their emotions. They just don't want to feel the fear that is so strong within them. Often strong Three-energy results in confusion over sexual preferences as well.

2. The Five-Energy influence—People with strong Five-energy in their Life Path, and of course that includes all of the Five Birth Cards, are here to express their personal freedom and to gather up as many different kinds of personal experiences as they can over the duration of their life. To most Five people, marriage is seen as a cage that will restrict their freedom to explore new experiences. Freedom is such a strong theme for a Five that it would be like taking away their reason for living. Marriage for them becomes the dreaded 'M-word.' They will have relationships, and many of them will last a long time. But they have to find a way to have it while avoiding the M-word. In many cases it is the concept or sound of it that they fear the most. Five people are often in conflict within themselves. Part of them wants the security and comfort that a long–term relationship brings while the other part is constantly fighting to break free of anything seen as a confinement. This inner conflict is very painful for some and reflects itself in the quality of their relationships—usually shallow at best.

3. The Saturn/Venus influence—In this scenario, which is experienced by a great many cards, the person comes into this life with a karmic debt to pay in the area of relationships. Often they were extremely uncaring in their previous life-times and hurt the feelings of others by being so inconsistent and free-wheeling in areas of love. Because of their lack of awareness of how much their actions caused pain in others, they make a date to come back, in this lifetime to see what it is like to be on the receiving end of such treatment. These people are often hurt very deeply by a love relationship early in their life. The hurt is felt so keenly that they choose to close up their emotions almost completely. In many cases they make an unspoken vow to never let anyone get close enough to hurt them again. In doing so, they cut themselves off from any chance of emotional fulfillment. These people have relationships but never allow anyone to get close to them. Emotionally they are dead—they never feel much joy or pain in love. Commitment to them has no meaning. They usually resign themselves to quasi-relationships with people of the number 1 and 2 categories listed above.

4. The Neptune influence—With these people,

love is a thing of grandeur and splendor. It is the panacea for all of their problems and if they could only find the right person, all of their troubles would be over. They inwardly know that love is the most powerful force in the universe and they see themselves as saviors of other poor souls that are without love and compassion. The thing that they will avoid at all cost is the feeling that they have hurt someone else. They often attract partners that are broken down—alcoholics, drug addicts, those that can't find jobs, and the like. They want to see their love heal and change someone, all the while completely neglecting their own personal needs as if they are some angel who has no personal needs of their own. However, those they love never seem to change. They create heavily codependent relationships and feel weighted down by the burden of all of those who sponge off of their energy constantly. If they do meet the person who seems to be the one of their dreams, they usually fall head over heels and get hurt much more deeply than the average person. Like those in category number 3, they then choose to never open up again to anyone, just to avoid the pain they felt. Another manifestation of the Neptune influence is when the person's ideals of love are so high that they can never find a partner who is perfect enough for them.

5. The Pride influence—This combines with the other factors mentioned above and adds a distinct quality to them. This is experienced by the all of the royal cards, the Jacks, Queens, and Kings and by other cards that have a strong connection to these royal cards. Among the others are the 8♦, 10♣, 7♠, 8♠, and 9♠. There are others as well but these are the main ones. These people place a lot of value upon 'looking good.' They have a certain amount of pride in themselves and never want to appear to lower themselves in any way. Part of lowering oneself would be to show fear or insecurity. Therefore, these people have a particular aversion to showing their vulnerable sides to their partners. This being the case, they never allow a free exchange of love in their personal relationships. They can give to their partner, but may have difficulty in receiving, especially if that receiving requires them to drop their pride and ask for help.

6. The Power influence—These people have a certain amount of charm and magnetism that makes it easy for them to find new partners for love. Because of this, they can always find someone new if their current relationship gets to be a problem. In most cases, they will choose to leave their current relationship and start a new one rather than face the problems that come up. This is especially true when the problems that arise start to show them their own faults and weaknesses. With so much power at their disposal, they have usually made it a habit to blame everyone else for problems that arise in this area. This influence is closely linked to the Pride influence just mentioned—many cards that have one also have the other. And why should they ever consider a real commitment when it is so easy for them to just find someone to take your place?

THE NATURE OF THE FOUR SUITS

The suit of our Birth Card reveals a lot about us and if we spend some time examining those people we know of the various suits, we find many patterns emerging that help us to better understand ourselves and the mysteries of our world.

Card-wise, the four suits are associated with the four seasons, the grand cycle of birth, growth, maturity, and death. Hearts are spring, Clubs are summer, Diamonds are Fall, and Spades represent winter. The four suits also represent the four seasons of life. Hearts, the suit of love and family, represent our childhood. Clubs, the suit of knowledge and ideas, represent our adolescent school years, lasting until we graduate from college and have completed our vocational training. Diamonds, the suit of money and values, represent adulthood and the time of amassing our fortune in the world. Finally, Spades, the suit of work, health, and spirituality, represent our final years on the planet as we prepare for the life hereafter.

Just knowing this much can tell you a lot about people who are one of these suits by Birth Card. We might say that Hearts are eternally youthful and child-like. Hearts enjoy children and are excellent school teachers. They retain their youthful nature their entire life. In one sense, they never grow old. On the negative side, these folks may retain a certain immaturity as well. Clubs are the eternal high school or college student. They are always inquisitive and interested in new ideas or ways of looking at things. They are avid talkers and are always learning new things in their life. They also love to read, more than any other suit in the deck. A Club is never too old to go back to school, where they usually find a great deal of satisfaction. On the negative side a Club can be overly attached to their own ideas and take what they or others say too seriously. Diamonds are the adults of the deck. For this reason, they usually do not like anyone to tell them what to do, especially if they feel they are being treated like a child. This would never do for a Diamond. By the same token, a Diamond may take on an adult or parent role in their relationships and associations. They want to be seen as mature and responsible for the most part to retain this adult image. Diamonds put special emphasis on the accumulation of value and will be the first to tell you about the importance of having a good job or occupation. They will also try to help you commercialize your skills and abilities, one of the major occupations of the Diamond period of our life. Spades can be seen as eternal old people. Even children and babies who are Spades seem to have that 'wise look' upon their face. Spade people tend to relate best to older people, at the least to those people who act more mature and responsible. Spades are the workers of the deck and tend to have strong wills. They also can be the most spiritually oriented people in the deck, but this is not the rule of thumb.

Just from knowing the connections with the seasons, we can see how this 'vibration' translates into personality traits that can be identified in those we know. However, there are more subtle manifestations of the suits that we can explore, some of which are connected to these same seasons, and others to the elements that go with these same seasons.

We can also learn a lot about each of the suits by studying the King and Queen of each suit as role models for the suit in general.

HEARTS

People who are of the Heart suit act young and look young too. They can be dramatic and entertaining. Hearts is the suit of love, youth, children, romance, relationships, and artistic expression. Astrologically this would tend to associate those of the Hearts suit with the sign of Leo and the 5th house. This is also the suit of sensual pleasure and delight. Hearts have special

affinity for the subjects just listed. Hearts women can be the ideal romantic partner or wife. They can also be overly interested in sensual pleasure and turn toward the lazy and self-indulgent side of their suit. Any person of the Heart suit runs the risk of becoming overly infatuated with the romantic, sexual, or pleasurable side of their personality.

It is said that every heart, at some point in their life, makes romance or having a child the major focus of their life to the exclusion of all other things. By diving deeply into the things associated with their suit, they hope to learn about themselves and their inner natures. This obsessive behavior will take over for a while, until they learn to find a balance between those sides of their personality and the other considerations of a healthy lifestyle. Still, we can find many Hearts that are focusing much of their life energy on these topics. Many become famous or successful artists, actors and actresses, or musicians. Others are the Playboys and Playgirls of the deck. On the negative side, many of those who abuse children are Heart cards. These are the ones whose obsession with children has been allowed to be expressed in an unhealthy manner.

Since the suit of Hearts relates to the childhood, there are other connections that we can see in Hearts people. Our childhood is where we develop our basic personality and where we achieve a certain level of self-esteem. We might say that Hearts are related to self-esteem in many important ways. What the Heart person can give to us as his or her gift is acceptance and acknowledgment of our value as a human being, the very same things that parents give their children in the first years of life. By the same token, a Hearts person can withhold acknowledgment if they want to hurt or control us in some way. These are the levels of communication that they most often work through. We might say that acknowledgment, acceptance, and approval are their domain. Any Heart person may choose to use or abuse the power they have in their domain. It is up to the individual how it is manifested in their life.

CLUBS

Clubs also retain a certain youthfulness in their countenance. Being like the eternal college or high school student, they retain a certain curiosity about life, people, and new situations. They are interested most in ideas, methods of communications, the quality of their own thoughts and ideas, and in making a mark on the world with these thoughts and ideas. To a Club, the idea is as good as the thing itself. The word is as good as the action. The intention is as good as the deed. A Club will tend to take you on your word and take your words seriously, sometimes to a fault. One of the major challenges that all Clubs must face at some point in their life is to separate what others say from who they really are and what they do.

Clubs are searching for the truth in all things and this truth does help guide them through the maze of experiences that life has to offer. For example, a Club person who has all the facts about certain experiences in childhood may be able to quickly recover from emotional injuries inflicted by a parent who was withholding acknowledgment and affection. In this manner, Clubs energy is superior to Hearts energy. To further explain, a Hearts person who is, for whatever reason, not in a loving mood, may use the withholding of affection and approval to try and manipulate or hurt us. However, the beauty of the Clubs energy is that when we know the truth about ourselves, that is, if we know that we are loving and wonderful inside, no assault from a Hearts person may touch us. One might say that mental truth, represented by Clubs, can overcome emotional injury, represented by Hearts. The tools that Hearts use on us, to either get their way or to try and hurt us, are only effective if we are not whole in our inner child, or Hearts part. Clubs energy can rise above these areas by seeing the facts and truth of the situations.

Every person of any suit will be tempted to abuse the qualities of their suit from time to time. When they do they will manifest the negative side of that suit. Clubs, likewise will abuse the facts and truth at times when they are under emotional distress. A Club, for example, could use something you had said earlier against you, much as an attorney would use your words in court after you have been sworn under oath. Another Club malady is that of trying to get at the truth of a situation based solely upon the facts and whatever their definition of fairness is, without taking into account their own feelings. Often their conclusions exclude their own emotional involvement, which can often be at the real root of the situation. Sometimes focusing on the facts can be a means of avoiding one's feelings.

A Club is interested in the details, facts, and reasons why a certain thing happened. However, reasons do not always make up for a person's actions. If someone hurts our feelings and then gives us good reasons for hurting us it does not make it okay. It is the challenge for the Club to learn that the spoken word is not always the final truth about something. Oftentimes our actions speak louder than our words.

Knowing the details of situations is generally a basic need for Clubs people. If you are dating or married to one, you have to get used to the fact that you need to tell them all the details of situations, not because they don't trust you, but because it is one of their basic needs.

Likewise a Club may take what you say to heart a little too often. They can be strongly identified with their ideas. If you shoot down their idea, you are shooting them down. We only need to understand that all of us are identified somewhat with the suit of our Birth Card to realize that it has both a liability and a benefit. The benefit is the power that the Clubs person has in their speech and expression, and in their dedication to learning. The negative is that they sometimes cannot separate themselves from their own beliefs and thoughts. In truth, we are not our ideas.

One last comment about Clubs is that many of them have issues centered around freedom and individuality. Like the wind that is connected with their element, air, they want to be able to move, come and go as they please. For many of them, this independent nature makes relationships difficult. They often see relationships as restricting their freedom in some way. Being so strongly identified with their ever-changing minds can preclude the possibility of a happy relationship. This is not true of all Clubs, of course, but we can see some of these elements in a great majority of its natives.

DIAMONDS

We Diamonds are big spenders. I say we, because I am a Q♦ Birth Card myself. All of us identify with our values and our possessions to some extent. As mentioned earlier, we are the adults of the deck and dislike being treated as children, being bossed around, matronized or patronized. We are the ones who are always asking how much things cost. To us, everything has a value, if not an actual price on it. I used to say in my presentations that if you are married to a

Diamond, you have a price on your head. Because we are so closely associated with values, we are constantly exploring what everything in our life is worth and not worth, both on a personal level and a more universal level as we observe the goings-on in the world.

Diamonds develop techniques to get their needs met in childhood. These often center around Skinnerian psychology, the concept of 'instrumental learning' and the 'token economy.' In short, this philosophy states that we do everything to either get a reward or to avoid punishment. Pavlov's dogs is what we are, or so this point of view states. Thus we can be manipulated by being offered pleasurable or valued things or altered by exposing us to things we do not like, as in the case of shock treatment and punishment. We are the greatest salespeople and the easiest targets for sales people. It is the task of every Diamond person to arrive at a higher set of values if he or she is ever to attain peace of mind.

Every Diamond person, at some stage in their life, is likely to try and make the acquisition of money and property their most important and cherished goal in life. This is how we learn about ourselves. It is by attaining this 'pile of money' that they realize just how meaningless it is and learn that true happiness requires more than money. Still, even after the lesson is learned, Diamonds like money and enjoy spending and shopping, two activities that they most enjoy.

When a Diamond is feeling bad, they will often want to go out and spend some money, just as a Club might want to read a book. Buying something is often just the remedy for the blues. Of course, this doesn't always work and in some cases, it is actually a bad idea. A Diamond is more likely than any other suit to spend so much money that they lose their own sense of financial security. When we spend, we like to get quality items. Remember that we are concerned with the value of things. To purchase something of low quality often means undermining ourselves. However, purchasing quality usually means spending more for things and this can develop into a vicious cycle that leaves a Diamond feeling worried about money most of the time.

Diamonds make the best sales people because they know how to bring out the value of things to others. Most of the advertising we see is created by Diamond people. Many of the sales people are Diamonds or those of other suits that have favorable Diamond cards in

their Life Path. Once Diamonds believe in something, they are the best promoters in the deck.

Diamonds will also try and use your values to control you, just as Hearts and Clubs will try and use the qualities of their suits. Diamond energy, or values, is superior to Hearts and Clubs only from the standpoint that our truth (Clubs) is really based upon what we want (Diamonds or values). My teacher, Amrit Desai, would often say that whatever we want in our life, our minds will try to make up good reasons why we should have it. This illustrates what I feel is a truth about life and the distinctions and relationships between the suits. Most facts that are presented in this world have some motive or reason for being presented when they are presented. This motive or reason is usually found within the values of the person who is presenting them. A Diamond person who is clear about his or her values would never be influenced by any one else's truth or philosophy, or emotional factors (Hearts) either.

Let's take some examples to illustrate this. Someone who smokes cigarettes will have some sort of philosophy or belief structure that makes smoking okay for them. They might tell you that "I have known lots of people who smoked every day of their life who lived to be 90," "Smoking is great, it doesn't bother me at all," "Many famous people smoke cigarettes" or other statements like that. Clearly their truth supports their smoking. Take this same person just after he or she has decided to quit smoking and you will find a entirely different philosophy present.

I was a celibate for five years while living in a Yoga ashram with my teacher, Amrit Desai. During that time we learned all the ancient philosophies about the benefits of celibacy. There were many truths about celibacy that we learned and practically recited in order to accomplish it. Among them were things like "Only a celibate can reach the highest stages of Yoga and meditation" and "Sex destroys the spirit of a person, his creativity and his chances for liberation." Then, I got married and began having sex. Now, all those beliefs came to haunt me, making me feel guilty and having me believe that I was a bad person for having sex. Later, I discovered an entirely new set of beliefs that actually supported having sex and being married. I literally changed my beliefs just as I would change a set of clothes to adapt to weather conditions.

This illustrates how values are stronger than beliefs. For every belief and truth you may find, there is another one, probably one that seems exactly opposite that also exists and is just as true for the person who believes it. This is what Diamonds, and Clubs to a lesser extent, are here to learn. Since Diamonds and Clubs make up approximately 66 percent of our population, it is not surprising that values are such a predominant part of our culture. The United States, a J♦, exemplifies much of the value-based motivations and activities that characterize this day and age.

SPADES

The Spade person, being associated with the last suit in the deck, operates in a much different manner than the other suits. In some ways, they have the ability to rise above the concerns of the other three suits. It is through the application of their will power that they can be untouched by the manipulations of the other three suits.

Spades are workers, concerned with getting the job done. They tend to be as interested in the quality of their work as they are in how much they will make financially from it. The Spade is the craftsman who takes pride in his or her work OR the laborer who drudges through life and never rises above the mire of slavery. The boss who is a Spade, regardless of sex, can be ruthless and hard driving. They will expect you to work for what you get just as they have had to do.

Spades is the suit of wisdom and experience, traits associated with the older generation and as mentioned earlier, Spades tend to relate to others who are older or more mature. They tend to take a more mature outlook on life. Most Spade birth dates fall in the winter between January and April. They represent that last period of life when we prepare for our own death and transformation. This tends to associate Spades with the sign of Scorpio, the sign of death, sex, and power. Spades are powerful people with strong wills. Spades are called the most powerful and strongest suit in the deck. For this reason, many Spade people have power issues to deal with in relationships. Power struggles and "who's in control" issues will surface in their lives until they find some resolution of their inner struggles in these areas. They won't like anyone's attempt to control them and will also try and maintain control of their life and relationships as much as possible.

Their powerful wills can make them impervious to the manipulations of other suits. But they are only able to maintain this high place if they themselves have learned to acknowledge the qualities of the three suits that precede them. Spades are said to contain all the other suits within them. If they refuse to acknowledge any aspect of another suit within themselves, they too can fall prey to the challenges and difficulties faced by the other suits. For example, as powerful as they are, Spades can have tremendous challenges in the area of relationships. It seems that the relative distance between the Hearts and Spades (three suits apart) makes dealing in those areas somewhat foreign to them. According to most Spades, working and performing one's job well are more important than catering to human relationships and emotional needs. This is not to say that Spades cannot have a good marriage or love life. It is just that this is a common challenge for those of this suit.

Spades possess the opportunity, by their suit, to align themselves to the will of God and by so doing, achieve the highest expression inherent in this suit. This involves a process of surrender of their wills to the higher will. When they do turn their attention away from their work and careers long enough to realize that they also possess a great spiritual heritage, they can tap into a huge reservoir of spiritual understanding that can benefit both themselves and everyone that they come in contact with. They represent souls on the stepping-off point, where matter touches spirit. By their example we can share in their wisdom and be lifted to new heights.

WHAT THE CONNECTIONS WITH OTHERS TELL US ABOUT OURSELVES

By now you may have realized that much of our success or failure in relationships depends upon who we choose to be with. We cannot change the way that two cards tend to interact when involved in an intimate relationship. We can make the most out of the way they interact but we cannot make a Saturn connection turn into a Venus connection. Thus, the energetic connections that are reflected in this book are fixed. So, where does our choice fit into this picture? It has everything to do with our success because we are the ones who choose who we are going to be with. We have been exercising this choice our entire life and we continue to exercise it right now. I am not saying that we are completely aware of our choices, but nonetheless we are making them deliberately. Thus, one of the purposes of using this book is to give you a tool to enlighten you to the choices you are making or have made in this important area.

No choice is all bad or good. In each relationship that you have been in, there was some vital reason for your taking part in it. Being as picky as we are, no two people get together unless there are important reasons for each of them to be there. By using this book, you will be able to look back at any and all of your past relationships and be able to more easily pinpoint what it was that you were getting out of that relationship. Even if that relationship had a very bad outcome in the usual sense, I am certain that you benefited from it in some important ways. Many times what we get from the most challenging relationships is important knowledge about ourselves, specifically knowledge about ourselves that we couldn't have gotten any other way.

If we examine the connections between hundreds of people and their current relationships, we find that most people are not together to live happily ever after. We find many relationships with a heavy Saturn or Mars influence that are just too intense for the partners to be at ease with one another.

The Moon Relationship

We choose a Moon relationship when we want a lot of intimacy in our life. Moon relationships are also chosen to create a foundation upon which to build a family so in choosing one you are saying that "I am ready for a successful long–term relationship." Since this connection is one of the most favorable for marriage, it is generally chosen by those who have reached that stage where they are ready for it. In a Moon relationship there is a giving and receiving of intimacy and security. The person who is your Moon Card supports you and will help you create a place you can call home. For this reason, your choice of a Moon relationship can be a signal that on some level you have decided that these things: home, security, and foundation, are very important to you at this time. Whether or not you remain in this relationship will depend a lot upon whether or not these things remain at the top of your priority list. If

so, you can look forward to a happy and long marriage, especially if you share other connections that have high compatibility.

The Venus Relationship

Venus connections produce friends and people who take great pleasure in being together. The fact that you have chosen a relationship with strong Venus connections is tantamount to your giving yourself permission to have fun and to enjoy some of the more pleasurable aspects of life. It is, in essence, a sign that you are loving yourself. For this reason it is also a favorable sign for marriage. Those who love themselves have an easier time within a marriage. The Venus connection is not any kind of guarantee that you will get married. That decision has too many other factors involved in it. But if you did, you can rest assured that you have made a wise choice for a mate, one that will reward you with years of friendship and enjoyable times spent together.

The Mars Relationship

When we choose a relationship with a lot of Mars energy, we are probably wanting, on some deep level, to work out some of our anger and sexual issues. I have consistently chosen Mars relationships and isn't it interesting that I have a Mars/Sun conjunction in my natal chart? Mars relationships, by definition, are highly energized, sexual, and often competitive. One or both of the partners has difficulty expressing needs and instead tends to get angry when they are afraid. It is a fact that all anger is actually fear that is hidden. So we might say that the Mars relationship will help us work out our fears that we cannot or will not express. Operating out of our fear in the aggressive manner that Mars energy seems to promote always causes a lot of destruction in our lives. Anger always perceives that someone else has deliberately hurt us. It wants to hurt, to conquer, or to get back at the other for what they have done.

Once we have learned to recognize our fears as fears and make the distinction between anger and fear, we can eliminate the destructive effects of such Mars energy in our relationship. Then the Mars relationship becomes a positive stimulus for us to work and do positive physical things in our life. A positive Mars relationship is one where the partners exercise together or work together.

The Jupiter Relationship

Jupiter does nothing but add to a relationship. It creates in the partners a sense of benevolence toward each other, and a desire to contribute in a positive way toward each other's welfare. The Jupiter connection works very well where one of the partners is the bread winner of the family. He or she would naturally enjoy giving his or her resources to their partner. Jupiterian connections are not always financial, but they usually are. In a higher sense, the Jupiterian relationship could represent a connection of higher philosophies or a spiritual connection where what is exchanged is wisdom and integrity. Choosing a relationship with strong Jupiter connections is a symbol that you are giving to yourself. It is obvious that on some level you have decided to give yourself a gift. That gift is a partner that loves to give to you. But it was you who gave to yourself first because you are the one who chose them.

The Saturn Relationship

The Saturn relationship will bring a lot of maturity and a sense of responsibility to the lovers involved. It will be one of the most difficult in the usual sense but the net result of that relationship will be that each partner will be more mature and able to have more success for the duration of their life. Saturn is not good for compatibility. It causes a lot of judgment and criticism to be passed between partners which makes being together unpleasant. This is what I call negative compatibility. But sometimes a Saturn relationship will teach us things that we really need to learn if we are going to have true happiness in our life.

It wasn't a pleasant experience when my mother caught me shoplifting at age 7 and turned me into the police. She actually got the police to pretend that they were taking me to jail as she sat there saying good-bye and lamenting that she wished I didn't have to leave. That experience was one of the most horrific of my life, a real Saturn experience at its best. But guess what? I never stole another thing in my life after that. In one five minute experience, orchestrated by my Q♣ mother, I was cured of shoplifting forever. Some may call it cruel but now I am glad for it.

This is how Saturn relationships are. They are difficult only to the degree that we need to grow up and learn the truth about life. We unconsciously choose a Saturn relationship just to help us mature in one or more important areas.

The Uranus Relationship

Those who choose a relationship with strong Uranus connections are people who either enjoy a certain amount of freedom in their relationships, or those who want to learn about unconditional love. The Uranus connection guarantees that either one or both of the partners will act in unexpected ways or need complete freedom of expression. It is likely that the people in this sort of relationship will have separate jobs or interests.

Sometimes a person chooses someone who is Uranus to them in order to learn lessons about trust. Their partner will act so unreliably and unpredictably that they will be forced to face their fears of abandonment on a daily basis. They will likely feel uncertain about the affections of their partner because he or she will seem to come and go without warning. In some cases it will seem that their partner does not fulfill their promises. This may be taken as a message that they don't love them. In any event a relationship of this sort will confront that partner with their fears of not being loved and prompt them to have more trust in their partner's love, in spite of their actions.

Uranus always demands complete freedom. It can produce a very advanced form of relationship, one where the partners are each other's friends first and where they give each other the space to express themselves fully. This kind of relationship is progressive because in order to have it, both partners must be at a place where they each love and find joy within themselves. Each must feel secure within themselves so that they have the natural desire to give freedom of self expression to their partner. These are the relationships of the Aquarian Age.

The Neptune Relationship

Neptune relationships can be great teachers for us. With Neptune we learn about dreams, fantasies, and ideals. When we meet someone who is our Neptune card, especially someone whose Birth Card is our Neptune card in our Life Path, we have met the embodiment of our hopes and fears, and our desire to merge into another on the deepest level. As the higher octave of Venus, Neptune can produce some of the most romantic pairings of any other connection. Each of us has dreams about the perfect love or mate. Even when we are married, we still dream. There is a part of us that is searching for some kind of 'soul mate,' another person who will in some way fulfill our every need and desire just by their presence. When we meet someone who is Neptune to us, we are standing face to face with someone who stirs up those dreams and who, for the moment, seems to be that person in the flesh.

Sadly to say though, there are very few times when these relationships have happy outcomes. To understand why, just imagine being the person that someone else projects all their fantasies and illusions onto. Imagine them looking at you and seeing you as the person who is going to fulfill all their dreams and who is going to take care of their every need. On one hand this can seem a heavy burden to be placed upon you. What if you really don't want to play that role for them? How will you ever be able to be everything for them? On the other hand, you may realize that since they are holding this fantasy about you, it gives you a certain power over them. Since they can't see who you really are, you could use this power to take advantage of the situation and get a lot of things from them. You can easily deceive them as long as you keep playing into their dreams.

In real life this is what usually happens. Either one of the partners gets tired of donning the masquerade costume for the other person every day or they use the illusion-oriented energy of this connection to deceive and take advantage of their partner. In either case, suffering is the result. Inevitably the truth comes to the surface. Dreams are broken, fantasies dashed against reality and in most cases, feelings severely hurt. When Neptune beckons at our door step, we want to drop all our defensive barriers so that we can really take in all the wonderfulness that is awaiting us within the relationship. When the relationship goes bad, as they often do, the pain is much greater because we have opened up so much more than ever before. With this pain eventually comes truth and wisdom. We develop the ability to see through our own self-projected fantasies. Knowing this we are able to prevent ourselves from ever placing the responsibility for so much of our needs on another person.

Having a Neptune connection as the 3rd, 4th, or 5th connection in a relationship can actually have a very positive effect. Neptune energy does help in compatibility. It keeps the romance alive. It is only when Neptune energy is dominant that we have the situations like those described above.

The Pluto Relationship

Those who choose a relationship with this connection are usually those who are working with their need to control or change others. Pluto is the God of destruction and death. Psychologically, a Pluto relationship may help us go through many inner deaths as we burn away the layers of illusion that we hold about ourselves or life in general. On a deep level, the fact that we choose a relationship with strong Pluto energy is a symbol that we desire a profound change within ourselves. It is a fact that those who are trying to change or control others are in reality desiring such a change within themselves. Whether this need to change is taken in a positive, optimistic spirit or a negative, pessimistic spirit will depend upon the consciousness of the person. This same consciousness will determine whether the relationship is seen as a positive, uplifting force in their life or a difficult and negative influence. All that is certain is that the relationship will produce great and much-needed change in the individual. The end result will be that they become a person who is confident, wise, and patient, someone who has learned from experience and who no longer expects the world around him or her to change. This person has found their inner power.

THOSE WITH BIRTH CARDS IN THE NEPTUNE LINES

Being one of the seven planets, Neptune has a profound effect on our lives. All of us have a Neptune Card in our Life Path and the planet Neptune located somewhere in our natal astrological chart. However, for some of us, Neptune assumes an even greater prominence as revealed by our Birth Card's position in the Mundane Spread. This position is not apparent by merely reading the Life Spreads in this book or *Cards of Your Destiny*. One must see each card's position by row and column in The Mundane Spread, which is located in the back of this book. Cards whose position puts them in a Neptune row or column such as the 4♥ and 6♣, have a strong Neptunian energy about them that bestows upon them certain gifts and responsibilities. Let's first list them in case you don't understand which cards I am referring to. In the Neptune row from right to left are the 4♥, 4♦, 2♠, 8♥, 6♣, 6♠, and Q♥. The Q♥ is also in the Neptune column. Other cards in the Neptune column from top to bottom include the A♠, 2♥, 8♣, A♦, 5♦, and J♦. We find certain patterns prevalent among these cards that are recognizable. These patterns come from the influence of Neptune, the planet of dreams, ideals, universality, escapism, and fantasy.

Neptune bestows upon its receivers a strong sense of ideals. Neptune would have us reach into the heavens for perfection and he shows us that all things are possible. This can produce a person who is highly motivated to achieve a great ambition for the benefit of the world. It can also produce those who are addicted to drugs or other forms of escape when these same dreams are dashed by the harsh conditions of reality. Any of the cards found in the Neptune row or column listed previously have the ability to project a vision of a better world and then to see it through to its conclusion. But Neptune energy is meant for the good of the world, not necessarily the individual. Look at Jesus Christ, the Avatar of the Age of Pisces, for an example of this. Pisces is ruled by the planet Neptune. Christ personified Neptune's cosmic love principle by allowing himself to be crucified. In this manner, he demonstrated to us that the highest form of love, the love that gives to the world unconditionally, often requires completely letting go of all personal concerns. This same law of energy that Neptune follows makes life very challenging at times for those whose cards fall under his jurisdiction.

One might say that the Neptune person can achieve great things in life, but not for personal gain. This holds especially true in the area of relationships. Neptune casts such an ideal glow on relationship matters that one is usually so swept up in the possibilities of what that relationship might become that they totally ignore what the relationship is. When Neptune energy is misused, it causes deception. We think that our motives are lofty and selfless when in fact they are based on our usual mundane fears of being abandoned or hurt. The trouble with Neptune is that it is very difficult to see through our own deceptions. In most cases, it takes a lifetime to unravel the situation and get back to the essential truth of what is going on. So, we find many, many people in the world going around getting themselves hurt repeatedly in love affairs and not knowing why such a wonderful, loving person like themselves should get hurt so much and so often. Martyrdom is a common result of misplaced Neptune energy. There is such a thing as pure sacrifice but more often than not what appears to be pure motives are actually hidden and disguised fears.

When a Neptune-influenced person misuses the energy, either consciously or unconsciously, reality has a way of catching up with them. Sooner or later, their deceptions run up against the truth, their motives are exposed or at the least, their fondest dreams are shattered. When this happens, the other side of Neptune, that of escapism, often is the result. This can range from alcohol or drug abuse to other, milder forms of escapism.

These Neptune ruled cards are not the only ones guilty of these sorts of problems. We also see a lot of this sort of relationship deception in those who have their Venus Card of their Life Spread in a Neptune column. This includes the 5♣, 9♣, 2♦, 8♠, 9♥, 2♣, and 6♣. When we mix Neptune and Venus together we usually get a great deal of self-deception in love matters, often masked by good intentions to help or save the other.

And yet, all of these Neptune-influenced folks retain the capacity for true love of the highest degree. They are fortunate in some respects because they have the opportunity to taste divine love at different points in their lives, something that most other cards may never experience. And a few of them allow themselves to be guided by this divine love into great work and great actions for the benefit of the world. We are fortunate to have them in our lives because they can show us a glimpse of unlimited possibilities for ourselves and our lives. They also serve as reminders that we are all connected on a soul level, that we are all part of a unified existence though we appear to be separate entities.

The Importance of the Sun/Moon Connection

I taught a small workshop recently and was surprised when four couples showed up. Usually my workshops will only have the women show up, or single people. The husbands usually do not attend. But what really amazed me was that every couple there had significant Sun-Moon connections between them. As I do readings for people and study people in the news, I see over and over again how the Sun-Moon connection is found among nearly all married couples. There is something about it that makes us feel that our partner is someone with whom we could get married, have children, or both. I now think that this is the number one marriage connection above all others. I think that when you start to investigate, you will probably feel the same way. It is getting to the point to where I find very few married couples who don't have this connection, now that I know where to look for it.

For those of you who don't know, the Sun-Moon connection occurs between two cards that sit adjacent to each other in either the Life (Mundane) or Spiritual (Natural) Spread. For example, the 10 of Diamonds and 10 of Hearts are adjacent to each other in the Life Spread, the 10♥ being the Moon Card to the 10♦. The 9♣ and 8♣ in the Spiritual Spread would be another example.

But, to really see how prevalent this connection is, we have to look for it not only using our Birth Cards, but also our Planetary Ruling Cards and Karma Cards. The Birth Card to Birth Card connections are easy to see and indeed many married couples have them. But when you don't see a Sun-Moon connection with the Birth Cards look a little further. There is a good chance you will find it with the other cards. Let's take a few examples just to illustrate this point.

Kim Basinger is a 10♣ and her husband, Alec Baldwin is a 5♠. We don't see any Sun-Moon connection between those Birth Cards in either spread. However the second Karma Card for the 10 of Clubs is a 4♠ and of course we see the 4♠ sitting right behind the 5♠ in the Spiritual Spread. This makes Kim an ideal wife for Alec, and he her ideal husband.

Here's another example. My first wife is an 8♦ Aquarian, making her Planetary Ruling Card the 5♣. That Five of Clubs sits right behind my Karma Card, the 3♦ in the Life Spread. This is an example where her Planetary Ruling Card is Moon to my first Karma Card. In this same relationship, my second Karma Card is a 9♦. Her Birth Card, the 8♦ is the Moon Card to the 9♦ in the Spiritual Spread. In this case, there are two Moon connections, which is not uncommon.

With Katherine, my third wife, it is easier to see. My Ruling Card, the A♦ is the Sun to her Birth Card, the K♣ in the Spiritual Spread (My birthday is July 3rd). Sun-Moon connections involving the Birth Cards and Planetary Ruling Cards are the strongest.

Sometimes a couple will have a double Moon connection, going both ways. One partner will be Moon to the other and vice versa. An example of this is a couple who came to the workshop I mentioned earlier. The woman is a J♣, Pisces, born 2/27. Her husband is a K♣ born 9/11. Her Ruling Card is the 4♦ and his is the J♦. Her 4♦ is the Moon Card to his first Karma Card, the 2♠. Likewise, his Birth Card, the K♣, is Moon to her J♦ Karma Card. Actually these two had so many connections it is almost confusing since her Karma Card, the J♦, is the same as his Ruling Card. At any rate, when each partner is both Sun and Moon, they have to sort of take turns being the leader of the relationship. Katherine and I have that because in addition to the Moon connection I mentioned earlier, my Karma Card, the 3♦ is Moon to her Ruling Card the 4♦. We can each nurture each other and both need to be the boss in certain areas of our life together.

The Sun person is usually the boss or leader of the relationship. If the Sun person doesn't have a clear direction or is noncommittal about the relationship it will not help to have this great marriage connection, the relationship will fail. The Sun-Moon connection works best when the Sun person knows where he or she is going. And it is not always the male in the relationship who plays the Sun role.

Another couple at the workshop I gave was a female Libra 10♣ who was married to a Scorpio 9♣. So immediately we see that he is her Moon Card in the Spiritual Spread. However, did you also notice that his first Karma Card, the Q♥, is her Moon Card in the Life Spread? I told her that she had found a good "wife." He said that he would be very happy staying home and watching the kids, if they ever had any. It is just a very unique thing. We know that most 10♣ women are strongly career oriented. For them, a 9♣ man makes a good husband who would readily assume the domestic responsibilities. This is especially true since the 9♣ person is such a devoted parent with of their Q♥ Karma Card. Many of them would enjoy that role.

So now you see the many permutations of the Sun-Moon connection and know how to find it. I believe that if you examine couples carefully, you will find this important connection in nearly all of the married couples you take a look at.

Picking a Good Day to Get Married

Just as you and I have a birthday that describes our karmic destiny, everything that has a new beginning in our life likewise has a birthday all its own. Marriage is no exception to this and is perhaps one of the most important events in our life. We are fortunate that we can consciously choose this day and by doing so, give it the best possible chance of success. Here are some techniques that I have used with success.

You may think that getting married on a 4♥ or Q♥ day would be the best. This is logical since those are the traditional marriage cards. And yet I have found that those are not the best days for marriage. Since our marriage is like an entity to itself, we must look at the Life Path and marriage karma of the day we choose in order to make the final determination. Actually the Q♥ is not a bad day. It has some fairly good marriage karma. But there are days with better influences that are usually available if you want.

My personal choices for marriage are the 6♣, K♣ 2♠, and 7♠. Why, you may ask? Because each of these cards has a good marriage influence in its Life Path. The 6♣ has the Q♥ in Venus—a wonderful love and marriage card. The K♣ has the 4♥ in Venus—another marriage and family card in a position of love. The 2♠ has a Q♥ in Jupiter—a marriage that is prosperous and based upon spiritual truth and philosophical similarities. Finally, the 7♠ has the 4♥ in Jupiter which is much like the 2♠ card.

The Q♥ card itself has an 8♦ in Venus. The 8♦ happens to be the most elevated card in the deck. It sits in what we call the 'Sun' position at the very top center of the Life Spread. A Q♥ marriage would likely be a popular event and very expensive, even a marriage based more upon financial considerations than love.

Using this technique you can also examine people's marriage dates and see what that tells you about their life together and the life of their marriage. Some people have intuitively chosen good days for marriage, while others have chosen very difficult days. One last thought is that you could also use this same technique to plan important days for other things, such as the start of a new business. Just choose a card that has a good Life Path for that particular subject and you are well on your way to great success in that enterprise.

The Life Spread, Spiritual Spread, and Our Life Path Cards

It seems like every person who studies this system and begins teaching about it comes up with new names and labels for the essential pieces of the system. The system itself is unchanged since before the days of Egypt. However, each new teacher brings their own experience and understanding to it and finds names for the various aspects of it that fit his or her understanding. This can make it confusing for the beginner. The problem is that no official names were given by Olney Richmond to many of the aspects that we use a lot in our readings today. So, like most everyone else, I have come up with my own set of names, choosing the ones that I think best fit the functions of the various parts. I apologize if this seems confusing. We will begin by discussing what I call the Life and Spiritual Spreads.

THE SPIRITUAL SPREAD

The Crown Line

		K♠	Q♠ ✡	J♠			
7♥	6♥	5♥	4♥	3♥	2♥	A♥	☿
A♣	K♥	Q♥	J♥	10♥	9♥	8♥	♀
8♣	7♣	6♣	5♣	4♣	3♣	2♣	♂
2♦	A♦	K♣	Q♣	J♣	10♣	9♣	♃
9♦	8♦	7♦	6♦	5♦	4♦	3♦	♄
3♠	2♠	A♠	K♦	Q♦	J♦	10♦	♅
10♠	9♠	8♠	7♠	6♠	5♠	4♠	♆
Neptune	Uranus	Saturn	Jupiter	Mars	Venus	Mercury	
♆	♅	♄	♃	♂	♀	☿	

342 ♥ Love Cards

		K♠	8♦ ✡	10♣	The Crown Line		
A♠	3♦	5♣	10♠	Q♣	A♣	3♥	☿
2♥	9♠	9♣	J♥	5♠	7♦	7♥	♀
8♣	J♠	2♦	4♣	6♥	K♦	K♥	♂
A♦	A♥	8♠	10♦	10♥	4♠	6♦	♃
5♦	7♣	9♥	3♠	3♣	5♥	Q♦	♄
J♦	K♣	2♣	7♠	9♦	J♣	Q♠	♅
Q♥	6♠	6♣	8♥	2♠	4♦	4♥	♆
Neptune	Uranus	Saturn	Jupiter	Mars	Venus	Mercury	
♆	♅	♄	♃	♂	♀	☿	

When the entire deck of cards is laid out in a certain formation, called The Grand Solar Spread, we have a visual display of the very basis for this entire system. The illustrations on the previous two pages show you the first two of ninety Grand Solar Spreads. These first two are the most important and are the ones that are used exclusively to obtain all the information in this book, including the descriptions of the Birth Cards and the Relationship Connections. If one knew these two spreads by heart and had an understanding of all the planetary energies, it is entirely possible that they could have the entire contents of this book at hand at any moment to do a personal or relationship reading from memory alone. However, this method requires some time and is rather complex. This book is designed to help you get the information you need without having to learn the complexities of the system.

I have named the first of these spreads, found on the next page, the Spiritual Spread. It has also been called the Soul Spread, Perfect Spread, and the Natural Spread, because the cards in it fall in their natural, or perfect order, beginning at the A♥ and ending with the K♠. I call it the Spiritual Spread because it is the spread from which past-life influences are derived and the spread from which we may read 'soul' qualities. I define soul qualities as those that are deep within us, below the reach of our conscious minds, that have accumulated from the summation of the influences of all of our past lives. We look in the Spiritual Spread for hidden qualities that show up in an individual's makeup through careful examination. More on this later.

What I am calling the Life Spread has also been termed the Mundane Spread and the Worldly Spread. The Life Spread shows all the cards 'mixed up' in an apparently random fashion, and yet, it is not random at all. The cards in the Life Spread are each located in their exact position, both relative to each other and relative to the planetary influences that govern each of the rows and columns. It is from the position of each card and from the interpretation of the ten cards in the Life Path that we derive our understanding of each of the 52 Card Personalities or Birth Cards. In this book you will find a description of each of the 52 Birth Cards, along with the Joker. On each of the 52, you will also find a listing of the Life Path Cards for each Birth Card. If you take any single card in the deck, look up its Life Path Cards and then locate each of them within the Life Spread illustrated on the previous page, you will see exactly where they have come from. These ten cards tell us much about a person's personality, karmic traits, highest potential, and what will happen to them a various stages of their life.

This book is not meant to be a complete study of these Life Path Cards. However, I want you to know that the interpretations given for each of the Birth Cards are taken from that card's position in the Life and Spiritual Spreads, and from its Life Path Cards. If you have studied *Cards of Your Destiny* and are already familiar with some of the meanings of cards as they are influenced by the various planetary periods, you should be able to get some meaningful information from the study of these Life Path Cards. For example, if you have a 5♣ in your Venus position of your Life Path, you could read the meaning of the 5♣ in Venus in *Cards of Your Destiny* and learn something about your personality and life from it. Here is some information about the Life Path Cards and how to interpret them, for those who wish to further their knowledge of this science.

The Moon Card

The first card in our Life Path is our Moon Card. It sits right next to our Sun, or Birth Card. This card represents those energies or things that make us feel safe and secure or nurtured. The K♣, for example, has a 2♣ as a Moon Card. This tells us that K♣ people always feel safer and more nurtured by having conversations with other people. They need (Moon) to talk (2♣). When we meet someone whose Birth Card is the same as our Moon Card, we have found someone who makes us feel supported and safe. This is a powerful connection as you will learn later, one often found among successful couples. The Moon Card does not govern any particular time of our life. Its effects are steady throughout our life.

The Sun Card

Our Birth Card is also called our Sun, or Soul Card. The Sun has long been a symbol for the Soul, or subconscious mind, that part of us that is always giving to us unconditionally and completely. Our Sun Card is a symbol, for this lifetime, of qualities and characteristics that shine forth with much brilliance. The Sun Card is actually a gift of sorts. It represents areas where expression comes easily to us, where we have a certain gift in abundance. Sometimes this gift comes through in such abundance that it needs to be carefully expressed otherwise it might cause some problems in our life. The 3♣ person, for example, has an abundantly creative and versatile mind. It is so versatile, in fact, that they have trouble making decisions and are often worried about everything. So, even our greatest gifts can become liabilities and must be handled carefully if we are to access our highest and brightest potential. One of our challenges in life is to use the energy of our Sun, or Birth Card in positive ways, thus keeping ourselves busy doing good things. This is how we minimize the negative qualities of our Sun Card.

Each Sun Card has a highest form of expression. Though it is not the only card in our Life Path, it is the most important. Keep in mind that it represents the card that governed the day of our birth. Within the pattern specified by that card are many secrets and wisdoms that apply to us personally and professionally.

The Mercury Card

Our Mercury Card in our Life Path is very significant and represents many things. First of all, you need to know that each of the seven cards, from Mercury through the Neptune Card, all govern a period of approximately 13 years of our life. Therefore, our Mercury Card governs the first 13 years of our life (ages 0 through 12), our childhood. This means that our Mercury Card can tell us something about the nature of our first 13 years of life. Scientists have proven that 90 percent or more of our personality and character traits are formed in the first 6 years of life. Therefore, we can see the importance of this Mercury Card, since it describes in some manner the events and experiences of our first 13 years. Take the 9♣ person for example. Their Mercury Card is the 9♠, which often symbolizes death or losses. It is common for 9♣ people to have lost a family member during childhood. There are often physical complications (9♠) at birth also. Other cards that have a Face Card (Jack, Queen, or King) as their Mercury Card will often report that their childhood was either dominated or highly focused upon some powerful person. All A♦ people have powerful mothers who were the main influence in their childhood as symbolized by their Q♦ Mercury Card. The same applies to the A♣, 2♣, and 5♦, to mention a few.

The Mercury Card is also a symbol of how our mind operates, what we think about and how we communicate with others. It can reflect just how successful we might be in publishing or public speaking. The 4♠ person, for example, has the 10♥ as their Mercury Card. This has them thinking a lot about social involvements and tends to bring them a certain amount of popularity.

The Venus Card

Our Venus Card rules the second thirteen-year period, or our life from ages 13 through 25. Those who have any of the Fives as their Venus Card, for example, probably did a lot of traveling during that period of their life, since Fives indicate travel and changes. It is during our Venus Period that most of us experience love for the first time and in that sense we set a pattern for the way we love for the rest of our lives. Therefore, our Venus Card reveals something about how we love others, what we are attracted to in a mate, how we relate or don't relate to marriage and commitment, and what things and people bring us pleasure and joy. Whenever we meet someone whose Birth Card is the same as our Venus Card, we usually like them and have good things in common with them.

Venus represents the pleasure principle. Therefore, our Venus Card tells something about what brings us pleasure in our life. Take the 9♦ person for example. They have the 2♣ as their Venus Card. This tells us that the 9♦ person enjoys conversations (2♣) and is most attracted to someone with whom they can have these conversations. They want someone they can talk to, whether they are friends or mates. Intellectual compatibility would be very important for such a person. The 4♦ person on the other hand, has an 8♥ in Venus. They would be most attracted to the Playboy type, or someone who has a lot of charm and emotional power. This same 8♥ tells us that the 4♦ person enjoys group associations and that they have a lot of charm and magnetism themselves, as indicated by the 8♥. So, with these examples you get to see that one card in a certain position has many different levels of meaning and often all of them apply at the same time.

The Venus Card is very important in terms of telling us something about the romantic or relationship nature of a person. However, it is not the entire picture by any means. A Heart Card of any number found elsewhere in our Life Path can also tell us something about our love life as Hearts are very much the suit of Venus. There are other considerations as well, most of these will be mentioned in the descriptions of the cards.

The Mars Card

Our Mars Card governs the third thirteen-year period of our life, from ages 26 through 38. It is during our Mars period that many of us really begin searching for our best occupation. It is typically an energetic period and one full of ambition and passion, two of the keywords for Mars. A powerful Mars Card, such as an Eight or Ten, can indicate a great deal of success during that period. Whatever your Mars Card is, it will somehow describe the general tone of those years of your life.

As far as our personalities are concerned, our Mars Card describes those qualities, things, and people that both motivate us to action as well as those that make us angry. We can even say that our Mars Card represents some of our own qualities that we are unhappy with at times. Mars also rules over legal affairs, since Mars is the God of War. Thus our Mars Card will tell us how well we fare in legal proceedings and battles. If, like myself, you have a not-so-strong Mars Card (mine is a 3♠), you would best avoid legal matters whenever possible and find other means to get what you want. Because Mars is the essence of masculine energy, it also says something about how we get along with men in general throughout our life. Your Mars Card says, 'this is how events will go for you when you approach them passionately or with anger.' It can also define the things that we are most passionate about and the things that get us motivated into action.

The Jupiter Card

Governing ages 39 through 51, our Jupiter Card is considered another of the 'blessing' cards. In fact, for most people, this Jupiter period of life is the one in which they accumulate the most wealth and property. By that time of life most people have figured out what they do best and have worked with it long enough that they make more money and begin to acquire property. This is a general rule of course. There are always exceptions. Usually, though, the Jupiter period is a prosperous time and our Jupiter Card may define just what it is that we will be doing during the period that brings us this prosperity and accumulation.

Our Jupiter Card represents a blessing in our life. For one, it tells us what sorts of activities can bring us the greatest financial rewards. It is sort of a given talent that we possess, whether or not we use it. The 9♦ person, for example, has the J♦ in Jupiter. Since the J♦ is the 'Salesman's Card,' we know that 9♦ people can make a lot of money doing sales and promotions. Not all 9♦ people end up doing sales work, but most of them have tried it and will tell you that they were pretty good at it. They might choose another line of work, but they know they can always fall back on sales or promotions if they want to make some fast money.

The Saturn Card

Saturn has always been one of the most feared planets or influences as far as astrologers and other readers are concerned. Even in this system, Saturn is usually associated with ill health or other problems. For many people, it is probably during the Saturn period of life, from ages 52 through 64, that they experience their first real challenges health-wise. In any event, the Saturn period ushers in old age which is often accompanied by health considerations. However, Saturn also has a lot to do with our reputation and career. So, it comes as no surprise that many people achieve some degree of prominence and reputation during this important period of their life.

Our Saturn Card is often a symbol of what our careers are, or that work that we are known for. My Saturn Card, for example, is the 7♣. This is a card of spiritual knowledge and of helping others to elevate their thinking patterns (as I elevate my own in the process) which describes the work I do fairly accurately. It is no secret that we often choose work that will help us overcome challenges that lie within us. If, for example, I want to overcome my fear of poverty, I may choose to help others overcome their fear of poverty. Thus, our Saturn Card also represents an area of our life where we have some major work to do. It usually symbolizes some area of our life where we have a habitual pattern of negative expression, an area that we will put much effort and discipline into during the course of our life in order to elevate and improve ourselves. Saturn is almost the opposite of Jupiter. If Jupiter is a 'given' talent that we possess, then Saturn is a talent that we must work hard and diligently for. Don't forget though, that this same talent is probably the one we will be known for as we progress through our Saturn period of life.

The Cosmic or Universal Planets and Positions

The diagram below illustrates how the 10 main planetary positions line up with each other. Each position in the lower row is a higher octave of the planet position in the top row. The first five planets are the ones that deal with the physical reality of the earth plane. Each one of these has a 'higher octave' or universal expression. For example, Mercury governs the mind and communications. Mercury in the normal sense is connected to Virgo and Gemini, the two signs it rules over. In astrology, if we have Mercury situated in the sign of either Virgo or Gemini, we have a good, logical mind, capable of making fine distinctions. However, if we have Mercury in Aquarius, which is the sign ruled by Uranus, we are a genius. We have risen above the need to be logical up to the 'super-logic' of the intuition and knowing level. It is no accident that the keywords for the sign of Aquarius are "I know." The Aquarian mind is able to tap into what is called the 'universal mind' where all the wisdom of the ages exists at all times.

Earth-Bound	Mercury	Venus	Mars	Jupiter	Saturn
Universal	Uranus	Neptune	Pluto	Cosmic Reward	Cosmic Lesson

Thus each of the positions in the bottom row are similar to their corresponding 'earth-bound' planets but they reach a broader perspective that is less personal and more universal. Keep this in mind as we discuss the last positions.

The Uranus Card and Neptune Cards

The Uranus and Neptune Cards together govern the last years of our life. The exact numbers of these years is not known since there is such a range of life spans today. It is probably best to look at both of them together to get a feeling for the last years of our life. Someone, like a 2♦ person, who has the 10♦ and 8♠ in Uranus and Neptune, will probably have a long life, signified by the 8♠ (good health) and money signified by the 10♦. Other Birth Cards who have challenging cards such as the 7♠, 9♠, or any other Seven or Nine in Uranus and Neptune will have challenges in the last years of their life, unless they have turned to the spiritual side of life for their answers. It is during the Uranus and Neptune periods of our life that we naturally become interested in the life hereafter and spiritual matters. It has been said that at the entry to the Uranus Period, we either turn to spirituality or we stagnate. Today's nursing homes are full of people who have stagnated. They talk like endless loop cassettes, saying the same thing over and over again, living in their own world, with little connection to reality. On the other hand, those who have turned to their spiritual sides are lively, keen, and intelligent, even if they are 90 years old.

It is a natural part of our life cycle to become more interested in spiritual matters and to be preparing ourselves for our death and what may lie beyond as we approach our death. Many people find a certain group or religion to identify with and join, one that reflects their own personal beliefs and desires. Perhaps this is why the Uranus Card also represents the groups that we hang out with in life, coworkers, and any other large organizations that we become a part of. A strong Uranus Card in our Life Path can mean that we have good fortune working with corporations and other large institutions. Our Uranus Card also has something to do with real estate. Once again, a strong card here, such as an Eight, Ten, or one of the face cards, could mean success in this area for the individual.

Our Neptune Card can be called the 'Hopes and Fears Card.' It often represents something or someone that we dream about over the course of our life. It may be a quality that we desire, something that we have wanted our whole life, or in some cases, it may be something that we are afraid might happen. On the most basic level, our Neptune Card represents the contents of our subconscious mind. When we look at someone's Neptune Card, we are looking at their deepest and most secret dream and desire. This is why meeting someone whose Birth Card is the same as our Neptune Card can be so seductive and addictive.

The Pluto Card

The rest of the cards in the Life Path do not govern any particular period of life. Instead they are all life-long influences. They are very important, each representing a different facet of our life. However, the ones from Pluto on are more universal in nature and are more difficult to understand without direct experience. The best way to understand them is to find someone whose Birth Card matches them and see how we get along with them and how they affect us.

The Pluto Card is one of the most important in the entire Life Path because it represents a quality or essence that will cause us to undergo one or more powerful transformations during the course of our lives. It can be said that our Pluto Card represents a part of us that must die and be reborn, a place where we must transmute lower energies into higher ones. It is much like the Saturn Card, but usually more dramatic in its effect. Whereas Saturn requires discipline and hard, steady work to improve ourselves, Pluto asks for complete annihilation of certain personality traits. We undergo a psychological death in whatever area is specified by our Pluto Card. This card is both frightening and fascinating at the same time. Like a moth to a flame we are inevitably drawn into this card to be destroyed and reborn anew. The Pluto Card may be considered one of the most important of the 'lifetime challenge cards.' We can see from the diagram that Pluto is a higher octave of Mars. Mars is the god of lust and war. With Mars we get mad, but with Pluto, we get even (ask any Scorpio). This again illustrates how any planetary position that is of a higher octave can manifest with more intensity.

The Cosmic Reward Card

The Cosmic Reward Card is like a second Jupiter Card, but this time taken to a higher or more universal level. It represents another one of our gifts but it is a blessing that takes a certain degree of awareness to actualize. I have also noted that for most people, the Cosmic Reward Card acts more like a second Pluto Card until they have met and dealt with their Pluto Card. It seems to stand to reason that we do not receive the full benefits of the Cosmic Reward Card until we have passed through the tests implied by our Pluto Card. One card follows the other in our Life Path like a natural evolutionary path for us to follow. Therefore, I have noticed that people who are relatively unconscious of the personal issues represented by their Pluto Card are also unable to access the blessings of their Cosmic Reward

Card. For this reason, the blessings of this card are generally experienced more as we get older. However, this card acts also like a destiny card in our Life Path. It can symbolize that which we will be rewarded with toward the end of our life for having passed through the trials of the Pluto Card. In this regard, one might say that we are 'destined' to have the qualities associated with that card at some time in our life. It's like a guaranteed pot of gold at the end of the rainbow.

The Cosmic Lesson Card

I have also called this the 'Cosmic Responsibility Card' and to understand it one must look back at the meaning of the Saturn Card and then mentally project this into a more universal realm. If Saturn represents lessons we are learning on the Earth plane, then the Cosmic Lesson Card must represent lessons we are learning in a more cosmic sense. Thus the lessons implied by this card may have more to do with how, in past lives, we have behaved with respect to our responsibility to our fellow men and women as a whole. For example, how aware were we that our actions affected not just those in our immediate surroundings, but also our society, country, and planet as a whole? In this lifetime the Cosmic Lesson Card may describe the role we must play in relationship to this more universal perspective. Take the 8♠ person for example. Their Saturn Card is the 3♣. This tells us that one of their big personal challenges is to overcome worry and fear and to transform all the negative worry and indecision energy of that 3♣ into creative expression. However, their Cosmic Lesson Card is the Q♠. This tells us that their responsibility to the rest of us is to develop the capacity to internalize their problems and master themselves, instead of trying to push everybody around, as 8♠ are inclined to do. So, the Cosmic Lesson Card represents a role we must play in order to be equitable and conscious of the needs of the world around us.

THE MAGIC CIRCLE OF 45 CARDS

In a certain fashion, the deck of 52 cards can be divided into two distinct groups. There are 7 that are part of a special family called the Fixed and Semi-Fixed Cards. We will discuss them next because they behave differently than the remaining 45 cards. For now, lets talk about the rest of the 45 because they are all part of a family themselves and are intimately connected in many ways. These 45 cards form a circle of sorts when they are all placed next to each other in a way that represents their karmic links to each other. The illustration on the next page shows you this. As you look at this circle of cards, imagine a group of 45 people all holding hands and facing the center of the circle. Find your card in that circle and notice which Birth Cards are sitting to your immediate left and right. This circle is a circle of never ending energy, constantly regenerating itself. The energy in the circle moves into your left hand and out of your right hand. If you look carefully you will see that the person on your left is your Karma Card that you receive from and the person on your right is the Karma Card that you give to. One step more in either direction reveals your Karma Cousins. From this circle we see that the energy that we give to the Karma Card that we owe eventually comes back to us after it passes around the circle through the 44 other cards in this family. There may be other peculiar connections with certain other cards in this circle, such is who is directly across from us and so forth. For now, all we know is that these 45 cards are bound together in a karmic circle of energy that flows from one to the next around and around. There are other special qualities that this family shares that we talk about in The Advanced Oracle Workbook that deal with what happens to each card every year of their life.

THE FIXED AND SEMI-FIXED CARDS

There are seven cards in the deck that have no karma cards in this usual sense. These are the K♠, J♥, 8♣, A♣, 2♥, 7♦, and 9♥. These seven cards comprise a special family of cards that are karmically linked only to each other. In essence, each of these cards has six other Karma Cards. This means that whenever we see two of any of these seven cards together, we know that one of the reasons for being together is to repay some past-life debt between them. As you study the cards of people you know, you will begin to notice that people of this special group are very often found linked up, either through love, marriage, friendship, or in business associations.

If we note the positions of these seven cards in both the Spiritual and Life Spreads, we realize that the first three occupy the same position in the two spreads. We also note that the last four merely change places with each other. These are known as the Fixed (K♠, J♥, and 8♣) and Semi-Fixed (A♣, 2♥, 7♦, and 9♥) Cards. This phenomena manifests as character traits in these specific cards and was discussed earlier in the descriptions of these individuals. For now, keep in mind that with these seven cards, different rules apply than with the remaining 45 Birth Cards. We cannot, for example, read the information given about the 8♣ person and expect that to apply to the K♠ or the A♣, or any other card in the deck. The three Fixed Cards are truly all to themselves as far as their character traits are concerned. The only thing they have in common is that they are 'fixed' in their natures.

However, the remaining four Semi-Fixed Cards do each have one other card that is like their alter ego. The A♣ and the 2♥ are replacements for each other, so are the 7♦ and 9♥. For this reason, an A♣ person could read the description of the 2♥ person to get relevant information about themselves and vice versa. The same applies to the 7♦ and 9♥. These four Semi-Fixed Cards also have a lot of fixed-ness to their natures. If you don't believe this, ask anyone who is either married to one or who has one as a child.

The Moon Connection—The Most Important Connection of All

As discussed on page 276, there is a great deal of significance to the Moon Card connection—one of the closest connections that can exist between two people. Not surprisingly, then, the Moon connection is consistently found in a great majority of marriages, and also in love affairs and all sorts of other relationships, which should tell us of its importance. And this connection, above all others, provides insight into the fundamental dynamics of any relationship, which, in turn, can predict how that relationship will turn out. It tells us, first and foremost, who the leader of the relationship is, which holds a lot of importance in wherever that relationship is heading. Even among competitors in any field, it is the Moon connection—if there is one— that will determine the winner. If you enter into any relationship, you really need to know if there are any Moon connections and if so, who is moon to whom. Sometimes there are multiple Moon connections. I have seen as many as four. Here I want to explain the significance of the Moon Connection, and exactly how it operates.

How Do You Find a Moon Connection?

Recall that a Moon connection occurs when two cards are sitting right next to each other in either the Spiritual or Life Spread in a horizontal direction. It does not work vertically or diagonally. Every card has two Moon cards—one for each spread. The card on the right is the Moon Card to the card on its left, which is the Sun Card. You can refer to the Spiritual and Life spreads on pages 342 and 343.

Let's take the 4♣ for example. In the Life Spread, on page 343, it is found in the center column. In that spread, we find the 2♦ to its left and the 6♥ to its right. So, the 4♣ shares a Moon connection with both of these. In the Spiritual Spread, it has Moon connections with both the 3♣ and 5♣. This card is fairly easy to do using these spreads. But some cards are more difficult unless you know exactly how the cards run in each spread, i.e. where they start and how they proceed in order.

For example, if we are looking at the J♦ in the Life Spread, we can easily see that the K♣ is one of the cards it shares a Moon connection with. But what about the other? Because the cards move from left to right and then down at the end of a row, it turns out to be the 4♥. And if you look again at the illustration, you will note that the direction of the cards is from right to left and then down a row when you get to the end of a row. You go down a row and back to the far right on the next row. When you reach the last part, where the Q♥ sits in the Life Spread, you move up to the top and far right, to the 10♣. Therefore, the Q♥ has Moon connections with the 6♠ and 10♣. In the Spiritual Spread, illustrated on page 342, it works exactly the same way. And in most cases, the cards that share Moon connections will be in the same suit and just one number apart. Like the 10♦, which has the 9♦ and J♦, as cards it shares Moon connections with. And by the way, when you get to the K♠, in either spread, the next card is the next row down, far right, which is the 3♥ in the Life Spread and the A♥ in the Spiritual Spread.

You only need to know all of this if you plan to look for Moon connections yourself. This book will tell you if you have a Moon connection, the abbreviation will always start with MO. If the connection ends with an S, it was found in the Spiritual Spread and if not, it was found in the Life Spread.

Planetary Ruling and Karma Cards Count!

We use not only the Birth Cards for Sun/Moon connections, but also the Planetary Ruling Card and the Karma Cards of both the Birth and Planetary Ruling Card(s). This of course can make the process more complicated, but we really have to include them all because of the importance of this connection. You may not think you have any Moon connections with someone, but when you examine the connections with some of these other indicators, you might find some. So, to be complete about any relationship you are looking at, you need to:

1. Find any and all Moon connections between Birth Cards, Planetary Ruling Card(s), and Karma Cards of the Birth Card and Planetary Ruling Card(s). Remember that Scorpios have two Planetary Ruling Cards and Leos essentially have none.
2. Determine who is Sun and who is Moon in each connection found.

The Moon Connection is the Best for Marriage

Though some marriages do quite well without a Moon

connection, Moon connections are usually found in marriages. There is something about a Sun/Moon connection that causes a couple to want to make the long-term commitment. They complement and complete each other. Whenever I evaluate a potential marriage, I always first look to see if there are any Moon connections. If I find one or more Moon connections, I know that this relationship already has a greater chance of success than if they are not present. Sometimes, when a Moon connection is not present, I ask my client, "Why are you with this person?" It is a good question in some cases, because it heightens the awareness of what is really going on in that relationship and whether it is actually a good one for the long-term.

What It Means to Be the Moon Card in a Relationship

If you are the Moon Card in any relationship, and if this is the only Moon connection found, you can assume:

1. You are playing the feminine role in this relationship, that of support person, homemaker, helper, nurturer, etc.
2. You bear the emotional burden. It is up to you to have and share feelings about what is going on.
3. You have to trust the direction that your partner is going, because that is where your relationship is going—where he or she says it is going.
4. You are more likely to "fall in love" with your partner.
5. It will hurt you a lot more than your partner if this relationship ends.
6. If you compete with the person you are Moon to, you will likely lose.
7. You find your partner's ideas and communications really interesting.

What It Means to Be Sun Card in a Relationship

If you are the Sun Card in any relationship, and if this is the only Moon connection found, you can assume:

1. You are playing the masculine role in this relationship. You are the leader and direction-setter for this relationship.
2. That you are responsible for setting the clear and specific direction for the relationship.
3. If the relationship fails, it is probably your fault.

4. You will naturally want to lead this relationship and to direct the other person into new areas that you think will be helpful or good for them.
5. Should you break up, it will be easier for you to leave the relationship than your partner.
6. Your partner cannot really hurt you in any significant way. And if the two of you compete in any way, you will win nearly every time, if not every time.
7. It is also your job to appreciate the support you get from your partner. A little bit of appreciation goes a long way here.
8. You may not find your partner's ideas all that interesting and you will not usually follow any of their suggestions.

These are the basic qualities of being either Sun or Moon in a relationship, but they only apply if there is only one Moon connection. If there is more than one Moon Connection and if they are not all the same, i.e. who is playing the Sun or Moon role is the same in all, your relationship will be a mixture of these roles. One partner will play leader in certain areas of the relationship and the other partner will have their place where they are leader.

The operation of the Moon connection is unconscious. This is very important to understand. You might be in a relationship where you are the Moon card to the other, and you might not want it to be that way. Maybe you don't want to be the follower or support person. But there is nothing you can do about this. You cannot change it, and it will play out in the ways described above regardless of what you do or think about it.

Men who are Moon to a Woman Lose Masculinity in the Relationship

The traditional roles of male and female are for the female to play the role of Moon. After all, the Moon is the feminine planet and the Sun the masculine. When a man plays the Moon role in a relationship, he loses some of his masculinity. We like to say he "sacrifices" some of his masculinity. And for some people, this can be a problem. There are some birthdays for men that are okay being the Moon card. They might be naturally more feminine or drawn to be the support person. And there are many birthdays for women that are very career-oriented and goal-driven. The 10♣ is a good example of this. Most 10♣ ladies are very career-driven. And most of them are not going to want to be cast into the traditional role of wife and helper to some man. For them, it is generally better to find a man who will be Moon to them, and hopefully one who will be okay not taking the lead.

Madonna, a famous Leo 10♣, first married Sean Penn, a Leo 9♣. He is Moon to her but the relationship failed because he was not comfortable being second to her, or any woman for that matter. Some men have a strong male identity and for them, being Moon to a woman is not an option. But a strongly male-natured woman, such as the 10♣, can usually find a man who will be happy to be their Moon card if they just look for them. There are other cards for ladies, such as Kings and a few others, who probably need a man to be Moon to them. And I have recommended many times to some of my clients, because of astrological considerations, that they only choose men who are Moon to them to date or marry. So, it does happen and needs to happen in many cases.

Some cards for men tend to be what we call "momma's boys." Usually these men have powerful mothers, and often they are Moon to their mothers. And this can cause them, as adults, to unconsciously seek a similar relationship with a woman because on some level, they feel that their role is to "please mom." In some cases these relationships work out, but more often they do not. The A♦ is a common example, and the cards show this with their Q♦ in Mercury, which represents the powerful mother they have. Our Life Spread Mercury Card is a symbol of what was predominant in our early childhood. But the A♦ is a very masculine card and will never really be happy being Moon to a lady.

But even when it is necessary, it is still true that a man loses some of his masculinity with such a woman. And he will need to regenerate that somehow. He usually has to do things outside the relationship from time to time. Or, he needs to have male friends that he can do male things with to recapture this lost masculinity.

WHEN YOU WOULD PICK A MOON CONNECTION FOR PLATONIC RELATIONSHIPS

Moon connections appear in all sorts of relationships, such as relationships with coworkers or health care providers. And it is equally important to know about them because sometimes the direction of the connection will either help or hinder your plans. Many relationships can benefit from a Moon connection, but depending on what you want from the relationship, it is important to know whether to be Sun or Moon. In general, you would choose to be Moon in a relationship if:

1. You want guidance or direction from the other person. This could be from a doctor, lawyer, or consultant. (See how OJ Simpson had two lawyers that he was Moon to, and they guided him successfully.)
2. You need some good ideas for your problems or to benefit in your future.

Likewise, you would choose someone who is Moon to you, if:

1. You know where you are going in life and want someone to follow your direction.
2. You want someone who would support or nurture you (like a secretary or massage therapist).

I once hired a woman to work for me as an office assistant. I found out very quickly that it would not work. She would not follow my direction. She would do things her way, disregarded my orders, and always had this attitude that she was superior to me. I realized then that I was Moon to her and quickly let her go. You cannot give direction to anyone you are Moon to.

CELEBRITY COUPLES EXAMPLES

Most couples who have Moon connections will have the male as the Sun Card and the female as the Moon. This is the most common. Here are some examples of famous Moon connections so that you can see how this system works in real life.

Examples Where the Woman is Moon to the Man:

- Bill Clinton/Hillary Clinton
- Tom Cruise/Mimi Rodgers (see page 357)
- Tom Cruise/Nicole Kidman (see page 357)
- Justin Bieber/Selena Gomez (see page 364)
- Whitney Houston/Bobby Brown
- Melanie Griffith/Don Johnson
- Alec Baldwin/Kim Basinger
- Prince William/Kate Middleton (see page 365)
- Justin Timberlake/Jessica Biel (see page 361)
- Javier Bardem/Penélope Cruz (see page 361)
- Gwyneth Paltrow/Chris Martin (double Moon connections)
- Howard Stern/Beth Ostrosky
- Ryan Seacrest/Julianne Hough
- Ellen Degeneres/Portia de Rossi (Ellen is Moon to Portia)
- Matthew McConaughey/Camila Alves
- Christina Aguilera/Jordan Bratman
- Barbara Streisand/James Brolin
- John F. Kennedy/Jacqueline Kennedy
- Abraham Lincoln/Mary Todd Lincoln

Examples where the Man is Moon to the Woman:

- Barack Obama/Michelle Obama
- Brad Pitt/Angelina Jolie (see page 358)
- Melanie Griffith/Antonio Banderas
- Madonna/Sean Penn
- Tom Cruise/Katie Holmes (see page X)
- Jennifer Aniston/Justin Theroux (see page X)
- Rebecca Romjin/Jerry O'Connell
- David Beckham/Victoria Beckham
- Jessica Alba/Cash Warren (see page X)
- Orlando Bloom/Miranda Kerr
- Gwen Stefani/Gavin Rossdale
- Alicia Keys/Swizz Beatz
- Sonny/Cher
- John F. Kennedy/Marilyn Monroe
- Maksim Chmerkovskiy/Kirstie Alley (see page 359)
- Maksim Chmerkovskiy/Erin Andrews (see page 359)

Other Celebrity Relationships

Here are a few examples of important celebrity relationships that were not marriages, but where the Moon connection still played an important role.

- Bob Hope/Bing Crosby: Bob was Moon to Bing, very successful partnership.
- Barack Obama/Mitt Romney: Romney is Moon to Barack and he lost to Obama in 2012.
- Tonya Harding/Nancy Kerrigan: Tonya is Moon to Nancy and Tonya made Nancy famous.
- OJ Simpson/F. Lee Bailey and Johnny Cochran: OJ was Moon to both.

Parent/Child Sun/Moon

In parent/child relationships, the Moon connection plays an important role. If you are a parent and you are Moon to your child, do not think for a moment that you are going to guide them. Even though they may be a child, the energy of the Moon connection will cause them to disregard your suggestions and direction. When you are Moon to a child, which is the best connection a mother can have with her child, what you offer is unconditional love, not guidance and direction. This can infuriate some parents because they think the child is intentionally disregarding their input. They take it personally and argue and fight with the child. It is not personal.

It is ideal for the mother to be Moon to a child. This is considered to be a blessed connection as far as the child is concerned. Moon means mother!

The reverse is true if your child is Moon to you. You can direct them. Just be careful that you don't overshadow them so much that they are never able to find themselves. It would be easy, in this Sun position, to dominate your child to the point of them never finding their own path in life.

I hope from what is written here that you will now take the Moon connection very seriously. It affects all of your relationships to some extent. Now let's take a look at another important relationship connection, the Neptune connection, considered to be the most romantic of all.

Of all the various connections we can have with another person, one stands out as the longest lasting and that is the Neptune connection. Neptune connections can only be found direct and vertical in the Life and

Spiritual Spreads. They are never diagonal or mutual. And all of us have several Neptune Cards associated with our Birth Card and Planetary Ruling Cards. The main one is the direct Neptune Card in our Life Spread. But there is also a Spiritual Spread Neptune Card and we can also get the Life and Spiritual Spread Neptune Cards for our Planetary Ruling Card and Karma Cards. So, the entire list can be quite long in many cases. And it is very likely that you have met and been romantically involved with someone who was one of your Neptune Cards. One word that describes Neptune Card relationships is "unforgettable." If the strength of a relationship connection were determined by how long its influence lasted, the Neptune connection would be the most powerful connection of them all.

Astrologically, Neptune is the highest vibration of Venus, the planet that generally governs love, sex, and marriage. With Neptune there is a sense of everlasting love that spans lifetimes. No matter what spread a Neptune connection is found in, the feeling or experience of it is always past-life. And with Neptune there is the feeling that, if necessary, one would make sacrifices on behalf of the beloved. If you fall in love with someone who is one of your Neptune Cards, it is likely that you will always love them and never forget them. We often hear stories about people who marry late in life to someone they had loved as teenagers or young adults. I can guarantee that most of these will have a Neptune connection involved.

But Neptune connections are not all good by any means. All energy in the universe is capable of a negative expression. And Neptune's negative expression can be just as powerful as the positive. Here we have things like deception and codependence, along with the victim/savior complex, and finally, addiction. The person receiving the Neptune energy in a Neptune connection is like someone who has just taken a powerful drug. They can be easily deceived by their Neptune person. They can be duped into things they would normally never do, on account of the power of their Neptune-induced experience. For example, if you are my Neptune Card, I will project onto you all my secret dreams and desires. I will see a fantasy version of you that fulfills some of my deepest longings, sometimes longings that my own conscious mind is not even aware of. For this reason, I can become addicted to you, thinking you are the one

and only for me, and that I absolutely need YOU to have any happiness in my life. You can see how this point of view can be damaging. And like a drug addict, I might do anything to have you or keep you in my life. This in spite of the fact that you and I might not even be compatible!

I myself experienced this firsthand. I met a lady when I was in my thirties with whom I fell in love. She was a 2♠ Planetary Ruling Card, which is Neptune to my 9♦ Karma Card. I went for it with her with everything I had but in the end she left me and broke my heart. It took me seven years to stop thinking about her every day; it took that long to search within myself to find out why I had become that addicted to her. I did finally gain some self-understanding and freedom from that addiction to her, and although I never forgot her, thankfully I moved beyond that addictive desire. Over twenty years later I was single and sincerely looking for a life mate when she magically appeared in my life again. This time she fell in love with me. And I still loved her. And now we are married. I could go on and on about how I feel about her. And we are in some ways not that compatible. But here we are, married. That's the amazing thing about Neptune: the feelings never die. They are as constant as constant can be. And in the end, isn't this what we are all looking for? A love that never dies?

I was recently doing some research on celebrity couples. I came across Ryan Gosling and Eva Mendes. These two met on the set of the movie, *The Place Beyond the Pines*. I was searching to see if they had any Moon connections. It turns out they don't. But they do have a powerful Neptune connection, from Ryan to Eva, along with a few other important ones. It is easy to say that Eva, who is a Pisces 5♠/6♥, and generally is not going to settle down with one man, has found her dream guy. Ryan is a Scorpio 8♣/10♥/Q♦. And his 10♥ is not only her first Karma Card, it is also Neptune from her 6♥ Planetary Ruling Card. The attraction here is mostly on her end. Ryan is her drug. Fortunately for her, he is fairly marriageable. And the fact that they are compatible Sun signs helps too. Right now the gossip magazines are full of stories about how romantic these two are together and what great chemistry they have on screen. I am not going to predict how their relationship will turn out, but I can predict that Eva Mendes will always love Ryan and always be in love with him.

When you meet someone who is your Neptune card, fasten your seat belt! The power of this connection will take you on an experience that may change you forever. And as Kahlil Gibran says in *The Prophet*, *"For even as love crowns you so shall he crucify you."*

Love that is the most powerful will teach you the most powerful lessons of all. And it is for this reason that we must respect and be mindful of the power of Neptune connections.

Chapter Eight
Examples of Celebrities and Celebrity Couples

Here we present some examples of celebrities and celebrity couples that illustrate how some of the cards and relationship connections work in real life. I am sure by now you have plenty of examples from your life and the lives of your friends and family. But since most of us are familiar with celebrities, these are good to study and learn from as well.

THE MANY LOVES OF TOM CRUISE

Tom Cruise, born July 3, 1962, is a Q♦ Birth Card and A♦ Planetary Ruling Card. Both of these cards are not considered to be very marriageable. So, why would he get married so many times? He has been married three times so far and I predict a fourth. In my opinion, the driving force is his Q♦. Because the Q♦ has a 3♦ first Karma Card, there is an inherent insecurity in all Q♦ people. This is usually related to finances but it can also extend to relationships, especially when we consider that Tom's birthday is a double-diamond. Being a double-diamond, everything in his life is considered to be something of value, so that even his relationships would be judged on some scale of worth. And that pesky 3♦ causes his sense of worth to be changing and unclear most of the time. And the Q♦ has the distinction of having every Three in the deck in their Life Spread. There's the 3♥ in Jupiter, 3♣ in Venus, 3♠ in Mars, and the aforementioned 3♦ first Karma Card. The 3♣ in Venus also affects relationships and for many Q♦, it means three or more marriages. Having a Three in Venus can cause a perpetual dissatisfaction in love, meaning that as soon as you have someone, you want someone else. I can't speak directly for Tom Cruise, but his relationship history says a lot.

Tom has been romantically linked with, which means he has had sex with, many women, including Rebecca De Mornay, Cher, and Penélope Cruz. He has married Mimi Rogers, Nicole Kidman, and his latest, Katie Holmes. Most people don't know about his brief marriage to Mimi Rogers. Mimi, born January 27, 1956, is a K♣/6♣. She is six years older than Tom. After the divorce, Mimi complained at one point that Tom didn't want to have too much sex. It was because of his beliefs

in connection with Scientology that Tom was trying to be married but also sexually conservative, which didn't sit well with her. Mimi is Moon to Tom Cruise at least twice and he is Moon to her once. It is interesting that both Mimi and Penélope Cruz have a 6♣. The 6♣ has a 2♦ Karma Card, which is strongly connected to both Tom's A♦ PR Card, as well as his 3♦ first Karma Card.

A friend of mine once mentioned that Tom usually marries women who are not as successful as him and that when they start becoming successful, he divorces them. That appeared to be true with his second wife, Nicole Kidman. Tom was still officially married to Mimi when he met Nicole on the set of *Days of Thunder*, his movie about NASCAR racing. Nicole Kidman, born June 20, 1967, is 10♣ and 8♦. Her birthday is double Moon to Tom's if you consider that Tom's Decanate Ruling Card is the J♣. Obviously they were very compatible. No one knows why he divorced her. They adopted two kids. Tom's marriage to Nicole lasted less than two years. It appeared his marriage record was that each was getting shorter in length.

Tom waited a long four years before he met Katie Holmes, born December 18, 1978, a K♥ with a 2♦ Planetary Ruling card, and sixteen years younger than Tom. Many in the media saw this marriage as a situation where Tom, and his cult-like religion, Scientology, basically controlled Katie. But what is not apparent is that Tom's A♦ Planetary Ruling card is Moon to Katie's 2♦. Tom had complete control over the ladies in his first two marriages since they were both Moon to him twice. That also made it easy for him to leave them. But with Katie it would be different. The fact that she was so young made her somewhat naive in the beginning, but it was inevitable that she would find her power in the relationship and step into it. This is especially true where children are concerned. Tom had his first biological child with Katie, and K♥ will do whatever it takes to make sure the children's interests are being considered. Katie finally realized that Scientology was just not good for her or her child, and she took charge. Once it became obvious to Tom that she wasn't going to take any crap from him anymore, he let her go.

This marriage cost Tom Cruise a lot, and not just financially. After Tom's infamous behavior on Oprah in 2005, and with his public rants against the validity of antidepressants, postpartum depression, and the like, Tom lost favor with the public. He has made several movies since then that have not done well at the box office. Now that the marriage is behind him, his career is slowly recovering.

Will there be a fourth wife? I certainly think so. But I get the feeling that Tom will have to someday cut his ties with Scientology if he really wants to regain favor with the public. Who will this fourth wife be and how long will it be before he meets her? It will be very interesting to see.

THE STORY OF BRAD PITT

Brad Pitt, born December 18, 1963, is a K♥ with a 2♦ Planetary Ruling Card. As a K♥, he had many relationships in his younger years. He became recognized as a "hunk" and "heartthrob" early on in his career, and no one expected he would ever settle down. But the cards always knew. Both his Birth and Planetary Ruling Cards are very marriageable and marriage-oriented. But being as young as he was, there were some wild oats to sow. But even then, most of the ladies he dated, including Robin Givens, Jill Schoelen, Juliette Lewis, and Gwyneth Paltrow, were ladies with whom he had strong connections and could have married.

But he didn't tie the knot until he met Jennifer Anniston, born February 11, 1969. They had a lot in common. Jennifer is an A♠ with a 9♠ Planetary Ruling Card. They shared many good aspects together, including a mutual Venus connection, direct Venus Connection, and a Uranus connection, which is regarded as a good friendship connection. (Funny that Jennifer was working on the *Friends* TV show back then.) They were both successful, young, and beautiful and seemed to be heading in the same direction in life.

The reasons their marriage ultimately failed are found in their cards: First, Jennifer's 9♠ has a K♥ first Karma Card. This means many things, including that Brad was her first Karma Card, which can cause a lot of intensity in a relationship. You see, our first Karma Card reminds us of something we tend to do negatively. 9♠ people are known to manifest the negative side of the K♥, which means they bully others and can be very demanding or domineering. Though it is not common knowledge, it is known around Hollywood that this is her basic nature. Her A♠, the second factor, contributes to the problem because it has the 7♥ first Karma Card, which represents emotional uncertainty and fear of being dominated, used, or abandoned by their partner. I am certain these two had a lot of really intense fights.

Then there is the matter of children. I wrote this about Brad in my newsletter, back in 2005 just after their split:

Brad is a King of Hearts. As such, the prospect of having a child would be of monumental importance in his life. With most King of Hearts, the child or children take preference over everything, including the wife. I believe it has been the issue of Jennifer having a child which has caused friction. Why, you ask? Because I believe Jennifer hesitated as she was beginning to realize that having Brad's baby would end their relationship. This is often the case with any woman who is married to a King of Hearts. Once the baby is born, the King simply regards their spouse as the helper to raise HIS children. I believe Jennifer could sense this coming. I imagine that it was obvious to her when they discussed it. She could already sense his attitude about the child and how she didn't rate as much to him personally.

It was the fight about having children that broke them up. I think the idea really scared Jennifer, and instead of showing vulnerability, she took the road of anger and fighting, which led to their breakup.

I also wrote back then that I didn't see a permanent break-up in their cards. However, I also said:

It would not surprise me if Brad has an infatuation for Angelina Jolie. She is a King of Diamonds, the first card in Brad's Life Spread. When we meet someone who is our Mercury Card like this, we find them constantly interesting and fascinating. This is a Moon connection, the one found the most in marriages, and one that Brad and Jennifer do not have. But there are no indications in either Brad's or Angelina's spreads that the two of them will get together. The press release that Brad and Jennifer gave about their split mentioned that it was not because of what the tabloids had been saying, which is that he was interested in Angelina. If Brad ever got together with Angelina, he would have met his match. Her birthday is much stronger than his and he would not be able to control her or dominate her; at least she would not have that fear with him.

The news that he had hooked up somehow with Angelina had been a part of the split from Jennifer, but it wasn't clear just yet how important she would become. Angelina, born June 4, 1975, is a K♦ and 6♥. K♦ women are very strong and somewhat masculine, even though their physical appearance can be very feminine. Think Sharon Stone, Faye Dunnaway, and Lindsay Lohan. If I can think of one defining characteristic that all K♦ people share it is this: they are completely focused on what they want—and they usually get it.

Even though Brad has a lot of connections with Jennifer Anniston, he has even more powerful connections with Angelina. Both Brad and Jennifer are in a Moon position to Angelina because the K♥ is the main Moon Card for the K♦. Being the Moon Card to someone means that they have the power over you, and that they are the leader of the relationship. Essentially Angelina plays the role of the man in her relationship with Brad. And yes, she did "steal" Brad away from Jennifer. But who can blame him? I don't think Angelina and Brad have the kinds of conflicts that he had with Jennifer. She is a much more balanced and happier person in general, and she and Brad share the same views on family and children. You will notice that when you see pictures of their family that Angelina is always out front and Brad is behind, lugging the children, luggage, etc. That is the unconscious expression of their Moon connection in action.

It is interesting that Angelina is also a 6♥, which is Brad's Venus card. It is common for Hearts Birth or Ruling Cards to have the same number of children as the spots on their cards, and Brad and Angelina have 6 children.

When a man gets involved with a woman he is Moon to, he usually is extremely enamored with her. But at the same time, he loses his masculinity to her. She is playing the masculine role in the relationship, not him. As such, to regain this, he has to separate from her somewhat. Brad lost a lot of his masculine power in the beginning of their relationship. You didn't see him doing as many movies in general. But now, he seems to be back in balance. And I am sure that making a movie helps him regain his masculinity just by being away from Angelina. I am not saying she is bad for him but being around her too much would cause him to lose himself. The prognosis is that these two will be together for a very long time. But who knows? All relationships are challenging and sometimes they only last for a while. But as Hollywood marriages go, this is definitely one of the longer-lasting ones.

As for Jennifer, her fiancé, Justin Theroux, is a Leo 3♦. This makes him Moon to her. And as dominating as she is, having a man she can boss around might just be the best thing for her. Hopefully it is, because recent reports suggest she is pregnant.

THE SAGA OF MAKSIM CHMERKOVSKIY

Maksim Chmerkovskiy, born January 17, 1980, 10♦/5♥

Maksim is the hunky pro dancer on *Dancing with the Stars*. He has come close to winning a couple of times but never finished in first place. But what I wanted to write about here was how he has been linked a couple of times with ladies he is Moon to. The first was Erin Andrews, a female sports-caster. She is a 2♠/6♣, born May 4, 1978. Because the 2♠ has a K♣ Karma Card and because the 10♦ has a Q♣ Karma Card, there is a Moon connection. Not only that, but Maksim's 5♥ Planetary Ruling Card has a 4♦ Karma Card that is also Moon to Erin's 2♠ Birth Card. This makes Maksim double Moon to her.

Now when you are the pro dancer on a famous television show and you have someone who never danced professionally as your partner, you expect them to listen to you and follow your every lead. However, when the teacher is Moon to the student, this doesn't happen the way it should. The teacher in this situation ends up following the student more, being more of a support person. And sometimes this support role doesn't go smoothly for the teacher. Maksim had a lot of difficulty during the season he danced with Erin. He threw several tantrums in frustration, as he tried to get Erin to do what he wanted. They ended up in third place, which was actually pretty good, but not without a lot of consternation on Maksim's part. I found it somewhat comical to watch. What is great about *Dancing with the Stars* is that they show a lot of outtakes of the two dancers as they practice. And Maksim was very vocal about his frustration. That 5♥ can really throw a tantrum!

Then, just two seasons later, Maksim was paired with another 2♠, Kirstie Alley. Kirstie, born January 12, 1951, has a 10♣ Planetary Ruling Card so with Maksim, he is Moon to her one time, not twice like with Erin. Kirstie is both tall and heavy so it was a challenge for the couple to do ballroom dancing. During one performance, Maksim slipped and Kirstie fell. Again, throughout the competition, we saw outtakes of Maksim's frustration as he tried to lead a woman he is Moon to. But despite several mishaps, they found themselves in the finals and earned a perfect score on the final dance. Even so, they ended up in second place, Maksim's best ever. I give credit to both Erin and Kirstie for their successes. If they personally had not wanted to win as much as they did, they both would not have lasted as long as they did in the competitions. And that is the way of the Moon connection. The leader—in this case, the two ladies—must be clear about their roles for it to work.

What is also interesting, as a side note, is that Fives often have issues with authority. Maksim, being a 5♥ Planetary Ruling Card, has often had very vocal objections to the judges in *Dancing with the Stars*. And this came out even more the two seasons where he was Moon to his partners. He was obviously protecting Erin and Kirstie from the harshness of the judges' comments. But after fifteen seasons, the latest gossip is that Maksim has decided not to be on the show any more. Being a Ten, he probably has some ideas of his own.

JAVIER BARDEM AND PENÉLOPE CRUZ

Javier, born March 1, 1969, 9♠/J♠.

Penélope, born April 28, 1974, 6♣/Q♥.

These two were married in July 2010. Both had numerous relationships before, but when they met, it was like love at first sight. Both were born in Spain, and both are Oscar winners. And, between their cards, they have three Moon connections. It is, from all points of view, a perfect marriage. The only potential problem would be Javier, whose Planetary Ruling Card, the J♠, is known to have issues with freedom and dishonesty. Time will tell if those characteristics appear in their relationship. So far, they have not. Penélope is very marriageable, and it is actually surprising that she did not marry sooner. Both the 6♣ and Q♥ usually do. I guess she just had to find the perfect guy.

Looking at their relationship, we see that Penélope is Moon to Javier twice, both through Karma Cards. First, Javier's first Karma Card is the K♥, which fits with Penélope's Q♥ Planetary Ruling Card perfectly. Then, Javier's second Karma Card, the 6♠, sits right between Penélope's 6♣ and Q♥. This means that she is Moon to him and he is also Moon to her.

Penélope had Javier's J♠ as her yearly Pluto Card the year they were married, and her Result Card, the 3♥, had the 4♥ underlying it. It appears that they both knew she was pregnant when they decided to get married.

On January 22, 2011, they gave birth to a baby boy, whom they named Leonardo. This makes Leonardo a 5♦/K♣. Javier had a 6♥ Result that year with a 5♦ underlying it. Leonardo will likely be much different in personality than either of his parents, but he does connect with them through Karma Cards. This is interesting because 5♦, as well as all Five Birth Cards, are known to have issues with their fathers. And the 9♠ is also known to be very controlling and dominating, especially in the home. Leonardo is likely to be very rebellious and to fight against his father's control. No Five wants any of their freedom taken away. With Penélope, Leonardo has love and friendship connections. I would say that the boy will be challenging for Javier as his values will be very different and he will have this aversion to being told what to do.

I think this couple will be together for a while. It is even possible they will have another child in 2015 or 2016. There are no strong signs of breakup in the next seven years but again, Javier is the wild card here. The J♠'s negative expression may creep in and cause him to want to abandon his beautiful wife and family.

Jessica Biel and Justin Timberlake

Jessica Biel born March 3, 1982 7♠/8♥

Justin Timberlake born January 31, 1981 9♣/4♣

This famous celebrity couple was married on Friday, October 19, 2012, after a cycle of dating, breaking up, and reuniting for several years. Justin had previously been in relationships with Britney Spears (3♦) and Cameron Diaz (9♥). Prior to his marriage, Justin never spent much time alone. I believe that due to his 4♣ Planetary Ruling card, he may have some strong security issues. Jessica, for her part, doesn't have such a colorful romantic history, but her birthday is a power birthday. Not only does her Birth Card (the 7♠) have a K♦ first Karma Card, but her Planetary Ruling Card is another power card, the 8♥. Though sweet and demurring on camera, I am sure she is a force to be reckoned with on a personal level.

They were married in her Saturn period where she has a 4♥ and 5♥ vertical. Very appropriate, because Saturn represents challenges and this will be a challenging marriage and also tells us that this wedding was very difficult for her. There had been some fallout over a guest's disturbing video that was shown at their wedding and then leaked to the Internet. It resulted in some negative press for both of them even though they had nothing to do with making it. The wedding was not quite as difficult for Justin as he was in his Uranus period, but I think the video and resulting fallout surprised him, too.

Sometimes we can look at incidents at the beginning of a relationship as indicators of future trends. Having that video leaked out to the world might be considered a negative omen for their marriage. However, both of these are fairly marriageable people with a tendency to commit. I think the real story will not be about either of these two cheating on the other, but whether their personal dynamics can withstand each other. Both of these two have control issues. And I am sure that control battles ensue in their relationship.

I think there is a very good chance that there will be a baby appearing in the next year. The A♥ and Q♥ appear in both their spreads. That would be a natural outcome and it will, at least for a while, give them both something positive to focus on. I do think that their incompatibilities will surface again and ultimately destroy their marriage. There are some indications in two to three years of that possibility.

Why would they break up? Jessica and Justin have no Moon connections between them and their cards are from different neighborhoods, card-wise. So, it is interesting that they have gotten together because they are not super compatible in the first place. However, both of their careers are in full gear and they are highly regarded in the film industry. So, if their relationship fails, they have their careers to fall back on—and for people in this stature of society, their careers usually come first anyway.

Even rich and famous couples get married for the same reason the rest of us do. Unconsciously we are all attracted to someone who can help us grow on the spiritual level. That means we could ultimately end up with someone who triggers all our fears and anger. On a spiritual level, it seems that these two are drawn together to work on their power and control issues. If they adopt an attitude of allowing the relationship to be their teacher, it could transform them both. But if they are just hoping for a "happy-ever-after" story to their lives, they will be disappointed.

Anne Hathaway and Adam Schulman

Anne Hathaway, born November 12, 1982, 8♣/10♥/ Q♦

Adam Schulman, April 2, 1981, 6♠/8♦

After looking over Anne's and Adam's cards, it makes me

wonder why they got married. It's not that they have no connections, but their connections are weak overall. Their cards originate in very different parts of the Grand Solar Spread. The strongest connection they share is that Adam's Planetary Ruling Card, the 8♦, has a 7♣ first Karma Card. That is naturally Moon to Anne's 8♣ Birth Card. Other than that, their connections are not strong at all.

Previously, Anne has not had the best success with men. She was dating Raffaello Follieri, born June 28, 1978, (2♣/7♠) when he was arrested for misappropriating $50 million in a Ponzi scheme. He was sentenced to four years in prison. Funny that she didn't have strong connections to him either, though she was Moon to him. One has to wonder why Anne would attach herself to men she is not that close to. And Adam's card, the 6♠, is known to be emotionally vacant. I suspect that some part of Anne is also absent emotionally.

Anne is more famous and important than Adam. She won an Academy Award in 2013 for her role in *Les Miserables*. She has appeared in many films and is known as a desirable Hollywood starlet. On the other hand, one of Adam's best known roles is that of Deputy Enos Strate in the 2007 film *The Dukes of Hazzard: The Beginning*. You can see there is a big difference here in social status. The fact that Adam is Moon to her suggests that Anne has chosen a relationship that is safe. It is always safer to be the Sun Card in a relationship. If the other person leaves you, it is not that big of a deal. It is always easier for the Sun Card to walk away from a relationship with a Moon card. It must have hurt her deeply when Raffaello Follieri was caught and it ended her relationship with him. She is a Scorpio and actually has four planets in Scorpio. Part of her really wants to find a very wealthy man to marry. This is the nature of Scorpio ladies. Adam certainly doesn't fit this description. But it is a safe haven for her for a while. It is hard to say how long this marriage will last, but I predict that eventually Anne will be ready to go out and seek a much more powerful man.

Anne has proclaimed that she has wanted to have a baby since she was sixteen years old. And rumors have been flying around that she is pregnant, but those are unconfirmed. Still, it could be true. Scorpios are known to be good at keeping secrets. There are indicators at present of a possible child in her cards in the near future. And it is apparent that she wants to settle down.

As an 8♣, Anne is fairly marriageable. However, both her Planetary Ruling Cards, the 10♥ and Q♦ have commitment issues. Both of those cards do get married, but often have trouble staying married. The 10♥ is a fun-seeker and the Q♦ just plain indecisive. I would estimate that people born on this birthday are about 10% marriageable. Being a Scorpio Sun sign helps too, because they tend to stay with one partner. But being famous does not. If and when they break up, it will be Anne that decides to leave. But for the present everything is good, and the potential baby could cause these two to be together longer than they might otherwise.

ELIZABETH TAYLOR AND RICHARD BURTON

Elizabeth Taylor, February 27, 1932, J♣/4♦
Richard Burton, November 10th, 1925, 10♣/3♥/3♥

Elizabeth Taylor and Richard Burton were Hollywood's most glamorous and notorious couple for over a decade. They were, in many ways, the quintessential couple of fame and set standards that have never quite been duplicated since. They were soul mates, lovers, and fellow actors who appeared together in eleven movies. The pair was married twice, from 1964 to 1974 and 1975 to 1976, and even though both had other marriages and romances, theirs was known to be the most memorable in every way.

One has to wonder what kind of connections that would result in such a strong attraction. And this is found by looking first at their two Moon connections. In both, Burton is Moon to Elizabeth. It is not normal for a J♣ to have eight marriages, but indeed Elizabeth did just that. But with Richard Burton, she had a man who she could respect intellectually, and one who adored her. But she didn't adore him, at least not at first, although she quickly grew to respect and desire him.

It was on the set for the movie *Cleopatra* in 1963 that they met. Both were already married at the time of their affair, but nothing would stop them being together. It took a year for the two to get divorced so they could marry. Elizabeth admitted she had a belief that if you wanted to have an affair with someone, if you had fallen in love with them, you ought to get married. And she was very fixed (J♣) about that notion.

The couple was known for their fights. Richard, being Moon to Elizabeth, likely rebelled against that connection that would have him always playing second fiddle to a woman. And, of course, J♣ enjoy arguing. Though I am sure that they had some great conversations too, there had to be conflict. And Elizabeth, being a Pisces, was an alcoholic. Actually both her Sun sign and her 4♦ Planetary Ruling card are connected to alcohol and drugs. Richard was also an alcoholic. He had the typical 10♣ insomnia and likely sought drink as an escape from his overactive mind. So I think their relationship had a good degree of codependence operating in it. And that same 4♦ has this propensity for seeking the ideal relationship, and yet are somewhat unwilling to put in the work required to make a relationship successful. With Elizabeth's fame and beauty, I imagine it was just easier for her to get divorced and remarried, rather than face the everyday challenges that appear in any relationship.

These two were also known for their passion. It was evident in all the movies they made, and their affection for each other was displayed frequently in public. Even though both had very successful careers, each considered the other to be the love of their life.

Jessica Alba and Cash Warren

Jessica Alba, April 28, 1981, 6♣/Q♥

Cash Warren, January 10, 1979, 4♠/A♦

I really like Jessica Alba. First of all, she is one of the most beautiful women in Hollywood and is a 6♣ and Q♥, two of my favorite cards.

I think many young men are in love with her, and we would all like to see her happy, but she is both married and a mother of two.

Cash (4♠/A♦) is quite the catch, or so it seems. He is decidedly handsome in an A♦ kind of way (think Tom Cruise). They met on the set of *Fantastic Four*, where he was part of the crew. He has gone on to become a producer, albeit small-time up to this point, but certainly pointed in the right direction. Their relationship so far has been rocky. In July of 2007, they broke up, with her telling him, "I am not in love with you anymore." Just a month before that, Spike TV had named Warren the "Luckiest Bastard" of 2007 at their first annual *Guy's Choice Awards*, due to his relationship with Alba. There is an obvious gap, however, between their star status, and that can always be the source of conflict. He is a long way down the Hollywood food chain from her. So what is it about these two? What is going on here?

The first thing to look at is that they have two Moon connections. The 6♣ has a 2♦ Karma Card and Cash's A♦ Planetary Ruling Card is Moon to that. A♦ men often end up with 6♣ women because of this Moon connection. Then again, his 4♠ has a 10♣ Karma Card and Jessica's Q♥ Planetary Ruling Card is Moon to that. These two Moon connections are what are making this relationship work. And having double Moon connections could be considered the best a couple could have. Jessica also is very marriage and family oriented. And unlike Penélope Cruz, who shares her same birthday, Jessica is following the "get married young and stay married" path. If there is a problem with this relationship at all, it will be Cash.

No matter the Birth Card, if a man has an A♦ Birth or Planetary Ruling Card, he can never have enough women. In other words, "So many women, so little time!" Even having Jessica Alba would not be enough. Now that he has her, being an A♦ Planetary Ruling Card myself, I can imagine him thinking about how many women out there would like to date him, the ex of Jessica Alba. I predict that their marriage will not last long. I just don't think a leopard can change his spots. I am betting that Cash will express his A♦ sooner or later, probably sooner, and play a role in the breakup.

So far, after two children, the couple is going strong. Jessica's career is also on track, though she hasn't starred in as many films now that she is a mother of two. It is interesting too, and this is just a side thought: I have met some A♦ who, for one reason or the other, profess that they would never cheat on their lady. And usually what happens is their lady cheats on them. This is what often happens when we repress something inside of ourselves—our partners will act it out. So, it will be interesting to see if one of them has an affair in the long run. Even so, I do not think this will happen anytime soon.

JUSTIN BIEBER AND SELENA GOMEZ

Justin Bieber, born March 1, 1994, is a 9♠ with the J♠ as his Planetary Ruling Card. The singer and performer is hugely successful, with a net worth estimated at $110 million and rising. He has the second largest following on Twitter, just behind Lady Gaga, at 30 million people. His double-spade birthday is known for many things, including:

1. Desire to help others (9♠)
2. Very creative and the ability to play any role successfully (J♠)
3. Accident prone (9♠)
4. Arrogance, bullying, and using other people (K♥ first Karma Card to the 9♠)
5. Dishonesty (J♠)
6. Problems with commitment and lack of boundaries (J♠)

Given his young age, we are bound to see some of Justin's negative traits come to light as his fame and fortune grow—especially because all of his actions, both good and bad, are in the public eye.

Selena Gomez is also a successful singer and performer—not nearly as much as Justin, but enough to be in his wealth/fame bracket for dating. Selena was born July 22, 1992, making her two years older than Justin. She is a 6♣ Birth Card and the 8♥ Planetary Ruling Card. Very pretty and talented, but also very competitive. Her birthday is known for:

1. Desire to reach a high degree of success in the eyes of the world (6♣)
2. Very competitive and revenge-oriented (6♣).
3. Very persuasive and charming (8♥)
4. Bullying others to get what she wants (8♥)

So, you can see that she and Justin, on account of his 9♠ which has a K♥ first Karma Card, are both very powerful and used to getting their way. However, one important thing to note about their cards is that Selena is Moon to Justin. Justin's second Karma Card is the 6♠, which is Selena's Life Spread Mercury Card. This makes her Moon to him and this is likely the main reason they hooked up and have the desire to be together.

They began dating in early 2011 and were considered a steady thing until November of 2012 when they allegedly broke up. Then, just two days later, they were back together and rumors were that Justin begged her to let him back in. It is hard to say just why they broke up, but rumors were that Justin was interested in other ladies. Selena is very marriageable, but Justin could go either way. It will probably depend a lot on the role model his parents are for him. But even so, the J♠ is known to have commitment problems. Time will tell. But as Justin gets to know himself, he may realize at some point that any commitment is just not what he really wants. And if that happens, he will lose the opportunity for this perfect marriage with Selena.

An interesting side note: the pop star Ke$ha, who is seven years older than Justin, recently announced that she would "totally have sex with Justin Bieber." What is interesting here is that she and Justin have the same birthday. If you look at Ke$ha and her persona, you might be looking into Justin's future.

PRINCE WILLIAM, DUKE OF CAMBRIDGE, AND CATHERINE, DUCHESS OF CAMBRIDGE (KATE MIDDLETON)

Prince William, June 21, 1982, 9♣/9♠
Kate Middleton, January 9, 1982, 9♠/K♥

What an interesting relationship we have here! Prince William is the eldest son of Prince Charles and is the heir to the British throne after his father. Kate then is heir to the throne after Prince William. And what a fine queen she will make. In essence, both William and Kate have King/Queen material in them. They share the 9♠ card, which has the K♥ as its first Karma Card. Kate has the addition of the K♥ as her Planetary Ruling card. Lots of K♥ here, and any King can handle being in charge. These two share so many relationship connections it is uncanny. Besides having the Birth Card/Planetary Ruling Card match, William is Moon to Kate twice. Like the marriage of Barack and Michelle Obama, the female is the one with the real power here. She is the Sun and the man is the Moon. And Kate is more powerful than William in other ways. She is inherently more stable and more marriageable. And she is likely to rule the household with an iron fist (many K♥ ladies do). Kate is also one of William's Mars cards. This makes for good passion and, later on, good fighting.

Their marriage took place on April 29, 2011. On December 3, 2012, it was announced by St. James's Palace that the Duchess of Cambridge is pregnant and expecting the couple's first child. When the child arrives, it will be Kate who takes charge in this area. And here is where the possible problems with this marriage can start. Though these are both two very beautiful and attractive people, who are very compatible, William's 9♣ Birth Card is known to have affairs. And being royalty is no deterrent to this sort of behavior. William's father Charles cheated on Lady Diana so he has that as a role model. Once their child is born and so much of Kate's attention is upon the child, or children, William may seek sexual and romantic fulfillment elsewhere. This will be interesting to watch unfold. K♥ are known to put the children ahead of their spouses so the spouses can feel left out or disregarded.

If this does happen, it is hard to say whether they will remain married. And this may not even occur, or it may occur five to ten years from now. It will be very interesting to watch. As fans of famous people, we often think they are exempt from the sorts of behavior we see in our friends' and families' lives. But in fact they are not. If anything, their manifestations of human behavior are often more dramatic. And the whole world gets to hear about it. I wish this beautiful couple well. I am hoping that the wisdom of Kate's 9♠ Birth Card can make the difference here.

THE MANY LOVES OF JENNIFER LOPEZ
Jennifer Lopez, July 24, 1969, 4♣

As a Leo Club, Jennifer Lopez is a natural performer. Her cards and Sun signs demand the attention of

others. Jennifer Lopez is a lot like Madonna. Both are Leo Clubs, Madonna being a 10♣, and both their cards and their Sun signs demand the attention of others. In all ways they are natural performers. Both have had success at music and acting and both have had many relationships. The 10♣ is usually viewed as a player in the relationship department, someone that cannot stay married long, if at all. But not the 4♣. The 4♣ are usually considered very marriageable. They are, after all, somewhat security conscious, being a Four, and marriage is a security institution if anything. But the Leo thing has something to do with it. Plus Jennifer is known to be challenging, in a demanding, controlling kind of way. This can make relationships difficult. I have also looked at JLo's astrological chart. She has a strong Mars/Sun connection that is often referred to as the "you don't own me, baby" aspect. And with that, she also has Venus being squared by Pluto. This aspect usually plays out as either being super controlling in her relationships or attracting someone who is super controlling. This has certainly played out in her love life so far.

JLo's first marriage was to actor/producer Ojani Noa, born June 11, 1974. Being a 6♦/4♠ he is both Jupiter and Saturn to JLo. Their rocky marriage lasted two years and ended in 1998. There are no Moon connections in their relationship. But to this day, there is still news from time to time about another legal bout between these two. I would say that Ojani is JLo's nemesis, if anything. 4♣ usually win in all legal proceedings, but since Ojani is her Saturn Card, that tends to turn the tables a bit.

After her divorce, Jennifer met rapper Diddy, then known as Puff Daddy. His birthday is November 4, 1969, making him a 3♦/7♦/2♥. It's interesting that their relationship also lasted two years, though they never married. Diddy was Moon to JLo through his 6♥ Karma Card. I am sure the two of them had mutual interests, but Sean Combs (Diddy's real name), as a 3♦, may never marry anyone, though he has five children so far. So, after two years together, it was time to move on. And now things begin to get interesting.

JLo's next relationship and marriage was to Cris Judd in 2001. Cris was born August 15, 1969, and is a Leo J♣.

They met while Cris was directing a music video for her and it was love at first sight. These two have no Moon connections at all but do have a strong Neptune connection. There are also two mutual Mars connections, but I believe it was the Neptune connection that was the glue here. Leos love romance, and Neptune can produce the most profound romantic feelings. The only problem is, it tends to mask the other feelings for a while, but they eventually reveal themselves. And all the Mars they had must have come out and destroyed the marriage. It was another two-year affair for JLo. She seemed to be following a pattern of two-year relationships, and most of them with no Moon connections.

And this brings us to "Bennifer," JLo's famous marriage to Ben Affleck. And here is what is really interesting about this one: Ben has the same birthday as Cris Judd, and they began their affair while Jennifer was still married to Cris! Wow, talk about instant replay. Their relationship, though it only lasted three years, was tops in celebrity attention. The entire world knew about them. The bookmakers in Las Vegas laid odds on how long their relationship would last. But here again, it was really a repeat for Jennifer of her relationship with Cris: the same aspects between them and the same results. The one thing that stands out about J♣ men is that once they are married, the wife is considered very controlling. Well, the 4♣ is also controlling for their own reasons. So, it is easy to see how the sparks can fly, especially with two mutual Mars connections. One Mars connection is quite enough for a healthy relationship. It creates passion and the desire to do things together. But to have two of them, and for them to be mutual, is probably too much. The relationship can easily turn to a constant conflict. And remember that J♣ actually enjoy arguing.

Jennifer didn't waste much time after her divorce from Ben Affleck. In 2004, she married Marc Anthony. I was somewhat surprised that she married him, because the first thing I noticed was the Mars connections. Marc was born September 16, 1968, making him an 8♣ with a 6♦ Planetary Ruling Card. His PR card is the same as her first husband's Birth Card. Maybe there is something about that 6♦ that makes for longer lasting relationships, because she was married to Marc for seven years. But again, the Mars is here and no Moon connections. What these two also had in common was that they are Latino pop stars. I am sure their cultural connection helped them stay together. They also had

twins! Mars and Pluto are closely connected, and JLo has strong aspects of both in her natal chart.

As of today, Jennifer has not remarried. She has been dating a dancer, Casper Smart, who is much younger than her. We don't know his birthday, only that he is currently twenty-five years old. The thing about Jennifer is that she has demonstrated a more or less constant theme in her choice of man: she marries men with whom she has strong Mars connections and no Moon connections, and these marriages just don't last long. I can predict that until she marries a man with whom she has different connections, her relationships will be short-lived. Perhaps by now she has learned a few things about her men choices. It will take a powerful man to handle JLo—someone to be the Sun to her Moon. If the right 2♦ or 5♣ guy shows up, that could mean that JLo is actually ready for something long-term. In the meantime, we all love her and wish her the best.

THOSE SEXY, BUT UNAVAILABLE 9♣ MEN

Al Pacino, Robert DeNiro, John Malkovich, Jack Nicholson, Paul Simon, Oliver Stone, Sean Penn, Donny Osmond, Prince William and Prince Henry, Quentin Tarantino, Leonardo DiCaprio, Justin Timberlake, and Donnie Wahlberg are all 9♣ men. What else do they have in common? Most of these men are dark-haired, handsome, and have a sort of "darkness" about them—along with a list of ladies they've bedded that is the "Who's Who" of Hollywood. What is driving these continual affairs?

The 9♣ has the Q♥ as their first Karma Card. The Q♥, like every card in the deck, has both a positive and negative expression. The positive expression is that of intuition, idealism, and power—someone devoted to his mate and children. But the negative Q♥ is often indulgent and very sexual in nature, and there is a marked negative expression of the Q♥ energy in the life of a 9♣. This compels them into sexual liaisons.

9♣ men also have the 2♥ in Venus. This is the card of the lovers and only the 9♣ has it. The 2♥ in Venus causes an innate love of sex and romance. In itself, this is quite positive. But the Q♥ first Karma Card brings the added addictive quality to these pursuits. The desire for satisfaction is so strong for 9♣ that they will find others outside their marriage if they are not fulfilled there—and they rarely are fulfilled. The final factor, and the real rub here, is that they have the 6♥ as their lifetime Saturn

Card. This speaks of difficult karma with relationships. 9♣ attract past life lovers, some of which return to them negative experiences from their past lives. And the 6♥ guarantees that they will know the full price of their indiscretions, sooner or later.

If you look into the personal lives of these men, you see that some tend to get married and then give that up to be a bachelor on the loose. Others don't get married until they are old enough to value a constant companion. It's not that all 9♣ men are unavailable. Many of them do the marriage experiment. And that could last for several years. Sean Penn was married to Madonna (Leo 10♣) for five years and to Robin Wright (K♦/2♣) for twelve years. I never thought this marriage would last, but it lasted longer than anyone thought. The two main reasons for this in my opinion are that Robin's 2♦ Planetary Ruling card is Sean's Neptune card in his life spread and that they had children together. Children helped to divert his attention away from his romantic life. They divorced in 2010, and it looks like Sean is catching up on all the sex he missed while married. His list includes Scarlett Johansson, Shannon Costello, Calu Rivero, Garcella Beauvais, Jessica White, Valeria Golino, Petra Nemcova, Elle Macpherson, Jewel Kilcher, and Brigette Nielsen. And he is just getting started.

The life of the perpetual bachelor is miserable in its own way. Men living this lifestyle can never really allow any woman to get too close to them. They learn this early on and keep their walls up at all times, moving on quickly from a relationship. I have had clients who dated Robert DeNiro and they all told me he was cold and aloof most of the time. But this lifestyle does get old, and especially when 9♣ get older, and they start looking for a companion relationship. This generally only occurs after age sixty or so when their compulsive sexual energy has waned. You will meet 9♣ men who seem happily married, but these are usually younger men. At some point, however, their karma kicks in and it's off to the sexual races for them. Will you be one of their conquests?

HARRY EDWARD NILSSON III: THE CLASSIC 2♦

Born June 15, 1941, 2♦/J♠

This book is not just about relationships—it is about the personality of each card, so we can learn a great deal not just from celebrity relationships, but also from their personalities. One such example is the performer Harry Edward Nilsson III, a classic 2♦.

In the early 1970s someone asked The Beatles, "What bands do you guys listen to?" Their unanimous response was Harry Nilsson. I grew up playing music and was professional for a number of years. I knew of Harry Nilsson but didn't pay much attention. Recently I watched a documentary about his life, *Who is Harry Nilsson? (And Why Is Everybody Talkin' About Him)*, and was amazed at this man and his talent. He looked and sounded like Paul McCartney and his voice and songwriting talent were equal or better. He wrote hit songs for many artists including The Monkees and Three Dog Night and won two Grammy Awards. At that moment, when he received his second Grammy in 1972 at the age of thirty-one, his life began a slow decline. He had peaked.

The 2♦, although terribly smart and talented, is also deeply insecure. Harry had an experience as a child where he performed and was made fun of. This experience caused him to never do a live performance for the rest of his life. He never toured or did concerts. Even a television show he did was prerecorded without an audience. His fear of rejection prevented that. His insecurity and neediness was prevalent in the lyrics of his songs. Many of his songs were about his own life experiences, such as his father leaving him and his mother when he was three years old. You can hear that loneliness in many of his songs. He was extremely successful, however, and had good friends, among which was John Lennon.

But his real downfall, which is also where his amazing creativity came from, was from his J♠. We see in Harry all the traits, good and bad, of the J♠. It accounted for his amazing creative gift. Just listening to his songs I can see that he tapped into a realm of music that was never ending. But many of his problems stemmed from how he used this creativity to avoid his insecurity. Plus, the J♠ has issues regarding freedom. You see, the J♠ wants no one to limit them. And for many 2♦/J♠ this combines with their insecurity to a point where they create an entirely fictitious world that they live in. They create illusions to explain away whatever they choose and in the end become lost in their own lies.

Harry's father left him and his mom when he was

three years old and Harry left his first son when he was three, as well. He repeated exactly what his father did and even wrote a song admitting this. And he divorced his wife. But that divorce was much harder on him than it would have been on most people. Again, that 2♦ suffered greatly, even though it was the J♠ that prompted it. That divorce, among other things, started Harry on a drinking binge that lasted until he died.

The success of his best album, *Nilsson Schmilsson*, was really great in part because of his producer Richard Perry. Perry agreed to produce him only if Harry would give him full creative control, to which Harry agreed. But during the making of the album, Harry fought against this supposed "authority," a typical J♠ occupation. At one point after a huge argument at the studio, Richard reminded Harry of their agreement to give him full control. Harry looked at Richard and said, "I lied." Fortunately, by this point the album was nearly done and produced three hit singles. But Harry decided that no one would ever control him from that point on. Without those boundaries, and refusal to cooperate or compromise, Harry's music and lifestyle tumbled. He never produced another album of that caliber, though he could have produced many.

His decision to never cooperate or let anyone stop him from doing whatever he wanted was Harry's downfall. His entire lifestyle degenerated along with the quality of his music. His great gift was wasted. I, for one, regret this. The music he did make, and his amazing voice, was truly God-given.

Friends say that Harry never thought he would live long. There was a history in his family of parents dying in their fifties as well. Harry died in his Saturn period at age 52 of heart failure (card students will note the critical year). One might say that he intended to die. Unconscious forces within him compelled him to the lifestyle that brought on an early death. This is important to see, card-wise, because 2♦ is one of the cards that generally live the longest. In the name of freedom from tyranny, Harry abandoned the advice of all who would help him. He was a Two who would not join forces with others.

CONCLUSION

Every day I read celebrity stories on the Internet. And each time I take the time to look up their cards, I am amazed at what I find. It appears we all are following some divine plan, much of which is predicted by our cards.

Chapter Nine

Bringing More Conscious Awareness into Our Personal Relationships

The following is a collection of articles about the inner aspects of personal relationships. Contained within these pages are some truths and observations that will help you in your quest for the perfect love affair or marriage. Much of this is from my experience as a counselor and reader of astrology and the Science of the Cards, and some of it is from my own personal experience. It is my intention that you get a refreshing new look at your personal relationships through the study of the cards. The Science of the Cards is a spiritual or 'sacred' science. That being the case, if we study it, it is bound to enlighten us in one or more important ways. May this chapter lighten your load and bring more light into what is usually the most challenging area of our life.

RELATIONSHIPS ARE A SPIRITUAL PATH

If we examine the lives of 200 people and look at all their relationships, we will undoubtedly discover that there are many reasons that account for why we enter into love affairs and relationships. We all yearn for that intimacy that a truly close personal relationship promises us. Each time we 'fall in love' we get a taste for just how great life can feel and be. It is those experiences, for the most part, that keep us searching for true love even after we have been devastated emotionally over and over again. We somehow cannot let go of this yearning for a deep, satisfying love.

However, each time we fall in love we run right into the things that prevent us from having this profound experience. It even seems that after we have had a few love affairs, the time it takes to begin confronting the problems that exist in relationships becomes shorter and shorter. That wonderful 'honeymoon period' that we so much enjoy seems to get shorter and shorter. Indeed, for some of us, the honeymoon stage disappears altogether and we nearly lose that dream forever. When we fall in love we become vulnerable to being hurt. After a few such hurts we may decide that we will never let ourselves become that vulnerable again. At the very least we become much more guarded about our feelings.

Taking one step back from all this drama of love relationships we can see that what is really happening in each relationship is that we are being confronted with our own emotional hang-ups. There is an old saying that "Love brings up everything unlike itself." This means that when we are in love, everything within us that is unloving or fearful is forced to come to the surface to be dealt with. Every time we love someone, we stand the chance of having to face those parts of ourselves that believe in love's antithesis—fear and self-rejection. We must find a way to realize and remember that these qualities live in ourselves first. It is impossible to attract an unloving partner if we are loving ourselves. It is only our inner self-rejection that causes us to believe that others are rejecting us. This is a truth that we must hold onto for dear life if we are ever to find our way out of the maze of relationship unhappiness.

This is why relationships are a spiritual path. Spiritual path implies a road that leads us back to our true self. Forget all the associations with the word spiritual that imply anything outside of ourselves and what is important in our lives. Knowledge of our true self is knowledge that will help us in every conceivable way, and should immediately benefit our personal relationships if it has any true value. If we hang out with all the feelings and emotions that come up for us when we are in a relationship, we have the opportunity to learn more about ourselves than in almost any other way. How we truly relate to others in our life is how we relate to ourselves.

Seeing our relationships as a spiritual path puts everything we do in relationships in a new, more positive light. We can now interpret all that happens to us in our relationships as lessons instead of problems and failures. There are no failures on the spiritual path, there are only things to be learned and understood. The path of relationship is one of the highest. Someone who is in a successful relationship is someone who is loving themselves. There are no two ways about it. Being in a good relationship is a symbol that we know how to love ourselves. And isn't this the goal of all spiritual practices?

RELATIONSHIPS ARE OUR PERSONAL MIRRORS

So many of us are so involved in the search for the 'perfect partner' that we forget one of the most basic and important truths about relationships. That is, that our partners are mirrors of ourselves—nothing more and nothing less. Many people get so wrapped up in trying to find out what their partner's motives are, asking whether or not he or she will be around later, and trying to find out whether or not their partner really loves them, that they forget who has the power in the relationship and who is responsible for making it work or not.

This is especially true of those with Libra sun-sign or other strong Libra planets and those whose birth cards are one of the Twos. Twos and Libras are a lot alike because they tend to see themselves as being one half of a pair instead of a single, whole person unto themselves. However, many more of us have Twos in our Life Path cards or have strong Libra or 7th house planetary influences that make us see ourselves the same way as a Two or a Libra. A big part of my work has been to help others see that they are the ones calling the shots in their relationships and to show them how they make their relationship decisions. Many of us need to unhook ourselves from the notion that we are victims in love and begin to get honest with ourselves and admit that we are constantly making decisions about our relationship that determine how it shows up for us and what happens in it. We need to take a look and see what we are doing and realize that we wouldn't have it any other way. In many cases, unacknowledged fear is lying at the core of our relationship problems and prevents us from seeing the truth. We usually don't want to look at our fears and for this reason, it takes us longer to get our power back.

For example, one of my clients is a K♣ man who is 40 years old and has never been married. During our initial reading he asked me why he always chooses women who can't make a commitment in a relationship. Later he told me that what he really wanted was a harem of women and that he couldn't seem to get the women he knew to participate in his harem experience. Now, when I hear anybody talk about their relationship and use the words 'they' or 'she' or 'he' and phrases like "why don't they ever want to commit," I immediately start asking myself what that says about the person asking the question. I

have learned a trick. I just put the word 'I' in place of 'he,' 'she,' or 'them' and I have the answer. I also know that most K♣ have some challenges around losing their personal freedom in a relationship. It is an issue for them personally but unless they are very aware, they will tend to project that issue onto their partners. Looking in my client's astrological chart I also noted that he had a very strong aspect that represented fear of abandonment.

So I began asking him why he has difficulty in making commitments in love and what it is about being committed to one person that is so scary for him. After he got over the initial shock of what I had said, he began to see the truth in it. His own feelings told him that he had a great fear of betrayal and that whenever he got too close to a woman, he became even more afraid of being hurt or abandoned. Thus, he would pull away and want some space, inadvertently creating the very situation he was afraid of, that is, being separated from his loved one. His other ploy was to try and keep multiple relationships going at the same time so that he would never have to worry if one of them hurt him or left him. On a deep emotional level, his drive to create a harem for himself was a defense mechanism aimed at protecting himself from ever being hurt or abandoned again.

Here he was, seeming to attract women who couldn't or wouldn't make commitments and thinking it was some sort of bad luck that he couldn't find anyone who wanted to be committed. In fact, he didn't want to get too close to anyone himself and used his harem idea to keep women at a distance. The truth is that he is a very sensitive person, especially when he is in an intimate relationship. Till this day he has never been able to create his harem.

When I see someone repeatedly trying to make something happen and being unsuccessful I always look at the person to find out why they are stopping themselves. The only reason my client was never able to create it is that his desire for that was based totally on his inner insecurity, which he was unable to face and acknowledge.

I have also had many female clients who are dating married men. I have also had clients who are married and having affairs with other people. This particular pattern has become so familiar to me that I just have to smile every time I hear about it. Anyone with common sense can figure out that a person who is having an affair with someone who is unavailable is also unavailable themselves. Aside from the dishonesty that usually accompanies these kinds of affairs, I see nothing wrong with married people dating unmarried people. The fact is though that these relationships are usually very painful and unfulfilling. They almost seem like something people do to punish themselves. A lot of pain could be avoided if these folks could just admit to themselves that they are not interested in a committed relationship. Then, perhaps, they could choose someone who was unmarried and side step all the dishonesty and hiding that accompanies these affairs.

Choosing a married person to fall in love with is 'safe.' First of all, they will never tell anyone because they are afraid their spouse will find out. Secondly, they will never want a commitment from you because they are already committed to someone. Usually they have children and this is a very strong tie that binds them to their current marriage. It is amazing how many women are doing just this thing, and then bitterly complaining about how little time they get with their lover, how jealous they are of his wife, and how tired they are of lying all the time and compromising their personal sense of integrity. First they consciously choose to have an intimate relationship with a married person, and then they complain about it.

Our relationship issues are 100 percent about our relationship with ourselves. It's just that relationships provide such strong mirrors that we often can't stand to look at ourselves so directly. There is pain in seeing the truth, often so much that we would prefer to live our lives ignoring what is true just to avoid it. The trouble is that only truth will liberate us from the pain, struggle and toil that we call relationships. So, we have two kinds of pain to choose from—the pain of living life ignorantly and the pain of seeing the truth. My master used to say that all we need to do is exchange our pain of living ignorantly for the pain of living in the truth and that little by little, our pain would disappear. The pain of living in ignorance will never go away. It always gets worse and worse.

The fact is that we all consciously choose our relationships. Not only that, but we are extremely picky about it. A person could be introduced to five people with whom they have great planetary aspects and great connections in the cards and they wouldn't be interested in even one of them.

Some who read the descriptions of their birth card in this book will say, "That is not me at all, but it does sound like my boyfriend." This is a common occurrence. Often the partner we attract exemplifies characteristics in ourselves that we either choose to avoid or ones that we didn't know we had. Often it takes an intense relationship experience to show us parts of ourselves that are locked far away from the reach of our conscious minds. It is one of the immutable laws of relationship that we attract others who represent and demonstrate qualities in ourselves. Usually these are qualities that we are afraid to look at or refuse to face.

One of my clients is a 5♣. She has been married three times and is now single again after divorcing her third husband. In truth she didn't really get married the third time. They had a ceremony, which appeared complete with everything, but they never signed a marriage certificate or got a license. The reason she gave was that they both decided that it was better tax-wise to not be officially married. After living together for 7 years and having all of their acquaintances think they were married, they broke up. Her reason: He was never available, never accessible to her. She said he couldn't open up to her emotionally and he had become apathetic about everything. So they broke up and she quickly met two new guys.

The first one lived 3,000 miles away. The second one was local, but they only went out once every two weeks. Occasionally they would take a vacation trip together. While there, he required that they sleep in separate rooms, not just separate beds. And they never made love. He refused to introduce her to his family, saying that he did not want to rush things. This went on for a year. Then, he began asking her to use her credit card to pay for the vacations. She complained that he was so inaccessible. I had given her a reading but she totally denied that she might be the one who was emotionally unavailable, except when a friend asked her, "What would you do if he called you today and asked you to marry him?" She hesitated and mumbled something about not being sure if she would marry him and then said that she would say no.

This woman is a 5♣. If any card in the deck has trouble with commitment, it is a 5♣. This was an unusual example, one in which she totally denied any hand in creating one unsuccessful relationship after another with the same theme. And yet, it was her own lack of commitment that caused her to attract men who were unavailable. Underneath her whole story was a common thread.

SHE was the one who didn't want to get tied down and because she couldn't accept this as part of herself, she created elaborate dramas in her life where the man in her life was always the bad guy—always the one who was unavailable, emotionally or physically. She could never explain why she stayed in these relationships as long as she did. No one was forcing her. Whenever you see someone who is not manifesting the qualities of the descriptions of the cards in this book, take a look at their partner. There, you may see the mirror.

As you study this book, you may discover why you have chosen certain people in your life and why others that are your friends or family have made the choices they made. Don't be surprised to discover that some of these choices were not with people that you shared much in the way of compatibility with. However, we all have very good reasons for making our choices in love. The cards merely help us to make them conscious. Consciousness accelerates our progress and lightens our load. If we are able to see our choices clearly and affirm the reasons for them to ourselves, we will be at peace within, regardless of what they look like on the surface. We all choose relationships that we think will make us happier or better at some level. Let's take a look in the mirror and be open to what it shows us. It might be the most important thing we ever learn in our life.

MAKING THE BEST CHOICE FOR MARRIAGE

If you are truly ready for a long–term relationship such as marriage, you are more likely to choose someone with whom you share a lot of compatibility and less intensity. High intensity in a relationship means that you and your partner seem to constantly challenge each other. There would be fewer times of peace and harmony between you and more of dramatic and emotional turmoil as the two of you deal with all the issues that are sure to come up. Intensity is like friction. It heats up the relationship and smooths out your rough edges. It is great for personal development but it wouldn't bring a lot of pleasure into your life unless you are masochistic.

Though not common, it is possible that a high intensity marriage might be best for you. In this case, you would have made a decision on some level to undergo intense

personal or professional development for an extended period of your life. You would be, in effect, asking for someone who would constantly challenge you so that you would be constantly faced with the areas in which you need to change and develop. Though it may not be a lot of fun, the changes that you would see in yourself as a result may be the most important changes of your life. Ultimately you would learn to love yourself, making a magical transformation that could not have been effected in any other way. This is the power of relationship when harnessed and directed.

In any case, each of us will eventually find that perfect balance of attraction, intensity, and compatibility that best suits us. In using this book you should become more familiar with yourself and your individual needs. Then you will be able to have more fun as you make your choices in relationships more consciously.

HAVING PERSONAL POWER IN OUR RELATIONSHIPS

My definition of having power in relationships is getting all the things needed in a personal relationships. This is especially pertinent in marriage or whatever intimate relationship a person is involved in. If you can have everything you need then you will feel that you have power in your relationships. If you are not getting what you want or need in your closest relationships, you will not feel powerful. You might even feel victimized by your relationships. You might even have many beliefs like "I will never have a truly happy relationship" or "I always attract the wrong person" that you may have accepted as the truth because of all the incidents you have had in your life. If you are having any of these symptoms then this chapter might shed some light on this subject in a way that can really make a difference. Truth is not worth much to me if it doesn't result in having more fun, pleasure, and peace in your life. Hopefully the words herein bring you the best kind of truth—the kind that makes a difference.

No matter how powerful we think we are in our current relationship, we could always use a little more power, especially if we are not happy with it. If you are not in the perfect relationship or if you don't have one, then you could use some of this power right now. But what is this power and how do we obtain it? How can we create a wonderful relationship right now, one that is both harmonious and fun? Read closely and you may discover the answer for yourself.

You already have tons of power ready to be used to achieve your dreams. If one of these dreams is a wonderful relationship, then you have plenty of power in which to create it. It can also be much better than you ever imagined. To achieve the relationship of your dreams, you only have to take this tremendous power that you already possess and move it in a new direction. It is already there but it is being scattered and misdirected. What we are going to do is focus it and aim it. Then, watch miracles happen!

The first step in this process is to get in touch with where your power is heading right now. It is entirely possible that you have made decisions in your recent or not so recent past that are now counterproductive to your finding a wonderful mate. You may have even decided that you would never allow yourself to get close to love again. Many people do and then later forget that they had made this decision. Then they wonder why they never attract anyone with whom they can trust and feel close. We often forget consciously the emotional decisions that we have made in our life. Many of them go unnoticed by our thinking minds but affect us just the same.

Since we are regaining the helm, as it were, in this area of our life, we must first see where our boat is heading and that leads us to the first immortal truth of love and relationships: Things are the way they are because that is how we insist they must be. We wouldn't have it any other way, even if it were offered to us on a golden platter so to speak. The first step here is to take a look at the way your life is in the relationships area and realize that it is exactly as you want it to be. Now that's a funny thing to say since you are probably reading this hoping to find out how to make things better in this area. For me to say that it is already just the way you want it is somewhat of a paradox. You may not believe this at all. However, you must believe it if you are ever going to have different results in your love life. There is no other choice.

It can be difficult for us to take full responsibility for our lives and say to ourselves: "I wouldn't have it any other way," but this is the starting point and the foundation of having power in our relationships. We are either the cause in our life or the victim of some more powerful cause outside of ourselves. This is really an area where we have a choice. We CHOOSE whether to be victims or creators. If you want to have more power in your life and in your choice of relationships, you have no choice but to believe that you have the power to create. This also implies that you are already creating your life just the way it is right now. There is no escaping this unspoken law of life. The question is, which will you choose? Now is the time to make that choice.

Jesus said that the Kingdom of Heaven is within us. If we are to access this Kingdom, we must affirm for ourselves that it is indeed there and that we are already rubbing the magic lamp. The Genie is already working overtime for us all, creating everything that you now see standing before you. Every single thing in your life, especially your relationships and the things that you own and call 'yours' are things that you specifically requested and received. Each of these things were visualized first and acquired later—your thought and manifestation power at work. Everything that you will have in the future likewise will be created by the things you are thinking right now. Realizing this puts you ahead of 99 percent of everyone else on the planet in terms of getting what you want in a relationship. You chose this person you are with, or you chose to not have anybody. Why did you do it? That is a better question than "Why can't I have what I want?" which is totally untrue.

As a professional reader and counselor, I have seen this power of choice at work and the consequences of believing that we did not make those choices ourselves. Much of my work with clients is to help get them back in touch with their power by showing them that they are the ones that made their relationship choices. Once they see this clearly, a certain freedom emerges in them. Having regained their power, they are now ready to use it to create something different in their lives.

For some reason, the process of realizing the truth about our choices is a fearful and often painful one. We just don't seem to want to know the truth about ourselves and what we are really up to. We seem to prefer to live in some sort of fantasy place where good and bad things just happen to us, a world where we are either blessed or cursed and we have nothing to do with our happiness or fulfillment. Yet, this is the furthest thing from the truth. We are the creators of our fate, the captains of our destiny and no one is to blame but ourselves if we are unhappy. Likewise we deserve all the credit for every good thing in our life. This first step, that of acknowledging our power and seeing how and why we have made all of our current choices in relationships and other areas is the most important and critical one of all. This awareness that we apply to our lives is the magic elixir that opens up a new world of possibilities. Though painful or fearful to the uninitiated, start asking yourself the following questions:

1. Why did I choose my current relationship?

2. What am I getting out of this relationship that makes it so important to have this particular person with all their positives and negatives?

3. What would I change about this relationship if I could?

4. What is the most fearful aspect of this relationship?

5. How would I feel about leaving this person and being alone? How do I feel about being alone?

The most powerful and addictive relationships of our lives, the ones that we fall into head over heels and lose control in, are the most revealing in terms of how we are in relationship and what are some of the deepest unfulfilled aspects of ourselves. Many of my clients have been embroiled in destructive, codependent, and addictive love affairs and marriages that have lasted years and that have taken even longer to understand. These key relationships hold the most profound information about the secrets of our own hearts. If we are ever to get our power back in our relationships, we must begin to understand ourselves. These relationships offer the biggest opportunity to get this invaluable information. I suggest that you ask the following questions about any of those relationships that you may have been in:

1. What was it about that other person that made me feel so good? What was the thing about them that caused me to fall in love with them when we first met?

2. How did I feel when the relationship ended? What was missing in my life at that time that I may have felt was irreplaceable?

3. What did it mean that I couldn't make that relationship work? What did that say about me?

4. What was it about that other person that made me the most angry? What made me the most afraid?

5. Sum up what that person is like in one sentence. Fill in the blank:

That person is _____.

6. Try these fill in the blanks if they seem appropriate:

That person will never be happy because

_____.

I could never trust that person because

_____.

I ended that relationship because

_____.

Now, go back over your answers to all these questions and look at them from another perspective. Assume for this next step that you are the one who was 100 percent responsible for the relationship and what happened in it. Assume for a moment that you are the one who created the relationship and that you are the one that ended it. Imagine that your partner had nothing to do with it, that they were just playing a role on your stage and that you fed them the lines that they spoke, that nothing was done without your permission, that it all happened as you had planned it. Review all the questions again from this point of view, even if you don't really believe it now. Once you have done that, answer these questions:

1. What did I choose that person for? What is it in myself that I choose them to awaken in me or to help me develop in myself?

2. What are the qualities in them that I liked so much that are really my own qualities?

3. What is it about myself that is so difficult to look at—the things that my partner reminds me of?

4. Why did I decide to end the relationship? (Regardless of whether they seemed to end it or not, assume that YOU ended it when you answer this question.)

5. How does this relationship remind me of the others that I have created? What pattern is revealed here in terms of my choices in love relationships?

6. What do these patterns tell me about myself? If all of these other people that I have been in a relationship with have similar qualities, what qualities in myself do these reflect? (For example, if you have attracted partners unwilling to commit themselves, why is it that you are unwilling to make a commitment?)

7. What did I learn about myself in this relationship?

8. How consciously did I choose this person? Did I acknowledge what I was looking for before I chose them? Did I have a list of what I was wanting? How specific was it? Did I get what I asked for?

9. What characteristics of my partner were not on my shopping list (things that I did not specify clearly)?

10. If I could improve on that last relationship, what new elements would I choose to create in my next relationship? How important are those elements to me?

If you have answered those questions, you are getting a feeling for having power in your relationships. The best approach to love is to consciously take charge of our choices, assuming total responsibility for all of our choices in the past.

This new way of looking at our life is may be a little unfamiliar to many people. It is not a popular point of view and few choose to look at life this way. The ones that are looking at life this way, though, are the ones that are successful in their life and in their relationships. A little practice with these principles brings great success.

There is nothing wrong with any of the choices you have made. You had good reasons for every relationship that you have been in. There is no guilt, there is no shame and no blame. Each relationship has brought you many blessings of one kind or another. We never fall in love with someone unless we are getting something extremely valuable out of it. The process that you are going through in this chapter is one of distinguishing what it is that you are getting out of your relationships. These are keys to you. Once we know what we are choosing and why, we can choose alternative and more constructive ways of fulfilling our needs. Let me illustrate with a small story.

I once had a devastating affair with a woman that I was very incompatible with. As an astrologer I knew ahead of time that we had little in common, but still, I felt that I had to 'have' her. I tried everything in the book to make her part of my life. I really pulled out all the stops and did things that I will never do again to keep her. But in the end it all failed.

It took me four years to get over the feelings I had for her. I would ask myself again and again, 'Why did I want her so much?' and 'What was it about her that made me feel so special and good inside?' I knew on some level that there was something important for me to learn about myself, so I persisted with the questions until some answers began to appear. I had been totally addicted to her and later realized that there were things about her that boosted my self-esteem. I considered her to be a very beautiful woman and I felt that I was a more special person when she was seen with me. She had high self-esteem. She was somewhat proud and confident and strong-willed. She was also very independent and I realized later that she represented a part of myself that wanted to be more independent in love relationships. She also took very good care of her body and herself and this was something else that I wanted in my life. Overall, it was the self-esteem aspect that was the strongest pull but it was the total combination of qualities that caused such a strong addiction in me.

After years of learning about myself and reflecting on that relationship I have found peace within myself. I have realized that each and every thing that I loved about her were things that I deserved to have in my life and things that I could give to myself personally. I learned that I could love myself in the same way I loved her and bring all that love back to myself. I now give myself the esteem, freedom, respect, and admiration that I once gave to her in the hopes that she would stay with me. It was a very painful process, but in retrospect that relationship was one of the most important and powerful of my life. It showed me what I most needed to give and create for myself. It showed me the areas within myself where I felt lacking and needy, where I held self-limiting concepts about who I was and what I could do. It is a beautiful process to take such a huge amount of love that was once reserved for some other person and give it back to ourselves. This is 'The Gift of the Magi' in the truest sense of the word.

Our entire society, its music, television, and movies are all centered around the big fantasy that we will find someone who will answer all of our prayers. You won't find much support for 'finding the love inside yourself' in all that is out there. Just listen to all the songs on the radio. Almost every one gives total credit for the magic in a relationship to the other person. "You make me feel so good" and so on. The other half of the songs out there give all the blame to the other person. "You tore up my heart and threw it away" and the like. That belief, that we are victims in love, is one of the most destructive and prevalent of our current age. However, it can be eliminated from our life simply by using our power to see the truth. We really are the creators of everything in our life.

The exploration of ourselves is the final frontier. This journey starts to get very exciting too, as we begin peeling back the surface layers and begin to see the beautiful person inside. It is like the best mystery movie you ever saw. We don't know just what is going to emerge from within us, but we know it is going to be good and that it is going to feel really good too. It all starts by asking the right questions and daring to believe that we are the creators of it all. We are created by God and we have God within us. If God is our creator and he created us in His image, then we must be creators too. It is this approach to life that leads us

back to our inner divinity. Our relationships can be one of the most important vehicles to lead us back to this rightful place in the scheme of things. Our relationships are our mirrors that help give us the truth and clarity to see through the illusions of life and to restore us to our thrones where we belong.

THE NINE GOLDEN TRUTHS OF RELATIONSHIPS

After doing over a thousand readings and counseling sessions I have found some essential truths about relationships that can serve as guiding lights during times of conflict. As a matter of fact, most relationship problems can be traced to violations of these truths by one or both of the partners involved. There may actually be more truths that should be on this list. You can add your own based upon your successes in love.

There is a lot of value in realizing these truths. Personal relationships are the hardest area in which to remain objective and rational. Relationship is the easiest area for us to blame others for our problems and escape responsibility for our actions and choices. It is the area where there are the most confusion and irrational words and actions, the area where most of us need the most help in clarifying what is going on and how we can have more success. It is likely that you may reject one or more of these truths at first glance. But I have discovered that these truths reign supreme in all successful relationships. For that reason, we can attain more success and happiness just by pondering over them. They can remove unclarity about our love lives and lead us to the place where we can make better decisions and choices in this vital area. So, if you are ready, let's explore some of these and see how we are doing.

Truth Number One

WE are the ones who choose our partners, not the other way around.

Many people would like us to believe that their partners forced themselves upon them or that they had no choice in whether or not to be with a certain person. They would like to blame their partner or blame God or blame their parents for who they are with. However, the truth is that they made that choice completely by themselves, and for their own reasons. Not only that, they chose that particular person and probably rejected many other possible choices in order to have that person. Our choices in the area of love are very specific. We may not be at all conscious of why we are with who we are with, but there is no mistake that we are extremely picky about it. Exploring our reasons for choosing those we do pick can reveal a lot of much-needed self-understanding in this important area. If you are currently in a relationship that doesn't seem to be working for you, consider why. Even if someone comes on to you very strong, all you have to do is say "no" and mean it and they will go away.

Truth Number Two

No one can make us stay in a bad relationship but ourselves.

Just like Truth Number One, we are the ones in control of our love lives. Whether or not we realize the true reasons why, we only stay in a relationship if we are getting something out of it that is very important to us. It might be our values, or beliefs, our family peer pressure or something, but there is always something that keeps us there and it is not anything that is beyond our control or ability to change. For this reason, no one has any right to complain about their current love lives. Anybody can do most anything they like anytime. Many people are in abusive relationships. Perhaps their partner is an alcoholic or may be physically abusive or unfaithful. Ask yourself why they would choose such a relationship—sometimes it takes some searching to come up with the answers. The answers are always there, however, and often they will surprise you. Some are there because they would rather be abused than have to be alone for any period of time. These are the ones that value security above all else. Others choose an abusive relationship because deep down they don't like themselves and they want someone to punish them. In all cases, however, we find that the relationship they are in reflects to them the places where they need to love themselves. This leads us directly into the next truth.

Truth Number Three

Though together, we each chose our current relationship for our own personal and specific reasons.

There is a prevailing fantasy that somehow there is some commonality between us and our partner that is more important than our personal reasons for being with them. Some of us undoubtedly believe that there are some 'special reasons' for being together that are more important than our personal feelings and issues. I am not denying that there are some couples that come together and achieve great things in their life, but you can also bet that each of them is getting each and every one of their personal needs and desires fulfilled at the same time. Your relationship is for YOU, not your partner or for those other people in your life. If it wasn't giving you something that you wanted, you wouldn't be there.

Truth Number Four

All we can see in our partner is our self.

This is probably one of the toughest of the truths. Not that the concept is that difficult, but putting it into working practice is one of the most challenging things we can do in life. Regardless of what you may think about your partner, whatever it is that you do see in him or her is YOU and nothing but YOU. If you like the way your partner is so mature and responsible, it is because you like that part of yourself. If you dislike the way your partner talks to his or her mother on the phone, it is because you dislike those parts of yourself that act in that way. If we sit down and take an inventory of all the qualities that we can recognize in our partners, and list them under two headings, "Those qualities that I love about my partner" and "Those qualities that I hate about my partner," we will have a pretty accurate map of how much and where we love or hate ourselves. I have found that often, we choose certain people to be with in a relationship who have certain exaggerated qualities that we dislike very much. We usually make these kinds of choices because we truly desire to develop some love for those same qualities in our self. If we just step back from our normal way of looking at relationships for a minute and start to see all people in relationship as being there to learn to love themselves, we will begin to have some incredible breakthroughs in our understanding of our own choices.

Much of what goes on in relationships is male-female stuff. Dr. John Gray's books go into great detail in this area and I would highly recommend all of them as survival handbooks for relationships. It is because so many of us have inner male-female conflicts that we are so attracted to relationships, and why these relationships are so difficult. If you are a man, your partner represents your inner female side. How you see her and how you treat her reflects just how comfortable you are with your inner female, your mother, and all expressions of femininity in the world. Likewise, if you are a woman, the man in your life personifies your issues centered around father and the male principle in general. None of us escape this mirror effect. And that is how it should be. We can learn more about ourselves by looking in the mirror than without it.

Truth Number Five

We cannot hurt others and others cannot hurt us. We can only hurt our self.

Boy, this is often a tough one to swallow! Not only that, but there are so many people who really believe they can hurt someone else. Not hurting our partner is a catch-all for so many lies and untruths in relationships that I cannot begin to emphasize just how destructive it can be. So many times I have counseled those who lie to their partners, stay in bad relationships much longer than is healthy for them, and allow their partners to perform all sorts of abuse on them, all in the name of not wanting to hurt their partner. One example is the person who is having an affair. They will use this excuse to have a reason not to tell the truth to their partner. They have already lost all the intimacy in their relationship by leading a double life and lying to their partner, but they are afraid that they might hurt their partners if they told the truth. The truth is that they are hurting themselves in a big way by compromising themselves and living a life of lies and shame. Another example is the person who is staying in a relationship that is going nowhere because they don't want to hurt their partner by leaving them. In all such cases, a closer examination reveals that the person is getting something out of being with such a codependent partner, a payoff, such as feeling worthwhile, or in control. The truth is that they don't want a REAL relationship with someone who is healthy because they are afraid, either of losing control or of having to face their own fears of abandonment and rejection. These are the real motivators under all such situations.

Anytime we withhold information from our partner about our self because we don't want to hurt them, it is time be honest with ourselves about our intentions. Telling ourselves that we don't want to hurt them is a lie. There is always another reason for lying or for any situation where we are using this excuse. It's not hard to find either.

We cannot hurt anyone, period. No one can hurt us either, unless we have created such an expectation of them being some specific way that we feel pain when they change. To see it more clearly, we set ourselves up for being hurt by creating unreasonable expectations of others or the world around us. Whenever I have a client who is stuck with this belief that they can hurt someone, I tell this story.

If I suddenly came up to you, with a painful look on my face and pleading eyes and said to you, "You must give me $5,000 or I am going to feel real hurt. I have to have that $5,000 and if you don't give it to me, you will be responsible for really hurting me so bad that I will never forgive you." Well, how would you react to this? Suppose this was just someone off the street, that you never met before. You would be surprised to see that some of these same clients actually entertain the notion of "Well, maybe I could give them the money." It bewilders me a bit, but as I tell the story, I watch the looks on their faces and see how they react. I can tell that this is just the kind of story that gets them. Not only that, but these are the kinds of situations that they get hooked into over and over again.

But what is it about these people that they would entertain the idea of handing over $5,000 to a complete stranger just so they wouldn't feel responsible for hurting them? Well, to begin with, let's state the facts and get that part of the story settled. If I approach you asking for this $5,000, it is obvious that I have set myself up to be hurt. In essence, I have created a structure in my mind and emotions that says "I promise to feel pain if I don't get that $5,000." Now, if I have made that promise to myself, is it anyone else's responsibility? I created the need and the expectation and I will be the one to suffer because I have told myself so. This is exactly what happens in relationships in many different forms. One of the partners has expectations that are unreal or at the least, beyond the capacity of the other partner to fulfill. Then they feel hurt and upset, etc.

But why would anyone fall for that sort of manipulation in a relationship? Why would anyone believe that they are responsible for something that someone else set themselves up for? Why would they believe that they can hurt someone else? My study of astrology has revealed that in every case of someone who falls for these sorts of situations, the person is afraid of being rejected by the other. All of those so called "kindhearted" people out there are invariably very afraid of being rejected or disapproved of by others. It is there in their chart and it is there in their behavior.

So, if you find yourself falling for any of these situations, stop and ask yourself what you are really afraid of. If you address that fear you will save yourself a lot of pain and suffering as you do things to prevent your partner from not liking you. In the end they will always reject you anyway. If you are not loving yourself, others pick up on it and are repelled by it. They will reject you sooner or later.

Truth Number Six

The best thing we can do to love and help our partner is to love our self.

Many of us try and try to help our partners and do things that we think will make them happy. This is a natural extension of our love for them. But the truly best thing we can do for them is to stay happy ourselves. This means taking care of our health and doing the things that we enjoy the most. If you are not happy within yourself, you will have a hard time helping or loving your partner.

Have you ever noticed that each time you get on an airplane to travel that one of the important rules they announce in the beginning of the aircraft safety spiel is to always put on your own oxygen mask before attempting to put masks on your children? Does that seem unloving to you? It is a simple matter to realize that if you are not breathing properly you will not be much good in helping your children get their oxygen masks on.

But in our relationships, we try the same thing. We try and help our partners and our children before taking care of our own basic needs. In doing so, we are less capable of helping or loving them. In addition, we give them a role model of someone who doesn't love themselves. This is perhaps more damaging than anything else we do. The weird thing is that we usually expect some sort of pat on the back for being so loving and compassionate in these situations.

The truth is that if you are not loving yourself, you are a model for unhappiness and no one wants to be around you anyway. Don't kid yourself about how kind and loving you are. If you are not loving yourself, you are not a loving person, period. Put yourself first and get happy. Then, no matter what you do, your energy will act like a generator to pull others around you up to your level, a level where life is good and prosperous.

Truth Number Seven

Love always wants more of itself and love always brings up everything unlike itself.

When we first fall in love, we so much enjoy that feeling of being appreciated and loved for who we are that we strive to experience it as much as we can. For many of us, this is such a special time, an experience that we don't have every day. The feeling of union and closeness that love brings is like a cool fountain of water in a hot desert. As we drink from that fountain, we want more, we want to dive in and drink our fill of the cool and rejuvenating waters of love. In order to experience the joy of love and lovemaking more, we open up our feeling side. Most people feel more alive when they are in love precisely because they have allowed their feeling sides to open up. They notice the smells in the air, the beauty of a sunset or a clear summer's day. Life suddenly becomes magical and joyous.

As we open ourselves up to take in this abundance of pleasure and good feelings, funny things begin to happen. Suddenly we find that we are more afraid than usual. Then we discover that we have become more emotional and touchy. Our feelings get hurt more easily. Finally, we realize that we are truly vulnerable, especially to our partner. The least little thing they say has so much meaning to us that it carries a big impact. We are so open to them that we now seem to be at their mercy. If they say the wrong thing they could destroy us. If they reject us now, we will be hurt worse than ever before. What are we going to do in this situation?

This is a typical scenario and most of us have experienced it at least once. This is the nature of love and as Kahlil Gibran says, we best not get too close to love if we are not ready and willing to be thrashed by it. It isn't the fault of love that we get so scared and get hurt so much, though. What happens is that when we are in love, we become much more aware of our own emotional blocks and negative beliefs. In truth most of us have some of what I call 'negative emotional programs.' These are basically automatic emotional reactions to certain stimuli that are negatively based. A negative emotional program is one where we don't have any conscious choice about it. Any time and place that X happens, we react with Y. Most, if not all of these negative programs are based upon something that is really true. We might even logically be able to look at the situation and tell ourselves, "Why did I do that? I wasn't in any danger." But emotionally, we are hooked in. It is a pattern that has been set in the past sometime, either in our childhood or in some former life.

What's important about these patterns is that we can structure our life in such a way that we can avoid having to deal with them for the most part. Anthony Robbins, in his book, *Unlimited Power*, says that people actually do more to avoid negative situations than they will do to achieve positive ones. In any event, it is plain to see that most of us will go to great lengths to get our lives set up in such a way that we do not have to deal with our negative emotional patterns. For example, I dislike being rejected by those in authority so I have structured my life in such a way that I never have to deal with it—I am self-employed!

However, when we fall in love with someone and begin opening up emotionally, guess what happens? You bet, all those areas where we have our life so well protected just melt away in the fires of our love. Now, everything within us that stands between us and feeling great all the time comes up for us to deal with. This is why I say that love brings up everything unlike itself. It always has and always will. When we are in love we are striving to feel that way all the time. Those negative emotional patterns that tell us that we are not loved must be faced again and again until we can re-program them to reflect the loving world that we so much want to keep going in our lives. Sadly most people don't get too far in this endeavor. Most relationships these days don't last very long beyond the honeymoon stage.

Truth Number Eight

Lying destroys intimacy.

Regardless of what we tell ourselves about why it is okay to lie to our spouse, the bottom line is that as soon as we lie to them, we lose that feeling of closeness that we are in the relationship to feel in the first place. Love requires complete openness. When we are in love we want to share all of ourselves with our partners. As soon as we hold back any part of the truth with our partners, to that extent, we have created separation. It goes against the nature of love to lie. We lie because we are afraid. Love says "Don't be afraid, everything will be fine." Our fears say, "Oh yeah, but what will happen to me if this or that happens?" When we lie to our partners, we make a commitment to our fears. We in effect make a conscious choice to take action (the lie is an action) based upon what we are afraid of instead of what we love. Each time we lie, we dramatically reduce our ability to feel the joy and pleasure of love. We may be able to enjoy the sexual stimulation, but the emotional intimacy is missing. Without that intimacy, we cannot really enjoy the sex or the relationship. As Kahlil Gibran says, in his book, *The Prophet*, you will:

> *"pass out of love's threshing-floor, Into the seasonless world where you shall laugh, but not all of your laughter, and weep, but not all of your tears."*

This is the place where over 90 percent of us live. Think about it. I am not saying that lying is the cause of this, but only that lying has this effect. There are some cases where withholding the truth can be a loving thing. But these cases are far too rare for any of us to tell ourselves that we are doing a good thing by lying to our mates. If we lie, we are creating distance in our relationship. We might as well get divorced or leave them, for in effect, that is exactly what we are doing.

Truth Number Nine

Marriage is not forever.

Much of what I learned as a child about marriage was that it was a life-long vow and that only bad people got divorced from each other. To get divorced was considered one of those nasty sins that only the lowest and most despicable people would stoop to doing. However, as I grew up, I noticed that a lot of people were getting divorced. My own parents broke up when I was 19 and many of my friends' parents got divorced too. Now, as a student of the science of relationships and a professional counselor, I can see that the role of marriage in our society is in a great transition. It is in the process of being redefined, a process that hasn't yet been completed. The reasons for marriage that existed 50 years ago or 100 years ago just don't apply today. Everything is accelerated in many respects. People get married and divorced more frequently than ever before. In striving for role models for marriage and relationship, many of us feel lost. All we have is television and movies and the role models we find there don't ever work when put into practical use.

I have arrived at some relevant ideas about marriage that fit most cases and that can help put it all in perspective. First of all, marriage is not forever. It only lasts as long as it is a positive and important aspect for each of the individuals involved. Once it loses its meaning or relevance for one or both of the partners, it is time for it to come to an end. Remember Golden Truth Number Six? Well, if we are not loving ourselves by being in a marriage, then we are not loving our partners either. No matter what we tell ourselves or them.

If two people truly love each other, then they must always be aware of the needs of their partners as well as their own. If the marriage is bad for your partner and you love him or her, wouldn't you want something better for them? Divorce can be very loving in some cases, an act that affirms the needs of the two people and sets each of them on their way toward a new life of joy and fulfillment. Perhaps someday we will have an entirely new association with divorce, perhaps we will call it a graduation from one stage and the beginning of the next one. That is exactly what it is anyway.

Of course, divorce can also be a convenient escape route, a means to avoid having to face our feelings or the consequences of our actions. There are many people today who would rather not take any responsibility for their choices or creations. For these people, divorce offers a convenient escape route. Since divorce has now become an acceptable thing to do, no one will blame us for it. In the end we have only ourselves to answer to.

Relationships of all kinds are opportunities to grow in our loving and understanding of ourselves. Nothing can cause us to face ourselves more directly and intensely than an intimate relationship. Whether we like what we see once we are there depends entirely upon how well we know ourselves and how much we can love who we are. Even what someone may call 'the worst relationship of their life' can be the most valuable in terms of what they learn. Learning more about ourselves increases our ability to be happy.

Ultimately being in a relationship brings us to a place where we can experience the most joy out of life. We can learn how to be in that blissful 'in love' state all the time, not because we have found the perfect partner, but because we have found ourselves. These Nine Truths can be very helpful in separating the truth from the lies that we tell ourselves. They can help us through the maze of emotional turmoil and give us some anchors in reality upon which we can depend. If we remember them in times of need, they will be of help.

SUGGESTIONS FOR CREATING OR HAVING A SUCCESSFUL RELATIONSHIP

Most of us will admit that we desire a good relationship. It is basic to our human makeup to want one, it is part of our genetic material. We cannot escape this fact any more than we can escape the fact that we need food or water. Of course we probably wouldn't die if we were without relationships, but once we have our basic needs met, the next thing we seek is to find intimacy and commonality with another person. In my personal and professional search for the truth about relationships and the knowledge to make one work, I have discovered that there are certain things that we can DO to accelerate the process of creating and maintaining a good relationship. Not everything in this life is accomplished through doing, but if you are looking for things to do to improve your chances, this list may spark some ideas in you. Just reading these chapters will give you a lot of good knowledge about the scope of what you are attempting. But now you may be ready to act. If so, read on for some suggestions.

> 1. Find a meaningful purpose for your life and make that your first priority.

It is interesting that many of the cards in the deck tend to lose the power of their Birth Card when they fall in love. The 8♣ is a classic example. An 8♣ person is, by birthright, one of the most powerful and successful cards in the deck. When an 8♣ woman falls in love and allows her relationship to assume a greater priority than her purpose or work, she inevitably suffers and loses her identity. This is because she then operates as the Q♣ who, though powerful herself, is not as powerful or successful as the 8♣.

I have found in my practice that a great majority of relationship problems are settled by simply being clear on our life's purpose and never allowing anything to come between us and that purpose. Even if your life's purpose is to raise children and be a good mother, this may have to take a higher priority than being a good wife or lover. Most Q♥ and 9♣ women can attest to this.

I have also noted that when a person is really clear about their life's purpose, they have much greater success in their choice of mates. Is this because they are

thinking more clearly? Not really. It is because they are now clear on their life priorities and know exactly what kind of mate would best support those priorities and directions. If I am committed to good health, for example, I would never attract a partner that had poor health habits. This is not a judgment about them, but simply a choice. It would not be fair to either of us to fall in love when we both are so different. But the real bottom line is not usually health issues but more importantly, what are each of your major life directions? If you are not clear about where you are going in this life or what you are really up to, how can you expect to find someone that fits together with you?

I learned this lesson the hard way. After two unsuccessful marriages I realized that I had not found my life's purpose yet. Once I did, I made a choice for a relationship with someone that is a better fit than I could have imagined. We are both joined by our purpose and each of us is clear that we would not sacrifice that purpose just to be with each other. We are together because being together enhances each of our life's purposes. This is the first time in my life I have made a relationship decision from this point and I can tell you it is a totally different feeling. I feel much more powerful and in my rightful place. I have much less fear of abandonment, perhaps because inwardly I know that I will not abandon myself, not even for the love of my wife.

> 2. When envisioning a person to be with, be specific.

If you are single or between relationships and have decided that you are ready to start a new relationship, be as specific as you can about what kind of person you want to have in your life. As strange as it may sound, you will attract a person who exactly meets your specifications. If you are hazy about your specifications, you will attract someone who is a little hazy in his or her ability to meet your needs. Several times in my life I had the opportunity to do just that. I was single and I wrote down a list of the qualities of the kind of woman I wanted to have in my life. Later, after I was again in a relationship, I found the list tucked away in a notebook and lo and behold I had gotten exactly what I had asked for. Each time I also wished I had been more specific. Though the person met every criteria on my list, I had failed to list certain other qualities that I now realized were very important and regretfully missing from the person I had attracted. I guarantee that the same thing will happen to you.

We are not used to being so specific and detailed in the areas of love. We would like to believe that we will just magically attract the perfect person by virtue of the goodness in our hearts. However, the truth is that we are the creators of everything in our life and bear the responsibility for what we have created. For that reason it behooves us to take some time and deliberate carefully when we envision in our minds just how our perfect mate would be. Remember that it is our thoughts that create our world. Everything in your world was once a thought or desire of yours. Use this power to create someone that truly fits well with you in important ways.

3. Once you're in a relationship, learn to communicate with your partner.

Communication is absolutely necessary in any relationship and even more so in an intimate relationship. The most important thing you and your partner can communicate with each other is your feelings. Feelings are the vital element that bridges the gap between unclear and clear communications. Feelings reveal what is really going on between you and your partner at the most basic and important level—the level of needs and fears. We all have needs and fears and our feelings tell us what they are and if they are getting met. If you are a person who is out of touch with your feelings, your chances of having a successful relationship are slim at best. Anyone can learn to get in touch and then communicate their feelings. It just takes intent and practice. All of the books by Dr. John Gray are excellent handbooks for those who are in a relationship and want to make it work. His books include *What You Feel You Can Heal*; *Men, Women, and Relationships*; and *Men Are from Mars, Women Are from Venus*. Go out and get one of his books and begin reading. They are some of the best books I have seen and I have used them myself for much greater success in communicating with my wife.

If you are completely out of touch with your feelings, you may require some other support or service to help you re-establish the connection. It is a very common condition in our society today, but it can be healed and changed. There are many ways to get this connection made with yourself ranging from therapies of different kinds to doing Yoga. To feel is to be alive and to taste the joy of life. When Christ said "Let the dead bury the dead," he may have been talking about all the people in the world who are no longer feeling anything because they have closed themselves off. If you think you are dead, it is never too late to live again.

There are some experiences that are available with a partner that cannot be had by ourselves alone. Beyond that even, are experiences of a blissful nature that can happen when two people really apply themselves to creating a successful relationship. After two marriages and other failed love affairs, I thought I knew what love was, or could be. I still had dreams of a wonderful marriage or bonding with another, even though I hadn't yet experienced it. I can honestly say now that I am experiencing things with my wife that I never even imagined before. In other words, I didn't even know what I was missing. I just kept working at it, hoping for something good at the end of my efforts. There are realms of love and caring and intimacy that can only be experienced by two people who have truly opened up and revealed their fears and weaknesses to each other. Sadly, most people alive today will never have these blissful experiences of being with another person. Many of them have already given up any hope of marital or intimate happiness with another. But this experience is where we all are destined to arrive someday, whether in this lifetime or the next, or the next.

Why not start now and take a chance on love? Reveal yourself to your partner fully. If they choose to not be with you just as you are, there is no blame in this. It only means that the two of you are not right for each other. There is always someone else who is right for you, if that is the case. But you will only find that person if you are willing to give the universe a chance, by being who you are completely. The potential rewards are great and you have only your misery to lose. Good luck!

The Cards and Relationships

5 hours of instruction, $74.95

This five-hour live recorded class with Robert is where you will learn everything you need to know about how to use the cards in all of your relationship matters. Listen and follow along as Robert covers these topics:

- The many ways the Science of the Cards can help you with your relationships.
- What is attraction between couples and how does it operate? What connections are most responsible for it?
- The most important thing to consider when you are looking at two people's possibilities for a good relationship.
- How the relationship connections are derived.
- The important difference between Life Spread and Spiritual Spread connections.
- The number one most powerful sexual connection, and why.
- Who is marriageable, who isn't, and why? Which cards should never get married?
- How to do a relationship reading without using the Love Cards book.
- How to choose the best people for work, legal, health practitioners, and others that are non-intimate relationships.
- The importance of the Moon connection and how to spot these people quickly.
- When Saturn relationships are desired and beneficial.

These and many more topics are covered and many examples are covered as Robert interacts with the members of the class. This class will make you a master of choosing relationships.

The Intermediate Workshop

Six hours of instruction and handouts, $89.95

Also includes the yearly spreads for the fourteen people discussed in the class. This video workshop is all about learning how to use *The Cards of Your Destiny* book to make more accurate predictions. Learn the "Rules of Interpretation" that help you decide which cards in your yearly spreads are the most important. Learn how to find information in the yearly spreads on specific topics such as money, love, health, and travel. Watch Robert as he reviews all the elements of a yearly reading and how you can get the real messages that are there to be found. Hear questions and responses from the class and learn to interpret your cards better utilizing the latest discoveries.

***

The Advanced Card Training Course

Four hours of instruction and The Advanced Oracle Workbook (ebook format), $89.95

This original and ancient method of reading the cards is what you will encounter here. It is, by definition, more complex. But at the same time it offers you a wealth of information that is not available using the basic methods. This is the system as it was taught originally to Robert Lee Camp. His books took this complex method and simplified it to make it easier for everyone to use. But you can learn this ancient method now and have two to three times more information about anyone you are reading for.

You will learn:

- How the Life Spread and Spiritual Spread are interconnected.
- How to create all of the 520 Yearly Spreads in the Cards of Your Destiny with only a deck of cards in your hand.
- How to Quadrate the deck to generate these yearly spreads and generate the Grand Solar Spreads.
- How to locate and identify every card in the Yearly Spreads while looking at the Grand Solar Spreads, including the Environment, Displacement, Long Range, Pluto, etc.
- How to locate and use the Underlying Cards that give more meaning to each card in a Yearly Spread.

- How to find the vertical Long Range Card, the Seven-Year Environment, Displacement, Pluto, and Result cards and how these become particularly important in certain years of life.
- How all the Auspicious Events listed in the Cards of Your Destiny book are identified in the Grand Solar Spreads.
- The particular significance of the Critical Year, Rise to the Pinnacle, Pinnacle, and Most Blessed Years.
- Why the Fixed and Semi-Fixed cards are connected and why they are immune to many auspicious events.

PERSONAL READINGS AND COMPUTERIZED REPORTS

http://www.7thunders.com/products-services/destiny-reports/
Book of Destiny Yearly Report
35–45 pages in color, $24.95
These reports are great for personal use or for birthday presents. Every card in your yearly spreads is laid out and described in an organized manner. Includes your yearly Environment and Displacement Cards and reports on your Birthday Card as well as your Planetary Ruling Card or Personality Cards.

Lover's Profile Report
20–26 pages in color, $24.95
From our new version of Love Cards Reporter, this report takes you and someone close to you and does a complete analysis of your compatibility as taught in the book *Love Cards*. Includes the affirmations and in-depth analysis of each of the seven most significant connections between the partners of an intimate relationship. You will have to see these reports to really believe how great they are. They incorporate many advanced features to present an easy-to-read and very informative analysis of two people in love. You can also specify this as a **Friends and Family Report** or a **Business Associates Report**, which has completely different interpretations for those kinds of relationships.

A Personal Reading with Robert Lee Camp
http://www.7thunders.com/personal-readings/personal-readings-with-robert/
60 minutes by phone, or in person, recorded, $300.00
Applying the Science of the Cards and astrology, my intent in giving you a reading is to open up the doors of your understanding of yourself. My readings are based upon the premise that you are the creator of your destiny. If I can reveal your power to you, along with the reasons why you have created your life to be the way it is right now, then you are free to make whatever changes you desire in your life and create a life that is closer to your ideals and dreams. I will do a complete analysis of both your Life Path Cards and your Astrological Natal Chart as you and I explore your deepest issues and reasons for being here on the planet. Includes the natal analysis, examination of your relationships, as well as the next one to three years of significant events. Once you know the cycles you are currently in, you can plan better for the future and take advantage of the influences.

Professional Destiny Software

http://www.7thunders.com/products-services/software/
We now have computer software for PCs and online software for all computers that do readings and create reports you can sell or share with others. The online versions, which are compatible with all computers that can browse the web, create Love Cards reports and Yearly Destiny Reports and are subscription based. Our desktop software for PCs only does the same but is a one-time purchase. People use the software for their personal use as well as a way to make money. How you use it is up to you.

The Book of Destiny Professional for Windows 3.7	$399
Love Cards Professional for Windows 3.0	$349
The Book of Destiny 4.0 Web-based software	$10-$35/month depending on which version
Love Cards 4.0 Web-based software	$10-$35/month depending on which version

Destiny Apps for iPhone and Android Phones and Devices

We have a basic app for cell phones that does daily, yearly, fifty-two-day and Birth Card readings. Just search in your app store for *My Destiny Cards*. These work on iPhones, iPads, and Android phones and tablets.

Free How to Read Your Destiny E-Course

Come to www.7thunders.com or www.e7thunders.com and sign up for our 17-day E-Course. This fun and educational course introduces you to all the concepts and methods found in the Destiny Cards system and includes some product specials as well.